THE SILVERTIP
OMNIBUS I

MAX BRAND

THE SILVERTIP
OMNIBUS I

MAX BRAND

CHANCELLOR
PRESS

The 'Silvertip' series was first published in Street & Smith's Western Story Magazine in serial form before being released as a novel. The books which followed some years down the line, published later volumes first and were thus published in a sequence different from the chronology within the narrative. This reprint of series follows the original order of the storyline, as written by the author, and keeps the series chronology intact.

The Stolen Stallion first published as a serial in 11 March, 1933 in *Street & Smith's Western Story Magazine. The Stolen Stallion* first published in book form in 1945 by Dodd, Mead & Company, New York. *Silvertip* first published as a serial on 25 March, 1933 in *Street & Smith's Western Story Magazine. Silvertip* first published in book form in 1941 by Dodd, Mead & Company, New York. *The Man From Mustang* first published as a serial on 15 April, 1933 in *Street & Smith's Western Story Magazine. The Man From Mustang* first published in book form in 1942 by Dodd, Mead & Company, New York. *Silvertip's Strike* first published as a serial on 20 May, 1933 in *Street & Smith's Western Story Magazine. Silvertip's Strike* first published in book form in 1942 by Dodd, Mead & Company, New York

This Chancellor Press edition published in 2017
This edition © 2017 Chancellor Press, an imprint of Hachette

This edition © 2017 Hachette India

ISBN 978-93-5009-053-4

Hachette Book Publishing India Pvt. Ltd
4th & 5th Floors, Corporate Centre,
Plot No. 94, Sector 44, Gurugram – 122003, India

Typeset in Manipal Digital Systems Private Limited

Printed and bound in India by Manipal Technologies Limited, Manipal

CONTENTS

THE STOLEN STALLION

CONTENTS

1 – Brandy

HE stood sixteen three, but his hoofs pressed the ground like the paws of a cat. Wherever the moonlight fingered him, shoulder or flank, it touched on silk. With head raised, he looked into the wind, and there seemed in him a lightness of spirit, as though he were capable of leaping into the air and striding on it; but the leather crossbars of a halter were fitted over his head and a lead rope trailed down into the hand of Lake, the half breed. The stallion, that looked as much king of the earth as ever a hawk was king of the sky, was tied fast to a brutal humanity.

Lake turned his savage face. The same moon that lingered on the beauty of the horse etched out the ugliness of the man with a few high lights and skull-like shadows.

"What's he called?" asked Lake.

Harry Richmond was grinning, for he understood the excitement that was making the voice of Lake hard and quick.

"Brandy's his name," said Richmond. "And that's what he's like, ain't he? A regular shot under the belt, eh?"

He moved to another position, so that he could examine the stallion anew with familiar but ever-delighted eyes. Richmond had the lean legs of a rider and a fat lump of a body mounted on them, so that he looked like a blue crane when it stands at the margin of water with its head laid back on its shoulders, readier for sleep than for frogs.

"Looks ain't the hoss," Lake was saying. "But where'd you get this one? You never had nothing on your ranch but mustangs that was rags and bones, and this here is a thoroughbred."

"Yeah," agreed the rancher, "he makes even Mischief look pretty sick, don't he?"

He pointed toward the big mare which stood near by. Mischief seemed nothing, after the stallion, but any good judge who narrowed his eyes could not fail to see her points. She had been caught wild off the range and never more than half tamed; but, like a wild-caught hawk, she seemed able to move without tiring. In every rodeo race where she was entered, the cowpunchers were sure to back her with their money, and she never yet had failed them.

"Maybe he has looks," reiterated Lake, "but looks ain't the hoss. Take and run 'em, and Mischief would likely eat him up."

"That's what we're goin' to see," answered Harry Richmond. "That's why I got you down here, Lake. I'll pay you ten dollars, if you'll run the mare a mile or two against that stallion."

Lake shook his head with a movement so slow that he seemed merely to be looking over each shoulder. "I won't run Mischief for ten, but I'll race her for fifty," he declared.

"For fifty!" exclaimed Richmond. "And me ridin' Brandy? Me givin' you more'n a pound for every dollar of the bet? I ain't such a fool."

"Then it ain't a go," said Lake. "I'll run Mischief yonder to the top of that hill, where the rocks stick out and back here for a finish."

"Two miles, and a lump like me ridin' against a skinny buzzard of a jockey like you?" protested Richmond. But then his eye ran over the silk and the shine of Brandy, and he said through his teeth, "I'll do it!"

He picked up a saddle and bridle, and began to prepare the stallion.

Lake made a cigarette and presently was blowing dissolving wreaths of smoke into the moonshine.

"Look!" he commanded, and waved his hand toward the rattletrap barn near which they were standing, and toward the broken-backed house beyond, and then to the hills and hollows of the ranch, naked as waves of the sea. "Look!" said Lake. "You never raised no horse like Brandy on this kind of a place, and you never paid for him out of your pocket. Where'd you get him?"

"I only got half of him," said Richmond, "but, if he can run the way I think, I'll have the other half, too."

"Who owns the other half?" asked Lake.

"You know Charlie Moore?"

"That old cowpuncher of yours? That cockeyed one?"

"That's him. He owns the other half," answered Richmond. "Three or four years back, Charlie Moore was over at the railroad station in Parmalee, and a train pulls in, and on that train there's the racin' stable of Sam Dickery, the big oil man and crook. And they take off a dead mare, a brood mare by the name of Mary Anne, that had had a foal before her time; the foal was carted off, too, not strong enough to stand. It was the get of Single Shot, that foal was, and the stable manager cursed the hair off the head of the veterinary who said he couldn't save the colt. Anyway, they got ready to knock the foal on the head when old Charlie Moore—that never did have no sense—said he'd like to have the colt. Dickery's trainer grinned and said the deal was on, and all it would cost Charlie was the price of diggin' the grave. But Charlie spent a week right there on the spot, and never moved until he got that colt onto its feet; and here it is today—Brandy!"

"Yeah," said Lake, "that's why Brandy has a kind of hand-polished look about him. Every fool in the world has got one good thing in him, I guess, and this is what Charlie Moore's done with his life. But how come that you got a half claim in the horse?"

As he spoke, Lake began to dig softly, with the tips of his fingers, among the India-rubber strands of muscles which overlaid the shoulder of Brandy.

Harry Richmond thrust out his head with a laugh, saying, "Moore's a half-wit, just about. He never has any money. The boys do him out of his month's pay before he ever gets close to a saloon. So when the colt got sick a couple times and needed a vet, I took a chance and paid the bills, and pulled a half interest out of Moore. That was when Brandy was more'n a year old, and I could see that he was goin' to be somethin'. It was like takin' half the teeth out of Moore's head, but he signed up a paper with me. And I'm goin' to get the other half of Brandy, too, if he can make a fool out of Mischief. Ready?"

They sat the saddles side by side, with Mischief already sensing the contest and beginning to dance for it, while Brandy fell to looking once more into the eye of the wind that brought to his nostrils so many tales from the unknown range.

That was why, when the count of ten was finished, Mischief shot off many a length in the lead; Harry Richmond, thinking of his fifty dollars, began to curse, calling Lake back for a "fair start." The words were blown off his lips. There is something in every hot-blooded horse that can sense a race, and Brandy went after Mischief like a hurled spear.

It was soft, sandy going over which Mischief dusted along lightly, while the pounding hoofs of Brandy broke through, flinging up handfuls of sand that puffed out into clouds. They had six furlongs of such going before they struck the steep slope of the hills, and Richmond waited for that ascent to quench the speed of the stallion. Instead, Brandy went up that rise like a bounding mule deer, and collared the mare at the rocks, where they turned.

A cry came suddenly out of the throat of Richmond. He struck the stallion with the flat of his hand. And then he found himself leaning backward, fighting to get into an upright position, for the mount seemed to be leaping out from under the rider. Brandy had twisted his head a little to the side, in the full

fury of his effort, as though he were about to turn a corner, and nothing
could have been stranger than to see him boring his head so crookedly into
the wind. One might have thought that he was looking back for orders from
his rider.

That was the end of the race. As Richmond went by, his heart lifted into
his throat by the prodigious striding of the stallion, he saw the face of Lake
convulsed with malice and disbelief. And when Richmond pulled up at the
starting point behind the barn, the mare was thirty lengths behind.

The half breed had nothing to say. He dismounted, threw the reins, and
then stepped back to watch the dropped head, the heaving sides, the sweat
that ran in a steady trickle from the belly of Mischief. As for Brandy, he was
merely polished black by the run, and seemed on tip-toe for another race.

Still in silence, Lake drew out his wallet to pay the bet.

"Wait a minute," protested Richmond. "Fifty dollars will break you. I'm
goin' to give you money, not take it away."

"She lay down and quit!" said Lake fiercely.

"She didn't quit," answered Richmond. "She'll go right on winnin' all
kinds of races at the rodeos; but, the way Brandy come wingin' past her, he
would a' beat pretty near any hoss in the world. He's goin' to get his chance,
too. Listen to me, Lake! You got the wool pulled out of your ears and your
brain tuned up?"

"What kind of a crooked deal?" asked Lake.

"It ain't crooked," declared Richmond. "You take a poor half-wit like
Charlie Moore, what would he do with a stake hoss? He wouldn't know.
But you and me would know. You hear me, Lake? This here Brandy has
gotta go East, and pick up a new name, and he's goin' to meet the best in the
land—for the biggest stakes. I can't leave the ranch—there's too much money
for me right here in beef—but you're free, Lake. You're goin' to take Brandy
tomorrow night, and you're goin' to start East with him. You're goin' to
clean up, and you and me go half and half!"

The half-breed looked at Richmond and grinned. Then he put back his
ugly face so that the moonlight flooded it, and laughed silently.

2 – Silvertip

THE plans which the rancher and the half-breed laid by moonlight were perfectly definite and simple. Lake was to come the following night, after Richmond had scraped together some money to cover expenses on the trip to the East. The half-breed was to steal Brandy and make for the railroad, not at the town of Parmalee, close at hand, but far to the north. On the road he could ship Brandy to the East, and inside of three weeks the big horse might be appearing on the tracks. It was a scheme that promised the greater success because the crime in which they shared would force them to a mutual honesty in their own dealings.

But next morning a message came. A messenger rode out from Parmalee with a brief letter from Lake to Richmond. The rancher read:

Dear Richmond: The game is off for a while. I've had a glimpse of Charlie Moore in town, and he was drinking with Silvertip. Why didn't you tell me that Silver was Moore's friend? Silvertip would as soon take a shot at me as at a mountain grouse. I'm laying low till he leaves this part of the range.

Lake.

The name of Silvertip was unknown to Harry Richmond. He burned the letter and went in search of information. Since the punchers were out on the range, he went into the kitchen with his questions; the cook stopped peeling potatoes while he answered.

"I never seen Silvertip no more'n I ever seen wire gold," said the "Doctor," as the cook was sometimes called, "But I've heard gents talk about him, here and there. He gets his name from a coupla streaks of gray hair over his

9

temples, but he ain't old. He ain't thirty. He's ripped the top ground off a fortune twenty times, but he never stops long enough to dig out the pay dirt, because he's always in a hurry. Trouble is what he hunts for breakfast, kills it for lunch, and eats it for supper."

"What kind of trouble?" asked Harry Richmond, gnawing his fleshy lip.

"Any kind," said the cook. "A hoss that pitches right smart is his kind of a hoss; a forest on fire is his kind of a forest; a gold-rush town is his kind of a town; and a two-gun fightin' man is his kind of a man."

"They ought to outlaw that kind of a hound," said the rancher angrily.

"No," said the cook. "He ain't any trouble to a sheriff; he's more of a help. Coupla years back, down in Brown's Creek, when the gold rush come and half the yeggs in the country flocked in, the regular, honest miners, they got together and they sent an invitation to Silvertip to go and settle down with them for a while. And he went. And that was a loud town, Richmond. That was a town that you could hear all the way across the mountains. But after Silvertip was there a week, he soothed it down such a lot that you couldn't hear a whisper out of it."

"He killed the bad actors, you mean?" asked Richmond.

"I dunno that he killed any. I hear that mostly he can shoot so straight that he don't have to kill; and when he comes in one door, the yeggs go out the other."

Richmond went off to digest this news, agreeing in his mind to despise Lake less than when the half-breed's letter had arrived. The rattling wheels of an approaching buckboard brought him out of the house, and he saw Charlie Moore drive up with a big stranger on the seat beside him. The stranger's mount, a big bay gelding with chasings of silver aflash on it, jogged behind the rig, which was loaded with the supplies which Moore had been sent to buy the evening before. It was the simplest way of getting him off the place while Lake arrived to test the stallion.

Charlie Moore drew up near the kitchen door and climbed to the ground; his big companion glided down with one step, as though from a saddle.

"Meet Silvertip, Mr Richmond—Harry Richmond," said Charlie Moore. He smiled with pride to be presenting such a famous man.

Harry Richmond stepped forward with a grunt and a grin, but the manners of Silvertip were rather more Latin than American. He took off his hat and bowed a little to the rancher, as he shook hands. Richmond saw, above the temples, the spots of gray, and an odd chill passed through him.

It was a brown face that he looked into, and the expression was full of such gentle peace as the rancher had never seen before. It was the look of one who daydreams, with the faintest of smiles continually about the lips. Never was a face more handsome, more honest, more open; and yet the chill was still working in the spinal marrow of Richmond. Brandy, and all the fortune that could be made out of the great horse, was as good as his own, until the arrival of Silvertip. Now he felt that good fortune had withdrawn many miles from him.

They began to unload the buckboard together. The flour sacks, the sides of bacon, the hams, were easily handled. But when it came to the big two-hundred-pound sacks of potatoes, which Richmond and old Charlie Moore struggled with together, Silver picked them up by the ears and carried the burden easily into the storeroom.

"He's strong," said the rancher.

"Aye," said Charlie Moore, wagging his head in admiration. "He's mighty strong. He's too strong. A gent like that is too strong to work."

There was a meaning behind this remark which Harry Richmond appreciated to the full, and he looked suddenly and sharply at Moore, as though wondering how far that simple-minded fellow could have looked into a man like Silvertip. But there was nothing to be seen in the face of Moore other than his usual expression, which was that of a child half dreaming over the world and half hurt by it.

Moore looked much younger than his fifty-five years, except for the pain which had worked in the lines about the mouth and in the center of the forehead. But his hair was still dark, and his eyes were still bright. His clothes were those of any hard-working cowpuncher, except that his boots were common cowhide—and where does one find a self-respecting cowpuncher who is without meticulous pride in his footwear? But there was no pride in Charlie Moore. He had gone all his life quite content if he could avoid trouble and understand the need of the moment, and the commands which were given to him. He was not, like Silvertip, "a gent too strong to work!"

To be sure, Silvertip was walking by again with the weight of another sack trundled comfortably in his arms. As he passed, Harry Richmond looked askance and saw the great spring of muscles that arched from shoulder to shoulder, the corseting of might which gripped him about the loins and swelled his torso above hips as lean as those of a desert wolf that can run all day and fight all night. That was what Silvertip seemed to Harry Richmond—a machine too flawless to be used on the mere mechanics of ranch work.

"Silvertip, he's an old friend of mine," said Charlie Moore, dusting the white of flour from his coat sleeves, as the unloading of the wagon was finished. "I guess," he added, with a sudden wistfulness, "that Silver's about the best friend that I got!" He blundered on: "Which ain't meanin' that Silvertip takes me very serious. Nobody does. But I guess he means more to me than anybody else."

Harry Richmond, watching very closely, saw the smile struck from the mouth of Silvertip; but at the same instant the hand of Silver went out and rested for a moment on the shoulder of Moore. The latter seemed to accept that touch as an assurance of all that he could have wished. He brightened; with an air of surprised happiness, he looked up at Silvertip, who avoided that glance by saying to Richmond:

"Charlie tells me that you and he have a great horse out here."

"Pretty fair—pretty fair," answered Richmond. With an air of thought, he pursed his mouth until the tip of his nose was raised, and his fat face was sculptured into a new and amazing design. "Soft—but I'll tell you what he's got, that Brandy. He's got pretty good lines. That's why I could use him with some mustang mares and get me some saddle stock. I'll tell you what, Charlie—I'll buy out your half in Brandy. He ain't much. He's too heavy and soggy, kind of, in the quarters. But I'm tired of this partnership business, and I'll buy him off you. I'll give you a good price for your share, too. Whatcha want, Charlie? Speak up and name your price."

"Sell my half of Brandy?" asked Moore, staring like a round-eyed child. He laughed a little, but the pain remained in his blue eyes. "I could easier sell half of myself," he concluded.

"Now, don't you be a fool," said Richmond. He stepped closer, so that the superiority of his bulk might impress itself on the eye of Moore as the weight of his words impressed itself on the simple mind of the puncher. He laid the tip of a forefinger like a dagger at the breast of his ranch hand. "Who knows more about business, you or me?" he demanded.

"Why, you do, Harry," answered Moore, instantly abashed. "Sure, you know a lot more than I do."

"Then don't be a fool," went on Richmond. "I'm goin' to pay you your own price. I'll pay you up to six months' wages. Not that half of Brandy is worth that much, but just because I wanta get rid of the argument. I hate argument. You know that. I'm goin' to give you a chance to pick up a price of good money, Charlie; I'm goin' to show you that I'm your friend."

For it seemed to Richmond that this was the time to strike, and strike hard, for the prize, before Silvertip laid his wise eye on the stallion and saw Brandy's real value. And Charlie Moore, amazed and baffled and somewhat agape as he listened to the impressive words of Richmond, rolled his eyes from side to side.

The quiet voice of Silvertip broke in: "No man will sell the blood out of his body, Richmond, and that's what Brandy is to Charlie. Let's put up the team and have a look at the horse."

Charlie Moore heaved a sigh of relief; Richmond bit his lip. But by those few words the matter seemed to be settled beyond appeal. If Richmond wanted the stallion, he would, in fact, have to steal him. And he cursed Silvertip with a silent fervor.

They put up the mustangs, ran the buckboard into the wagon shed, and went to the big corral behind the barn, where Brandy was grazing. He could have had his name for his color; he was a golden fire, red-stained and sun-burnished. At the whistle of Moore, he picked up his head from his grazing and turned suddenly about. Black silk covered his legs to the knees and the hocks; black velvet covered his muzzle; and between the eyes there was a white wedge, like the hallmark of the Master Maker.

"Kind of soft all over," said Richmond. "Kind of heavy and soggy in the quarters, ain't he? But sort of good-lookin'; picture-book hoss, that kids would be crazy about. That's all."

But a faint cry had come out of the throat of Silvertip. He was through the bars of the fence and stepping across toward the stallion with hand extended. Charlie Moore made so free as to grasp the arm of Richmond with a frantic hand.

"Look! Look!" said Moore. "It's even the kind of a horse for Silvertip. It's the kind of a horse he wants, and he's never wanted a horse before."

"How come?" asked Richmond angrily. "How come you say he never has wanted a hoss before?"

"Look at what I mean," muttered Charlie, keeping enchanted eyes upon the picture of Silvertip approaching the stallion. "What I mean is that Silver, he never finds nothin' that he really wants. That's why he never stops still. There ain't no girl pretty enough to stop him for a week. There ain't no house right enough to be his home. There ain't no mine rich enough to keep him diggin'. There ain't no man big enough to be his friend. There ain't no horse fine enough for him to make a partner of it. No horse before Brandy, maybe! But look at Silver now! Look at the way he's steppin' around him. Look at him measurin' and measurin' and admirin'—"

"There ain't much in this world that Silvertip's interested in except a fight—is that it?" asked the rancher.

"That and danger," said Charlie Moore absently. "There's danger been put into the world, and there's men been put to love it, I guess. Why, he ain't even satisfied with Brandy—not even with him! Look at Silver shakin' his head a little and shruggin' his shoulders. And here he comes back to us. Hey, Silver!" he called. "Don't you make up your mind till you've tried him. Don't you damn Brandy till you've tried him, will you?"

"Of course I'll try him," said Silvertip. "And he's a grand horse. No wonder you're proud of him, Charlie. He's the finest for his weight that I ever saw. Just for a minute I almost thought—well, no matter about that."

He broke off with a sigh, and his eyes went regretfully back toward the stallion.

"You thought what? You almost thought what?" asked Moore eagerly. "You thought almost that he would be the horse for you, Silver? Ain't that what you almost thought? Try him, Silver, and maybe he is the horse for you. If he is, you can have him. I'll give him up. It'd be better to me than ownin' him to think of you and him out together, like a coupla kings, like a coupla hawks flyin' over the mountains. You try him, and if he is your horse, you can have him. It'd do me good, day and night, to think of you two together."

The hand of Silvertip rested again on the shoulder of Moore, and his glance went deeply into the face of the cowpuncher, for an instant.

"You're a kind fellow, Charlie," he said. "One of these days I'm afraid that you'll give away your heart and soul—because you'll find somebody else who could use 'em!"

"About givin' Brandy away," said Richmond angrily, "that's a kind of a joke, ain't it? Or maybe I don't own half of him."

The quiet eyes, the quiet voice of Silvertip turned toward Richmond, as he answered: "I can buy your half of the horse, Richmond. A half interest is only worth six months of Charlie's pay, isn't it? That's the top price that I heard you put on him."

A hot retort swelled the throat of Richmond, and died in it. For suddenly he knew, not by reputation only, that this man was dangerous.

"I'll get a saddle on Brandy. You try him," Moore was saying.

So saddle and bridle were put on the stallion, Brandy opening his mouth for the bit as though it were a thing to eat. Then Silvertip mounted, sliding into the saddle as though he were stepping onto the back of a pony. This man made all things seem small and easy.

Afterward, he rode Brandy out of the corral, down into the hollow, jumped the dry ditch there, and brought the horse swinging back. Charlie Moore was white with eagerness and questions when the big man dismounted. A gentle consideration appeared in the face of Silver as he regarded Moore.

"It's a glorious horse; it's a wonderful horse, Charlie," said Silvertip. "It's as fine a horse as I ever had under me—or finer."

"But not for you?" asked Moore huskily, working at the cinch knot with fingers that seemed suddenly too weak to handle the strap.

"You know how people are," answered Silvertip, more gently than ever. "It's only when a thing fits into the mind like a word into a line—it's only then that a fellow will give up his blood to get what he wants. That's the only time. But if Brandy were just a hair different, I'd give my soul for him; I'd trail him down on foot to get him!"

His head and his voice had lifted. He seemed to be looking into the future. And, in fact, he was making a phophecy, though not exactly of the sort he had in mind.

"Well," said Charlie Moore sadly, "he fits into my ideas, all right. He suits me well enough. Poor old Brandy! Poor old boy!"

He put the stallion back into the corral, while Richmond, with a breath of relief, turned on his heel and went back to the house, satisfied that Silvertip would not try to buy the stallion. His satisfaction would have been much less if he could have overheard Silvertip at the corral fence saying to Moore:

"Mind you, Charlie, Richmond wants that stallion, and he's going to have him unless you look sharp. I won't be around here very long, but, while I'm near, I'm going to help you watch. The hand is faster than the eye, Charlie, and this fellow Richmond has the look of a thief about him."

3 – Lake Takes the Chance

RICHMOND went into the town of Parmalee that same day, and found the half-breed, Lake, hidden out in a little Mexican tavern at the edge of the village. In the dimness of the back room they talked together; their eyes and their whisky glasses glistened; their voices were so soft that they melted into the shadows of the place.

"I've seen Silvertip," said Richmond, squeezing his fat fingers around his glass. "And he's plenty to look at."

"He'd go in the dark into a hole in the ground and rip the heart out of a mountain lion with his bare hands," said Lake. "That's all he would do. I've seen quarters throwed up into the air, spinning, and I've seen him shoot 'em, with never a miss."

"Can he do that?" said Richmond.

"He can," said Lake.

After that, in a silence, they drank their whiskies. Something more than the rankness of the drink made Richmond shudder. Then he went on:

"Silvertip don't like me. He looked me in the face like a buzzard at a dyin' steer. Seemed like he wanted to be at me. He's workin' on that fool of a Charlie Moore, too, tellin' him how much money Brandy is worth. And the thing to do is to act right now. Lake, you're goin' to sneak over to the place this evenin' and take Brandy, and skin out with him. Understand?"

"I hear you talk," said Lake. He laughed with a light hissing sound. "I hear you talk like a fool!" he added. "While Silvertip's around? No, no, brother! I'm goin' to lay low like a chipmunk in a hole till that hombre is out of sight!"

"What you so scared of him for? What you ever done to him?" demanded Richmond, angry with impatience.

"I never done nothin' to him," said Lake. "I ain't such a fool to try my hand on Silvertip. But one night I was havin' a time for myself in a saloon— and it don't matter where—and he come and dropped in and seen what I was doin'. I got away by divin' through a window and takin' the glass with me."

He raised his hand to his face and delicately traced the course of a scar with the tip of his finger.

"Listen to me," said Richmond. "You're broke. You're flat. I'm goin' to stake you to five hundred bucks. Understand? Five hundred iron men!"

He pulled out his wallet.

"Feed your money to swine," said Lake. "I don't want it. It's only goin' to choke me—while Silver's around."

But Richmond began to lay out the greenbacks, one after the other. They made a soft and secret whispering.

"Five—hundred—dollars!" said Richmond, pushing the stack across the table. "That'll see you all the way East with Brandy. And after that—the big money for the both of us!"

"Take it away. I don't want it. I won't risk my neck. Not while Silvertip's around!" groaned Lake.

Suddenly he clutched the pile of soft paper and crunched it into the palm of his hand.

"It's cuttin' my throat," he said through his teeth, "but I'll take the chance. While you're sleepin' soft, I'll take the chance. You'll be dead asleep, and I'll be dead on the ground. That's the way it works. The gent that has the money always gets the best deal. I hope you rot!"

"Do you?" said Richmond, with a yawn. "Have another drink."

"I don't want no more. I've had too much already. I don't want no liquor on board of me while I'm within fifty miles of Silvertip. Go on and get out and leave me alone. I gotta do some plannin'."

The planning of the half-breed kept him motionless in that dark little room through most of the remainder of the day. He sketched in his mind every detail of Richmond's ranch—the house, the barn, the corral, the devious ways among the naked hills. If there had only been a growth of trees, how much more securely he might have approached the thought of the stealing of Brandy!

It was almost dusk when he left Parmalee and rode toward the Richmond ranch; it was in the thick of the night when he saw the light from a bedroom window throwing frail yellow spars of brilliance against his eyes.

He came up like an Indian, making a complete circle about the place, then drifting in at angles until he had reached the corral behind the barn. The moon would be up before long; yes, the pale hand of it was already climbing in the east.

The thought of the brightness that would soon flood the earth made the heart of Lake twist and shrink in his breast. But now, out of the ground shadows, arose the form of a great horse, and he knew that it was Brandy, standing up to sniff at a stranger in the night.

Lake remembered suddenly how the stallion had breezed past him, making Mischief seem to stand still. There was money—there was a fortune in that horse. Mischief was no thoroughbred, but she could last like patience; and yet she had been run off her feet and worn weak by the stallion. What would Brandy do, then, with a perfect track under his hoofs, and a mere feather of a jockey in the saddle?

Across the eye of the half-breed rolled a picture of turreted stands, bright with flags, white with massed faces. He felt along his nerves the vibrancy of ten thousand voices cheering; he saw the field of horses sweeping toward the finish; and then a chestnut stockinged in black silk sweep out from the throng to finish by himself. Brandy! The cheering—the curious and envious gentry—the presentation of the silver cup—the stake money—the flattery from the rich and the great!

He—half-breed Lake—had always known that he could make as good a gentleman as another, when occasion offered. It was merely a matter of money, clothes, and a certain coldly distant manner. But the money was the chief thing—easy money that would take wings again easily.

He slid from the saddle, threw the reins of his mare, and, taking his coiled lariat from the pommel of the saddle, he advanced to the corral and slid between the bars of it. Something seemed to strike at his head, like a hand of darkness. It was merely the flight of an owl, slanting close to the ground. But, with guard still raised, his body still crouching, Lake turned his snarling face and stared for a long time after that night hunter.

He recovered after a moment. Every instant he wasted was a chance for life and success thrown away—for Silvertip might be somewhere near. He might be watching at this moment, smiling his faint smile at the figure of the horse thief caught behind the black bars of the corral fence.

For one thing Lake was profoundly thankful—that the stallion had been handled to the point of absolute docility; for now, as Brandy stood at the farther side of the corral with raised head and shadowy arching tail, he looked capable of bounding in three strides to the distant rising moon. Lake shook out the noose of his rawhide rope and swung it in a widening circle. Carelessly he threw the lariat, still from the corners of his eyes hunting for an enemy that might rise out of the ground. But, even if he had been totally alert, he might have missed, for Brandy leaped sidewise and sprang swiftly across the corral.

The reata, cutting the empty air, struck the ground with a rippling fall, and a slight tremor ran up the hand and arm of Lake. For suppose that the stallion fought? Suppose that the great horse made a sound of trampling and snorting? Suppose that the noise reached the house?

Lake gathered up the frail and snaky shadow of the rope. Hastily he advanced toward the stallion in the corner. Brandy leaped aside, the starlight glancing dimly in the polish of his flanks.

"Now, you high-headed fool!" muttered Lake, and started to whirl his rope as he stepped in for the throw.

That cast was not made. Instead, Lake dodged for his life, as an avalanche of horseflesh hurled suddenly at him, with a glint of eyes and yawning teeth, and a flag of mane blown above.

Right across the corral and around it galloped the stallion, with every stride making the enclosure seem smaller and smaller; and as Brandy ran, he flung his head up and sent through the night a neigh that rang like the blast of a thousand copper horns in the ears of Lake. The blood rushed upward through his brain. He seemed like a child gathering a string into his hand—a foolish child attempting to snare a monster. That challenging call from the stallion would be sure to rouse all the punchers in the house. Most of all, it might reach the ears of that consummate man-slayer, Silvertip!

Yet the half-breed did not run for his life. He shuddered, his very heart quaked in him, but all the Indian of his soul had now rallied to that game of horse stealing. He ran forward, keen-eyed, sure of hand, and snared Brandy with the swift, underarm fling of the rope.

Against the taut lariat the stallion would not pull; Lake ran up the line, hand over hand. Near by, he heard a door slam. It seemed right in his ear, yet he knew that it must have come from the house. A voice called; other voices answered; and, above all, came the beat of hoofs.

Aye, and there in the east, white as frost, brilliant, the eye of the rising moon glanced at him. There was no time to flee now. There was not even time to run to Mischief and be off on her. The danger that approached was a wave whose head already curled above him.

Lake caught the mane of the horse with his left hand, jerked the reata into a noose over Brandy's head, and leaped onto his back. Under Lake, the silk and steel of Brandy flinched, and off to the side, rushing at full speed, was a big rider on a big horse, the brim of the man's sombrero blown flat up by the wind of the gallop. By the width of those shoulders, by something dauntless in that bearing, Lake knew that Silvertip was at him, and with the steel rowels of his spurs, Lake gripped the tender body of the horse.

Brandy groaned, but with his groan he started; he was running away from the pain that burned into his flanks; he was running from a new fear of humankind who never before had harmed him. It was that fear which lifted him at the lofty bars of the corral fence. He skimmed it with his elbows, with his belly. His heels struck so hard his head tipped down.

A yell of fear exploded upward in the throat of Lake. It died as it reached his teeth, for Brandy landed on sure feet and fled straight forward. Mischief, by the startled upfling of her head, tossed the reins across her back and rushed in pursuit.

Lake glanced back. All of this had happened, yet only half of the shining face of the moon was showing above the eastern horizon. Yet that mighty lantern would soon be high, striking him with its rays, showing him to the big rider on the big horse that strode behind. But let him ride with all his cunning, let him be ten times Silvertip, if only Lake could keep on the back of Brandy for another five minutes, he would be out of pistol shot. The wind of the gallop burned his eyes, and still that speed increased.

A shout struck his ears; a bullet pierced the air beside him; the sound of the explosion shook him as though by a strong hand. The half-breed flattened himself along the back of Brandy and clutched the flanks of the stallion anew with his spurs. Right through the velvet of the hide, into the rubbery sheathing of muscles, drove the rowels. Brandy did what he never had done before; he bucked high in the air and landed on stiffened legs.

They were flying down hill at the time. The sharpness of the slope snapped the whip for Brandy and shot Lake off of that smooth bare back. He rolled skidding across the sand. As he got to his knees, he saw Silvertip coming like a giant of wrath, with a revolver poised in his hand. The half-breed screamed. He fell flat on his face, yelling for mercy. Hoofbeats fell near him. Sand squirted into his eyes. But there was no thunderclap of an exploding gun at his ears.

He half rose. Up the farther slope raced Brandy, the snake-like shadow of the lariat flying above him, Mischief laboring in vain pursuit. And yet farther behind them was Silvertip, losing ground at every stride.

The whole body of the moon had risen in the east. Lake turned from that accusing light and threw out his hands before him like a child fleeing from a nightmare. That was how he raced to find shelter, dodging as he ran.

4 – The Victor

FOR three miles Silvertip raced behind the fugitives. Then he gave it up and settled down to a steady, cautious hunt. The stallion, he was sure, he could have snared at any time, but Mischief made the trouble. Wild-caught, she seemed to have reverted to the wild again. It was she who stood on constant watch; it was she who herded Brandy away at every near approach of the hunter.

On the first night she stepped on a trailing rein and dragged the bridle from her head; on the next day she broke the saddle by rolling, then rose in a frenzy and bucked it off. No sign of man was on her, now, except the brand on her hip.

It was no blind flight. She had a direction in her mind, as surely as a migrating bird. North and west, north and west, she led the way into a region of naked mountains; of great valleys that seemed to have been carved out by the wind, since there were no rivers to flow through them; of plains where the grass grew not at all, or only in scattered tufts. Only the eye of an artist could wander with pleasure among the colored mesas, or from the white of the sands to the blue of the distances. A horse had to rove for miles in order to pick up a meager bellyful, then lope twenty miles in the evening to find water—sucking it out of a muddy hole. But there was one advantage that made the region a paradise for wild horses; if it was a bitter country, burned bone-dry in summer, frozen by terrible winds in the winter, it was all the more free from man. Here and there a prospector voyaged like a snail, sighting his course between the ears of his burro; but no farmer, no cattleman, not even a sheep-herder, would enter this range willingly. And the wild horses knew with a sure instinct that it was better to go half starved in a land free from the tyrant, man, than to fatten for a little while on green pastures in constant danger of rope and gun.

21

It was on the third day of the hunt that Silvertip, from the brow of a low-running ridge, saw the mare go down the further valley with Brandy at her side, while a dust cloud rose in the distance and rolled against the wind toward them.

They halted. The dust cloud dissolved into a band of twenty loping horses. Brandy stood his ground uneasily, occasionally turning his head to look at the mare. And, meantime, from the rear of the herd, the king of it came sweeping. He was a buckskin with silver mane and tail. He looked like a patch of bright gold in the distance, with a pair of silver flags to blow over him.

The watcher pulled his Winchester out of its saddle holster, and took aim. But right into the circle which his sights covered the buckskin galloped, so that Silvertip dared not fire. At such a distance, his bullet might as well strike one of the swerving, plunging fighters as the other. He lowered the gun and sat, grinning with agony, waiting for the inevitable. He did not even try to rush his horse forward and so interrupt the combat, so certain he was that the wild stallion would kill the tame one out of hand.

He had seen the leaders of the ranging bands struggle together long before this. Like tigers they fought, each toughened by a hundred battles, kicking, striking, above all striving for a throat hold which would end the strife with one wrench and a tear. How could Brandy, no matter what his superiority in size, stand for an instant against such a trained combatant?

In came the buckskin like a dancer, swerving to this side, then to that, before he closed, lunging to take hold on the throat. Missing that vital point, nevertheless the weight of his charge behind his shoulder was enough to knock Brandy head over heels.

That would be the end. Silvertip closed his eyes, unwilling to see that wild beast of the range leap on the fallen body of the thoroughbred and knock it to pieces. But when he looked again, Brandy was up, the buckskin leaping far off to avoid the drive of the reaching hind legs.

Brandy whirled to meet the next charge, and Silver could have sworn that the buckskin got the throat hold, only to have it broken as the taller stallion reared. Upon the crest of the buckskin fell a shower of strokes from the armed forefeet of Brandy. The wild horse fell to his knees, swayed staggering to his feet, and fled before the victorious charge of the stranger.

Silvertip, agape, laughed with joy. He saw the buckskin halt, far off, while Brandy kept his place with a lofty front, as though disdaining to pursue a beaten enemy. Mischief came to his side and touched noses with him. The mares and the younger colts of the wild herd advanced by degrees. Curiosity drew them inexorably. Sometimes the scent of man or the sight of the rawhide lariat about the neck of Brandy sent them scampering, but again and again they returned, until a thick cluster had formed about their new companion.

Mischief broke up the cluster. She advanced up the valley at a steady lope. Brandy followed her; he ranged ahead and the whole herd flooded after; and far to the rear, with fallen crest, came the deposed buckskin leader at a slow trot.

Silvertip watched them for a long time through the clear mountain air. Not a sound came to him. The dust cloud thickened. Finally, it was rolling without a sign of the life that thronged beneath it, and Silvertip shook his head.

If, as he had told Charlie, the chestnut stallion had been a trifle different, he would have given years of his life to secure the horse. But there was something lacking. In Brandy was not the spark that could set the soul of the wanderer on fire, and already he had given three priceless days to this pursuit. He looked toward the horizon. Somewhere beyond it, the great adventure was still waiting for him. Reluctantly he turned his horse, and jogged steadily toward the south.

5 – The Horse Hunt

THE letter which came for Charlie Moore to the Richmond ranch was very crisp and brief. But Charlie read it over and over, sitting in the twilight on the steps of the house while the other cowpunchers sat around their poker game inside. It was near the end of the month, and they were gambling, therefore, in futurities.

Harry Richmond, noisily stalking through the room, more like a fat-bodied, long-legged crane than ever, plucked the paper out of the limp fingers of Moore and read:

Dear Charlie: I was ten seconds too late, the night that Brandy was stolen. That Indian half-breed, Lake, is the rat that ran off with him. Brandy bucked him off before I had a chance to shoot him off. I should have killed the brute while he rolled on the ground, but it's hard to finish off a man who's yelling for mercy. So I went on and trailed Brandy and the mare, Mischief, up into the Sierra Blanca desert. I saw them meet up with a herd of twenty head of wild mustangs and I saw Brandy lick the buckskin leader and take charge of the lot. You know it's no easy business to run down a wild herd. At least, it's about as hard for one man to do the trick as it is to run a flock of wild geese out of the sky. I gave up the job. I have something to do a good bit south of here, and I'm headed in that direction. In the meantime, I thought I'd let you know where Brandy is wandering. Sorry that I couldn't bring him back on a rope to you. But you'll probably need a big outfit of men and horses to run that herd down and get the stallion back. Best of luck to you. I'll try to see you on my way north. If you run across Lake, let him know that his trail means a good deal to me, and that I hope to spend some time on it before long. The yellow hound!

Yours,
Silvertip

When Harry Richmond had finished reading this document, he balled it in his hand and hurled it into the outer darkness.

"Sierra Blanca!" he groaned.

Charlie Moore nodded his head, and swallowed slowly. At last he said, "He's gone. I'll never see Brandy again!"

"If you took care of what you own," shouted Richmond, "if you didn't let sneakin' half-breeds steal everything you've got, you might amount to somethin', some day. Now Brandy's gone. You've let him get away—and half of him was mine."

"Aye," said Charlie Moore, "half of him was yours. And half was mine. And he's gone. I'd give up my half for the chance of seein' him inside the corral once more, liftin' his head when I talk to him, comin' when I whistle. But he's gone into the Sierra Blanca, and nobody'll lay eyes on him again."

A thought struck into the mind of Richmond, deeper than the sound of a bell.

"You'd give him up—your half of him?" asked Richmond.

"I'd give him up," said Charlie Moore, "but that won't bring him back here. I might as well just give up a wish as to give up a horse that's runnin' wild in the Sierra Blanca."

"I dunno," said Harry Richmond. The greatness of his desire and his hope raised a storm in his breast. His eyes burned. "Suppose that you and me and a bunch of others, with some fast horses, went up there and campaigned for Brandy. Suppose that we caught him—you'd give up your half?"

"Sure," said Charlie Moore, "but there ain't any hope."

"There's hope enough to make me try," said the rancher. "Besides," he added, "it would be the same as though he was part yours, anyway. You'd have the handlin' of him!"

* * *

It was Mischief that smelled the scent of men and iron and gunpowder before any of the herd. She had been as wild as any of them during half her life, and the other half had familiarized her more profoundly with man and his ways. So her hair-trigger senses found the danger while it was still far off. Her neigh gathered the herd into swift flight that she led, while Brandy ranged at the rear, swinging back and forth, nipping at the old mares, at the ancient, blundering stallions, at the clumsy colts that made up the rear guard. So the herd was partly led and partly swept out of the dangerous narrowness of a valley, and as it ran, the wild horses saw riders streaming down the slope on their left.

On out of the ravine, exploding like a shell in the midst of rolling dust, the herd poured into the more open desert. Behind it the pursuit sagged down, and failed.

But that was only the beginning. For ten days the pursuit continued. Mysteriously, horsemen appeared at the water holes toward which the band headed. Deprived of water and with little time to graze, on account of constant alarms, the whole band lost flesh and strength and spirits—all except Mischief and the new leader. Her iron-hard constitution saved her, and in Brandy there was an unfailing fountain of strength; the greatness of his soul seemed able to supply the needs of his body. Even so, he was drawn fine indeed on that day when the herd had been led into a pleasant valley by Mischief, so that the older and the younger animals could find easier grazing. Here the grass grew almost thick, and two springs threw out rills which joined in a delightful stream before the thirst of the ground sucked up the running water. It was high time that the band should find rest and food; the older animals were beginning to stumble and the knees of the younger colts were continually a-tremble.

They had grazed for perhaps three hours, undisturbed, when the accurate nose of Mischief detected trouble in the offing; her neigh was a clarion that gathered the herd suddenly around her. Brandy joined her on the slight hummock from which she was sweeping the landscape.

"There's no danger," said Brandy, as he touched his nose to hers. "I haven't your eyes, but there's no danger. No horse and rider could manage to sneak up on us, here. Common sense will teach you that."

"Trust a mare's instinct rather than a stallion's common sense," said Mischief, flaring out her nostrils, and stamping suspiciously. "I found the scent of man in the air, and that means trouble."

"A man on horseback—yes," said Brandy.

"Horseback or afoot, it doesn't matter a great deal," said Mischief. "The smell puts the taste of iron back in my mouth, and I feel the rope burn again, and the halter flaps once more on my head. Don't try to tell me, because I know."

"You're afraid," said Brandy.

"I'd rather be afraid ten times than to be caught once," said Mischief. "There!"

As she snorted, Brandy saw a man on foot step out of a patch of brush hardly a hundred yards away. The stallion flinched in turn; the entire herd swerved to flee with Mischief, for the others had learned to defer to her cleverness, her constant watchfulness. More than once the real leader of a herd has been a mare; Mischief was filling that role now.

"Come on!" she called to Brandy.

But he remained where he was. He had lifted his magnificent head, and was studying the slowly advancing figure. A faint wind came from the man to his nostrils.

"There's no scent of a gun," said Brandy. "There's no smell of iron, you know. And there's no rope about him. Why should you be afraid, Mischief?"

"As long as a man has one hand, he's dangerous," said the mare. "Are you coming, Brandy?"

"I'll come presently," said Brandy. "Get the herd down the valley a little. Something makes me want to look at this man a little more closely. I think I know him."

Mischief instantly fled a furlong farther down the valley, the other horses packed closely around her. There she paused, and sent her call after her mate. But Brandy was standing his ground. Once or twice he flinched, when Mischief whinnied for him. Yet still he lingered in un-decision, for there was something very familiar about that form which came toward him, with hand extended. And now he could hear the voice that passed with a singular magic through all the nerves of his body, soothing him.

It was Charlie Moore, who had come down to try his single hand, where all of the others had failed; the starved, hollow-eyed men of the hunt, the staggering horses, remained high up among the hills, while Moore went down by himself to see what his luck might be.

"Run while you can!" called Mischief, from the distance. "The snake can hold the bird with its eye—and some men can hold a horse, when they come near enough. Run, Brandy!"

Brandy whirled about, tossing his head and then his heels. He slashed his tail right and left, brilliant in the sunshine, before he paused once more. But the half circle in which he ran, had not taken him farther from the approaching figure.

The voice went on. It spoke in sounds which were mostly meaningless, but others were as familiar to Brandy as the speech of his own kind. And, above all, there was the name repeated over and over:

"Brandy! Stand fast, Brandy! Brandy, good boy!"

The stallion let Charlie Moore come straight up to him. When the hand of the man was a yard from his nose, Brandy stretched out his head, sniffed at it, and then bolted at full speed.

Down the valley before him he saw the rest of the herd flying, he heard the rejoiced whinnying of Mischief, and turning in a great circle, Brandy came back almost to the spot where he had confronted Moore before.

His senses were so alert that he could see everything; two buzzards that circled, near and far, in the thin blue of the sky; the thick shadow that dropped along the side of the mesa; the smoke of greasewood that straggled across a nearby hollow; the mist of dust that hung in the air after the passing of the herd. But, most of all, he was aware of the man, the voice, the outstretched hand, the eyes.

What had Mischief said about the eyes of man? These were filled with understanding and gentleness as well. Above all, there was the voice that kept running through his being like a river, and always pouring contented music about his heart.

Far off, Mischief was calling on the highest note of fear and warning.

Brandy shuddered with apprehension, but suddenly he stretched his head to the hand of Moore, saw that hand go past it and grasp the tattered end of the lariat which still hung from his neck. A sobbing noise came out of the throat of Charlie Moore, a sound which Brandy had never heard before. He turned his head to nuzzle the man's shoulder. Still the grip of Moore was on the end of the rope. Freedom had passed from Brandy at that instant, but he hardly cared, for the caressing words dulled him like an opiate. And what was all the wild freedom in this world, compared with the touch of that hand, as it ran down along his neck, and the penetrating, reassuring music of that voice, filled with promises that green pastures and bright waters alone could not fulfill?

6 – Parade

THAT was how Brandy went back to the hands of men, while Mischief led the herd far off into the intricacies of the Sierra Blanca. Sometimes, in the dawn and in the dusk of the day, she ran out from the rest, or lingered behind them, waiting and watching; but she knew, nevertheless, that there was no real hope, and that what men have taken they will not surrender again. They hold what they put their hands on, and no power except that of other men can remove the prize.

There were more things for Mischief to give heed to than the disappearance of Brandy, however. The buckskin leader was still with the herd, but after his downfall his authority could never again be complete.

There was now no voice that the band followed readily except the whinny of the mare. Her tossing mane was what they looked toward in flight, and her way was that which they followed when, in times of drought, the whole group hungered for water.

One old mare died of water famine. That was the only casualty in the band that Mischief led through the summer and the winter, and into the pale green of spring that spread over the desert like a thin mist. She was great with foal of Brandy, long before; and it was fortunate that, as the gentle season came, no horse hunters appeared with it. For the State had put a price on the wild horses, a bounty, as on so many wolves.

By small marches, the herd wandered where the grass was springing and where water flowed at hand. And on a day when the Sierra Blanca stood white indeed under the western sky, and the sun was already beginning to burn with the full promise of the summer's heat, the foal was born that men afterward called "Parade." He was a golden chestnut like his father, Brandy; he was stockinged like him in black silk to the knees and hocks; he had the

29

same sooty muzzle, and, above all, between the eyes, the white sign of his race was printed.

But there were differences, also. Never was there a gentler spirit among horses than Brandy; and never was there a prouder or a fiercer one than that of Parade. When first he stood braced on his long, spindling legs, already his head was high, and his tail arched; already, too, the fire was kindled in his eyes. Mischief, looking him over wisely, knew that she had brought into the world a lord of their kind.

In three days, he could keep up with the galloping herd, and proved it, for on that third day a group of bounty hunters came with racing horses and with crackling guns. For good shooting the reward was fairly high, for the ranchmen were tired of having their saddle stock swept off the range into the band of some wild stallion, to be lost permanently, or else worn out by constant hard traveling. They were striking at the root of the trouble—the stallions themselves. And on this day it was that the buckskin stopped in his stride and squealed with pain.

Parade, looking back, saw the beautiful animal crumble to its knees, then fall flat upon the ground. The wind brought up the sickening odor of blood, and his mother ran beside him, snorting as she ran:

"It's the Great Enemy! It's Man! Whenever men come, there'll be the smell of blood! Look! The pinto mare is down. See how her shoulder is covered with red? The Great Enemy kills from far off. Fly for your life, oh brave, oh noble son of mine!"

Four of the herd were killed on that day, when the band was safe, the long legs of Parade were shaking under him. He lay down in the shadow of his mother, and every staggering beat of his heart thrummed home in his brain the newly learned lessons:

"Man is the Great Enemy! Man kills from afar! With the scent of Man comes the smell of iron and powder, and the latter scent is that of death. There is no wind so cold, there is no sun so hot, as the wrath of Man. Therefore, Man is the Great Enemy."

He would not forget those lessons. Through that summer and that autumn, he had the point brought home to him more than once. If he learned to run as never a horse on the range had run before him, the bullets of men were what gave him wings. The herd dissolved. Half were dead, half were scattered. There remained only Mischief and her foal, lurking in the great wilderness of the Sierra Blanca, in fear of the very ground on which they trod.

"We must go in a straight line, on and on," said Parade to his mother. "There is fear all around us! We must go straight on until we leave it behind us."

She answered: "Fear is a thing that can never be lost, except by slaves. The stupid beasts which wear saddles and carry men in them may be safe, but all the rest of us are afraid. Every wild thing is afraid. Even the wolf goes in fear. The mountain lion sneaks out of its lair to hunt. The grizzly skulks through the brush and hides among the rocks. You want to escape from fear, but it would be easier to escape from yourself. You want to run over the edge of the horizon and find a new world, but all you can ever find is a new skyline. Trouble will rain down on you everywhere out of the brightest heaven. And the wise horse, my son, is he who makes the best of the grass and the water at hand, no matter how far he may have to range for it."

They went into that winter alone, and it was a bitter one. It began with a norther that whitened the desert and the mountains alike. They had to paw through the snow to get at the scanty grass beneath. Then the Chinook blew. Dark flags flew from the peaks, and the warm wind melted the snow for a day. Afterward the frost congealed the water to ice, a transparent coat of armor through which hoofs could not break.

Even wild horses would have starved then, but Mischief was wise among her kind, and she showed the colt how to forage in the lee of the bluffs where the chinook had not melted the snow, and where it could still be broken away for the sake of the sparse grass beneath.

They lived, but with death fingering their ribs and looking them in the eye every day. Men had hunted them all through the year until winter; now winter itself reached out for them with hands of ice.

Then the wolves hunted them down the Wainwright Valley. Seven great lobos—gaunt skeletons whose loose hides waved and rippled as they ran, red-eyed, with teeth that shone like ice—hunted the mare and her foal through the narrow pass, and out through the plain, and around in a great circle. For three days, they hung to the trail, far slower of foot than the horses, but patient as hunger itself.

The starving colt would never forget how he ran when his legs were numb, of how his mother, when he staggered, came beside him and nipped him cruelly, hip and flank, wringing his tender flesh with her teeth until the torment spurred him into a stronger gallop.

With snorts and with whinnyings, with half-human moans, she scolded him through the length of that frightful three-day run.

"There's neither heart nor pride in you!" she would say, "and yet you are the son of a king! The blood of a king is in you, but you let a pack of filthy timber wolves run you down! If you were the son of Brandy in spirit as well as the flesh, you'd make the wind whistle so fast for ten minutes that all the skulking flesheaters would give up and stand to howl at the sky."

Those taunts were more to Parade than the cruel nippings that drove him forward; and now, for the first time, the picture of his father began to loom in his eyes, growing greater and greater with time, a picture of a horse like a winged, golden flame. Pride and blood kept Parade running through those three days, until the wolves slunk away and their angry voices rang with hollow echoes down a long ravine, to say that they had surrendered the contest.

Parade would have fallen, but Mischief put her shoulder against him so that he could stand; well she knew that, once down, the ice on the ground and the ice in the wind would soon freeze the blood that ran in her son.

A week after that, the spring came suddenly, and the first great ordeal had ended. It left Parade with a gaunt belly, a roached back, and a coat shaggy and weather-faded. But it left him all hammered steel in body and in spirit.

That year the grass was good, the water holes were freshened by many rains, and Parade grew with wonderful speed. They picked up a few of the wild strays, willing enough to follow the leadership of the wise mare, Mischief; and again the herd was the salvation of the mare and her foal, for when the horse hunters came with their rifles, Mischief and Parade were always first away, and the rifles did their work on the rearmost members of the band.

It was at this same time that the legend began of a young stallion, a mere yearling, that ranged through the Sierra Blanca with the beauty of a golden thunderbolt. That legend grew. Old prospectors forgot their quest when they heard of it; old cattlemen looked with squinted eyes at the picture that formed far off in their minds; and many a boy on the range planned against the future when he might ride a peerless horse.

By winter, the band had been dispersed once more. Again Mischief and Parade went lonely through the season of ice that was beating the colt with white hammers into the metal that was to make him lord of the range.

When he was a two-year-old, men began to hunt him, not with rifles but with relays of fast horses.

A wild hawk flies better than any tame-bred one because it has to live for twenty hours a day on the wing, and Parade was running constantly. No trainer of horses would have dared to work a colt as the hunters in the Sierra Blanca worked that fugitive.

That autumn, Hammersley, the English rancher, brought up three dozen horses and eight riders, and worked Parade for a month. Mischief had to turn out of the way. He ran for the first time alone; and for a month his keen ears, his blazing eyes, and above all, his sense of smell, keener than the nostrils of a wolf, studied all that lay between him and the horizon. And fear crept beside him, rose like a ghost out of the ground, became such a familiar presence that it no longer sapped his strength or filled his lungs with a breath of icy mist. He had been tested a hundred times, and always he had won. Confidence was born. He had the wariness of a grizzly, that wisest animal, but he had the courage of a grizzly, too.

So he endured Hammersley's famous running, about which men will tell you still, yonder in the Sierra Blanca, and wherever celebrated horse hunts are talked about. For a month, Parade stood off every challenge and then was able to leave the dispirited hunters and go free.

They had lost one man, killed instantly by a fall from a mustang which put its foot into a hole. They lost five horses; three because of broken legs received in the frantic races through the mountains, one through sheer heartbreak of fatigue, and another so worn to the bone that it was not worth while to drag the poor brute out of the desert.

Afterward, legend increased those losses, multiplying them by three. Men said that Hammersley had spent twenty thousand dollars on the hunt. Parade became a lodestar to attract every lover of great horseflesh.

When the Hammersley hunt ended, Parade went up the Wainwright Valley, found his mother and went off with her.

That was only the beginning of things.

Half a dozen outfits tried for Parade the next year. The most celebrated effort was that of Wilton Parker and Champ Rainey, who clung to the task for six weeks, with an army of horses and a small host of expert riders and ropers.

They failed, for Parade had learned and mastered the most difficult lesson of all, which is that a hunted horse must not run in a circle, but in a straight line. They might start him in a curve, and herd him into it for a time, but eventually he recognized the circle and broke away like a hawk across the horizon. Then they had to plan on his probable lines of retreat, and place relays of horses and hunters along them. It was during this year that Joseph C. Curry ran Parade a hundred miles with eleven relays, and killed six good horses on the way, but Parade escaped with a greater fame than ever. And about this time some of the men on the range began to declare that Parade would never be taken. The best brains had been used against him, yet he always escaped, always with greater and greater ease.

Also, half a dozen fine marksmen started out, in the fall of this year, letting it be known that they would attempt to crease the stallion, since he could be captured in no other way. To crease a horse is to shoot a bullet across the nape of the neck, jarring the spinal column sufficiently to stun the animal; but for one horse captured in this way, a hundred are killed. And Sheriff Tom Crawford published far and wide the fact that with his own rifle he would "crease" the man who shot the famous stallion dead. The creasing experts, at that, gave up their attempt.

Parade's name was known far and wide by this time. Newspapers had taken him up as front page material. Travelers from distant lands begged to be brought within eyeshot of the famous horse. But even this was becoming more and more difficult. He and Mischief had learned how to hide themselves like foxes; they had learned the value of making hundred-mile marches from one good grazing place to another.

And then calamity began. It was not the fault of Parade, but the weakness of Michief, that brought the final great trouble on them in the same year when Parade began to be called the "Hundred-thousand-dollar horse."

7 – The Great Enemy

THAT winter was given a spark of excitement by poor Hammersley's second great attempt to catch the golden stallion whose beauty had become a devouring fire of his mind. Hammersley was being ruined by his prolonged horse hunting. It was not so much the money he spent on the task as the way his ranch went to ruin during his absences, for everyone he trusted was taking advantage of the placid, good-natured Englishman. Hammersley hunted Parade for three furious weeks of effort during the cold season, only to find that his well-shod horses could do no better over the frozen ground than could the bare hoofs of the stallion. Mischief, as usual, was simply shunted to the side, and the hunt flew past her, but Parade could not be taken.

In the spring, Parker and Joe Curry combined. They tried a new project, which was to starve Parade with a water famine by fencing off all of the water holes over a considerable district, using tough barbed wire for the task. When the holes were fenced, Curry and Parker made the rounds eagerly and found three of the fences broken down in a singular manner. The horses had not been able to handle the barbed wire, of course, but they had worked at the slender posts, usually of crooked mesquite wood, until one or two of the posts went down. Then the fence was soon flat.

Once Mischief and her son learned the system, a barbed wire fence was no more than a trifle to them, unless the posts were big and sunk deep in firm ground. So that laborious effort on the part of Curry and Parker became history, and the legend of the golden stallion grew more formidable than ever. The time had come when tens of thousands of ardent sympathizers prayed that the great horse would never be captured. And at that very time, trouble was preparing for Parade, a mysterious and unexpected danger.

35

It came about in this way. He and Mischief had gone to the northern limits of the range of the Sierra Blanca, not by chance, but because they were taken with a longing for the grass which grew rank and heavy on the slopes of the hills that reached like fingers into the desert. Here were scrub trees, too, and masses of shrubbery whose green tips made delectable provender to the tough palates of the desert-bred horses. Sometimes the pair ventured to remain among those pleasant foothills for as much as a a week at a time, though as a rule caution made them change their place of residence after a two- or three-day halt.

They had come up off the sands to relish this earthly paradise; in half an hour they had cropped an abundant meal of the long, rather salty grass. They had drunk deep at a rivulet of cold, pure water, and then began to pluck at the green, tender sprouts that tipped the branches. Mischief lifted her wise head, after a few moments, and snorted.

"Do you find that scent in the air?" she asked.

"I do," said Parade. "As foul as a dead body; nothing but a buzzard could like it!"

"Yes, a buzzard," said Mischief, "or the Great Enemy, or a bear."

"The Enemy?" said Parade. "Will Man like such a thing as that?"

"All meat eaters are foul," said the mare, "and even if you know very little about the matter, you understand that Man is a meat eater."

"That is true," said Parade, "but I can't understand it."

"You are young, my son," said Mischief, looking over the bronze and rippling strength of the stallion, "and you must learn that that which is not understood is always strange, but the horse of much understanding is the lord of the herd. The horse that cannot understand, at least should be silent. There was your father, Parade. He was a king of horses. I shall never see his like again. But he understood that it was best in everything to defer to my experience, and that was why he led the herd gloriously for the time he was with it. As for understanding that Man could enjoy such a scent as that one yonder, let me tell you the fact. Man himself puts out those horrible odors in order to attract the four-footed meat eaters—wolves and bears. I have smelled it before, and there is always a trap near it!"

She began to work cautiously up the wind, with Parade moving beside her, a little to the rear. Now that age had dulled the edge of her speed, she liked nothing better than to show off her superior experience. She moved like a cat, her knees bending with readiness to spring to one side or the other. And Parade kept one bright eye on her movements, the other on the ground they passed over.

Presently, she paused.

"There's the bush that the smell has been put on by Man. What a stench! And somewhere near us there is sure to be a trap."

She pawed lightly at the sand in front of her. A bright thing leaped up out of the ground. A huge mouth had opened, and powerful teeth clanked together—a jaw without body or head, a very incarnation of evil!

The thing lay still on the ground, now. Parade had covered a hundred yards in the twinkling of an eye, but the whinny of his mother called him back. He came prancing and dancing, feathering himself on tiptoe.

"That is the trap," said the mare calmly. As a matter of fact, she was trembling inwardly with excitement, thinking how close that terrible engine had come to her foot.

"Mother," said Parade, "there is more courage in you than in a whole herd, and more wisdom in you than in twenty old mares whom time has eaten away like the mange."

"Well, well," said Mischief contentedly, "there is very little wisdom in the management of this world, I fear, but after all, I dare say that it is wisdom that makes courage bright. Not that I should be saying such things of myself. But it is a cruel pupil that denies credit to a teacher, and experience has taught me, my son. There is a sample of the work of the Great Enemy. You can see what it would do."

"It would smash the leg of a wolf. It must be meant for a bear," said Parade, snuffing at the thing from a distance, staring at it with his great, bright eyes.

"Yes, for a bear," said Mischief. "And one day a bear would have stepped into it, perhaps, and then there would have been a crashing and smashing and a roaring and snarling, until the hills trembled."

"I would like to see such a thing," said Parade. "The cunning devils have eaten enough horseflesh!"

"Aye," said the mare. "There is a living brain in the forefoot of a grizzly. It is delicate enough to pick a small grub out of rotten wood; but it is also strong enough to smash in the ribs of a grown horse. Well, if men are near enough to have set this trap, it is time for us to leave this place."

She started to swing around.

"Back up! Back up!" exclaimed Parade. "Put down your hoofs where you stepped before or—"

"So?" said Mischief angrily. "Has the time come when you are to start teaching your mother what—"

The ground seemed to lift to meet her right forefoot, as she spoke. She sprang back on three legs; to the fourth clung a naked pair of iron jaws like that which already had been snapped shut. But this time the trap had closed with only a horrible crunching sound.

Mischief did not struggle, but a sweat of agony spotted her neck and her flanks. She bowed her head and sniffed at the engine that clutched her. Behind the jaws appeared a heavy chain, lying snakelike upon the ground.

"Go, my son," said the mare. "They have taken me now."

"I shall never leave you," said Parade, all dark and shining in a moment with sweat. "I shall stay here——"

"And be caught with a rope and be turned into a slave?" exclaimed Mischief. "As for me, I am old. I have no great time left to me. Besides, this is only a right judgment. I have been proud, and, therefore, I was blind. Age ought to kill pride before it kills the body, but I have remained as high-headed as a young filly in her second spring. Parade, leave me. Will it be a comfort to me to pass under the saddle and bridle again and know that you are suffering with me? What? You haven't felt spurs! Listen to me and don't be a fool."

A quiet rustling approached them, no louder than the small sound of a wind that walks among green leaves. From among the shrubbery appeared the clumsy body of a grizzly bear, with a vast rounded head, and the wrinkles of wisdom cut deep between the eyes.

Mischief, with a groan of fear, lunged back. The long chain rattled out its length and then held firm. The mare sank on her haunches.

"My son!" she neighed.

Parade sprang before her. He seemed ready to hurl himself at that formidable monster, that creature made for war.

The grizzly stood up with its paws held together, very like a prize fighter stuffing his hands deeper into the gloves.

"A little closer, my son," growled the bear, and his red eyes shifted in his head. A drool of saliva dripped from a corner of his mouth.

"Away from him!" commanded the mare. "He looks clumsy, but he can charge like a rock jumping down hill, and with one stroke he can smash in your skull!"

Parade drew back, slowly, unwillingly.

The bear dropped forward on all fours, with a rolling motion, at once wonderfully clumsy and with the grace of infinite strength.

"Horse meat," said the grizzly, "is good for a working bear. This bit looks old and tough, but there will be a few tender places along the back. And if a fool has a soft heart, then hers should make good eating!"

He waddled closer to Mischief. With a dull eye of despair, she saw destruction approaching. Parade, in futile agony, galloped around and around them, while a cloud of dust rolled upward toward the sky. All that ground might be sowed with traps, but in his frenzy he forgot. If he could dart in and strike with his forehoofs—but he knew that the paws of the grizzly were a subtle pair of thunderbolts from which he could not escape.

Mischief lurched to her feet, suddenly, as though she wished to take her death standing.

"And what a fool you were," said the grizzly, "to walk on ground where a bear feared to tread. But it will soon be over now. There is one lesson that every fool must learn, in the end, and that's the lesson that I'm about to teach you. This is a lucky day. I've almost forgotten horse meat—and here it is in a fine lump for me! I would rather have a colt half your size, madame, but I shan't look a gift horse in the mouth."

"Parade! Away!" neighed the mare suddenly. "They're coming from behind you."

The stallion looked back, and he saw three riders galloping straight at him over the ridge of the hill. Terror sent him away in a bright golden streak.

Behind him, he saw the grizzly scuttling off with a speed wonderful for such a loosely jointed body. He heard the rifles clang like sledge-hammers beating together, face to face. He saw the bear halt, turn, and charge in. He saw it pause again, and slump slowly to the ground. Then the dust of his own raising veiled the picture from the eyes of Parade.

He ran on, and he ran alone. He would run forever alone, he felt. The Sierra Blanca became suddenly more lofty and more vast, and he shrank to a lonely speck that crawled aimlessly across it and trailed behind a little wisp of dust.

8 – Reunion

IT WAS Dave Larchmont, cattle king, horse breeder, and great hunter, who took the pelt off the dead grizzly, and then led Mischief limping to his ranch. It looked as though that torn foreleg would never heal properly, and he would have killed the mare, but he had recognized that streak of golden lightning which had dashed away from the scene. The mother of Parade was worth having, even if she could only stand on three legs. If she could give the world one foal like the famous stallion, might she not give another, and another?

He took Mischief back to his ranch, not far from Parmalee, and straightway his place was deluged with visitors. They came in floods, with cameras. The corral where Mischief stood was constantly surrounded. Not that she filled the eye more than many other horses, but because an aroma, a glamour of great romance, clung to this mother of Parade, this companion of his many adventures.

Her wound healed. She could walk, trot, canter, and even run, but at every gait she limped, and she would always limp. The tendons had been frayed by the steel teeth of the trap, and now they were drawn a vital bit shorter.

Big Harry Richmond, fatter of body, more like a great blue crane than ever, came and stared at her, and with him came Charlie Moore. He was close to sixty now, but it was not the passing of the years that had suddenly turned his hair white. Grief had done it, and the knowledge that he was still bound inexorably to Richmond.

"It's comin' close to the end, Charlie," said Richmond. "Now they've got Mischief, they'll be gettin' hold of Parade one of these days. And there'll be a lot of whoopin' then. Larchmont," he said to the other rancher, "look at the way she's marchin' up and down that fence, lookin' out at the evenin' as it

40

comes over the hills. You reckon she's lookin' for Parade, too? You reckon that he might show up, one of these days?"

Larchmont shrugged his shoulders.

"You been hearin' a lot of talk about that Parade horse," he said. "You got him all built up. Think he'd have the sense to come all the way down here from the Sierra Blanca? Even if he had the sense, think he'd have the nerve? No, sir, that Parade knows enough to be scared of men, and he's goin' to stay on his own campin' grounds, where he knows the howl of every wolf and the hoot of every owl. He ain't no miracle horse, Richmond."

But that same evening, Parade came over the naked hills toward Parmalee.

He moved like a soldier who has passed inside the lines of the enemy; and, in fact, all around him there were signs of the Great Enemy, and the scent of iron was never out of his nostrils. Half a dozen times, before this, he had ventured farther and farther over the trail by which Mischief had been taken from his ken. He knew how it pointed, and now he was determined to follow it to the end.

But every step was a mighty peril to him. On the trail there was the smell of iron from the hoofs of shod horses. Iron again breathed at him, new or rusted, from the fences. And through the air came the scent of such food as the flesh eaters could relish, mingled with smoke, and again the poisonous breath of hot iron.

There was iron everywhere. The stain of it filled the air. And then again he would pass a huge barn, a dark blotchy outline in the distance, out of which the wind carried to him such fragrances as must be found in the heaven of horses: the sweetness of sun-cured hay, and delights that Parade could guess at but could not know.

He went on at a trot or a swinging lope, most of the time, only slowing to a walk when the way led too close to a dwelling of man. And so he came across the hollow and up to the horse corral of Dave Larchmont.

There were full thirty head of mares and young colts in that corral now. Mischief stayed there alone, during the day, in order that the curious might satisfy their eyes by gazing upon her; but at night, all the best of the grazing saddle stock was herded back to this place of security. Dave Larchmont had invested many thousands of dollars in working up that nucleus of a saddle string which was to be the delight and wonder of the range. He could not afford to let horses worth five hundred a throw wander abroad, where careless fellows might "borrow" them here and there.

He penned them up at night, and let one cowpuncher ride night herd over them.

Parade, from the deep darkness of the hollow, saw that rider pass and repass, and his strength of will loosened in him. He studied the wind that blew to

him from the crowd in the corral, but there were too many conflicting scents
for him to pick out Mischief from the lot. Only a premonition, an instinct,
warned him that she might be there.

He whinnied. It was a mere whicker, a shadowy whisper of sound. Out
of the entangled shadows of the corralled horses, it brought one form that
moved rapidly up and down the line of the fence.

Now he knew for certain that Mischief was there. The rider passed. He
paused on the farther side of the corral to roll a cigarette, and as he smoked,
he sang, softly, as a good puncher will do when he rides night herd; and as
he sang, he looked toward the yellow-lighted window through which the
murmuring voices of his companions drifted, as they sat at their poker game.
Chance can play cruel tricks, but none so evil as when it sends out into the
night a fellow who has plenty of money in his wallet when a poker game is
at hand!

Parade, in the meantime, went up the slope like a great cat, with the stars
striking dull sparks out of his lustrous coat. Mischief followed him down the
inner side of the fence. There were eight feet of that fence, and the bars were
close, until they came to the gate, which was built of far lighter stuff, so that it
could be handled more easily. Not because it was a gate, but because the bars
here were farther apart, Parade paused, and thrust his head between them, and
touched the tremulous muzzle of Mischief.

"Be quiet—hush! There is a man on guard," said Mischief. "And he carries
a gun, which you know about, and a rope, also. He will be at you like a
mountain lion, if he guesses that you are here. Oh, my son, I have told the
others that you would come. It is terribly rash of you, but love is greater than
mountains and stronger than rivers. What have you done since I left you?"

"I have been alone," said Parade. "I have been alone in the desert, afraid of
shadows that seemed to be dropping out of the sky. The Sierra Blanca is ten
times as great as before, and I am ten times as small. How has it been with you?"

"I am lamed," said Mischief. "I can run, but not as I ran before. Men come
every day and look at me. They speak a great deal in the voices which we
cannot understand. I am sad, but now I must pay for my pride and folly."

A tall colt with a great white blaze on his forehead came curiously toward
them.

"Go back!" commanded Mischief, swinging toward the interloper.

As the mare swung away from him, Parade pressed harder against the gate
to come nearer to her. The wood creaked and groaned. A sudden sense of the
weakness of that barrier ran tingling to his brain. One thrust might down the
gate; one effort might set the door wide for his mother.

The guard had heard the sound.

"Halloo! Halloo!" he called. "Steady, boys! Don't crowd that gate, you fools!"

He started his horse at a gallop, and came swinging around the corral. Parade could see the hat and the head sailing past the horizon stars.

Should he recoil, and bound down the slope of loosened rock? He snorted with the desperation of fear and hope commingled, and with one thrust of his shoulder he burst the fragile lock of the gate. It swung in, and before Parade himself had recovered, Mischief was through the gap. Not she alone, but the tall colt with the white blaze followed, and Parade, as he turned and shot down the slope, sent his mighty neighing blowing like a red flag to call the others.

They came, for in that neigh there was the promise of freedom, the defiance of masters, the whole band of Dave Larchmont's chosen horses burst through the gateway and hustled down the slope after their leader.

Right at them, from the flank, charged the guard.

He had drawn a revolver and was firing it repeatedly into the air to give the alarm. His wild shouts rang back to the house, and brought the other punchers in a fury of haste.

But they were far too late. By the time they had saddled their commoner horseflesh from the other corral, the stream of the liberated was pouring far off toward the Sierra Blanca.

The cowpuncher vainly spurred behind them. He was able to overtake Mischief, but what was she, compared with the fortune in horseflesh which was streaming away into the night? Desperately he rode, but when the dawn came, he had merely succeeded in tracing the fugitives to the edge of the desert.

There he paused because his mustang was exhausted. And far off to the north of him, Mischief jogged contentedly on. She knew where to find her son, and in the Wainwright Valley, sure enough, she discovered him before noon of that day, with such a herd gathered around him as never another wild stallion ever was lord over.

Up and down ranged Parade, eying his new possessions, mastering them with a kingly eye, and keeping a wary lookout for the dangers that would surely come rolling over the horizon before long. When Mischief came, he went to greet her, and they moved together up and down.

He exulted: "Men are not the great masters, after all. They can be met. They can be beaten. I have beaten them, mother!"

She quaked as though a strong wind had cut at her.

"You saw how they put teeth in the ground, teeth that will bite though there is nobody behind them? Ah, well, there would be no fools, except that

they rejoice in their folly! My son, I have told you of the danger in the tooth
of the rattlesnake, and the wiles by which a wolf will hamstring the greatest
stallion in the world, and the cunning of a hawk in the air, and the wisdom
of an otter in a stream filled with fish, but now I tell you that all of these
are nothing compared with man. I have felt his hot iron burn into my skin.
Twice he has reached into the wild desert and taken me. Will you still be a
fool and rejoice in your folly?"

For answer, Parade neighed loud and long.

Every head among the stolen horses snapped up from the grazing; every
eye shone with new brightness, turning toward the master.

"Do you see?" said Parade. "They are mine! And they can run over the
ground like birds gliding down the sky. When the horse hunters come, how
will they be able to catch such horses as these, with your wits to give us the
warning, and my heels to show the herd the proper way? We have been
wandering like foolish little hunted things. Now we can live like lords of
the earth!"

9 – The Rodeo Race

IT WAS not long after this, far south from the Sierra Blanca, far south from Parmalee, that the horses lined up for a rodeo race. There was not much of a purse to be run for, but the betting was high. Nearly every cowpuncher in that section of the country had put up all he had; guns had been sold and spurs pawned to raise cash, and all around the little half-mile track there were tense spectators.

A dozen horses had lined up for the start. There was a long, low mare from the Indian country, and she had her share of betting; there was a dappled gray out of the Pecos region, a picture-horse that made many a cowpuncher reach for his wallet; and among the rest there was a brown stallion, rather time-worn, his hip bones thrusting up at sharp angles. Nevertheless, at least half the money had been bet on him, for that was Brandy and on his back was the meager body and the ape-like face of Lake, the half-breed.

Upon Lake and the stallion, one man stared with a peculiar intensity of interest. He forgot the race impending, he forgot the fluttering flags, he forgot the lowing of cattle in the distance. Suddenly the sun seemed to press on him with a greater heat. He took off his sombrero to wipe his face, and showed the features of a man who might be anywhere from twenty-five to thirty years of age, with a spot of gray hair over each temple. As he settled the hat back on his head, a man near him said:

"What you pick, stranger? My money's on the gray. I never seen such a hoss."

"If looks could win, he has the race before it starts," agreed Silvertip. "But looks won't beat Brandy—not if he gets an honest ride."

"Honest ride?" said the other. "You think that that half-breed would—"

45

The starting gun tore that sentence off short. The yell of the cowpunchers seemed to strike the sky and fly back from it in echoes. Madness of joy and hope set the watchers dancing. Only Silvertip remained aloof from the excitement, with the faint smile touching the corners of his mouth and his glance wandering calmly from face to face of the spectators, with hardly a glance at the racers.

The old melancholy had suddenly dropped on him in the midst of all this turmoil. These were men who wanted to win. To lose their money would be almost like losing their blood. Their eyes were wolfish, their nostrils flared. They struck at the air with their fists, or with open hands they pulled on invisible wires to draw their favorites forward in the race.

But Silvertip stood outside of all this. He had put down fifty dollars on Brandy as a mere gesture. He had a little silver outside of that sum, and that was all. But he was still more interested in the people than in the race. And, as he glanced from man to man, he was wishing with all his might that he could commit himself so utterly to a moment and lose every other thought.

It was a good moment for Silver, in a sense, for he was able to probe deeply into the minds around him, while they were regardless of his eyes; it was an evil moment in that it made him realize, more than ever, the strange gulf that separated him from other men. And suddenly he told himself, through his teeth, that if he could not gain an interest in any other way, he would resort to crime. There, at least, one could be assured of sufficient excitement to stir the blood.

People began to shout the name of Brandy. Silver saw that the field had completed the first round of the track and that they were well along the second and last lap, with Brandy running second to the gray stallion from the Pecos. Easily the long strides of Brandy covered the ground; he seemed to slide along as though he were the shadow trailed by a kite.

But in spite of the ease of his striding, he did not gain on the gray. And now the mare, the long, low-built mare, came streaking up on the outside. The stallion drew ahead. The gray and the mare fought nose to nose, while Brandy dropped gradually back.

A wail of dismay broke upward from the crowd; when men groan, they lift their heads.

"He's too old; he's worn out; Brandy's done for!" men were saying around Silvertip, but Silvertip knew better.

He had seen the pull of the half-breed, something more than that weight on the reins which steadies a horse and helps it to stretch out to full speed. Now the whip flashed into Lake's hand. It rose and fell methodically, while with his left hand Lake jerked at the reins. One would have thought that he was working with all his might to get the utmost out of Brandy, but the keen eye of Silvertip saw that those pulls on the reins were exactly timed to unbalance the stridings of Brandy. More rapidly he fell to the rear. Four horses in a cluster swept up and past him.

And then a dull heat began near the heart of Silvertip. It spread through his body. It flushed his face. It burned in his brain. This was not the first time that he had seen Lake at one crooked trick or another, but to cheat a horse seemed much more horrible than to cheat a man.

The gray stallion and the mare, still running head to head, rounded into the stretch. A furlong off, down the straightaway, was the finish, and both riders went to the whip.

Far, far back, was Brandy, but coming again as if with a second wind—a cunning trick on the part of Lake to give himself a chance honestly to ride out a horse that he himself had hopelessly beaten in the course of the running.

A yell ripped into the ear of Silvertip, the harsh, sudden outcry of many astonished men. Something had happened, and it was to Brandy. The right-hand rein had broken away at the bit, and, no longer troubled by the pull of his jockey, Brandy came up the track as if on wings. He rounded the sharp corner at the head of the stretch, swinging wide to clear the cluster of horses which was struggling there.

They fell behind. The track seemed to flow back against them, carrying them to the rear. Only Brandy it allowed to speed ahead.

Lake was no longer using his whip. It would have been like flogging an avalanche.

But far away, the gray stallion and the long mare were fighting toward the finish. Now the head of the gray began to bob. The mare shot ahead. Victory brightened the eyes of her rider.

Then the thundering of the crowd gave him warning as the chorus shouted for Brandy. There came the stallion on the outside, with enormous strides. The rider of the mare yelled with fear. The mare strained to her utmost under the rapid cutting of the whip. Very different was that picture from the sight of Lake, clinging to his place with a distorted face, one hand twisted into the flying mane of the stallion.

They seemed to strike the finish line at the same instant, though Brandy was immediately half a length ahead before the pair began to ease up. Perhaps that was what influenced the judges, and the name of Brandy was posted as winner.

The favorite had won, and so had Silvertip, but he collected his bet with an abstracted air. Drifting to the verge of the group that was packed around Brandy, he heard Lake explaining in a sullen voice:

"He kind of sulked. He dodged it all the way through the start. Then he got hold and run away on me. I never seen such a fool hoss."

How much had Lake and Harry Richmond stood to win by pulling Brandy in that race—wondered Silvertip. What had been the life of the fine horse during these years? Unless he was very much mistaken in horseflesh, long ago Brandy's name should have been among the winners of some of the great Eastern stakes; but still he seemed unknown, except in the pickup races of Western rodeos and fairs.

Silver drifted with the crowd, afterward. He was not a part of the rejoicing. All life seemed flat and savorless to him. The only fire that burned in him was one of steady horror that such a horse as Brandy should be in such hands as those of the half-breed and the crooked rancher, Richmond.

Silvertip was not drinking. He was merely wandering with the crowd, preoccupied. He had one pleasant surety, which was that in this place he would not be recognized. But even in that he was wrong, for a man with a square, lined face came up to him and tapped him on the arm.

"My name's Dodgson," said he. "I'm the sheriff of this county. I know you, Silvertip, and I wanta say that I'm watchin' you. If there's any gun play in this town, self-defense ain't goin' to be worth anything for you to talk about."

He gave Silvertip a glimpse of his badge, and went on.

Silvertip, in disgust, turned into the first big saloon and took a whisky at the bar. Men were crowding up to the rail. Voices were shouting. Half of that crowd was already drunk, and their jolly condition seemingly was envied by the other half. But the liquor was no more than a sourness in the throat of Silver, a foul smoke in his brain.

He passed on into the big back room where a dozen groups sat at the tables, playing poker; the half-breed, Lake, was at one of them. The sight of him made the jaw muscles of Silvertip bulge. He came near, but not too near. He saw the progress of the game at once, and that all the flow of money was toward Lake. In ten minutes, one of the men pushed back his chair and slammed down the cards with such violence that one of them skidded into the air and dropped near the feet of Silver. The latter picked it up.

"It's no good," said he who had risen. "I've seen more cards here than I ever seen before in a whole night, but I can't win. It ain't my day, and I'm licked and busted. So long, boys!"

"Wait a minute," said the voice of Silvertip.

He approached, holding the blue-backed card which had fallen to the floor. On the back of it was what he had expected—a faint blue smudge, almost indistinguishable to an inexperienced eye, and located half way between one corner of the card and the center of it. The card itself was a jack, and it was not hard to guess that every honor card in the pack had been similarly marked by Lake, by this time. Perhaps the entire pack was tampered with, and to the half-breed it would be as if the faces of the other hands were turned toward him.

"Wait for what?" asked the man who had left the game.

Lake, twisting about in his chair, saw Silvertip and turned a yellow-green. Fascinated, he watched while Silver threw the card back onto the table.

"Wait for Lake," said Silvertip. "You don't want to carry the joke any further than this, Lake," he added. And to the other bewildered players he went on. "He takes a hand with the boys, now and then, but nobody ever loses through him."

"What's all this lingo mean?" demanded a fiery youth at the table.

"It means that Lake is shoving back the pile he's won, and leaving the game," said Silver. "That's all. Take your table stakes, and come along with me, Lake."

He saw the lips of the half-breed twist away from yellow teeth, but no words came. Then, selecting one stack of coins, Lake dropped them into his pocket, and stood up. His eyes were fighting those of Silvertip every instant.

"Is this gent a crook?" asked the youth of the party. "Is that why you're hooking him away, big boy?"

But Silver gave no answer.

"Walk ahead of me," he commanded Lake. "Go out the back door, and don't try to get away. The spots are still on that pack of cards. I suppose you've still got the crayons on you. And if I split your wishbone for you, nobody will care a bit."

10 – Silvertip's Discovery

THEY stood between the back of the saloon and a woodshed, with a pair of dusty-leaved cactus plants nearby. Lake was shaking like a bulldog that wants to hurl itself at a jungle tiger, despite all differences of size and fighting talents. But if the red fury was in his eyes, the green sickness of terror was in his face. The greatness of his emotion made his voice and his entire body tremble.

"There was twenty thousand bucks in that game," he groaned. "I could a' had the whole of it. It was the best chance that I ever had, and I could a' had the whole of it! I'm goin' to have the heart out of you for this!"

"Why don't I march you back inside?" demanded Silvertip, looking Lake over calmly. "Why don't I take you back inside and show the boys the smudges on the backs of those cards?"

The half-breed was silent. But as he breathed, his nostrils kept working in and out like the nostrils of a panting horse, and the muscles of his ugly, frog-like face kept pulling at, and distorting his features.

"I brought you out here to get some information out of you," said Silvertip. "The last I saw of you, you were trying to steal Brandy. How does that happen?"

"Ask Harry Richmond," snarled Lake.

Silvertip smiled at him, and then made a cigarette. It was very dangerous business, for Lake had been tormented to the point of madness, and as he saw both the hands of Silver occupied, his own hands jumped and jerked several times in the direction of the guns that he wore under his coat. Yet something held him back; an invisible thread bound his strength and kept him helpless; with every moment the mastery of Silvertip grew more complete.

He was saying: "I won't ask Richmond. I'm asking you. What happened after Brandy got away?"

"Richmond hunted him, and old Charlie Moore caught him."

"Charlie still owns half the horse?"

"No. He gave up his half because Richmond made a big job gettin' Brandy back."

"Richmond made the big job of it, and Charlie caught the horse, eh?"

"Yeah. That's it."

"What did Charlie get out of it?"

"He got a chance to groom Brandy every day and talk baby talk to him, and feed him, and set on the edge of the manger and rub his nose."

"That's what he got out of it?"

"Yeah. He's a fool. But that ain't my business."

"What happened to Brandy then?"

"I took him East, and we put him into a coupla races."

"You took him East? Then Richmond arranged with you to try to steal him, before that?"

"I dunno nothin' about that," said Lake sullenly.

The eyes of Silvertip shrank to points of brightness.

"Did Brandy win his races?" he asked presently.

"Yeah. He won a coupla. He was goin' good."

"What happened then?"

"He got off his feed, or somethin'. He quit winnin'."

"He couldn't win at all?"

"The dirty crooks, they went and double-crossed us! They throwed Richmond and me and Brandy clean off the tracks. Just when we were ready to haul in the big dough, they ruled us off."

"Because you pulled Brandy in a race?" suggested Silvertip. "Because you bet against him, and pulled him in a race, eh?"

"He was off his feed," muttered Lake.

The faint smile of Silver twisted at one corner of his mouth only. "You threw away your big chance, eh?" said he. "You wanted the quick money—the dirty money. You got one taste of it, and you threw away your chance of the long green, and you threw away Brandy's chance of becoming a famous horse. Ever since that time, you've been dodging around the country, racing Brandy under different names at little rodeos and country fairs. Is that the story?"

"You think you know everything," growled Lake. "What's the good of me tryin' to tell you anything?"

"What a dirty, sneaking lot you are!" said Silvertip calmly. "Where's Moore now?"

"I dunno where the old fool is. Somewhere singin', I guess, because Brandy won the race."

"He wouldn't have won if you'd had your way," observed Silvertip. "I suppose you and Richmond lost a good deal of coin today, betting against your horse?"

The face of Lake worked. He made no other answer.

"And where would Charlie be?" insisted Silvertip.

"I dunno. Out in the sheds at the rodeo grounds, maybe, coolin' off Brandy. Always takes the old fool two or three hours to cool off Brandy after a race. Cool him off and rub him down. You'd think that old skate was a pack of diamonds, the way Charlie works over him."

That was why Silvertip went back to his horse, mounted, and returned to the rodeo grounds. Everyone else had left. It was nearly sunset, and the golden waves of light that rolled across the earth showed only the white head of Charlie Moore, as he walked back and forth, followed by Brandy.

There was no halter on the stallion, but he kept his head close to the left shoulder of his handler all the time. Now that the saddle was off him, he seemed to Silvertip older and more timeworn than ever. Still, he was a horse in ten thousand, with a certain lordliness about even his walking gait.

When Charlie Moore saw Silver, he cried out in a loud voice, and came running; the stallion trotted softly behind him. A moment later, Silver was on the ground, shaking hands.

"All these here years—doggone my soul!" said Charlie Moore. "Where you been, Silvertip?"

"I've been here and there," said Silver.

"I know," said Moore. "We get rumors and whispers, now and then. It ain't newspaper stuff. But sometimes we run into a gent that starts talkin' about a big gent that he knew, somewhere down in Mexico, or up in Alaska, or off in the South Seas, or down in Nicaragua, say. And he'll tell a terrible yarn about what the big gent done, and then he'll say there's a coupla gray spots in his hair."

"That's a lot of talk," said Silvertip. "I've been hearing from Lake a little of what you and Brandy have been through."

The face of Moore darkened.

"He could a' been a great stake hoss, Silver," he said huskily. "He could a' been one to have his picture in the papers, for a coupla years, and when he was retired to a stud farm, he would a' had visitors comin' to see him. He oughta be in a fine green pasture all to himself, and he oughta be eatin' the best oats, and nothin' to do for himself but pose for a camera, now and then. But they throwed him away, Silvertip. They throwed him away."

"He was ruled off, eh?" said Silver.

"It was at Aqueduct," said Charlie Moore. "He'd won a coupla times. The wise gents was watchin' him. They was timin' his moves in trainin'. Tips was beginnin' to float around about him. There was a kind of whisper in the air that a great hoss was on the track. And those crooks didn't want that—Lake and Richmond. They wanted to bring him on slow. They wanted to enter him in some big stake with long odds agin' him, and then they'd clean up and make a fortune. So they decided that they'd spoil his reputation by puttin' him in an overnight race and pullin' him. And they pulled him, all right.

"I ain't goin' to forget how I stood there and watched from the rail, and seen Brandy try to eat up that field and swaller it, and how Lake pulled him double and jammed him into a pocket, and brought him around on the outside, and jammed him into another pocket. And then he came again, with the bit in his teeth. And even the way he was rode, the winner only beat him by a head. And the stewards throwed the whole lot of us off the track. We couldn't race no more anywhere in the country, on a regular track. And since then, we been a lot of bums, travelin' from place to place. Lake handles us, and Richmond sends down a flock of money, now and then, to bet."

He turned away from Silvertip, a little, and let his hand wander over the face of the thoroughbred.

"We won today," said Moore, "but you seen how. And Richmond is goin' to be crazy mad. He must a' lost three or four thousand, because he bet agin' us."

He sighed, and added: "Where you bound now, Silver?"

"For the Sierra Blanca," said Silvertip. "I want to take a look at that Parade horse."

"There's a lot that's had a look at him, but there ain't any that's had a hand on him. There ain't goin' to be any, either. Not even you, Silver, I reckon, because now they're huntin' for him with guns."

"Guns?" cried Silvertip. "Hunting for him with guns, did you say?"

"He run off with the fine saddle stock of Dave Larchmont. Ain't you heard about that? There was ten or twelve thousand dollars' worth of stock in that outfit. They started chasin' him to get those hosses back. Dave has worked hard, but he runs more hosses to death than he catches. He caught up eight of 'em, at last, and he took 'em down and corraled 'em with Steve Barrett's hosses.

"And in the middle of the night, Parade come and busted down the fence, like he done at Larchmont's place, and he run off with Larchmont's nags, and all of Barrett's too, and they say he's got seventy head of good stock with him out there in the Sierra Blanca, now. Well, ranchers ain't goin' to stand for losses like that, so now they've put a thousand dollars on the scalp of Parade, and the boys are out with their rifles—bad luck to 'em!"

"It's not possible!" said Silvertip. "Nobody would do it. Not even for a thousand dollars. Why, Charlie, it's not in the game—it's not in the cards! Look here! Men started driving that horse—men started hunting him—they drove him for years—and now he's finding out how to hit back—and you mean to tell me they're going to use guns on him?"

Moore nodded. "There's gents alive," he said, "that would cut off an arm for a thousand bucks in cold cash. Don't you make no mistake about it! And they'll have the scalp of Parade, right enough."

"It's murder," said Silvertip quietly.

"Aye," said Charlie. "Murder pays pretty big, if you know the right gents to kill!"

That was how Silvertip started for the Sierra Blanca as fast as a good horse could take him.

When he reached Parmalee, he found talk of very little else in the air. All was news of the last outfits that were to try their hands at capturing the great stallion, or of the hunters who were going out singly, expert shots who carried high-power rifles to end the career of the horse.

Silvertip carried a rifle himself, but it was not to be used on horses, when he rode into the white-and-purple land of the Sierra Blanca.

He rode for four days, and then what he wanted to see came suddenly on his vision. He had hobbled his horse and slept out on a tarpaulin in the hollow corner of a small ravine, and he was wakened about dawn by the sound of hoofs thrumming rapidly over the ground, beating up musical echoes almost like the swift fingering of a tambourine.

So he sat up and saw for the first time in his life a sight that made his heart rush out in an ecstasy of delight. For there was a whole river of horses pouring down the ravine, and at their head ran a creature made of golden fire, a thing of blinding beauty. His trot kept the tide of horses at a gallop; when he swung into a flowing gallop, the others had to race to keep up. It seemed to Silvertip that the stallion barely touched the ground with his hoofs; it seemed to him that there was a beat of invisible wings, supporting and prolonging the striding of that monster. It was not by size but by magnificence that he dwarfed the retinue that poured behind him.

And afterward, when they were gone, Silver remained for a long time, staring before him. He had seen a kingly thing. All his being flowed outward with a desire to possess it.

This was what he had been searching for all his life, one object which he could desire with all his might. Battles with other men had not given him the ultimate thrill, the full madness of joy. In all his days he never had set his hands upon an object utterly capable of filling his heart. And now, at last, he had found it.

When he thought back to the picture that he had seen, it seemed to Silvertip that there had been only one horse running down the valley like a creature of molded flame, and behind the stallion had run futile little shadows.

He stood up and looked his own horse in the eye. It was a good, tough gelding, but it looked to Silvertip like a worthless rag of horseflesh.

He glanced around him at the immensity of the mountains. He felt that the game was lost before he commenced to play it. For that very reason, his heart swelled, and he set his teeth for the great endeavor.

11 – Desert Meeting

SILVERTIP rode sixty miles the next day. twice he came within rifle shot of the horse herd; once he saw in the distance the flash of a golden star, gliding rapidly across the earth. But these animals had become, by dint of constant flight, more wary than so many antelope. Each time he drew close, he heard the signal whinnying, faint and far; and then the herd dissolved into the distance and sent back to his ears only the subdued thunder of trampling hoofs.

He was not surprised by the difficulties. He would have been amazed had they been less. And the resolution of Silvertip hardened like steel when it is properly tempered in ice water.

It was close to evening when he saw smoke rising in a thin gesture across the sky. At the base of that smoke he found two men camped in a small mesquite tangle, with a muddy blotch of a waterhole near by. They gave him a wave of the hand and continued their cookery.

His gelding was thirsty enough to have drunk the filthy water as it stood, green scum and all. But Silvertip kept him back until a trench had been dug beside the water hole, a foot or so from the edge of it. Slowly that trench filled with liquid filtered through the intervening wall of sand, and out of that Silver let the weary horse drink its fill.

In the meantime, he took note that his was the first filter hole that had been dug beside the water, and that the little lump-headed mustangs of the other two men were hardly of the gear or type that would be expected to come within speaking distance of Parade. It was apparent that the two were on the trail of the great stallion; it was equally clear that they were hunting, not his body but his scalp.

With his gelding hobbled to feed on the wretched rags of grass that grew among the mesquite, Silvertip went over to the camp of the strangers.

They looked like brothers. They kept the hair on head and face conveniently short by means of clippers that had left the marks of their cutting. They wore, also, grease-blackened canvas coats, in spite of the heat of the desert evening; and they had bright, small, squinting eyes. One of them was cleaning his rifle. Silvertip sat down cross-legged and began to eat his supper.

They could have offered him some of their food, when they saw that he was chewing parched corn only. But it was only after a long interval that one of them said:

"There's a drop of coffee here. I'll give it to you. The rest of our chuck, we're goin' to need it, maybe."

"I don't want the coffee," said Silver. "On a trail like this, I want to cut right down to the essentials, for a beginning. Parched corn is good enough for me."

"Maybe a sage hen could live on that dead feed," said one of the bearded men. "It don't look human nor right nor nacheral, to me."

"It takes some chewing," said Silver. "That's all it needs."

"Look here," said the other man, "you're a long ways out to be havin' nothin' but that. You mean to say that you ain't got no bacon or salt or coffee or flour or nothin' like that along with you?"

"A man can travel a lot better light than he can loaded," answered Silver. "I'll stick to the corn till I catch my horse."

The two looked sharply at one another.

"What hoss you lost?" they asked.

"A chestnut stallion with black points," said Silvertip.

"He's lost a chestnut stallion, Chuck," said one of the men gravely.

"Yeah. With black points, Lefty," said "Chuck." He asked Silver: "You might be meanin' Parade?"

"That's the one," said Silvertip.

He looked away from the others, as though the sudden keenness of their eyes meant nothing to him. The sun was down. All the hollows were filled with blue dusk; a black mesa, rimmed with light, stood in the west, and out of the east marched purple headlands. Far above, like clouds in the sky, hung the white heads of the mountains.

"You say he's your hoss, partner?" asked Lefty, as he paused in the cleaning of his rifle.

"He's my horse," said Silvertip.

He saw the eyes of the others glint as they exchanged glances.

"Buy him or trade for him or breed him?" asked Chuck shortly.

"I looked at him," said Silvertip, "and he's mine."

Suddenly Lefty broke into laughter.

"He looked at Parade, and Parade belongs to him," said Lefty.

"Bought him with a look," said Chuck. "Cheap at the price, eh?"

"Dirt cheap," said Lefty. "What would you do if you had him, stranger? Show him to folks at a nickel a look?"

"When I catch him up," said Silvertip, "I'll know what to do with him, all right."

"Yeah—when you catch him up," said Lefty, sneering.

Chuck pointed.

"You usin' a one-hoss outfit to catch Parade?" he asked.

"That's my outfit," said Silvertip.

The two men looked at one another and broke into fresh laughter that ended suddenly, as though they were unused to the sound and it had startled them somewhat.

"There's some," said Chuck, "that've come up here into the Sierra Blanca with twenty men and fifty hosses, all to try and catch Parade, but they ain't caught him. Maybe you'll have better luck with one hoss. Maybe brains'll make up the difference.'

"Maybe they will," said Silvertip. "All I want is a chance."

He rose, having finished the munching of that difficult meal. From the dying fire he picked out a small stick of wood, the end of which was a glowing coal. He flung it far into the air, drew a Colt, and fired. A puff of sparks flared dimly in the evening light and died out. There was no sound of the wood striking lightly on the ground, afterward. Chuck and Lefty stared at one another.

"What's the idea of that?" asked Lefty suddenly, and with a changed voice.

"I have to keep my hand in, that's all," answered Silver. "There's likely to be trouble before me."

"You goin' to crease Parade? Is that your idea?" asked Lefty.

"No," said Silvertip. "That's not the idea. But the fact is that people tell me about a parcel of skunks who are out here in the Sierra Blanca hunting for Parade, not because they ever want to sit on his back, the way I do, but because they want the thousand-dollar reward that's been put on his head."

He paused, and put up his revolver. The silence was perfect, except that the fire crackled dimly.

"If you should run into anybody of that sort," said Silvertip, "you might tell 'em that the man who shoots Parade will have to shoot me afterward. Otherwise he won't have a chance to enjoy the thousand dollars he pulls down."

"You'd go after him, eh?" said Lefty.

"The way I'd go after a mad dog," agreed Silvertip. "I'd shoot him on sight, and no jury in this neck of the woods would ever convict me for doing it. Not to the man who kills my horse."

"What I ain't quite figured," said Chuck softly, "is just how you come to own Parade."

"I'll tell you how it happened," said Silvertip. "He was made for me, and now I've come to get him. That's the reason."

12 – The Pursuit

THERE was no plan in the mind of Silvertip any more than there is in the mind of a wolf when it settles to the long trail behind an elk, in winter; there was simply a consuming hunger that drove him on. He got sixty miles a day out of his gelding, for six days. Then he saw that the limit of endurance had been reached, and he abandoned the animal in a spot where there was both good water and good grass. The saddle had to stay behind, of course, and so did everything else of weight, except the main essentials. These were a forty-foot manila rope of the closest weave, a quantity of parched corn, a bridle, a Colt with a few rounds of ammunition.

The heavy gun would have been left behind, also, but Silver had to keep in mind the statement which he had made to Lefty and Chuck. By the grace of fortune, they might have spread the news of his threat far and wide, by this time; and in the Sierra Blanca the law is thinner than the clear mountain air. It might well be that some of the headhunters would combine to drop down upon him and wipe him out, before they went ahead with their hunting of the stallion.

Many men, of course, were crossing and recrossing the desert on the trail of the famous horse; but no one before had been mad enough to attempt the pursuit on foot.

He walked fifty miles the first day, in his narrow riding boots. After a five-hour halt for sleep, he could not force his bleeding, swollen feet back into the boots.

He cut them up and tied the pair of leather soles under his feet, as sandals. They made wretched footgear. His feet overlapped the narrow soles; blisters began to rise. But he tramped forty miles that day, and came right up with the herd in the dusk of the evening. He was a scant hundred yards from the outskirts of the horses before the alarm sounded.

They went away like a flock of geese volleying through the air. Behind them, from the left, the golden stallion swept across the rear, brushing the stragglers before him; and to the dazed eyes of Silvertip it seemed that fire flew from the feet of the horse.

Into the gathering night they charged, and Silvertip went on, in spite of the tormenting pains of his feet. Twice more, through the dark of the night, he roused them, for they must not sleep or rest at ease. That was the main point of his plan. He had ridden far enough to wear out their first strength, but only constant nagging would suffice to reduce them to the point where he could have his chance at the golden horse.

In the dawn, he fashioned a new pair of sandals out of the tops of the boots. They were rudely made. They allowed his feet to slip and slide. Sand worked into them and cut at his skin like gnawing rodents. But he forced himself to walk on. Only by maintaining a marching gait could he ever win.

Over the horse herd he had one vast advantage—that the horses had to pause for hours every day in order to pick up enough grazing to support them while, for his own part, he could eat and still march along. And they could only carry water in their bellies, whereas he could keep the canteen at his hip well filled. But all of these advantages were wasted unless he could keep up a steady, forcing march.

He went for three days of torment, until the improvised sandals had been worn to rags. Then a coyote came imprudently near to his camp, one evening, and got a bullet between the eyes. Silver made new sandals out of part of that hide. The rest of the skin he stretched on mesquite twigs, roughly tied together to make a frame, and when he started the march this day, he carried the frame across his shoulders, so that the skin might cure in the sun. At intervals, when he paused, he rubbed the coyote's own fat and brains into the drying leather.

Baked all day, and all the next day, in the fierce sun of the Sierra Blanca, that hide had become fairly good leather before he cut from it another pair of sandals and fitted them to his battered feet.

Every step was now a torment, and still he forced himself to the swinging stride. He dreamed of shoes. Even the battered old flopping shoes of a crippled beggar would have been heaven to him. The strain told on the unsupported arch of his instep. The muscles up the shin and the back of the calf revolted against this new pressure. When he permitted himself to rest, shooting pains darted through his legs and up into his body. When he rose to walk again, he could literally hear the blood crushed out from his wounded feet.

He began to tear up his underclothing, his shirt, even his outer clothes, to make bandages.

In those few days, he had grown thin. At the end of eight days of marching, he looked at himself in the stagnant surface of a water hole and saw a starved face, lips chapped until they were white, eyes buried in shadows. His ribs stood out, and when he dropped his chin, it struck against the great bony arch of his chest. Every ounce of fat had been whipped away from him—and still his diet was parched corn, and his work was almost twenty hours a day of steady marching.

He went on. He knew, with the close of every day, that this was the end; but the next morning he was gone again on the trail, and the vision of the stallion drew him forward almost from step to step.

Results began to show now. Those fine horses from the Larchmont place, which had been so hunted before, were the first to fall to the rear. He passed them, one after another, gaunt, failing skeletons. It was a bitter temptation to put a bullet through the head of one of them and use the incalculable masses of hide to make for himself new, capacious moccasins; but he knew that such theft is worse than murder, and he had to let those beaten horses fall back past him.

Then, one day, he found himself listening to a laughing, raving voice. It was his own. The realization shocked him out of the trance into which he had walked. He found his lips twitching, his hands opening and shutting convulsively, and in his brain the streaming of a vacant wind that would contain no thought.

He needed better food than parched corn, that was clear, so he used two valuable bullets to kill two mountain grouse as he struggled through the foothills that day. He spent twenty-four hours marching slowly, pausing now and again to build a fire and roast portions of the flesh. When that food was consumed, he lay down and slept ten hours. On rising, he was a new man.

His feet now pained him less. They were scarred, deformed, swollen into horrible things; but they were not tormenting him so much. New callouses were spreading. There were few germs in this air to infect the wounds, and gradually they dried up. At every halt, he exposed them to the burning strength of the sun, and the sun itself seemed to be a miraculous healing agent.

It became less a matter of the torment in his feet than of the strength of his body. That strength never had failed him before, but it was doing so now. Still he kept the same swinging stride, no matter how his muscles yearned to shorten it.

And the horses of the herd were dropping out, day after day, day after day. The mustangs now failed continually, and he saw them fall past him to the rear, gaunt creatures, often standing with eyes closed and heads hanging, as though they had decided to wait for death to strike them down and free them from the torment of this pursuit.

But there remained, at the last, an old mare and the shining stallion. She was thin enough, and she went with a limp in one foreleg, yet she managed to keep going. As for Parade, sometimes it seemed to the bitter heart of Silvertip that he had marched all this distance in vain, seeing that the great horse appeared as rounded and smooth and filled with power as ever. Only now and then, when luck brought him quite close, could Silver discover that the stallion was stripped finer than before. The whole outline and splendor of the animal were unaltered; but when the sun fell at a certain angle, the shadows between the ribs appeared.

Sometimes, also, it appeared certain to Silvertip that, even if he came within rope-throw of the horse, he would not be able to accomplish anything. Unless he managed to catch the stallion by a foot, how could Parade be thrown? Silver was no master with a rope. With knife or gun he was at home, but he had not invested many of the days of his life in the dull, honest work of a ranch.

In fact, he was not thinking a great deal of what he would do in the end. The goal that drew him was quite blind. Somehow, in some way, he would finally be able to touch the golden stallion with his hand. That was all. That was the end of his desire. After that, a miracle would give the possession of Parade to him. It was, he told himself, a sort of gigantic game of tag. When he touched Parade, the game would have ended!

There was little or no difficulty in keeping to the trail now. In the beginning, sometimes the stallion would put a great many miles, suddenly, between him and his pursuer, and on every one of those instances he would have dropped the hunter for good and all, except that the course of Parade, when he bolted away, was always straight; by an air line it could be followed. Now, a dozen times in a single day, the vision of the old mare and the shining horse would come into the eyes of Silver, but never without making his heart swell suddenly, never without lightening his step.

He had gone on for thirty days, through the burning sun of the Sierra Blanca. He was blackened to the color of a half-breed, when he came, at last, to what seemed to him the suicide of Parade.

It was a thing that he could not believe, at first. It was his understanding of the thoroughness with which Parade knew the entire Sierra Blanca that made the thing more grotesque. But the fact was that, when he followed the stallion to the mouth of Salt Creek, he saw the old mare drifting sluggishly south, away from the entrance, while the hoof marks of Parade went straight on into the mouth of the ravine.

Suicide—for a horse in the condition of Parade, it certainly seemed no less, for Salt Creek was a narrow cleft that led through the foothills, straight into the heart of the Sierra Blanca, for a hundred and twenty miles. And through the course of all those miles it was fenced on either side by time-polished cliffs, hundreds of feet high.

There are greater canyons than Salt Creek, but all have water flowing through them, the visible agent of the visible work. Yet water was nowhere near Salt Creek. Through a hundred and twenty miles of it, the traveler could wander, the sand underfoot as white as salt, the heat confined and focused by the cliffs, the air almost always unstirred by any wind. And not until the head of the terrible valley is reached is there water.

These things must have been known to Parade, and yet he had entered the gap willingly. That was why the heart of Silver stood still, and he groaned to himself incredulously: "Suicide!"

13 – Salt Creek

TO THE stallion, it had been a struggle as bitter, almost, as it had been to Silvertip. Parade had been hunted before, but never like this. He had been challenged by whole troops of fine horses, ridden by the craft of the Great Enemy. He had met those challenges, thrown off those troops, beaten the brains of the Enemy.

And now came this other thing that hardly seemed a danger, that seemed no more, in fact, than the shadow that trails under a cloud. It had been a mere nothing, at first. The herd had been reluctant to run from the poor creature that walked alone in pursuit of them. Only by degrees, the leader realized that the same solitary form which so often dropped beneath the horizon, was always reappearing. On the wind he had studied the scent of this man a thousand times. He had been close enough to know something of the gaunt body, too, and the tireless, swinging stride, and the ragged clothes that blew in the wind like feathers.

They had endured. The whole herd had endured, but always the strain was telling. If they ran fifty miles in a straight line, exhausting the younger and the older members of the band, nevertheless, within half a day, before the legs of the colts had well stopped shaking, the man was again in sight. At last the Great Enemy seemed personified in that terrible, lonely figure.

From Parade to the youngest colt, not one of the herd dared to drink in peace, but all lifted their heads with a jerk after a few throatfuls. None of them dared to graze with quiet minds, in spite of the sentinels which were scattered on every side to keep the lookout. It was not that they feared that the stalker could actually run up on them, but because the danger had appeared so often that it was lodged in their hearts and minds.

65

When the Great Enemy drew near, it was as a ghost appears to children, a thing that froze the body and the soul.

Then, after long endurance, the herd began to melt away. It was, to Parade, as the destruction of his army is to a warlike king. He had gloried in his power. He had reveled in the many heads which lifted at his call, in the bright eyes that watched him for commands, in the sleek, swift bodies that fled with him over the plains and through the valleys of the Sierra Blanca. Now they were deserting.

The better bred horses went first. Their bodies were worn; they had lost spirit; the strength went out of their resolution; they stumbled even when they went at a walk; they refused to lie down, because the alarm might come again at any moment of the night or the day.

They melted away and fell to the rear, first of all. Then the toughest of the mustangs followed, one by one, or in little groups. Surrender was in the air, except for the pair of them, Mischief and Parade himself.

As for Mischief, she had kept up to the last because her nerves had been trebly tempered by dangers of this sort long before. She could graze undisturbed until the Great Enemy was actually upon them. She could lie down to sleep by day or night, with a quiet mind. In spite of her lameness, she was ever with the leaders.

Then even Mischief began to give way. She was "tucked up." Her belly drew to a gaunt line. Her back roached up. Her head sank. Her forehoofs were beveled at the toes by constant scraping against the sand and the rocks over which she wandered. That was her condition when she and the stallion came opposite the mouth of Salt Creek, on that day.

And Parade, naturally turning away from the entrance to that death place, was stopped by the whinny of his mother. She stood pointing her head at it and saying: "This is the way to escape!"

Parade snorted the dust from his nostrils.

"Look at the bushes at the top of the cliffs," he said. "Even the sage-brush is dying. It means two days of travel to go through that place. We tried it once, long ago. Do you remember the spring when the rains came so hard, and we went in here, thinking that there would be water everywhere? But we were wrong. There was nothing except a puddle here and there, and we were glad of the puddle water, even before we came to the water hole at the head of the valley. Now it's the middle of summer, and how could we live through it?"

The old mare sniffed at the ground, then raised her head and smelled at the air.

"He is coming," she said. "The Great Enemy has followed you week after week, but even he walks more slowly through the heat of the day. And his feet cannot move so quickly. Go through the valley of fire, my son, and when you come out on the other side, he will not be behind you. If he enters, he will die on the white sands, of thirst and the heat. You will leave him behind you, like a wolf caught in quicksands. Then we shall be free again. This is not freedom that we have now. Better to be closed into the corral of the Enemy than to have his shadow falling across your feet every day. Go quickly. I shall turn the other way. You know where we meet!"

The golden stallion turned, and he saw, rising out of a swale in the desert, the Great Enemy himself, the ragged clothes blowing in the wind like many tattered flags. Certainly it was better to pass through the fire than to let this creature like a leech cling to the trail. So he gave to Mischief a farewell whinny, and jogged straight forward into the jaws of the valley of death.

His was no longer the light, swinging trot that sprang across easy going or hard with such infinite ease. Instead, his hoofs trailed, and his hind legs seemed to be sinking away from beneath the burden they had to bear.

Presently, as the sand grew deep, he fell back to a walk. The heat rose like fire from the white surface of the sand, and like walls of flame it burned along the polished faces of the cliffs on either side.

Sweat rolled out on his hide and dripped from his belly. Not a breath of air came to cool him, only stirrings of warmer and warmer currents, like the ripplings of hot water in a pot. Where the sand rose above his hoofs, it burned him to the fetlock joints, and higher still.

It wound like a snake through most of its course, this valley of despair, and, coming out into a straighter part of the passage, he looked back and saw that the Great Enemy had indeed come into the trap. Exultation filled Parade. He arched his proud neck again and sent down the valley a neigh that was a challenge indeed.

So it was accepted by the man.

"He thinks I'm beaten," said Silvertip to himself. "And maybe I am. I don't know. Maybe I am!"

He freshened his pace. The muscles across his stomach began to ache. He bent his body a little to favor them. His legs were numb. Breathing was difficult. And always in the looseness of the sand his feet kept slipping back.

The stallion broke into a trot that carried him swiftly out of sight around the next bend.

When Silvertip came to that corner in turn, he could look more than half a mile straight ahead—and Parade was not in view!

Then Silvertip got to the shadow of a rock that had fallen from the edge of the cliff above him, and he slumped down where his head and his half-naked body would be protected from the sun.

The arm on which he leaned shuddered with weakness. Dizziness kept his brain turning, for it seemed almost hotter in the shadow than it had been in the full blaze of the light.

He took off his sandals and looked at his battered feet. His right foot was twitching with every pulse of his blood, and the red stain was continually growing from some new wound, or from an old one that had recently been chafed open.

He told himself that he was beaten. The neigh of the stallion still grew up in his mind and echoed freshly. He was beaten. He was trapped. What lay before him he could not tell, but he knew that it was more than twelve miles to pass on the rear trail to get to water. Twelve miles—and a pint of water to get him there!

He took his canteen from his hip and swirled the water in it. It was a liquid that had now arrived at almost blood temperature. But it was moisture, and moisture he must have.

He looked down at his hand, and it seemed the hand of an old man, trembling as with an ague, so great was his weakness. If his hand shook like this, of what use could a heavy revolver and bullets be to him?

He took out the Colt, aimed at a near-by rock, and fired. The bullet missed! He tried again, steadying the weapon with both hands, but again the shaking of his muscles made the shot fail.

Suddenly he hurled the gun from him, and caught out the extra ammunition and threw it after the gun. Every ounce of extra burden that he carried was an ounce of life-blood drawn from his heart.

He stood up, and the blaze of the sunshine covered him as with fire. That blasting heat scorched him through and through. It cast a fume up his nostrils; all the landscape wavered before his eyes.

It was only common sense, not weakness, that determined him to turn back to cover the known twelve miles to the water hole. He would only go forward to the end of this straight stretch, and from the next corner try to take his farewell glimpse of Parade.

So he went on to the next bend, and, looking down the exposed ravine for more than a mile, he found no trace of the stallion—there was only the trail that went straight ahead, and vanished. Now, those hoof marks were not entirely straight, but here and there they meandered, as the sign of Parade never had wavered before, in all the miles he had followed the horse.

This gave him the flickering gleam of a new hope. It was the way of Parade to move as straight as a bird through the air; and if he were faltering now, might he not be near to dropping out of the fight?

The thought made the big man forget all his troubles, the heat of the sun, the anguish of his feet. If the great horse were near to failing, he, Silvertip, would be on hand to see the last moment. He would strive to get there at least in time to see the last light of life in those wild eyes.

So Silvertip found himself stumbling vaguely, feebly forward and continually straightening his leaning body to save himself from pitching down on his face.

After that, the best of his senses left him. He walked on. All he knew was that he was continually walking. He could hardly tell in which direction he was going, but he was walking on and on.

Once he came to himself with a hand of fire laid across his face, and he found that he was staggering, his head swayed far back on his shoulders. He was frightened. He dropped on one knee and put the knuckles of his hand on the burning sands.

"I'm going out on my feet," said Silvertip to himself. "I've got to do something about it."

And then, with laughter that cracked his lips, he remembered that he actually was carrying water with him! The canteen had gone out of his crazed mind.

He took a tablespoonful to moisten his mouth. He took more, and more, in swallows so small that they would hardly have sufficed for a bird. But he knew that this was the proper economy. Small drinks, and many of them.

The sun dropped. He dropped with it, flat on his back, and watched the angry fires climb the sky, and wane again toward darkness. But the heat still radiating from the ground scorched him and made his head ache.

He sat up, stripped off his rags, put them on the warm sand, and stretched out on this bed, naked. Then he went to sleep.

He dreamed that he had fallen into a river of ice; he wakened to find that the heat of the day was gone, and in its place a wind off the mountain snows was cutting through the ravine. His body was congealed to pale iron, so he dressed, and went on.

The pain in his feet shut out all other thoughts presently. He could forget the cold, because of that greater agony. And now the cold was gone, and the pain from the feet was gone, also, since the aching of his entire body recommenced. It was strange that mere walking should be an act that required such an effort of the volition. He began to swing his arms, so that the forward momentum of his entire body would be increased, and in this way he strode on, until he was stepping out at the ordinary pace to which he had forced himself all through the hunt. Once that pace was established, it maintained itself, as it were.

He rounded a corner. Something dark struggled a moment against the pale starlight on the sand; then the figure of a horse lurched to its feet not ten yards aways, and went cantering down the valley, each stride longer than the one preceding.

It was Parade, and not until the horse was out of sight did Silvertip realize that he had been near enough to make the cast with his rope, and try to end this frightful chase!

14 – The Pool

THE darkness thickened, at last. No, it was only that the mountains in the distance and the rock walls of the valley appeared to be growing more black. Something in his memory recognized that effect and connected it with a dim hope, a thing of pleasure. And after a moment he realized that the dawn was beginning.

Looking up, he was like one sunk in water, staring through the thick film of the sea toward mountain heights that now loomed closer. At first, the fire of the day seized on the snows, then glinted on the stone flanks of the mountains, and finally slid down into the hollow of Salt Creek itself.

He knew that he was exhausted, but he knew that he dared not halt; that he must use the blessed coolness of these early hours, while he could still keep his legs swinging in rhythm. Thirst was no longer a part of heat; it was a part of cold, and seemed to help the ice of the air to pass through him.

But it was not long until a blaze of pale light flared in the east, so brightly that he had to blink his eyes a little. And a little later the sun was looking down at him. The very first stroke of it went to his heart, like a touch of fever. His knees shook. He had endured much during the day before, but he knew that he could not pass through this day.

Out of that certainty, he told himself that he would simply go on until he could go no longer, and then find a place among the shadows where he might lie down and die. And so it was that, making a turn of the sinuous valley, he came upon view of Parade.

But he was on parade no longer. That glorious head was sunk at last. The shimmering tail hung straight down, the hocks knocking it back and forth at every step. The head of the stallion bobbed with each stride, and about his hoofs, never lifted clear, the sand was swishing. Silver heard the

71

sound of it, like water, and he shouted, waving his arms wildly, running forward.

The stallion lurched into a trot, with labor, like an old plow horse. Finally, with a supreme effort, Parade swung into his gallop. It was a mere caricature of his usual wind-free gait, but a gallop it was that drifted the horse swiftly away from the pursuer. As Parade strained forward, the pulling muscles of his flanks, and his laboring lungs, made the bones of his ribs thrust out. His hips were two up-thrusting elbows. His withers were a great lump. His back sagged. The velvet and the sheen were both gone from his starving coat.

"He's dying," said Silver to himself. "He's dying, and I'm dying on my feet, too. But, before I die, I'm going to have my rope around his neck!"

He took another swallow of the water. There was less than a cupful remaining, and the sound of it swishing lightly in the canteen was death music to Silvertip.

A queer sense of doom came over him—that he would not be permitted to die until he had placed his hand upon the body of the horse. Therefore, he strode on and on. The fear was gone from him. It was not hope of life that sustained him, but that other strange hope.

He came in sight of the stallion again. The horse had halted, head down once more, feet braced. This time, thought Silver, he would surely be able to put the rope on the tall skeleton.

But he was wrong. At his nearer approach, Parade was able to lift himself into a trot, and then to a reeling gallop.

Sudden pity struck through the heart of the man as he saw that unhappy sight, but the pity was crushed by the sterner emotion. If they were found dead, the two of them, it would be with his rope around the neck of Parade, and the end of that rope tied to his hand, in sure sign that he had conquered the stallion before death destroyed them both.

That would be something of a monument to leave behind him. Enough people had come into the Sierra Blanca with their outfits of men and horses to appreciate the supreme thing that he would have accomplished.

The heat of the day grew. Long before noon, delirium attacked his mind, and he was never in his right senses for more than an hour at a time during the rest of that day. In that madness of the mind, sometimes it seemed to him that the horse which staggered before him was not a skeleton, but the full beauty, the full power of the great Parade. And he himself was pursuing the speeding monster on wings.

He could not know that they were involuntarily trying to save one another—that the stallion did not lie down to die merely because the man pursued him, and that Silver himself did not drop because the haunting vision of the horse was continually in the corner of his eye.

Twice that day, he tried the rope. Once he missed completely. Once the loop slapped on the hip of the horse, and sent Parade off at a blundering, swaying trot. Galloping was now impossible, and even a trot could not be sustained for more than fifty yards at a time.

If bitter compassion at times poured through Silvertip, thinking of the wreck of the beauty of the horse, he looked down at his own skeleton body, and set his teeth again.

A sane man would have doubted his senses, if he had observed that picture. But there was no sanity save the lust for power in Silvertip now, and in the horse there was a fear of the Great Enemy, greater than the fear of death.

More than their bodies could accomplish, they now performed. The day went on, bitterly, slowly, hour by hour, until the sun had gone well beyond the zenith. Then the stallion halted, and, for all his desire to close in, Silvertip had to slump down in the shade of a rock.

There he gathered his strength, bit by bit, summoning his force, breathing deep, snorting like an animal to clear his nostrils of dust.

At last he could rise and go on with shaking legs; but, as he came near, again Parade went lumbering forward. And the fiercest heat of the day began, burning them, scalding them both. The canteen had long been empty, and for two days the stallion had gone through that oven without water.

The afternoon wore through. The blaze of the sun was less terrific, but the contained heat of the valley seemed thicker and deeper than ever. There was no oxygen in the air, and the mouth of Silvertip opened wide, though he knew that it was fatal to breathe that dusty atmosphere through the mouth for any length of time.

And then, in the twilight, he saw far before them a beautiful mirage of a blue pool, with two trees standing beside it, and a green fringe of grass.

If it were a mirage, it was strange that the stallion should drag himself toward it at a lumbering trot. If it were a mirage, it was stranger still that the birds should dip out of the sky to cut the surface with their beaks.

It was no mirage at all, he realized with a sudden wildness of joy. It was water, beyond doubt. It was honest water, which God had placed there at the end of the trail for the suffering.

Silvertip on staggering knees, began to run in turn. His legs turned to quicksilver. He fell on his face, rolled, crawled forward on his knees and on his hands, with his elbows bending beneath his weight, until his fingers were in the wet margin of the pool.

Already the stallion had thrust his muzzle into the surface, sending small waves across the water, and Silvertip, stretched out on his gaunt stomach, drank like an animal, and lifted his head to breathe, and drank again.

By a greater miracle than the actual presence of the water, it was cool. Silver thrust his arms into it, and it rippled over his flesh like a blessing over the soul of the damned. He laughed, and choked, and drank again and again.

Then he pushed himself back, and saw the stallion on the farther side of the water, watching him with red eyes. Knee-deep stood Parade, and the dust was washed from his face almost to the eyes, he had plunged in his head so deeply.

Silvertip coiled his rope.

The stallion flinched—then he lowered his head to drink again, blinking as he did so.

Now Silvertip stood erect, the noose ready, strength rapidly beginning in his body, the certainty of victory in his soul. He swung the rope—and still the horse drank, with the shadow flying in circles across that very mirror into which he had dipped his head.

The hand of Silvertip dropped. The rope struck lightly against the green of the grass.

For suddenly it had seemed to him that this was a sacred spot, removed from the strifes of the world and hallowed by some more-than-mortal law.

He stared at Parade, and saw the great horse in the hollow of his hand, yet he could not throw the noose. It was not water that he had drunk; it was not water that the horse was still drinking; it was life.

Silvertip looked up with a groan to the darkening twilight in the sky, and when he glanced down again, Parade was drawing back from the verge of the pool, drawing back from the range of the rope, moving again into a world of freedom. And still Silvertip stood entranced, and could not lift his hand.

15 – The New World

PARADE, withdrew from the reach of the rope, blundered only a few steps before he lay down beneath a tree. He saw the man come a few uncertain, wavering steps after him, then sink to the ground in turn. The thicker night, more perfect in silence, drew over them, with stars in the heaven above them, and more brightly in the water at their side.

Still the two rested, motionless, like two heroes of some legendary combat who battle together from dawn to midday, and in the heat withdraw from one another a little and lie down to rest, by mutual consent, well knowing that they will soon rise again and join the struggle once more.

The man lay on his face, his head pillowed in his arms. Parade could see that, and something out of the human face spoke to him continually through the dark of the night. Eyes were on Parade, passing through his body, it seemed, and finding the spirit within. He could not believe that he was actually lying there, prone and passive, while the Great Enemy, personified in one man, lay near by, a danger ready to spring. Yet the agony of weariness controlled him. The eyes of Parade closed, and his mind wandered in sleep, constantly broken as his eyes winked open again and again.

He heard a sound of regular, loud breathing from the Great Enemy. Sometimes it seemed to him that the man was gathering, and rising to his feet; and again, as he jerked his own head high, it seemed to Parade that the Great Enemy was merely sleeping.

There was enough of the savage beast in Parade to make him think of lurching to his feet and charging that frail body. One stroke of a forehoof should be enough to shatter the life in it. And there was not the formidable scent of iron and gunpowder, warning him away. But Mischief had always declared that there is in man a mystery of power, incomprehensible and vast,

75

so that, for all his fragility, the Great Enemy is always dangerous. Moreover, in the heart of Parade there was welling a strange sense of fear, and something that was different from fear.

It was like that emotion which comes between day and night, or between night and morning; it was like standing on a high hill and looking at a new country. There was the sense of something infinite, and infinitely worth exploring.

The hours went by like a swift river. The mountains began to darken in the east, and Parade knew that the day was coming. He got to his feet, with an effort. There was no returning down the length of Salt Creek, he knew, because of the fluid weakness which coursed through him. One more day without water would be the end of him, in his condition. There remained only one way, and that was ahead, up the trail that wound dimly into the higher mountains; for he was now at the very head of Salt Creek.

Would the man rise, also?

Yes, Parade had hardly made three steps when Silvertip stirred, groaned, and then rose to his feet, and stood swaying.

He drank from the pool again, put something from a pocket into his mouth, and stepped out limping on the trail of the stallion. It seemed to Parade that it would always be like this—that, as he struggled through the world, this two legged creature would follow him, with the snaky rope in his hand.

More hope came to the horse when he found that he had regained some of his lost strength after water and rest. He struck forward at a trot. The ground lifted. He wound rapidly up and up through a maze of rocks. Before him, above him, the sun struck on polished boulders never been able to accomplish what this Great Enemy had and flamed on the blue-white ice of the summits, half lost in the sky.

There was another land beyond those peaks, and Mischief had told him of it. The passes were narrow and dangerous, but if he could get through them, he would come out into a green world, and his strength would soon return to him and his limbs be robed with power, as before. All that those men who had striven to catch him had done was drive him at last out of the hot fastnesses of the Sierra Blanca.

As he climbed, he had many a glimpse behind and beneath him of the lower country. He could see the whole course of Salt Creek winding away toward the open desert. Through that crystal morning he could make out small forms; and, in a valley close to Salt Creek, two horsemen were striking in toward the mountains.

Well for Parade that he had met no horsemen during these last terrible days! They could have run him down in a moment, and ensnared him with their ropes.

He seemed to have climbed, now, into the heart of the dawn itself, and the morning light was seeping down from the higher levels over a darker earth beneath. Then the sun itself poured over him like a warm liquid.

He stood out on a projecting point, for an instant. It was like the prow of a ship, and he, as the lookout, stared far away through the sea of mountains. He had risen, now, to the level of the snow. A gray bank of it lay along the ledge, at one side. Beneath the stunted pines there were bits and sparklings of it. It was the first promise of the region of wind and ice that lay above him.

Then the Great Enemy came up around the bend below. He had a stick in his hand, and leaned some of his weight on it. He climbed stolidly, with slow steps, his head swaying a little from side to side. A sort of angry despair came over the stallion, made him toss up his head, and brought a trumpet-sounding neigh from his throat. The violence of his call made his knees tremble. But the man did not even look up. He came on, slowly, steadily, step after step, as remorseless as time.

Parade turned and fled as fast as he could up the next rise. He looked back. The rocks had blotted out the form of the man, but, of course, he would be coming. Like a wolf, he seemed to have a nose that told him the way, and the fear of the stallion grew into a blind panic that scourged him wildly forward.

He gained a height. He fled down a steep-sided hollow. He rushed the rising ground beyond, and found himself trembling and already exhausted on the bitter upward slope that seemed to have no ending. Far beneath him, he saw the man coming, plodding with the stick, head down, swaying slightly from side to side!

There was no wind on these heights, though usually the storms must have flowed like invisible rivers, to judge from the manner in which trees were blown back at timber line. And immediately above was the white world of the snow. Later in the year it would shrink upward and upward, until there were glistening caps on only a few of the loftiest peaks, but now the mountains were drowned in it, and the passes choked. A crunching and squeaking sound kept coming from the pressure of his hoofs on the snow crystals.

It was slow going. There were few levels; it was always up and down, with need to step like a cat for fear a false step on the treacherous snow would hurl him over the lip of some vast canyon.

It was a new world. A mountain sheep, almost as big as a pony, ran across the path of the stallion and hurled itself over the edge of a cliff—to be dashed to pieces beneath, it seemed! But no, it was caroming from side to side of a narrow crevice, seeming to strike on its head at the bottom of every jump, rebounding sidewise and ever downward like a great rubber ball.

The horse, eying that descent, felt suddenly weak and helpless. Then the snow before him became alive, and white ptarmigans rose on purring wings and shot away in a long, low flight, arrowy fast.

All creatures here were new, and their newness brought home to the stallion a sense of doom. To be in such a fantastic world was almost like being dead.

And the man? He was still coming. Step after step, at the unvarying rhythm, he climbed the steep way, and the footmarks which he left behind were spots of his own crimson blood. The stippled trail moved far away behind him before it dipped out of sight. The wind blew softly from that direction, and the stallion distinctly smelled the freshness of new blood.

Another panic overcame him, at that. Slipping, sliding, groaning with fear, he rushed along the narrow trail, regardless of the thousand-foot gulf at his left, and so came out on a small platform of rock, slicked over with an incrustation of ice. Here all progress stopped. At the right, the cliff went upward at the pitch of a rising heron. At the left was the gulf. And across the ledge on which the horse had been traveling had spilled a mass of snow, mixed with ponderous boulders of ice. The sun shone full on this trap, dazzling the eyes of Parade.

He turned. He knew that the time for the final battle had come, and already he was eying the gorge at his side. Better to die there, he felt, than to pass into the mysterious hands of the enslaver, Man. He imagined the outward spring, the downward rush, the cold sweeping of wind against his belly. Perhaps he would begin to turn over and over, like a great stone. Then one last crushing blow, and life would be over.

Around the corner of the icy rock stepped the Great Enemy, and confronted him, leaning on the staff. Parade lifted his head, and sent a great neigh, a death cry, ringing through the echoing mountains. Far below, across the canyon, and on a different trail, two riders with clipped hair and close-clipped beards heard the call, and looking up, saw, in part, what happened.

16 – The Capture

THE snaky shadow of the rope was deploying in the hand of the Great Enemy. It slid out through the air, and hovered an instant. The stallion, trying to dodge, almost shot his weight off the slippery rock and into the abyss. As Parade regained his feet, he felt the noose whip home with a burning touch about his neck. It closed up on his windpipe. It was a cruel hand that relentlessly throttled him.

There was no chance for flight, or for pulling free. Parade did the next possible thing—he charged straight home!

Before him, he saw the man shrink aside, and the way of escape opened. Then the burly wooden staff whirled, a blur of speed before the eyes of Parade.

The blow took him between the ears and knocked him to his knees. He was at the very feet of the Great Enemy. The smell of the blood from them was a stench in his nostrils; the scent of the body of the man was terribly near; and, above all, the voice of man was ringing out at his ears, in savage victory.

Parade shrank back as he came to his knees. A loop of the rope whipped under a forefoot. He barely managed to disengage the hoof before it was jerked up toward his throat.

Again the two faced one another. Laughter came out of the throat of Man, laughter, detestable to all animals, because it is a sound which otherwise has no existence in nature. The whole mind and difference of man is expressed in that half-gasping and half-singing noise.

And seeing the Great Enemy shaken for the moment, Parade charged again. He came with teeth bared, ears flattened, his head thrust out like the head of a snake. The club whirled up. He dodged. Instantly his feet shot out from beneath him. His whole body skidded over the ice-polished rock.

79

Beneath him was the dreadful, empty glimpse of the chasm, the white dance of water that foamed through the bottom of the ravine.

With his forehoofs, as a cat with paw and claw, the stallion clung to the verge of the cliff. His hind legs, reaching frantically upward, struck at the massed ice that underlay the ledge and knocked it away in great chunks. Then his forehoofs began to slide slowly outward.

He stopped struggling. The shuddering cold of death was already in him. And then Man leaned above him, reaching far down. The smell of blood was ranker than ever in the nostrils of Parade. The ragged clothes of the Great Enemy brushed his face, and the dust of Salt Creek filled the nostrils of the horse. It would be easy, now, to seize one of those fragile hands and crush the bone in his teeth—but miracles were happening!

Of all the mysteries of man, his hands are the most wonderful. It is they which work with fire; it is they which use iron and gunpowder; but now the hands of the Great Enemy had laid mighty hold upon the noose that encircled the neck of Parade.

Man was lifting with a power incredible in so small a thing. Man was swaying back, every instant in danger of losing his foothold and slipping out into the void. Man was pulling with such a force that the forehoofs of the horse no longer slipped outward, but worked in to gain a better grip.

The rear hoofs struck up to gain some purchase on the under ice, below the ledge. Again those striking feet merely managed to knock away great lumps. Utter despair came upon Parade. Not even the miraculous hands of Man could save him.

But Man still struggled. It was plain that the Great Enemy was risking life to save life. And how could that be true? Yet he remained there on the brink of death for them both, tugging, straining; and out of the throat of Man came new sounds, never heard before.

Man is a whooping, yelling monster. He rides horses at frantic speed, goring their flanks with terrible spurs. Man yells, in a voice that strikes through the mind like a stone through thin ice. But this time Man was speaking in a tone of sympathy and encouragement as plainly decipherable as ever was the soft whinny of a mare to its foal. Groaningly the words came out, forced and strained by the physical effort that accompanied them.

New strength came into Parade; despair left him. With head and forelegs he pressed down on the rock; his struggling hind legs beat upward until one of them found an instant's lodgment.

That instant was enough. The pull of the man was greater than ever. Parade swayed upward; his whole body trembled for an instant in the crisis of the strain; then he lurched forward onto the safety of the little platform.

The man staggered back before him, without ever letting go the rope which encircled the throat of Parade. And the face of Man was horrible. Out of his distended jaws came the hoarse, panting breath of exhaustion. His breast heaved in and out against the very muzzle of Parade. His eyes glared, bloodstained as those of a beast of prey. His whole body swayed with weakness, and the magic hands which had saved the stallion now quivered as they retained their grasp on the noose.

There was an equal weakness in Parade. Only the wide bracing of his legs sustained him, for the time being. Then, gradually, power returned. Out of the haze of exhaustion he recovered, to realize more fully how he was bound to the man.

What he had felt the night before returned to him. He had then been on the verge, as it were, of a vast, undiscovered country, and now he felt that he was in the midst of it. The mere crossing of mountains could not be to him what this moment with the Great Enemy had meant.

He had been struck to his knees—such was the force of the magic of this puny creature—and then he had been drawn from the brink of death.

Now the hands of Man left the rope and passed upward along the soft under parts of his throat, and came over the tense muscles of the jaw, and moved with infinite delicacy across the face of Parade.

He stood entranced, for electric happiness flowed out of that touch, and the voice of Man, recommencing, made through the soul of the stallion such echoes as sing and murmur quietly down the ravine of a small mountain brook.

Danger, and starvation, and long labor, and the torments of heat and cold were forgotten; but fear, most of all, was the ghost that disappeared in this new sunshine of understanding. Years of quiet living cannot reveal our friends to us as can the cruel light of one moment of danger and need. Then the many fail, and the one is found, and to have such a one is better than all the throngs. There is no bitterness like full knowledge, and there is no such glorious happiness. And one friend is the bread of life, if his friendship has been proved.

The wisdom of the old mare, his mother, had been to the stallion a profound thing. Suddenly it shrank. It became obscure and worthless, compared with this new knowledge.

The hand of Man was laid across his forehead, then both hands blinded his eyes. But he stood without a jerk of the head, without a tremor of the body. Into the darkness of that moment, Parade was pouring his faith and his trust that no harm would come.

He heard joy come bubbling like spring water out of the throat of Man, and the flow of it invaded his own being. The hands were removed. He looked with his unblinded eyes, curiously, with only a faint comprehension, into the face of Man. And the dead centuries worked in the blood of Parade, surely—all the generations through which his race had served Man, the master, and had known Man, the friend.

The Great Enemy drew back, and pulled gently at the rope. Parade drew back against the weight. And Man stood beside him, now, softly pressing forward on the noose until Parade yielded to the pressure.

There was no harm in that. There was no harm, surely, in walking with his head at the shoulder of Man, while the voice made music in his ears.

Mischief had said that in time even some of the sounds of the voice of Man can take on a definite meaning. Parade wondered if that time would ever come for him. Even as it was, the speech had a meaning of contentment.

They went on slowly down the icy way. Parade slipped. The hand of Man, strongly sustaining, steadied him again. A little later, Man slipped in turn, and the full weight of his body dragged down against the rope until he was in balance once more.

The ears of Parade pricked forward. He was walking, not on rock and snow and ice, but into a country of the spirit, where every step was a marvel beyond calculation.

They wound down out of the region of white snow. They passed the distorted willows and aspens of the timber line that stretched like a dark water mark, level and straight, along the sides of the mountains. They came to the kinder going beneath, and where a small dale opened, there the Great Enemy made a pause.

Deep, rich grass grew here, but Parade was regardless of it, watching the face of Man as a child watches the face of a summer sky. And Man plucked a handful of the grass, and offered it at the lips of Parade. Curiously he sniffed at it. The taint of the flesh of Man was on it, yet he gathered a little under his prehensile upper lip. The taste was not spoiled. He ate, suddenly, with eagerness. Again and again that hand was filled, and again and again Parade took the grass from it. Then handfuls of seeded grass, carefully chosen; richer food than ever Parade had been able to sort for himself.

They remained there for more than an hour, and during that hour, the voice of Man would speak, and then the silence of the wilderness would flow gently in upon them, and unutterable peace began to steal like happy sleep over the stallion.

Far away, he saw two riders moving. But what of that? He would have fled, if he had been alone, but now he was with a mighty companion, stronger than all other men, more patient than time, more enduring than heat or cold.

If other men came, they were his lesser fellows, like colts in a herd to the great wild stallion that rules it.

Presently, the riders were no longer in view, but two men on foot moved carefully among the rocks and shrubbery, obviously stalking, and coming straight in the direction of Man, the Great Enemy!

This was strange! But all-knowing Man would surely know this.

Perhaps it was a game, as when colts play together in the happy summer of the year.

Then one man was kneeling, and the long line of light that ran down the barrel of a rifle narrowed and shortened to a single winking eye of light.

Well did the stallion know guns, and now he started violently, throwing up his head, staring in the direction of that new danger.

Man arose, also, and turned, and as he turned, an audible blow struck his head and knocked him flat on his back. A thin mist had appeared around the mouth of the rifle, and now the report clanged softly against the ears of the stallion, coming vaguely through the thin mountain air.

Parade looked down. Red covered the head, red streaked the face of Man. He lay with his arms outstretched, and his eyes partially open, and a smile was on his lips. The hot, thick, sweet scent of blood filled the nostrils of Parade.

He stared toward the place from which the shot had been fired, but now there was nothing to be seen of the two men.

Parade lowered his head, and sniffed at the face of the fallen man. There was no response. He stamped. It brought no answer, though sand flew from the stamping of the hoof into the face of the Great Enemy.

A moment later, a shadow crossed near by. Parade, tossing up his head, was in time to see one of the strangers snatch up the end of the fallen rope and snub it around the point of a boulder. And Parade himself, rushing off at a gallop, came to the end of that line only to be flung heavily on his side.

He lay senseless for a moment. Meantime, both of the men were leaning over Silvertip.

"You got him, Chuck," said one of them. "You got him good, too. Right through the bean, old son."

"He's goin' to bump off the gent that takes the scalp of Parade," answered Chuck. "But he won't be doin' no bumpin' no more. Get your rope on that hoss, Lefty. He's goin' to raise the devil when he gets to his feet again. Shall we roll Silvertip down into the ravine?"

"Leave him be," answered Lefty. "The buzzards'll spoil his looks so's nobody would know him. In half a day, they'll spoil him."

17 – At Parmalee

THEY took the stallion on two lariats and half led, and half dragged him away, looking back a few times, contentedly, on the body they left behind them. It was not until they were out of sight that Silvertip's head turned slightly to the side, and a groan came through his parched lips.

If they had heard it, they would have come back like tigers to finish their work, or else they would have loosed the stallion and fled away like carrion crows to a distant region. They would have separated, changed their names, shaved their faces, and striven in a new life more completely to bury themselves from the eye of Silvertip. But they went on in happy ignorance that the rifle bullet had glanced on the skull of Silver, instead of boring its way straight through the brain.

They had Parade delivered into their hands in exactly the state in which they could work on him. Half dead with fatigue, more than half starved, he looked more like an ancient caricature than the king of the Sierra Blanca desert. So one of them hauled at him from in front, and the other fed a quirt into him to urge him across the desert. He tried more than once to fight back. His spirit was not dead, but his body failed him.

When they came in sight of Mischief, hardly in better shape than her son, in spite of the fact that she had not made the frightful journey through Salt Creek, it was easy for Chuck to catch the mare, while Lefty held the stallion.

At this stroke, they exulted beyond words. They were bringing in both the stallion and the mare, where the ablest men in the West had failed. Perhaps it was true that more than a hundred thousand dollars had been spent in time, horseflesh, and other ways, in order to capture Parade. All of that money had been spent in vain. And now they were bringing him in!

There was reputation in it, in the first place. There was enough reputation to last a dozen men the course of their lives.

There was money in it, too, for what would not some rancher pay to get hold of this famous animal in order to improve his saddle stock? Besides, Parade could be showed at a quarter a head, and people would throng to see him, close at hand. His very picture would have a good cash value.

Lefty and Chuck were thrifty souls, and they talked over these prospects with a calm determination to miss no tricks. Even Mischief was of value, as the companion who for so long had gone limping at the side of Parade. She was the stamp and seal of his identity.

"It ain't what you do," said Chuck. "It's the way you do it, that counts. There's poor old Silvertip now. There's a gent that's been talked about and wrote about and sung about. And he takes and burns himself up, and he does what nobody else can do, and he gets as thin as a crow, flyin' after Parade. And what does he get out of it?"

"He gets a bullet through the head," said Lefty, grinning. "And we get Parade."

"It ain't what you do," Chuck repeated. "It's the way you do it that counts. And we've done this the right way. If that Parade don't fall down flat before we get him to a corral and some good grass."

"There ain't any hurry about that," said Lefty. "We got him weakened and we're goin' to keep him weakened till he's broke."

In this there was the sort of sense that could not fail to appeal to such a mind as that of Chuck. That same day, they put a saddle on the back of the exhausted stallion, and Lefty mounted.

There was one minute of violent bucking, one flash in the pan, one faint suggestion of the explosion that would have taken place had Parade possessed his strength, and then the big horse crumpled to the ground.

For a time they feared that he was about to die. But his body was not dead. It had been toughened through too many years of famine and pursuit to give way so suddenly now. He was able to rise again, and stumble on. And when they came to grass and water, the men spent two whole days letting the stallion and the mare recuperate.

In the olden time, Parade would have recovered with amazing speed. But now his progress was very slow. His body was still intact, but the heart and the pride in him had been almost fatally wounded.

It hardly mattered that the saddle was placed on him every day. It hardly mattered that his flanks felt the goring stroke of the spurs, or that the quirt bit into his hide, or that his tender mouth was sawed by the savage grip of the Spanish bit. The chief indignity already had befallen him. He had been mastered!

And every inch of the Sierra Blanca was an insult and a reproach to him. The ragged summits of the mountains that he had viewed so many times with a feeling of kinship and companionship, now seemed to stare down at him with scornful eyes. Behind him followed the ghosts of the fine horses which had been at his command. They were gone with his freedom, and there was no heart left in him.

Vainly Lefty and Chuck waited for a return of his magnificence, as they drifted him slowly south. Flesh appeared once more over his ribs. He was as he had been before, but the horse which responded to whip and spur was far other than the old king of the Sierra Blanca. The spring was gone from his step, the arch from his neck, the fire from his eyes. Weariness was always in him, the weariness of the spirit.

That was how they brought him into Parmalee.

The great Parmalee rodeo was about to commence; in ten days it would start, and in the meantime, visitors, cattle buyers, cowpunchers, were beginning to pour into town. It was a perfect opportunity for the showing of the stallion, and Lefty and Chuck made the most of it.

Harry Richmond had his stallion, Brandy, in a corral near the race track. Adjoining it was a high-walled inclosure used sometimes for the breaking of very refractory mustangs, with a snubbing post in the center. Here the mare and the great Parade were placed. It was a simple matter to hang cheap canvas around the enclosure so that people could not peek in. It was equally simple to build a little platform against the side of the fence, and there, for twenty-five cents, a man could stand as long as he wished to stare at the famous outlaw.

Dave Larchmont came and stood there almost half a day, with that poor Englishman, Hammersley, beside him. Hammersley was almost ruined now, men said. He carried his head as high as ever, and his back as straight, and his mustache bristled as fiercely, and his eye was as stern as when he had spent thousands upon thousands in the pursuit of Parade. But it was said that his fortune had melted away. He had spent too much time horse hunting, and not enough in the management of his place.

There was a long silence between him and Larchmont, and then Hammersley said:

"D'you know what it's really like, Larchmont?"

"It's like seeing a ghost," said Larchmont.

"No," said Hammersley, "it's like seeing the poor relation of a great man. The name may be the same, and the face may be the same, but the great heart's gone, Larchmont. The heart's gone, and nothing will bring it back again!"

Even to see the ghost, the fading relic of what Parade had once been, people were willing to come, not once, but many times. It was a poor day when Chuck and Lefty did not haul in from twenty to thirty dollars, and this was money so sweet and so easily come by that Chuck took a bit to drink, and Lefty to poker. They managed to spend their winnings in that way, easily enough.

"Suppose that Silvertip could see us now," said Chuck, one evening, as he leaned against a bar beside his partner. "He'd doggone nigh rise out of his grave, wouldn't he, Lefty?"

"Him?" snapped Lefty. "I kind of half wish that we'd left him alone."

"Whatcha talkin' about?" demanded Chuck. "Ain't it the best day's work that we ever done in our lives? Or you got an idea that murder will out, eh?"

Lefty pointed before him, at the mirror, and seemed to be squinting at his own image in the glass.

"We went and murdered Parade," he said. His face puckered.

"What kind of fool talk is this here?" demanded Chuck.

"You wouldn't understand," answered Lefty. "I was just thinkin'."

"Quit your crabbin' while the coin is rollin' in," said Chuck.

"What I mean to say," remarked Lefty, "that hoss was plumb satisfied with Silvertip. Account of bein' hauled back up over the edge of the cliff, maybe. I thought that fool of a Silver was goin' to slip over the edge himself, for a while." He shook his head.

"Are you tryin' to get mysterious, or something like that?" demanded Chuck. "Whatcha mean—the hoss bein' plumb satisfied with Silver? Didn't Silver wear Parade down? Didn't Silver nigh onto kill the both of them, he chased that hoss so long?"

"You seen Parade eatin' out of Silver's hand," said Lefty gloomily.

"Well, he'll eat out of our hands, too," said Chuck, with a grin.

"He won't," said Lefty. "I been and tried him, and he won't. You'd think that there was poison in my hand. If I take and stir up the barley or the oats for him in his feed box, he'll smell at it, but he won't eat. You try the same thing, and see."

"I've tried it—and he won't eat what I've touched," agreed Chuck. "What's the matter with him?"

"I was sayin' a while back," answered Lefty, "that he took and ate out of the hand of Silvertip. That's all that I was sayin'. He was right friendly with Silver."

"He was dead beat, and he couldn't help what he did," argued Chuck.

"He took and ate out of Silver's hand," said Lefty.

"What's the idea? Was that crook of a man-killer—was he any better than us?" demanded Chuck.

"I was just thinkin' about Parade eatin' out of his hand," said Lefty dreamily. His friend glared at him.

"The main thing is right here in this," said Chuck at last. "Can we get Parade in shape to run him in the big race?"

"At the rodeo?"

"Yeah, at the rodeo."

"I dunno," said Lefty. "He ain't hardly got ambition to eat his oats. How would he come to run in a race?"

"We could stick a shot of somethin' into him," suggested Chuck.

"Yeah, we could do that," said Lefty. "But he'd have Brandy to beat, and I guess there ain't any hoss beatin' Brandy. He's a thoroughbred."

"Nothin' that ever lived," said Chuck, "could beat Parade. Everybody knows that."

"Not on a fifty-mile run," answered Lefty. "Not out there in the desert. But he ain't made for a one- or two-mile sprint. There's too much of him to get goin'. Who's this old codger?"

"It's Charlie Moore, that's been takin' care of Brandy a long time. Hello, Charlie."

Charlie Moore came slowly up to them, smiling vaguely.

"Gents," he said, "I been fired by Mr Richmond. Seems like him and Brandy don't need me no more. I was wonderin' could you use me to take care of Parade?"

"What should we need of a man to take care of that hoss? Ain't we got a pair of hands apiece and ten minutes a day to work on him?" demanded Chuck.

"All right," said Moore. His vague old eyes steadied on them for a moment. "I just sort of cottoned to him, was all. And ten minutes ain't hardly enough to polish the hoofs of a horse like Parade, was all I was thinkin'."

He turned and went slowly out the door.

"Maybe we missed somethin'," said Lefty. "Maybe he could wake up Parade better'n a shot of dope."

"You talk like a fool today," said Chuck. "Leave off your thinkin', and let's have another drink."

18 – The Old Stallion

IN THE evening of the day, as soon as the stream of visitors stopped flowing up onto the platform—at twenty-five cents a head—in order to see Parade and the old mare, the canvas screen that turned the corral into a showroom was taken down, so that the wind might freely blow across the pair of captives. And on this evening, Parade and Mischief stood head to shoulder, she facing away to the northwest, the direction of the Sierra Blanca, and he looking in the opposite direction, into the pen where Brandy was kept. The sun was hardly down; it was still flinging up an abundance of fire that clung to the clouds in red and gold, and it would be long before the twilight ended. This is the time when cowpunchers lounge, between day and night, and forget the hard day, and try to make every moment an eternity before it is necessary to go to bed again—which means one step from breakfast and the saddle.

"I can see all the peaks of the Sierra Blanca," said the old mare.

"All of them?" asked Parade sadly.

"All white and blue against the red of the sky—it's as red as firelight shining on smoke."

"Can you see old Mount Blanco, itself?" asked Parade.

"I can see it clear to the shoulders," said Mischief, "and below that it turns blue and melts into the other mountains."

"If we had gone up there, into the ravines," said Parade, "then, perhaps, they never would have run us down."

"You can feed on regret like moldy hay," said Mischief, "but it will give you indigestion and pain, afterward."

"Perhaps it will," said Parade, "but what else is there to think of?"

"Think of the time to come," said the mare. "Prepare for the moment when you may be able to strike one blow for freedom. Be like a coiled snake.

89

It's better to die trying to get back to the Sierra Blanca than it is to live a slave all the days of your life."

"That may be true," said Parade, "but even if we escaped, he would come again and walk us down."

"You said that and you meant it," said the mare, "but you saw him fall dead."

"Yes," said Parade.

"And there is no other man in the world who ever tried to do such a thing as he managed. Now that he is gone, there is no other."

"You want me to play the king again," said the stallion. "I know the ways of the business now. That's true. I've learned how to shoot the bar that holds a gate, even. I could open this big gate here, for that matter, except that besides the bar there's a padlock on the outside. And if I were free, I could gather the best horses from the ranches, I could go and raid their corrals and their ranges, and run off with what I want. But there's no heart in me to do these things, mother. Man would come again. The Great Enemy would find me; I would fail; I would be hunted down."

"I can see the other mountains fading," said Mischief. "There's only one mountain left for me to remember, and that's the way with my memory of this life, Parade. I have thought you were a king, but I was always wrong."

"There's only one mountain left for me to remember, and that is your father. He was the king!"

"You said," answered Parade, "that Man simply walked down into the valley and led him away. At least, I fought harder than that!"

"It's not by reins and saddles and spurs and ropes that men control some of us," said the mare, "but Man puts his will on some of us, and then we can never escape. And your father was raised by a man he loved. He used to talk to me about the touch of his hand and the magic of the voice. I heard that voice calling out to your father, and he could not move. But if he had been raised wild and free, like you, Man never would have been able to break his heart as your heart has been broken!"

"Tell me more about the mountains," said Parade. "Can you see them now?"

"Only Mount Blanco, and the blue is growing up from the earth and covering it more and more; now to the shoulders, and the summit is all that remains, like a white cloud. Look for yourself."

"I'd rather hear about the mountains than see them," said Parade. "I look down at the ground all day long, because when I see the Sierra Blanca in the distance, I begin to think of the great days, and of the great runs, and I can taste the water of every water hole, and the grasses, and the tips of the shrubs on the foothills. But most of all, how we left Man struggling behind us, like little foolish pools of dust that the wind has raised and then run away from."

"You can think of those days," said the mare, "but still you haven't the heart—"

"You never passed two days staggering up the Salt Creek," said Parade. "If you had, you would have left your heart on the ground there. Hush! The old stallion in the next corral wants to talk to us."

"Let him talk to himself," said Mischief. "I'm tired of horses. I want to be alone. Ah, the day you were foaled, when I looked at you and saw you leading all the herds in the world, blackening the valleys, sweeping over mountains—but there is only one horse, after all, and he is dead—or so old that death is only a step from him."

She moved off to a far corner of the corral, and Parade went to the fence, and touched the nose of the old horse, half of whose head was reached through the bars.

After touching noses, they went through the rest of the formal greeting which two well-bred horses always exchange. That is to say, they withdrew half a pace from one another, tossed their heads high, stamped, and returned to look at one another with bright, half-mischievous eyes.

"I have watched you and heard your voices," said Brandy, "and there is something about your companion that reminds me of the one happy moment of my life, long, long ago. The one really happy moment, because it was the one free moment."

"Have you been free?" asked Parade.

"There was a time when I ran free," said Brandy. "That was longer ago than a colt like you could remember. But let me tell you, I have not always been like this, with staring hips and gaunt withers, and a scrawny neck, and sunken places over my eyes. Before Time had moth-eaten my coat, I shone almost as you do. Well, it's a foolish business to boast about the past!"

"It is," said Parade. "I have seen the time when a hundred horses followed me, and the men who hunted us might as well have hunted a flock of wild hawks in the sky. But those days are ended, and now I'm like you—a beaten drudge, a slave of man."

Suddenly Mischief came across the corral and stood at the side of Parade.

She said to Brandy: "There is something about you that reminds me of an old companion of mine. I wish that I could hear you neigh out with your full voice. I think it might have a meaning for me."

"There is nothing for me to neigh out loud about," said Brandy. "Not unless I fall to thinking of the past, and that's a melancholy business."

"And what do you think of most in the past?" asked Mischief.

"One glorious time on which I don't dwell," said Brandy. "And for the rest—I'm a race horse, you see. And I think of races. I wonder if either of you ever faced the barrier?"

"I don't know what it is," said Mischief.

"A webbing," said the old stallion, "and the other horses stand beside you. The youngsters are on tiptoe. You can hear the crowd of people screaming higher and higher. The starters are trying to get the horses perfectly in line. The webbing flies up. There's one deep groan from all the people—and the race is on. And every start is another pull at the heart. It makes me young to think of it."

"You're old," said Mischief, "to still be racing. Do you win, these days?"

"Age doesn't matter so very much, up to ten or twelve," said Brandy. "That is, it doesn't if your blood lines are right. So I'm told, at least."

"For my part," said Mischief, "I always hold that one horse is as good as another!"

"I didn't mean to hurt your feelings," said Brandy, "in case you don't happen to be a thoroughbred."

"Thoroughbred, fiddlesticks!" said the mare. "I can tell you that I've been on deserts where a silly thoroughbred, with his paper skin and his soft ways of living, would wither up in a single day."

"I've no doubt you're right," said Brandy politely. "I didn't mean to claim any superiority. We were simply speaking of—"

"Thoroughbred, my foot!" snorted Mischief, interrupting. "For my part, I'm a democrat, and I don't care who knows it. I never believed in an aristocracy, and in a free country, there's no place for one. You're a thoroughbred, are you? Your long legs and your narrow chest, I suppose. I'd like to see those long legs climbing among some of the rocks that I've scampered through. Oh, it would do me a precious lot of good to see you trying to haul yourself over ice-coated rocks in the middle of winter, to get through a frozen pass—or else starve on the desert side!"

"Hush," said Parade. "You're insulting him."

"Thoroughbred, is he?" said Mischief furiously. "Well, I never laid eyes on a thoroughbred in my life, that I ever had any use for—barring one. And that one didn't look like this poor, skinny wreck."

"Go off and leave us alone," said Parade. "You've disgraced us both."

"I'm glad to leave you," said Mischief, "though what you can find to talk about to a conceited, overbearing, rude, intolerant boor of a worn-out thoroughbred, I can't tell."

With that, she stalked across the corral, and Parade apologized at once.

"The fact of the matter is," said Parade, "that it's a tender subject with her. But I'll tell you that the only horse she ever respected was a thoroughbred, who was my father."

"Was he, indeed?" said Brandy. "What were his blood lines, then?"

"You must understand," said Parade, "that my mother was a simple soul, and at the time she met my father, I dare say that she didn't know a blood line from a forty-foot rope."

"I understand you perfectly. She simply didn't ask," said Brandy. "And what a pity that is, because all thoroughbreds are more or less related. If you could dig down into your past, you might be able to find that you and I are cousins. My father was Single Shot, and my mother was Mary Anne; no, you wouldn't be able to place her very well, but, of course, you've heard of Single Shot?"

"No," said Parade. "I'm sorry to say that I haven't. I've lived away from race tracks."

"And a lucky thing for you," said Brandy. "There's no good comes to a young horse from such a business. I want to talk to you about it, but here's my friend, Man. I must go talk to him."

The rather bowed form of Charlie Moore was approaching the corral, his gentle voice sending a greeting before him.

19 – Silvertip's Return

CHARLIE MOORE opened the gate and entered the small corral. He began to walk up and down, his hand lying against the shoulder of the thoroughbred, as Brandy moved beside him, led only by the pressure of that hand.

The mare said quietly to Parade: "There you see it! There's the slave that loves his slavery! You may be like that, one day!" she predicted.

"Never," said Parade.

Another figure loomed through the twilight.

"Moore!" bawled the voice of Harry Richmond.

Poor Charlie Moore started, and hurried out of the corral. He stood shrinking before Richmond.

"I told you you was fired," exclaimed Richmond. "What do you mean comin' back here in the middle of the night? Whatcha tryin' to do?"

"I was sayin' goodbye to Brandy," answered Moore. "That was all. I was goin' to say goodbye for the last time. It's quite a spell that him and me has been together."

"I don't wantcha no more," declared Richmond. "Get out, and stay out."

"I was goin' to say," muttered Charlie Moore, "that if you didn't want to pay me no more, I'd be pretty glad to go on workin' here for nothin', and takin' care of Brandy."

Another figure could be seen by Parade, moving dimly in the background of the dull light. The new man lingered beside a ragged mesquite, his outline blurring with that of the bush. He was within easy earshot.

"Hold on," exclaimed Richmond. "You ain't that kind of a fool, are you? You wouldn't work for nothin', would you?"

"I'd work for nothin'," answered Charlie Moore. "There wouldn't be much meanin' for life, if I lost Brandy for good and all."

He held out his hand in an unconscious gesture through the bars of the corral, and the stallion put his soft muzzle against it.

"You'd work for nothin', and what'd you live on?" asked Richmond curiously. "Because I wouldn't be feedin' you. You can count that I wouldn't be wastin' no money on an old scarecrow like you."

"I'd manage somehow," declared Charlie Moore. "I dunno just how, but I'd manage somehow. I don't need much to eat. I'm getting sort of dried up, and I don't need much. I could live on stale bread—and Brandy!"

He laughed a little, as he said this. Richmond laughed, too. He said carelessly:

"Well, if you're that kind of a fool, you can stay on. I don't particularly hanker after feedin' and curryin' the hoss every day. And I guess Lake don't, either. You can spend as much time with Brandy as you want."

He turned and went off through the twilight, and his loud, snarling laughter came trailing back behind him.

The man who had paused by the mesquite bush came slowly up. He stood by the corral that held Parade and Mischief, and Parade suddenly lifted his head high in the air.

"What is it? What's the matter?" asked Mischief.

"Can the dead come to life, mother?" asked the stallion.

"What nonsense are you talking about?" asked Mischief.

"It's he—it's the Great Enemy—it's he!" snorted Parade.

And he stood alert, like a horse at the start of a race, frenzied with eagerness to be gone.

"How are things, Charlie?" asked the voice of the stranger.

Charlie Moore whirled about.

"Hi! Silver!" he breathed.

They shook hands.

"It's he!" groaned Parade to the mare. "I know his voice. I could tell about him in darkness!"

"What if it is?" answered Mischief. "Does that mean you have to tremble like a foolish colt when it first smells green grass in the spring of the year? What is any man to you?"

"His hands never touched you!" said Parade. "He never drew you back out of death into life. You never drank from the same water with him when thirst was killing you. Listen to his voice speaking! Doesn't it call to you? Don't you feel a madness to come to the touch of his hand?"

"Bah!" snorted Mischief. "The touch of his hand? I have no madness to come to the touch of anything except the good open wilderness of the Sierra Blanca."

"I'll come to him!" neighed Parade. "I'll jump the bars or break them down and come to him!" And his whinny rang long and loud across the night air.

Charlie Moore was saying: "It got so's Harry Richmond, he couldn't afford to keep me on, so he turned me off. I don't get no regular pay, no more. But I'm managing to keep along. Where you been, Silver?"

"Out in the Sierra Blanca."

"Have some bad luck? I see you got a bandage around your head."

"I had some—bad luck," admitted Silvertip. "You can call it that. Bad luck!"

He laughed a little, softly, and the neighing of the stallion broke in wildly upon his words.

"What's the matter? What's wrong with Parade?" murmured Charlie Moore. "Look at him prancin' up and down. Like he'd want to smash through the corral fence. What's drove him crazy?"

The neigh of the stallion shrilled through the evening like the shriek of a bagpipe and the thunder of a great brazen horn. It shook one's soul to hear that battle cry.

Up and down past the bars rushed Parade, swinging rapidly back like a caged wolf, now rearing, now beating at the fence with powerful hoofs, until it seemed that the barrier would surely be beaten down.

Lefty came running, yelling as he approached.

"There comes Lefty," explained Charlie Moore. "He's one of the two that caught Parade."

"One of the two that caught him?" said Silvertip. "I'm glad to know that. The other one was Chuck, eh?"

"That's right. You know 'em?"

"I know 'em," said Silvertip. "I'm going on, Charlie. I'll see you again tomorrow. In the meantime, remember that you haven't laid eyes on me. There's something that I want to do. Understand?"

"I understand," agreed Charlie Moore.

"You're broke, I suppose," said Silvertip, drawing back farther from the corral as Lefty drew near to the frantic stallion inside it.

"I got a quarter," said Charlie Moore. "I ain't broke."

"Here's five dollars," said Silvertip.

"I ain't worked for it," answered Moore. "I can't take it."

"You take it, and maybe I'll be able to show you how to work for it later on," said Silvertip. "So long, Charlie!"

And so he was gone, stepping quickly away through the night.

Lefty, in the meantime, was striking at the fence of the corral with a stick, and shouting and cursing Parade, but he might as well have called to a storm wind. Parade, every moment, grew still more violent, still rearing, still beating at the fence with his forehoofs, and sending his ear-blasting neigh across the night.

Chuck came. Others gathered. Lantern light fell through the bars of the corral and through the rising mist of dust that kept boiling up from the ground, showed Parade flashing here and there.

"It was that fool of an old Charlie Moore!" yelled Lefty. "He was out here. He done something to Parade! I'm goin' to take it out of his hide!"

Chuck went to Charlie Moore and grabbed him by the shirt at the throat and flashed lantern light right into the blinking old blue eyes.

"I didn't touch Parade," said Charlie Moore. "I wouldn't do nothin' wrong to a hoss."

"Who was out here talkin' to you?" demanded Lefty.

"A gent that come to look at Parade—but it was too dark to see nothin' and he went off."

They could get nothing from Charlie Moore, but they cursed him from their hearts and fell back upon the task of taming the fury of Parade.

Suddenly, it left him as it had come, in a flash.

He stood at the corner of the corral, facing steadily toward the direction in which Silver had disappeared, and the men, climbing onto the fence, looked down on him like explorers upon new lands.

"Something has happened," said Lefty, at last. "Look at him quiverin' Look at his eyes. Look at the way his tail is standin' up. Look at the bend in his neck. By thunderation, that's the hoss that drove gents mad—the look of him—when he was rangin' through the Sierra Blanca. His heart's come back to him!"

"His heart's come back to him," said Chuck. "I guess he'll be quiet now, for a while. Maybe he smelled somethin'."

They left the horses to darkness.

Still, in the black of the night, Parade remained standing as before, looking out at the southeastern stars.

"What is it now?" said Mischief, at his side.

"Nothing!" said Parade. "He's gone, and there's nothing left. But somehow I'll find a way to tear down this fence with my teeth and hoofs and get out and follow him till I find him."

"You act," said Mischief, "not like a horse at all, but like some starved beast of a meat eater. I've never seen a horse behave like this, Parade. Not even your father when he was first tasting freedom and ranging the Sierra Blanca like an eagle in the sky. Lie down, be quiet, and remember that tomorrow is another day."

20 – The Sheriff Talks

THAT new day brought the beginning of the rodeo. Parmalee, already overcrowded, was now filled to overflowing, and all day long the air was trembling with the lowing of cattle and the neighing of horses, the clashing of horns and the beating of hoofs, until the very earth seemed to come to life. It was early in the morning when Lefty and Chuck brought saddle and bridle to the corral where their stallion was housed. They found Parade wandering restlessly up and down the fence, hunting ceaselessly, hopelessly, for a means of escape.

"It wasn't no shot of dope that was shoved into him," said Chuck. "It wouldn't a' lasted this long, Lefty. If this here hoss has come to life, we're goin' to have a chance of doin' somethin' with him in the rodeo race."

"Agin' Brandy there?" Lefty sneered.

"We could bet on him for second place," answered Chuck.

They entered the corral, unnoticed by the stallion. Lefty roped him; Chuck saddled and bridled him, and mounted.

He had barely settled into the saddle, he had barely gathered the reins, when the horse beneath him exploded with incalculable savagery. It seemed to Lefty that the air was filled with a dozen images of that horse and rider. Then Chuck was hurled from the saddle and sent crashing against the fence. His head struck a post; his loose body thumped against the ground.

Lefty dragged out the senseless Chuck beneath the lowest bar of the fence. He dared not enter while the maelstrom continued to rage. Mischief was backed into a far corner, pressing herself into as small a compass as possible, her legs bending under her with fear. Old Brandy had even retreated to the opposite side of his own corral. And still Parade fought, twisted, bucked, until the girths loosened and the saddle fell from him.

98

At the saddle he went with insane fury. With teeth and hoofs he battered it to a mere blur of what it had been. Then galloping with a ringing neigh around the corral, the loose ends of the reins caught over the top of a post, and the bridle was promptly ripped from the head of the big horse.

He was free, again, sweat-blackened and polished, flecked with froth here and there, magnificent beyond expression.

Lefty looked at that glory of horseflesh with a snarling lip, and then he glanced back at his companion.

The eyes of Chuck had just opened, and they were the glazed eyes of a very sick man.

"Shoot that killer," said Chuck. "He's smashed me up. I'm all broke inside. The life's runnin' out of me, Lefty!"

But the life did not leave the body of Chuck. They carried him—Lefty and two strangers who happened by—into the barn, and cared for him there. And when a doctor came, the man of medicine made a careful examination and reported that there was nothing to fear if Chuck were kept quietly in bed for a few weeks.

"He was almost smashed in twenty places," said the doctor, "but being tough stuff, he only bent instead of breaking."

Chuck was carried on a stretcher to the hotel, and put to bed. By the time he was installed in his room, Parmalee and all the crowds in it had heard the story of the return of the stallion to wildness.

A still more important thing happened to Lefty, as he left the hotel. For he saw a tall fellow walking down the street with a peculiar swing to the shoulders, and to Lefty it was as though he had seen a ghost moving in the open light of day. The figure turned a corner. Lefty saw the white streak of a bandage that passed across the forehead.

Lefty stood transfixed. He said aloud, finally: "If I'd only taken one more look—if I'd only listened to his heart—but I seen where that bullet busted right through his brains!"

He went into the bar-room and took three big whiskies in a row. Soon the fumes of them had reached his brain, and the crazy specter of fear was subdued a little. He could think for the first time.

A mere tap on the head with the butt of a rifle would have ended Silvertip, on that other day, when he lay prostrate, his arms flung wide, and his eyes slightly open, exactly like the eyes of the dead. But now he was up and alert.

It was only wonderful that he had not found Chuck and Lefty before this, and put bullets through them. Chuck would now escape—the lucky devil was confined to bed, and according to reputation, Silvertip was not the sort of a man to pick on a helpless enemy.

But he, Lefty, was not helpless! Not only was he up and about, but he carried with him his own reputation as a fighting man. Yet he knew the distance, the infinite gulf, that separated his talents from those of Silvertip.

When the whisky had brought some calm to his mind, Lefty went out to find the sheriff. It was walking in a new world, to go down that street hunting every doorway with his eyes, coming to every corner as though to the mouth of a cannon. But there was no sight of Silvertip, and so Lefty came at last to the office of the sheriff, a little one-room shack where that square-faced, savage man of the law lived by himself.

He was at his desk, laboriously writing a report. He looked at Lefty with bright, impatient eyes.

"I been and heard that your partner was laid out, Lefty," he said.

"That ain't why I'm here," said Lefty. His thin face grew thinner still, as it lengthened with gloom. "I'm here," he said, "because there's a gent on my trail that's goin' to get me before the day's out, I reckon. I mean Silvertip is back in Parmalee!"

"I know he is," said the sheriff. "I've heard that talked about, too. How come Silver and you to have bad blood between you?"

"It don't take no effort to make Silvertip start on a gent's trail," answered Lefty. "You know what he's done in the world. There's more'n twenty dead men scattered down his trail, and that's a fact. And them that they count are only the known ones. Maybe there's twice as many more that ain't accounted for."

The sheriff twisted his mouth to one side and grunted.

"When killin's get more'n five or six," he said, "I always start in and doubt 'em a good deal. You better do some doubtin', too!"

"It ain't the arithmetic that makes Silvertip dangerous, anyway," said Lefty. "All I know is that he's after my scalp and I ain't ready to lose my hair."

The sheriff began to rub his knuckles across his chin. "I gotta remark," he said, "that I been and talked to Silvertip some time ago and told him that I was watchin' him. I gotta remark, too, that for all I've ever heard of him, I've never heard of anybody sayin' that he went for his gun first."

Lefty sighed. He answered: "Look at here. Suppose that you was a bird. Suppose that you met a rattler. Suppose that you tried to get away, and the eye of that snake caught hold of you and held you tight. Why, you'd be swallered, the first thing you knew, and you wouldn't say it was a fair fight, no matter whether the snake made the first move or not."

"You mean he kind of hypnotizes gents?" the sheriff asked.

"Sure he does," said Lefty. "Not with his eyes, but with the rep that he's got. You take and look at him, and you can see the dead men in his face. If you look at his hands, you can see those hands wishin' the gun right out of the air. He can shoot quicker than a wasp can sting. And a man has nc mcre chance agin' him than a spider has when a wasp up and sings in the air over it. The spider, he just lays down and gets ready to die. He's too scared to run. And that's the way with most of us when Silvertip is around. We know what he's done before; we know that he can do it ag'in."

"There's folks that have fought him," said the sheriff. "There's stories of plenty of folks that have stood up to him."

"Sure," said Lefty. "There was a good plenty of 'em in the early days before he got known. And even after that, there was gents that would get together, two or three of 'em at a time, and try their luck with him. There was the whole Harris family that jumped him up north in Montana. There was old man Harris and his five sons, and a coupla cousins throwed in. They cornered Silvertip in a box canyon, and he had to fight his way out. Well, old man Harris stayed behind in that canyon after Silver got out, and there's only four of the boys left, and most of 'em limp, or something. They used to raise a lot of trouble, the Harrises did, but now they're the quietest family in Montana."

The sheriff nodded. "I've heard tell of that fight," he said.

"What I want," said Lefty, "is to get Silvertip bound over to the peace, or somethin', while he's around this here town."

"There ain't anything to bind him over for," said the sheriff. "He ain't done nothin', and he ain't said nothin'. Not that nobody has heard. But I'll go and give him another talkin' to. What's this I hear about Parade goin' and wakin' up and turnin' wild ag'in?"

"I dunno how it is," said Lefty. "Queer things is in the air. I've seen what Parade's turned into, but I dunno how it come about. I'm goin' to get that Mexican, Jaurez, to ride Parade and gentle him before the race."

"Jaurez can ride anything that wears hair," said the sheriff. "He'll tame Parade, all right. But you ain't goin' to win much out of that race, Lefty— not if Parade was twice what he is. It's a shame to put him into a race like that. It ain't more'n a mile and a half, and he couldn't stretch himself out and get warmed up in that kind of a run. It needs one of these skinny, spindlin' thoroughbreds to sprint a race like that. Like Brandy is, maybe. And besides, there's a gent here that calls himself Steve Jones, and he's got a long, narrow, washed-out lookin' chestnut mare with him—and if he ain't a jockey, and if she ain't a ringer right fresh off the big tracks, I'm a sucker. You keep Parade right outta that race. If he had the lot of 'em out in the desert, he'd run their hearts out three times a day, but a race track is different."

He left the office at the side of Lefty.

"I'll find big Silvertip," he said, "and I guess he won't make no trouble while he's around here."

He found Silvertip, in fact, sitting in the long line of loafers whose chairs were on the veranda of the hotel, tipped back against the front wall. He beckoned the big fellow to him, and Silvertip came down into the street. He was making a cigarette and he offered the tobacco and wheat-straw papers to the sheriff.

The sheriff refused them with a gesture.

"You're here after Lefty," said the sheriff. "Is that right?"

Silvertip smiled.

"You're here after Lefty," said the sheriff. "It ain't me alone that knows it. Understand what I mean, Mr Silver?"

Silvertip lighted his cigarette.

"Silence ain't goin' to do you no good," said the sheriff, raising his voice angrily. "I'm givin' you warnin' right now to get out of this here town. Move on, and leave Parmalee, and stay out of Parmalee. Hear me?"

Silvertip smiled again.

At this, the sheriff took half a step back. There were many eyes watching him, and he could understand that he was being quietly, silently tested in the minds of all those men who beheld him. Something was demanded of him, some sort of action.

But what could he do?

He could not, after all, pick up Silvertip on a charge of vagrancy. He had ordered the man to leave Parmalee, but since there was no charge against him, he could not force him to move on if Silvertip were minded to resist. He looked up at the white bandage around the brow of Silvertip. He looked beneath that bandage at the face which had been recently reworked in deeper lines, and with a finer, closer modeling. It was not the same man to whom the sheriff had talked not so many weeks before. It was a new soul, encased in flesh which had altered, also. The steel had been given a finer tempering; it possessed a sharper and more remorseless edge.

"I've told you," shouted the sheriff suddenly, "that this ain't the town for you. Get out!"

It was the crisis. The men along the veranda of the hotel leaned forward, or slanted to one side, and all narrowed their eyes to make sure that they observed every particle of this historical event.

They saw the right hand of Silvertip slowly convey the cigarette to his lips. They saw the end of the cigarette turn red with fire; they saw it lowered; they saw the lips of Silvertip part a little, and rippling tides of white smoke drawn inward, disappearing; and with the exhalation, they saw the cloud of smoke blown with careful aim straight into the face of the sheriff.

The sheriff did not move until every whit of that smoke had been blown in his face. Then the others could see that he was gray and drawn and looking weary, as if with a burden of new years laid on his shoulders.

At last he said: "All right, Silvertip. You've called my bluff. I ain't man enough to lick you. I swaller this insult, but the minute that you step a quarter of an inch across the line of the law, I'm goin' after you. Every man has gotta die once, and I reckon that my time is pretty close to up!"

21 – Juarez, the Horse Breaker

IN THIS singular scene, it was felt that both men had come through the crisis with undiminished reputations. Silvertip, without lifting a hand or speaking a single word by way of threat, or doing anything that would have, in a court of law, more weight than a puff of smoke, had quietly defied the sheriff and all that the sheriff represented.

The sheriff, on the other hand, had endured the strain of a superior force without weakening, and a great deal of sympathy and respect were felt for him, accordingly.

After that meeting, half a dozen men went to the man of the law and quietly suggested that they would make themselves into a committee to look after Silvertip while he was in Parmalee. The sheriff promptly swore them in as deputies, and they went off to find their man.

They found him where the rest of Parmalee was to be found—out at the rodeo grounds where Parade was to be ridden this day by Jaurez. Everyone in town knew by this time that the stallion had suddenly gone wild again, and that the real Parade was now to be seen, as he had been when he reigned over the Sierra Blanca. And the six deputies, ranging quietly up beside big Silvertip, found him staring toward the shed out of which the stallion would be brought into the big inclosure. He was rapt. The coming of the deputies seemed to mean little or nothing to him.

And now all other matters were forgotten by every man and woman and child in that crowd, for out of the shed, and through the gate into the rodeo grounds that occupied all the ground inside the race track, burst Parade.

He came as if he wished to exemplify his name, rearing, plunging, swerving like a bright sword blade. Two cow-punchers with strong lariats and competent horses were controlling him, but he seemed to be dragging

104

them along as though they were stuffed toys. He was a thunderbolt newly forged and polished, and every heart shuddered, and every heart leaped, at the thought of sitting on the back of that monster.

Lefty was one of the cowpunchers. He had Parade take the complete circuit of the field, inside of the big fences, and when he came opposite the benches which had been built under a shed and which were called the "grandstand," he made a little speech.

"This here hoss," said Lefty, "has pretty near killed my partner. When I seen him skyrocket, I figgered that there was hardly no other man that would be able to set him out. But Jaurez thinks he can do it. He's bet me a hundred dollars that he can; and I've bet him three hundred that he can't. Jaurez, if you're anywheres about, step out and show yourself, because Parade is plumb ready!"

It seemed as though Parade exactly understood that speech, or perhaps it was because he could see the far-off peaks of the Sierra Blanca shining like spear points against the sky. At any rate, his head went high, his tail swept out in a loftier arch, and his neigh sounded like a trumpet of challenge across the field.

There came to answer it a tall Mexican, who slithered through the bars of the fence, and went on, carrying a saddle and a bridle. His face would have been handsome, but smallpox had ruined it as life had ruined the soul of the man. Existence was to him a sneer. The years had battered him. He walked with a slight limp, but in his mouth and in his eyes he expressed his contempt for the world.

At this moment, he made a splendid picture for mind and eye, as he moved out across the field toward the savage beauty of the golden stallion. For an instant, everyone forgot what was known about Jaurez the savage, and saw him only as Jaurez, the peerless horse breaker. Some men were accustomed to say that after Jaurez had broken a horse, not even a veterinary surgeon could put the poor beast together again. He was known to have ridden twenty famous outlaws until their hearts were gone, and though he had had his falls, as his limping proved, still in the end he was always the conqueror. But it was felt that now he was going to meet as fair a test as ever would be found.

It was the sort of a contest that the West has always loved—man against nature, with the dice loaded on nature's side, for when the Mexican had reached the side of the stallion, he looked a mere wisp, a mere stripling beside the glory of Parade.

Parade was blindfolded by Lefty; the saddle and bridle were slipped on, and in a moment Jaurez was smoothly up and in the saddle. Lefty, his hand on the blindfold, was seen to speak for an instant to the Mexican. No doubt he was rehearsing the terms of the agreement—that the attempt would be limited to three falls. If by that time the stallion had not been mastered, then Jaurez lost his bet.

Jaurez was seen to agree to those terms with a slight gesture. Lefty, leaning from his own saddle, jerked off the blindfold. Parade sprang like a released fountain into the air.

There was something more than the hands of Jaurez to control him, in the last emergency, for with a sixty-foot rawhide lariat, Lefty still had a hold on the horse. But now he kept that rope slack, and allowed Parade to fight as though for freedom.

And Parade went mad.

Have you seen a cat fly into a passion because it loses the mouse with which it has been playing? Have you seen it bound here and there, striking, and leap into the air, and hurl itself down, rolling over and over? So Parade turned his great body into the body of a cat, and seemed to grip the earth with claws.

And there was this blood-curdling factor of interest, that with every twist and turn and fall, he was continually striving to put teeth or hoofs on the Mexican. He wanted to get that burden off his back, and once off, he wanted to smash the life out of it.

The thing was appalling. The women began to look down at the ground. Children opened their eyes and their mouths. And even of the men who thronged the fences, there was hardly one who could find voice.

What gave point to the awfulness was that Jaurez himself seemed to be daunted for the first time in his reckless life. His whole face was as white as the ghastly silver pockmarks that were cut out of it. He kept on grinning, but there was no life in the smile; it was like the grimace of the punch-drunk boxer who still keeps stretching his mouth toward a smile of indifference, as the blows make the hair leap on his head, and cause his knees to sag.

Jaurez, plainly, was afraid. He was a dozen times out of the saddle and onto the ground as that huge wildcat flung itself down and turned and twisted. And always he was back into the saddle again at the critical instant as Parade lurched up to his feet.

Then came the end. Everybody could see that it was coming. Parade began to leap at the sky and come down on one stiffened foreleg. It was wonderful that even whalebone and sinew like his could withstand such frightful shocks. And every time, Jaurez was snapped like the lash of a whip. His chin came down on his chest, or his head banged over on his shoulder. His sombrero went off. His hair exploded upward with every shock.

And then the red flag of danger showed on his face, as he started bleeding from ear and nose and mouth.

He was done. Men began to hold their breath and stare as though they saw a man toppling on the brink of a cliff. Up in the grandstand a woman was screaming in a terrible voice, calling out to shoot the horse and save Jaurez.

That was what everyone felt. Once Jaurez struck the ground, Parade would finish him. Parade would turn him into red pulp in one second, unless Lefty with his rope and his cow horse could manage to hold the stallion.

Jaurez was holding by spurs and hands. He was "pulling leather" for all he was worth, but nobody blamed him for that. He was in the center of a tornado, and fighting for his life. The quirt which he had swung so gayly in the beginning now hung down, flopping like a dead snake from his wrist.

Then human nature could stand no more of that punishment.

He knew well enough what lay in store for him if he were flung to the ground, and he determined to shoot Parade dead beneath him. One wild yell burst from all throats together, like a shout from a chorus when a conductor strikes down his baton; for everyone saw the flash of the revolver as Jaurez drew it.

The stallion seemed to see it, also. Instead of leaping at the sky again, he dodged cat-like to the side, and Jaurez sailed out of the saddle, diving at the ground.

He put a bullet into the dust, and then his body struck on the same spot. It was something like throwing a stone into the water and then diving at it. People spoke about that, afterward.

And Parade?

As he whirled to dart back at the fallen man, Lefty did his part well and nobly. He threw his cow pony back on its haunches and jerked the lariat tight. The poundage of the stallion hit the end of that rope like a freight train going down a sharp grade. There was no more danger of that rawhide breaking than of a steel cable coming apart, but Lefty and his horse went over with a crash.

Lefty was flung far to the side, rolling; the horse rolled, too, and as the pommel of the saddle snapped, Parade came clear of the wreck with the length of the lariat streaming almost straight out from his neck.

That was the speed with which he was hurling himself forward, and he went straight at the fallen body of Jaurez.

No man would ever forget how Jaurez, stunned and broken as he was, turned like a worm that has been half crushed under foot. He still had his gun in his hand, and now he fired it twice, right at the charging stallion.

He missed. Almost of course he missed, for his hand must have been shaking and his eyes half blind. Then the Colt went wrong. The hammer dropped, and there was no explosion to answer its fall.

The stallion was almost on the fallen man by this time. Around the fence, perhaps a hundred men had drawn their guns, when a very odd thing happened. One voice broke out above the tumult in a great, wordless cry, and as Parade heard it, it seemed to strike him like a volley of lead.

He plunged suddenly to the side, veered off in a circle, and then started once more for his victim.

Poor Jaurez had turned again. He was trying to drag himself on his hands toward the fence and safety. The lower part of his body dragged like a limp sack behind him. He had his face turned over his shoulder, watching the rush of Parade, and he was screaming. Other voices were shrieking, too, and all the screams did not come from women, either.

Those poised revolvers along the fence were about to come into action with a roar that would have blown Parade into kingdom come, but the shooting was stopped by a stranger thing than any man ever had seen before. For a big fellow with a bandage about his head came running out straight toward Parade.

It was suicide, but it was such dramatic suicide that people forgot even about Jaurez and fastened their minds on this madman.

What they saw was Silvertip standing astride Jaurez, and Parade hurtling down on him. Silvertip put out a hand, and incredulous eyes saw that there was no gun in that hand. It was open. The palm was turned up. The fool seemed to be treating this equine tiger like a friend.

What actually happened was that Parade sheered off at the last instant. He turned around and around that motionless central group, where Jaurez now lay flat with his face in his hands, shutting out the sight of destruction, and where Silvertip kept moving just enough to face the wild horse.

Then Parade put on the brake by skidding all four hoofs through the dirt and coming to a halt in front of Silver.

The horse put up his head and sent his ringing neigh across the field and through the stunned brains of the spectators. They could see that the hand of Silvertip already was caressing the polished neck of Parade!

That was not all, but that was the picture which remained when everything else was finished.

There was the carrying of Jaurez off the field, and the long wait before the doctors announced that he would walk again—but never ride horses any more!

Then they had picked up Lefty like a limp sack, but all he needed was a dash of water in his face, and a slug of whisky down his throat. He came to, and could not understand, with his stunned mind, the strange story which men were trying to tell him.

These things had their interest, but what were they compared with the manner in which men saw Silvertip mount Parade and ride him with loose reins across the field, leaning forward in the saddle, keeping his hand on the neck of the great horse, while Parade turned his head a little, as he jogged softly on, and listened, and listened, and seemed to understand?

22 – Lefty's Proposition

WHAT brought back the full use of his wits to Lefty was the information that Parade had been ridden away by Silvertip. He cried out in an agony that the horse was gone forever, and rushed out to pursue the trail.

Six good citizens of Parmalee went with him, and the sheriff was also in the group. They had changed some of their opinions about Silvertip since they saw the manner in which he had handled the horse, but if he had stolen Parade—well, it might be a long trail, but they intended to undertake it.

What was their amazement when they traced Silvertip straight back to the corral where Parade always had been kept by Chuck and Lefty? And there stood Parade, now, with Silvertip beside him, rubbing the sweat out of his hide with twists of hay, and bringing up the true golden color.

They stood outside the fence, all of them, and stared. Then the sheriff went quietly away; his posse followed.

But before he left, the sheriff said to Lefty:

"You've been wrong about that hombre. There ain't any killing in his head, or he would a' left Parade to polish off Jaurez and bash in your own head. We're goin' to watch him, still—but I guess you're wrong!"

Lefty himself remained by the fence. He was trembling with excitment. He was terribly afraid, and yet he could not drag himself away from the spectacle of that horse which had changed so suddenly from tame to tiger, and back to tame again.

"Silvertip!" exclaimed Lefty.

"Well?" said Silver, without turning.

"It's this way," said Lefty. "Either you're goin' to go after my scalp, or you ain't!"

Silvertip said nothing. Lefty wiped the water from his forehead and flicked the drops from his fingers into the dust. They fell in thin, straight lines of darkness.

"Silver," said Lefty, "the fact is that that hoss waked up and got wild after seein' you. Ain't that the fact?"

Silvertip went on with the grooming of the stallion, silently.

"I'll tell you what," said Lefty, "after what I seen today, I ain't goin' to try, ever, to ride the devil. Nobody else will try, either. He wouldn't be no good to me except as a show hoss, nor to Chuck, neither. What I wanta do is to make a proposition to you. You ride that Parade in the rodeo race, tomorrow, and you'll sure win it. And if you ride, I'm goin' to bet my socks on him. And if you win, Silver—why, you take the hoss, and that's that! Is it a go? He wouldn't be any good to me, anyhow!"

Silvertip, at last, raised his big head slowly. Then he turned toward the fence. With his hand, he kept on automatically stroking the stallion's brightening side.

"Have you seen that mare, that ringer, that the tough little mug called Jones has brought into town, Lefty?" he asked.

"Yeah. I've seen her. She looks like she could split the wind," agreed Lefty.

"And there's old Brandy right here beside us. He can still move," went on Silvertip.

"He can," said Lefty, "but there ain't nobody that seen Parade move today, that don't think that he can beat the world, if there's a man to ride him."

"There's two hundred pounds of me, Lefty," said Silvertip. "Mind you," he added in a different voice, "I'm going to have Parade one of these days. If I have to wipe out the murdering pair of you, I'll do it. Because I'm going to have Parade."

The calmness with which he spoke did not deceive Lefty, and the tremor of mortal fear went through him again. But he said, still sweating violently: "Look at it my way, Silver. You got an easy chance to get Parade, if you'll do what I say. There ain't no murder in it, if you'll do what I say, and we'll all have a chance to clean up. I'll clean up the coin, and you'll get Parade."

Silvertip looked aside at the horse, and the stallion turned his head and stared into the mysterious face of Man.

Silver sighed.

"It's no use, Lefty," he declared. "Suppose that I ride him? My weight would kill him. Besides, he's not meant for sprinting. I wouldn't shame him by letting him be beaten. If you want a match against Parade, take anything in the world out into the desert and then run 'em against Parade, and he'll laugh. But a race track sprint, that's a different matter. That chestnut mare—she can move. I know her lines, and they're meant for speed. Jones is a featherweight in the saddle on her. And Lake is not much more on Brandy. Parade would be giving them seventy pounds. He couldn't do it. No horse could do it."

Lefty looked from the man to the horse. It seemed to him, suddenly, dwarfed and deformed as his soul was, that he could see a similarity, a sort of kinship between the two; the same lordliness about their heads, the same calm fearlessness in their eyes, and something formidably big and wild about them both. Now that he saw the picture from this angle, it seemed to Lefty not strange that the man should have won the horse, but that it would have been mysterious indeed if that kinship had not worked out.

"Silver," said Lefty, "I ask you this here—ain't it worth the try? Ain't it worth it? I'll make a few thousands if Parade wins, and you'll get Parade himself. Look at it that way, and figure it for yourself!"

"And what about Chuck?" asked Silvertip. "How does he come into the deal?"

The narrow face of Lefty sneered.

"Never mind Chuck," he said. "He got himself smashed up, and he ain't in the game, no more."

Silvertip looked the little man over carefully. Suddenly he nodded.

"I'll take the chance of shaming Parade for the chance of owning him," he said.

"Now you're talkin'!" cried Lefty. "I'm goin' to clean up on this. But listen to me, Silver—you gotta ride him till he's right in the palm of your hand. You better ride him today. Get him ready for tomorrow. It ain't long away—it ain't hardly long enough away for me to get my money down."

"I'll have him in the palm of my hand when the race comes around," said Silvertip. "Go off and lay your bets!"

He turned again to the grooming of Parade, which he continued till the big horse was dry.

He left, and again Parade began to move restlessly up and down behind the fence, whinnying, stamping at the ground, sometimes rearing and striking at the bars with his forehoofs.

The old mare, Mischief, came out of her corner of the corral, where she had been standing sullenly, and muttered at him:

"What's the matter, now, Parade? Why are you stamping and raging? He'll come back. You can depend on that. Men will keep on returning like winter. The great heavy brute! I'm thankful that I don't have to carry him on my back. Why are you hysterical?"

"You have never found a man," said Parade. "But I have found one. You've never had a hand on your shoulder that seemed to lie on your heart, also. And you've never had a touch on the reins that ran into your blood. You've never heard a voice that made you feel free, even under saddle and bridle. But I have heard that voice."

Mischief began to nibble at one of the posts, breaking off splinters of the wood, and pretending that she had not heard, but she knew that her son had been taken away from her at last. She could dream of the great wild freedom of the Sierra Blanca, but she would have to dream of it alone.

And she remembered how the man had come down into the valley and taken Brandy away, by the mere sound of his voice.

The old stallion spoke suddenly from the next corral: "I have heard a voice, also. I have known a touch, too."

"Bah!" said the mare. "A fool will still be a fool when he's old, and so are you. Who cares what you've heard and what you've felt? But my son has been king of the Sierra Blanca! Why do you compare yourself with him?"

"The Sierra Blanca? I know it very well," said Brandy, patient under this abuse. "I've been there!"

"You've been there under a saddle or a pack," said the mare. "Who cares where you've been? Who cares a whit? Not I!"

"I care," said Parade.

He went to the fence and pushed his head a little between the bars.

"I'd like to hear what you did in the Sierra Blanca," he declared. "I'd like to know what you've seen of it."

"I have talked enough," said Brandy stiffly. "There is an old proverb— when the mare is angry, never talk to the colt."

He turned away as he spoke, and now the pleasant, husky voice of old Charlie Moore came toward him, singing, and the old stallion ran to the gate of the corral.

"A disgusting—shameful—degrading sight!" said Mischief. "To stand and wait for a man, like a dog! And you, Parade, storming up and down again, whinnying, dancing like a little fool in its first May days! What shall I think of you but shame?"

23 – The Crooked Three

THERE were only three men in the back room of the saloon, and they looked as sordid as the atmosphere of the place. There had been a lamp on the table, but now it was moved to an adjoining one, because not one of the three wanted too much light to play over his features. The liquor in the whisky bottle was black, with one trembling highlight in it, blood-red, and in the glasses the drink appeared dull amber. They nursed these glasses with their hands, slowly turning them, drinking, not to one another but out of turn and out of order, their mouths twisting into sneers as the terrible bar whisky burned its way home.

Richmond was one of them, his swollen face creasing and dimpling as he spoke. The frog-faced half-breed, Lake, sat beside him, rarely talking. And opposite them was a lean little brown-faced man, that certain "Mr Jones" who had brought to the rodeo the chestnut mare that looked fit to cut the wind like a knife.

Mr Jones talked with a certain amount of dry humor, and frankness.

"You take birds like us, that've been barred off the tracks," said he, "and we can't pick and choose. We gotta enter our nags where we can, and pick up a livin', one way or another. That mare of mine has worn fifty different names in fifty different races. She's worn three or four different complexions, too. She's been a bleached bay, and she's been a red-brown. She's had all black stockin's, and she's had 'em all white. But no matter how she's dressed, she always runs like a lady."

Lake, at this, grinned down into his glass and suddenly sipped at the contents. Richmond lifted his big head and turned his fat face from side to side, making sure that there was no one near enough to overhear these confessions.

114

"It ain't any use to cry over spilt milk," said Richmond. "But I'll tell you something worth more than that old sayin'."

"Fire away," said Mr Jones.

"It ain't any use talkin' about spilt milk, either!" added Richmond.

Jones put back his head and his leathery, thin face convulsed in silent laughter.

"You look scared enough for the prison shakes," he said. "Ever done time, Richmond?"

Richmond scowled at the words. "Whatcha mean by that? Time? Sure I never done time."

"You never done time?" said Jones, still laughing a little. "No, I guess you never have. Some gents are lucky, like that. Sometimes it's more than luck; sometimes it's just brains. Somebody else does the job for 'em—blows the safe—or rides the crooked race!"

He was still laughing, but the laughter was only a pretense. It was apparent that Jones was as ready for trouble as a bird is ready for a grain of wheat.

Richmond, therefore, made a broad, sweeping gesture.

"Lemme just tell you somethin'," said he.

"You been tellin' me plenty, right up to now," said Jones, dropping his head a little, and looking up from under the brows.

"Lemme just tell you this," said Richmond. "You and me, either we can do business together, or we can't. And bar-room arguments, they don't buy you anything, and they don't buy me nothin', either. What do you say?"

"I dunno," said the other. "I dunno what you got in your head, brother. I dunno what your style is, yet, or how you sell on the open market."

"I get a pretty good price, maybe," said Richmond. "But that ain't the point. Do we do business, or do we just finish off this drink and bust?"

"Either way," said Jones. "I don't care. I put my cards on the table, and I don't care a whoop. You do what you please."

"All right," said Richmond, and he pushed back his chair.

Jones sneered down at his glass of whisky and made no move.

"Wait a minute, chief," said Lake.

He put his hand on the arm of Richmond, and the big man readily slumped back into the chair from which he was rising.

"Whatcha want, Lake?" he demanded.

"I was just thinkin'," said Lake. "You two, you oughtn't to bust up like this here. There's money for you two to make."

"There's bullets for us to get in the neck, too," said Richmond, "if anybody happens to see us in here together, tonight. They'll know that we're saltin' the race away for tomorrow."

"Sure they'll know," said Jones. "And who cares? Who wants to make crooked money without havin' somethin' to flavor it? I wouldn't steal a dime, if there wasn't a chance for me to get caught."

"That's right, too," said Richmond, stirring in his chair.

"I'm not backin' up none," said Jones. "If you wanta do business, all right. If you don't all right. I'm not backin' up none, is all I say."

"He ain't backin' up none. That ain't what you want—for him to back up, chief," suggested Lake.

"Sure it ain't," said the rancher.

He looked suddenly into the keen, small eyes of Jones, and said: "We could do business together, you fool."

Jones merely grinned. "You sound more nacheral, now," he said.

"I been nacheral from the start," answered Richmond. "The point is, this whole town is nuts about the race tomorrow. It's crazy about the race, ain't it?"

"Crazy? Listen!" suggested Jones.

He lifted his hand.

It was well past the hour at which Parmalee was ordinarily asleep, but this was a night of nights, and a steady uproar rose from the place, higher than the flying dust. In the street there were two big parties of whisky-maddened cowpunchers who were sweeping back and forth down the long street, yelling, shooting off their guns, whooping. And when either of these groups came near, the thundering of hoofs and guns, the screeches of the riders, made talk impossible. Afterward the wave of tumult sudsided, but it was always present in the air.

Besides these climaxes, there was a steadier undertone of noise that moaned and laughed and roared its way out of Parmalee. There were two improvised dance halls, with two very improvised orchestras blaring out tunes well out of date, and from those halls came the laughter, the waves of sudden outbreaks of heavy voices of men, or single, piercing notes of women; and again the silence would be so profound that one could hear, even across the street, even behind flimsy walls, the whispering of the many feet upon the floor.

"Crazy? I'll tell you the town's crazy for tomorrow," said Mr Jones.

"If they got an idea that anything crooked was pulled in that race, they'd take us out of the saddles and hang us up," said Richmond.

"They won't take you out of the saddle," said Jones, sneering. "You won't be ridin'." He looked at Lake, and sneered again, and nodded his evil head.

"That's all right," said Richmond hastily. "They'll know that I was behind the hoss and the arrangin'."

"Well," said Jones to Lake, "how good are you, kid?"

"I can put the mufflers on," said Lake, "and you wouldn't know a thing. Besides, I've rode Brandy every race he ever run. What I mean, though—he can run."

"So can the mare," said Jones. "And I can ease her down to a whisper, and make it look like she was just plain played out."

"The thing to do," said Richmond, "is to put our money on the mare. Put it up to her, to win, and a little to place, because the favorite is goin' to be Brandy. The boys around here know Brandy. They've seen him win a lot, and the odds are goin' to be favorin' him."

"Some are bettin' on Parade," put in Lake.

"Yeah? The fools!" commented Richmond.

"I seen the big guy out on Parade today," said Jones. "That nag can gallop."

"Silvertip is the only man in the world that can ride him, and Silver weighs two hundred pounds, and more," said Richmond.

"Yeah," said Jones, "but that nag can gallop."

"The race is a mile and a half. No horse can carry two hundred pounds a mile and a half and beat Brandy," said Lake.

"No?" persisted Jones. "I'll tell you somethin' else. Silvertip is full of brains, and brains take off weight. Brains don't weigh nothin' in a race."

"Silvertip can go hang," said Lake savagely.

Mr Jones licked his lips, and laughed. He filled his glass, sloshing off the whisky out of the bottle, and tossed off another drink. Then he laughed again loudly.

"You two birds are scared of Silver, ain't you?" And still he laughed.

Lake said, with slow emphasis: "Yeah, we're scared. Everybody's scared of him."

"Listen to me," said Jones. He lifted a crooked brown forefinger. "I ain't scared of Silvertip."

"Then you're just a plain fool," said Lake.

Richmond jerked his glance suddenly toward Lake and then back toward Jones. It looked as though Mr Jones were about to draw a gun. He had half risen from his chair, and his eyes burned. But presently he settled back again.

"Maybe you're right," said Jones. "Maybe I ought to be scared of him."

"Sure you had oughta be," persisted Lake.

"Let it go!" commanded Richmond. "The thing to do is you and me declare the mare to win."

"She'd beat Brandy, anyway," said Jones. "She's younger, and she can go like the wind."

"She couldn't beat Brandy," said Lake calmly.

"Shut up!" ordered Richmond. He added: "The mare wins, and we split everything two ways."

"And me?" said Lake.

"I'll take care of you," growled Harry Richmond.

Lake turned on his employer a yellow, sour grin. "Yeah, you'll take care of me," he muttered.

"That's fixed," said Jones. "You can't bet agin' yourselves, so you hand me the money, and I bet for you."

"I have to hand you the cash," agreed Richmond slowly, and he drew out his wallet.

Then his hand paused. His face turned bright with perspiration.

"I give you the cash—" he muttered.

"When I play a game with a gent, I play the game," said Jones. "But I don't care. You can all go hang, for all of me!"

Richmond opened the wallet, took out three small bills, and pushed the rest of the money across the table.

"Listen," said Richmond. "It's everything I've got. I used to have a ranch. All I got now is a mortgage—since I followed the racing business. This is the last that I could get together. Listen—put some down on the mare to place. We gotta make sure."

"I'll do that," said Jones. "I'll write down the bets and the odds. I'll show you the list, afterward, and we'll split everything two ways. You trust me?"

Richmond sighed. "Yeah, I trust you," he answered.

"Then there's Parade," said Jones. "We gotta fix Parade."

"Why, you couldn't buy Silvertip. You dunno what you're talkin' about," retorted Richmond. "You couldn't buy him. He's one of those honest fools. He'd kill himself sooner than turn a corner short. Besides, you don't have to think about him, unless that crazy stallion of Lefty's runs amuck and kicks the daylights out of the mare at the post. And that ain't likely."

"Parade can gallop," said Jones scowling. "I watched him, and I seen him gallop."

"He's got two hundred pounds up," argued Richmond patiently.

"Take off fifty pounds of that for brains," said Jones. "Silvertip ain't anybody's fool."

"Well—just in case," remarked Lake, "we could box him."

"That's what I mean," said Jones. "No matter what Silvertip may do at the finish, the mare and Brandy have got the early foot. The last half mile—suppose that the stallion comes along pretty fast—you and me, we box him. I guess I'll be on the rail, and we'll box him! Understand?"

Lake chuckled at that. "Whatcha think?" he demanded. "Understand? Sure I understand. I'll nail a lid right down over Parade; if he tries to sneak up between us. I'll ride wide of the mare, and get ready to box off, if he tries to slip through."

24 – Out of the Past

THE night was warm and perfectly still, and the stars kept burning down closer and closer to the earth, until no man could keep them out of his eyes, and heads were sure to be lifted toward the zenith and the Milky Way.

Inside, not outside, the corral fence, Silvertip was putting down his tarpaulin, and then unrolling his blankets; Parade, near at hand, kept sniffing at everything. When the bed was made, he caught the edge of it with his teeth and tossed everything into confusion. Silver shouted at him. He fled across the corral and came romping back. His great eyes glowed bright through the starlight.

"Yeah, he knows you, all right," said Charlie Moore. "How come?"

"How does it come that Brandy knows you, Charlie?" asked Silvertip.

"There was a question of him livin' or dyin', a long time back," said Moore, "and a hoss ain't like a man. A hoss never forgets."

"Well," said Silver, "it was a question once of both of us going over the edge of a cliff—or both being saved. He was sliding, and I wouldn't let go my hold on him. I couldn't let go. Something inside of me kept saying that it was better to go together, or live together. I couldn't let go—and we had the luck, together."

"I know," said Charlie Moore. "You goin' to sleep out here all night?"

"I am. It'll keep Parade quiet. He raises the devil if I'm not around, and he needs to be himself tomorrow."

"Silvertip," said Charlie Moore, "I want to wish you luck. I'd sure like to see you win and get that hoss. But you know how it is—you know how Brandy can run, and you know what you weigh."

"I'm not thinking," said Silvertip. "I'm only praying, Charlie. Let's not talk about it. It means too much to me. What are you going to do, old

119

timer, after this race—if Richmond moves out of this neck of the woods? They say that he's broke, and that he may have to move. About all that's left to him is Brandy, and I don't suppose that he'll take you along with the horse."

"He wouldn't take me along," agreed Charlie Moore, "and what I'd do without Brandy, I dunno. You take a life like my life, there's been only one thing in it."

"Come along, Charlie," agreed Silvertip. "Back yonder, in the old days—there was a girl or two, eh?"

"Never no women," said Charlie Moore. "You see how it is? I didn't have no tongue to talk to 'em. You gotta have a tongue, to talk to a girl. She can't see you by what you do, same as a man can. She's gotta have talk. No, there never was no woman. There never was nothin' else, except days of work, and pay at the end of the month, and that sort of a thing."

"That's hard," agreed Silvertip. "But you've had your friends, Charlie."

"I've had you, Silver," said Charlie Moore. "I guess you smile at me, a good deal, but to be smiled at is a lot better than to be laughed at. You're the closest friend that I've ever had."

Silvertip could not answer. He wanted to say something pleasant, but pity choked him.

Charlie Moore went on: "There's only been Brandy. It seems like the time before I had Brandy, I didn't have nothin'. Come here, Brandy, and talk to me."

Brandy came rapidly across the corral and pushed his head out between the rails. The hand of Moore began to wander over the fine, bony head.

"And when Brandy steps out," said Charlie Moore, without bitterness, with a sort of calmness of acceptance, "I've been havin' a feelin' that I'd step out, too. Just a sort of a feelin', if you know what I mean, but I guess I won't. The days'll go on, one after another, like walkin' down a long road, with no home at the end of it. You know how it is, Silver."

"Aye," said Silver. "I know something about that."

"So long," said Charlie Moore. "Good night, Brandy. Run like a three-year-old tomorrow, you old tramp!"

He turned and disappeared into the darkness. Behind him, Silvertip set for a time on his blankets, hugging his knees. Then he turned in.

He looked at the frosty brightness of the stars for a moment. He thought of the test which was coming on the morrow. He thought of Parade as his own horse, bearing him through a greater, a freer, a nobler life. His heart leaped, and yet a moment later he was soundly asleep.

A little after that, Brandy lay down, with a groan.

"So, so!" exclaimed Mischief. "That's the way with old horses. They can't keep their feelings to themselves. They have to grunt and groan and maunder, and make themselves disgusting and life ridiculous for everyone else!"

Brandy had endured much. Now he started lightly to his feet.

"I'm only about nine years old," said he, "and I can run within a step as fast as I ever ran in all my days, just now. Don't talk to me all the time about old horses. There have been horses three times my age, for that matter, before they died."

"Nine years of slavery!" exclaimed Mischief. "Nine long years of slavery!"

"I was once as free as any of you," said Brandy. "You can talk down to me, if you please, but I was once as free as any horse in the world."

"Were you?" The bitter mare sneered. "Free in a pasture—free in a corral—free in a stall—that's the only freedom you've ever known."

"You were speaking a time ago," said Brandy, "about the Sierra Blanca. Well, I ranged through that, one time."

"A very short time," said the mare.

"I wish it had been longer—except for the hand and the voice of the man I love."

"It sickens me to hear that sort of talk," said Mischief. "A precious lot Man ever did for me, except to feed a spur into my side and a Spanish bit into my mouth! You talk of love and Man? I can love my foal, and my free country, and that's the end—except for such a horse as the king of them all was!"

"And who was the king of them all?" asked Brandy calmly, because his disposition was able to endure worse spite than that of Mischief, even.

"The king of them all," said Mischief, "was such a horse as was only once in the world. How am I going to tell you about him? Imagine yourself! You're a good horse. You have lines, and bone, and you can gallop. Imagine yourself sleeked over, beautiful, and fast as the wind. Imagine yourself just escaping from captivity and running out into the desert for the first time. Imagine yourself on the sides of it. That's the sort of a horse I mean, and he was the king of the world, and he was the father of my colt here!"

"Well," said Brandy, "I can't imagine all of the things that you say, but I can imagine the time, well enough, when I got away from captivity, and ran out with a fine mare, a fine, wise, tough-minded, clever mare, right into the Sierra Blanca."

"You ran—with a mare—into the Sierra Blanca?" said Mischief.

"Yes."

She came slowly up to the bars, and sniffed at the head of Brandy. Then she asked:

"You went into the Sierra Blanca with a mare? What sort of a mare?"

"Oh," said Brandy, "she had run wild there. She had been wild-caught and she was still wild, on the inside."

"Come closer to me, Parade," said Mischief. "Come closer, and listen. Something is being told to us now. He escaped into the Sierra Blanca, and there was with him a mare that had been wild-caught off the desert—years before."

"Years before," said Brandy.

"Then tell me what happened after that!" Mischief demanded of Brandy.

"We came to a herd of wild horses, and there was a leader with them of course—a stallion."

"What color?" snapped Mischief.

"Cream-colored," said Brandy. "And I'll never forget how his tail flashed like metal, when he came sweeping around from the rear of the herd. And then—"

"Neither shall I forget!" exclaimed Mischief.

"You?" snorted Brandy.

"And how you fought, and how he caught you by the throat—and how you beat him to the ground, and then let him go! Parade, come closer to me! It is the king—it is your father! Time has marred him, but it is he. I should have known him by his gentleness and his forbearance. It is the king!"

"What do you say to me?" asked Brandy.

He touched noses with her; he touched noses with Parade. Out of the past the wild days came over him, the wild and happy days when he had been a king indeed.

"And then a man came," said Mischief, "and called to you. When I was calling to you, too. I would have taught you how to run free, always! Why did you stand and wait for him to come?"

"You never will know," said Brandy. "But he understands!"

"Steady, boy!" called the voice of Silvertip suddenly, and Parade turned and went rapidly toward the blankets of the speaker.

"It is true," said Mischief. "But we have this moment. Here are the three of us. Now let tomorrow bring whatever it will!"

25 – The Great Race

MEN bet their past wages, and their future. Men bet their spurs and saddles, and a saddle is the last thing that a cowpuncher places in jeopardy. Men bet with borrowed money, and with stolen money, too, for when a Westerner makes up his mind about the winner of a race, he makes it up with a violence, and with a perfectly firm conviction. They would have bet the skins off their bodies, if there had been money value attached.

And nearly half of those bets went down on Parade.

Common sense might say that the slenderer lines of the mare of Mr Jones, and Brandy, meant greater speed over a distance as short as a mile and a half. But common sense is not the virtue of the great West. And when those cowpunchers looked upon Parade, his beauty and his fame joined in their souls and stirred their hands toward their pocketbooks to place their wagers.

There were plenty of others, calm and crafty-minded people, who laid their money with what seemed greater discretion, and these bet on the "dark horse" of Mr Jones, or on the celebrated speed of Brandy.

There were other entries, but they hardly counted. Eight horses danced and pranced at the post, with Silvertip towering head and shoulders above the rest, both on account of his own stature and the almost seventeen hands of Parade. Next to him was Brandy. And this strange thing was noticed even by the excited, abstracted eyes of the bystanders—that the two stallions actually touched noses more than once, in the intervals of fiddling for the start. But presently they were as wild as the rest of the horses. Only the long, rangy mare of Mr Jones remained alert, but without wasting an effort, at her end of the line, and she was the farthest from the inside position.

As for Brandy, he was exclaiming: "We're going to run! We're going to race! Parade, try hard to keep close to me. I can feel the wind in my heels.

I'm going to run faster than a storm. Stay as close to me as you can and try to be second. Watch the mare. She has the lines of speed, too. Watch the mare, and follow me, and you won't be disgraced!"

Then a gun boomed, and as the others lurched away from the start, Parade was left half-turned, standing flat-footed.

He got away like a wildcat, with the wailing cry of despair from his supporters ringing through the air.

He saw the mare sweep with wonderful speed right across the face of the field, and then settle down to the best position, on the rail, where she ran easily, with no effort, and kept the rest at bay. Brandy came up to her and looked her in the eye, and would have gone ahead, but the firm hand of Lake held him back.

"Make a race of it! Let her go!" called Lake.

There was nothing around them. The best of the range-bred horses were already laboring well to the rear, only able to fight it out for third-place money, and Parade was among them.

"There's plenty of time!" called back Jones. "Bear out a little, and watch Parade!"

"Parade's sunk already!" called Lake.

That was how they swept around the course for the first round. It was a three-quarter-mile track, and they would travel about it twice. And going by the little grandstand, where most of the people were thronged on the outside of the inside of the track, the voices rose up in waves, and smote the horses and riders in the face. There was the high, joyous staccato of the supporters of the mare and Brandy. There was the groaning despair of those who had bet on Parade.

He was out and away from the other range horses now, but a great distance from the leaders. And yet Silvertip was making no effort to urge him. He swung his body low along the neck of the stallion, like a jockey, and he had a high, strong grip with his knees, to keep his weight off the running muscles that come up under the saddle; but outside of position, and a firm but light grip on the reins, he was making no effort.

That was why they yelled at him. That was why some excited men called him a fool and a crook, and threatened to have it out with him after the race.

But he knew that whatever was in the body and the brain and the soul of Parade was his, and in his hand, ready to be poured out when he pleased. He told it by that electric current which quivered up and down the reins. He told it by the slight turn of the head of the horse, that showed Parade was studying his rider, waiting for him, ready for the supreme effort. And so Silvertip waited still. He was not exactly tense. It was something beyond tenseness, this pull on the strings of the heart, and this knowledge that he was riding for possession of the horse.

He remembered Lefty, pale-faced, keen, saying: "I've bet everything on Parade. Maybe I'm a fool, but I've bet more on you than on the nag. I don't have to tell you to do your best. You get Parade if you win!"

"And Chuck?" Silvertip had said.

"If Chuck opens his mug, I'll tell the true story—how Chuck put a bullet into you after you had Parade in your hand!"

That was how it would go—if he could win!

And little by little, as he hung quietly, in perfect balance, over the running machine beneath him, he saw that they were creeping up on the leaders—not rapidly, but little by little.

He knew it was unfair, this test. He knew that Parade could maintain this speed for an indefinite time, and run the others into the ground if there were ten miles to cover. But what would happen when he asked for everything that Parade could give, and entered the stretch with the leaders—those narrower, clipper-built sprinters?

That would have to be seen.

They rounded into the back stretch, and Parade was coming closer up. Silvertip saw Lake turn his head—a single flash of that ape-like countenance, and then Brandy moved faster, and the mare moved faster beside him. Like a team, the mare and Richmond's stallion were keeping together, while the crowds went mad with excitement.

Not only the voices of their supporters, but now the majority of the men, who had bet on Parade, were beginning to yell also. For they saw the favorite creeping up with every stride.

The horses rounded the turn toward the head of the stretch, and then Silvertip set his teeth, and made his call.

The answer took his breath away. It was like leaping from a height. It was like being caught by the race of a river that is all white water. It was like being hurled from the hand.

The lurch of increased speed threw Silver back a little in the saddle. He had to struggle forward into the better position. And with that first rush, as they rounded the turn into the stretch, he came straight up on Brandy and the mare.

The two stallions jarred together. Brandy lagged; Parade, thrown completely out of stride, fell well to the rear, and the mare went winging on alone.

A screech of rage and disappointment went up from those at hand, along the fence, and murder flashed from the heart of Silvertip into his brain. They would die for this—Lake and Jones! He saw the plot as clearly as though he had sat at the table where it had been hatched.

And Parade? Could he come again, with that crushing burden on his back? Could he loose again that long-bounding stride, that seemed to be buoyed up by the beat of invisible wings?

He called, with his heart in his voice, and Parade answered. He swayed a little, but found himself, and shot ahead.

Brandy, running with wonderful strength, was beside the mare again, but bearing well out toward the middle of the track, and the gap was plain and free before Silvertip. That was why he tried to put Parade through it, instead of passing around to the outside. It seemed impossible that Lake would attempt to foul him twice.

The finish was not far way. The two white-washed posts gleamed nearer and nearer. The frenzy of uproar did not come, it seemed, from human voices, but from wild beasts, and from blaring brazen trumpets.

Men were standing up on the rails, and pulling their favorites ahead with foolish gestures; and here and there someone with a weaker heart looked down at the ground, white-faced and overcome.

But the same rush of speed came pouring out of Parade, the same dazzling outburst as before. It would not endure long, this time. By a certain tenseness and brittleness in the body that labored beneath him, Silvertip recognized that fact.

Then he saw an odd thing, for as the ultimate strain was placed on both Parade and Brandy, as they stretched their heads out, they twisted them a little to the right, and bored into the wind of their own gallop, as though they were about to turn a corner. They were identical in style—and chance could not make this! There was only one great difference, and that lay in the greater sweep of the stride of Parade. It bore him rapidly up. The head of the stallion was on the hip of the mare, when suddenly Brandy was swiftly swung in again to close the gap.

It was too patent. Everyone in the stands, everyone in eyeshot along the fences could see the dirty device, and a howl of rage went upward.

But that was not what stopped Lake.

He would risk the rage of the crowd, knowing that every penny of money that Richmond possessed had been bet on the mare. He would risk everything, hoping to get his percentage, if only he could shut off Parade.

But now, as Parade came up, something happened in Brandy. The head which usually gave so easily to the slightest pull of the reins, now stiffened. The mouth became iron. There was a sudden outthrust of the neck of the stallion that tore the reins through the strong hands of the jockey, and Brandy was running straight and true toward the finish line, leaving plenty of space between him and the mare.

It was like the opening of a gate of hope, to Silvertip. The rage vanished from his heart.

He shouted again to the stallion. He saw the ears of Parade shudder as the horse heard the voice. He felt the final, desperate effort come out of the quivering body. That stride could not be made more rapid, and yet it beat more rapidly. That stride could not be lengthened, and yet actually it was extended!

The long, lean mare drew back in jerks. Those jerks represented the strides of Parade, one by one.

Then the sardonic face of Mr Jones turned. He seemed not in the least degree excited. His whip worked rhythmically. Still something like a smile was on his face as he fell behind.

But the head of Parade was not in the lead. It was Brandy, running like a nimble-footed three-year-old, running as he never had run before, perhaps. Still his head was in front, while Lake, his frog face contorted, screamed out curses and plied the whip.

And then two great pulses, and Parade was ahead. The white posts flashed past. Had he gained that vital ground in time?

Silvertip did not know. It might still be Lefty's horse that he bestrode, he thought, as he turned back toward the grandstand. But then all doubt left him as men leaped over the fence or crawled through it, and came pouring toward him, and as they ran, they kept screeching out one name:

"Parade! Parade!"

There is only one sort of madness that pitches the voices of men as high as that, and that is the madness of victory.

Movement became almost impossible. The throng pressed closer and closer. In vain, Silver shouted to beware of the teeth and the heels of the stallion. The winners did not care. They wanted to touch that gleaming piece of victorious horseflesh if they had to die for it the next moment.

In a vast huddle, growing every moment, they attended Parade down the track.

Only one thing could part them, and that was a small man with a thin face and blazing eyes.

"It's Lefty—it's the owner!" men called, and gave place, meagerly, to Lefty.

He came up and gripped the right hand of Silvertip with both of his, and put his foot on Silver's, and so hoisted himself until he could speak in Silver's ear.

"I've made a fortune!" he shouted, "and you're goin' to have a share in it. You're goin' to have Parade, too. And welcome, too, because there ain't another man in the world worthy of settin' on his back. And it was the greatest race ever rode!"

26 – Settlement

ALL THAT Lake could think of, after the defeat, was whisky. He went back to the same obscure little saloon which he favored, and took what comfort he could, until his eyes blurred, and his senses were dulled.

Afterward, Richmond would come—Richmond ruined, Richmond in a frantic rage. That would be that. Lake hardly cared. A savagery was in him. He had spent these years with Richmond, always waiting for the big clean-up and the time had never come. Now there would be some sort of a settlement.

The door opened from the rear, and Jones came in. He leaned over the chair of Lake to say briefly:

"Better get out of here. Richmond is clean nutty. He can't take it, the dirty welsher. You get out of Parmalee and stay out, or there'll be trouble. He thinks you double-crossed him. He can't see that Brandy took that race in hand at the finish. And what did I tell you? That Parade could gallop—and well he did!"

He laughed, his sneering, mirthless laughter, and went on into the front of the saloon.

He had hardly closed the door behind him when Harry Richmond came in from the rear entrance. Lake looked up askance, and saw the drawn gun in his hand, the big pulpy face thrust forward, the working of the mouth.

It was twilight. The fields and sky were blue outside the open doorway.

And this was to be the end. Lake knew it. He knew it by the fact that the light did not tremble on the gun of Richmond. The hand of the man was steady, and the murder would be done.

They said nothing. Richmond kept inching forward, his gun leveled. Lake got up from the table. He knew that the instant he tried to pull a weapon, he would be shot down. His own hand would give the signal for his death. But

128

while he hesitated, Richmond was edging nearer, making sure of his aim, getting to a range at which he could not miss.

Suddenly the hand of Lake flashed across his coat and up under the flap of it. The Colt boomed in the hand of Richmond. A forefinger of fire stabbed through the murky air at Lake.

The shock of the bullet knocked him backward. He struck a chair. It went over with him. He turned a somersault and landed on his face with hands still clutching the gun he had drawn.

Richmond was still firing, and life was running out of the body of Lake with every throb of his heart. But he lay there stretched on the floor, making a rest of one hand to support the long barrel of the revolver. And from that rest he fired. After Richmond fell, he was not contented.

He wanted to get up and stand over the man and blow his face off. He wanted to crawl to him, and put in a final shot. But he knew that even the effort of getting to hands and knees would make the last of life burst out of him.

Even now, a dimness was being drawn across his face. The agony was entering his throat, closing off his breath. And still he fired.

Richmond began to shriek. He got to his hands and knees, screeching for help. Another bullet knocked him flat on his face.

There was no more firing, as the men broke in from the front of the saloon. Lake lay on his face, dead, smiling; and Richmond was two gasps from death, also.

It was only marvelous that he could exist long enough to speak words, and Jones and the barkeeper leaned over him.

There was an expression of stunned surprise on the face of Richmond. His lower jaw had dropped to his chest.

He kept saying, thickly: "Tha's a'right. Tha's a'right," and a drool of blood spilled over his lip and kept sliding down on his coat.

Jones said, calmly, almost with enjoyment in his voice: "You're a dirty dog. You're dying like a dirty dog. But if you've got anything to put right, tell me, brother, and I'll do it for you!"

Harry Richmond looked up at him with vague eyes.

"Old Charlie Moore," he said.

Bubbles of blood formed and burst on his lips, snapping rapidly.

"Moore—he gets Brandy. I got Brandy away from him—and I got nothing but trouble. Give Brandy back to Charlie—and tell him—"

He put his head on his shoulder as though he wanted to wipe his bloody lips on his coat, but the head kept on sagging down, for Harry Richmond was dead.

When justice is done, sometimes it is not done with a feeble hand, but with a certain flourish. That was the case with Charlie Moore. The whole story came out. It had been known before, but dimly. Now the long story of injustices stood up darkly against the bright light of the race and the tragedy that had followed it. And Charlie Moore got Brandy.

He got another horse, too, because when Brandy was led out of the corral, Mischief tried to climb the fence and follow him. Big Silvertip bought Mischief on the spot and presented her to Charlie Moore.

Charlie was leaving Parmalee. He was going into the Northwest, where a comfortable job had been offered him as timekeeper in a big mine.

"Because," the mine owner had said, "the world's given the simple old fellow a bad break. Now he can have his horse, and peace, to the end of his life."

That mine lay on the edge of the Sierra Blanca, among the foothills, and Silvertip rode all the way with Charlie Moore to his new job.

What they said to one another made very little difference, but from horse to horse there was much talk. It was somewhat annoying to the riders because, while Mischief ranged here and there, without so much as a bridle on her head—it would be a simple thing to run her down, if she tried to bolt—the two horses insisted on walking shoulder to shoulder.

"You see," said Brandy, "that we return to the old places."

"We return," said Parade.

He lifted his head, and looked at the white spearlike tips of the Sierra Blanca range.

"Some day," he said, "perhaps we'll run together through the valley again, and gather a herd behind us."

"Never!" said Brandy. "To be free is a great thing; to be loved is a greater thing still. If there had been no whip on me, the other day, perhaps I would have beaten you, Parade, if I had loved my rider as you loved yours. Did he touch you with a whip, from the start to the finish?"

"A whip?" said Parade. "Why should he do that? A whip stroke only makes you twist to the side to escape from the pain. He never has touched me with more than the flat of his hand."

"And that," said Brandy, "I understand. But your mother never will. Where are you traveling now?"

"A great ways off," said Parade. "All I know is that with my master in the saddle, I keep looking at the horizon, because I know that he always wants to be somewhere beyond it. Look at him, father. He is the Great Enemy turned into a friend."

"Therefore," said Brandy, "you will be of one blood and one bone with him, all your life. See the man who rides me. He keeps a loose rein. His eye wanders. He trusts me, my son. And the greatest joy in this life is to trust and to be trusted."

And old Charlie Moore was saying to his companion: "Look at 'em rubbin' shoulders as they walk, rubbin' our knees together, too, the old fools. Now, I'll tell you somethin', Silver."

"Fire away," said Silvertip.

"You seen them in the finish of that race, boring their heads into the wind?"

"I saw them—and their heads twisted out the same way, when they were putting everything they had into the running."

"D'you think that's chance?" asked Moore.

"It was a queer thing," admitted Silver. "What's the answer?"

"When Mischief got away, long ago, she got away with big Brandy, here, and there's no doubt in my mind—Brandy's the father of Parade."

"Hold on!" exclaimed Silvertip.

"It looks like a long shot, but I think it's a true one. Two horses don't run in a queer way like that, unless there's the same blood in 'em, likely. And look, at the cut of Parade—and then look at Brandy. Years make a difference, but I can remember when Parade and Brandy would've been almost blood brothers at a glance. They got the same cut, but Brandy's finer, and Parade's bigger—and there you are!"

"You'll be telling me," said Silvertip, smiling, "that they know that they're father and son, and that's why they walk together, like this!"

"There's strange things in this here world," said Charlie Moore, "and that's exactly what I believe."

"All right," answered Silver, good-humoredly. "I'm happy enough to believe anything, today."

"Old son, where might you be bound?" asked Charlie.

"Over yonder!" said Silvertip.

He waved before him toward the shimmer of the desert, alive with the rising of the heat waves, and toward the rugged waves of the mountains, that gave back on either side from a pass.

"Over the pass?" said Charlie Moore.

"Yes, over the edge of the world, somewhere," said Silvertip. "I've spent a life, so far, trying to find one thing that I really wanted. I've got it now, and I'm going to use it. I don't know for what!"

Old Charlie Moore looked on his companion with dreaming eyes for a moment.

"Give a boy a sword, and the man will be a soldier," he murmured. And then he added: "I'd need to be a younger man, and a stronger man, and Brandy a younger horse under me—but if I could follow you, Silver, I know that I'd find what you're goin' to find—the other side of the horizon, and the reason the sky is blue!"

SILVERTIP

CONTENTS

CONTENTS

1 – Beckoning Lights

"SILVERTIP" was what men called him, since the other names he chose to wear were as shifting as the sands of the desert; but he was more like a great stag than a grizzly. For he was built heavy to the waist; below, he was as slender as any swift-running deer. Yet the nickname was no accident. Above his young face, high up in the hair over his temples, appeared two tufts of gray that at times and in certain lights had the look of small horns. For this reason the Mexicans were apt to call him "El Diablo," but Americans knew him as Silvertip, which they shortened often to Silver, or Tip.

On this day, he had ridden out of the green of the higher mountains, and now, among the brown foothills, he sat on his mustang and looked over the gray of the arid plains below. The day had hardly stopped flushing the upper peaks with colour, but night was already rolling in across the plain beneath. It covered the river; it covered Cruces for a few moments also, but then the lights of the town began to shine through.

The place glimmered in the thickening welter of shadows, and as Silvertip watched the gleaming, he remembered the little garden restaurant of Antonio Martinelli, down yonder in Cruces. He remembered the taste of the acrid red wine, and the heaping plates of spaghetti, seasoned with Bolognese sauce and powdered with Parmesan cheese.

He knew, then, why he had ridden down through the upper valleys. It was not only because the law did not threaten him, at the moment, but because he was a little tired of venison or mountain grouse roasted over a camp fire. It was dangerous for him to leave the fastnesses and descend into the plains, for even when the law did not want him, there were always sundry men who did. If they could not pull him down single-handed, they would try in

137

numbers. They had tried before, and his body was streaked and spotted with silver where their grip had touched him.

But just as an old grizzly rouses from the whiter sleep in the highlands and looks off the brow of some mountain promontory down into the shadows of the plains, — remembering the danger of guns and dogs and men, feeling his ancient wounds ache, but recalling also the taste of fat beef and, above all, the delight of the dangerous game — so Silvertip looked down into the shadows and smiled a little. With an unconscious reaction, his right hand went up under his coat to the butt of the six-gun that hung beneath the pit of his left arm, in a clip holster; then Silver started the gelding down into the night.

It was not long before his horse was slipping and stumbling over the water-polished rocks at the bottom of the ford; then the close warmth within the streets of the town received him, the half-sweet, half-pungent odors. The children were still playing, flashing through pale shafts of lamplight and turning dim in the darkness beyond; the house dogs ran with them; only the pigs had gone to sleep.

A sense of comfortable security began to come over Silvertip. He fought against that as a traveler in the arctic struggles against the fatal drowsiness of cold. He sat straighter in the saddle, shrugged back his shoulders, expanded his nostrils to take a deeper breath. As he rode on, his head automatically kept turning a trifle from side to side while his practiced eyes, with side glances, studied the houses at hand and all the street behind him, as well as the way before.

He had to go most of the way through Cruces before he came to the jingling sound of a mandolin and the noise of jolly laughter that told him he was near Antonio Martinelli's place. It stood off by itself, surrounded by the olive trees and grapevines, which only the pain of Italian handwork could make flourish in the dry West. The two windmills which gave life and greenness to that spot were both whirling their wheels high overhead with a soft, well-oiled clanking.

He did not go directly in, but first rode past the lighted front of the saloon, hotel, and restaurant; for Martinelli's place was complete. He rode close, piercing the windows with his glance, peering over the top of the swinging doors of the saloon through the smoke wreaths at the faces within. All seemed friendliness and cheer; the dangerous feeling of security welled up in him, again, irresistibly. His taut mind relaxed as a body relaxes, after labor, in a warm bath.

He rode straight back around the building to the stable, and led the mustang inside. The horse drew back, cowering a little. It snorted and stamped; it trembled at the unfamiliarness of inclosing walls, for it was as wild as the mountains among which Silvertip had caught it.

High up on the mow, a voice was singing. Hay rustled and thumped down into a manger.

"Hey, Piero!" called Silvertip.

"Hey? Who's there?" called the voice of a man from the top of the haymow. Then, as though the tones of Silvertip had gradually soaked deeper into his memory: "Oh, Silver! Is it Silvertip?"

"Yes," said Silver.

"I am coming—quickly!" panted Piero Martinelli. "Oh, Silver, this is good! Is it safe for you to be here? Are we to hide you? Must I talk softly? How long will you stay? Father will be happy—mother will dance and sing. Ah, Silvertip," he finished, as he came breathless to the bottom of the ladder and gripped the hand of the larger man, "how happy I am to see you again!" said Silver. "And I don't have to hide, this time. Look out—this is a wild devil of a horse."

"I know," said Piero, laughing. "You don't like tame things; you like them wild. Oh, we all know about that. I won't come near those heels. Does it bite and strike?"

"Like a mountain lion," said Silvertip, stripping the saddle from the round, strong barrel of the horse. "There's plenty of hay for him. Will you come in with me? Are you through here?"

"Of course I'm through," said Piero. "The work ends when you come. I'll tell everyone that—"

"No," cautioned Silvertip. "Don't do that. I want a corner table in the garden; to be *as* quiet as possible; to hear the singing; to eat pounds of spaghetti. You know, Piero, that the day has passed when I could walk into a crowd and be comfortable. It's bad medicine for me to have anyone standing at my back."

"Ah, ah," groaned the other. "I know! Well, we'll go in the side door."

They walked out into the open, following a curving path covered with gravel. The step of Piero was a loud crunching, but the foot of Silver, in spite of his weight, made hardly a sound.

"Tell me who's inside," said Silvertip.

"All good fellows," answered Piero. "All except one."

"Never mind about the others, then. Tell me about him."

"The Mexican, Bandini, he—"

"You mean Jose Bandini?"

"Yes, that one—with the record of killing so many men—that same Jose Bandini."

"He's a bad hombre," remarked Silvertip, pausing. "And there's an old grudge between us."

"Hi!" exclaimed Piero under his breath. "Is there an old grudge? And will he face you? Will he really dare to face *you*, Silver?"

"He'll face anybody if he has to," answered Silver. "But he'd rather shoot from behind. Bandini's there, is he? Well, that's bad." He walked on, slowly, saying in addition: "I know him and I know his record. But his killings are mostly talk. Like mine, Piero. You know what they say of me, and it's mostly talk."

"Ah—yes?" murmured Piero politely. Then he went on, with a touch of passion: "That Bandini is with another Mexican—a young man—a very fine-looking young Mexican. They are eating together in one of the small rooms. Bandini is making trouble. We hear their voices jump up high, for a minute or two, and then drop away, again. There is a lot of trouble between them. My mother is worried."

"If Bandini's talking," said Silvertip, "you don't need to worry. That sort of snake doesn't rattle before it strikes."

They went in through a side door into a kitchen filled with smoke and whirling wreaths of steam, for all the cooking was done at a great open hearth, with black pots hoisted on cranes in various places above the flames. Two women were working, one slender and young, one overflowing with fat and energy and high spirits. Her rosy face grew redder still when she saw Silvertip. She threw out her arms as though she would embrace him, and then with moist hands, took both of his and struck them softly together.

"Ah, Silver," she cried, "I speak of you, and you come. But I am always speaking of you, and you are seldom here. Look, Maria! Do you see him? He is bigger than I said, eh? See the gray spots in his hair? See how brown he is, too, and how his eyes laugh. See how he smiles, exactly as I said; mostly with his eyes. Look at him! You'll never see such a man again, so good and so bad and so gentle and cruel and so much of everything that we love. We have reason to love him; I've told you the reason, too."

The girl began to blush and laugh. Silvertip, with that faint smile of his, picked a handful of smoke out of the air and made as though to throw it into the face of Mrs Martinelli.

"What do you have, Silver?" she asked him. "Antonio has a bottle of red wine saved for you. It is the last of the old wine, that you liked. It is down in the cellar, covered with dust, old with waiting for you. But what will you eat? Look—here are Spanish beans—yonder is roast kid—here's roast chicken. Look at the brown of it, Silver! And here—"

"Spaghetti, that's what I want," said Silvertip.

"Spaghetti of course, and then?"

"Spaghetti first, with that meat sauce, and lots of Parmesan cheese to sprinkle on it. I can't think about what I'll want next until I've looked at that spaghetti."

"You see, Maria?" said Mrs Martinelli. "I told you that he was true Italian. He will have his *pasta*. And if—"

"No!" cried a voice from beyond the wall on the left. "No, Jose!"

That cry struck a silence through the kitchen, and banished all the smiles except that quiet smile of Silvertip which was so often on his face.

"There! There!" whispered Mrs Martinelli. "You hear, Silver? It's Bandini. There's murder in the air. It's Bandini—and he means to kill, I'm sure."

"Tush," said Silver. "He's talking too much. There'll be no shooting."

"Ah," said Mrs Martinelli, "you may say that, but I tell you, Silver, that a man's eyes—even your eye—can only see what it falls on. But I see something more. And there is death in the air tonight. Someone will die before the kind daylight comes back."

A door opened, with a sudden bang, and Jose Bandini stood on the kitchen threshold.

2 – The Shot in the Dark

EVEN without the force of his reputation, Bandini would have given pause to the eye and the mind of any observer. He was one of those tall men with narrow shoulders and long fingers, who are strong as apes inspite of their slenderness. Of the meager width of his shoulders he was very conscious, and usually wore, as he was doing now, a cloak with a wide-flaring collar. He was dressed like a Mexican cow-puncher on holiday, with a silk shirt and a colorful scarf tied about his hips. But nothing mattered, on second glance, except the face of the man. For it was built back from the chin in a series of steps, all rugged. Chin and mouth, nose, brow, receded in due order, and yet there was plenty of brain capacity in that head. It was a handsome face, in a strange way, time-battered, life-worn; and at will Bandini could be either charmingly pleasant, or savagely dangerous.

He was dangerous now. He thrust forward his head a little and blazed his eyes at Mrs Martinelli.

"You woodenhead!" he shouted. "Where's the pepper sauce for those frijoles? And send me a waiter with another face, because if I see the fool again, I'm going to scramble his brains on the floor!"

Suddenly he was silent. He had seen the face of Silvertip, and the faint, small smile on it. The fingers of the right hand of Bandini made a sudden movement which could hardly be followed; it was the sign against the evil eye. The glance of Bandini lifted to the small gray tufts, like incipient horns, high above the temples of Silvertip. "Senior Silver," said Bandini, and made an ironic bow. Then he came across the room, deliberately. It was plain that he was afraid, but a devil of the perverse in him forced him on into the danger. He stood right in front of Silvertip, and eye to eye.

"Have you come to see me, senior?" he asked. Silvertip said nothing. He kept on smiling, and looking. The moment lasted ten grim seconds. Suddenly Bandini turned white, and shouted:

"Have you come here to insult me? You know where to find me! Bandini does not run!"

"I want to talk with you," said Silver. "Come outside into the dark for a moment, will you?"

Bandini turned yellow-white about the corners of his mouth.

"Only for talking; I want a word with you alone," said Silver.

"Dark or light and day or night, I avoid no man," said Bandini, and went out through the door with a swagger that brushed his cloak against both sides of it.

Silver took heed of the round eyes of fear that were fixed upon him from both sides, and he reassured them with a smile. Then he stepped behind Bandini into the darkness, and pulled the door shut behind him.

There was only starlight here, and the stars were dim lanterns by which to follow the movements of Bandini.

Silver became just a trifle more alert than a hunting cat.

"Now!" breathed Bandini. "And what do you want?"

"I want some news," said Silver. "I want to know about the fellow who's having dinner with you. I want to know what's in the air."

"Just a fool of a boy—that's all he is," said Bandini. after a moment. But there was that in his eyes that made Silvertip yearn to see the face. A single glint of light would have helped then, to reveal a story. "And what business is it of yours?"

"It ought to be every man's business," said Silvertip, "to watch you. No good ever came out of you, Bandini."

"Do you insult me?" snarled the Mexican.

"You don't understand me, Bandini," said Silvertip. "I don't insult you. A man doesn't insult a rattlesnake; he shoots it. And that's what will happen between us, before the wind-up."

He heard no answer—only the heavy, irregular breathing of the Mexican. Bandini was afraid—sick with fear—and Silver knew it.

"Every man who has ever seen you at work has reasons enough to wish you dead, Bandini. That's why I'm asking you what deviltry you're up to with that other young Mexican, tonight?"

No matter what fear there was in Bandini, he exclaimed suddenly: "Is every man to tell you his secrets—or be murdered?"

Silver, gritting his teeth slowly together, mused on that answer before he said: "I've seen you deal crooked cards; I've seen the scar of your knife left on a man's back; *I* knew some of the dead men you've left behind you. Now you're at some deviltry again, and you're not going through with it, if I can help it. I'm going to give you time to think it over. Pull yourself together and make up your mind.

"There's no reason why we should spoil our dinners about this. But by nine thirty I'll look for you in front of the restaurant—anywhere on the street in front of it. If you're there, I'll know that you want to have it out with me. If you're not there, I'll know that you've left town. But if you're neither in the street nor out of town, I'm going to start looking for you, Bandini, and I'll break down doors until I get at you. It was never intended that rats like you should go about the world gnawing at the lives of honest men!"

There was another moment of pause; he heard, again, the hurried breathing of the Mexican, like that of a man who has been running hard. Then Bandini turned on his heel. His cloak swished with a whispering sound through the air, and he passed back into the kitchen. As Silvertip entered in turn, the farther door banged behind Bandini, and Silver stepped into a strained moment of silence in the kitchen.

Silver turned with a sudden cheerfulness to Piero.

"If there's a corner table in the garden, I'm going to have it, Piero."

"Come!" said Piero Martinelli.

"No," said Silvertip. "Quietly does the trick. I'll find my way. I'm hungry for that spaghetti, Mrs Martinelli."

Then he went out toward the garden. The bustling in the kitchen began again, behind him.

"Wake up!" cried Mrs Martinelli to the kitchen maid. "Get the pepper sauce for that Bandini devil. Fan that charcoal and bring it to life. Do something! What's the matter with you?"

Maria looked at her with wide, dark eyes.

"You were right," she said. "There will be a killing. And Bandini will be the dead man!"

Then she fell to her work again.

But out in the garden, there never was a more tranquil face than that of Silvertip as he passed under the high grape arbors until he found a small corner table. All the rest of the little garden was filled with family groups, Americans, flavoring their food with hearty portions of the red, home-made wine of Martinelli. No one paid any attention to Silvertip as he passed. Americans lack the public curiosity of the Latins, and only unhappiness makes them aware of the outside world. A contented party is surrounded by an unpenetrable wall of its own pleasure, as it were, and that wall is rarely peered over. So those ranchers, miners, town tradesmen and shopkeepers of Cruces, with their families about them, talked high or low, and paid no heed to Silvertip as he went by.

He, apparently, had no more eye for them, and yet he studied every face in turn, analyzed it, shaved a mustache here to see if the naked skin might bring out a dangerous likeness; put on a beard there for the same reason. By the time he had reached his corner table, he was fairly well convinced that he knew none of them, and that none of them knew him.

Still, as he sat down, he was by no means willing to relax. He measured the height of the wall behind him.

He regarded the thickness of the arbor foliage, behind which a man might easily hide.

For Bandini was near, and Bandini would kill him by courage or by craft, if possible.

Antonio Martinelli came hobbling on his crippled leg. He embraced one of Silvertip's hands in both of his. He leaned over Silver's table, and beamed upon him.

"How are things?" said Silvertip.

"How can anything be bad with me? How can I ever complain?" said Martinelli. "I have a leg and a half, instead of no legs at all. Therefore we all thank God and Silvertip every day of our lives. Look! Here is the wine. If it is not beautiful, every drop, you shall have the blood out of my heart."

Silvertip made him sit down at the table. They tried the wine together, Martinelli smacking his lips.

"What's happening in there between Bandini and his friend?" asked Silvertip.

"It's no friend that's with Bandini," said Martinelli. "All I know is that Bandini wants something out of that young Mexican, and can't get it. But there'll be trouble! There'll be trouble!"

"I think so, too," said Silvertip, with a voice filled with quiet meaning. "I wish you'd watch and listen as much as you can. And let me know if a break seems to be coming on."

"You would help? You would stop the trouble?" asked Martinelli. "You know what one gun fight does—it spoils the name of a place. It takes away the cheerfulness. If people say: 'Martinelli's, where the man was killed the other day'—if they say that, they will come to me no more. I'll go and watch them like a hawk. I would give twenty dollars to have them under my eye as well as under my ear. I can only hear mumblings through the door, and very few words."

He went off, and Maria came, bearing a plate, the grated cheese, the Bolognese sauce, and a great platter of spaghetti. She put all the dishes down, deftly, and arranged them without making a clatter, and yet all the time her thoughtful eyes were on the face of Silvertip, not on her automatic work.

She paused one instant, watching Silvertip lift from the platter the first white-dripping forkful of spaghetti and bring it over to his plate.

"You think of him still," said the girl, "But he will not harm you if you keep away from him."

She hurried away, as though frightened by her own boldness in giving an opinion, and the hazel-gray eyes of Silvertip watched her out of sight, before he moved his hand again.

He finished the spaghetti slowly. The goodness of the food to one who had eaten little except meat for many weeks, filled him again with that sleepy content against which he had to be so on guard. Finally he roused himself, as Martinelli came hobbling up the path, ducking under the trailing green of the arbor.

His face beamed a brighter red than before, as he exclaimed: "It is all finished; it is all well; and they're in the saloon drinking together like brothers!"

"Are they?" said Silvertip. "Then the trouble is right on the verge of breaking. I know the sort of brotherhood there is in Bandini!"

He looked at his watch. It was nine thirty.

He finished his wine with a gulp, and rising from the table, with a swift, secret gesture he touched the revolver that hung under his coat. Martinelli gaped vaguely at the form that strode so quickly before him, and started to hobble in pursuit.

But Silvertip entered the barroom far ahead. One glance showed him that Bandini was not there, in the long irregular line of noisy drinkers. He called the bartender with a crooking of his forefinger.

"Bandini?" he said.

"Bandini's just gone out with a young fellow, a friend who—"

Silvertip waited to hear no more. He felt sure that the young fellow was now indeed in grave danger, so he slipped out of the swinging doors onto the street. He whipped that street from end to end with a rapid glance, and saw the mere fluttering of a cloak as a man passed from view. Bandini, after all, was awaiting him in the street!

That was enough for Silvertip. He ran like a greyhound to that corner. A dark, narrowly winding alley moved away on his left. He winced back a little from that darkness, as a kennel terrier might wince from the black tunnel of a fox's earth. Then he hurried straight forward, stepping long and light, every nerve in his body made acute, every sense working with electric surety and speed.

Something moved before him. Heels ground against the earth. He saw the swaying of a cloak, dimly seen through the shadows.

"Are you ready?" cried Silvertip. "Then fill your hand!"

The form whirled toward him, the cloak fanning well out to the side. One hand rose, as if to let go with the gun it seemed to hold. The other did not rise.

"Take it then, damn you!" muttered Silvertip, and drawing, he fired.

The finger of red fire flicked out of the muzzle of the gun, as though pointing the way for the bullet with the death it carried. That flash showed Silvertip not the face of Bandini, but a dark-skinned, handsome youth. The horror in those wide eyes flashed at Silvertip for an instant, and then the inflooding darkness covered the falling body.

Silvertip could not move; he could not catch that weight before it struck solidly against the ground. The dust that puffed out under the impact rose in a cloud, acrid against the nostrils of Silvertip.

He kneeled and put his hand over the heart of the fallen body. There was no beat. The coat was wet and warm with blood.

Silvertip, still kneeling, lifted his head as though to listen, but he was not heeding any human sound, far or near. He had killed the man he would have protected. A vow was forming in his heart, filling his throat.

3 – Cross and Snake Brand

W HEN Silvertip rose, he was carrying the loose weight of the body in his arms. He felt the sway of the hanging head, the swinging of the feet with every step he took. There was still the warmth of life coming out of the body. The weight made his own step loud and heavy, like the footfall of a stranger, to his ear; and already his heart was heavier, too, with the double burden which he had taken upon himself.

He rounded to the rear of the restaurant of Martinelli, and through a side door carried the dead man straight into the small room where, only a few minutes before, this youth and Bandini had been at dinner. Two crumpled napkins lay on the table, now, and a scattering of soiled dishes, and glasses dimly stained by wine.

He put the body down in a chair. The form sagged helplessly against him, the head hanging, the arms dropping straight down toward the floor. Still supporting the inert thing, he cleared half the table with a few sweeps of his arm; then he laid out the young Mexican in the free space.

The puncture in the coat was a neat little round hole. There was not much blood anywhere on his clothing. He straightened the legs and the arms. They did not seem to lie naturally along the side, so he folded them across the stomach of the dead man. The lips were still parted, as though in a gasp; the eyes of horror stared upward, unwinkingly, at the ceiling.

A footfall paused at the door; then Mrs Martinelli's scream rose in shrill, endless waves that cut ceaselessly through his whirling brain.

Other people came, running. He regarded them not at all. He closed the eyes, and they remained closed. He touched the tip of the chin, still soft and warm, and brought the lips together.

It was as though he had dragged the soul of the dead man up from hell to heaven, for it was a faintly smiling face, a happy, dreaming face. He was not more, this handsome young Mexican, than twenty or twenty-two; and the features were beautifully carved. There was strength and manliness in the face, also; and Silvertip felt that Fate, with sinister malice, had driven his bullet into one of the chosen men of the earth. If there had been a garden of weeds with one priceless flower blooming, he, like a blind gardener, had felled the once choice plant.

In a hundred years of striving, what could he do for the world that would equal the value of the life he had canceled?

Silvertip, stirring from his dream, took a handkerchief, and wiped the dust from the black, silky hair. There was still warmth in the brow, also. With every touch it seemed to Silvertip that the life could not actually have gone, that the forward running of the years could not have ended, as a river ends at the sea.

Silvertip himself was not so many years the senior of this dead man, yet he felt like an old man beside a child. What would that child have grown into? Upon what labors would it have set its hands?

He regarded the soft, slender tapering of the fingers—far unlike his own hands.

And now, as he looked down at the still face, he laid his grip on the two hands which he had joined, and groaned.

Some great purpose burns in every soul; if only he could penetrate into the dead mystery of that mind, he swore, in that solemnity of silence, that he would undertake the unfinished labor of this life.

A voice broke in upon him. He looked up. People were staring at him, not at the dead man, for there was something in the face of Silver that filled them with awe.

It was the sheriff speaking.

"Silvertip, can you tell us about this?"

"I found the dead body in the alley one block down from the restaurant," said Silvertip.

"Bandini!" cried the voice of young Piero Martinelli. "Jose Bandini was with him all the evening, right here in this room. Bandini did it."

"Bandini?" said the sheriff. "Where is he?"

"Not Bandini," said Silvertip firmly. "I saw him going down the street a minute or two before the shot was fired. It certainly wasn't Bandini."

"No," said the bartender. "It couldn't have been Bandini. He may have been arguing with this poor kid, but he stopped the arguing before they left the barroom. I seen them make up and shake hands. I seen Bandini go and take off his cloak and put it around the shoulders of this dead kid. I seen him do it, kind of like a gift, to show that he meant to be friends, honest and straight."

Silvertip looked up, slowly, into the eyes of the bartender. The trick of Bandini had been too simple for belief. By that simple change of dress he had made another man walk in his own footsteps to meet a death that should have been his own.

It was not just chance that had killed this victim. It was not the hand of Silvertip, either, though he had fired the shot. It was Bandini's craft that had performed the murder!

Silvertip drew in a great, slow breath.

The sheriff said again, slowly: "Silver, I know that it ain't like you to be shootin' gents in dark alleys. It ain't your style or your cut. But you've used guns, plenty. Where was you, all the evening?"

"He was in there in the barroom," said the bartender. "When the gun went off, I heard the shot. I heard it, but I didn't think much about it. Silvertip hadn't hardly got through the door."

Silvertip looked into the broad, red face of the bartender and silently thanked him for that lie.

"It's goin' to be one of them mysteries," said the sheriff sadly. "Does anybody know who he is?"

No one knew. So the sheriff started a careful examination of the pockets.

They revealed very little. There was a small pearl-handled pocket-knife which made some of the men smile a little. There was a little .32-caliber revolver of a bulldog model that would fit neatly into almost any pocket. There was a bill fold containing a hundred and forty-seven dollars. There was a gold watch of a fine Swiss make, with a delicately worked gold chain that had been simply dropped into the pocket that held the watch.

The sheriff pried open the back of the watch, examined it with care, and replaced it with the little heap of belongings.

He turned his baffled eyes upon Silvertip. "Silver," he said, "you look kind of cut up. Wasn't he a friend of yours?"

"No," said Silvertip. "He's just so young—that's all!" He added: "Have you looked at his horse?" They trooped out to the stable and found the horse. It was a high-headed queen of a mare, a blood bay with four black silk stockings on her legs and eyes like liquid diamonds that turned and shone in the lantern light. On of her quarters was burned a cross with a wavering under it. "That's the Cross and Snake brand of old Arturo Monterey, down in the Haverhill River country," said the sheriff. "I know that brand! Maybe down there I could pick up a clue to the name of this gent. Why, it's a fifty-mile ride."

Silvertip touched the sheriff's shoulder.

"I'll go," he said. "I've never been down there, but I know the way. I'll take the outfit of that poor fellow; I'll take his horse along, too."

"Would the outfit and the horse arrive if you started with 'em?" asked the sheriff tersely.

Then, under the steady eye and the faint smile of Silvertip, he flushed.

"I didn't mean that. It just sort of come popping out," he explained. "Silver, no matter what some say about you, I'll trust you around the world and back. When will you start?"

"Now," said Silvertip.

"You mean in the morning?"

"I mean—now!"

The sheriff nodded slowly. "Something about this job has sort of burned you up, Silver, eh? Take the lot and start now, then, if you want to. Find old Arturo Monterey if you can. They say he's a hard case; I dunno in what way. But find out if he remembers selling a hoss like this to anybody, and the name of the hombre that got it. That's all. Then you'll come back here and let me know?"

"I'll come back," said Silvertip.

He was lifting his saddle off a peg as he spoke, and the sheriff, after pausing for a last glance at his messenger, went back to the restaurant and the dead body, the curious crowd following him. Only the red-faced bartender remained.

"I would have been in the soup," Silvertip told him curtly. "Thanks for that lie."

"You did the job, eh?" said the bartender, leaning against the manger on one hand and peering into the face of Silver.

"I did the job."

"Thinking it was Bandini?"

"Yes."

The bartender nodded his head slowly. "A kind of an idea come over me," he said. "A kind of an idea that there was a dirty trick in the brain of Bandini when he give that kid his cloak. He ain't the kind that gives something for nothing."

"You saved my neck," said Silver.

"That's all right," said the bartender. "But I'd kind of like to ask you a question."

"Anything you like."

"You got something in your mind, Silver. What's dragging you down into that hell hole, the Haverhill?"

"Because there's a brand on the boy's horse; and the brand come out of the Haverhill Valley, they say."

"Yeah, that's all right. But there's something more on your mind than that. What's on your mind, Silver?"

"I've killed a man," said Silver.

"According to yarns, he ain't the first."

"I've had fights with men who were born with guns in their hands," said Silvertip. "I've fought in the dark, too, as far as that goes. But this was no fight. It wasn't murder, either. There can't be a murder except when there's murder in your mind. I was sure he had drawn on me. What was it, then?"

"It was just a kind of a wiping out of the poor young gent," suggested the bartender.

"I wiped him out," said Silvertip slowly. "And by the look of him, he was a better man than I'll ever be. What can I do? Two things, partner, and, by heavens, I'm going to do them!"

"Two things?" said the bartender.

"If I can find out his name and the lives that he fitted into, I can find out at the same time what he was meant to do in the world. By the look of him, that would be something too fine for my hands. But whatever his job was, I can *try* to do it, partner."

The bartender shrugged.

"I see what you mean, Silver," said he. "And a doggone strange thing it seems to me. Now, supposing that this here gent, maybe, has got a wife and a coupla brats stowed somewhere? What would you do? Marry the widow?"

"Work for her and the youngsters," said Silvertip solemnly, "till I rubbed the flesh off the bones of my hands."

"Would you?" said the bartender. "Well, you beat me. But that ain't queer. You beat most people. Well, that's the first thing you wanta do. Mind telling me the second?"

"I'll tell you," said Silvertip, through his teeth, and suddenly in a cold rage. "You ought to be able to guess, though."

"I know," agreed the bartender, "Bandini is the bird that fixed up this job on you. You never would 'a' picked out the kid for a gun play except that he was wearing the cloak—and Bandini must 'a' known that. Are you going after him?"

"Before I die," said Silvertip, "I'll see Bandini in front of me, and I'll get at him with a gun or a knife or my bare hands."

"Yeah," said the bartender. "You will! I can see it like a picture in a book, Silver, I'm goin' to wish you luck. You're a cut different from all the rest of us—but I'm goin' to wish you luck. But fit yourself into the skin of another gent's life? Man, man, nobody in the world ever had an idea like that!"

That was all he said before he went out from the barn.

Silvertip, in the meantime, finished saddling and bridling. He saddled and bridled the bay mare, also, and tied her lead rope to his pommel. Then he brought the two horses out into the open and mounted.

He wanted, above all else, to go back into the restaurant and look once more at the delicate, olive-skinned beauty of that dead face, but he kept that impulse in check.

He gathered the reins for the start; inside the house he could hear the high-pitched, excited voice of Mrs Martinelli, babbling out her woes.

The broncho moved suddenly and set jingling all the possessions of the dead man, which the sheriff had poured into one of the saddlebags. So Silvertip rode from Cruces into the night.

4 – The Haverhill Country

IT was early morning when he got through the Haverhill pass and looked down along the valley of the Haverhill River. As far as his eye could reach, from the height, the bright water was running in wide, sweeping curves, silver-clear just below him, and a dull-blue sheen far off, with winkings of highlights on it now and then.

Men had told him that there was a curse on this country, and, in fact, he had always heard strange tales of it.

So had everyone. Very few exact reports came through, but there were mysterious murmurings. Now and then someone was pointed out as a "Haverhill man," and that fellow was sure to be avoided by all other people on the range. At least, until he had proved himself anew.

There was always talk about the Haverhill country, yet it was odd that so few people had accurate knowledge.

It was not simply that the high mountains encircled it.

Mountains cannot fence any place from a Westerner. But those who went into the valley seldom came out, and if they did, they were not easily drawn into talk. One might have thought that it was a hellish place—but never had Silvertip looked on pleasanter country.

There was plenty of water, for one thing. He had ridden up out of a plain where the grass was all dust-gray, but what he looked on now was a soft green comfort to the eye. And from the highlands on both sides he had glimpses of brooks running silver and white down the slopes to the Haverhill River below. Moreover, there were trees. There were big, roundheaded trees in groves that hung against the more brilliant green of the grass hillsides like dark clouds against the blue sheen of the sky. A heavenly place altogether, he decided. Nothing but gossip could poison it.

He made a cigarette, lighted it, began to inhale smoke in great whiffs.

He laughed, threw his hat in the air, and caught it again in spite of the frantic dodging and bucking of the mustang beneath him. He had changed from saddle to saddle all the way during the night. The horses were still fresh, especially that deer-shaped, wing-footed bay mare; so he made no longer halt, but rode down the trail toward the little village that lay at the side of the stream in the central valley beneath.

The trail was very winding, and he never could endure to push a horse going downhill. It meant ruined shoulders too often. So it was nearly prime of the morning before he came off the trail onto a beaten road near the town.

A man in a buckboard came past him from the village. Silvertip lifted his hat and called good morning.

The fellow kept his reins in one hand and his stub of a buggy whip in the other. He kept jerking at the reins constantly, and tapping at the down-headed span of mustangs with the other, without in the slightest degree altering their gait. He returned no salute or gesture or word. The wind tipped the brim of his felt hat up and down, but there was not even a nod of actual greeting.

Silver turned in the saddle and looked back. The stranger had turned also, and was staring. He was a gaunt man, of late middle age. The stubble of his beard gave a gray sheen to his face. His eyes were set in dark hollows. It was a craggy face. It was to the faces of other men as a rocky upland farm is to the rich green acres of a smooth river bottom.

At length Silver faced the town again, frowning. He had been through a great part of the West, and he had been through it on horseback or on foot. He had used his eyes, too, simply because he *had* to use them to save his scalp. But he could never remember encountering behavior like this.

All that he had heard of the Haverhill country swept over his mind again like clouds across a sunny day.

He rode on at a walk, because he wanted to digest this town as well as he could with his eyes before he entered it.

It looked like any of a thousand other Western villages. There were the same flimsy shacks that seemed to have been thrown together at random— mere tents to be occupied by an army that would soon pass on. For Westerners have had something to do other than lavish time on places to eat and sleep and sit. They have had business to do, and their business has been the whole outdoors.

This was like all the rest, in so far as Silvertip could see, and there was little that his keen eye missed. He hunted every board, every shingle, every window like a hawk searching for game.

As he came into the single winding street, he heaved a sigh of relief. Everything was the same. The signs in front of the shops, and the stores, and the hotel, and the saloons —all were the true Western pattern.

Then he saw a small boy of eight standing in an open doorway with a grown-up's shotgun in his hands.

"Hello, son!" called Silvertip.

The boy made no answer. He turned his grave face to stare after Silvertip, but he spoke not a word, made not a gesture. It was a broad, roughly made face with an expression far older than the possible years. And the eyes were set in deep hollows filled with shadow!

The chill struck again through the blood and up the spinal marrow of Silvertip.

Men may be different in varying parts of the world, but the children should all be the same.

Then he heard the cheerful beating of hammers on an anvil. Yonder was a blacksmith's shop with horses tethered before it, waiting to be shod. And through the open doors drifted thin puffs of blue coal smoke.

Silvertip breathed more easily again. The noise of the hammers rejoiced him, at that moment, as much as the sound of human voices could have done.

He halted in front of the shop, dismounted, and looked inside. A cowpuncher sat just inside the door, making a cigarette as he sat on an upturned tempering tub. The elderly blacksmith was holding a bar of iron with a large pair of pincers, and as he turned it and tapped it with his light hammer, a powerful striker banged on the indicated spots with a twelve-pound sledge.

The head blacksmith spoke two words, or three—no more. And then both turned full on Silvertip. He saw their faces were broad, their eyes set in deep, shadowy hollows!

5 – The Silent Men

THERE had been something of a nightmare ghastliness about the farmer passing down the road silently, and the sight of that lad on the porch, gun in hand, silent, also. But now the dreamlike quality departed from the scene and left to Silvertip a most absolute sense of reality. A grim reality, but one with the full sun of truth playing on it. He had simply run into a backward lot of sour men who had migrated, no doubt, from some single section of the East or of the Old World, and had developed a common surliness of manner just as they had grown to be similar in features. That cow-puncher who sat by the door, at least, was a distinct type. He was small, wizened, with a birdlike beak of a nose and birdlike eyes. But there was no more friendliness in him than in the others.

"Morning to you all," said Silvertip cheerfully.

A nod of greeting is an inclination of the head; the head blacksmith merely jerked his up a trifle. His striker did not move at all. Their heavy, obstinate, unlighted eyes weighed down upon the face of Silvertip in silence.

He ran on briskly: "I've got a mare out there with a brand that I've heard called the Cross and Snake brand. I've heard that the brand comes out of this valley. Is that right?"

He was incredulous when silence greeted this direct question. Anger burned up in him with a gust, like flame through dry tinder. He mastered it at once. He had learned, by hard lessons, that a quick temper must not be allowed to flare—no, never!

However, there is such a thing as standing up for one's rights. And he said coldly: "I asked a question. Did any of you hear me?"

He smiled as he said that. There was something about that smile of Silver's that cut like a knife edge through the most obdurate stupidity and the most sullen resentment. It never failed to point his words.

The elder blacksmith jerked a thumb toward the cow-puncher who sat by the door.

"You talk to him, Ed," he said.

The little man by the door pushed back his sombrero, scratched his head until a bushy forelock fell down across his eyes, lighted a cigarette, threw the match away, inhaled and exhaled the first smoke cloud.

"I dunno much about brands here," said Ed.

"Well," answered Silvertip, "suppose you come out and take a look, partner?"

"I dunno that looking would do much good," said Ed. "I ain't a brand expert."

He became aware, then, of the small, cold smile of Silvertip, and rose slowly to his feet.

"Ain't any harm in taking a look, I guess," said he.

He stood by the mare. The sight of the brand did not seem sufficient to him. He had to run a forefinger across the lines of it. Then he had to thumb up the gloss of the hair to see the print of the scars on the hide.

At last he stood back and shook his head.

"Never saw that brand before?" asked Silvertip.

"A man sees a lot of brands here and there," said Ed, looking at his cigarette.

"How long have you been living in Haverhill Valley?"

"Why, quite a spell," said Ed.

"What do you mean by 'quite a spell'?" asked Silvertip.

"Why, quite a heap," said Ed.

"Oh, you've stayed here quite a heap, have you? Ever heard of a Mexican called Arturo Monterey?"

"Arturo Monterey?" asked Ed, looking still at the fuming point of his cigarette.

"Yes, Arturo Monterey."

"Well, it seems to me," remarked Ed, "that I've heard the name somewheres. I ain't well acquainted around Haverhill Valley."

He turned and walked back into the blacksmith shop slowly, dragging the heels of his boots in the dust, and sat down again in the shadow within the door.

Silvertip took a deep breath and let curses flow out silently with the exhalation. It was a new experience for him. He had been through many difficult times, and through many dangers among savage and brutal men; but he had never been badgered like this before. Something about him usually prevented light treatment at the hands of others.

He went back to the door of the blacksmith shop and made for himself a new cigarette. The clangor of the hammers on the iron had recommenced, and every beat of the metal on metal sent a savage pulse through his body and through his brain.

Slowly he made the cigarette, and slowly he lighted it. He was aware—as if through the back of his head— that Ed had smiled at the blacksmith, and that the blacksmith had smiled at Ed. The poison of anger invaded every portion of Silvertip's being.

And yet his hands were tied. Besides, he had been forewarned. Men had told him that there was danger and death in the very air of the Haverhill Valley. He could understand that now. He had a strong feeling, amounting to surety, that if he attempted to discipline any one of these three, they would all be at him, like so many wolves of a pack. No matter what else could be said of them, they all seemed capable of giving a good account of themselves with their hands. They were made to endure shocks and to give them.

So he stood there, trying to think, but unable to connect one idea with another.

And then he told himself, suddenly and grimly, that this was as it should be. He was trying to find the unfinished life of a dead man and complete it, and therefore every step of the way, from the beginning, was sure to be hard. It was better so. Only with pain could he pay his debt, and far bitterer pain than this must be his before the end.

Ed stood up presently, and sauntered out of the shop and up the street. A butcher—wearing the badge of a red-stained apron—walked out with a bucket of slops, which he threw into the dust of the street. It made a great black triangle of mud in the midst of the white. Ed paused by him, spoke to him. And the butcher turned sharply around to stare at Silvertip.

Then he laughed.

That whip cut made Silvertip tremble as though a cold wind had struck him.

Ed and the butcher went into the shop door together, the butcher still laughing. The sound of his laughter came braying down the street even when he was inside his shop again.

Silver turned his head. The blacksmith was grinning, too. He looked steadily back at Silver, all the while busy with both hands at his work, and continued to grin. Silver glanced quickly back at the street.

Out of the distance a sound of a herd of cattle driven on a narrow trail had been growing, a thunder of lowing mingled with sharp, clashing sounds, such as horns make against horns, or splay hoofs clacking together. Now the river of noise entered the street, was confined by the houses, and doubled and redoubled suddenly.

He looked back and saw the swaying fronts of the steers coming, big, wide-shouldered, deep-bodied animals. Two Mexicans rode before them, slender, graceful fellows with enormous hats set over the darkness of their faces. They rode proudly, as all Mexicans ride.

They went by. The steers followed. The wide wash of that crowded herd almost scraped against fences and posts on either side of the roadway. They came in a thin smother of dust, like a blowing sea mist that rolls over the waves. Silvertip saw the red shining of the eyes, the sheen of the long, lyre-shaped horns, the glistening of the wet noses.

They were fat, these great brutes. They showed the green grass they had been battening on. Rolls of heavy flesh were bouncing up and down their flanks. Their tails swung like great flails. They beat up a clashing uproar with their feet, and the dust squirted out in thickening clouds.

But in a moment more Silvertip saw something else to take his eye. For on one of the quarters of every one of these animals there was the big pattern of a very distinct brand—a cross with a wavering line beneath it!

This was the brand about which Ed was not sure—not sure whether he had seen it or not—not sure that it belonged to the herds of Arturo Monterey or no!

He turned and saw the blacksmiths laughing in unison, boldly, openly, laughing Silvertip to scorn, laughing in his very face. And still he controlled himself.

The end of the herd poured past in thick dust masses; the mouths of the steers were hanging open; they crowded against those in the lead, just like fish swarming in a shoal. Close behind them came more riders.

Silvertip stepped out through the billowing mist and waved his hand before a rider. The man drew up with a jerk. His gray-powdered face turned impatiently toward the questioner.

"Partner," said Silvertip, "I want to know where I can find the house of Arturo Monterey?" The teeth of the Mexican flashed. "Gringo swine!" he yelled, and sent his mustang ahead again with a slash of the quirt.

Silver turned, and saw that the blacksmith and his helper were both standing at the door of the shop, swaying with delighted laughter.

Another rider galloped up the street, the last of the lot. Silver sprang before him with raised hand. The horse dodged.

"Out of my way, gringo!" yelled the Mexican with a curse.

The refined steel of Silvertip's patience parted with a snap. With one long bound he reached that Mexican's side and caught him by the wrist and the collar. The speed of the horse did the rest. It tore the Mexican from his saddle and rolled him with Silvertip in the deepness of the dust. Something winked before Silver's eyes. He reached at the flash and caught the wrist of the Mexican's knife hand.

One twist and the knife dropped. Silver stood up, lifting the cow-puncher with him. Dust poured down like water from the clothes of both of them. The roar of the herd departed; the shouted laughter of the blacksmiths began to predominate.

Suddenly that laughter had increased, not diminished in volume, and Silvertip was more bewildered than ever. Was it a common thing to the people of these parts to see a dashing Mexican caballero, a man with the shoulders of a bull, plucked from his horse and disarmed as he drew a knife?.

He laid the point of that knife against the shirt of the herdsman.

"Now, amigo," said Silvertip, "we talk."

The Mexican glanced over his shoulder at the diminishing cloud of dust that was the herd. And Silver could read the thought. How long before the fellow's companions saw a riderless horse coming after them and turned back to learn the fate of their companion?

"We talk," said Silvertip. "I ask you, first, if the Cross and Snake brand belongs, really, to Arturo Monterey?"

The vaquero stared into his face with eyes yellow and red-stained by fury. He said nothing.

"Tell me," said Silver.

The body of the Mexican was shaking with rage. His hands kept flexing and unflexing.

"Yes," he said at last.

"Very well," said Silver: "And where is the house of Monterey?"

Even fear of the knife could not prevent the Mexican from shouting savagely: "In it's own place, gringo!"

And he swayed forward a little, as though expecting the thrust of the knife.

"Look at that bay mare," said Silvertip. "Did you ever see her before?"

The Mexican glanced at the high-headed beauty. His eyes widened; his jaw dropped; his very color changed, it seemed to Silvertip. Then the big head of the man swung back, and he scowled at his questioner.

It was plain to Silvertip that he had reached the end of the rope, that he could extract no more words from this fellow. It was equally plain that the mare was known to the Mexican intimately. Yet it seemed that all the men of the Haverhill Valley would rather die, almost, than talk.

"All right, hombre," said Silvertip, and tossed the knife to him carelessly. The Mexican caught it out of the air with a hungry hand. He had the air, for an instant, of one about to leap forward; but again there was something in the faint smile and the steady eyes of Silvertip that discouraged attack. Presently the big man turned and strode off down the street, making violent gestures, cursing volubly to himself.

The two blacksmiths had stopped their laughter. They remained in the doorway and watched with brutally inexpressive faces while Silver remounted and rode down the street to a hotel. He found stable room behind the place; when he entered the hotel itself, a lowering clerk seemed unwilling to give him a room at first, but eventually he was shown to a dingy corner apartment that overlooked a side lane and the back yard. There he sat down and took his head between his hands. He was sleepy from his all-night ride, but the jumping of his nerves kept him from lying down.

He was half beaten within an hour of his arrival in the Haverhill Valley. All the self-confidence had melted from him, and he felt that he was leaning the weight of his mind against an impenetrable wall.

6 – The House of Monterey

HE stretched on the bed at last, for he could find no solution to his problem, and he knew that he needed sleep. When he wakened, a few hours later, a whispering air fanned his face, and he saw the door slowly swinging open.

When it was wide, Silvertip was already sitting up, at watch, and he observed on the threshold a man whose face was of the brutal type which he had seen so often before this in the Haverhill Valley. He was making a cigarette, leaning one shoulder against the jamb, and dripping tobacco unconcernedly over the floor. He was big, like most of these Haverhill men; and, like the rest of them, he stared heavily and steadily, without a shift in his eyes.

"You're the gent that slammed Juan Perez, are you?" asked the stranger.

"Who are you, brother?" asked Silvertip.

"Chuck Terry. Alligator sent me down to get you."

"Get me for what?" asked Silvertip.

"For the ranch."

"I'm not looking for a job."

"Sure you ain't," agreed "Chuck" Terry. "The job's looking for you. Grade-A pay, and the best eats in the land. Is that the sort of a picture you wanta step into?" Silvertip stood up.

"Look here," said he. "Who's the Alligator? I never heard of him."

Chuck Terry came suddenly to life, stepped into the room, and closed the door behind him.

"You never heard of Alligator Hank?" he repeated. "You never heard of Drummon?"

"No," said Silver. "Never heard of either of 'em."

With amazement, with long-drawn-out disgust, Chuck Terry regarded him.

"Well, what's the use, then?" said Chuck. "What're you driving at in the valley, anyway? You slam a greaser, and yet you ain't throwing in with Drummon?"

"Should I?" asked Silvertip.

"You know your own business better'n I do," replied Chuck Terry.

"What I want to do, first of all," said Silvertip, "is to find the place of Arturo Monterey."

This announcement was so interesting to Terry that he came a step or two closer to Silver, peering earnestly at him all the time.

"You wanta find out where Monterey lives?" he asked.

"I've asked a lot of people already," said Silvertip, "and they laugh at me."

Terry himself began to grin.

"All right," he answered. "I'll tell you. You want to see Monterey, do you? Well, ride right on down the valley and take the first road that forks over to the left. Keep down that left fork till you sight a house that looks like a doggone old castle out of a fairy-story book. And somewheres around there, likely you'll run into this gent, this Arturo Monterey, all right."

Terry struggled with a grin that would not be totally suppressed. It worked and twisted at his face.

"So long, brother," he said. "You go and find Don Arturo."

And, striding to the door, Terry cast it wide, slammed it behind him, and hurried down the hall. A noise of suppressed laughter, then a roar of it, came echoing back to Silvertip.

He went to the window and looked out at the brightness of the day, at the roofs of the town with quivering heat waves dancing over them, and beyond were the muscular knees of the mountains and their bare upward shoulders. For the first time since his childhood he felt the cold fear of this physical world reach him and finger his very heart. He seemed to have entered a region of ironical Titans. Among them he was reduced to an absurdity, and that purpose which had brought him to the place became more dreamlike than ever.

But his trail, he was sure, would take him far out of the Haverhill Valley. If he felt like a stranger in the place, it was certain that the slender fellow he had killed could never have lived here. It was merely to pick up some clue of him and then to be gone on the out trail that Silver lingered in Haverhill Valley. And with all his heart, he yearned to be gone at once!

He went down to the stable, saddled his own mustang and the mare, and rode down the street with grinning faces at watch on either side of him. They knew where he was going. They knew all about it. And they foresaw disaster, which pleased them to the heart. A group of boys tumbling in a vacant lot jumped up and shouted and pointed at him. Even the children understood things that were curtained away from his understanding.

He was glad to be out of that town, as if escaping from a curse, into the green, open arms of the country. The bright running of the river washed away some of the shadows that were pouring up in his mind. To his desert-bred eyes, the green undulations of the valley were more than waves of gold, and peace came to him as he watched the cattle grazing or lying in dim shadows under the trees. The strength flowed back, and that self-confidence which never had been lost to him for so many years until he entered the town of Haverhill.

He found the branching road that ran to the left. It was worn more by hoofs than wheels, and it mounted into the throat of a narrow valley. Great walls of rock went straight up on either side, one blue with shadow, one on fire with the sun, and through the middle of the canyon a creek ran with a sound of rushing, like a wind. The way up the valley was half blocked by the house of Arturo Monterey.

He knew it by Terry's description, for the road wound up a steep slope toward the entrance; on the other side was a precipitous fall of rocks, and above rose old adobe walls and one blunt tower of stone.

Up the winding way, Silvertip came to the house itself, and a great stone arch across the entrance to the patio. A big Mexican appeared suddenly and stood in his way. Silvertip dismounted.

"Amigo," he said, "I've come up here to find out, if I can, if Senior Monterey ever owned this horse, and who he sold it to. Maybe you can tell me and save me a lot of trouble?"

The Mexican regarded him with a long side glance in silence. Then he turned toward the mare with a sudden start, as though there were something about the animal which had jarred home upon his memory.

"Wait!" he said to Silver, and hurried back into the patio.

Silvertip looked curiously about him. Chuck Terry's description had been a little from the point; the place was more like a fortress than a castle, and the weather-worn adobe had the look of immense age. The patio was flagged with great stones and surrounded by an arching arcade, under the shadow of which he could see doors of heavy oak. The faces of those doors were seamed and cracked by dry old age.

His Mexican reappeared now, and not alone. Two other men walked briskly through the entrance arch, went by Silvertip, then halted suddenly. The man to whom he had spoken came up more slowly, with the look of a hunter who has marked down prey. A door opened on the farther side of the patio; more footsteps approached; and Silver knew that he was trapped.

White men or Mexicans, the Haverhill Valley seemed to be filled with madmen! He glanced over his shoulder toward the first pair who had passed through the arch; they faced him now, one with a drawn gun, one with his hand on a revolver butt. He thought of mounting and trying to break through, and cast that hope away even as it entered his mind.

Two newcomers loomed now at the side of the patio entrance. One of those he knew by the bull face and the sleek round of the neck, that same fellow whom he had pulled from a horse that morning, and to whom Terry had given the name of Juan Perez. He opened eyes and mouth, then grinned gapingly with joy.

"The gringo!" he cried, and reached for his gun.

Retreat was thoroughly blocked; Silvertip followed his normal instinct by advancing. He jumped like a scared cat at his first interlocutor, who had called out all this show of strength against him. The fellow's face convulsed, reaching for a weapon.

"Stop!" cried a woman's voice. "Juan Perez, stop!"

Nothing, could have nullified the motion which Perez had begun. There was a Colt already in the hand of Silver, but he held fire, and saw the fingers of Perez open, so that the revolver he had drawn flicked away and went spinning and rattling and slithering over the pavement of the patio.

Other guns were burning in the keen sunlight all around Silver. If he had been in danger before in his life, it was never a greater danger than that which surrounded him now. The voice of the woman had saved him. The mellow sound of her words still lingered in his mind, tasted and retasted.

She had suspended all the murderous action that had been in progress.

Then Juan Perez was crying out as he turned to the side, gesticulating violently: "This is the man with the horse of Pedrillo! Look! Look for yourself, señorita!"

Past the arch of the entrance a girl came into view. She wore sandals and a wide-brimmed hat of cheap straw, like any peon woman, but her dress was the white translucency of fine linen, and there was a dark Latin beauty in her face. A careless glance might have passed her over in a crowd; but a second look would be sure to dwell on her, and little else.

She came straight toward Silver, and paused at a distance which maintained her dignity.

"What is your name?" she asked.

"Silver," said he.

He took off his hat before her. The brilliance of the sun struck a dazzle across his eyes. He put on his hat again and looked steadily at her through the protecting shadow that fell across his eyes.

"You have the horse of Pedro Monterey," said the girl. "How did it come to you?"

"He is dead," said Silver.

He heard them all cry out. He saw them all surge in toward him and stop again, as though his words had first drawn and then repelled them, as the edge of a cliff draws frightened men. Only the girl remained motionless and well poised, though he could see the pain had gone through her wide eyes and was still working in her.

He added: "I say that he's dead. I only know that the man who rode this horse was middle height, slender, handsome, dark, about twenty or twenty-two years old."

"That was Pedro Monterey," said the girl. "His father will see you."

She turned about. One of the vaqueros hurried to take her arm, but she paused and said in her distinct, quiet voice: "I can walk very well by myself. Call the senior."

Then she passed out of view with the same unhurried step.

7 – Don Arturo

SILVER looked around on the stricken faces of the Mexicans who surrounded him. That sorrow was not strange to him, nor the blow which the girl had received so calmly and so deeply. It was right that the man he had killed should have come from such a place as this, with the air of a manor about it. Perhaps the girl was his sister, and these were the adherents of the house. The dead face had been that of an aristocrat, and it was from such a setting as this that he must have come. Long generations of breeding and culture will carve the features with more delicacy, and refine the body itself.

And the very soul of Silver expanded. If he had undertaken a great task, it was in a worthy cause. But more than ever he was baffled and bewildered. For how could he set his great hands to any task that had been important in the life of that dead man who now had a name—Pedro Monterey? Pedrillo, the vaqueros had called him, with an affectionate intonation.

They still pressed close, watching Silver like so many wolves about a helpless elk. He had put away his useless gun. Against such numbers it was a folly to show any sign of resistance. The least gesture in such a moment as this would bring the end of him, he knew that perfectly well.

He made a cigarette, lighted, and began to smoke it.

The news he brought had entered the house. These vaqueros who stood on guard about him had endured the shock steadily enough, but there were women in the big, sprawling house, and now voices rang out here and there in wild peals of grief that came through the walls as though through compressed lips.

The vaqueros began to be moved by those audible signs of woe. Some of them started swaying a little from side to side. Voices rose half audibly, bubbling and moaning, struggling in their throats, wordlessly.

But other words came. He heard them say: "The gringo!" and again: "The gringo dog! The dog!"

He was the messenger of bad news, and that was enough to insure him a bad reception. Lucky for him if the reaction consisted of words only.

The hinges of a heavy door grated. And then a slow footfall came across the patio.

"It is Don Arturo—God help him! God be merciful to him!" Silver heard one of the men murmur.

All of the Mexicans drew back a little, as though in respect, and in sympathy, while an old man with sweeping silver hair and a pointed gray beard came out into the patio. Time had pinched his shoulders a little, and perhaps it was the flow of hair that made the head seem disproportionately large. All his features were accented, together with the whiteness of his hair, by a band of black cloth which passed across his forehead, to be lost immediately under the flow of his hair. He would be a more imposing figure seated than standing; but even as he stood, he was a man of mark. He walked with a slim cane in his hand, his meager fingers spread out on the round head of it. And as he came to a halt, he stood very straight, as if at attention.

The blow had fallen on him, and, like the girl, he had received it calmly. The weight of it had not broken him. No doubt there was a deeper shadow under his brows now than there had been a few moments before. Perhaps his lips were pressed more tightly together. But his voice was calm as he said:

"You are Señor Silver?"

"I am," said Silver.

"You come to tell me that Pedro Monterey is dead?"

"The man who rode that horse—a young man—dark, handsome—" began Silver.

But the other lifted his hand.

"What was the manner of his dying, Senior Silver?" he asked.

The girl had come out from the house. She stood in the shadow of the arcade that surrounded the patio. One fold of her linen skirt thrust forward, and flashed like snow in the sunshine that touched it. She looked like the dead youth; she must be his sister, in fact. But what manner of people were these, when a father and sister could take the news of a death in such a way?

"May I speak to you alone?" said Silver.

Arturo Monterey drew himself up a little.

"In twenty years," he said, "no American has entered this house. May it be another hundred years before one of your race passes through my door. You stand in my patio; and even that is very much, indeed! But come closer to me, if you will. My sons, fall back."

The vaqueros moved off a little distance, their spurs rattling. Silver moved forward until he was close to the older Monterey. And just at that moment the opening of a door, as it seemed, allowed a wild cry of lament to break out from the house, a single dreadful note of grief, shut away to dimness again, as though the door had been suddenly closed once more.

Silver saw the chin of the old man jerk up, as he endured the thrust of that keening. But nothing seemed able really to shock Arturo Monterey.

"It was in Cruces," said Silver. "Do you know the place?"

Arturo Monterey made a slowly sweeping gesture.

"The mountains of the Haverhill," he said, "are the boundaries of my life."

"It's a small town," said Silver, "fifty miles from here, beyond the mountains. I was there, and I met an enemy of mine, who was with your son."

"What was his name?" asked Monterey.

"Bandini."

"Bandini is an enemy of yours?"

"So much so, that we agreed to meet at a certain hour, and fight out our arguments together. At that time, I went into the street to find him. I saw a man wearing Bandini's cloak. I followed him, and stopped him. Señor, a man does not pause to ask many questions, at such a time. I was sure that it was Bandini. I challenged him with enough words to give him a chance to draw a gun. It seemed to me that he drew. Then I pulled my gun and fired. And the fire that spurted out of the gun showed me not the face of Bandini, but that of a stranger. He fell dead! I took his horse and his possessions, and traced him through the horse to this house. And what I wish to say is—" "Perez! Juan!" gasped Monterey. He gripped his walking stick with both hands, and leaned a little on it.

"Take him!" groaned Monterey through his teeth, as the men came running to him. "Take the cursed gringo! God told me, twenty-five years ago, that nothing but evil could come to me from them, and here is another proof! Take him—away from my eyes—out of my sight—where I shall not hear the death cry! Make of him what my son is—a dead thing!"

They closed on Silver from either side, suddenly. Many pairs of hands gripped him with a force that ground the muscles against the bones, and paralyzed the nerves. In an instant he was as helpless as though he had lain for a month in benumbing fetters.

What a savage joy there was in their eyes, in the twisting of their mouths as they grasped and shook him! The grip of their fingers on his body seemed to feed them, like so many dogs tearing at living flesh.

And then he heard the girl calling out, not loudly: "Uncle Arturo, what are you doing?"

"I am finding justice, justice, justice on the gringo!" cried Arturo Monterey. "Quickly, my sons—quickly! Juan Perez, you will take charge, for you have seen this man before, and know a little about him. No torments—let death kill with a sharp edge, suddenly!"

There was bounding joy in the eyes of Perez, as though he looked upon a bright treasure, in beholding Silver.

They swung their prisoner about. They began to sweep him down the roadway that led up to the house.

Behind them, Silver heard the girl saying: "A man who trusted you, brought you the news of the death, and the horse of Pedro for the proof! Uncle Arturo, what has come of the honor of the Montereys?"

"Where is there honor among the gringos?" thundered Monterey in answer. His voice swelled out enormously, from that withering body. "Do you speak to a Mexican of honor in dealing with them? Honor, in handling a brute who brings me the horse of my dead boy, and the word that *he* has killed him? Honor?"

The Mexicans had come to the horse of Silver, and now they flung him upon it. They had taken his guns, his knife. Some held the bridle of the horse; others gripped the legs, the arms of the prisoner. Still more were riding up horses from the patio, coming on the gallop. But the voice of the girl, like a meager hope of salvation and life, still found the ears of Silver, dimly, through the tumult.

She was saying: "He had faith in you. If you betray faith, God will never forgive you. What a man does innocently is not done at all. Uncle Arturo, you have only this moment to decide. They are taking him away—it will be too late—you will be shamed—and you will let in the law on us all. If you let him be killed, it is murder in the eyes of Heaven, and in the eyes of the law, also. Oh, if the ghost of Pedro is near us, it is giving an echo to what I say!"

But now the cavalcade had formed, half on horseback and half on foot, bearing Silver with them resistlessly, carrying him forward toward the quick ending of his life. He could see the big barrier of the mountains surging in steep-sided waves across the sky before him. His horse was shaking its head, and making the bridle ring. One of the Mexicans had a broad red stain on the shoulder of his white shirt. A wild jumble of detached observations came flooding into the brain of Silver. And through it, the voice of the girl, raised by desperation as distance made it fade.

Afterward, a dull cry reached them, calling Juan Perez. The man turned.

"She has persuaded him," said one of the escort. "Perez, what do you say? Shall we sweep him away? Aye, or kill him here in the roadway! Kill him here, and have it done?"

Perez, looking back up the road, saw something that made him fix on Silver the eye of a maniac. Then, with a gesture of despair, he halted the troop.

"Take him back!" he commanded. "The señor calls for him. The girl has won again. She always wins. We are only dogs to be barked back and forth. Perhaps this gringo fills her eyes; perhaps we shall have to lick his feet before long!"

The whole escort turned, gradually, and Silver could see again the stern old man standing as erect as ever, with his two hands resting on the head of his cane. The girl was beside him, withdrawn a little.

So they came straight back to confront Don Arturo. The passion was working in his face, still, and he was paler than before.

He cried out in that great voice which seemed to make his body smaller than ever, by contrast: "He has come to me, Juan Perez, and I must take thought before I put hands on him. But for his sake I shall forget the vow I made twenty-five years ago. He shall enter my house! He shall be taken into it now. Perez, carry him down to the cellar, to the lowest and the darkest room. There are irons to fit on him. Load him until his body is safely held. You, Perez, are his keeper, and shall answer to me for him!" "Uncle Arturo—" cried out the girl. "Be still—be still!" exclaimed the old man. "Do you talk to me of honor and kindness? They have shamed me, they have dishonored my house, they have ravaged my lands, and now they have slain my son, and leave me a dry, dead stalk! Juan Perez, do as I command!"

8 – Imprisoned

THEY carried Silver rapidly into the house. The last he heard from the sunlit outdoors was the voice of the girl, raised higher than before as she passionately implored Don Arturo to remember himself, and the loud, stern cry of the old man as he bade her be quiet.

Out of a big corridor, they turned through a high and narrow doorway down a steep flight of steps. Lanterns were carried. Their swinging light began to flash far ahead, glimmering along damp walls, or throwing a dull sheen across the water that lay on the stones they trod, as they penetrated story after story, deep and deeper into the rock.

Juan Perez went first. Of the crowd, perhaps only half a dozen remained to hustle Silver along. And it seemed as though they were not descending through the cellars of a house, but through the galleries of some old mine, that had been worked for centuries, drill and pick and shovel digging into the living stone to find the treasure. It was a wilderness. Silver had attempted to keep track of the turns, the descents, the stairs, the sloping passages, but he gave it up. And three or four times even Juan Perez, who seemed to know the place well, came to a halt and swung his lantern from side to side before he made a choice between one gallery or another.

Once he stopped at a corridor hewn to a great size, and Juan Perez commented to his awed companions, that this was the place where the heart of the great lode had been found.

It was, in fact, through the galleries of an ancient mine that they were passing. But now they paused and took from a room a set of manacles brown with time. With these they went forward only a short distance until they came to another door, and opening this, the lantern light revealed a little room perhaps three steps by two in dimensions. On the irregular floor of it

173

water had gathered, which had been scummed over with green; the air itself was very foul; and the odor of the slime was like a throttling hand on the throat.

There they fitted the irons to the body of Silver. Juan Perez, with a key, opened and locked them again. Then he stood back and lifted a lantern until the sheen of it fell upon the captive.

Half in dry stone and half in slime sat Silver, and met the eye of Juan Perez calmly. There was no word spoken. He heard only the softly inhaled breath of Perez, and saw the flash of his eyes and teeth as he grinned. Then the Mexicans left him. The door slammed shut with the booming noise of a cannon shot. And far away he heard the departing troop. They were laughing and shouting; even that laughter and derisive shouting seemed to Silver a precious thing to be harkened after with an eager ear. He strained his senses to hear every scruple of it; and when at last he could make out no more sound, the darkness was suddenly trebled about him, and a weight fell crushingly on his lungs.

It was the impure air that sickened him and made breathing almost futile. Presently he forgot the slime in which he lay, and, stretched flat on his back, did his best to calm the insane fear which was working in his brain. Then began the first eternity, black, still, foul, breathless. He secured hope out of one strange thought—that he had appointed himself to redeem the lost life of Pedro Monterey, and that therefore he must suffer worse than death, and then be given the chance to use his hands and his brain. He must nearly die, but some life would surely be left to him.

When we are in bed, clean, clear reason departs from us. And it departed, now, from Silver, as he lay in the stifling black of that prison. His second occupation was to employ his mind with dreams of what the life of Pedro Monterey must have been in this house with the stern old man for a father, and with all the fierce vaqueros ready to ride or to fight at his bidding. The girl, however, was not his sister. She was merely a cousin, more or less distant. And there was mercy in her which the pure strain of these Montereys seemed incapable of feeling.

She kept moving across the close velvet blackness that filled the eyes of Silver. She moved like a light before him, and filled his mind with a singular happiness.

Now, at the end of that eternity, there was the faint sound of footfalls. The lock of the door turned. A lantern flashed, blinding bright, throwing intolerable diamonds of brilliance into the eyes of Silver. By that light, dimly, he saw a jug put down beside the door, and a lump of bread was thrown toward him. It splashed in the slimy water. A voice laughed, and the door shut heavily again.

But he found himself forgetful of the spoiling of the bread, and of the contents of the jug, though he was starving for food, and famished for water. All that he bent his attention on was the noise of the retreating footfalls.

When it had dissolved, still a faint echo worked in his brain, as though to reassure him that there were human beings left in the world. Then he started toward the door, dragging his body along with great difficulty. He found the jug and sniffed at it. He had hoped for something better than water, but when he lifted the pitcher with his manacled hands, it was water alone that he tasted. Yet it flooded his hot throat with wonderful relief.

When he had drunk, hunger returned to him with new force. He had seen the bread fall into the rotten slime, but revolting as the sight had been, he sought for that bread now, and found it, and tried to eat it, but the repulsive taste made the walls of his stomach close together in nausea. He threw the food from him and stretched himself again to wait.

The cold of the stone was sinking into his body, reaching the bone. He knew that weakness caused by lack of food was making him more and more susceptible to the cold. He must use his muscles to gain heat from them, no matter how the efforts increased his hunger. So he devised a regular system, getting painfully to his feet, bowing, forward and backward, swaying to the side, stretching his loaded arms as far as the chains permitted, then squatting and rising, squatting and rising until he was numb with the efforts.

Those exercises kept his blood coursing in the veins. And afterward it was easier to sleep. But sleep occupied only a small portion of the second infinity of darkness before he saw more light. When he wakened, there was a new, pungent, horrible odor in the air, a sort of sickening sweetness, and a moment later he heard the pattering of infinitely light feet, the squeak and gibbering of sharp voices. Rats were in the room with him! He felt a sudden blind horror, a horror of squeamishness. He actually parted his lips to scream out; but the man in him came to his rescue and sternly throttled back that weakness. Yet what would he be in the course of a few weeks or months? But were there not men who had lain for long years in darkness, like beasts, and still endured? Hope came to him with the rats. If they had entered, it was by some hole, and if there were a small hole, he might enlarge it. He began to work with his finger tips across the entire surface of the wall, knowing that touch would give to him the effect of sight, in a sense.

What he found, at last, was a narrow crevice, so small that it seemed impossible that even a mouse could have come through. But it was not in masonry that might be crumbled gradually away from this small start; it was a rift in the living stone, strong as iron on either side of the little aperture.

He gave up that hope slowly, and his spirits and his strength seemed to ebb away from him for a long time afterward.

He went through the exercises again, as he had devised them. And now he sat in a dry corner and waited.

At last the steps came again, the door opened, and again a light shone on him. The lantern was raised high; he saw the face of the girl beneath it, as she saw him.

"Phaugh!" she cried. "Rats, and slime, and filth for a Christian man. In the name of mercy, Juan Perez, what—"

The voice of Perez answered sullenly: "Any sort of life is too good for him. The rats keep him company. Some day I hope they'll eat him!"

She stepped in, and pushed the door shut behind her. And her coming poured upon Silver wave after wave of incredible comfort and joy. He had hardly thought her more than pretty in the sunlight; in the dark, damp room she seemed to have the radiant beauty of an angel.

Perez was calling out, beyond the door. She silenced him with two or three sharp words of command. Then she came closer, picking her way between the puddles of slime. Silver struggled, and rose to his feet with a clanking of chains.

He towered above her, and she with a lifted face looked at him with pity and with pain.

"Have they given you food?" she asked.

"They threw one lump of bread—into the slime," he said. "They knew I could not eat it, after that."

"No food, then? Three days without food?" she cried. "Three days?"

"Three years, it seems to me," said Silver, "of this darkness."

She hurried to the door and pulled the weight of it open.

"Perez," she gasped, her voice shaking with anger. "Quickly! Run to the kitchen. Bring meat—a good meal— a huge meal—and wine—and bring it with your own hands—quickly!"

Juan Perez snarled like a dog, but his footfall departed.

9 – Señorita Julia

SHE came slowly back, a step or two, and then paused. "They have treated you like a dog," she said, "and I knew when I first saw you, that you are an honest man. You're weak. Sit down and—Great heavens, you've nothing to sit on but the damp of the stone! Phaugh! The rats want to come back!"

They had scampered through the crevice in the wall, as she entered with the light, their naked tails flicking like whiplashes out of view. Now their eyes glittered from the mouth of the covert again.

"God forgive Uncle Arturo," she said. And then she broke out: "Yet there's no kinder or more gentle man in the world. But his son is dead, and his hope is dead, too, and he's half insane with grief. He had to put his hands on something, and there were you in his grasp! And then Drummons—what's left to him now for the fight with them? Only his own hands, and mine, and only half my blood is that of the Montereys! You can understand him a little, and forgive him a little?"

He said nothing.

"I came to ask you one definite thing," she said, when she saw that he would not speak on the other subject. "What was in your mind when you came to this house to tell us that you had killed poor Pedro?"

"Have they sent for his body? Will he be buried here?" asked Silver.

"They have sent for him," she answered.

"When I saw by the flash of my own gun that I had shot the wrong man," said Silver, "I don't think I would have cared so much if he had been older. But he was at the start of everything. He hadn't had a chance to prove himself. And—well, it's a hard thing to talk about. I really can't tell you what I thought."

He ended abruptly, but she was watching him with such studious and yet such gentle eyes that presently his words began again, as if of their own accord.

177

"I thought," said Silver, "that I could try to fill in some of the gap left by his death. I was a fool. I couldn't tell that he was the only son of this old man. I thought that I could do something about him. And somehow," he added, his voice swelling as the old resolution burned back into his brain hotter than ever, and more inwardly bright, "and somehow, I think I'll manage to put my hands on something that he left unfinished, and complete it for him. I suppose this sounds like crazy talk to you. And I won't beat about the bush. I've killed other men—more than one or two! But this time it was different. To kill a man is bad enough; but to finish a life that's hardly begun to cut its own way through the world—that was what made me sick, then! And—"

He paused, with a gesture. He felt that he had talked absolutely in vain.

She merely said: "I believe you, and I understand you. And for that bigness of heart, you've been thrown into this blackness and treated like a murderer! Ah, but my uncle shall hear about it from me! I'll make him understand!"

Then, turning, she exclaimed: "Here's Juan Perez back again. You shall eat, now!"

The door was pushed open, and it was Juan Perez indeed. He carried a small half loaf of bread in one hand and a jug of water in the other. He put down the jug, laid the bread across the mouth of it, and then straightened to face the girl with a grin.

That smile made him look more like a hungry tiger than ever.

"Señorita Julia," he said, "the señor forbids the prisoner to have more than bread and water."

"You went to him?" exclaimed the girl. "You went to him, after I had given you my orders?"

"We serve you, señorita," said the politely sneering Perez, "as we would serve an angel. But there is only one master in the house of Monterey!"

He made a little bow to her, and lifting his head again, he stared not at her but at Silver, with unabated hatred. The girl was instantly calm.

"I shall see my uncle," said she. "And some changes will be made. You shall have a bed. I think I can make him change your room. Perhaps there will be decent food, after a little while."

She went to the door and turned suddenly. Her eyes flashed. Her voice flared up. Color burned into her face. "Day and night," she exclaimed, "I shall try to serve you, señor!"

She was gone. Perez, lantern in hand, looked after her, toward the door, and then shook his forefinger in the air. He began to laugh, in a silent convulsion of mirth.

"Those words will undo everything else she may say to the master," he told Silver. "Day and night she will serve you, gringo. Is that the truth? Señor

Monterey shall hear what she said. I shall see to that. And afterward—hai! You'll feel the spur as well as the toe of the boot!"

He laughed again, this time out loud, and left Silver in the black darkness.

And there Silver crouched, chewing eagerly at the bread, while the rats swarmed over his feet, leaped up on his clothes, in their eagerness to come at the food. The air was foul with the smell of their vile bodies, but the ravenous hunger of Silver stilled all the other senses. He ate, drank the water to the last drop, and then lay down and slept. Something would be done for him. The girl had promised. And he would believe her more than the oaths of a hundred men.

But nothing was done!

Bread and water were brought to him regularly, once a day, and that was all. The cell was not changed. Not one item of comfort was added to him. And two days later, Juan Perez came again, alone. He unlocked the door, put the lantern on the floor, and made a cornucopia-shaped cigarette, which he lighted, and then blew the smoke toward Silver, to make sure that the full flavor of the tobacco would reach him. The very heart of Silver quaked with yearning, but he made his eye calm, and kept it fixed on the Mexican.

"So I repeated the kind words of the Señorita Julia to the master," said Juan Perez. "And you see what has happened? You see the comfortable bed you lie on? You see the warm sunshine that streams through your window? You taste the good tobacco that is given you to smoke? You breathe the pure air? You relish the fine roasts and the stews and the dried meats that are brought to you? For all of those things, Señor Fool, Señor Dog, you can thank Juan Perez!"

Silver slowly dragged up his legs until they were half doubled under him. A plan was forming dimly in his brain. Now he merely smiled at Perez. That smile seemed to strike the Mexican like a blow. He started, and then scowled.

"You think that you've tormented me, Perez," said Silver. "As a matter of fact, I have to stay here for another day or two. That is all. Then I shall leave. Before I go, I shall have certain words to say to you, certain blows to strike you with a whip, certain speeches that I shall listen to you making on your knees, while you grovel before me, and beg for your life."

"Dog!" breathed Juan Perez. "You mean that I, Perez, shall be on my knees before you? You mean that in a day or two you'll be gone? Ah, I see— your mind is touched, you are losing your wits in the long darkness!"

"Poor Perez!" said Silver. "You cannot understand?"

"Understand?" said the Mexican, coming a stride closer. "What is there to understand?"

"That you have been a fool from the first! You can't understand that?" said Silver.

"I? I a fool? I who walk with free feet and eat and sleep as I will, and breathe the fresh air—I am the fool—and you are the wise man?"

He drew a shade closer.

Silver leaned his head and shoulders back against the wall. And he smiled at Juan Perez as if out of the deeps of a profound contentment.

"Poor Juan Perez!" he said, and shook his head a little, as though words could not fit the matter.

"Gringo beast!" gasped Perez suddenly, and striding one step nearer, he struck Silver full in the face.

The next instant the legs of the Mexican were knocked from under him, for the two manacled feet of Silver had shot out with a true aim and a desperate vigor. Perez, falling, pitched straight forward at the prisoner. Silver, with both hands raised, met the dropping body with a club stroke over the head. The weight of the irons on his wrists helped home that blow, and Juan Perez lay face down on the stones, without a quiver.

Silver went through the man's pockets. He knew, he thought, the very look and face of the key that fitted into his manacles. And he found it in the pocket of the deerskin vest of Perez. It was clumsy work to fit that key into the lock of the hand irons, and it was impossible to turn it with his fingers. He had to go to the little crevice in the wall, and there laboriously fit the handle of the key into the base of the crack, and then turn his arms until the lock was sprung. But a moment later he was free, both in arms and hands and feet.

A wave of half hysterical delight shot through him, and centered in his throat.

It was dashed away, a moment later, by the fear that he heard footfalls hurrying down the corridor outside his room. Then he realized that it was merely the beat and flutter of his racing heart.

Juan Perez groaned, and sat up. He saw Silver standing over him, with the gun of Perez himself in his hand, and he groaned. In the rage of his despair, he cast himself back, and the slime into which he fell was flung out in a fine spray on either side.

"You see, Perez?" said Silver. "After all, you were a fool, and sooner than you expected. But be patient, my friend. When you leave this room, a good many things may have happened, and, above all, the whole world will know that Perez is a fool!" He took the lantern, and left the Mexican groaning, beating his head with his hands. He left the room. A small, cold draft was stirring in the corridor, and as Silver locked the heavy door behind him, and pocketed the key, it seemed to him that all the freshness of spring and the sweetness of spring flowers were in that air!

He went up the hallway. There was no plan in his mind. He must simply pray that it was night, that he could be able to reach the outer door that led into the patio, that he could pass from the patio into freedom.

And leave behind him the great task unfinished, and poor Pedro Monterey doubly dead?

His heart failed him, when he thought of making such a surrender. Have not men said that nothing is impossible to the resolute mind? He thought of that saying, also, as he roamed up the corridors beneath the house of Monterey. But it seemed to him that it would be almost a sufficient miracle if he could save his life from the hands of the old man.

But the thing persisted in him. He had set his soul on the purpose for too long. And the completion of the life of Pedro Monterey had become a spiritual necessity to him. That was why, as he roved through the passages, he began to deny in himself the thought of mere flight and to take to his heart a greater steadiness.

If he were to remain near Monterey, another miracle must happen, greater than any which had gone before. But Silver determined to let the events of each moment dictate what he was to do with himself in the immediate future.

There was the problem of getting up from the cellars at all. And that seemed enough to fill his mind. For hours he wandered, and always he was coming to the end of passages that stopped against solid stone. The flame in the lantern burned low, flickered, died. He was left in a horror of darkness that seemed to keep flowing past him.

A man might pass days, fumbling through that blindness, and never come to an exit. He might be so far lost that not even the faintest echo of his voice would reach to any ears.

Silver leaned against a wall and closed his eyes, and tried to find in his mind some solution, but all his thoughts were whirling, spinning like foolish squirrels in a cage.

He was still standing there when something clinked like the lock of a door. He looked up, and a flash of light entered the passage just before him, and footfalls came clumping down steps. Then light shone again, swinging out from behind the voluminous skirts of a woman.

Silver crouched close to the floor, with hope once more in his heart The light disappeared. The woman was singing softly as she went on some familiar errand, her wooden heels bumping on the stone.

But what was important to Silver was that door through which she had come, for it seemed that his lantern had failed him when he was a very few steps from salvation.

He hurried through the darkness, spreading his hands far out before him. Then his feet struck the steps. He climbed. He came, at the top of the steps, to the kind touch of wood, and fumbling, he soon found the knob.

Softly he opened the door, and peered out. At once the rattle of many voices in laughter and raillery struck on his ears as if with open mockery of all that he was attempting.

10 – In the Garden

HE shrank back, then thrust the door wide in a sudden desperation. And springing out into the hall, he discovered to his amazement that it was empty.

Still the voices persisted, but plainly they must come from some adjoining room, beating through a thin partition.

He went rapidly to the end of the hall. The clinking of his spurs followed him like an accusing voice, so he drew off his boots, and left them in a corner.

He tried the nearest door. It opened with a dull groan of hinges and let him into a big room. He knew its bigness, only, by the faintest of high lights that glimmered here and there in the chamber. It was a bedroom, and crossing it to the stars that filled a window, he looked out and down.

Beneath him, he saw still another drop of twenty feet of unbroken wall, with a garden spread over the ground under the window. He must be on the first floor of the house, but on this side another story was added below. It was just the garden that a Mexican would conceive in happy dreams—a little flat of ground with a canal of water lilies driven through it, and a rectangular pool at one end, with a fountain rising over it. That was the chief feature, together with a semicupola, a sort of open-faced summer-house raised on narrow columns, so that one would have both shade and wind.

Silvertip saw this by the light of a big yellow moon which was tilting over the eastern mountains with its cheeks still puffed beyond the full. And this light showed him, moreover, a table laid in the cool beside the canal of water lilies. The girl, Julia, sat there, and opposite her old Monterey, rigid with dignity. The moon gleamed faintly on his long hair and his pointed beard.

There was no escape by that window. So Silvertip turned, and, crouching low so that no light might strike up and outward through the window, he scratched a match. Cupping the flame securely in his hands, he threw the dull flash of it here and there about the room. He saw, at once, a small door to the right; he saw the big bed, like a mahogany house, the fireplace, and above it a portrait that drew him suddenly across the room. He ventured rising and passing the light from the match across the face in the picture. It was Pedro Monterey, younger, and alive and smiling.

The flame of the match seared the fingers of Silvertip before he dropped it on the hearth, and still in the darkness he remained staring before him as though he could still see the portrait. The bitterness he had been feeling toward old Monterey now vanished. It was only strange to him that the slayer of the son had not been slain out of hand.

He fumbled his way with outstretched hands through the darkness and came to the little door that he had seen on the right. When he opened it, a cool breath of air moved upward into his face. And he had a sense, though no sight, of steps descending through the shadows before him. With his foot he reached and found, as he had expected, a stairway that led down. He shut the door behind him. The draft no longer blew. A close dampness of moist stone surrounded him as he descended a winding way until one outstretched hand told him of another door.

He opened it with great care, and instantly found the outdoors before his face, the yellow of the moonlight striking directly against him. It was the garden where the girl sat with Monterey.

The silhouette of a man moved before him, close enough to touch. But the figure did not pause at the partially opened door. It went on, bearing a large tray with glasses twinkling on it, and a luster of half-seen silver.

Silvertip ventured outside. Other people moved here and there, but all at a sufficiently safe distance, so he stole for the nearest shelter. It was a bank of shadow that looked to him like brush, but turned out to be tall flowers, which were hedged up here as a margin and border to surround the garden.

Delicately he moved forward, putting the great, rank stalks aside until he had made for himself a covert of darkness. There he crouched, and parting the branches before him, he could look out on the garden scene and the table with a more intimate eye.

They spoke suddenly, and then turned their faces directly toward him.

"There is something in the flowers," said the girl.

"There is the wind," said the voice of Senior Monterey.

"Something moved in there, slowly," she Insisted.

"A snake, perhaps," suggested the old man.

He dismissed the subject with a wave of his hand. The wind stirred his long hair, and his beard, and the moon glittered over him till he looked to Silvertip like a patriarchal form that had walked out of a distant age.

"You think of him still," said Monterey suddenly.

The bowed head of the girl lifted slowly. And a touch on the heart of Silver told him that it was of him that Monterey was speaking. That was hardly strange.

"I think of him," she answered. "I keep thinking. I keep trying for words that will move you, Uncle Arturo."

The old man answered: "You would not need to whisper to me, Julia, if I dreamed that he is what you say— honest! But he can't be honest. There is no honesty in his race. I have suffered at their hands enough to have broken the hearts of twenty stronger men than I, and only my hope for revenge keeps life in me. Now that my boy is gone, you will wonder that I can still hope even for revenge, but let me tell you that the dream has been in my heart so long that it cannot die as quickly as Pedrillo did.

"I think that even bullets could not kill it. If my body came to an end, the hate for the gringos would still live. It would take a bodiless form; it would walk the earth like a ghost. But no matter how I hate his race, if this man were honest, I would set him free, reward him, beg for his pardon."

"He is honest, if I ever saw honesty!" said the girl. "And now he lies in a pen where you would not even put swine!"

"He is like his people—a liar and a traitor!" exclaimed Monterey. "How many times they have betrayed me, Julia! You know only a little of it! And now I think of how he tried to deceive you, of how he told you that he came here only hoping that he could fill the place of my dead boy, in some way. Oh, my child, it was the sort of a story that a man might use to a woman, but never to another man."

"Uncle Arturo," said the girl, "he came with the horse, he told the truth of the death of poor Pedro, and he put himself in your hands. How could he have done those things unless he meant honestly?"

But there was no response to her plea. After a pause of silence, the girl stirred.

"To the good, all creatures are virtuous," said Monterey, "and there is such a well of goodness in you that you could forgive the devil himself for his craft and his fiendishness. You would pity him for the pain that he lies in. But let me tell you that I shall never again believe well of a gringo until his virtue is established more plainly than the mountains that stand by the Haverhill Valley!"

She looked steadily at the old man for a moment. Then she sighed.

"It's time to go in," said Julia. "Onate and Alvarez have been quarreling again, and you'll have to see them."

"I can see them out here," said Arturo Monterey.

"It's not safe," she answered. She leaned a little across the table. "The men of Drummon are bolder every day; how can you tell how bold they'll be at night? They may slip up here. They have a moon to show them their way. They may be here now. What I heard there among the flowers may be one of them lying still and watching, and listening."

"Let them watch, and let them listen," said Monterey. "I have a feeling, Julia, that I've come to the end of my day. Let it close as soon as it will. I'm ready for it."

The girl waited an instant. Then she said: "You're tired today, Uncle Arturo. And when a person is tired, the gloomy thoughts are the ones that come up in the mind."

He answered: "I've been marked by my shame long enough, and if I am to die, I am ready for it."

He touched his forehead significantly as he spoke, on the band of dark cloth that crossed his forehead.

The girl would have spoken again, but he stopped her with a raised hand, saying:

"There is nothing but cold and emptiness in my heart. And I should die even gladly, except that there is the one great purpose of all these years unaccomplished."

"But if you stay out here," said the girl, "if you throw yourself away into the hands of Drummon's brutes—is there any chance, then, of doing what you promised yourself?"

He answered: "If the hand of God is against me, why should I attempt to defend myself?"

11 – Brand of Shame

OLD Monterey was asking to have Onate and Alvarez brought before him. They must have been attending close at hand, for now they came in together, escorted by two vaqueros who had bound the hands of the pair. And they stood with bowed heads before the master. One was young, one a grizzled veteran. They were peons of the field, not cattle herders; they wore huarachos on their bare feet, and they were dressed in white cotton that shimmered in the moonlight.

"Now, Tonio?" said Arturo Monterey.

One of the vaqueros made half a step forward. He was a solid fellow with a grave, steady look.

"Their houses are side by side, as you know, señor," said Tonio. "They have always been friends. Onate is a good man, and he has helped Alvarez. He's older, this Onate, and he has a head on his shoulders. But now, all at once, they are enemies. They run at each other with knives. We ask them why they quarrel. They give us no answer. They will not speak to each other. They will not speak to us. So we have brought them to you, señor."

"Who began this quarrel?" asked Monterey.

The two peons looked at one another, and were silent, staring again at the ground.

"Answer!" cried Monterey, lifting his voice suddenly to thunder.

They both started violently, and with one voice, both exclaimed: "I started the trouble, señor."

Then they were mute, and again gaped on one another.

"You both began the fight?" said Monterey, amused and interested. "How could you both begin it?"

"It was I, señor," said Onate. "I am sorry, and I repent."

"I am sorry, and I repent, also," said Alvarez. Then, losing his control for an instant, he exclaimed: "But this Onate is a liar and a fool!"

Onate, grinding his teeth, said nothing. He continued to look merely at the ground.

"You both began the fight; you both repent; and one of you is a liar and a fool. How, Onate? Are you the liar and the fool?"

Onate jerked up his head savagely. Then something from within gave him pause. He drew a breath and gasped, "Yes, señor."

Monterey regarded them both soberly.

"They have seen you; perhaps it is enough. They will not fight again, senior," observed Tonio.

Monterey hushed him with a gesture.

"Fire can burn underground, but it will always break out when a wind blows," he said. "Why did you quarrel, you two?"

Again the pair regarded one another, gloomily.

"Speak!" commanded Monterey.

Onate said slowly: "I, señor, said a foolish thing. I am sorry. I angered Alvarez. I ask him to forgive me. I am—a liar—a fool!"

He brought out the last words with a bitter effort.

"There is no more lying in you, Onate, than in a blessed saint," declared Monterey. "What was it you talked about?"

There was another pause, but not so long that Monterey had to lay the whip of his impatience on either of them again. For Alvarez muttered:

"About you, señor, and God forgive us!"

"God will forgive you and so shall I, probably," said Monterey. "What was it that you said about me?"

This time the full pause lasted so long before an answer, that the silence itself became more of a threat than any words from Monterey could have been. It was this quiet pressure that made Alvarez say:

"I asked Onate if he knew why the señor wore the cloth band about his head, always, day and night. And then he told me such a great lie that my knife got into my hand. But even a good man will lie, sometimes, to make talk. I am sorry. But the señor is my father; he is the father to us all."

Monterey was so moved by something in this speech that he stood up from his chair, suddenly.

"What did you say, Onate?" he demanded.

"Señor," he said, "if you ask me for my words, I shall seem to you a traitor and a scoundrel. In the name of Heaven, do not make me speak, and forgive me!"

Monterey bowed his head for a moment in thought.

"The time has come, Onate," he said, "when secret shame should be bared before the world. My son has gone from me, Onate, and I fear that he will not return. Perhaps the secrecy with which I have kept that shame of mine is the reason that God chooses to punish me. Speak out, freely. What did you say to Alvarez?"

Onate flung himself suddenly on his knees.

"Señor," he groaned, "it is a foul story that has been in the air for many years, since the night when Señor Drummon and his men poured into the house. And it is said— forgive me for repeating it!—but it is said that on that night the brand of the Cross and Snake was burned into your forehead with your own branding iron by the gringo devils!"

He put up a hand before his face, as though to shield himself from an unexpected blow.

The girl sprang up and hurried to the side of Arturo Monterey, anxiously, as though to be a shield to any object of his wrath. But the old man, after a moment, cried out:

"It is the will of God that the whole world should know. Onate, you spoke the truth."

With that, he suddenly tore the cloth band from about his head, and the brightness of the moon showed to them all, and above all to the straining eyes of Silvertip, a small cross printed in a shadowy furrow in the brow of Monterey, and beneath it a wavering line—the complete brand of the Cross and Snake.

The Mexicans, both the prisoners and the vaqueros who had guarded them, slowly drew back from that sight, then turned, and fairly fled. Monterey slipped back into his chair and the girl, lifting the cloth circle from the ground, fitted it carefully over the bowed head again. She was weeping, stifling her sobs as well as she could. Then she sat beside him, watching his bowed face.

"The whole world had heard of it," said Monterey. "You have heard of it also, Julia. Drummon has talked of it and boasted of it among his men That is why the gringos laugh, when they look at me, and laugh, also, when they speak of me."

"The cruel, savage dogs!" sobbed the girl. "I had heard of it, Uncle Arturo, but I would never believe. None of us would ever believe. Why did you show it to them?"

"The will of God," repeated Monterey. "Who can avoid that? And yet perhaps, before the end, I shall be able to strike one blow at Drummon. I have prayed for that. I have yearned for it, since that night when Drummon and his men broke into this house and lashed me to a chair in my own hall, and heated the branding iron in the coals of my own fire."

"No!" cried the girl. "No one could do that to you! Not even a beast like Drummon, or the brutes that follow him!"

"He told me," said Monterey, "that since I fought with him about the cattle in the valley, and since I claimed more than was mine, he would put my own brand where the devil himself and every man could always see it. And then he took the branding iron with his own hands. It was white-hot. It threw out snapping sparks, and the heat seemed to drip away, in shining water. He stamped the brand in the middle of the forehead, and burned the flesh through, to the bone. Then he left me, and I heard their laughter go like a roaring wind through the house. He left me with the brand on my forehead, and a ruined right hand, so that I could never strike back."

He lifted that hand, and Siivertip saw for the first time that it was a withered, twisted, inturned claw.

"Do you wonder, Julia," said Monterey, "that I raised Pedrillo to be a warrior, and that I taught him very little besides riding and shooting with rifles and revolvers? Do you wonder that I brought in the gun fighter and man-killer, Jose Bandini, to be a tutor to him, at last? For I had sworn that when he reached his twenty-first year, he should have to leave my house, and never return to it unless he had fulfilled my promise to Drummon. I swore to him, Julia, as he stood back from me—I swore to Drummon, when the pain had blinded me, that I would do to him as he had done to me, but more, and lay this brand of mine on the door of his house, on his forehead, and over his heart. Do you understand why I have waited these years? I married in hope of having a son; when he was born, I gave my life to raising him for that one purpose. And he is gone, Julia. He has been swept away. So I remain alone, with only this to perform my task!"

And he lifted, again, the withered right hand which was his only tool for labor.

12 – Drummon's Men

IT had come to Silvertip like a thunderstroke of revelation. The sense of folly and of wasted effort departed from him; the whole cloud of obscurity was not lifted, but he could see his major purpose emerge clear and straight before him. He knew to what end the life of Pedrillo Monterey had been aimed; now he had before him, clearly, the definite goal. On the door of the Drummon house, on Drummon's brow, and over his heart to place the brand which had been stamped so brutally into the forehead of Monterey—that was to be the task. The joy that swelled suddenly in the heart of Silvertip could not be contained by the cold constriction of fear that also gathered about it.

And as the bewilderment left him, as the purpose became clear before him, he was struck again with wonder as to how he should be able to approach Monterey, to offer his services. His face was known in the house—and the Mexicans were prepared to hunt him like a beast.

He heard the girl saying: "We must go in, Uncle Arturo. It's growing very cool, now. And it's late."

"It's late," said Monterey, "and it's too cool for you out here now But I want to be alone, Julia. I have to be alone for a time. Go in, my dear, and I'll stay out here for a few moments."

"Then let me call some of the men," said the girl.

"So that they can guard me under the wall of my own house?" asked Monterey angrily. "So that they can stare at me, and whisper to each other because of the shame they've seen stamped on my face forever, this evening? No, I'll stay here alone. And if Drummon's hunting wolves come near enough to nip me, they will not be taking a great prize. Go in, Julia."

She lingered for a moment, then, as though persuaded by some inward impulse, she left him silently, and passed into the house.

Arturo Monterey, when she had gone, walked to each side of the terrace, and peered across the hollow of the valley. Then he returned and sat at the table, staring north. A gust of wind, iced from the mountain snows, struck coldly across the garden, making the tall perennials around Silvertip whip up and down with a rushing sound. The breeze fell away, and old Monterey remained at his place unmoved by the cold, lost in his thoughts. Again the wind fanned his silver hair, ruffling and raising it, sending through the flowers rustlings that seemed to continue even after all the breeze had died.

It was time, Silver knew, to step out and confront the Mexican. Sooner or later he had to face him and make his offer, in whatever words he could find. But still he delayed. One shout from Monterey would bring men pouring out from the house; and perhaps the shout would come before he could explain himself.

So he waited, irresolute, and now heard the rustling among the tall flowers again, though it seemed to him that there was no wind at all. Something pulled his glance suddenly up, and he saw two figures rise almost beside him. The back of Monterey was turned toward them; it did not need a glimpse of the shotgun one carried or of the revolver that shimmered in the hand of the other to tell Silvertip that these were the men of Drummon. They were black against the sky, their faces darkened under the wide brims of their sombreros as though they had been rubbed with charcoal.

Silvertip's Colt was in his grip as he rose, shouting: "Monterey!"

The old man leaped up; a revolver spat twice. To Silvertip the gun seemed to make hardly a sound; he was more aware of the shotgun, which was being swung toward him; and at that fellow he fired.

The man dropped his weapon. He ran stumbling forward, stretching out his arms before him as one who has lost balance. Right between Silvertip and the second of Drummon's men he ran, and lurched into the flowers at Silver's feet with a crash. Silvertip was already firing over him, as the body fell, but the second stalker had taken to flight and ran like a snipe flying down wind.

Already he was through the opposite border of flowers, and racing down the slope beyond. Silver, running in pursuit, saw old Monterey standing by the table with a small pocket pistol raised to an attitude of attention, like a duelist in another day, waiting for the word to fire.

When Silvertip gained the edge of the terrace, he saw his quarry already in a cluster of tall shrubbery, out of which the fugitive sped away on a horse. There was no purpose in pursuit. The moon flashed for an instant on the striding of the mustang; then it was lost among great trees, like a hawk in a dark cloud.

Silvertip whirled back, to find that Monterey already was kneeling beside the fallen body, trying to turn it over. That task Silvertip performed for him, and as a door of the house crashed open, as wild voices poured out at them, Silver turned on its back the powerful body and the wide, brutal face of Chuck Terry.

His mind flashed back to the picture of young Pedrillo Monterey, lying smiling at the ceiling, and Silver felt that at last he had made one long stride down the trail on which he had set his foot.

They were all around him now, Tonio and the girl among the first, with others filling in the background. Every man of them was armed. They would have pulled down Silvertip like a pack of hungry dogs, if the voice of Monterey had not stopped them.

"That is the gringo who brought the mare, señor!" shouted some one.

"By the grace of God!" said Monterey. "Otherwise I should have lain where this one is lying. He has saved me, my children. He has killed this murderer, and made another run like a deer. Do you know the face of the dead man, any one of you?"

They came up to look at that immobile face, and as they passed by Silvertip, they looked with fear, with wonder, with hatred, also, upon him. He felt the shifting of their eyes upward, to the two gray tufts of his hair, like incipient horns rising. Tonio made the sign against the evil eye.

"This one is called Terry," said Tonio. "He is one of the leaders for Drummon. He is one who hires others. We have seen him before come near the house, like a buzzard sailing in a clear sky. And now he's caught and down— caught and down! Gringo! Hai! You grin at us now, eh? But we are laughing. If all—"

"Be quiet, Tonio," said Monterey. "Do you forget that this man who has saved my life is also an American?" He went up to Silver and faced him closely. All of Monterey's visage was old, the lines down-flowing from the brows and the mouth, but the eyes remained unflattened and undimmed by years, like the eyes of an artist.

"Take the body away," said Monterey to the peons. "And leave me alone with this man."

He remained standing close to Silver. The girl had come up beside him. And the servants rapidly picked up and carried away the dead man. One of his arms hung down, and the loose, dead fingers trailed along the ground.

"Sit down," said Monterey suddenly. "Sit here. You are weak. Julia, pour some wine. Here, señor. Sit down!"

He made Silver take the very chair in which he had been seated. He took the glass of wine from Julia, and passed it to Silver.

"I cannot drink alone!" said Silver. "You shall not," said Arturo Monterey, and put a little wine in two more glasses.

The old man held up one of them as high as his head, until the wine sparkled in the moonlight.

"I see you in clothes covered with the slime of the cellar water," said Monterey. "I see you with a haggard and unshaven face, señor, and for every hair that grows upon it, I know you have had a bitter thought about me. How I wish, now, that I could have seen you with the clear eyes of Julia! But I can only drink to you now out of the gratitude of my heart. Gratitude, señor, to the man who killed my—"

The words disappeared in a groan.

"I ask your forgiveness," went on Monterey, suddenly, as Silver rose from the chair. "I drink to kindliness between us, and perfect trust!"

"To the trust between us!" said Silver, and drank the wine. And over the edge of the glass his eyes found the eyes of old Monterey, and held them.

They lowered the glasses, all three.

"Were you here when I spoke to Julia of the past?" asked Monterey.

"I was here," said Silver.

"You have seen the Drummons," said Monterey, "and everything that I said about them is less than the truth. One of them you have killed. Therefore the whole tribe will hunt you down. You must leave the valley. You shall have guides and fast horses. Once beyond the mountains, you will be safe. In five minutes you must leave!"

"Not unless you gather your men and have me tied into a saddle and make them lead me out," answered Silver.

"Do you hear?" said the girl softly. "Uncle Arturo, do you hear? He will not leave you!"

"He *must* leave me," answered Monterey. "He has been treated like a dog. There must still be hatred in him."

"The wine has washed it away," answered Silver. "Señor, I am bound to this valley by an oath."

"To whom?" asked Monterey.

"To a dead man," said Silver. "It is a promise I made to Pedro Monterey as he lay dead. I swore then that I would never give up his back trail until I found what purpose he had in life, and that I would try to fulfill it. Tonight I've heard of the thing he was to do. I shall stay here in the Haverhill until there is the Cross and Snake brand on the door of the Drummon house, on the forehead of Drummon, and over his heart."

The words were somewhat magniloquent; the voice that spoke them was perfectly quiet and subdued. Arturo Monterey stared at the speaker, and then at the girl.

"I understand," he said at last. "And now that you have spoken, there is no word fit to make a reply to you. You have spoken to Juan Perez. Even Perez could believe you, and that is why you were free to come here?"

Silver smiled faintly.

"Perez is lying in the room where I was kept," he answered. "He came to see me. I managed to knock his feet from under him, stun him, get the key, and free myself. After that I locked the door on him, and it was mostly chance that brought me here."

"Chance?" cried Monterey. "Chance? There is no chance in it! If ever God showed His hand, it is in this."

Monterey turned to the girl.

"Do you hear, Julia?" he asked.

"I hear," she said, watching the face of Silver all the while.

The old man lifted his voice, suddenly and loudly: "I believe! Do you see a justice in this? The very people who wronged me have sent me a champion. Providence is working. In every way, this surpasses ordinary human accident. The man is sent to me as a helper; he is attacked in front of my house; he is imprisoned; he breaks out to save my life, and offers me his own good right hand to help me in the fight. Do you see, Julia? It is a stroke out of the sky!"

He lifted his hand over his head as he spoke, and Silvertip saw the grisly distortion of it, a black, twisted thing against the brilliance of the moonlit sky. The voice and the hand of old Monterey fell at one moment. The strength dissolved out of him. He took the arm of the girl on one side and the arm of the gringo on the other, and so went slowly into the house.

13 – Accepted

MONTEREY himself led the way to a closed door and paused before it. He said to Silvertip: "When a man comes closer to the grave, he comes nearer to a belief in many things formerly deemed incredible. I am old, my friend, and therefore I am superstitious. I take you as a great gift out of the hand of fortune. Senior Silver, for twenty-five years nobody of your race has entered this house, but now I am opening a room for you. I open this door for you, I open my hand and my heart and my faith to you, also." He cast the door open. A servant carried in a lighted lamp before them to reveal a big chamber. Silvertip saw a gleaming of dark, polished wooden chests of drawers and a huge wardrobe, and the slender, shining posts of a big four-poster bed. The servant pushed open the heavy shutters of two windows and let the thin dappling of the stars be seen. They looked both close and dim, except one burning yellow eye of light. Old Monterey took Silver's hand. "In everything you say and everything you do," he said, "you are now as the master of the house. Señor, good night. An old man gives you his blessing."

The girl went out with him. The servant remained for a moment, moving slowly here and there to open the bed, to dust the window sills, which were covered with fine silt. Before he left, the fellow paused at the door and looked at Silvertip out of narrowed eyes. He continued to stare, unwinking, for a moment, then he nodded, and, with a muttered good night, left the room.

Silver could not settle down at once. He had to walk between the hall door and the windows, back and forth, back and forth, struggling with the thoughts that worked like moles under the surface of his mind.

As he looked back on the events that had occurred since that evening when he rode down from the mountains into Cruces, it seemed to him that miraculous influences had been working on him all the while. He had been

196

seized upon like driftwood by a powerful current, and brought straight down to the moment he desired. Now he was accepted by the family of the man he had killed. All the strength of Monterey and his men would be focused to help him in his work, and he was given freely his opportunity to step into the shoes of the dead man. In a sense, the ghost of young Pedro Monterey was most certainly walking up and down with him.

Other things, small problems, remained to be explained. For one thing, if Bandini had been retained as a tutor to educate Pedro as a fighting man, it was odd that the teacher and the pupil should have been so obviously quarreling when they were in Cruces together. But this was a minor point. The main fact was that at last he was confronting the unfinished life work of the dead man. He could not falter now. But though that work was exactly where his strength was the greatest, he felt assured that there were odds against him too great to be overcome. Monterey, with all of his men, had struggled vainly these many years. It would be strange indeed if he could succeed where so many had failed utterly.

Even when he had been imprisoned he had hardly felt a more intimate sense of peril than that which followed him coldly up and down through this room. And in the background of his brain the thought of the Drummons rose up like thunderheads in a winter sky.

He was still pacing the floor when a tap came at the door, and he opened it on Julia. There seemed to be no light whatever in the hallway. The black hand of darkness held her in sharp relief.

"Is your uncle still holding a stiff upper lip?" asked Silver. "I've never seen a stronger will."

"He's shaking like a leaf now," said the girl. "But he won't let himself think about Pedrillo. He keeps poor Pedro out of his mind. That's the reason why he's able to bear up. And he'll keep fighting back the sorrow, because that alone would be enough to kill him, and he won't die until he's made the Drummons suffer."

Silver nodded. "Señorita," he said, "I want to know a few things."

"I thought you would," she answered. "Ask me."

"About you first. Who are you?"

"I'm the waif, the orphan, the poor relation. My name is Monterey, also."

"You're no more Mexican," said he, "than I am."

"My mother was American," she told him. "That's all about me."

"Your father and your mother died, and Don Arturo took you in?"

"Yes."

"And you've been happy here?"

"Who can be really happy in the Haverhill? There's a curse on the entire valley."

"How close a relation are you of this family?"

"A third cousin."

"And you want to leave the Haverhill and the Casa Monterey?"

"Not until Uncle Arturo is either happy or—dead."

"Tell me about Pedro. Sit down and tell me."

She sat on the edge of a chair. He sat down in turn and took his unshaven, unclean face between his hands. "Pedro was handsome—but you saw him."

"The finest-looking lad I ever saw. And he was the true steel all the way through. He laughed a little too much to please his father. But he had the making of a fine man."

"I knew it," said Silver bitterly. "There was no flaw in him, and I—" He finished with a gesture. "Tell me more about him," he urged.

"You only shortened his life a little," she answered. "He was to go against the Drummons in a short time, and they would have crushed him at once. Pedro was not clever. He was not very wise or strong-minded, either. He was simply honest and cheerful and brave. He would not have known how to meet the Drummons. He would have ridden straight at them—and that would have been the end."

Silver lifted his head and looked at her, but he was seeing the face of the dead man again. He felt that it was true—that young Pedro would have charged a mountain blindly.

"There's another thing—Bandini," he said.

"Bandini is a rascal."

"Does Monterey know that?"

"No. Uncle Arturo loves him—simply because he can ride well and shoot straight, and because he pretends to have a deathless devotion to my uncle and his cause. But as a matter of fact, all that he's interested in is in lining his wallet with more money. I'm sure of it. He worked here teaching Pedro how to ride, how to shoot, even how to fight with a knife. It used to be a savage thing to see them fighting, even although the knives were wood! But Uncle Arturo believes in Bandini almost as he believes in the Bible,"

"Where will Bandini be now?"

"Taking charge of the body of poor Pedrillo, seeing that it's embalmed, bringing it back toward the Haverhill."

"He'll be here soon?"

"Yes. What else do you want to know?"

His eyes surveyed her face curiously. She was not beautiful, but something from the mind spoke in her face. The lips and chin were modeled with the tender delicacy of childhood still; but across the forehead and eyes she was a woman.

"Only one other thing," said Silvertip. "That's about the servants. They hate me. But will you try to tell them that I'm not a monster?"

"You're wise," she answered. "You're so wise that you'll add a few days to your life, perhaps."

"A few days?" said Silver. "I'll live to be as old as Monterey."

She looked up at him and smiled.

"I hope so," she said, and almost immediately she said good night, and walked off into the thick blackness of the hall with the surety of one born blind and stepping through a familiar place.

Silver closed the door, stripped, took a sponge bath in cold water, and went to bed. The coolness of the sheets soothed him. All the blood of his body seemed to be gathered in his head, and to be whirling and churning there.

He looked to the side out the window. Now that the room was thoroughly darkened, the stars were both brighter and more distant. He watched the patterning in which they were set. By degrees it grew confused. The points of light seemed to be moving a little. They softened, blurred, and Silver was asleep.

14 – The Sheriff

THE sheriff came up with the sun, so to speak, and old Arturo Monterey and Silver had to go out and meet him on the terrace garden behind the house. Silver had risen to find that fresh clothes were laid out on a chair beside his bed. When he had shaved, he looked at a face four shades paler than it had been for years, and chiseled lean and hard by pain. And then he tried on the clothes and found that they fitted almost miraculously.

But they were Mexican type. There was a tightly fitted jacket, with his big shoulders exploding out above the narrowness of the waist, and there was a sash that went about the hips, and all the middle of his body was incased as in armor, though the trousers flared out at the bottom a little. His own old sombrero looked sadly out of place with such an outfit. There was another hat with the clothes, one with a silver band of Mexican wheelwork girdling the crown, but he could not induce himself to put this on. It was bad enough to be Mexican to the neck; his head had to remain in an American fashion.

He had barely finished dressing when he received the summons to join Monterey in the terrace garden behind the house. He went uneasily, wondering about the cat-footed one who had been able to enter his room unheard during the night and place that outfit at his hand. There the body of Chuck Terry was laid out among the tall flowers exactly where the imprint of it had fallen the night before.

The sheriff considered the situation with a sour eye. He was a true Haverhill man, with the jowls, the blunt jaw and nose, the huge brows that kept the eyes in shadow. And, like the rest of the tribe, it seemed as though the sun could have no power to influence his skin; very few of those men were tanned. The majority, and the sheriff was one of them, kept an unhealthy white, like that of things which seldom see the day. Those Haverhill men all looked as though they were freshly out of prison.

He listened to the story with angry eyes that shifted from the face of Monterey to that of Silver.

"How would you know?" challenged the sheriff. "How would you know that poor Chuck here wasn't just comin' up to make a friendly call?"

"Perhaps that was all he was doing. In that case, we made an unhappy mistake," said Monterey.

The profound irony of this remark influenced even the mind of the sheriff. He kicked the ground and stamped on it impatiently.

"You gents," said the sheriff, "oughta take your time about things. There's been too much shootin' around the Haverhill. And it's gotta stop. *I'm* goin' to stop it. You all hear me? Here comes Chuck. Just kind of curious. He was only a kid. He was younger than his years. Everybody knew that. Just a great big, open-hearted, fine kid. Just curious. Like the way an antelope is curious, the poor fool! And he comes up here with a friend, and they wanta have a look at the great Arturo Monterey. That's all they wanta do. And by thunder, I'm goin' to jail the pair of you for murder, is what I'm goin' to do! There ain't any sense. There ain't right in it. There ain't any judge, and there ain't any jury that wouldn't call it murder!"

"When a fellow's so curious that he and his pal start sneaking up behind a man at night," said Silver, "and when they start shooting as soon as they hear someone behind them sing out—"

"Just kind of startled, maybe," suggested the sheriff.

But presently he was scowling at the ground.

Monterey, in that moment, let his eyes run over the new clothes on the body of Silver, and at the new face which had been revealed by the shaving away of the shaggy growth of beard. He seemed to find much that was worth seeing, and his glance wandered intently from feature to feature. To Silver, aware of the survey, it seemed as though the old man were weighing him in a fine balance and accepting him as a thing of price.

"All right," said the sheriff. "I oughta take up the two of you, but there's enough trouble already, and this'll just make more. I'll leave you go free. You, Monterey—and you're the gent called Silver?"

"Yes," said he.

"You're the one with the white horns, are you?" said the sheriff. "Well, young feller, if you'd keep your horns out of this business here in Haverhill

Valley, you'd be a lot better off, and so would we. You been makin' trouble, and you're goin' to make a lot more trouble, and before the end, maybe you'll wish that you never seen the Haverhill River, or the Haverhill men that the whole valley had oughta belong to!"

After that he had the body of the dead man placed in his buckboard and drove off, but his venomous eyes dwelt continually on Silver all the time that the preparations were going on; particularly after he had stared for a time at the red spot on the left breast of the coat of Chuck Terry.

"They've laid their eyes on you now, señor," said Monterey, "and that means that the air you breathe in this valley is poisoned from this moment on. But you have a horse, and yonder is the nearest way to the first pass. And in two hours you can be safely over the hills. Think carefully, my friend. Every chance is against us. They have numbers. They have craft. They have the cruelty of devils and the persistence of hungry beasts. Nothing but the last chance is left to you if you remain!"

It was not half-hearted persuasion. As in the eyes of the girl now and again, so in the eyes of Monterey, something came up from the spirit and spoke to Silvertip.

But he slowly shook his head and smiled.

Julia came suddenly out to them from the house. Her glance found Silver and dwelt on him with a smile. He knew that she had picked the outfit, by the look she gave it.

"I have stopped trying to persuade him," said Monterey. "If he is to stay here, Heaven knows it is of his own free will; and like a gift from Heaven I take him. You have news in your face, Julia. What is it?"

"Juan Perez is a madman," said the girl. "He has bitten his lips till they bleed. I tried to speak to him. But he lay on a bed and kept beating his head with his hands. He says that he is shamed forever. Something will have to be done about him. You must go to him, Uncle Arturo."

"No," said Silver. "I'll go myself."

"You?" she cried. "He will try to kill you! There is a wild devil in him. It's more dangerous to rob a man of his self-respect than to take the cubs from a she-bear."

"I'm the man to see him," said Silver. "Let me go to him."

"Perhaps," said Arturo Monterey. "But I shall go with you. Juan Perez is the most faithful of the faithful, but there never was a more dangerous man."

"Show me to the door of his room," said Silver. "Then leave me there."

The two of them conducted him. They went across the patio and into the long wing where the servants were housed. At the end of the long and narrow upper hall, Arturo Monterey stopped before a door.

"Go back now," said Silver. "Or else stand here quietly. I know how to handle this case. And if I don't manage him now, he'll put a knife in my back later on. Stand quietly, and don't argue. I have to have my way about this."

He knocked at the door. A faint groan answered him. He opened the door and stepped into a naked little room with only the mask of a grizzly hanging on the wall, and the claws of the great bear strung on a half necklace below the head. On a cot lay the tall form of Perez, face down.

"Juan Perez!" said Silver.

The Mexican came to life with a bound. He said nothing. The devil that was in him needed no sound for expression. The writhing face of Juan Perez expressed him fully enough.

The Mexican had thrown off his belt. Now he caught from it the long hunting knife whose handle projected from a leather sheath. The steel flashed in the dim room as Perez leaped.

But Silver put his hands behind his back and waited. The left hand of Perez caught at his throat. The knife trembled with the tense strength of the arm that wielded it. But it was not driven home.

"Will you listen to me?" said Silver.

Juan Perez thrust himself back to arm's length. The gringo was in his power. The point of that knife could find the life with a single slight gesture. But though the Mexican was half mad with shame, there was manliness in him that made it impossible to strike an unresisting enemy.

"Now, gringo—now, dog," he groaned. "Take your gun and fight me man to man!"

"We are serving the same master, Juan Perez," said Silver. "Will he gain very much if we kill one another? The Drummons will laugh; they will be the ones to gain."

"You tore me from my horse in the town; you have beaten me senseless and left me in your own prison; and the people are laughing at me!" cried Juan Perez.

"And you," said Silver, "have thrown me into the slime of a dark cellar, and tossed my bread into the foul water, and left me there to starve and go mad in the dark. Which of us has suffered the most from the other?"

The logic of this statement was so convincing that the left hand of Perez fell away from the collar of Silver's jacket. He retreated a step, breathing very hard. His teeth were set. He seemed striving to work himself again to the height of his passion, but an increasing calmness appeared in his eyes.

"If I forgive you," said Silver, "it will be a greater thing in the eyes of every one than if you forgive me. And that is what I have come to say to you. Let us forgive one another. Let me have your hand. We are each wise enough to know that the other man is worth fear. Therefore he is worth respect. I respect you, Juan Perez. I want you for my friend. That is why I have come here. That is why I humble myself and take the first long steps. They told me that you would kill me the instant I appeared, but I knew that you are an honorable man. Here is my hand, Perez. Give me yours!"

"And how about my shame?" muttered Perez. "The smiles? The sneers?"

"I have seen a great many brave men in the world," said Silver, "but I don't know one brave enough to sneer or smile when he sees Juan Perez and Silver walking shoulder to shoulder as friends."

Juan Perez suddenly clasped the hand of Silver. The other hand of the Mexican was struck against his forehead.

"What am I doing?" he exclaimed. "Have my wits gone?"

"Is it a foolish thing," said Silver, "to turn an enemy into a friend? Are you afraid of what old women will say, or do you want the friendship of true men?"

"You are right," said Perez, taking his breath in great gulps. "There is no more truth in all the blue sky than in what you have said. But let me be alone for a little longer. Let me prepare myself. Then I shall walk out into the open day and take your hand where everyone can see us. And if there are smiles—"

He ground his teeth together at the thought. Silver dropped a hand on his shoulder.

"This is the beginning, brother," said he. "Before the end of the trail, we shall have ridden through some strange places together. Come when you wish. Call for me if you please. I am in your service and you are in mine, and we shall fight for the same master. Adios!"

He went out of the room, and down the hall he saw the Montereys standing side by side. To their astonished eyes, he smiled and waved; and when he joined them, old Monterey exclaimed:

"What has happened?"

"We have shaken hands," said Silver. "We are now brothers. We shall go to one another whenever we are called, and we shall serve one master."

He went down the stairs before them. And he heard Monterey saying:

"You understand, Julia? As I said before, it is not chance. There is fate in it. If Juan Perez is won over, then all the others will be ready to follow him. They will ride behind him just as though he were my own son and wore my proper name!"

Silver went back to his own room, and there a servant brought him fresh chocolate, and bread, baked in small brown loaves, with butter. He ate and drank hungrily. There was a full pot of frothed chocolate, and he drained it to the last sip. Then he smoked a cigarette and watched the wreaths of blue-white rising up against the ceiling. He could think of nothing except the round, brown face of Tonio for the purpose he had in mind. Tonio today— Juan Perez on other occasions.

So he went out into the patio and sent for Tonio. The minute the man appeared, Silver knew that his interview with Perez had become known, for there was no hostility in the big eyes.

The eyes of Tonio were pale and a little prominent. They blinked twice as he greeted Silver. Then he began to smile.

"Tonio, will you help me today?" asked Silver.

"There is nothing every one on the place wishes except to serve the señor," said Tonio. "For my part, no trouble would be too great; we know what service was done the night before in the garden terrace."

"You'll help me then, Tonio?" asked Silver. "The first thing is to take me out riding and show me the way to the house of Henry Drummon. Will you do that?"

Tonio's round fat face wrinkled like the skin of an overripe apple.

Then he sighed and nodded. But he added: "This is war now, señor."

He waved his hand at the breadth of the valley, the pale-green of the grass, with the wind and the sun giving it a shimmering life, and the trees rolling in darker clouds across it.

"War now," said Tonio. "There has been almost peace for these last years, but now there is another death, and the war commences once more. If we go to look at the Drummons, be sure that the Drummons are coming to look at us. There will be cattle rustling, horse stealing, and every rock, and every stump, and every bush will have a rifle behind it, perhaps. But if you wish to ride to see the Drummons, I'll show you the way."

They went to the stable, where Silver found his mustang. In the patio, the girl came out to watch them leave. She had on a wide-brimmed straw hat, tipped so that the brim was a halo for her face; and she wore a blue dress with yellow Mexican embroidery spilling across it.

Silvertip waited for her to say something, but she said nothing at all. She merely came out to the patio entrance and watched them go through the arch. The sun flamed on the whitewash of the wall behind her as she watched them pass. Silver turned suddenly to speak to her; the words stuck in his throat; he rode on silently. There was something fixed and still about her smile, and a pallor around the mouth that told him she was smiling merely as a soldier smiles when he faces the firing squad. Perhaps she was guessing what errand he rode on with Tonio. Perhaps she was assuring herself that neither of them would ever come back again.

Juan Perez was gone with Monterey; Tonio was with Silver; no one remained in the house to give guidance to the ignorant, clumsy peons, and the unruly vaqueros who could protect her in case the Drummons, in fact, were reaching out at that moment toward the house of Monterey.

But he went on.

"Gallop, Tonio!" he called, and they raced down the slope and swung down the easy pitch toward the middle of the valley, then out from it into the broader expanse of the Haverhill Valley itself.

Presently, when their horses were black with sweat, they drew rein at a signal from Tonio. His lifted hand pointed toward a group of cattle that seemed to Silver a smaller and a scrawnier breed, less square in the quarters than the stock of Monterey.

"You see the brand? You know it?" asked Tonio.

Silver singled out a steer and drifted slowly down toward it, until he made out the loom and strike of the brand against the skin of one of the quarters.

"Bar 17 Bar" called he to Tonio. "Is that the brand?"

"That's it. That's the Drummon brand."

Silver looked around him with an appreciative eye. He could understand that in the Drummon range it was necessary to go on more carefully.

"Where did the men of this valley come from?" he asked.

Tonio made a great gesture toward the east. "A long time ago they were in England, some people that looked like beasts, I suppose," said Tonio. "Then they move out and go to Carolina. They go back up into mountains. They stay there till their neighbors begin to hunt them like beef. They leave that country and they go West. They come to the valley here. They kill the Haverhills, who own half the valley. They start fighting the Montereys. They keep on fighting the Montereys. Now there is one old man left to us, and there are plenty of Drummons remaining. They stay all the same. When strangers come into the valley, the Drummons ride them down. They burn the houses the squatters build. Sometimes they burn the squatters with the houses."

"And nothing is done to 'em?" asked Silver.

"The sheriff is Drummon, the jury is Drummon, the judge is Drummon," said Tonio calmly.

Then his eyes rolled, and his teeth flashed in something that was not a smile.

"Before I die, I shall do something!" said Tonio. "I have already done a little bit in my life!"

He held up one finger as he spoke, and drew in his breath through his teeth, as though he were drinking.

He had killed at least one Drummon; that was fairly clear.

"How many have gone down in the fighting?" asked Silvertip. He took off his hat and ran his hand over his head as he waited for the answer.

"Who knows?" asked Tonio cheerfully. "Fifty years— and who knows? When I was a boy there were two other little towns in the valley. They were both Mexican towns. Now they are gone. The fire caught hold of them on windy nights, and they're both gone. Look there—by the edge of the river— yonder!"

Silver could see it—a curious dark smudge, covered with small mounds.

"That was one of them. That was the last one. The grass hasn't begun to grow on them yet," said Tonio. "There is only Haverhill now. But who can tell? Some night the wind may blow *up* the valley, and there may be fire in *that* wind; and then there will be no Haverhill town, either."

He began to laugh and nod. And Silvertip saw the picture of the flames whirling, and the houses dissolving, and the people running into the night, dragging with them what they were trying to save from the ruin, and clouds of sparks exploding up into the sky.

Perhaps he would have to see that picture painted brightly in before he came to the end of his days.

15 – The Drummon Place

THEY came to the verge of the bright water, with its currents running like half-luminous shadows beneath the surface.

"This is the limit," said Tonio. "This is as far as we can go. Over there is the home of Henry Drummon— beyond that hill, with the trees covering it. If any of the men of Monterey are found across this river, we are shot like dogs. It is the dead line."

"We could ford the stream right here, I think," said Silver.

"Yes," said Tonio, "and we could be shot on the other bank."

Silver scanned the wooded head of that hill and knew perfectly that he would have to cross to the other side of it. He knew, rising in him, the peculiar force of the temptation, and he set his teeth against the surge of it in vain.

At last he said: "We'd better go over to have a bit of a look, Tonio, don't you think so?"

Tonio stared at him.

"This," he said, making an appropriate gesture, "is the dead line." He indicated the river with the sweep of his hand, and continued by drawing the edge of the hand across his throat suddenly. "Besides," he said, "this is the daylight. And they are all hawks and owls. They can see miles and miles even in the half light. What do you wish to do, señor?"

Silver drew up his belt a notch, as though he were hungry.

"I'll go over and take a look at the house," he said. "Go back in there among those trees, Tonio, and wait for me. If you hear guns, and don't see me come pelting back over the head of that hill, you'll know that they've got me, and you won't have to wait any longer."

Tonio shouted in rapid protest, but Silver was already riding into the water. He would not look back, in spite of the heated arguments that Tonio poured into his ears from a distance. But when he gained the farther bank, he turned and waved his hand. Tonio, with both arms moving, was indicating to heaven and earth that he abandoned the cause of a madman. Silver cantered his mustang up the easy slope and made straight at the hill.

As he came to it, he swung the horse to the side, and well away from a road that cleft through the trees. He had barely changed direction when he heard the beating of many hoofs, the creaking of leather, the notes of raised voices. And as the trees began to spread their branches above him, he saw a cavalcade of half a dozen riders sweep over the top of the hill, with a cluster of dogs racing about the horses, or frolicking in the lead.

It was a group of the Drummons. He could have known them at a greater distance by the way the big, blocky heads were set on the thick necks, and by the way the necks grew out of the shoulders. He could have judged, too, by something devil-may-care in the free swing of their riding. The very dogs had a look that to Silver seemed harmonious in the entire picture. They were huge brutes, all of a type, and the type something between wolfhound and mastiff.

When he came to a good thickness of brush, Silver dropped from the saddle, threw the reins, and made sure that he was well hidden from the eye of any observer. With a rattle and a roar, the group went by down the road.

He breathed more easily, and was about to toss the reins over the head of the sweating mustang again when a hound gave tongue on a note that approached him rapidly. A voice yelled out of the distance: "Belle! Hey, Belle, you brindle-faced fool, stop running that rabbit track! Come back here, Belle!"

But the baying of the dog still approached, and now a great brute with a brindled head and a white-and-tan body broke through the shrubbery, hesitated, then hurled itself straight at Silver.

He aimed at the head of Belle a kick that missed but made her swerve. Her bared teeth almost gripped his leg. As he turned, she was swerving, leaping full at his head. Instinct made him reach both hands forward, and luck gave him a double handhold just under the jaws. He let the big dog swing with the impetus of its own leap and flung her heavily on her back, his own weight behind the fall.

She lay still, on her side, with her long red tongue lolling out onto the dust and no sign of motion in her sides. He was afraid for an instant that she was dead, and if her master found her stretched out, he would not pause until he had found the cause that had brained her.

Through the trees, through the shrubbery, a horse was crashing its way, and the voice of the master was roaring:

"Belle, you woodenheaded fool! Belle! Come here! Hey, Belle! I'm going to have the hide off you; I'm going to have it off with a whip!"

The dog revived all in an instant. Once on her feet, she stood swaying for a moment, her red eyes fixed eagerly on Silvertip; then she swung to the side and went hurtling away toward the calling voice.

Silver heard the man cursing. They were so close that he could even make out the whistling of the whip with which he struck at the dog. Then all those noises receded. He heard the pounding of hoofs, and the high-pitched halloo of the rider, hastening after his mates.

Silvertip took the loop of the reins over his arm and walked on among the trees slowly, scanning the vistas which opened among the trunks, and swerved away and closed to either side. He went on until he reached the brow of the hill. The trees stopped there suddenly. Through the verge of them he glimpsed a picture still obscured and brown-striped by the tree trunks which intervened between him and the open.

He saw a shallow valley, with a crooked flash of water streaked across the center of it, trees clustering here and there, and a long, low-fronted house that had once been painted white, though now the weather had scraped the wood bare in most places, and left merely a look of wet dust. The tramping of many hoofs had worn away all grass near the house, and across the face of the building stretched a hitch rack whose beams had been gnawed thin in many places. The front door was set off by an ornamental hood of carved wood, and there was a brass knocker that looked foolishly out of place.

Silvertip left his mustang and rounded to the rear of the house. A narrow veranda ran along it. A workbench had been rigged here by laying a few long boards across two sawbucks. On the bench appeared the keel and the ribs of a sharp-ended rowboat which was probably intended for the stream that ran down the hollow near the house, and not for the Haverhill Valley itself. There was a litter of wood shavings on the floor, and spilling off onto the ground. From pegs along the outer wall hung bits of harness, and coats and hats mostly green with age, as though they had been hung up one day and then forgotten for years.

Silvertip tapped at the open kitchen door. He could see no one inside— only the worn tatters of some linoleum on the floor, and a broom with half the straw scrubbed from it, and a big rusty range on which a few pots were steaming idly. But a stifled voice called from an unseen corner of the room, and Silver went in.

In a corner near the sink, at a little kitchen table, sat a lad of fifteen, chewing at a big mutton bone, ripping off the shreds of flesh, or gnawing at the knuckle with strong, white teeth. He kept on gnawing, his eyes half closed with content, half buried by the upward snarling of his face muscles. Even at fifteen, he had the perfect Drummon features beneath a ragged mop of hair. He continued to chew at the bone, mumbling around it:

"Who're you?"

"I'm a new man," said Silver, and walked over to the stove, where he lifted the lid, replenished the fire box with wood, and thrust the heavy poker into the rising of the flames. With the lids replaced, except one which the poker shaft lifted askew, Silver turned toward young Drummon and found that the latter, having put down his bone for a moment, was licking his chops and staring with insolent eyes. He looked as dangerous as a half-grown mountain lion; and one could be sure that he was far more formidable than that.

"You're the new man, are you?" asked young Drummon.

"Yes. I'm the new man."

"The devil you are. There *ain't* any new man."

"You ask your old man," said Silver.

"Whatcha mean? That a way of telling me to go to the devil?"

"Why? Is he dead?" said Silver.

"Yeah. Sure, he's dead. The greasers got him. But I'm goin' to get me a coupla yaller skunks to make up before I'm a lot older. What's your name? Who are you?"

"I'm a fellow that keeps my mouth shut," said Silver, "and never asks a lot of questions, and doesn't answer 'em, either."

"You don't, don't you?" asked the lad, rising. He showed six feet and an inch of tough muscle laid over a burly frame. His neck was already as thick as a wrestler's; and his pale Drummon eyes glared at Silvertip. "You're goin' to talk, or you're goin' to get out," said young Drummon. "If Alligator Hank was here, he'd know if you was one of the real men. But he ain't far away, and I could call him. But I don't need to call him. Whatcha doin' with that poker? Back up and lemme hear you chatter! I mean it. Turn around here and talk or I'm goin' to sock you."

The voice of the lad was rising as he spoke. It reached a high-pitched snarl at this moment, and he leaped with no further warning at Silver. Silver was loath to strike. But it was not defending himself against a boy so much as against a dangerous young beast of prey. He let the hard-driven fist of Drummon go past his head, and clipped him on the chin as he swayed forward.

The hair flew up on the head of the youth. He stood rocking, with blank eyes. Silver took him under the armpits, led him to the door, and thrust him outside. He walked away with drunken, fumbling steps, and Silver, turning back to the stove, drew out the poker.

It was white-hot, throwing out a shower of coruscations. He went through the house and opened the front door. On the solid face of it he fulfilled the first vow of old Arturo Monterey by searing into the wood the sign of the Cross, with the wavering line of the Snake underneath it.

16 – The Pursuit

HE retraced the line of the Snake with the tip of the poker, now a dull red, and heard from the rear of the house a loud shouting, answered from not far off. Silver threw the poker away and ran for the woods where his mustang was left. He had hoped that all the Drummon men would be in the party which he had watched ride out hunting. But, as in a hornet's nest, there appeared to be a continual reserve of warriors about the camp. For now he heard the thudding of hoofs, and he looked back as the big youngster, running on foot, turned the corner of the house with three horsemen sweeping up behind him.

They were Drummons, every one, and the central figure of the three bore a face which Silvertip would never forget. It was the true Drummon type, with fleshy, battered brow, and skull-like eyes, but the neck and the features of the man were flushed over and swollen with whisky bloat, like a raw sunburn.

He led the way, and, pointing to the side, toward the front door of the house, uttered a sudden wild yell of rage. For he had seen the newly crawn brand!

Silver was already inside the brush. It crashed and crackled around him. A rapid fire of bullets searched it, also. One of them nicked the mustang as Silver mounted. It reared, struck out at the air, then fled unmanageably among the trees. There was more danger from its running than from the gunfire to the rear. The branches of the trees seemed to reach out and then stoop suddenly at the head of the rider. The tree trunks threatened to strike him on either side and fling him with a broken body to the ground.

At last, sawing savagely at the reins, he managed to get the head of the frightened horse under control. They were already nearing the edge of the woods; now they swept out into the open, and Silvertip saw a cavalcade coming up on the farther side of the river, the same rout of horsemen and dogs that had streamed past him not long before. But there was one difference now. For in the midst of them, his hands tied behind his back, rode Tonio.

The distance was still great, but by the horse Silver knew his companion. The little mustang went proudly along, as though feeling that it was a guard of honor that accompanied its master. But the sight was a stroke to the very heart of Silvertip. For Tonio had protested; he had not come blindly into the region of danger, but had been persuaded and drawn on against his will.

Retreat in the direction of the river was impossible.

Silver turned the horse back into the trees. The three riders, yelling loudly, poured into the open, had a glimpse of him, and hurtled in pursuit again.

He ran the horse hard, so that the brush cracked noisily about him. Then, making a sudden halt, he turned to the side and walked the mustang a few quiet steps into high brush.

It might be that he could lose them in that way. He heard them come with a sweep; he saw, through the screen of branches, shadowy forms leaping past him, two of them in succession. But a third drove straight at his place of concealment. Only chance was aiming that course; but it came near to being the death of Silvertip. He had to get his mustang under way with a rush, swerving it well to the side.

It was the man of the bloated face, looking redder than ever because of the white flash of his bared teeth as he fired on Silver. The first bullet sang at the ear of Silver; the second knocked the hat from his head.

"Alligator—hey, Hank—you got him?" yelled a voice from in front.

"I've nicked him. Turn to the right and we'll bag him. We got him! He's the one that killed Terry!"

But Silvertip's mustang already had taken him clear of the woods. He took an angling course to the right, down the slope of the hill. The guns began again behind him. Then the trees of an open grove received him, flicking back in a shadowy throng, like the pickets of a fence.

That patch of trees shielded him from gunfire for a little distance. He reached the small stream in the center of the hollow at a narrows, and the mustang leaped the gap. On the farther slope he gained another cluster of trees.

The Drummons were not gaining. They had been too eager with their guns, and a man cannot shoot and ride his best at the same time. They gave up gun work now. Their hat brims blown and flapping like open jaws, they came now with a rush; and off to the side, from the big barn behind the house, the youngster was quirting a mustang into full speed, trying to cut across the line of the flight.

Silvertip angled again to the right. There were more trees in clusters that received him as clouds in the sky receive a fugitive bird when the hawks are flying near.

Then the mouth of a narrow canyon opened to his left. He shot into it. A yell of frenzied delight rang behind him, to give warning that he was in a trap, and, scudding around the next corner, he saw the very face of the danger. For the ravine ended against a sheer wall of rock fifty feet high, with a dribble of water dropping into mist from the lip of the rock.

He snatched the rifle from its saddle holster and leaped to the ground while the mustang was still running.

To the left the wall of the ravine went up like the flat of a hand; to the right a rubble and scattering of great boulders climbed in broken stairs toward the sky line. Silver was instantly in the heart of that rocky confusion.

The Drummons were already at the spot. They were out of the saddle; they were pouring in among the big boulders, calling directions.

Silver lay out on the flat forehead of a rock and waited. A head bobbed at the side of a great stone twenty yards beneath him.

He knocked the hat off that head. Another man lurched into view and dodged back to shelter again with a yelp; a bullet from Silver's gun had slipped through his arm.

Then Silver continued his retreat, for he knew that they would not press him too closely. Twice he came into the open; twice they salted the rocks around him with splashes of lead. But he was not touched in body. He had lost a hat; his coat was torn with a great gash close to the pit of his right arm; and that was the only mark he bore.

He reached the top of the divide. Beneath him was another valley; or he could go up or down the divide itself. But he chose, as an alternative, to double back down the hillside which he had just climbed. He could hear the gritting of heels among the stone. So he pulled off his riding boots and feathered his way among the boulders in his stockinged feet.

Just before him he heard the grunt and stifled gasp of a man doing hard labor. Silver dropped to a knee with his gun ready. The sun beat on him with sudden strength. He was aware of the gleaming of the rocks around him. For an instant all of that great face of nature was still, and all its eyes seemed to be focused upon him.

He waited with his teeth set behind that faint smile of his. If the fellow who puffed and panted among the rocks so close to him came in view, there would have to be a death. His own position among the rocks would be revealed, and the others could take him from above and hunt him down with ease.

But the hurrying climber went by on the left, out of view. And Silvertip continued to work down among the rocks.

Above him he heard voices ring out; then the sounds grew dim, as though the Drummons had clambered into the valley just beyond them.

He reached the floor of the ravine. Looking up, he saw one form looking gigantic against the sky, rifle at the ready, as the lookout turned gradually, scanning all about him.

Yet he never looked down into the floor of the canyon, where Silvertip was now stealing toward his mustang.

He gained the saddle before a yell from the middle of the sky, as it seemed, floated down to him; then bullets. Those bullets merely helped him. Nothing is harder than to shoot accurately from a height at a running target. The gunfire aided Silver to rouse the four other horses to a frenzy of panic, and they scattered at full speed before him down the canyon, out into the pleasant, open green of the valley.

There was no more pursuit. There *could* be no more. He caught up those four Drummon horses, fastened their lead ropes together, and trotted straight back toward the house of Monterey.

Nothing happened on the way. He saw not a soul. Nothing lived in the valleys except the slowly browsing cattle, or the bright wind riffles that ran over the grass.

So he came up the narrower valley into view of the fortress house of Monterey. It seemed to him like a picture of a gallant last stand, a great castle without a garrison. There were armed men within, to be sure, but at their head was a tired, grim, despairing old man.

He came up to the patio gate; and there a house *mozo* greeted him, stared at the horses, then saw the brands on their sides, and gave token of news to the entire household with a yell.

17 – In the Night

IT was like the alarming of a garrison, indeed. Distant shouts, distant footfalls beat inside the house; doors slammed like muffled reports of cannon; then the torrent of humanity came sweeping out into the patio. Male and female, they gathered about the four captured horses; they examined the bleeding cut where a bullet had nicked Silver's mustang across the quarters. They laid their fingers on the shot-torn cantle of his saddle. They noted the absence of his hat, and they looked with a deep interest on the torn side of his coat. But even more than these signs of battle, they regarded the horses of the Drummons with a sort of startled awe, at first, but afterward with a joyous laughter.

Julia Monterey came out, last of all, and Silvertip told her, shortly:

"Tonio's gone. We got to the river, and I wanted to go across to see the Drummon house. Tonio hid and waited for me. I went on to the house, and burned the brand on the door of it. The Drummons chased me. The head of the gang was with the rest. They hunted me up to the rocks.

"I managed to get around 'em and bring back the horses. And I saw a whole herd of the Drummons leading Tonio up to the Drummon house. It's a bad business, Julia. And there's the whole of it."

Tonio? It seemed as though his life or death were of no interest at all to the other Mexicans, compared with the immense fact that the first step of Monterey's vow had been performed. That vow was known to the whole world, it appeared. It was the battle song which the Monterey faction followed. They were like happy children. Three of the vaqueros rode in from the upper valley, heard the news, and turned the demonstration into a frenzy.

Silvertip escaped into the house. He went out onto the garden terrace at the back of the house with Julia, and a house *mozo* brought out a decanter of strong wine and another of rye whisky. Silver took the whisky. He drank it in small sips, letting the sick burn of it fume in his nose and up like a mounting smoke into his brain. It was bright and hot on the open terrace, but he would not move into the skeleton shade which the pergola offered to them. Instead, he chose to soak in the sunshine, relaxed, inert.

The girl sat opposite him with the same broad hat on her head. At a distance, it buried her features in shadow. At close hand, the color burned through from her cheeks, and her eyes. Her eyes were not Mexican black. They were paler, clearer. There seemed to be more of spirit and less of race in them.

Arturo Monterey walked back and forth across the terrace. He had not spoken a word to Silver about the branding of the door of the Drummons. What he felt about the accomplishment of the first portion of his vow was too great for speech. But as he walked back and forth, once he paused and dropped his hand on the shoulder of the American. Then he continued pacing, and halting at the farther end of the terrace, he stood staring over the lowlands beyond, lost in a dream of hope.

"He even forgets Pedro," said the girl softly. "Don't doubt that he loved his son, but a thousand children would be nothing to him compared with the filling of his vow. Twenty-five years of hating and hoping!"

"And Tonio?" said Silvertip.

The sun that blazed on his head made the gray tufts above his temples glisten like metal indeed.

"Tonio? What does he matter?" asked the girl. She laughed bitterly. "Tonio was simply an old adherent, the wisest and the best man in the whole valley, the kindest to me, the truest to his master, the most faithful to his friends. But it doesn't matter. What does the life of one man mean, compared with putting the mark on the door of the Drummon house? Oh, nothing at all!"

She fell silent. He watched the pinching of her lips and the slight flaring of her nostrils. The battle spirit was in her, also, he could see. And in the distance, he could hear the Mexicans singing. The noise sometimes drove close to them with the opening of a door, then receded, and grew as far away as a thought.

Her chin was dropped on one brown fist that was whitened at the knuckles by the force with which she gripped it. His head was far back; she watched the faintness of his smile.

She looked at him with a queer mixture of horror and admiration.

"You want trouble," she said. "You live by it."

"I'll die by it, too," said Silvertip gloomily.

"What gave you the gray markings in your hair?" she asked. "That wasn't just chance, was it?"

"No. It's a long story," he told her. "Stop talking about me. I want to know about Tonio. What'll they do to him?"

"He'll disappear, that's all. He'll never be seen by his friends again."

"They'll kill him out of hand, eh?"

"Not at all," she answered. "He'll simply be riding through the woods, and he'll brain his head against a bough of a tree. Or else he'll fall off his horse and drown in the rapids. Or he might even have an accident with his own revolver. There are lots of ways. The Drummons won't know anything about it."

He nodded. "Tonio," said Silvertip, "you think quite a lot of him, don't you?"

"He taught me to ride," she said. "He taught me to shoot. He taught me the old Mexican and Indian legends of everything. Whatever I know that's worth knowing, he taught me."

Silvertip nodded again.

"That means I have to get him back," he said. At this, she looked him over quizzically, dropping her glance from his eyes to his smile. Then she seemed to rally to a sudden realization that he meant what he had said.

"How could you do it? How could you even try to do it?" she asked.

He looked at the horizon line, where it slid up and down the ragged sides of the mountains, across the valley.

"You can't go with numbers; they'd be seen," said she. "And if you go alone, how do you dream you could take Tonio away from them? They know that he's important to Arturo Monterey. They'll keep him caged and watched all the time."

"I'll go off and think," said Silvertip. He went to his room to be alone. But the four walls looked in upon his mind like four faces.

He went up to the roof of the old house, where a low wall was built around an open promenade. There he remained for hours, smoking cigarettes, staring at the mountains, growing constantly more nervous and tense. Something was gathering in him, as water gathers behind a dam; something was kindling in him. His smile was seen no more. As the evening came nearer, he began to pace the roof restlessly with a step longer and more silent. He watched the evening begin, the color burn up in the west like a red thunderhead.

Then he went down to the dining room and sat silently at one end of the long table, Monterey at the other, the girl between. She tried to talk; Silver answered in murmurs. The windows grew black with night, the yellow image of the table lamp sitting deep in the glass.

At last he left her, suddenly, and felt the drift of her eyes, as her glance followed him across the room. He knew that she understood where he was going, but she said nothing. An American girl would have had to speak, but the Mexican blood was enough to keep her silent. He felt, at that moment, that to look into her mind would be to look into a greater darkness than the night.

Outside, he went to the stable. Two vaqueros appeared from nowhere and attached themselves to him. Their attitude was a queer mixture of suspicion and respect. He wanted a horse, a fresh horse. They took him with a lantern into the corral behind the stable, and flashed the light for him over the string of mustangs that were kept on hand. He picked a bay gelding, built long and low, with a pair of fine shoulders. He had not made a mistake; he knew that by the way the two looked at one another. They roped that mustang, together with another, at his request. They wielded long, rawhide lariats, heavy and supple as quicksilver, and made their casts with a queer underhand flick, effortless and sure. The rawhide noose stuck with a report, like the slap of a hand.

The pair were saddled. Silvertip's rifle was brought, examined by one of the vaqueros, and slid into the saddle holster. The Mexicans escorted him to the gate of the patio. They held up their lantern to light him on his way; he saw the flash of their teeth and their eyes, and the gleam of perspiration on their dark faces. Then he was gone down the road.

A voice called after him. As he halted, Juan Perez galloped up and drew rein with a jerk.

"You are riding alone, amigo," said Juan Perez. "How is that? It is too dark to see anything. It is too dark to find anything except trouble. Let me go with you!"

"No," said Silver. "This is a case, Juan, where two men are too many, and where one is almost too much. But when the right time comes, I shall call on no one but you, amigo."

He left Juan Perez sitting the saddle disconsolately, and went on along the road.

He passed a small group of bushes. A figure rose out of it.

"Who goes?" called a voice. And it added instantly:

"Señor Silver?"

"Yes!" said Silvertip.

"Good fortune!" called the voice.

Silver rode on. At the mouth of the ravine, two more shadows arose, hailed him, let him pass. It was clear that the men of Monterey would keep good watch.

He kept steadily on across the valley of the Haverhill. The stirrups had been tied up so that they would not flop and make a noise. But as he drew near the ford of the river, the hoofbeats of his mustang seemed to grow louder and louder, for they were entering the domain of the Drummons, and armed men might grow up out of the ground at any moment.

He rode into the ford. The water dashed about the two horses; it seemed to burn with a white fire, to the excited eye of Silvertip. His long-geared mustang grunted as it climbed the farther bank, and it seemed to Silvertip that the sound must reverberate to the very edge of the hills. But still there was no sign of an enemy. So he reached the trees that covered the hill before the house of Drummon. There he dismounted, and led the horses slowly through the double blackness beneath the branches until, from the brow of the slope, he saw the long line of lights across the face of the Drummon house. It was not so much like a private dwelling as a hotel.

Many men had gathered; it was no wonder that every room seemed to be lighted. More than a dozen horses were tethered at the hitch rack, hanging their heads patiently, each of them pointing one rear hoof.

He saw the details as he went forward, after throwing the reins of his own pair. He had to move slowly enough to allow the casual eye small chance of seeing him, but there were eyes far from casual now sweeping the night. He saw one dull silhouette of a man move against the wall of the house. Another approached from the left and joined the first at the corner. Silver lay flat in the dust and waited. A tall clump of grass sheltered him.

He heard the voices challenge one another quietly: "All well?" and the answer: "All well." "It ain't so well for the greaser," said one, and chuckled. "And is he goin' to hold out?" "Not when Hank Drummon gets working on him." The two separated, and drifted away, passing dimly down the wall of the house again. Silver, setting his teeth, contemplated a retreat, for it seemed obvious that he would not be able to come closer to a place so well-guarded. He turned his head and looked back; it seemed to him that the ground over which he had wormed his way was clearly lighted by the stars, and that retreat was almost as dangerous as to advance. Twice more, he saw the sentries meet at the corner, and separate again; and now he got to feet and hands, and went rapidly forward.

The fellow who moved to the right, toward the back of the house, was his goal. The ghostlike footfall of Silver followed him to the end of his beat; and as the man turned, swinging carelessly about, Silvertip laid the muzzle of a revolver against his breast.

"What kind of a fool game is this, Jerry?" asked the guard. "What kind of tricks are you up to, you fool?"

"Hoist your hands, and keep walking," said Silvertip, "and don't speak out loud again. I'm from the house of Monterey."

He heard a sound out of the choking throat of the other. The hands went up slowly. When they were shoulder high, they paused; and the fellow groaned, faintly, as he struggled between fear and a desire to fight back.

But at last he surrendered, and walked on toward the corner of the house. The rapid hand of Silvertip already had taken the gun that hung in the thigh holster.

"To that other hombre you meet at the corner, I'm Jerry," said Silvertip. "You don't stop to talk to him. You turn around, and walk back with me. We've something to talk about."

Beyond the dark line of the corner of the house stepped the second guard.

"Thought I heard you sing out, Bud?" said he.

"Yeah. Here's Jerry got something to talk over with me," said Bud, and turned on his heel, with Silver swinging around beside him.

"Jerry?" exclaimed the first guard. "Looks like Jerry had growed a few inches since supper time. Hey, wait a minute!"

But they walked on slowly. The left hand of Silver kept a firm grip on the arm of his companion. He felt the big muscles slip up and down, like snakes moving beneath the skin. He felt the tremor of shame and disgust that worked in his companion.

"Stop here!" commanded Silver.

They were just under a lighted window, shuttered fast, the lamplight working dimly through the cracks. But one leaf of the shutter was broken out, and since it was fairly close to the level of the eye of Silvertip, he could look into the room. It was fairly crowded with a dozen or more men. He saw first the red of the whisky-bloated face of that Drummon who had helped to hunt him on this same day. And now he saw Tonio, tied to a chair and directly confronting the window outside of which Silvertip stood.

The man of the red, swollen face stood beside the prisoner, with his arms folded.

"Who is it?" asked Silvertip. "The older one—with the red mug?"

"Him?" muttered Bud. "That's Hank. That's Hank himself."

Silver looked into the puffed brutality of those features with a lingering and curious horror.

He heard a thick voice, husky and powerful, that matched the look of the man, saying: "All right, Tonio. This is the night when we ride at the house of Monterey. You go along and show us where the guards may be, and save your hide. We been handlin' you with gloves, Tonio, but now I'm goin' to cut deeper'n the skin. Are you swingin' over to our side?"

Tonio leaned his head back a trifle and laughed in the face of Drummon.

18 – The Torture Job

IT seemed to Silvertip incredible that any human being could shew such immense assurance, such carelessness of his life, as to insult Henry Drummon at such a time. The whole roomful of men surged toward the prisoner, but the older man and leader held up his hand and checked the advance.

"You ain't goin' to help us, eh, Tonio?" he said.

Tonio was silent.

"It wouldn't be much to do," declared Drummon. "All we want is to have the posts of the guards pointed out to us. And the entrance to the cellar under the house. That ain't much to do. We don't ask you to help in the fight, because we want all of that for ourselves. You hear me, Tonio?"

Tonio yawned. A bystander lifted a gun butt to strike into the captive's face, but again the chief of the clan checked his followers.

"This ain't a time or a place for us to make any hurry, he said. "We gotta think this over. We gotta get the best ideas to use on Tonio. He's goin' to be worth 'em, and he's goin' to last for a while. Get the Runt in. He's the one that will have the best ideas."

Some one laughed loudly—a long, braying sound of pleasure—and strode out of the room slamming the door behind him with such force that it sent a deep vibration down the slender iron chain which supported a lamp above the center table. The table was large and massive, and looked as though it could seat twenty men; and the varnished surface shone under the glare from the great double burner above.

Silvertip, marking that slender chain that held the lamp, felt, for the first time, that perhaps he would not be forced to stand as an idle spectator of the horror which he knew was about to come. For he had no doubt that Henry Drummon intended to torture Tonio to death by the most lingering means

223

possible. And now, as he studied the place where the iron chain met the ceiling, between the two white circles of light above the lamp, there was the glimmering of a hope in him, a vague and far-off thing.

A footfall came toward them from the left; it was the second guard come to inquire into the reason that kept his companion still.

"Send him back," said Silver to Bud. "Curse him out, and send him back."

The other had come almost up to them, when Bud turned fiercely on him.

"Get back on your own beat," commanded Bud. "What the devil you doin' on my side of the house?"

"What's the matter with you?" asked the second guard. He recoiled a little as he spoke. "You act crazy, Bud! What the devil has Jerry put into your head? Has he been talkin' about me?"

"Never mind," growled Bud. "Get out of here, and leave my side of the house, or I'll climb your frame."

"You will, will you?" said the other angrily. He paused for a moment, swaying a little forward, as though he were about to hurl himself at Bud. But caution came gradually over him.

"I'll be seein' you tomorrow about this," he declared. "If somebody finds out that you ain't been walkin' your beat, you'll have your explainin' to do, first, and your fight with me, afterward."

He retreated, however. And Bud, leaning against the wall of the house, groaned softly, in his anguish; the muzzle of Silvertip's gun was constantly pressed against his ribs.

Inside the room, the Drummons were waiting for the coining of the "Runt." The pause was filled with odd conversation.

"How much Spanish in you, Tonio?" asked Hank Drummon.

"Yo soy puro Indio," said the Mexican, lifting his head a bit.

"I thought so," said Drummon. "It takes an Indian to stand what you're goin' to have to stand. But listen to me —Monterey ain't Indian. There ain't no blood in him except Spanish. Why do you stick to him in a pinch like this? Can you tell me that?"

Tonio's round face grew flushed, and his eyes glimmered.

"Because the Señor Monterey is father and uncle and brother to me," he answered. "And if all the gringos, and all their lands, and all their money were offered to me instead, I would rather be a slave to the Cross and Snake brand."

Two or three of the Drummons cursed Tonio savagely, but Hank Drummon merely laughed. He seemed to gain a great contentment out of this scene, and now he walked up and down and back and forth, chuckling and rubbing his great red hands together.

With fascinated eyes, Silvertip regarded him. For this was the man on whose brow the brand of Monterey was to be planted, the Cross and Snake.

The thing seemed hugely impossible. The man himself was a Titan; and around him were gathered the brutal ranks of the Drummons, those great-shouldered and heavy-jawed fighting men.

"You know the dog who put the mark on my door?" asked Drummon. "That mongrel called Silvertip? That fellow they say has the gray spots in his hair, just like horns?"

Tonio nodded. "I know him."

"What sort of a man is he?" asked Drummon.

"A man," said Tonio, "who is worth knowing. Most things—they are nothing to him. He finds life very dull. The taste of it is like flat beer to him. But there is one thing that amuses him a little. That is to hunt a Drummon, and kill him; or to lead them like blind dogs across the country, and take the horses from six or seven of them, and send them home on foot. When he is ready, he'll come to the Drummon house and run them down as a cat runs mice."

Drummon stepped to the prisoner, swung his hand back, and struck him heavily, squarely, across the face.

The head of Tonio bounced back from the blow. A thin stream of blood broke from his nose and mouth, and descended across his chin.

Then the door opened, and the Runt came in.

He was like all the other Drummons in his main features, but he was qualified in two important ways. His bulk was condensed into a height a head shorter than most of his clan; and a frightful event in his youth had stripped the skin from his face, so that it was a silver white, streaked here and there with a grotesque patterning of red. All his features had been pulled slightly awry by the same accident, and the resultant draw of the skin. He walked with a distinct waddle and a sway of his broad shoulders, entering the room.

Coming straight up before the prisoner, the Runt said:

"There ain't more than one way to handle him. Fix him the way the Apaches fixed me. Take the skin off of him."

The whole clan applauded. And Silvertip would never forget the face of one man, the mouth gaping, the eyes closed with mirth, as he staggered this way and that, howling his glee.

"Who'll do the job?" asked the Runt, turning his head slowly, this way and that.

"Who but you?" answered Hank Drummon. "You oughta know how to work a skinning knife on human skin. The Indians done it on you, Runt. And this here is a pure Indian. He's just been gloryin' in it. Take a hold on him, and work slow, because I'm waitin' for him to break down —and you're the gent to do the trick."

The Runt, when he heard this, looked once more around the room, but this time with a frightful air of satisfaction.

He fastened his gaze, at last, on Tonio, drew out a knife, and commenced to whet the glistening edge of it on the sole of his boot.

All the while, he looked not at all at his work, but at the face of Tonio.

The Mexican was daunted, at last. That courage which had enabled him to endure the prospect of the torment, began to fail him when he saw the preparations in progress. For nothing in the world is so revolting to the man of Indian blood as is the thought of mutilation before his death. Christianity cannot dim the old legendary pictures of the unhappy warrior who goes broken and maimed to the happy hunting grounds, to perpetuate his shame and sorrows.

So Tonio looked at the bright flashing of the knife, and strained at his ropes, and leaned forward in his chair, in an agony of terror. No sound as yet had come from him, but he was white about the lips, and his nostrils flared with the beastly breath of fear.

The Drummons gathered close before him, shouting, laughing, pointing to his distorted face. And the Runt, having finished his preparations, took Tonio by the nose with the whole of his hand, and raised the blade for the first incision.

"Around the forehead first, right by the roots of the hair," said the Runt. "Then we'll peel it off in strips. I'll give him plenty of time to feel everything. Oh, I ain't goin' to hurry any more than the swine done when they worked on me."

He leaned closer over Tonio, and a shriek came tearing from the Mexican's throat.

Silvertip, with a groan, jerked up his revolver and fired. The chain that held up the lamp snapped in two under the impact of the bullet. The great double lamp fell, the flames leaping up brilliantly.

19 – The Second Branding

THE round holders that supported the lamp were of strong iron, like the chain which had held up the heavy weight, but the body of the lamp itself was glass that shattered suddenly and completely. Flaming oil spurted to all sides; fire leaped in sparks, in crimson and yellow globules, in long streaks of brilliance, as high as the ceiling and far out to the walls. The whole room flared up with one might of illumination that died, suddenly, and left only dim welters of blue fire clinging here and there, spilling across the table, dripping in fits of flame to the floor, and on the floor itself giving out smudges of smoke, and rolling fire from whole pools of the liquid.

The chamber was filled with a mad dance. Shadowy bodies sprang, here and there. One man hurled himself against the door, trusting to the impact of his body to cast it open, shattered. But the door held and flung him flat down in a pool of the flaming oil.

His shriek went upward shriller than the rest, as he scrambled to his feet.

Other hands tore open the shutters of the window. One, and then another fugitive flung himself wildly out toward safety, and the first man began to roll on the ground like a dog, to rub out the fire that stung him.

Then Silvertip swung himself through the open window and ran forward. He had no knife. But that which the Runt had been prepared to wield was in plain view on the table. He snatched it up and made Tonio a free man with a stroke.

He heard the names of saints come grunting from the throat of the Mexican. The oil already had caught on the woodwork, and snakes of the fire were working up the walls and creeping along the floor.

They could not return by the window through which Silver had entered. Other men were fairly sure to be watching that exit. Tonio led the way toward the door that opened into the hall.

He swerved out into it with Silvertip running at his heels. Before him Silver saw the length of a narrow corridor. Women were in it, running forward, carrying buckets of water. Men came, also. Voices and footfalls thundered. There were hands brandished, and frantic faces of rage. Silvertip fired three shots over the shoulder of Tonio as they ran forward.

He fired above the heads of the Drummons, because the women were there; because of the women, too, those shots were enough. Panic takes faster than fire in dead grass. The whole rout turned and poured back, yelling. Into doorways, down the next hall they ran, while Silvertip and Tonio held straight forward toward the opposite end of the hall.

The window was open there and promised them escape. They dived through it as into water, tumbled on the ground, lurched to their feet again, and confronted a gun spitting fire, and a mighty voice that boomed through the night.

It was the voice of Hank Drummon, and Silvertip knew it. Something in the greasy huskiness of the sound was unlike the speaking of any other man. Tonio knew it, also, and as though convinced that no human power could avail against the power of this man, he threw up his arms in despair.

Silvertip, instead, was shooting.

He intended the bullet for the heart; he thought, when the silhouette toppled, that he had struck his mark; but then he saw the form struggle on the ground, and leaped at it.

He took Hank Drummon by the hair of the head, jammed it back against the ground and, in the dimness of the starlight, cut quickly, but surely. He felt the edge of the blade grate against bone.

"The second branding, Drummon!" he shouted, and sped away with Tonio into the dark.

There was no need for very great haste. Behind them, even the mighty voice of Drummon, shouting orders, could not bring order out of the chaos that had seized the household.

Some of them ran here and there, probing a feeble distance into the darkness. But the majority, men and women, were laboring to extinguish the fire. Nothing, not even peril to human lives, seems as terrible and as important as the destruction which a fire works on a home. Bucket lines had been formed; both men and women, and children as well, were swaying the buckets forward, shouting to one another. The hiss of the water could be heard as it pulsed with a regular rhythm into the burning room. And huge clouds of steam and smoke expressed through the windows.

From the shadows at the margin of the trees, the two watched the scene; and now and then a sudden flickering light within the house told that the flames were by no means conquered, as yet. Tonio, swaying from side to side, thumped his fists against his face and his breast.

"Now for ten good rifles, and we shoot them by the light of their own fire. Ah, Señor Silver! Now we could sweep them away!"

Silvertip said nothing. There was nausea in his heart and a tingling and shuddering up his arm; and still it seemed to him that he could feel the grating of the knife against the bone of Drummon's skull.

But he had accomplished the second part of Pedrillo's threefold task. One step remained. He might have made that, also, before aid came to Drummon in the dark of the night. He might have literally cut the brand of Monterey into the heart of his old enemy. But he could not have done that. He felt that he *never* could do it. He would have been glad enough if his bullet had struck the heart of Drummon; but he could not murder a man already wounded.

He brooded gloomily on that, as he stood beside Tonio watching the gradual subduing of the fire.

Then he said: "We'd better go back, because they're putting out the fire, Tonio, and they'll come straight for the Monterey house like so many hawks. It's war to the finish, now. Because the Cross and Snake is on the forehead of Hank Drummon."

They hurried back to the horses, mounted, and fled through the darkness, down the slope to the tarnished silver of the ford, with a few bright stars burning in the quiet waters of the margin. They put out those stars as they entered the stream. They came out on the farther bank and galloped, while Tonio shouted through the wind of the riding:

"Is it true, senior? Have you put the mark on Drummon?"

Silvertip waved his hand in acquiescence. He heard the Mexican break out into a wild, drunken song, swinging himself from side to side in the saddle with the rhythm of the music. It was a sort of laughing madman that accompanied Silver across the darkness and into the stern ravine which the house of Monterey overlooked, now with a few lighted windows.

Only when Tonio came near to the house did he master himself, and as he dismounted in the entrance patio, he was as calm as ever. The same two vaqueros who had helped Silver depart, were now on hand to welcome him. But they gave him hardly a glance. Their gaping, their startled eyes, were all for Tonio. They insisted on touching him with their hands.

Then they heard the story of the brand that had been cut on the forehead of Drummon and seemed to go mad, as Tonio had during the ride across the valley.

Some of them began to dance and yell on the spot. A few more reckless ones burst open the wine cellar and rolled out a keg which they staved in, ladling out great dripping portions to all who asked.

The sleeping children, wakened by the riot, began to run down into the patio. The domestics were already there.

The fierce, slender vaqueros poured in. Someone began to ring the great wide-mouthed bell which gave the signal of alarm and joy to the lands and the people of Monterey. Festival rang through the air; and in the midst of it, Silvertip saw the girl come out into the patio with Monterey.

She had on a black mantilla. She had on a black dress, too, with a red rose at her shoulder. As Silver watched her, he thought she was coming toward him—that she had singled him out, so that she could praise him for what he had done. But she paused, meeting him with her eyes only.

Monterey went to the first horse that stood nearby, and swung up into the stirrup, standing there at ease in spite of the winces and prancing of the mustang which felt its withers wrung by the twisting weight.

He called out, and the crowd fell silent.

He was saying: "This is a good time for drunkenness and noise making! The brand is on Drummon now, and he'll be here soon. He has the law in his pocket. He can do as he pleases, unless the men of Monterey are wide awake. Tonio! Drive them out of the patio! Whip them out, if you have to. Get them back to watch posts. You fellows who have sworn you would die for me—you, Juan —you, Jose—Orthez—do you want the house knocked down about our ears? You knew there was reason to be on watch, today; there is a hundred times more reason now. A million times more!"

They obeyed him suddenly and cheerfully. Nothing could cool their spirits now. They were like an army which has been trembling on the verge of defeat, and which is now restored to a hope of victory.

Silvertip saw them scurry away, each to an appointed post, to take turn and turn about during the watch. For his own part, he felt that Mexican eyes and ears could be trusted more than his own.

They went into the big hall together, Monterey and Silver and the girl. They entered the library, where two lamps threw yellow pools on the floor without really penetrating the gloom. The girl had paused by the door.

"Come in, Julia," said Don Arturo.

"I am going to bed," she said.

"Going to bed before we hear from our friend the full story of what he has done?"

She kept drawing back a little as though she were afraid. There was something about her that made Silver want to go straight up to her and look into her face. But an odd constraint held him back.

"I don't think he'll talk about it," said Julia Monterey. "And I have to go to bed. I have a headache."

"Headache?" exclaimed Monterey. "Headache? Where's the Monterey blood in you? Now that you know the Drummon wears the mark—you talk of headache? Haven't you—"

He broke off suddenly, and then added: "Well, my dear, go along then, and good night."

"Good night," she said. "And Señor Silver, good night."

She went out; the door closed noiselessly behind her.

"What's the matter?" asked Silver. "There's something wrong with her. What is it?"

Monterey shrugged his shoulders. "What does it matter? I want to talk with you of the great thing you have done, my son. I want to know every step you made, and every gesture of your hand. Tonio is telling the peons his story, and the vaqueros are there, too, listening. Let me sit here and listen to you? Glory comes back to my house, and you have brought it!"

"I've told what happened," said Silver. "There's no more than that, and I'm no good at descriptions. But what's the matter with the Senorita Julia? Do you know?"

"She is afraid," said Monterey.

"Afraid? Of what?"

"Of you," said the old man.

The body of Silver jerked straight in his chair.

"You don't know why?" asked Monterey.

"I've no idea. What have I done to her?"

"Fair women, and brave men—that is the old story," said Monterey. "She has gone away for fear her eyes should tell you things that she would not speak with her lips. My friend, suppose that you seek her tomorrow, it would not be hard for you to learn what she knows."

Silver sat like a stone, staring.

Old Monterey stood up, moved to another chair, and sat again, leaning far forward.

"You have no real name—you hardly seem to have a country. What is it that drives you around the world?" asked Monterey.

"A hard thing to name," answered Silver. "The hope of what lies around the corner. You understand?"

"A little. Tell me more."

"The other side of the mountain always seems to be best; the man I haven't met is the fellow I want for a friend; the town I haven't seen is the place I want to go to; and the house I'm not in is the one I want to live in. Does that give you an answer?"

"That gives me an answer," agreed Monterey, frowning. "And of women, also? I would not offer you Julia, except that she seems ready to offer herself. But now I can say that I am old, that the name of my family dies with me, and that your blood, senior, though it is not that of my race, would be nearer and dearer than that of any other man. If you marry Julia, you can be as a king on a throne, and in her there is nothing but courage, faith, and truth!"

He paused, and Silver fought to find an answer. He could live here, it seemed, a baronial life, freed from all care. The grandeur of old Monterey and the beauty of the girl moved him.

But suddenly he was saying: "You offer me everything that a man can give. But I can't take it. I can't change the fever in the blood, senior. I have to keep hunting; there always seems to be something waiting beyond the rim of the horizon."

"It's a foolish thought," said Monterey gently. "One person is about as good as another, and one place is about as good as another, also."

"I know that, too," said Silvertip. "That's common sense. But it doesn't keep me from chasing around the world hunting, and hunting. That's why I've left my name behind me. It would tie me down. I have a father and a mother, a brother and sisters. If I used my name, they'd locate me, before long. They'd look me up. It would tear my heart! They've looked me up before this, and I've gone back home and loved it for a week or a month. But then one day I wake up in the middle of the night, and the four walls of the room take hold of me like four hands, and hold me down. Then I know I have to go, and I go—before morning. I can't tell when the impulse will come. It simply grabs me—and then I've got to move on."

"No friends?"

"No close ones," said Silver.

"No family."

"I've lost it for good and all now."

"No home?"

"No, only a wish for all those things that keep me scampering. I'm a fool. I know that. But something has hold on me. I have to keep going on."

"Like the wandering Jew," said Monterey gravely.

"Well, I suppose there's something in what you say. Is there a curse on me, too?"

"You'll get over it," Monterey answered. "You think that you're condemned for life and as a matter of fact— Why, you're not thirty!"

"No," said Silvertip.

"Then you're simply being young—that's all. Good night! Go to your, room and rest. The minute that there's so much as the stamp of a horse or the whistle of a bird, we'll call you. But we're all brave and strong now, because we have you with us."

Silver went to his room, closed the door and threw himself, dressed as he was, on the bed. The lamp still shone, but he was not troubled by that light in his eyes, as he began to think into his past and look blindly forward into his future.

He remembered what Monterey had said—that he was simply young—and it was like a promise of happiness and security to him. Under that influence he went suddenly to sleep. When he awakened, the rose of the day was pouring through the window, gunshots were sounding in the distance, and a hand was beating furiously against his door.

20 – Bandini's Plan

THE gunshots no longer boomed distantly on the ear, by the time Silvertip had raced down to the patio. An outcry came from the watchers beyond the house; hoofbeats crackled over rocks or beat more dimly on the ground. And here came Jose Bandini with a small cavalcade, and a horse litter that bore a large, swathed burden.

Through the wide arch of the patio gate Jose Bandini came first, lean, erect, graceful in the saddle.

Utter loathing brought a faint smile to the lips of Silvertip. He turned his back on that new-come hero, and went into the house.

He did not see Jose Bandini again until just before the burial ceremony, when with all the other adherents of Monterey, Silvertip entered the chapel and filed past the body of the dead youth.

There was no alteration, it seemed to him, since he had last seen that face. It was still gray marble with a faint swarthy tinge of yellow in it, and about the eyes a shadow of blueness. There was the same sense of defeated weakness about the features; there was the same smile.

The hands were crossed on the breast. He touched them, and the thrill of mortal cold ran up through his fingers to his heart, as he recalled the vow he had made over the dead man.

Two parts of it were fulfilled. But before the third part was accomplished, all the mourners in this room might be dead.

He turned, and encountered the steady, strange glance of Julia Monterey, reading his mind as she had read it more than once before.

He saw Jose Bandini, watching him like a bright-eyed snake, and Arturo Monterey with head borne high and blank, dreadful eyes.

Afterward, they went down into the crypt beneath the chapel floor, where all the Montereys had been buried for generations. There they saw the coffin inserted in the wall, and the small door sealed over with cement. Even then, Arturo Monterey did not break down. And directly that they had come up to the patio, he called Silvertip and Jose Bandini to him. He took one of them on either arm, and walked up and down the patio with them.

"My friends," he said, "I know that there is bad blood between you. But this is the time to forget it. This is the last moment of my life. I know, with a very clear knowledge, that I shall not endure long. There is only one purpose remaining for which I can exist. You understand what that purpose is. I have made a vow, and you understand its nature."

He freed one of his hands and touched the black band of cloth that encircled his forehead.

"Two parts have been accomplished," he went on. "You have done both things, Señor Silver, and it is a kind miracle of Heaven that lets you be still alive to walk here with me. But for the last of the three parts of my vow, no one man can suffice in action. It will need the strength and the wisdom and the courage of all of us. I don't know how I have deserved to have such friends gathered about me. But here you stand, and there is only one way for us to meet success. You must join your hands, my friends."

He took their right hands and tried to draw them together.

Jose Bandini murmured: "Everything at your will, Señor Monterey."

But Silvertip shook his head.

He answered: "There are reasons that even you would not understand, Señor Monterey, why I cannot take the hand of Bandini. Let me walk aside with him, and I'll explain matters."

So he went off, with Bandini walking slowly at his side.

"I have no wish to take your hand, Silver," said Bandini. "I'd rather see the hand rotted off your arm by fire than take it in my own. Only, to please the old man—"

"You murdered Pedro Monterey," said Silvertip.

"You lie," said Bandini. His lean face wrinkled with a sneer. "Your gun killed poor Pedro," he said.

"My gun did the work, but you did the managing of it," said Silvertip. "How did he come to have your cloak?"

"We had been arguing a little," said Bandini, with detestable smugness, "and I gave him the cloak, at the end of the argument, as a sign that we were reconciled friends again. That was all, in fact. A gift out of the kindness of my heart."

"Bandini," said Silvertip, "you knew that I'd look for you at that special hour that night. You were afraid. And you passed the cloak to young Pedro Monterey in the hope that I'd mistake him for you, during the night. And your idea worked out."

"You say this, Silver," answered Bandini, shrugging his shoulders. "But what you say means nothing. Every gringo is a natural liar."

"I am going to kill you, Bandini," said Silvertip gravely. "I warn you again. I'm going to kill you the moment Monterey's work is done."

"Why do you wait?" asked Bandini. "Here is a time now. I am ready for you, Silver, night or day!"

Silvertip looked at him with curious eyes. "No," he answered, shaking his head. "You're not ready, Jose. You'll never be ready. There's a curdling of your heart when you think of having to stand up to me."

"Do you think so? Try me now, eye to eye!" exclaimed Bandini.

Silvertip smiled. "You know that I'm tied to my place here, with Monterey," he answered. "That makes you feel safe. But don't be a fool, Bandini. Sooner or later I'll have it out with you, and the sooner the better! Not here. Monterey wouldn't allow that. But one of these days, we'll meet outside the house."

"The minute you say," answered Bandini, "I'll be ready for you!"

They parted on that note.

Old Arturo Monterey moved calmly through the day. The sense of destiny about to be achieved never left him. There was in him a perfect surety that his vow would be accomplished, and Drummon delivered into his hands for the final vengeance to be taken. After that, he himself would die.

And he was ready for the end. Twenty-five years of brooding upon one purpose had perhaps unsettled his mind a little, and now the death of his son, the pinching out of the line of Monterey, left him ready to hurry to his grave after his great purpose had been accomplished.

For some time, there was no sign of danger from the Drummons. Perfect peace seemed to fill the bright days, and when scouting parties went out beyond the grazing grounds of the cattle, they rarely sighted so much as a herdsman attendant of Drummon.

No one was deceived. The danger was present, but merely delayed, and the Drummons were preparing their blow.

To Silvertip, it was a strange time. He had become, in the house of Monterey, a great figure. The Mexicans could not accept him as a friend; the age-long prejudice was too compelling for that. But they could look up to him as a force without which they could hardly win their war. So they attended him with respectful glances whenever he appeared, and he could not stir from the house without having two or three of the half wild vaqueros appear to join in his company of their own volition. Above all, Juan Perez was his shadow.

It was the second day after the burial of Pedrillo that Jose Bandini encountered Silver in the patio and said to him, with a glance that moved grimly up and down his body: "Señor Silver, there is one great thing true in this world—that we hate one another. A gringo, like a swine, is able to lie in the mud of his passion; but I am not. I cannot sleep at night, Senior Silver, for thinking of the moment when you and I shall be face to face. And I have made a plan."

"Go on," said Silvertip.

"It's a simple one, and a good one. If the two of us fight near the house, the one who survives will be known as the killer. That is bad. When I have killed you, I lose my chance to get a reward out of the money box of the mad old man, Monterey. If you kill me, he will detest you, because he thinks that Pedro loved me. But suppose that we ride out, today, and come onto the lands of the Drummons—onto the verge of them. And suppose that we fight out our fight there, Silver? Why, then the one of us who remains alive can gallop back and talk about an ambush laid by the Drummons, and how *their* bullets killed the man!"

Silvertip scanned the face of Bandini with care. And then, suddenly, a fury of passionate hatred subdued all the sober part of his mind and made him throw away suspicion.

"Bandini," he said, "get your horse, I'll saddle mine. And in two hours one of us will be finished!"

21 – Tonio's Warning

OUT in the corral, the horses swept in waves, back and forth, as Silvertip advanced on them with his rope. He singled out the one he wanted, that same long, low-built bay which had carried him so well before, and dropped the rope on it at the first gesture.

Tonio came to him as he was saddling the broncho. There was concern in the big, round face, and the wise brow of the Mexican.

"You and Bandini, señor, you are riding out together?" he said.

"Yes," said Silvertip. "What's the matter?"

"He hates you so much that he groans when he hears your name," said Tonio.

"I know it," answered Silver.

"Hatred," said Tonio, "is a food that breeds thought. A great hate will make a fool wise. And Bandini is not a fool. I shall ride out with you."

"No," said Silver.

"Then keep eyes in the back of your head," went on Tonio. "I saw the face of Bandini, just now, and he was laughing to himself."

That warning from Tonio should have put Silvertip on guard, but the thought that he was about to confront Bandini face to face and so accomplish a great purpose, or end all things in the effort, worked like fire in his brain, and clouded and smoked over his better judgment.

He joined Jose Bandini, therefore, and they cantered side by side down the narrow ravine below the house of Monterey.

It was easy to believe that Bandini had been laughing before. He was still in the midst of a smiling humor, and when he turned his glance toward Silvertip, repeatedly there was a gleam in his eye and a chuckle from his throat.

"You gringos," he said to Silver, "think that you are the greatest fighting men in the world; and you, Silver, think that you are in the front rank of them. Now I'm not a distinguished man among my people, particularly, but—"

"No," said Silvertip. "Only distinguished for murder, not for fighting!"

"I am not particularly distinguished," went on Bandini, smoothly overriding the insulting interruption of his companion, "and yet, Señor Silver, this day I am going to eat your heart!"

"You're sure, Bandini," said Silvertip, "because you've learned a new trick in the pulling of a gun. Or you have a better revolver, and think that it'll act of its own accord. But that is only how you feel *before* we fight."

"Another lie!" said Bandini.

"No, it's true," said Silver. "The fact is that when you stand up to me, Jose, you'll turn into a snowman, and melt the strength out of your knees, and your hands will be shaking, and your heart will be beating in the hollow of your throat. How many times have you really stood up to a fighting man? You have a little reputation, but how many times have you earned it?"

He was amazed when Jose Bandini answered, with perfect cheerfulness:

"Never once! I've never had to. Most of the men I've met could be outmaneuvered. And any fellow's a fool if he thinks that it's dishonorable to take an enemy from behind. What does the lion do, for that matter?"

Bandini made a sweeping gesture to the sky.

"As the lion, so is Bandini," he said.

"And you're the rat that Monterey hired to teach his son how to fight?"

"If I'm a rat," said Bandini, who seemed willing to endure any epithet, "Pedro was only a mouse. He thought me a hero. I laughed continually behind his back."

They came out of the Monterey ravine, and thence rode across the valley of the Haverhill. Suddenly Bandini pointed out a group of low hills, though that was too large a name for them—they were mere swales of land, and over them grew entanglements of shrubbery.

"There's the place for us," he said to Silvertip. "When we get into that scrub, no one will be able to see us, and we can fight it out. Not an eye will fall on us, and afterward I can ride back to Monterey and tell him that unlucky Silvertip has been killed by sneaking, murdering assassins."

Silvertip said nothing. He merely smiled, and looked straight ahead as though already he were seeing a death— and not his own!

So, at the side of Bandini, he entered the brush and found himself in the midst of a small hollow around which the shrubbery gathered in what was almost a wall.

"Now!" cried Bandini, cheerfully, and sprang down from his horse. Silver followed that example, instantly.

"What'll you have?" demanded Silvertip. "Turn back to back and take ten steps? Or fire at the drop of a handkerchief? Take your choice—one way or the other—or anything else that pleases you better?"

"The first idea is a good idea," said the Mexican. "We turn back to back, and take ten steps."

"I take ten steps, and you turn at the fifth and shoot me through the back," said Silvertip. "That would be the way of it, and you know it, you yellow rat."

Again the insult slipped away from the easy mind of the Mexican.

"Well, then," he said, "you can tell me what next way you want. We can face each other—and the first man to go for his gun gives the signal?"

"Perfect!" said Silvertip.

He stood back a little. His shoulders dropped forward; his body flexed a trifle; a smile twitched at his lips, was gone, returned again; and his eyes shown. "Are you ready, Bandini?" he demanded.

To his amazement, Bandini laughed loud and long, once more.

"Ready for what?" asked Bandini.

"Ready to stand your ground?" asked Silvertip, bewildered.

"But why should I stand my ground?" asked Bandini. "You fool, do you think that I brought you out here to put my life in your hands?"

And still he laughed, putting his hands on the red and yellow scarf that was bound about his slender hips, and swaying rhythmically from side to side.

Silvertip stared for one more moment. Then a shudder of apprehension went with electric suddenness up his spine. He turned his head, slowly, and saw, standing head and shoulders above the line of brush behind him, the grinning faces of four men—a Drummon every one. Two held at the ready double-barreled shotguns, one of them with sawed-off barrels. The others covered him with rifles.

And still the laughter of Bandini rang and beat against his ears.

In a dream, Silver turned his body toward the line of guns. He heard one of the men say:

"Take him from behind, Bandini. Rope him, boy!"

And the thin shadow of a falling noose flicked past Silvertip's eyes; the lariat drew taut, and he was jerked to his back.

22 – Doomed!

THEY dragged Silvertip at the end of the lariat. Through the brush they pulled him, while the thorns and the tips of the sharp branches ripped his clothes, and the flesh beneath them.

Then they paused to confer with Bandini, and let Silver get to his feet

The conference was not long.

"Here's half your money," said one of the Drummons. "You get the rest from Hank, when you come to the house."

He was counting out greenbacks into the hand of Bandini.

"It's a pity to take the money," said Bandini, still chuckling. "I ought to pay you for this job. But now I have to ride back to the Monterey house like mad, and give the alarm: 'Silver is taken! The Drummons came down in force and mobbed him. I tried to help. But it was no good.' Here—put a few bullets in this!"

He pulled off his jacket and tossed it into the air. Three rifles cracked before he caught the garment again. Holding it up, he exhibited three holes that had been drilled through it by the volley.

"That is how bravely Bandini stayed and fought," said the Mexican. "Monterey will thank me for that. There is only one trouble—that flat-faced Tonio loves the gringo so much that he'll be apt to suspect that I had a hand in his taking. However, we have to take these small chances. For I have to keep the confidence of Monterey friends, if I'm to do the important work for you."

They spoke little more. Bandini merely lingered to say:

"Keep him alive until I get there. I want to see the finish of him. Tonight, if I can, I'll go out by myself, like a hero"—he still was laughing—"and go all alone into that dangerous house of the Drummons—to rescue Silver, or die for him!"

241

The Drummons could appreciate a joke of this nature. They greeted it with a hoarse thundering of mirth. And as Bandini rode off, they started toward their own place, in triumph.

Like a band of wild Indians they galloped, dragging Silvertip on the ground behind them; and when they slowed enough to enable him to regain his feet, they were soon off again, jerking him flat.

His body was raw, his wits half senseless, by the time they reached the river. Through it they dragged him, and brought him senseless indeed to the farther bank.

When he recovered, they were working his arms and his legs to get his breathing started again. And he heard one say:

"If old Hank gets a dead man, out of this, instead of a gent that he can work on, he's goin' to skin us, and don't you forget it. Throw him up there on a horse, will you?"

They flung Silvertip into the saddle of the bay gelding which he had ridden from the house of Monterey. The lariat still bound his arms. His feet were tied into the stirrups. And gradually his mind cleared.

It was the end, he was sure. There was a sense of perfected doom that gathered over him. He had known in the beginning, he felt, that he would find his death in the Haverhill Valley. Julia Monterey had told him the same thing in clear words. He had guessed at defeat and at death when he was first in the village of Haverhill and endured the jests of the brutal clansmen.

Now they were gathered around him. His body was covered with a thousand cuts and bruises the sting of which set him on fire; and the warmth of his own blood covered him. His clothes were practically ripped from his body. He was a ragged statue, soaked in crimson, as they led him up the trail toward the Drummon house.

Their yells and the noise of their gunshots sounded far before them. A flight of hard riders came lurching down the way, men first, and then a scattering of half-naked boys riding bareback, all screeching like Indians.

They swarmed about the captive and the captors. They were like the creatures of a lost and barbaric age. One lad came near enough to plaster the blood of Silvertip over his hands, instantly all the others had to do the same. Here and there they galloped, yelling, waving their bloodstained hands, filling the air with their ecstasy.

And so Silvertip was brought over the brow of the hill and into sight of the house of Drummon.

The whole corner of it was blackened and charred by the fire which he had kindled. That in itself was a warning of what might happen to him at the hands of these savages.

He was dragged from the horse and hauled into the house to a room where Hank Drummon himself sat in a chair, with his wounded leg extended on another. Silvertip stood wavering before him, while Drummon ran his eyes little by little over the battered figure.

He was very angry, this chief of the clan.

"You done this for yourselves, eh?" said he. "You took and helped yourselves to him, did you? Why, you might 'a knowed that it wouldn't be enough for me if there was twenty of him. I got that in me that could eat twenty like him! But you helped yourself to the cream, did you? You bring him in here half dead? Well, I'll see that you pay for it! Here—some of you throw him on the couch there, and some of the rest of you go and get cloth for bandages. Are you goin' to let the lifeblood all run out of him before I have my chance at him?"

It was done as he commanded, briefly and with rough-handed speed. They brought water to wash his wounds. Some thoughtful spirit had poured a cupful of salt into the dishpan, and the brine searched every crevice of the wounds with bitter fire. The sweat of agony rolled from Silvertip, as he endured, his jaws locked.

Then the wounded flesh was bandaged, and he was allowed the privilege of stretching out on the couch. His head rang still; and a hammer seemed to be tapping regularly at the base of his brain.

"Give him a shot of whisky," ordered Drummon. "I'm goin' to talk to this hombre. He oughta be worth talkin' to before he's bumped off. Hey, sheriff."

For the front door had slammed, and now the grizzled, sodden face of the sheriff appeared in the doorway. He came in slowly, his eyes fixed on the swathed body of Silver.

"Here's the one that the greasers call Señor Silver," said Drummon. "Take a look at the murderin' hoss thief, sheriff, will you?"

The sheriff stood over Silver with his hands on his hips, and grinned and chuckled. "Kind of had an accident, brother, eh?" said he.

Silver looked up into the face of the man of the law, and said nothing. There was no help to be expected here, of course.

"I been lookin' into his record," said the sheriff. "It's a long one, Hank."

"What's he been and done, outside of the trouble he's made in the Haverhill?" asked Hank Drummon, and pressed his hand lightly against the white bandage that ran around his wounded forehead.

One of the younger men lifted the head of Silver and poured a glass of whisky down his throat.

He heard the sheriff saying: "He's one of these here self-defense boys. When trouble's in the air, he never makes the first move. He don't have to. One of them chain-lightning gun-trick boys. You pick your hand, and he fills it for you—with lead. One of them gents that are outside the law except on Sundays and holidays. One of them that keep movin', and move alone. That's the sort of a bird that you've caught here, Hank. How'd you get him?"

"Brains," said Hank Drummon, who never moved his eyes from the face of Silvertip. "Brains, and a little spot cash, and a dirty sneak of a traitor to deal with."

"You pry one of the greasers loose from Monterey?" asked the sheriff, astonished. "That's about the first time that was managed, ain't it?"

"The first time, but it ain't a Haverhill Mexican. It's that slick greaser from the outside, that one called Bandini."

"I know him," said the sheriff. "I'd like to have the hangin' of him one of these days."

"Maybe you will," said Drummon. "But take 'em one at a time. I ain't through usin' Bandini. That lad's bright. He's goin' to show us the easy way into Monterey's house, I reckon, sheriff. And once we get inside that place, we're goin' to wash down the walls with blood! Understand?"

"I hear you talk, Hank," said the sheriff, "but you take an honest sheriff like me, and I can't listen to talk of killin' like that. It kind of rankles inside of me, to hear you talk like that, Hank!"

He roared with hearty laughter as he said this. Everyone in the room joined in the pleasant jest.

And Silver, looking up at the ceiling, drew a slow, deep breath.

It was going to be hard, and very hard; but he kept his mind fixed far forward upon the future, when they would be bringing him toward the moment of his death.

He would have been sure of himself even if there were wild Indians to complete the tortures, he thought. But these devils were different. He could remember the Runt standing over the horrified face of Tonio; he could remember the frightful yell that had burst from the lips of the stolid Mexican at the mere thought of the thing that was about to be done to him. And how would he endure? He feared death far less than he feared the loss of his self-control.

"How many laid up?" asked the sheriff of Drummon.

"Five," said Drummon. "There's two of 'em down bad. The oil soaked into the clothes and kept the fire burnin' right into the skin, and down deep. And there's three more that's burned enough so's bein' up and around is pretty miserable. And there's me that's down, besides!"

He leaned forward a little and stared heavily at Silvertip.

"Yeah," said the sheriff. "He's done a job, all right. I dunno, Hank, but what we could make a *law* case out of this agin' him, except that you boys was about to skin Tonio, the greaser. That would kind of stand out agin' you in a court of law."

"To the devil with the law," said Hank Drummon. "The cursed Cross and Snake has been carved on *my* hide, sheriff. It's carved on there so deep that it ain't goin' to come off. And old Monterey is goin' mad with pleasure every time he thinks that two of the things he promised to me twenty years ago has been done. There's one more left to go!"

"Yeah," said the sheriff. "The door, the forehead, and the heart. I know!"

He looked suddenly over his shoulder, and his face puckered with horror and with disgust.

"I been shamed," said Hank Drummon slowly, the words bubbling huskily up out of his throat. "I been shamed and made a fool of, and every Drummon in the Haverhill has been shamed and made a fool of alongside of me. And it's been a swine of a white man that sides with greasers that's done it to me. When I start thinkin' about it, I pretty nigh lose the head off of my shoulders!"

"You'll keep your head on your shoulders," declared the sheriff, "until you've had your chance at workin' on him." He added: "What kind of ideas might you use, Hank?"

"I dunno," said Hank Drummon with a sigh.

He touched the bandage that made the round of his head, and sighed again.

"I dunno," he repeated. "Fact is, sheriff, that for twenty-four hours I been turnin' the thing around and around in my head. It might be that I could set by and see him stretched out on an ant heap. We got some red ants around here that sting like poison. They might start and work on him."

"Well," said the sheriff, "I always held to the idea that a gent sewed up in green rawhide, and left to be squeezed as the stuff started shrinkin' in the sun, would sure know he was dyin' for a long while before he finished off."

"It's an idea," agreed Hank Drummon almost tenderly. "I didn't think of that one, but I thought of other things, all right. I thought of leavin' him out where the bluebottles would get at him. I wouldn't mind seein' him turned into a pile of fly-blowed meat."

The sheriff struck his hands together with a grunt of admiration. "You got ideas, Hank," he said. "You got a pile of ideas, and nobody can take that credit away from you! You got some of the best ideas that I ever heard about! Or hangin' a gent by the arms with a weight on the feet—that ain't a bad thing. The Indians, they used that idea often."

"They done that same thing," agreed Hank Drummon. "But I reckon that I'm goin' to improve on what the Indians done before I start to work on this gent."

"Yeah," agreed the sheriff, "suppose that you was to work on him and finish him off—you'd feel pretty sick if you thought of a better way afterward."

"I sure would feel pretty sick," said Hank Drummon. "He's put the mark on me. There won't be no way of takin' the scar off. When I get to hell, they'll take me for one of Monterey's beefs. They'll take me for one of the greaser's men when they see the sign on my face."

He groaned, and, closing his eyes, he allowed his great head to fall back against the edge of the chair.

"Whisky! Gimme a shot of whisky!" exclaimed Drummon, and held out his hand.

One of the younger men who had remained in the room, still feasting their eyes on the picture of the prisoner, instantly picked up a jug, filled a glass with pale moonshine, and offered it to Hank Drummon. Hank tossed it off. "'Nother!" he ordered.

His cupbearer had seemed to know the drinking habits of the head of the clan, and the jug had been maintained in readiness. Another glass was filled, and the liquor poured down the throat of Hank.

"Now get out of here," said Hank Drummon. "The whole flock of you haul out of here and leave me be."

"Better have somebody around to fetch and carry for you, chief," said one.

"Get out and stay out! I'm goin' to be alone," said Drummon. "I'm goin' to lay here and look at this here skunk of a Silvertip. And I'm goin' to turn over ideas in my head. And it's goin' to be like listenin' to music to me to set here and think of what I'm goin' to do to him. It's goin' to be like a poet settin' and pullin' his hair, and waitin' for words, and lookin' at the sky, and admirin' of the birds. Get out of here, the whole tribe of you. Get out and stay out, and if I want anything, I'll beller at you fast enough. Just keep inside of call!"

23 – Bandini's Price

SILVERTIP lay in a spider's web. He kept thinking of that. The pain of his wounds, bathed as they had been in brine, did not cease, but grew steadily. Hammers beat in his brain; torment writhed in the pit of his stomach. He kept closing and unclosing his hands.

Conversation was forced on him now and then. For Hank Drummon, as he lay in his chair, brooding with eyes of insatiate evil, sometimes asked questions. He seemed to have an almost tender curiosity about the life and the character of this man whom he intended to destroy. And Silvertip told him stray bits about his adventures, about men he had known and fought with, about strange places he had visited.

Silvertip had no hope, and yet he felt that he was pushing the inevitable moment away from him little by little.

The evening came nearer. The strength which had run out of the body of Silvertip with his blood was diminished further by the long pressure of the pain. Here and there ragged rock edges had cut deeply into his flesh; but worst of all were the bruises which had hurt him to the bone.

Now and again a spell of dizziness nearly carried his senses away. And in every one of those moments he remembered suddenly the face of the dead man, Pedro Monterey, sallow, gray as stone, and smiling.

After all, the third part of Monterey's vow had been unfulfilled, and it would probably remain unfulfilled. The life of Pedrillo was lost; Silvertip, who had stepped into his shoes in the strangest of all manners, was about to die; and old Arturo Monterey would quickly follow them to destruction.

This brute of the fleshy forehead and the yellow-stained eyes had overthrown them all—he and the treachery of Bandini. Silvertip could forget even the pain of his wounds and his weakness when he considered how the consummate trickery of Bandini had twice succeeded.

It was dark, and the chief of the Drummon clan had not yet chosen definitely among the thousand schemes of torture which had been drifting through his mind.

Many a rare device had made him grin and smack his thick lips with laughter; but when he stared again at the big body of Silvertip and thought of what this man had accomplished already in the Haverhill Valley, besides uncounted exploits in other places, it always seemed to Drummon that his best ideas were inadequate.

Besides, there was no hurry.

There was no danger from the Montereys, for he had tied their right hand; he had paralyzed them by taking Silvertip.

Now he could sit back at his ease, like a spider that has lashed its victims in the sticky silk from its spinnerets, and contemplate in advance the joy that would be his.

He was still contemplating when Bandini arrived, at the very moment when the supper gong was booming like a church bell, calling the Drummons to their food.

Silvertip, turning his head, saw the slender Mexican walk into the room, laughing, and, still laughing, come to stand over the prisoner.

"You see?" said Drummon to the traitor. "Silvertip's wearin' out. I been waitin' a good long part of the day for him to give up and start groanin', but he ain't quite weak enough yet. When we washed him in salt water, you could see the flash of his eyes as he rolled 'em from side to side.

"But all he's been doin' since then is to open his hands and shut 'em, like a fish workin' its gills. He's in hell, Bandini."

"That's where he belongs," said the Mexican. "That's where he'll stay. But what do you mean by letting him stay alive this long?"

"What do I mean by—" began Drummon, his voice rousing to a roar of anger. Then he stopped himself and sat with his swollen face, puffing and glaring. "Well, Bandini," he said, "you've done your share of work for me, and you been useful. But don't start tellin' me what to do. I ain't used to it, and I won't stand it."

"You'd better stand more than that," said Bandini. "I can tell you things about this devil that you won't believe. I can tell you that where a snake can slip, he'll pass, also. I can tell you of pinches he's been in that would have cost the lives of twenty men, but he always gets out. The harder you shut your hand on him, the farther he pops away—like a wet watermelon seed."

"Yeah?" growled Drummon.

He swung his heavy head and glowered at the captive. "Silver!" he commanded.

"Well?" said Silvertip.

"Your legs is free enough. Stand up," directed Drummon.

There was no point in opposing him. Silvertip swung his legs from the couch and put them on the floor. The move was an agony. He rose half to his feet, but there his bruised leg muscles refused to support him, and he pitched to the floor on his hands. His arms were strong enough, but the rest of his body was inert as a worm.

Both Drummon and the Mexican laughed loudly. "You see?" said Drummon in triumph.

"I see," said Bandini. "It's all right if it's real, if he's not pretending."

"I'll answer for that," said Drummon. "If he wasn't made of whalebone and India rubber, every bone in his body would a' been busted by the dragging that they gave him on the way here. He's done for. He's as good as in a grave. All it needs is for me to pick out the right way of layin' on the finishin' touches."

"Lay them on soon," advised Bandini, shaking his head and frowning. ' His hands are still strong enough, and there's magic in them."

"You been useful to me," said Drummon, "but advice is something that I don't like and I don't want, no matter what you done for me."

"What I've done is nothing," said the Mexican. "What I'm *going* to do is the important thing."

"More important than catching that piece of wildfire?" asked Drummon, pointing to Silvertip.

The captive turned his head as he lay on the floor, and regarded Bandini. The Mexican stepped to him and kicked the prostrate, helpless body, not hard, but as a gesture of infinite contempt.

"Aye, Silver," he said. "I can do more than handle you. Brains, Silver; brains, Señor Silver. That's what a man needs to beat you. You have a fairly good head—but not strong enough in brains, Silvertip. And that's why I've picked you up in the hollow of my hand and closed the fingers on you one by one. You can listen to what my brains are working on now. Monterey—you came to fight for him. You'd take the place of his son. You'd be the hero, eh? Oh, you're a hero, well enough—but Bandini undoes all that you've tried to do—in one day!"

He turned back to Drummon, who was leaning forward in his chair, scowling with incredulity.

"I give you the Monterey house and all the people in it—at my own price! You understand?" said Bandini.

"Price?" shouted Drummon. "Price? I'll sell my soul and give you the price of that! Open the house of Monterey to me? Can you do that?"

"Aye," said Bandini, "and all that I want is part of the price of the things that are inside."

"Tell me what," said the other. "Speak out, you fool, before I burn up!"

"The price," said Bandini, "is all in one room. An old safe, Drummon. I want the lining of it!"

"You'll have it," said Drummon. He paused suddenly with a groan of distress.

"I know what you mean," he said. "It's the safe where the old man has piled up his money for twenty-five years. And you're to get that? It'll make you rich—it would make the whole Drummon tribe rich, too. But that's no matter.

"What I want is to put an end to twenty-five years of waitin'. And the end may be comin' now! You mean what you say? You can open the house to us?"

"You give your word?" demanded Bandini.

"Give my word? Yes, and my hand with it! Here!"

Drummon stretched out his massive arm, but the other pushed it aside rudely.

"Call in the rest," he demanded. "I want witnesses. I want the crew of 'em to be witnesses."

Drummon's voice rose to the bellow of a bull; and all the pattering of feet and the noise of voices that had moved toward the house at the summons from the supper gong now focused like the sound of a storm toward the chief's room.

They came in a flood to answer him, the big, burly, heavy-faced men standing shoulder to shoulder, thronging around their wounded leader. And they stared hungrily down at Silvertip, stretched on the floor.

They seemed to think that the moment for ending him had surely come at last.

But Hank Drummon was shouting: "Here's Bandini wants witnesses that I swear to give him the safe of Monterey and every dollar that's in it, and I swear it now, in front of the whole of you. You hear me talk? Here's my right hand!" He raised it. "I'll give the safe to Bandini if he shows us the way into the Monterey house!"

"Into the house?" rumbled the chorus.

"Yes, into the house!" said Bandini. "There's an old door that leads to the cellar at the bottom of the cliff. It was walled up. But it's not walled up now, my friends. It's ready to be opened from the outside. I worked a few hours today, and the wall that used to block it up is gone."

They shouted. They smote each other on the shoulders. They looked about them with glimmering, drunken eyes. And the outcry which they had raised spread as if in strangely distorted echoes through the house, where women and children began to laugh and shout.

Presently Drummon cried: "We'll start now!"

"It's the best time," said Bandini. "They're weak as children over there at the Monterey house. They're expecting the sky to fall, and they're ready to run at a whisper since they've lost this Silvertip, this Señor Silvertip, as they love to call him. Bah! The girl's white as a sheet, and shaking. Loves you, Silver, does she? Lost her heart to the great gringo, eh? Well, if you ever see her again, it will have to be in another world. Because you'll kill him before we start?"

He turned to Hank Drummon as he spoke the last words.

But Hank Drummon pursed out his lips and then shook his head.

"There ain't time to do the job right, and when this gent dies, he's goin' to die right."

He added, rolling from side to side in the chair: "Take me out of this. Rig that litter up. I'm goin' to be on hand when the Monterey house goes down. I'm goin' to be there. Here, Runt. You stay and take care of this gent— this Silvertip. Make sure of him."

"And leave me out of the big party?" shouted the Runt.

"Listen, Señor," said Bandini to the Runt. "To take care of Silvertip might be a harder job than to capture the Monterey house."

24 – The Time to Die

THE rage and the despair of Runt was a thing frightful to watch when he saw the rest of the Drummons throng out of the room. Hank Drummon himself could be heard cursing violently all the way to the outside of the house, where the horse litter was brought up for him, and the yelling of the Drummons went up through the brain of Silvertip like so many towering columns of flame.

It was the end of the Montereys, he knew. Suddenly he looked up to the ceiling of the room and wondered, desperately, how Heaven could permit him to lie there helpless while the Drummons rolled on, like so many wild beasts, to the accomplishment of their purpose.

The Runt stood over him with hands that moved and twisted like two great, hairy spiders.

"I ain't goin' to stay here!" said the Runt. "I won't be left out of the killin' of the Montereys! I'm goin' to get over there if I gotta wring your neck before I go—your damn neck!" he repeated through his teeth, and, leaning, he fixed his grasp on the throat of Silvertip.

The whole massive body of Silver was lifted lightly in the frightful grasp of the Runt.

But as the shoulders of Silvertip were heaved high, his long arms gave him the chance he wanted. Too late, the Runt felt the weight of the revolver slipped out of the holster on his thigh.

He released his hold, and Silvertip fell heavily back upon the floor. A shower of red sparks flashed in front of his eyes, but through them he was seeing the Runt and covering him carefully. And the Runt moaning, trembling with eagerness to attack, hung on tiptoe, controlled by the small, dark mouth of the gun.

"Pick me up," said Silvertip.

"You mean it?" asked the Runt.

"I mean it. Pick me up and carry me in your arms."

"I'll see you damned first," said the Drummon.

"D'you think I'll hesitate about shooting, Runt?" said Silvertip. "Pick me up, and handle me with care. You're strong enough for the job. Put me astraddle on your back, because I can't stand. And move slowly—my finger's on the trigger all the time."

Cursing through his teeth in long, whispering, frothing sounds, the Runt lifted that burden and shuddered under it. But the pressure of the muzzle of the gun against his body ruled him.

He opened the side door and carried Silvertip out into the open night.

There was little danger for the moment.

The men of the Drummons were, without exception, journeying through the night; slowly, because the horse litter that supported Hank Drummon could not be moved rapidly. And as for the women and children, they were gathered inside the big house, celebrating in anticipation of the ending of the long feud.

So the Runt got Silvertip safely to the barn. His back against the manger, Silver directed the choice of a horse and the saddling of it, and finally he was lifted up and his feet fitted into the stirrups, and then tied there, and the rope passed beneath the belly of the horse.

If there were a fall, he would be killed by the rolling of the horse; but there must be no fall.

At the door of the barn he gathered the reins and let the Runt step back.

"Don't follow me, Runt," he said. "It's no use. I'll be safely off before you can have a nag saddled and get a gun. Run for your own life, because when Hank Drummon knows that you've let me get away, he'll flay you again the way you were flayed once before. But this time you won't live through it."

Then he loosed the reins, and the horse fled through the dark.

Every swing of that gallop was a torture to the rider. And his battered legs refused to take and sustain a hold, so that his weight kept slipping to one side and then to the other. With his hands on the pommel, he had to right himself, and the strength even of his arms began to give way.

He reached the river. Its bright face was a blurred flash, tarnished by the pain he endured.

The dashing of the water wet him to the shoulders, and was a blessing of assuaging coolness.

And then he went on, until faintness kept him gasping for breath. Twice he lurched far to the side, and the exquisite pain that he felt was all that rallied his senses.

But his head was bowed on the mane of the horse when, at last, he heard voices not far away, and looked up with amazement to find himself directly before the house of Monterey.

It seemed to him that there was a roaring of tumult in the air, and he thought that the battle must be in progress. But then he realized that it was only the pounding and the thundering of the blood in his own ears.

He came closer to lights. A voice shouted, and then many others joined in a chorus. Men walked beside him, supporting him. Others led his horse. He tried to stare through the bright mist and make out faces vainly. Then he heard the shrill, musical cry of Julia Monterey as the peons lifted him tenderly to the ground.

At that his brain cleared suddenly.

He could not stand. His whole body below the shoulders was limp.

"The outer door at the bottom of the cliff—the cellar door—Bandini has unwalled it from the inside today! D'you hear me, Julia? Bandini, and the whole crowd of the Drummons are down there, or almost there. Call the men and turn them loose. Start Tonio—where's Tonio? Where's Juan Perez?"

There was a rush of the party for the house, a storming of footfalls wending down into the cool dimness of the cellars.

He saw Arturo Monterey come for an instant into sight, then disappear into the house, calling orders loudly to his men. He saw Julia Monterey from a corner of his eye, he hardly knew where.

Those who supported him had dropped his body to rush after their master, Monterey. He lay sprawling. He raised himself to his hands and shouted out the name of the one man who, he felt, might come to him before all others.

"Juan Perez! Juan Perez!"

There was no answer.

It seemed to Silver that all the vast effort had been in vain, and that the oath he had breathed silently above the dead man in Cruces had been taken to no end, for now that the greatest need of Pedro Monterey's aid had come, his substitute had to sit sprawling on the pavement of the patio of the house, helpless.

"Juan Perez!" he screamed.

Then he looked up and saw Perez standing by him. Other feet were running close by. That was Julia Monterey. He looked at her face as through a fog. There was no need of women at a time like this. Men had died in this cause, and more men were about to die unless the premonition in his mind were very wrong indeed.

"Lift me, Perez—help me!" he said.

The strong hands of the Mexican raised him suddenly to his feet. Where the hands touched his wounded body, they burned him with fiery pain. But he was all one wound, and therefore the pain was not strange.

"I shall take you to a safe place," Perez was saying. "And I shall not leave you. Have no fear, senior!"

"Safe place?" groaned Silver. "Take me down into the cellars. Take me down into the old mine. I have a gun and I can still use it. Perez, lend me your strength and take me where I can help!"

"I shall!" cried Juan Perez. "Oh, that there should be such a man in the world!"

"Perez! He's dying now!" cried the voice of the girl.

She tried to break in between them.

"Leave him—only help me take him to a bed," she commanded.

"Away with her—she's only a woman—there's no place for 'em now!" shouted Silver. "While we talk the fighting has started!"

"He shall have his way!" cried Perez to Julia Monterey.

"It will be murder, not fighting, if you go down among the guns!" she pleaded, turning to Silver.

"I tell you," said Silver in a frenzy, "this is the time to die!"

"It is the time to die!" echoed Perez, and began to help Silver strongly forward.

More help came to that wounded, half-naked body from the other side. He looked in bewilderment, and saw that it was Julia Monterey who had passed an arm around him and placed her strong shoulder beneath his. A good part of his weight was supported by her.

They passed through the door of the house. She it was who picked up a lantern, never relaxing her efforts to help sustain the half-benumbed body of Silver.

Juan Perez pulled open the tall door that led to the cellar. Out from the dimness came a medley of departing shouts that sank deeper and deeper into the gloom.

"Go back, Julia!" commanded Silver. "You're not needed. I don't want you! Go back!"

"No," she said. "Steady, Juan Perez! The steps are slippery."

"Julia, go back!" shouted Silver.

"It is the time to die," she answered. "Heaven knows how willingly I come to that time!"

"Perez!" cried Silver as he was taken swiftly down the first flight of the steps and into the gloom of a great gallery.

"Yes, señor," said Perez, already panting.

"Send the girl back! It is no place for her."

"Alas, senior," said Juan Perez, "she is a Monterey, and their women are as the men, ever ready for death."

Before them, out of what seemed an infinite distance, came explosions that struck with rapid impacts against the ear of Silver. And he knew that he was too late to be in the forefront of the battle. The men of Drummon already had come through the river door, and the shooting had commenced.

25 – The Battle

AS the sound of the firing stopped their progress, Silver said: "Julia, you know a place, perhaps, where they're apt to come if there's a retreat of Monterey's men. Is there one place they're apt to pass?"

"Two places, where big shafts join together," she said. "Ah!"

She cried out at a nearer echo of a death yell that rang out far away.

"Take me to one of the two places. No, tell Juan Perez how to go there, and then run back!"

"Turn to the right—here," said the girl. "Quickly, Juan Perez! There may not be time. The Drummons are so many devils, and our men cannot stop them. Quickly— quickly—if we are to reach the place in time where we may fight. Now to the left—now down these steps."

"Julia, tell us the way and go back!" shouted Silver.

"Am I a child?" she panted. "I shall not leave you. If you die, there is one of the Montereys ready to die with you. Juan Perez—faster—faster!"

They reached the bottom of a long descent, and then hurried forward to a place where several galleries converged in a meeting point powerfully sustained by great buttresses of the living rock. The lantern light glimmered brightly over the moisture that covered the stone.

"Now!" said the girl breathlessly. "If we place the lantern here in this gap—so!—the light shines down the passages they may come by. And we are left in shadow. Juan Perez, have you a second gun? I can shoot, also!"

They had placed Silver where he sat with his back against a wall, his legs sprawled out helplessly before him. With the lantern put in an adjoining corridor, it flung its light straight on down a mighty hall, where the pick marks showed on all sides, and left the three of them in the darker shadow.

"I have a second gun," said Juan Perez, "but that is for the señor. There is no way for you to help us now. Go back, señorita."

"Go back! Go back!" yelled Silver desperately. "There is no way that you can help here. Go back to the house— they are coming, Julia! Are you to stay here and drive us mad?"

"I am going," answered the girl quietly. "Juan Perez, guard him with your life!"

She was gone from the sight of Silver.

He heard Perez murmuring: "I have already sworn it. My life for yours, señor, and your life for mine. And that is the way that dying is easy. They are coming! Now we shall mow them down!"

"Look sharp!" answered Silver. "It may be that they are the men of Monterey retreating. Listen!"

For wild cries in Spanish now broke on their ears as the approaching tumult swept around an adjacent corner of the tunnels. And then the lantern light struck on a mob of frantic faces—the men of the house of Monterey in headlong flight, reaching out their hands before them as they dashed through the gloom, screeching out the names of their patron saints.

"Curse them!" groaned Juan Perez. "Oh, dogs who betray the hand that fed them. Look—the master is among them—he beats them—but they will not turn and fight!"

For yonder was the silver hair and the white beard of Monterey as he was borne headlong by the current of the flight.

From the rear came the bawling voices of the Drummons in the height of their victory.

Now, behind the place where Silver sat, with a gun in either hand, and Juan Perez kneeling beside him in desperate readiness, he heard the shrill voice of Julia crying:

"Turn back! There is help here! Señor Silver is here— and Juan Perez— and great help! The fight is ours! Turn back, cowards! Turn back and face the bullets with me! Señor Silver is here, and he cannot die alone!"

He heard the girl's shouting as the leaders of the Drummon throng poured around the next bend of the hallway. He saw their faces gleaming white in the dull light of the lantern, like sickly creatures of the sea seen deep down in the shadowy water.

Right into the faces of those charging men Silver and Juan Perez poured a deadly fire.

He saw one man fall. He saw another pitch sidewise. He saw a third leap upward like a wounded deer, yelling. And the whole rout slowed, wavered.

A gap opened. In the rear he had a glimpse of the great form of Hank Drummon, borne on his litter by several pairs of hands. He had stripped himself to the waist, naked, like a sailor going into action on a battleship of the old days, and as though he expected to bathe in blood. In his hands were weapons. About his head was the broad white bandage. He seemed like a pirate picture out of the past.

"Jose Bandini!" he was thundering. "Show these cowardly fools the way to go forward. Charge the dogs! Charge 'em home and they'll vanish. Come on, boys!"

Into the van leaped the brilliant form of Jose Bandini. If he were a thousand times a villain, he was a thousand times a hero, also. He ran straight forward to lead the rest, and as he ran he laughed with the joy of the conflict, and waved a revolver above his head.

Behind him, the men of the Drummons rallied and surged ahead in a wave.

Silver, leveling his revolver, was about to fire with a deadly aim at Bandini when another form intervened before him.

It was old Arturo Monterey, running straight at his enemy, with his white hair blown back from his head. He shouted a wordless battle cry as he ran.

The moment was lost to Silver. The next instant he saw vast forms bulking above him, and loosed the fire of his gun among them. Half lighted by the lantern, but only enough to make them jumping, swaying, whirling silhouettes, he saw the men of Drummon rush at him.

He saw the fine form of Jose Bandini lead the others. At that body he fired as Bandini leveled a gun and rushed at him, guided by the darting fires from the mouth of Silver's Colt.

It seemed a bitter shame to meet that moment seated.

With a vast effort, Silver struggled to one knee. A bullet struck his body, he knew not where. The weight of the impact flattened him back against the wall.

A swinging foot kicked the gun from his left hand— that in the right was already empty. He was caught by the hair of the head and jerked forward on his face. And, turning as he fell, he saw Bandini lift a revolver by the barrel. That gun must have been empty, also, but a stroke with the butt of it would crack his skull.

His own hands were empty. But beside him lay Juan Perez, senseless, his face covered with blood that poured from a scalp wound, his arms outflung; and in the nearer hand, held out as though it were an offering in time of need to his friend, there was a Colt lying.

Silver threw up his left arm. The falling heel of the gun that Bandini wielded crushed the flesh against the bone, and beat the whole arm heavily down against his face.

But at the same instant his right hand had caught the weapon from the hand of poor Juan Perez.

"Take that!" cried Bandini. "I wish there were a thousand lives in you that I could beat out one by one. Gringo —take this! And—"

Silver fired upward, the muzzle of his gun inches from the body of Bandini. And the man fell forward on him, a loose, soft, warm weight.

The brain of Silver reeled.

He could hear two voices. The first was that of the girl, who was still crying out to the men of Monterey. And they had rallied. That was the meaning of the trampling and the stamping all around him. That was the meaning of the curses in Spanish and in English, one mixed with the other.

And the second voice was wailing not far away: "The Alligator's dead— save yourselves! Hank Drummon's dead!"

It was that yelling voice of dismay that beat the Drummons more than the sudden, fierce, and unexpected rally of the Mexicans. The cry that one man had started was taken up by others. As Silver worked the weight of the dead Bandini from his body and sat up, he saw the gallery filled with the thronging flight of the Drummons, the big men fighting to get one past the other. After them ran the victorious men of Monterey, yelling insanely with their victory.

Behind them were the dead.

It was amazing that so few had fallen in a fight so close and hot. Bandini was dead, to be sure. And two of the men of Monterey. And yonder sat the great Drummon in his litter, bloodstained about the breast where a great cross had been slashed with a knife, and under it a wavering line—the brand of the Cross and Snake!

On the floor beside him was a small body, with a head of white hair, but that body stirred, moved, stood up, staggering.

Juan Perez, who had recovered consciousness, was leaning over him, asking how he was. And then the girl slipped in between them and caught Silver in her arms, saying:

"Do you ask questions like a fool? He's shot through the body! He's dying! Call for help! If he's lost, there's no glory left in this day for the house of Monterey!"

26 – Geese Across the Moon

IF Silver did not die, it would be because, said the two doctors who worked over him by day and by night, he obstinately refused to give up life, even when all that remained to him was only a little handful of the immortal fire.

But he lived, and when he could sit up in the bed, he learned the great tidings of events that had happened while he lay senseless, near to death.

The Drummons were gone. Their long fight, for generations, to win and hold the Haverhill Valley for themselves, had failed. Their leader was dead. Their spirits were broken. And they had sold out their lands for a song and left the Haverhill in a great procession of horses and wagons, like a picture of emigration out of an earlier day. Farther west and farther north, they would try to find a new home for themselves.

In the meantime, old Arturo Monterey, at the end of his life, had swept in for little cost all the lands that he had fought for so long. As for the village, it was gone. On the morning of the day when the Drummons moved out, a fire had started mysteriously, and in a few hours it was uncontrollably sweeping the place. Now rains were beating and winds blowing the black ash heaps of the spot where the place had stood.

All of these things Silver heard. And he could have guessed them, he often thought, merely by the sounds of song and laughter which, all day long, flowed through the house of Monterey—now near at hand, now sweet with distance.

He began to recover rapidly. The day came when he could walk, and then he could ride out with Juan Perez. And the peons in the fields ran to the fences and shouted and cheered him like a hero.

It made Silver laugh with joy to hear them.

Every day he rode out, and every day, when he returned, he felt that he was being brought nearer and nearer to the crucial point of his life. Monterey had said nothing; the girl had said nothing; but he knew that their eyes were waiting for him to speak. And the question that he must answer was as to whether or not he chose to spend his life here in Haverhill, now that it was purged of its plague.

If he spoke, he knew without vanity that the girl would marry him, and that old Monterey would leave the whole estate to her. But neither of them spoke, and he, day by day, tried to face the question, and could not.

His thought was totally in solution, and something from the outside was needed to precipitate it in the form of action.

It was turning cool now in the evenings, but still they dined on the garden terrace and in the twilight of this day a big golden moon came up out of the east and climbed softly up the sky.

A streak of shadow moved across it. Silver stared, and could not understand, for no cloud could be at once so narrow and so dark a line, nor could the wind blow any mist with such speed, he felt.

A breeze cut at them from the mountains. And Julia went into the house to get a heavier cloak. But old Monterey remained seated in his chair, his eyes rarely leaving the face of Silver.

It was the night when some word must be spoken, Silver felt. There was a warm and happy flow of temptation when he thought of the quiet days of contentment which could stretch before him if he married the girl and settled to life in the Haverhill.

And yet something checked him, and he could not tell what.

More often, day by day, he thought of young Pedro Monterey, to whom this place should have gone in right succession. He could think without sharp pain of the dead man now, for the vow he had made silently in Cruces had been discharged. And still Pedro Monterey remained the shadow on his mind.

So on this night, as he sat with old Monterey in the garden, he heard a vague sound come out of the upper air, and looked up, startled.

He could see nothing.

It was a cry that he had heard before, he could not tell where. His inactive brain would not place the note that had reached his ears. But it stirred infinite echoes within him.

"What is it, my son?" said the gentle voice of Don Arturo.

"Nothing," said Silver briefly.

But his heart began to throb uneasily. A melancholy desire for he knew not what possessed him.

He stood up and began to walk the terrace with rapid steps, feeling the glance of Monterey swing back and forth with him.

Again the dark, triangular line swept across the face of the moon, and a moment later the cry came out of the sky again.

Wild geese! Wild geese flying south! Now he knew what it was that stirred in his blood. He, also, wanted to be on the wing to another land. And suddenly the mountains on either side of the Haverhill rose for him like prison walls.

Again that half melodious, half brazen call came tingling out of the upper air and ran through all his blood.

"I'm going inside," he said thickly. "I'll get—something to put on!"

That was how he left them.

It was not many minutes afterward that Julia Monterey came down and looked eagerly, anxiously, but saw that Silver was gone. Monterey answered her look.

"He has gone inside to get a heavier coat," said the old man. "He is very restless. He has been walking up and down the terrace. Tonight, my dear, he is surely going to speak. And after that we shall be happy together forever."

"Restless? He may be restless to leave us!" she exclaimed. "What did he say when he went in?"

"Only that he was going to get something to put on. The wild geese had flown across the moon; when they called out of the sky, he looked up suddenly. And then I suppose that he felt the cold as he heard them, and he went inside."

"The wild geese?" she murmured.

And she in turn heard the distant chorus swept down from the chilly regions about. Between her and the moon the unseen hosts were flying and sending their harsh music toward the earth.

"The wild geese—and he has gone! He has gone to follow them. He has gone to—"

She fled suddenly from the terrace. Arturo Monterey stood up, started and amazed. He cried after her.

But she, unheeding, ran on into the house, and hurried to the room of Silver. There was no answer to her knock. She threw the door open, and the darkness seemed to roll out just like a thick mist across her eyes.

She fled down to the patio.

"Señor Silver!" she cried to one of the house *mozos*. "Have you seen him?"

"Going toward the stable," said the servant.

"The stable!" moaned Julia Monterey, and ran on, breathless with fear.

It was near the stable that she met with Juan Perez, walking with his head thoughtfully bowed.

"Juan!" she cried. "Juan, have you seen Señor Silver? Has he been here?"

"Here and gone again," said Juan Perez. "There was trouble in his face. And he left this for you and the señor."

She snatched the letter and tore it open, to read:

My Dear Friends: It came over me all at once, tonight, that I must go. I wanted to stay and say good-by to you, but I knew that you would be kind, and ask me why I should leave, and then I would be able to give no answer.

Forgive me for leaving like a thief in the night.

Some day I shall surely come to you again. From wherever I light, I shall write to you everything.

Adios, Adios.

She crushed the paper in her hand and ran across the patio to the great entrance arch, crying out his name. The sound of her voice passed down the road and echoed back to her emptily from the hillside.

It was dawn of the next day. High up in the center of the northern pass, Silvertip turned in the saddle and looked back on the blue of the river and the green, rolling lands that swept up from the stream. He could see the cattle as dull spots of color, and the distant house of Monterey was like a child's toy that one could have picked up between thumb and forefinger.

He looked at it until a certain mistiness came over his eyes. Then he turned and walked the horse little by little over the ridge.

He knew that he was leaving a glorious chance of happiness behind him; but he closed his eyes to it.

The chance was so great indeed that he felt it pulling at his heart with hands.

He would not surrender to it. The old unrest moved in him like new blood. The wind of the mountains vainly caused his new wounds to ache.

He set his teeth firmly and aimed his course toward the blue and crystal-white of distant mountains.

THE MAN FROM MUSTANG

CONTENTS

Chapter – 1

ON THE brow of the last hill that spilled from the knees of the mountains toward the prairie, under the last tree, Silver sat with his knees hugged in his arms and watched the rider in the distance, and the prairie fire behind him.

Parade, with bridle off and saddle on, grazed nearby, biting off the short, sweet grass close to the roots, eating greedily, as though he knew that the taste of this pasturage was much sweeter than the tall, dry grasses beneath him. Now and then he jerked his head and looked suddenly at his master, and then all about him, with pricking ears, for he understood perfectly that to the wolfish keenness of his scent and to his quickness of ear and eye, Silver looked for warning if any danger came his way. Parade was a combination of stallion and sentinel, the guardian and the servant of the man.

The day was hot and dry. Silver had taken off the big sombrero as he sat in the shade, and thereby exposed the two marks of gray hair above his temples that looked like incipient horns sprouting, and had given him his universal nickname of "Silvertip." Now he made himself at ease. He had been long enough in the mountain wilderness which he loved, and it seemed to him a typical irony of fate that as he turned his face back toward the dwellings of man he should see a rider on the plain and a grass fire at the same time. For among men there was always danger.

The fellow who jogged his horse quietly along seemed unaware of the coming fire for a long time. It had begun as a small point, like a dust cloud rolling. It increased. Evidently a wind was favoring it, and finally a gust of that breeze went whispering through the leaves above the head of Silver.

By this time the grass fire had gathered both speed and frontage, and was leaving behind it a widening wedge of black against the pallor of the prairie grass. At the same moment the lone rider became aware of the danger behind him. Silver laughed to see the man bring his mustang to a gallop and flatten out along the neck of the horse.

It was high time, but time enough, for the horse could move a great deal faster than the fire itself, though that was now galloping like a thousand wild beasts, wallowing, plunging, throwing forward a leaning wall of smoke, as though a dense mass of skirmishers were running forward with rifles firing constantly. Fast as the wind blew, pressing the smoke forward, the speeding flames ran almost as quickly. Now they rushed down a hollow with a slower gait. Now they leaped up a slope, and at the crest hurled upward a gigantic cloud of fire, as though in excess of strength. A god seemed to be rioting in that flame, bounding between earth and heaven, trailing his cloak of smoke high up in the sky.

The fugitive, in the meantime, was gaining rapidly on the wall of danger, when all at once, as he came close enough for Silver to make out that the horse was small and the man big, the mustang went down and hurled its rider far away, spinning head over heels.

The horse tried to rise at once, but a dangling foreleg prevented it. The man, on the other hand, lay perfectly still, face down, twisted as though his body had been broken in the middle.

Silver had the bridle on Parade almost before he had finished noting these things. For both horse and man lay directly in the path of the fire.

With the throatlatch unfastened, he sprang into the saddle. The big golden chestnut got under way like a frightened deer. Down the hillside he streaked across the green like a meteor down the blue arch of the sky, and struck the level, where the tall prairie grasses whipped like splashing water about his shoulders. That impediment could not slow his speed or shorten his stride.

And angling straight toward the danger point, Silver rode him between the fallen horse and the fallen rider.

It would be a near thing. Already the running flame put out an arm of crimson and smoke that enveloped the struggling horse. The poor beast screamed with agony. Silver, twisting in the saddle, put a bullet through its head from his revolver.

Right behind him came the sweeping fire. The wind that hurried above the flames dropped a shower of sparks and whole bunches of burning grass that seemed to have been uprooted by the force of the draft! And little new fires caught hold on the dryness of the grass even before the main body of the flame had rolled to them.

One of these spots of fire was spreading at the side of the fallen rider as Silver came up. He called out. Parade stood on braced feet, and Silver, without dismounting, leaned far down from the saddle.

He took that burden under the armpits and hauled it up. The head fell back as though on a broken neck, to show Silver a young, brown face, almost absurdly homely. There was enough nose and jaw for two ordinary men, yet what the face enjoyed in length it lacked in width. But the forehead was good, and what Silver saw first and last was the frown that lingered on the brow. A dead man's face would have been smooth, he told himself, but there was the promise of life!

With that limp body in his arms, he called again; and Parade went like a flashing gesture through the tall grass, back to the shorter growth on the hillside.

There Silver deposited his burden. He had to spend a minute beating out sparks that had begun to ignite his clothes. Parade was dancing because of a smoking place on his mane. When that was out, there were more burning spots on the clothes of the stranger.

In the meantime, the roar of the prairie fire went by, leaving acres of glowing red behind it, and a black, smoking heap where the mustang lay dead.

The unconscious man now stirred suddenly, and sat up with a gasp. He said nothing for some time. First his eye marked the distant rush and roar of the conflagration. Then he looked down and actually patted the short green of the grass on which he was sitting. At last he marked the place where the dead horse lay.

At that he started to his feet with an exclamation. It seemed to Silver that he was about to run down into the grass toward the dead horse, though there were still flaming bits that far behind the head of the fire. Silver caught his shoulder and held him.

"You'll burn your boots, and spoiled leather won't help that dead horse," said Silver.

"No, you're right," said the other slowly. He looked at Silver with a dull eye of suffering. "He's eaten enough right out of my hand," said he. "And now the fire's eaten him—right off the ground."

He smiled. His whole face twisted with grief that he fought again.

"He was a good-looking horse," said Silver gently.

"He was a right good one. He was a cutting horse," said the stranger, wiping his hands on his leather chaps absently. "You put him on the tail of a calf and he'd follow that calf to kingdom come. Yes, sir, and head it off before ever it got there, in spite of anything. That's the kind of a cutting horse he was. But the fire got him—fire!" He shuddered as he said it.

"I put a bullet through his head just before the fire ate him," said Silver.

The stranger looked up and down, but saw no gun. A gleaming gesture made a big Colt with three extra inches of barrel on it appear from beneath the coat of Silver and disappear again.

"I'm thankin' you," said the stranger. "And you didn't have no lot of time on your hands, neither."

He looked down at the spots on his own clothes, some of which were still faintly smoking. Then he eyed the damaged costume of Silver. Suddenly he grinned.

"I'm goin' to be owin' you a suit of clothes in exchange for the skin that I'm still wearing," he said.

"All right," answered Silver.

"Poor old Jerry!" said the man under his breath. "I'll tell you what he was," he added suddenly. "He was a partner. You know?"

"I know," said Silver.

The stranger glanced toward Parade.

"Yeah, you know, all right," he agreed. "Maybe you know even a lot better'n I do. When I was camping out, he'd watch over me at night like a dog. We've been on desert marches when he ate half of my bacon and drank sugar and milk. We been on marches when I've boiled his oats and halved 'em with him. Jerry," concluded the stranger with a broad sweep of his hand, "was a horse!"

"He was," said Silver. "Right up to the end, he was trying to get to you and tell you that the fire was coming."

"What happened?" asked the man.

"He put his foot in a hole in the ground, I guess," said Silver. "He broke his leg when he fell, and he couldn't get up."

The stranger took off his sombrero and wiped from his face sweat that was never produced by the heat of the sun. He swallowed hard. Then suddenly he faced Silver.

"I don't know your name," he said. "Mine is Ned Kenyon."

Silver shook the hand.

"People call me Jim," he said, "or Arizona Jim, or Arizona. I don't care much what I'm called."

A slight shadow passed over the face of Kenyon, but it was gone at once.

"Any name is the right name," he said, "for me to tell you that I've had my hide saved by you. The day before my wedding day, too!"

He grinned broadly, and the ugliness disappeared from his face, it was so lighted.

"The luck stays with a plumb happy man," said Kenyon.

"It does," agreed Silver.

"Look," said the stranger impulsively. "I want you to see her right away. I want that you should know you've done more than save my hide; because maybe you've kept a lot finer person than me from trouble. I want you to see her."

He jerked a flat leather case from his inside coat pocket, and then paused, and his blue, small eyes lingered wistfully on the handsome face of Silver, as though asking for permission.

"I want to see it," said Silver. "Let's have a look."

That was enough.

Ned Kenyon opened the leather case and displayed the picture.

"It don't do her justice," he said, sidling around to Silver. "But you just get a sort of general idea, is all."

A small, stinging shock had passed into the brain of Silver as he looked. A queer numbness spread in his mind. For as he stared, he told himself that there was only one thing under heaven he could be sure of, and that was that such a girl as this could never marry Ned Kenyon.

Silver saw her in profile, but he could tell the bigness and the straightness of the eyes, and the refinement of the mouth, and the proud lift of the chin. A king could have married her proudly, and not for her beauty only, but for things of mind and spirit that spoke out of her face.

Half squinting, Silver called up the image of the man beside him, the long, gaunt body, the long, gaunt face.

No, he decided, the thing could not be. Perhaps the poor fellow had this mania that being unattractive to most women, he had picked up the portrait of some reigning beauty of New York or Paris, and carried it about with him, to boast pathetically of his triumph.

"She's very beautiful," said Silver gravely, giving back the picture.

Kenyon took it in both hands and shook his head.

"It ain't beauty that counts. It's the heart underneath it," he said. "She's a clean-bred one. Oh, she's as straight as a string, let me tell you!"

"I'll put money that she is," said Silver.

"Brave, and honest, sort of simple and quiet, and about perfect," said Kenyon slowly.

He put the picture back inside his coat.

"Tomorrow at noon," said he, "we're going to be married in Mustang. And I wish that you were going to be there, partner. That's what I wish. That you were going to be there, so that she could thank you face to face. I'd like to have you hear her voice—just once. Because it's the sort of a thing that you'd never forget if you lived for a hundred years."

Silver looked at the vanishing smoke of the prairie fire, far away, for it had been running like wild horses all this time, cleaving a greater and greater wedge of black through the pale prairie grass.

The thing could not be. Every instinct in him spoke against it. She could not, being what she was, marry this lean grotesque of a cow-puncher.

"How far is Mustang?" he asked.

"Only twenty miles!" said the other eagerly.

"Then I'll go there with you," said Silver. "It's a long time since I've seen a wedding."

Chapter – 2

THERE was no doubt of one thing—that just as firmly as Silver was convinced that the wedding would never take place, just so firmly was Ned Kenyon assured that on the morrow he would be the happiest man in the world, and that this girl would be his wife.

He was ready to talk of her. Words about her overflowed his lips.

She was only twenty. Her name was Edith Alton. All the perfections that God could give to a woman had been showered upon her.

Perhaps, thought Silver, it might be an old acquaintance, one of those deep affections that grow up from years spent together—as, for instance, Kenyon might have been for long the foreman on her father's ranch. Or perhaps there were hidden qualities in this man—he might be, for all his rather ungrammatical language, an artist, an inspired poet, or a philosopher such as Silver had met in the west more than once, filled with wisdom that seems to rise like sap from the ground.

"You've known her a long time?" asked Silver.

"Seven days!" said Kenyon.

Again the numb incredulity spread through the brain of Silver. Seven days!

"That's not long," remarked Silver. "Love at first sight, I suppose?"

"No," answered Kenyon. "Not for her. For me, yes. But not for her. I saw her at the railroad, and I drove the stage that brought her up to Mustang. I hardly kept the wheels on the road, because I was turning all the time to look at her. And then the next day was my day off the driver's seat, and I went to a dance, and there she turned up, and I danced with her, part of a dance.

"But she wanted to talk more than to dance. And she asked me to take her outside. We walked up and down under the pine trees, into the black of the trees, and out into the white of the moon. Mostly talking. Mostly me talking.

And she listening, with her head a little on one side. It's dead easy to talk to a girl like that!" he exclaimed. "And there was me, that never had found a girl in the world that would pay no attention to me! And there was me, with the queen of the world, as you might say!"

Silver, as he walked along at the side of his companion, the stallion following without the need of a lead, sighed a little. The problem was beginning to grow more and more unfathomable to him. Behind it there lay a mystery as profound as a pit, a darkness which his eye could not penetrate. But with every step he made at the side of this man, the more convinced he became of the man's steel-true honesty and worth. There was not a crooked bone in his body, not a shadowy thought in his brain.

"You talked of a lot of things?" asked Silver.

"We talked about me," said the stage driver. "She seemed a lot interested in that. I told her about being a kid on the farm in Dakota, and about the way the winter lasted, and the way the spring came up, and the way the snow first melted, and the spring skating, and a lot of things like that, and how I came farther west, and about prospecting, and all that, and how I started to drive the stage, and got along at that because I got a way with horses. And she listened like a baby to music all the time, with her head a little over on one side, and now and then turning her head, and smiling at me a bit. In a way," said Kenyon, "that I couldn't tell you about it. Just a kind of a smile that soaked into you, like spring sunshine!"

He was no poet, either, thought Silver—just a fine, honest, decent fellow, with unprobed virtues of courage and decency. But a mate for that girl in the picture, with her lifted chin and her straight-looking eyes, and the sensitive nose and lips?

No! Whatever happened, it could not be that she intended to marry Ned Kenyon.

"You go on and ride," Kenyon was saying. "I don't mind walking. I'm pretty good at it. And with Edith to talk about, I could walk to the end of the world."

Something jerked at Silver, something pulled him up in revolt even to hear Ned Kenyon call the girl by her first name—and yet he was to marry her on the morrow!

"If you could ride half the time while I walked," said Silver, "it would be all right. But this horse doesn't like most people, and he'd be fighting every minute to get you out of the saddle."

"Would he?" murmured Kenyon.

He gave the brim of his hat a jerk.

"I ain't boasting," he said, "but the fact is that I'm pretty fair with horses my own self. I'd like to try him, if you don't mind, stallion or no stallion!"

"Would you?" said Silver, smiling. Then he laid a hand on Kenyon's bony shoulder and added: "Don't do it. He's a trickster. He knows a thousand ways of getting a man out of the saddle, and the worst of him is that when the rider drops, he has a way of trying to savage the unlucky fellow. I'd be on hand, but I might not be close enough to call him off in time. I don't doubt that you're a good rider—but I'd rather not have you try him."

Ned Kenyon looked wistfully at the golden stallion, and then he sighed.

"You know your own self and your own horse better than anybody else," he observed. "And it's the seeing of a man like you, Arizona, with a horse like that, that makes me wonder how Edith can look at me once and want to look at me twice. But I remember folks saying years ago that the likes of men for women and women for men there's no accounting for. Only, when I think of you, riding on a horse like that—well, I can't help thinking that Edith may shake her head a coupla times. Only I know that there's nothing in her but faith. For what would the world amount to, Arizona, if there was anything behind a face and an eye and a voice like hers except truth and honesty, and the kind of love that won't die in a long winter?"

Silver, listening to this speech, which was drawled out with a good many pauses, while Ned Kenyon found proper words to express himself, looked several times down to the ground, and several times with his narrowed eyes peered into the horizon like a hawk.

He said at last: "A man or a woman that lied to you, Ned, would need a hanging; and I'd be glad to pull on the rope!"

"Would you, Arizona?" asked the simple man. "I think you mean it, too. I think it's been a great day for me, Arizona. Because, look here—a man can't live by a woman only, but he needs a friend, too. And I don't know that I've ever had a real friend in all my born days."

"Never a friend?" asked Silver. "Do you mean that, Kenyon? Do you mean that you've seen through the lot and found them all a worthless gang?"

"Looked through them?" echoed Kenyon. "Man, man, who am I to be looking through folks? No, no! There's three out of four or four out of five that I would be glad enough to have as friends. I'm no one to make big pretendings. Any right man is a good man for me to talk to and keep to. It's not my choosing, but the choice of the other people, that doesn't fall on me. Unless they want to cheat me out of money, or talk kind to me today just in order to make a fool of me tomorrow. And so it's come about that I've never had a friend in my life, until today it sort of looks as though you might be a friend to me, Arizona!"

He slowed his step and turned his frank, open eye on Silvertip; and the heart of Silver swelled in him.

He put his hand again on the thin shoulder of Kenyon and said carefully, weighing his words: "I've had few friends, too. And most of those I've had are behind me somewhere." He made a gesture, as though dropping something over his shoulder. Then he went on: "But I think that you and I could pull together as long as we're traveling in the same direction. I'd like to tell you this, Kenyon, that I hope you'll be able to trust me in any pinch—as long as I'm around your part of the world."

Kenyon held out his hand. It was taken in a firm grasp by Silver as they looked fixedly into the eyes of one another.

Then Kenyon began to laugh out of pure pleasure.

"It's been a lucky day for me—a right lucky day—if only poor Jerry hadn't gone! But Jerry was twelve, and every year it was harder for him to do what he wanted and live up to himself. Well, there he was, out fighting on the danger line, and that's the way that he would have chosen to die, I guess. And I'll tell you what, Arizona—the Indians all used to believe that when a brave went up to the happy hunting ground, he was sure to find his best horses there before him, waiting."

He laughed again in some embarrassment, as though he disclaimed a belief in any such superstition. But for a time, as they walked along, his eyes went upward and roved the sky with a blowing rack of clouds, and with such a smile on his lips that Silver knew suddenly what thoughts were running in the mind of his simple friend.

Silver made a fierce and a deep resolve to give mind and heart and hand to this man until that call which moved him irresistibly across the face of the world reached him again, and drew him he knew not where across the sky line.

He was still thinking of this hours later, when they came over a hill into sight of a town, and down a trail not far from them a woman was riding.

"Look!" cried Kenyon. "There's Mustang—and there's Edith Alton! Do you need more'n a sight of the way of her to tell that there's no other woman like her on earth?"

Chapter – 3

MUSTANG was a flourishing centre of trade, as was proved by the five roads that led into it, all whitened by constant travel, to say nothing of the irregular trails that were traced threadlike over the surrounding hills. Mustang Creek darted through the midst of the town, with two bridges over its narrow banks, and scattered groves of pines came down from the hills and right into the town itself. What more could the heart of any mountaineer require than such profusion of wood and water? Moreover, the town was placed where it could serve the great mountain region that tumbled behind it to the north and west, and also send out its freighters through the plains beyond the southern and the eastern hills.

But Silver gave that picture only a glance. Neither did he regard the huge wagon, drawn by fourteen mules, that was rolling down one of the white roads toward Mustang, sending the screech of brakes, like the screaming of hawks or bagpipes, through the still air toward him. What he watched was the girl who came pitching down a trail on the other side of the valley, swerving her horse through brush and among boulders, with the wind of the gallop fanning the brim of her sombrero straight up, and her bandanna fluttering behind her neck like a flag.

"And that's Edith Alton?" said Silver thoughtfully, shaking his head a little. "She's a Western girl, then, Kenyon?"

"No more Western," said Kenyon, grinning, "than Boston and New York. But she's the sort that knows how to do what other folks do, wherever she goes. She could ride Eastern, and it don't take much for them to learn to ride Western. I've stood and seen her, Arizona—I've stood and seen her thrown four times hand running from a pitching broncho, and get up and take the saddle, and never pull leather till that mustang fitted to her like a silk glove and said 'Yes' and 'No' just the way she wanted! And there she goes, sailing. And that black mare of hers is a piece of silk all over, too. I'd know that mare, and I'd know that girl, by the sassy way they've got about them!"

Silver let this talk slip easily through his mind while he studied the disappearing rider. She rode, in fact, as though she had been raised in the saddle. Some of the dark suspicion went out of Silver's heart, for what Western man can resist the sight of a woman who knows how to ride "straight up and hell bent"?

"She looks like one in a million," he said to Kenyon. "I suppose you've wanted to paint her or do her in words!"

"Paint her? Me? I can paint a barn; I wouldn't aim to even paint a house except on a bet. Words? I've written ten letters in my life, I guess, and that's about all!"

It seemed to Silver that the last possible way of understanding Kenyon's hold on this girl had been removed. If there had been mystery before, it was doubly dark now.

They came down into the village, Kenyon explaining why he had been riding across country. He had gone to the nearest railroad to telegraph to his distant parents the news of his approaching wedding, and to buy in a larger town a suit of store clothes that would be a credit to him when he "stood up in church." But when he and Silver had examined the pack behind the saddle of the dead Jerry, they had found it almost totally consumed.

"It don't matter so much," declared Kenyon. "She ain't the kind to care much about clothes. They wouldn't make much difference to her! It's the other things that count with her."

Every word he spoke, every expression of trust and faith, pulled at the heart of Silver as though he heard them spoken by a child who was about to be disillusioned in this savage world of facts.

They went to the hotel.

"The time you get straightened up," said Kenyon, "I'll tell her that you're coming in to eat supper with us in the dining room. She'll be right glad. There's only one other thing. She wants the wedding to be a surprise to everybody back home; everybody that knows her. She don't want it to be talked about here. You'll understand how it is, Arizona?"

Silver nodded and smiled, but his smile was very faint; and as he heard this, something rang like a bell in his mind, and made him surer than ever that the whole thing was a cruel illusion which was being built up around his companion.

After watering the stallion, Silver put Parade into the stable behind the hotel, and saw that he was well fed with clean hay of barley and wild oats. After that he took a room in the hotel and went up to shave and wash and brush his clothes clean of the dust of the long walk.

He was not tired. That body of his was furnished with steel springs so tempered that no ordinary strain could make an impression on him. And now, with a light step, he went down into the lobby and waited in the little square hall.

The girl came first. He watched her walk down the stairs. If all the features of her picture had been blurred, he told himself that he would have known her by something high and proud in the carriage of her head. And though she wore a plain khaki riding skirt and the most ordinary of blue silk blouses with full sleeves that ended at the elbows, she seemed dressed for the pleasure of the most critical eye in the world.

She was a smiling girl, of the sort that people like to see even in a stage or a railroad carriage, or in a ballroom, or on a street, merely. Glances trailed after her, and strange expressions of homesickness appeared for a fading moment in the faces of the men in the lobby.

She seemed to know the names of most of them, and she spoke to them all. In another part of the world she would have been surrounded at once, but in the West a woman generally "belongs" to some man, and outsiders are not in haste to rush in and make fools of themselves. She came straight across to Silver and held out her hand.

"Ned told me about you," she said. "You're Arizona, and you don't bother about other names except Jim. And he told me how you saved him from the fire, and that you're going to have supper with us so that I can thank you."

He looked straight back into her eyes. As far as he could penetrate them, there was nothing but candor. And yet there was a trick somewhere. It could not be honest. It must be a sham. She had blue eyes, a little stained with shadow on the lower lids, almost as though with a cosmetic. Her brow was as clear as a sculptor's marble. He could not find a place to put his finger and say that this or that might be the sign and the symbol of deceit. And her beauty drew at him like the first day of spring after a long, white winter.

"I don't want thanks," he said. "I've had a chance to talk to Kenyon, and I've learned to know him a little on the way here. That's better than having thanks."

She sat down beside him, explaining that Kenyon would be with them later. It seemed to Silver that perhaps she had turned to her chair a little too quickly, when she heard this deliberate praise of her fiancé. She went on to say that it generally took Ned a good bit of time to get his hair in order.

"It sticks up like fingers around the crown," she said, and laughed a little.

Silver did not laugh. He was looking back into his brain, running over his memories of other women. There had been none that gave a clue to her. There was an air of perfect calmness, of self-possession and strength, that set her apart from the rest.

She was talking again, in spite of his silence. Her whole attitude was one of gratitude and almost of reverence, though she would not touch again on the thing he had done that day for Kenyon.

Outside, the sunset was drawn red across the window. He wished that the full light of the day were striking about them, and that he could keep studying her face. But perhaps it was better this way, for he could face almost away from her and still regard her from the corner of his eye. That is an art. The cultivation of it had saved the life of Silver on more than one day.

She was saying: "Ned tells me that you don't talk about the past; that it's all future with you, Arizona. But I suppose that you've been what every one is out here, part prospector, cow-puncher, lumberman?"

He turned up the palm of his hand. The fingers were straight and lithe, as the fingers of a child. There were no callouses. Labor never had deformed that supple hand.

"No," he said simply.

And for the first time he had touched her. It was only a single upward flash of her eyes, and perhaps she felt that she was shielded from his observation because he was not directly facing her. But in that flash he thought he read suspicion and sudden fear.

He explained his simple negative. "I'm one of the drifters. I'm one of the idlers. I've daubed a rope on a cow now and then; and I've chipped rock with a hammer, too, and swung an ax now and then. But business never has interfered with pleasure."

"And pleasure?" she asked.

"Pleasure?" said he. "Oh, it comes in its own form. I never can tell where I'll find it, or what it will be like. Tomorrow I ought to find it, though, when I see you stand up before the preacher with my friend Kenyon."

She did not wince. She did not blush. She began to nod a little, and she kept on smiling. But he felt that the smile was a trifle too fixed.

All of his suspicions took him by the throat. What she could possibly gain from a marriage with Kenyon he could not guess. But in that instant he was convinced that it was not the man she wanted, but something else that she would reach through him.

And all her beauty seemed to drop away from her suddenly, as though a hailstorm had swept across the spring day of which she had reminded him, darkening the skies in a moment and battering grass and flowers into a common mud. So it was for Silver in that instant, and he could face her now with his own faint smile, that seemed to come from nothing except content of the heart. It would be a contest between them, and in the angry mood that possessed him, he almost pitied the girl who sat there, still smiling, still making pleasant conversation. The ice already must be entering her heart. She had guessed that he was hostile. She must be choosing the weapons with which she would fence.

Far back in his mind he cast, to find some possible goal of the deception she was practicing on poor Ned Kenyon. Silver could think of none unless it was a matter of property. And what property would a man like Kenyon be apt to have? He must make inquiry about that.

Kenyon came down. They went into the dining room together. They sat at the table, and made conversation amiably until poor Kenyon fell into a silence and merely stared hungrily at the girl.

If she were embarrassed, Silver helped her at that moment, for he began to tell stories of old Mexico that soon had both of the others agape with excitement.

Afterward they went out onto the veranda to watch the moonlight that poured down into the valley, making the upper branches of the pines a luminous mist. Kenyon went to buy tobacco for his pipe. And she said to Silver, in the shadow that covered them:

"Why are you against me? Why are you hating me? Why are you getting ready to crush me in the palm of your hand?"

He merely looked down at her and said nothing. Then he drew on his cigarette to complete, in this way, the perfection of the insult, and so that by the glowing tip of the cigarette she would be able to see his face dimly lighted, and his smile.

Chapter – 4

AFTER Ned Kenyon returned, the girl remained with them only a short time. When she had excused herself and said good night, Silver was left alone with his new friend. He found Kenyon overflowing with questions. It was not that the man doubted the beauty, the grace, the wonder of the girl, but it was simply that he preferred hearing Silver reassure him, because there was no other subject in the world of half so much importance to him. It was for the moment the subject that was most on the mind of Silver, also; but he wanted silence to think the thing over. He was glad when Kenyon suggested a drink.

They went across the street diagonally into the Lone Star Saloon and found a dozen men leaning their elbows on the bar. Luck favored them in finding a vacant space at the extreme end. Silver put his back against the wall.

It was the ordinary type of saloon, the room long and narrow, with a few tables against the wall, and a strewing of sawdust on the floor.

Silver had barely taken his place when he heard a voice say:

"Is that Kenyon?"

"That's him," said another. "Wanta be introduced?"

"I don't hanker to have nobody introduce me to a skunk," said the first speaker. "I'll introduce myself with the toe of my boot. Because I'm goin' to kick some new wrinkles into his spinal column."

By this time the attention of the entire saloon was focused on the fellow. He was one of the "picturesque" Western types, with blond, saber-shaped mustache, and a lean face a little too pale to belong to an honest man in this part of the world, unless he had just risen from a sick bed. He wore the finest of shop-made boots; his shirt was of yellow silk; and above all, his revolver had a handle of shining pearl. Yet it was apparently not a tenderfoot's gun

284

worn for show, but a useful tool. The way the holster was buckled about the thigh showed that, and the low pitch of the gun, angling forward a trifle so that the butt would be conveniently ready for a whip-snap draw. If ever this fellow worked, it was fairly apparent that his business must have to do with Colt revolvers.

He was coming forward now, and Silver took heed of Kenyon as the acid test was about to be applied to him. There are few grimmer moments than that in which a man is asked to defend his personal dignity and life from the attack of an armed stranger.

Ned Kenyon turned gray with fear and shuddered, so that the heart of Silver sickened. He closed his eyes for an instant, to shut out the picture of that terror.

And this was the man that Edith Alton had said she would marry the next day?

The bartender glanced at Kenyon and then shook his head.

"What's the matter, Buck?" he asked gently. "Kenyon never makes no trouble for nobody!"

"Buck" kicked a chair out of his path. It caromed across the floor and crashed against the wall.

"That's what you say, you square-headed fool of a beer-drinking Dutchman!" cried Buck. "But I say different. And I got in mind right now to ask Mr Kenyon to up and say is he a sneaking skunk or ain't he?"

Ned Kenyon turned around slowly. Silver half expected him to bolt for the door. Instead, his voice came out thin and sharp through the nose, but with a tone steady enough.

"I don't know you, Buck," said Ned Kenyon. "And I guess you don't know me. But anyway you look at it, I'm a peaceable fellow. I don't want trouble."

"I'm askin' you," said Buck, "are you a hound, or ain't you a hound? And if you ain't a hound, how you goin' to prove that to me? Hey?"

He thrust out his head. His lips twitched back to show the yellow line of his teeth. He was cold sober, and he was doing his best to work himself into a fighting rage.

Kenyon sighed very audibly.

"Well," he said, "I take everybody to witness that I'm not hunting for a fight. I never have in my life. I never so much as pointed a gun at any man. But on the other hand, I guess I never took water, that I can recollect, and I don't aim to start taking it now."

Silver, bewildered and delighted, could hardly believe his ears. Buck, also, was so amazed that he halted for an instant. Then a swift flash of joy crossed his face. For after this speech of Kenyon's, the fight that was to be would be in the nature of a fair battle, fairly accepted—the sort of thing which too often passes as "self-defense" west of the Mississipi.

At the same time, the men along the bar who had been looking on curiously, now scattered rapidly back toward the wall, to be out of the line of a possible gun play. The bartender prepared to duck.

It was strange to see how calmly everyone took this incident. Mustang, to be sure, was "wide open"; but even if the inhabitants had not seen gun fights before, they had heard of them often enough to brace their nerves for the shock.

Ned Kenyon stood straight and stiff. The straightness pleased Silver. The stiffness told him beforehand that his friend would die.

He took Kenyon by the shoulder and gently, irresistibly, pulled him out of the way. His left elbow was leaning on the bar. He continued to lean there, at ease, with his right hand resting on his hip.

"Buck," said Silver, "if you want to talk, talk to me, will you?"

"There ain't anybody that I won't talk to," said Buck. "Who in the devil are you?"

"I'll tell you a part of what I am," said Silver. "In a way, I'm your sort of an hombre, Buck. I spend a lot of time every day practicing with my guns, just as you do. I'm an expert. I'm such an expert that I know the average fellow, who does honest work with his hands, can't possibly stand up to me. Ned Kenyon, for one instance, probably couldn't stand up to me, any more than he can stand up to you."

It was perhaps the oddest speech that was ever heard in a Western bar-room. It struck every whisper out of the air. Winter frost could not have stilled all life more completely. Only the mouth of the bartender gaped and closed again, like a fish on dry land, making its last gasp for air.

"You're goin' to put yourself in his boots, are you?" said Buck. "You're goin' to prove that he ain't a skunk? You'll have some proving to show me what you are!"

"Wait a minute, Arizona," said Ned Kenyon. "This here is mighty fine of you, but I aim to fight my own fights when they come my way."

"Take your hand away from my shoulder!" snapped Silver, sharply, so that Kenyon jumped back. "And don't speak to me again. This rat here is likely to try his teeth on me the first instant he thinks that I'm off guard. Do you hear me, Buck?"

"Hear you? Well, yes!" shouted Buck. He smote the floor with the flat of his foot and swayed forward a little. Then curses began to spill out of his mouth.

"Were you hired to do this?" asked Silver.

The cursing stopped.

"Because," said Silver, "every time you swear, it's going to be harder on you. I thought at first that I might have to pull a gun and put you to sleep, Buck. But I can see now that I won't have to go that far, because you're only cursing to keep yourself warm, and you wish, this minute, that you were out there in the street in the kind darkness."

Buck tried to laugh. "Just a big bluff and a blowhard," he cried. "And when I break him in two, you'll all see yaller!"

But no one nodded. No one smiled in sympathy with Buck's laugh. It had been too hollow and manifestly false.

"I'm going to ask you a few questions," said Silver. "If you don't answer them, I'll give you a quirting. But in the first place, I'll have to take your gun away from you. Put up your hands, Buck."

He said this so quietly, with such assurance, that the spectators gaped and craned their necks, and could hardly believe that Silver did not have his man covered.

"Why, you fool!" shouted Buck. "You think I'm crazy?"

"You don't think that," said Silver. "You know I'm right, and that I'll do what I say. You know that I'm a faster hand and a surer shot than you are, Buck. And your poor little soul is shrinking and dying in you. There's a sort of pity that grows up in me when I see you turn white around the mouth, as you're doing now. And a disgust when I see your eyes begin to roll."

He stood straight, and commanded in a harsher voice.

"Put up your hands!"

It was a frightful thing to see that armed man, that gun fighter, that slayer of men—Buck—standing wavering as though a whole regiment of soldiers had drawn a bead on him. But all that threatened him was the empty hand and the pointing finger of Silver.

"You hear me?" said Silver, and took a half step forward.

A queer, bubbling sound broke out of the throat of Buck. His mouth yawned. His lips started to frame words, and could make only a hideous gibberish.

And before the eyes of the crowd the miracle happened, and his hands started to rise from the level of his pearl-handled revolver to his hips—would he try to whip out some hidden weapon, then?—and so on to his breast, and up to his shoulders, where they fluttered for an instant in feeble revolt, but then continued until they were above the top of his head.

The sickening thing was not finished. Silver stepped forward and pulled the pearl-handled gun out of its sheath, and as he drew it, a great groan of despair came from Buck. He had allowed an act of shame to be performed on him that would make him a very legendary figure of shame, a horror of which no man would gladly speak.

Yet all of those men who watched with pale, fascinated eyes, stared less at Buck in his disgrace than at the terrible face of Silvertip as he pulled that gun out, and then laid it on the bar. And more than one man wondered, if the face of Silver were before him, if he would have had the nerve to do anything other than Buck had done.

Hypnotism was what it seemed like. No man exchanged glances with his neighbor. Each man hoped that his own horror was not being observed, and each knew that the coldness of his skin meant a definite pallor.

"You can get the gun afterward," said Silver. "I'm not going to take it and keep it. And I'm not going to harm you in any way, Buck, so long as you tell me, frankly, the name of the man who hired you for this job. You were hired, I take it?"

The jaw of Buck dropped. He gasped, "Yes! Hired! Oh—yes, I was—"

One long breath was drawn by all the men in that room. The bartender stood straight for the first time since Silver had begun speaking.

"Who hired you?" demanded Silver.

"Who? A gent by the name of Alec Wilson."

"You lie!" said Silver. "Kenyon, get me your quirt, will you?"

"Not Wilson!" groaned Buck. "What I meant was, the gent that hired me was really—"

There was an open window at the side of the room. A gun glinted beyond the sill, now, and the explosion of the shot tossed the mouth of the revolver a little up into the air.

The head of Buck dropped over on his shoulder. He slumped into the arms of Silver, slipped out of them, and spilled onto the floor.

Chapter – 5

SILVER went out of that room like a cat after a bird, but as he turned the front corner of the building he heard the rapid beating of hoofs begin behind the saloon, and knew that the quarry was on the wing.

Oh, for five minutes of Parade, then to loose the golden stallion like an arrow at the mark—or for any horse, for that matter. But there were none except down the street, at the hitch rack on the farther side of the hotel, and that was too far away.

He went gloomily back into the saloon. Half the men had scattered to look for the murderer; half had remained to look at the victim.

He was dying, beyond doubt. The bullet had cut straight through his lungs, and Buck was already in his death agony. He kept rising on one hand, and turning his swollen face and his terrible, starting eyes from one man to another, mutely asking help.

But there was no help to be given. The finest doctor in the world could not assist, though messengers had gone to fetch all the physicians in Mustang. Buck himself seemed to realize that there were only seconds to him. Then he tried to speak, and that was the worst of all.

Silver, the indirect cause of his death, was the man he wanted most to talk to. He came clawing across the floor and reached up and caught Silver's hand in his. He tried to speak, but only a rapid succession of red bubbles burst on his lips. He was strangling. He was biting at the air, and getting none down to his lungs.

Others drew back from that sight of agony, but Silver slipped to the floor and sat by the struggling body.

"Write it, Buck!" he called loudly. "Write it on the floor! Write the name, and I swear that I'll try to get him for you!"

Buck was beating on the floor with his feet and hands, in the last struggle between death and life, but he understood Silver. He flopped heavily over on his side, dipped his right forefinger into the thick pool of his own blood, and commenced to write. Then death caught back his red-stained hand and turned him on his back. He seemed to be making a last effort to speak as he died. One long shudder ran through his body, and he was gone.

On the floor beside him was written: "Nel—" followed by the sweeping stroke of crimson where his finger had been snatched from the writing.

Silver folded the hands of the dead man across his breast and closed the half-open eyes. When he looked up, he saw that men were standing by with their hats in their hands, and with sick faces.

He stood up and took off his own hat.

"Does anybody here know a woman named Nell, or a man named Nelson?" he asked.

"There's a woman that does laundry," said the bartender, instantly.

Silver shook his head.

"There's Digger Nelson, the prospector," said another in the room.

"What sort of a man?" asked Silver.

"A regular rock chipper. He patches the seat of his pants with flour sacks and—"

"No!" said Silver. "He's not the man I want. He's not the man who hired Buck to pick a fight with Ned Kenyon, and shoot it out. He's not that sort."

The first of the doctors came hurrying in. The sheriff was just at his heels. Silver took Ned Kenyon by the arm and led him out of the bar-room into a back room, closing the door behind them. They sat down at a table.

Mustang was now well awakened. Scores of footfalls were padding up the street, or pounding loudly over the board sidewalks. Horses snorted in the distance under the spur. Voices were gathering toward the saloon like buzzing bees toward the hive. Presently the sheriff would be sure to want both Silver and Kenyon, but Silver used this interim to pump Kenyon as well as he could.

"Ned," he said, "do you know what to make of all this?"

"I'm flabbergasted," said poor Kenyon. "I can't make head or tail of it. But it looks as though you know the inside workings of everything!"

"I wish I did! I'm only guessing. I'm reaching into the dark and getting at nothing. That's all! Nothing! Ned, listen to me!"

"The way I would to a preacher," said Kenyon, with a naïveté that made Silver faintly smile.

"What does this fellow Buck hitch with?"

"I don't make that out, either. I never saw him before. I don't suppose that he ever saw me. He says that he was hired—"

Into this stream of meaningless words Silver broke sharply.

"What's the thing we can catch on?" he asked. "There's something you have, or that you're about to have, that other people want—or want to keep you from. Now tell me out and out—have you anything worth money?"

"Not even a horse," said the stage driver sadly. "Not even Jerry, now!"

"You have some land, somewhere," suggested Silver.

"Father has a patch—a quarter section. That's all there is in the family."

"Where? In the mountains? Some place where pay dirt may be found? Gravel, for instance? Near an old creek bed, perhaps?"

"Pay dirt? The clay runs down about a thousand feet. The old man works that ground about sixteen hours a day, and he hardly makes a dollar a day, clear. I never saw worse clay. We've dug wells. We know how far that clay goes down."

"Wait a moment," said Silver, violently readjusting the course of his suspicion. "There's another chance. You've been around the world a good deal, partner. And you're sure to know a good lot. You've looked in on some queer things in your time. You've seen men in odd positions. You have up your sleeve something that someone would be pretty glad to hush up. Think, now. It must be that!"

Kenyon thought. After his fashion, he took his time, fixing his eyes on distance, and thoroughly combing his memory. At last he said: "No. There's nothing that I can put a finger on."

"There must be," insisted Silver. "There has to be something! Think again."

"No, Arizona—or Jim, if I can call you that—there's nothing. Nothing ever happens to me—or nothing ever did happen until—"

"All right," said Silver. "That brings us back to Edith Alton, as far as I can see. You're going to marry her tomorrow morning. And someone hates the idea of that. Somebody wants to stop you. Somebody with a first or a last name beginning with Nel. Who could it be?"

Again Kenyon shook his head. "I don't know. It beats me."

"It beats you? It'll kill you before you're many days older!" said Silver. "Man, man, are you sure that you don't know anyone whose name begins with those three letters?"

"Well, Jim," said Kenyon, "don't be mad at me. I'm trying to think, but there are not many people whose name begins with those letters."

"No," said Silver. "There are not many. That's good point in the deal. It'll narrow down the hunting field."

"You look like a hunter," said Kenyon, rather overawed. "But by the jumping thunder, Jim, I'd hate to have you on my trail with that look in your eye and with that set to your jaw!"

"I'm not on your trail. I'm on the trail of murder," said Silver. "I can smell the murder inside my nostrils. I can taste it against the roof of my mouth. Murder—phaugh!"

The door opened. There stood on the threshold a man with a stocky body and a long, triangular face.

"Murder is what we been talking about, in there," he said. "Maybe I can talk to you two boys in here about the same thing."

Others were about to follow this stranger inside the room, but he closed the door in their faces, and they did not try to open it behind his back.

He came across the floor, opening his coat to show the badge that was pinned inside it.

"Name of Philips," he said. "Or maybe you'll introduce me, Ned?"

Kenyon started up and sawed the air with his hand, embarrassed.

"This here is Sheriff Philips. Bert Philips," he said. "And this is a friend of mine that's got into a lot of trouble on my account, this day. He's Arizona Jim, sheriff. And he—"

He paused. The inadequacy of that nickname seemed to fill the throat of Kenyon, at the moment that he spoke to the man of the law.

"Glad to know you, Arizona," said the sheriff. "Ned, who killed Buck?"

"I don't know. I wish—"

"Ever had a grudge between you?"

"Never. I never saw him before he—"

"Ned, you walk out and buy yourself a drink. I want to talk with Arizona."

Ned Kenyon went out hesitantly, as one who feels that he may be deserting a friend in a time of need, but the calm smile of Silver reassured him until the door was opened and closed again.

Then the sheriff pulled out a chair and sat down opposite Silver. He said: "You know what I've got on my knee?"

"Yes," said Silver. "A gun."

"Does that mean anything to you?"

"It means that you're rather young," said Silver.

The sheriff frowned. Then, suddenly, he grinned.

"You're all they say about you—Silver," he said.

Silver said nothing at his identification by the man of the law.

"A dead cool one," continued the sheriff. "Now, you tell me who killed Buck."

Silver smiled.

"Go on!" urged the sheriff.

"Otherwise you'll shoot?"

Suddenly Philips raised the gun into view and shoved it back inside his coat.

"Maybe I've been a fool," he said. "I thought for a minute that I'd call your bluff. But now I almost think you mean what you've been saying. That right?"

"It is."

"You're Kenyon's friend?"

"Yes."

"Do you make anything out of this mess, then?"

"Only guesses."

"Let's have them, Silver. I don't know just how to take you. There's some call you a crook and a man-killer, and others say that you're the whitest man on earth. Anyway, you have brains, and you've been a friend to poor Ned Kenyon. Now, tell me everything you think."

"I think," said Silver, "that some one wants to stop a thing that's due to happen to Kenyon tomorrow."

"What?"

"I can't tell you. I've promised Kenyon not to tell."

"Stop him by killing him?"

"Gladly, if there's no other way."

"Silver, how much do you know?"

"Hardly more than a baby."

The sheriff laid hold of his chin with a big brown hand and gripped hard, staring over his knuckles at the face of Silver.

"It's hard," he said, "but I'm going to believe you. I want to know this: Are you working with me?"

"With all my might!"

"Good!" said the sheriff. "And if you have an idea, you can call on me night or day."

"I'll have an idea before the end of tomorrow," said Silver. "And then I may call on you to blow up half this town!"

Chapter – 6

SILVER went to his room, dipped a towel in cold water, tied it around his head, and waited for the whisky fumes to disappear. He had had only two drinks, but he felt that they were too many. He sat in the darkness, without a lamp, watching the moonlight inch its way across the floor, reach the feet of a chair, and crawl up the varnished legs.

But still he could find no answer to the questions which were whirling in his mind.

He took off his boots, left his room, and went down the stairs. The outer doors were all locked. He opened a window, got onto the veranda, and stole down it until he stepped onto the pine needles beneath the grove beside the building. There he sat with his back to a tree, not even smoking, and watched the moonlight shine on the windows of the house as on pools of black water.

The moon grew dim. Its shadows no longer made a pattern of jet and white on the ground. The dawn came, with a chill that started his flesh quaking, and then he heard the loud rattling of iron on iron, as some one began to work at the kitchen stove. Immediately afterwards, a door in the back of the hotel groaned faintly.

Silver got up, and walked behind the trees until he could see the small form of a woman hurrying toward the barn. He knew her by the walk—the girl who was to marry Ned Kenyon before noon of this day.

He rounded to the back of the stable. Two seconds after she led out the black mare he was on Parade. He was saddling as she turned down the main street of Mustang, and he was able to note the direction. A half minute later he was riding west, also, but keeping behind the most outlying houses of the town. In that way, he rounded into the head of the valley in time to see the rose of the morning bloom on all the snow-clad peaks of the distance.

A solitaire was singing as though the beauty of the dawn had filled its heart. And in the distance he saw the black horse slide into the shadows of a big grove of pines.

He followed only a short distance up the valley, for he was reasonably sure, for a definite reason, that she would ride up the same trail by which he had seen her descend the evening before. Kenyon had told him that she loved to ride out by herself—generally toward the west. That was her favorite, the zigzag trail down the western hills, Kenyon had remarked.

But it would be very odd if she preferred that trail to others that were ten times more beautiful. And if she was, as Kenyon said, merely a girl tenderfoot trying to see the west for herself unimpeded by too much chaperonage, it would have been more natural for her to take all of the trails, one by one. Some singular attraction had kept her until deep into the evening of the day before among those western hills. Perhaps the same thing—not the beauty of the morning—was taking her out there before the day had well begun.

Silver rode up the slope to the left of him to the water divide above. The black mare was fast, but she could not keep pace with the cat feet and the winged stride of the golden stallion. Parade was well over the ridge and coming through a group of trees, when Silver saw the girl swinging her horse at an angle across his line. And he sighed with content. He was on the right trail. And if she were ten thousand times more beautiful than she was, he would find her share in the mystery and lay it bare.

So he shadowed her, moving Parade with care from one covert to another, half guessing the probable course of the girl a dozen times, and always hitting it correctly.

She dipped into a narrow ravine, at last, and Silver had to halt his horse on the brink of the steep ground, then rein it well back to wait for the black mare to climb out up the farther bank.

He waited a sufficient time, until a pinch of suspicion stirred him. So he dismounted, put Parade in a clump of tall brush, gave him the word that would tether him in place more strongly than ropes, and went forward on foot to investigate.

He had to lie flat and peer over the rim of the canyon, before he could see what he wanted. But the sight was reward, and a rich one. For in a clearing among the trees in the middle of the ravine he saw the girl walking up and down with a young man in a gray felt hat with a brim foolishly narrow for Western weather, and with a quick step, and nervous gestures. That was all that Silver could make out.

The stranger seemed to be pouring out a tirade, to which the girl listened most of the time with a bent head. She seemed then to be making gestures of denial, and at this he fell into an attitude of earnest argument and persuasion, until the very ears of Silver ached to hear the words.

Whatever they were, they were sufficient. Presently she was nodding in agreement, and then she was putting her head up in its characteristic fearless poise, as though she were ready to outface the world.

A few minutes later, the two disappeared under the trees, and then the black mare mounted the farther slope and tipped out over the rim of it beyond his view.

There remained the fellow in the ravine. Silver worked down the sharp slope toward him, moving more like a snake than a man. It was hard to make that descent with any surety that he was unseen, for a dozen times he was without real cover. He was perhaps twenty steps from the bottom of the valley when a rifle clanged, a bullet spat against the ground beside his face, and he had to dive into the shrubbery before him as into water.

He was worming his way through that cover, with his revolver in his hand, when he heard the rapid thudding of hoofs that ranged up the ravine, and knew his quarry had taken to flight.

Gloomily he went on until he came to a small clearing in which a mere dog tent was pitched. There was a heap of empty cans, at one side. There was a rudely put together fireplace built of stones. And under the cover of the tent he saw a bed made down, the blankets rumpled, together with a book or two and a few magazines.

Silver went around the camp with a furtive step. This camper had been on the spot for a week, at least. He was not used to a life in the open, or he would have built his fireplace better. He was no fisherman, for he would have worn a trail along the side of the little brook, and particularly down to the edge of the broad, still pool not far away. He was, in fact, nothing but a tenderfoot.

Silver sat down on a stump and smoked a cigarette. He had plenty of facts, and he could make a few deductions.

The girl who was betrothed to Kenyon came to this place daily, so it seemed, in order to talk with a light-stepping, active young man who apparently was able to persuade her against her will on matters of importance. This young gentleman, instead of going to the hotel in the town, preferred to live in the wilderness, though he had neither talent nor apparent liking for that life—for no one who liked it could have put up with the arrangements of that camp. In addition to these things, there was the further fact that the stranger actually had tried with his rifle for the life of a man who was stealing upon his camp!

The component parts made the picture of one who could not be other than a criminal, it seemed to Silver. And if he were, it was a fact that threw keen light upon the character of the girl.

But with this much gained, Silver had to return to Mustang. He went back to Parade, and took a leisurely way to the town, his mind crammed with thought every inch of the way. In the stable behind the hotel, he put up the stallion and paused to look over the mare. She had been taken flying home. She still was head down, panting hard, and the sweat was still running on her sleek body. It was apparent that the girl had wished to be away from the hotel for as short a time as possible.

Silver went up to his room, undressed, slipped into his bed, turned on his face, and slept soundly for two hours. Then the striking of the breakfast gong roused him.

A wash in cold water wakened him thoroughly. He dressed, and went down the stairs humming softly, and into the dining room, where the girl and Ned Kenyon were already having bacon and eggs, with a sooty pot of coffee beside them, for service in that hotel was not of the most polite.

"A good night, Arizona?" asked the girl cheerfully.

"One of the best," said Silver. "Did you sleep right through?"

"Like the dead!" said she, and smiled at him.

It was a good, direct smile, with open eyes that met his, easily. He wanted to say to her: "You lie well. I know the types of liars, and you're one of the best!"

Yet, as he sat there with them, as he heard the softness of her voice, as he watched the clear beauty of her face, he found himself saying, against his better judgment, that she must be all right. It would be an irony, a sarcasm of nature, if she were other than honest and true.

Poor Ned Kenyon, who dwelt on her with his eyes, who devoured her every gesture, every word from her throat—what would he say if he knew of that visitation to the stranger over the hills?

Silver had a chance to find out, a few moments later, when the girl finished and excused herself from the table. As she rose from her place, her glance lingered for one serious, penetrating instant on the face of Silver. Then she went out hastily, as though not trusting the words that she was tempted to speak.

Afterward, Silver said, to the rapt face of Ned Kenyon: "You love her, son."

"More'n breath," said Kenyon simply.

"If she turned out to be a counterfeit would that stop you?"

Kenyon did not smile. He merely looked out the window for a moment, as though to contemplate the immensity of that suggestion in a calm seriousness.

Then he said: "You're a swimmer, Jim?"

"Yes," said Silver.

"You know what it means," said Kenyon, "to fetch under water for a long distance?"

Silver nodded.

"And the way your lungs burn—and all? Well, suppose that you came up to the surface and there was no air to breathe! And it's that way with me. It ain't what is right or wrong about her, any more. It's just that I couldn't live without her in every day of my life either having her, being with her, knowing all the time that she belongs to me. You see?"

"I see," said Silver.

"Murder," said Kenyon quietly, "not even if she'd done murder, it wouldn't stop me. It'd matter, but it'd matter as though I'd done it myself. That's all. But what was in your mind, partner?"

"Well, I was just thinking, was all," said Silver. "I simply wanted to know how you felt."

"In a couple of hours," murmured Kenyon, "there's a new life waiting for me. I'm not thinking about that. I don't dare. It's like thinking of walking on water, or walking on blue air. But you'll be there, Jim. You'll be there to steady me. That's what I'm counting on."

Silver got out of the room like a blind man, fumbling. For he knew that to tell his friend of what he had seen this morning would be like pouring acid on a man already incurably ill. He could not speak!

Chapter – 7

THE church was a little frame box with a steeple tacked onto one side of it, like a forefinger lifted above a fist. The preacher was a good, hardworking man who covered all parts of his parish both winter and summer, climbing among ice-clad rocks in winter to places that no horse or mule could ever reach. Only a small percentage of Mustang attended his Sunday services, but there was not a man in the district who would not have fought for the sky pilot.

Silver looked on him with wonder. He was regarding all things with astonishment, at that moment, for he could not believe that Kenyon and the girl were actually standing in front of the man of God, about to be joined in wedlock. The hotel proprietor was one witness. The keeper of the general merchandise store was the other. As for Silver, he had dodged the duty. In case he served, his real name would have to be written down, and that name he preferred to keep unknown.

He stood in the back of the empty little church, acutely aware of the four windows that looked in on the scene, and prepared any instant to see the gleam of a gun outside the glass, for if they had killed one man in the cause of preventing the marriage, did it not stand to reason that they would kill another?

So, with a sense of the two revolvers that hung beneath his armpits, Silver waited, and watched, and was all eyes rather than ears. Yet he could hear the responses, too, and he could be aware of the surprised face which the minister kept continually turning toward Kenyon. Even that unworldly man could see the absurdity of such a match.

All had been done quietly. Not a soul in the village knew of what was to take place. That was the reason why the church was not crowded.

He heard the preacher saying: "You promise to love, honour and obey—"

Silver saw the girl turn her head suddenly, and flash her eyes at Kenyon before she answered in a forced, barely audible voice: "I do."

"Poor Kenyon!"

It was over, suddenly. In turn, the witnesses bent to sign the little book. The preacher was shaking hands with the bride and groom. And out of a few spoken words there had been established a bond which should last until death. But would it last for even a day?

Silver watched them come down the aisle. Kenyon was a man walking above the surface of this earth. The girl was pale, with a frozen smile. A careless eye might have put her pallor down to mere timidity, but Silver saw, or felt he saw, that it was an agony of the mind that moved her.

Silver himself avoided shaking hands with them, first by opening the door for them, then by saying that he would hurry to the hotel, and see that the buckboard was ready. For the plan of Kenyon was to take her at once out of Mustang, and then over the green plains and up to the little town where his mother and father lived. It would be a simple honeymoon, but it was all that his purse could afford.

At the hotel, Silver harnessed the span of mustangs which Kenyon had bought to the small buckboard. He heaped in the baggage behind the seat, while Kenyon came out of the hotel to help where he could. But his hands were helpless, and his small eyes were continually lifting to the sky, and being dazzled until they filled with moisture.

The girl would be down in a moment from her room, Kenyon said.

But she did not come for five minutes, for ten minutes, for half an hour.

"Women have always got fixings to go through," said Kenyon. "It don't matter, I'd rather wait for her here than dance with anybody else while a band was playin'."

Silver said abruptly: "Perhaps I can help her about something."

"No. Leave her be. Let her take her time," said Kenyon.

But Silver was already through the door of the hotel. Once out of sight, he moved fast, up the stairs, and to the door of the girl's room. He knocked. There was no answer. He pushed the door open, and no sign of Edith Alton was inside. Only a wraith of white smoke hung in the air above the little round-bellied stove that stood in a corner. And on the table was an envelope, sealed, and addressed in her handwriting to Edward Kenyon.

Silver went down to the back of the hotel and found the cook.

"See Miss Alton go out toward the barn?" he asked.

"Half an hour ago she rode her black mare out of the barn and went up the valley," said the cook. "She was traveling fast, too, like she wanted to catch a train."

Silver came through the hotel to Kenyon and took him by the arm.

"Ned," he said crisply. "You've got bad news. She's left you."

Kenyon straightened. It reminded Silver of how the man had stood the night before, in the saloon—straight, ready to meet his fate, but unable to struggle against it.

"She's left a letter for you upstairs," said Silver. "That may do a little explaining. I'll wait for you down here."

The stone-gray lips of Kenyon parted stiffly. He put a hand on the shoulder of his friend.

"If you wouldn't mind, Jim," said he, "if it wouldn't be wrong for me to ask, I'd like to have you come up there with me."

That was why Silver climbed the stairs again, suddenly feeling old and weak.

Yet there would be a sufficient strength in him, he thought, if he could lay his eyes on the girl, or on that fellow in the hills, who moved with that alert and springing step.

It seemed to Silver now that he had done everything wrong. He should have spoken his suspicions to Kenyon at once. At least he should have demanded from the girl an explanation of her morning visit to that rifleman in the hills—that young fellow who was so ready to try his hand at murder!

But now there was a ruin, and it was entirely in the life and the heart of poor Ned Kenyon.

When they got into the room, Kenyon paused a moment at the door, and took off his hat, breathing deeply.

"Kind of fragrant, Jim, ain't it?" said he. "I mean the air. Kind of like her. Like flowers, eh?"

He actually smiled at Silver, to invite his agreement. But Silver, jerking his hat a little lower on his head, stalked to the window and looked down to the ruts in the dusty street, and across the roofs of the houses, above which the heat waves were shimmering and dancing. He could have drunk hot blood.

He looked sideways, curiously, at the stove, above which the wraith of smoke was dissolving. In winter weather in Mustang there would be plenty of need for stoves, but hardly at this time of the year. He opened the door. On the fire grate there was a ball of gray-and-white fluff, the ashes of small bits of paper which had been wadded together. Now the draft took hold of them and blew them dissolving up the chimney.

He opened the lower door to the ash pan and pulled the pan out. As he had expected, several of the small bits of paper had dropped through. He picked them up. It was contemptible to read them, but the girl was no longer fit to be treated as a decent human being. She was a criminal, and she had committed her crime in the most detestable fashion, against the most helpless of men.

So he stared at the few words which he found. Several of the scraps were covered with words written in the more smoothly flowing and smaller hand of a man. None were in her own writing. But of them all there was only one out of which he could make any sense. It contained the words:

"out fail in Kirby Cr"

That could be pieced out a little. "Without fail in Kirby Creek," was perhaps the true sense of it. Suppose one went back a little and filled in: "Meet without fail in Kirby Creek."

If that referred to the past, it was nothing. If it referred to the future, it might be everything.

"Maybe you better read it," said Kenyon. He was holding out a letter toward Silver. Then he drew back his hand, murmuring: "I dunno, Silver. Seems to me maybe it wouldn't be fair to her, hardly, if I was to show her letter to another man?"

"Fair to—her?" asked Silver hoarsely.

"Ah, but don't be too hard on her," said Kenyon. "She ain't very old, Jim. And she ain't very used to the world, and you'll see that the world's been hard on her, poor girl."

"Well," said Silver, in a voice of iron, "do you want me to read the letter, or not?"

"Not if you talk like that," said Kenyon, drawing back his hand.

Silver laughed, in a sort of despair.

"Give me the letter," he said. "I need to read it. I have to read it."

"Well," said Kenyon, "I don't think that she'd mind. Only this morning she said to me that I must always stick to you, because there was no other friend that I'd find like you, in the whole world."

"Did she say that?" asked Silver sharply.

"She did, and she had her heart in her voice, and a kind of a pity and a kindness for me in her eyes. Jim. So I guess she wouldn't mind you seeing what she wrote to me. Here it is."

Silver, taking the letter, for a moment could not look at it. His mental preoccupation was too great, as he pondered over what the girl had said. For she could not have been in doubt that he was her enemy, heartily and forever.

He went back to the window and saw, first of all, pinned to the top sheet of the letter, a check made out to Edward Kenyon for ten thousand dollars and signed Edith Alton Kenyon.

Ten thousand dollars!

Some of his walls of reservations were knocked flat as he saw the sum. If she had done Kenyon harm, she had intended to do him good, also.

The letter ran:

Dear Ned: Tomorrow I expect that we shall be married, unless your friend Arizona Jim finds a way to prevent the ceremony; because he loves you, Ned, and he guessed from the first moment when he saw me that I was not honest.

And I'm not. If you're reading this letter, it is because I have married you, and left you, and this is the farewell message.

I suppose that it's human nature to wish to defend ourselves. That's why I'm going to say that I don't think another woman in the world could have stood out against the terrible necessity that was pressing on me. It was a question of life or death. Not my life or death, but that of another person, infinitely of more importance to the world than I am.

I can't even explain farther than this. I only knew that I had to be married, at once. I knew that I had to be married to a kind and honest man who might never forgive me for having wronged him, but who would not pursue me.

That was why I knew I had found someone who could be of help to me when I found you. I thought of even telling you what I wanted and of asking you to marry me, and then forget me, and divorce me. But I couldn't risk that You might say no, and then there would be no time to find another man. I had to talk with you, persuade you into asking me to marry you, and then go through with the ceremony.

Then it seemed to me that you were really growing fond of me. And my heart ached to think of it. But I've rushed through with everything, hoping that God would understand that I meant what is right, even if kind, honest, gentle Ned Kenyon would not be able to understand, ever.

I'm leaving a check with you. It isn't hush money. It's simply that I want with all my heart to help you to the thing you wish to have—a small ranch and a chance to lead your chosen life. I would make it five or ten times as much, but I know that you would never take the money.

Forgive me, forgive me.

EDITH.

Chapter – 8

SILVER, as he finished the second reading of that letter, ground his teeth together in a helpless rage. There was a certain ring of honesty to the words. But he would believe nothing. Her troubles were unknown, distant. The grief of Ned Kenyon was a present and immediate thing. Behind her there was certainly a power of wealth. Ten thousand dollars —which she could have made fifty thousand, she said, if she had dreamed that Ned Kenyon would accept it! It argued piled treasures somewhere in her background.

He gave back the letter to Kenyon.

"What do you think, Jim?" asked Kenyon.

"I think," said Silver, "that you're the straightest fellow I ever met. I think, Ned, that I could cut her heart out, and enjoy the job. As for the letter—man, it's easy to write words! Dead easy, I tell you!"

"You won't believe that she's honest?" asked Kenyon.

"Never in the world," said Silver. "She knew that you loved her. A woman can never go wrong about that. And still she went ahead."

"There was a matter of life or death," argued Kenyon.

"Bah!" said Silver. "You'd believe that a frog croaks in a marsh!"

Kenyon shook his head, picked up the letter, detached the check, and put the letter itself into his pocket. The check he tore into small pieces, and threw into the stove.

"She knew you'd do that, too," said Silver bitterly. "She knew that you'd never take the dirty money. Ah, Ned, you're going with me to find her, if we have to travel around the world. You understand? I'm staying with you until we find her, if it takes the rest of my life!"

"Follow her?" said Kenyon, with a look of mild surprise. "No, no, Jim. I can't follow her. She doesn't want me, and I can't bother her. I can't go after her."

"Are you going to sit down and take your licking—from a pretty little female crook?" demanded Silver.

Kenyon turned slowly toward him.

"You're bigger, stronger, and faster than I am, Jim. But if I ever hear you say a word against her again, I'm going to try to knock your head off! I'm sorry to say that, but it's what I mean."

Silver groaned. "What are you going to do, then?" he asked.

"I don't know," said Kenyon. "Back to driving the stage, I guess, and take up where I left off. The boys will guy me a little, when this marriage is known. But I come from the part of the world where they grow good hickory, Jim!"

He smiled, as he said this, and tears suddenly stung the eyes of Silver.

He took the hand of Kenyon and gripped it hard.

"You're a better sort than I am," said Silver. "I'm getting out of Mustang. One of these days I'll see you again. I'm going on a trip and—so long, old-timer!"

He walked out of the room quickly. When he reached the head of the stairs, he could hear the voice of Kenyon calling after him, but he ran down rapidly. His trail was outward. There were many things to fill his mind, from that man who had hired Buck, whose name began with "Nel," to that light-stepping friend of the girl, and there was the girl herself, and that matter of life and death about which she was so wrought up.

He paid his bill, went out to the stable, and saddled Parade. He was outside the barn before he heard the voice of Kenyon raised high in the distance, calling: "Arizona! Oh, Arizona!" But he put Parade into a hard gallop.

He cut back into the main street of the village, after a short distance, and stopped in front of the blacksmith shop to make his inquiry, for blacksmiths, next to bartenders, know more news than anyone else in the West.

The blacksmith came out, busily tying a bandage about a bleeding finger.

"Where's Kirby Creek?" asked Silver.

"Kirby Creek?" said the blacksmith. "Never heard of it."

"There's a place of that name," said Silver.

"Kirby Creek? Never heard of it."

"Anything else that sounds like Kirby Cr—"

The blacksmith grunted with the profundity of his mental effort. Then he said: "There's Kirby Crossing, if that's what you want to know."

"I do want to know," said Silver. "Where is it?"

"Fifty mile back into the hills. Yeah, right back into the mountains. You take the northwest road. You follow along it for twenty mile, and then you come to a trail that branches off to the left and—"

Silver listened to the directions carefully. He repeated them after his informer and was pronounced letter-perfect. After that, he would never forget. The words would stick like glue in his memory.

So he took the northwest road, keeping Parade along the edge of it where there was no dust and the footing was therefore firmer. Gradually the hills rolled up about him in greater and greater dimensions. He was climbing into the mountains when a rider with a pack mule tethered to the pommel of his saddle came down a cross trail toward the main way on which Silver was traveling.

He was a very big man, with a shag of beard covering his face almost to the eyes. And one of those eyes was covered with a great black leather patch. The size of that horseman made the mustang he rode look hardly bigger than a goat.

Silver, seeing that he was noticed, drew rein, and waited. He had reason to wait, he felt, unless he wanted a bullet through his back, for he had recognized "One-eyed Harry" Bench, from whom, not so very long before, he had taken two good riding horses by dint of not so much of the cash he paid down for them as of a bullet through the soft of One-eyed Harrys' shoulder.

So Silver waited at the crossing, in doubt.

Those doubts were scattered in a moment, as big Harry Bench let out a whoop and spurred his mustang to a canter, the mule dangling back grimly on the end of the lead rope. Pulling his tough pony to a halt, One-eyed Harry reached far forward and caught the good right hand of Silver in a grip that threatened to break bones.

"Silver!" he shouted. "Curse me black and white if I ever thought I'd lay an eye on you ag'in. How come, you old rattler, that you're in this part of the range? I thought you was away far north, or away far south. What brings you around here?"

"Just drifting, Harry; just drifting. How are things with you?"

"Better'n ever before," said Harry Bench. "The grouch I had at the world was all let out with the blood that run when you slid that chunk of lead through me, Silver. I done some hating of you, for a spell. But when the news got around to me, and I found out that it was Jim Silver himself that had nicked me—why, there ain't no shame in being put down by Silver himself, is there? Not to my way of thinkin'. The day has been, since then, that gents have seen me stripped and wanted to know where I got the scar on the shoulder, and when they hear that it was a bullet out of Silver's gun, I get a considerable pile of attention, Jim. And the boys, they most generally tell me that I'm lucky not to be wearin' that scar right through the heart, and make no mistake about it. Where are you bound?"

He poured out the words in a hearty torrent, and in a thundering voice that plainly had been rarely confined to the echoing walls of a room.

"I'm bound for Kirby Crossing," said Silver.

"Kirby Crossing?" exclaimed the giant. "And what would a gent of your size be doing in a place like Kirby Crossing, I'd like to know?"

"I'm a lot smaller than you are, Harry," said Silver.

"Across the shoulder, maybe, but not across the brain," said the big man cheerfully. "It would sprain Kirby Crossing in the small of the back and both ankles, to have a gent of your size of name inside of it, man!"

"I'm not wearing the same name," answered Silver. "I'm a Mexican, when I go in there."

"Hold on!" cried One-eyed Harry. "You mean that you're a bare-footed greaser in rags, like you were when I first seen you, Silver?"

"That's it. Something like that."

Harry grinned. "What's the little game in the wind now?" he asked.

"Would you help me?" asked Silver curiously.

"Me? And why not? Sure I'd help you. And how?"

"By being my boss," said Silver, "and letting me drive that mule into town for you, as though it were my job."

The mirth of One-eyed Harry thundered through the air like a roaring cataract in a narrow valley. "Me with a servant?" he said. "Me with Silver for a servant? And why not? But hold on, Jim Silver!"

"Well?" said Silver.

"There's another way of lookin' at these things. What kind of hurricane are you goin' to raise when you get into Kirby Crossing? And after you raise it, how you goin' to ride it? Have I gotta sit on top of the same kind of a wind that you like?"

Silver smiled. "I don't know what's ahead of me," he declared.

"Something like Barry Christian and his thugs?" asked One-eyed Harry.

"I hope not."

"No," said the big man, "it ain't likely that you'll ever crash into anything as tough as Barry Christian, if you live to be a thousand. They ain't hung Barry yet. You know that?"

The face of Silver darkened. "I know that," he agreed.

"And it doesn't seem likely to me," added One-eyed Harry Bench, "that they ever will hang him, because it don't seem likely that the rope was ever braided or wove that'll hang a neck like his. But about the things you're after in Kirby Crossing—tell me, Jim Silver—ain't it a blood trail?"

"Why do you ask that?" said Silver, frowning.

"Because," answered Bench, "I've heard more'n one gent say that you never ride on no trail at all unless it's a blood trail? Is that true?"

"I hope not," answered Silver. "I hope I'm not such a devil as that, Harry."

"Well," answered Bench, "there's a good many men have seen you at work here and there, and they all say that they never hear of a trail of yours that wasn't spotted with red before the end of it. Is there a killing in your mind, in Kirby Crossing?"

"There is!" said Silver, suddenly and grimly. "And you can count yourself out of the party, Harry. It may be more than you'll want to swallow."

"A mean gent that you're after?" said Bench wistfully.

"A man whose face I wouldn't know," said Silver.

"Not know," cried Bench. He groaned with curiosity. Then he exclaimed: "Ah, well, I can't live forever. I'm goin' to be a fool for once more in my life. Count me in, Jim. I'll stay as long as I can!"

Chapter – 9

THEY expected to get into the town that night, but when they reached the place they found that Kirby Crossing was no crossing at all, for the bridge had gone down in the flood that was still roaring through the ravine. Disappointed teamsters were piling up on the two sides of the stream, waiting until the bridge could be built again, and helping earnestly in its construction. It would be another week before the flimsy structure could span the creek, though the big stone foundation for the central pier was still in place and undamaged, and though the biggest trees were being felled and dragged down to build the under-structure of the bridge.

The only other way of getting over Kirby Creek was to go nearly another fifty miles up Kirby Run, and then come down it on the farther side of the stream, after reaching the ford. However, that ford was only practical for men and horses, and active men and horses at that.

Silver and big One-eyed Harry camped for the night opposite the little mining town, and then went upstream the next morning. It was nearly sunset of the third day before they got into the place. A strange outfit they were, and no one had a glance for anything other than One-eyed Harry. His picturesqueness took all glances away from the big-shouldered, long-shanked Mexican who trotted along bareheaded, a mop of shaggy black hair falling down over his forehead, as he led on a shambling mule and a chestnut stallion that looked fit for riding, but which carried nothing but a big pack saddle.

The big horse had the legs and the look of speed, if one cared to examine closely; but it was covered with dust and had a very sad limp in a foreleg. Not a man in all of Kirby Crossing but would have laughed if he were told that this was that famous outlaw stallion, Parade, which had defied capture so long and caused such a wastage of money in the hunt for him that at last he became known as the hundred-thousand dollar horse. It was too incredible.

The little group paused in Kirby Crossing only long enough to buy flour, bacon, a few canned goods, and get the latest papers. But the newspapers were far less important than the word that ran from lip to lip.

The State penitentiary, hardly eighty miles away, had been the scene of a cunning escape. One David Holman, then lodged in the death house, had cut through the bars of his cell, gained the prison yard, and climbed over the guard wall by the aid of a ladder of silk equipped with fine aluminium grapples at one end. Finally he either had drowned in the lake in the middle of which the penitentiary stood, or else had swum the long distance to the shore on a night when a veritable hurricane was blowing. Only one thing was certain—that some of the guards must have been bribed to look the other way. But so far the investigation had convicted no one.

It was One-eyed Harry who spent an hour or more buying the food and getting the gossip. Silver, in the meantime, was slipping along securely in his Mexican disguise from group to group and from window to window, until at last he had peeked into every saloon, and examined the people in the dining room of the hotel, and in the restaurant. He was searching for a man with a peculiar birdlike alertness of head and manner, and a singular lightness of step. Or if the man could not be found he hoped to get a glimpse, perhaps, of Edith Alton Kenyon.

But he was disappointed. He had to rejoin One-eyed Harry, who, in the presence of a few yawning spectators, cursed him as a lazy greaser for being late, and threatened to flay him alive if he were ever tardy again.

Then they went up the valley, and camped between the edge of Kirby Run and the trees that crowded the valley. They chose the site of some old diggings. Gold was everywhere in the sands of the creek. The only trouble was that it was scarce, and there were few places where a man could wash a day's wages with any ease. However, One-eyed Harry Bench was willing to stay there as long as Silver needed him.

"If it hadn't been for you routing me out with a bullet," said Bench, "I'd still be out there in the desert, eating sand with my bacon and hating the whole world! I'll camp anywhere you say. And what could be better than this here?"

It was a good camp, with plenty of food and water, and a view of big mountains before them and behind. Kirby Crossing was only a little over a mile away.

They built a lean-to the next morning, and Silver left his friend arranging the stones for an outdoor fireplace, while he slipped up into the town again. There were other Mexicans in the town, and one saloon at the end of the street was their gathering place. Into the brown horde Silver went, to let his disguise be thoroughly tested. But he had few doubts that it would pass muster; a dozen times he had used it in old Mexico itself.

In the saloon he kept his eyes down and his ears open, while he drank tequila. But he heard nothing that had any bearing on his quest. There was only talk and more talk about the prison break. It pleased the Mexicans to know that the government and the law had failed. Their rattling voices rose to crescendos; they laughed heartily, flashing their eyes at one another.

But what was the prison break to Silver? He left the saloon and resumed his search through the town. His eye was so trained that half a second's pause in front of a window could show him all the faces inside. And a few side glances were enough for his study of whole groups as he passed among them. But he had worked up and down the street twice before some one caught his eye.

It was a man he had seen before, seated in the back room of a saloon, playing poker and chewing nervously at a cigar. But only when he walked out onto the street did the attention of Silver fall seriously on him. For he had a quick, lightly rising step, like that of a sprinter in the pink of condition for a race. As he walked, his head had the same birdlike alertness that Silver had noted in the unknown companion of Edith Alton, that morning in the ravine. The farther the man drew into the distance, the more convinced was Silver that he had found his quarry.

A warm little glow ran through him. He had to set his teeth to keep from laughing aloud.

The stranger mounted a horse tethered in front of the saloon, and rode out of town at a dogtrot that freshened to a lope as he gained the open space beyond. But Silver was not far behind. He kept among the trees that bordered the narrow road closely on either side, and his long legs flew over the ground with the easy stride of a natural runner.

He had a chance to note several things on the way. The first was that he was behind a good horseman. The second was that the stranger was by no means used to the Western style of riding. And finally his conviction was that in spite of the cow-puncher outfit, time-rubbed as it was, his quarry was quite a stranger to the West and Western ways.

He was inclined to take the reins in both hands, for instance, instead of reining across the neck. And when they came to a runlet that ran across the road, the rider pitched forward in the saddle and hunched over, as though expecting the mustang to jump the barrier. Instead, being Western, that cow pony calmly trotted through the water.

It was not a long run. In twenty minutes or less the rider turned off toward the creek, and halted in front of an old, disused cabin, on the front of which a flap of canvas had been hung to take the place of a door. A burly young Mexican with a mustache that glistened like black glass came to take the horse of his master, throwing down the ax with which he had been chopping wood.

The rider disappeared into the cabin, while Silver sat on the edge of the woods and watched the Mexican put up the pony in a lean-to that was attached to the end of the cabin. This was only until saddle and bridle had been removed, and hobbles fitted. After that the mustang was turned loose to graze on the good grass.

When this had been done, the Mexican returned to his ax. Silver, who was now breathing easily again, came out from the trees and stood to watch. The other gave him a wave of the hand, and then went on with his swinging of the ax.

"There is no chance to talk, amigo," said he. "That gringo has the eye of a hawk and the ear of a grizzly bear. He keeps me working all day. Except for the good pay, I am only a slave. If you have something to say to me, wait for me tonight in the saloon in Kirby Crossing, where all of our people meet."

"The fact is," said Silver, "that this work is too hard for you, friend. It needs a stronger man."

"A stronger man?" said the Mexican, scowling. "Who sent you out here to trouble me?"

"I came of my own accord," said Silver. "I have a kind heart. I never want to see a man working beyond his strength."

"You, perhaps," said the Mexican, "could do this work very easily?"

"No doubt," said Silver.

"You could cut the wood, do the cooking, wash some gold out of the creek sands? You could wash the soiled clothes and sweep out the cabin, and then find spare time to shoot fresh meat for his table?"

"I could do all of those things," said Silver. "What's more, I shall do them."

The Mexican stared. Then his eyes glassed over with rage. His chest swelled, his chin sank. "Fool of a stone-faced half-wit!" he roared. "Get out before I cut you in two with the ax!"

"Don't lift the ax," said Silver, "or I'll have to take it away from you."

A voice spoke suddenly, sharply, from the cabin doorway, and there was the master of the house.

"What's the matter out there, José," asked he.

"Matter, Señor Lorens?" said José. "Here is a crazy man who says that this work is too hard for me, and that he is going to take my place!"

Silver turned to Lorens and gave him a deep bow.

"A bright day to you, señor," said Silver. "May the sunshine fall on your heart; may the gold gather for you in the sands."

This flowery outburst, in swift Mexican, set Lorens chuckling.

"This fellow is a poet, and poets are the devil, José," said he. "Does he say that he is going to take your place?"

"He may be a devil," said José, grating his teeth together, "but even a devil will feel the edge of this ax."

He gave it a swing as he spoke.

"What's your name?" asked Lorens.

"Juan," said Silver.

"Juan, I like the look of you," said Lorens. "Your hair might be mowed or tied back from your eyes, but you look able to do something."

"I can do everything that that man can do, and then twist his neck," said Silver.

"Do you hear, Señor Lorens?" said José, trembling with rage. "This is one of those fools who boasts and thinks that his loud talking will be the thing that weakens the heart of another man! Away with you, you lying, stealing, ragged thief! Would an honest man wear such clothes? Look, señor! His trousers are not long enough to reach his ankles, and therefore, he keeps them rolled up to his knees. There is nothing on his body but that cheap shirt. See the sandals on his feet! Señor, let me send him on his travels again!"

"If you can," said Lorens calmly. "Drive him as far as you please—if you're able!"

Chapter – 10

JOSÉ, when he had received this permission, gaped at Silver with a sudden joy. Then, weighing the broad-bladed ax in both hands, he advanced at him with short, quick steps, like a boxer.

"Hold on!" called Lorens. "An ax against a man with empty hands?"

"Señor," said Silver, "I have a knife, but I shall not use it. Who will use weapons on children, señor?"

José uttered a short howl, something like that of a dog when it starts to bay the moon. Then he came, with a skip and a leap and a swing of the ax, right at Silver.

In José there was no such folly as would lead him to try a downright blow that might be side-stepped. Instead, he feinted at the head, and then swept the ax around in a mighty circle. The edge of the blade flamed with keenness. It could have cloven deep into the body of Silver if it struck fairly home. Instead, it merely brushed through the top hair of his black wig as it swished by, for he had crouched suddenly close to the earth. The weight of the stroke turned José half around. He knew that he had missed, and that his failure was apt to be his ruin. Even while his arms were carrying his body around, his head turned toward Silver, and his face was desperate. But there was nothing that he could do. The blow that found him had the weight of Silver leaning straight behind it. José fell in a heap.

Silver took the ax from those numb hands and swayed it lightly into the air.

"This poor rascal," said Silver, "may come back to steal, señor. But if I tap him across the back of the neck until the bone snaps, then I can weight him with stones and drop him into the river. With this current he will soon be rolled to bits. In five days, if they have dragged the river, they would be able to find no more than a finger bone of all of him."

Lorens began to laugh heartily. He was a handsome fellow, a little too thin of face, a little too bright and active of eye; now he was alight with appreciation.

"Don't kill the poor rat, Juan," said he. "Do you think he'll come back if you tell him that you don't want him around?"

"I must talk to him in a special way," said Silver. "Permit me, señor, and his face shall never be seen around here again!"

"Talk to him any way you please," said Lorens. "I have an idea that you're going to work for me, Juan."

"Ah, señor," said Silver, "to hear you say that is already as good as roast kid and frijoles in my stomach. Hey! José!"

José, coming to his senses by degrees, was startled by this cry to his feet. He stood wavering, looking wildly from Silver to his master.

"The honorable and rich señor," said Silver, "is tired of wasting his money, tired of spending the kindness of his heart on a poor thickwit, a wretched fellow who knows nothing of cooking, who leaves the floor of the house dirty, who has no luck in finding gold, and who cannot make the smoke of the fire blow away from the house. He sends you away, José. And he tells you that if you are seen near this house again, to beg or to steal, he will make you disappear—like this!"

At that he picked up a small stone from the ground, hurled it far into the air and when it spun, hovering, at the height of its rise, he flashed a revolver into his hand and fired. The glimmering stone and the bullet met with an audible impact, and the stone disappeared.

José still was blinking in the direction of that spot where the little rock had hung in the air. Now his mouth opened slowly.

He had seen something that was worth more to him than a thousand hours of explanation and lecturing. He backed up a few steps, turned, and fled dodging, like a snipe when it goes winging against the wind to avoid the gun of the hunter.

"You see, señor," said Silver, "that when we deal with children, we do not need weapons except to frighten the silly fools!"

"Juan, you speak good Spanish," said Lorens, standing in the doorway, with his chin on his fist and study in his eyes.

"I learned it, my master," said Silver, "in Mexico City itself. I was in service there."

"What sort of service?"

"Shining silver, and taking the small dogs out for their walks."

Lorens smiled, but there was still dubious thought in his eyes.

"How do you wear that revolver?"

"Here under my left arm," said Silver. "Most people don't expect it to come from that place. So I have a chance to surprise them, and to please myself, and that means that everybody is happy."

"Or dead," suggested Lorens.

"Or dead, señor," said Silver, bowing.

"A fellow with your talents," said Lorens, "ought never have to work with his hands."

"Observe my palms," answered Silver. "They are smoother than the hands of a young maiden, señor."

"Ah?" said Lorens. "Then why are you taking a job here with me?"

"I am not in my own country, where I would be known," said Silver. "If I were there, señor, there are villages where the men would stop everything the instant that I appear, and the women, without being bidden, would at once begin to cook. One would roast a kid. Another would seethe a chicken. Another old woman would bring out her finest cheese, packed in wet salt grass, delicious in the mouth with wine. I should sit, señor, in front of the fonda, and drink with the head men of the town, and then eat and ask one of two of the notables to sit down with me and taste my food. And when I had finished eating, I should pay them all ten times over by telling them three true stories of three days of my life. They would give me their blessing, follow me to the edge of the town, fill my saddlebags with food, press a canteen of good red wine into my hands, place a little bottle of tequila in my coat pocket, and tell me to hurry back to them again!"

He delivered this long speech with a sort of lordly flourish.

"Well," said Lorens, "Mexico is still in the old place. Why aren't you there?"

"Because all of my countrymen are not so kind and so true," said Silver. "There are some rude fellows that you may have heard of."

"The rurales, perhaps?"

"The señor," said Silver, "sees at a glance to the heart of everything. The rurales know that there is a price on my head. Therefore they hunt me with more passion, señor, than the Americanos of your country will hunt a wild duck—though they may have plenty of tame ducks waddling about in their back yards!"

Lorens laughed again, but very shortly. "Look here, Juan," he said. "You won't want to be working for me very long as a cook and a hunter and a fire tender."

"Señor," said Silver, "you will not very long be camped by this river, pretending to hunt for gold. And before you leave this place, you may have found better ways to employ me."

"What do you mean by saying that I only pretend to hunt for gold?" asked Lorens.

"What do I mean? Nothing! If the señor is angry, I mean nothing. I know that the señor has eyes enough for two, and ears enough for two, also, and a tongue that is capable of speaking for all his affairs."

"No, but tell me why you think I only pretend to look for gold?"

"Because I saw you playing poker, señor. And after I had watched you shuffle the deck three times, I knew that you could dig more money out of the hands of men with a pack of cards than strong miners can earn by digging and blasting at a mountain of rock all their lives!"

Lorens tapped his rapid, slender fingers against his lips, looking over his knuckles at Silver critically.

"Juan," said he, "you're an impudent rascal, and you see too much."

"It is true," said Silver calmly, "the señor does not want a blind José, but a Juan with two eyes, perhaps. Yet if you tell me to close them, I am blind!"

"I know what you mean," remarked Lorens. "You're able to see anything and remember only what I want you to know."

"The señor understands," said Silver.

"Juan, you have killed men in your time."

"I have had that joy, señor," said Silver. "I have seen the faces of my enemies turn black under my hands."

Lorens shrugged his shoulders as though to get rid of a feeling of cold up his spine.

"What money do you want?" he asked. "How will you have it?"

"I shall be paid according to my services," said Silver. "If it is to cook and clean and hunt for the señor, the scraps of food that are left will be food and pay for me. But if more important matters come, and they are put in my hands, then the señor himself will know how to reward me. It is not for money alone that I work, but for pleasure, señor, and to fill my hands with the name of a man!"

This speech seemed to please Lorens more than all the rest put together.

"You're a hard bit of steel, Juan," said he. "You'll take an edge and keep it. I want to know one thing from you. Did you ever hear of a man named Silver—an American?"

"The Señor Silver?" said Silver, looking down. "I have heard of him and seen him."

"Tell me what sort of a man he is?"

"A man to beware of. He has done certain things. He shoots very straight, and he shoots very quickly. And he has killed men, señor—a great many of them."

"A fellow like that, Juan—a fellow who answers the very description of this man Silver, may be on my trail. I don't know. I'm not sure that he will follow me. But he's one that I should like you to have in mind. Dream of him as he was, Juan. Look for him in the shadow under every tree. Listen for his voice. Watch for the flash of his gun!"

"He shall be more in my mind than my own self," said Silver.

"Tell me this," said Lorens. "Would you stand up to a fellow like Silvertip, do you think?"

"Perhaps he is a larger man than I am," said Silver. "But I should hope to stand up to him. A brown hand can be as quick as a white one, and a white skin does not turn bullets."

"Juan," said Lorens seriously, "you and I are going to get on together. You don't need to make a slave of yourself. If you can shoot fresh meat and cook it, that will be enough for me, along with some coffee. And I suppose you know how to cook frijoles?"

"You shall be glad I am with you," said Silver, "every time you eat the food I cook."

He bowed again, and, looking up through the overhanging of his forelock, he studied the face of the man who within this week had sent a rifle bullet inches from his head. There was murder in that thin, handsome face. There were infinite possibilities of treachery in the uncertain brightness of the eyes. And behind all, there was a quick flame of intelligence. If he were to pull the wool over these eyes continually, Silver knew that he would have to be on guard constantly. He would have to live like a dog with a wolf, never knowing when the teeth would be in his throat.

But behind this man, somehow and somewhere, loomed the form of the girl. Perhaps it was in the handwriting of Lorens that the words had been written: "-out fail in Kirby Cr—" And perhaps through this man, also, Silver could come in touch with him who had encompassed the death of Buck, and whose name began with "Nel—"

Danger breathed now out of the very air, but opportunity was in it, also.

Chapter – 11

LUCK favored Silver in the execution of his first domestic duties for Lorens. He took the rifle of Lorens, a beautiful weapon, and walked ten minutes, straight through the woods, when a stag sprang out of a covert hardly twenty yards from him. Silver let it run until his bead was perfect, and then sank the bullet behind the shoulder.

The stag was young, but when all the less choice parts were discarded, there remained more than two hundred pounds of good, edible meat. Silver loaded himself with half of it and brought it close to the shack of Lorens. He went back and got the other half. After resting, he put the whole crushing burden on his shoulders. He stepped out from among the trees and came up to the shack with a swinging stride.

Lerons was sitting cross-legged under a tree, smoking a pipe. He sprang up with an exclamation.

"Venison, man? Venison, Juan?"

"It is not veal," said Silver, putting down the load.

"That's something Jose could never get for me," said Lorens. "He said that the deer were all frightened out of the valley, long ago."

"You know, señor," said Silver, "that we never find what we do not hope for. But I, Juan, will keep you in venison."

"There's enough there for a whole camp!" exclaimed Lorens.

He tried to pick up the burden, and it slipped out of his straining hands.

"Great guns!" said Lorens under his breath, and with profound awe stared at Silver askance. He had heard the rifle crack in the far distance; he had seen his new man come swinging in with a light, long stride, carrying that weight and hardly breathing under it. He began to look now at the lean shanks of Silver.

"Some men are different," Silver heard him mutter. "The way mules are smaller and stronger than horses, or cats are stronger than dogs!"

On venison steaks broiled to crust outside and of a melting tenderness within, they dined that night, with potatoes fried crisp, and cress from the edge of the running water, and thick, strong black coffee. And Lorens declared that he had not properly eaten since he had left—

The name of the city remained unspoken, but Silver did not think it would be hard to fit in the name of the metropolis where this gambler had been plying his trade. For all his good looks, the man had the manner and something of the look of a rat that had lived underground most of its days.

He said, as they sipped coffee—Silver sitting farther from the fire than his employer as though out of respect, but in reality because he wished to have his face studied as little as possible: "Juan, tell me something of your old life down there in Mexico, will you?"

Silver pretended a distress which was not altogether unreal. Then he said: "Ask me for my blood, señor, but do not ask me for my past. The old days are rope that is made: the new days are rope that is in the winding; my past may not please you, but the new rope may be what you want."

"For hanging myself?" asked Lorens.

The question was so apt that Silver started, but Lorens was already laughing at his own remark.

"You're right, Juan," said Lorens. "The fellow who talks about his past is not likely to have much of a future. Here's a poor devil who's had a past, I suppose. A batch of these posters came to town today. Fast work on the printing press, eh?"

He put on the ground before Silver a picture of a man of not more than thirty, with a strong, dignified, even a refined face, with every capacity of thought and feeling indicated in it. But the big print offered a reward of five thousand dollars for the apprehension of this man dead or alive. The name was David Holman, and Silver remembered hearing that this was the criminal who had recently broken out of the penitentiary, less than a hundred miles away.

"What d'you think of that face?" asked Lorens.

"He is too strong to be only a little good, or a little bad," said Silver. "He must be everything or nothing."

Lorens picked up the poster, and looked from it suddenly and piercingly at Silver.

"You're no fool, Juan," he said.

Then he added, half to himself: "Dead or alive! Dead or alive! Think of that! These fellows around here will hunt for a week, every day, for the sake of bagging a timber wolf that only has a ten-dollar bounty on his scalp. Dead or alive, and five thousand dollars for the lucky fellow who draws a dead bead and pulls the trigger! Eh, Juan?" he said, making his voice suddenly cheerful. "That would be a handsome bit of money to have down yonder in Mexico, where things are cheaper!"

Silver shook his head with real distaste.

"Blood money, señor!" said he. "I have killed men, but never for money."

"No?" said Lorens.

"No," said Silver. "Never for money. And I never shall."

"But five thousand dollars! That's a fortune!"

"It would all taste of blood!" said Silver.

Lorens began to brood again, the lower part of his face propped up in the flat of his hand, and his eyes lifting suddenly, now and again, to his companion. At last he said: "Juan, I have to be in two places at once tonight."

"Yes, señor," said Silver.

"One place is in Kirby Crossing. One is right here in this camp. Understand?"

"A man's body cannot be in two places at once," said Silver.

"One of me will have to be you."

"Yes, señor."

"Juan, I've known you only for a few hours, but I'm going to trust you. I want you to go into Kirby Crossing and at ten o'clock stand across the street from the hotel. You hear me? At ten o'clock. And stay there the rest of the night if you have to. Can you do that without closing your eyes?"

"Once," said Silver dreamily, "for four days there were men around a little nest of rocks. If I so much as nodded, they knew it and crawled closer."

Lorens grinned, a quick contortion of the face that became still again at once.

"As you wait there," said Lorens, "two or three times an hour you'll be smoking a cigarette."

"Yes, señor."

"Well, then, every time you light a cigarette, take two matches under your finger and scratch them both—so that the two will burn at the same time."

"I hear you, señor."

"After a time—I don't know when—I think that a woman will come up to you. She will ask for Charlie. You'll tell her that you come in his name."

"Does she speak Spanish, señor?"

"Enough to understand that."

"How shall I know that she is the right woman?"

"If she's young, pretty, and holds her head high, with her chin up a bit, you'll know that she's the right one."

"I understand," said Silver, his heart beginning to beat fast. For who could it be except Edith Alton Kenyon, that cunning trickster? And he wished, in a sudden moment of savage rage, that poor Ned Kenyon could be sitting here to listen to the words from Lorens.

"You can go now," said Lorens. "Buy two horses and two saddles. How much will they cost—two mighty good ones?"

"Five hundred dollars apiece," said Silver.

Lorens grunted. "That's worse than blood money. I mean something around a hundred and fifty dollars."

"It can be done, señor. There are horses for gentlemen and there are horses for Juan. I shall buy two horses for Juan."

"That's it. Put the girl on one of 'em, and bring her out here."

He took out a wallet and counted the money, while Silver scowled at the fire. He liked this very little. The man was, in fact, trusting him. And to betray the trust even of a fellow who had tried to put a bullet through his head, went sore against the grain.

"Here's four hundred," said Lorens. "And that's a lot of money for me just now. Do your best with it."

"I shall bring a hundred dollars back," said Silver, "And still you'll be satisfied."

"I don't want a hundred back. Spend all of it. Or if you can satisfy me with less, put the change in your pocket. You can go now. Buy the horses, and be opposite the hotel at ten o'clock, ready to wait there until the morning, if it should so happen you have to."

"In all things, as you please, señor," said Silver.

He took the money and counted it, and rose to his feet.

"One more thing," cautioned Lorens harshly. "I'm giving you enough money to tempt you a little, perhaps. But you remember this: You've been a big man in your own country, but you're not a big man in this one. And if you try to run out on me, I'll have the scalp off your head and the marrow out of your bones—I'll have it, and there are plenty who'll help me to get it!"

His thin face wrinkled like an old leaf with sudden malice as the mere thought of his promised vengeance passed through his mind.

"Señor," said Silver, "only a fool promises. A wise man waits to have judgment passed on his deeds."

"All right, all right," muttered Lorens. "You sound like a copy book. I'll see what you bring home to me from Kirby Crossing!"

Chapter – 12

SILVER went back to Kirby Crossing on the run. He only slackened his pace to walk with his long stride through the town, and he lingered an instant to watch the strange spectacle of the building of a bridge by night, for the work was being pressed twenty-four hours a day. Lanterns hung in a long festoon over the timbers. The great underlogs were being wedged and bound in place, and the bridge began to look like a skeleton of what it would finally appear.

Silver went on past it. He entered the dark of the open country in the lower part of the valley, and here he sprang again into his Indian trot that shifted ground rapidly behind him. When he was not far from the lean-to which he and One-eyed Harry had put on, he whistled. And from the dark of the brush sprang Parade, and came racing, with a whinny.

He went round and round Silver like a bird in the air about to settle on a nest. He was dancing and snorting, with the hand of his master on his shoulder, when big Harry Bench came out of the lean-to. In the dark he looked more gigantic than ever.

"Silver?" he called. "Man, man, that hoss has been about crazy while you was away. He's come smelling around the shack, and he's still-hunted your trail down the valley. Where you been, brother?"

Silver went into the lean-to and sat on a home-made stool in the corner. The stallion stood with head and shoulders intruding through the doorway.

"I'm up the valley on the other side of the Crossing," said Silver. "Take a look at me! I'm Juan, the greaser, who works for a fellow named Lorens. I've got two minutes to spend here, and no more than that. I have to get back. I'm working for a fellow with an eye like a hawk and the wit of a prairie coyote. One day, when I was wearing a white skin, this same Lorens put a bullet inches from my ear and then ran out on me. Just now he doesn't know me, but if he guesses that I'm lying to him, or that my skin is not as dark as it seems to be, he'll take the first good chance to shoot me in the back."

"What in the nation do you wanna waste your time on him, then?" said One-eyed Harry, lifting his huge voice.

"Because," said Silver, "I'm on the outside edge of a regular whirlpool, old-timer. Lorens is the edge of the whirl, and if I stick to him, I think I may be drawn into the middle of the pool."

"And who the devil wants to be drowned in a whirlpool?" demanded Harry, staring.

"Call it a dance instead of a whirlpool," said Silver, "and all of the dancers wear knives, and I'm blindfolded, and I never know what tune they'll strike up next, or where they'll step. But there's a lying crook of a woman, a murderer, and somebody who's tried to murder me. They're all elements in the job, and I don't know how many other forces are behind 'em. You can see that it's a pretty picture, Harry!"

"You like it!" exclaimed One-eyed Harry Bench. "Doggone me if you don't like it a lot. Kind of makes your eye shine just to think of that dance, eh? That kind of a job is just like pork and beans to you, ain't it?"

"Like it?" said Silver. "Of course I don't like it. I'm likely to lose my hide any minute, and my head along with it."

"You like it," said Harry Bench, pointing with his huge, grimy hand. "That's the game for you, the way poker is the game for the small-time gambler. You ain't happy, by thunder, unless your life is on the table as the stakes."

He took a step toward Silver and shook his hand at him. A sort of horrified realization came over that rugged face as Bench said:

"You're goin' to keep after them, you're goin' to keep playin' that game till you're killed. You know that, Silver? You're goin' to play with the fire till you're burned to the bone. What makes you such a fool? You can't keep ten knives in the air all your life. One of 'em is bound to fall sometime and stick right into your heart. Hear me talk?"

"Hear you?" said Silver, apparently irritated. "Of course I hear you, and you're talking like a half-wit, Harry. I'm not up there with that tiger cat, Lorens, for pleasure. I'm up there because there's a crooked game in the wind, and because a friend of mine has suffered on account of it already. That's why I'm there!"

"If you're not in that mess, you're in another one. It's always the frying pan or the fire for you, Silver!"

Silver started to deny the charge, but as he parted his lips to speak, his glance went inward upon his life and showed him the crowded story of his past in such pictures that he was suddenly mute. It was true. All of his days he had played with fire. He could tell himself that he was simply following the courses which chance led him into, but why was it that every trail he put his feet on was a trail of danger?

So he was mute for an instant, seeing those pictures, and out of the past reading the future. For what big Harry Bench had said was indubitably true. No man could continue to play with fire without being finally burned to an ash.

Gradually he drew himself out of the dark humor and scowled up at One-eyed Harry. Bench was pacing back and forth, taking the breadth of the little room in three strides, and whirling on his heel and toe. For all the size and the bulk of that man, he as as active as a big cat. Silver vaguely admired the magnificence of that physique, so swift and yet so massive. He himself had the strength of two men in his arms, but he knew that in the grasp of this giant he would crumble like sand.

"Somebody has oughta watch out after you," said Bench. "There had oughta be friends to keep you hobbled. Even your hoss has to stay and worry about you!"

Silver looked toward the sooty muzzle, the beautiful, deerlike eye of the stallion, and smiled. "Harry," said Silver, "maybe there's a lot in what you say. The more I think about it, the more I agree with you. I've got to stop my crazy ways. And I'm going to do it. Believe me, partner? This is the last job that I take over on my hands, no matter how the luck tries to drag me into trouble."

"Sure!" growled Harry Bench. "That's what you say now. But you'll be changing your mind one of these days. If you got sense, you'll stay here and let Lorens go hang."

"He won't go hang, and I want the job of the hanging," said Silver. "If I don't hang him myself, I want to point him out to the hangman, and turn him over with his hands tied behind his back, if he's the sort that I think I can prove he is! Now stop talking about me. I want to ask you a question."

"Fire away."

"There's a fellow named David Holman—"

"That just escaped from the death house at the prison. Yeah. I know about that."

"I've an idea that my friend, Lorens, up the valley, has a sort of an interest in Mr Holman. What put Holman in the death house? What did he do?"

"Oh, nothin' much," said One-eyed Harry. "He come out from the East to be a cashier in a bank over in Tuckaway. Pickin' up experience, you see? But he wanted to pick up some hard cash, too. And he took it out of the vaults. After a while he was pretty far in the hole, and so this here Holman, he planned to have the bank robbed, and, of course, the robbery would cover up what he'd stole.

"So he got a pair of yeggs to work with him, and one night him and them robbed the bank, all right. But it happened that Sheriff Bert Philips was riding back into town that night, after chasin' a half-breed hoss thief a coupla hundred miles and never sighting him. And he seen three men sneakin' out from the rear of the bank, and he hollered out to them. They ducked away to their horses and run for it. He followed and yelled for help, and some gents who were havin' a late night of it at a saloon, they come out and joined in the chase. And then there was a long run and the three of 'em got away for the time being.

"But the chase was so long that this here Dave Holman didn't have a chance to fill in his plan, which was to be back in his home in bed when the day begun, with his split of the swag stowed away somewhere safe. He was still on the run at sunup. And then he says to himself, that as long as he's goin' to be found out, he'd better be caught for a sheep than for just a lamb. So he ups and murders them two gents, and takes their share of the loot, and lights out with it. And the sheriff and his posse comes along while there's still a spark of life in one of the dyin' gents, and this feller tells about the holdup, and how Holman had planned it, and how Holman had murdered them. And the sheriff, he follers on, and gets a sight of Holman on a dead-beat horse, and runs him down and hauls him in.

"When it comes to the trial, this here Holman, he puts up a cock-and-bull story about how the two thugs had come to his house in the middle of the night and forced him at the point of a gun to go to the bank with 'em and open the safe, and how they'd kept him under their guns, and made him run with 'em, and how he'd taken the first chance to get hold of a revolver and shoot the pair of 'em. And why did he run when the sheriff came up after him? Well, it was because all of the swag was on him, and he seen that it would be hard to explain things away and prove that he was an honest man. It was a pretty far-fetched story, and the whole jury, it busted out laughin' in the middle of the yarn, they say. So they made him guilty of murder, and there you are!"

Silver had listened attentively to this story, and now he nodded his head. "What that has to do with Lorens," he said, "I don't know. But Lorens has a lot of interest in that fellow Holman, I think. Now, Harry, there's one thing more for me to say to you. I'm going back up the valley. I'm going to be in Kirby Crossing for a while, and then I'm going on. Every day I'm going to try to get in touch with you. If I don't manage that, I want you to start on the trail for me, because it may be that I'll be needing help. Will you do that?"

"I'll do it glad and willing," answered One-eyed Harry. "You're going back into the fire, are you?"

"This one job is the last one, but I've got to finish it," said Silver uneasily. He stood up.

"Try to keep people away from Parade," he cautioned. "There are more men who know that horse than there are who know me. And if Parade is spotted, people will know that I'm not far away—and that will complicate everything. This disguise business is thin ice to skate on, and it won't take much to make me break through. I'll put Parade in the woods, and he'll stay there till I come back. Just see that he has water and grain. And so long, Harry."

Harry followed his friend out into the night.

"I hate to have you go, partner," said he. "It seems to me that there's a lot of trouble pilin' up in the air around us."

"Perhaps there is," said Silver. "But this is the last time for me, Harry."

"The last time you hunt trouble?" echoed Harry. "You couldn't stay away from it. No more than a dope fiend can stay away from his dope. But so long, Jim. Will that hoss stay there without no hobbles, even?"

They stood together in the dark of the trees near the lean-to, and Silver spoke to the horse and patted the silk of the neck.

"He'll stay here till he hears me call or whistle," said he, "I think he'd stay here if the brush were set on fire. But your job, old son, is to keep people away from this neck of the woods during the day. Mind you, if anybody puts an eye on the horse, I'm next door to a gone goose!"

Chapter – 13

SILVER ran back to Kirby Crossing and went to the biggest horse dealer's yard. It was out on the edge of the town—a little shack of a house, a sprawling shed, and a tangle of corral fences all within sound of the flowing river. The proprietor was eating his supper alone in his kitchen when Silver tapped at the open door and saw a face swollen with fat and red-stained by whisky lifted from a platter of jumbled food.

"How much of a pair of horses do you want?" asked the dealer sharply.

"Four hundred dollars' worth," said Silver simply. "Horses and saddles."

The dealer ducked his head and coughed to cover his grin of satisfaction. Five minutes later Silver sat on his heels with his back against a corral fence, and watched a wrangler run half a dozen horses into the lantern light of the inclosure.

"No, señor," said Silver. "It is not four hundred dollars' worth of horse meat that I want, but two horses at two hundred dollars apiece."

"Here!" exclaimed the dealer. "There ain't a pair of this lot that ain't worth two hundred bucks."

But though he blustered, he realized that he was not dealing with a fool. He brought in new selections. It was not until twenty animals had been brought before him that Silver elected to try one. He took the one he tried. And twenty more went before him before he selected its mate. Then he had a good gray and a roan. Neither of them was a picture horse, but each promised to be full of service. It rather amused Silver to note that he was using his best endeavors for Lorens, who would eventually be his open enemy. But the instinct of the bargainer had control of him.

By the time the horses were secured, the dealer lifted his lantern and shone the light of it into the eyes of Silver.

"If everybody bought horses like you do, stranger," said he, "I'd have to go out of business or turn myself into an honest man!"

Silver took the horses with the flimsy, battered equipment that was included in the sale price, and led the pair to the long hitch rack in front of the hotel.

It was nearly ten o'clock, so he went to his designated post opposite the hotel and sat down on his heels again, with his back leaned against a wall.

There were few people in the street. Only about the doors of the saloons appeared the forms of men entering or slipping away. Those lighted doors seemed to be attracting the inhabitants as lamps attract insects on a summer night. But most of the houses down the street were already darkened, because the town dwellers of a small Western community retire early and begin the day betimes. Even in the hotel, only three windows above the ground floor were lighted. And at ten o'clock the veranda was empty, and the hanging lanterns that illuminated it were put out.

Silver stood up, stretched his cramped legs, and settled down on his heels again. He was perfectly content. Sometimes invisible whirlpools of dust brushed against him, and the taste of alkali came into his mouth. But in his nostrils there was the fragrance of adventure, and the light in his mind was more than lamps could shed.

The minutes went by him like stealthy feet. It was eleven, or close to that hour. Only a single window in the facade of the hotel was lamplighted. One of the saloons had closed for the night. And Silver, for the third time, lighted a cigarette, scratching two matches, so that both came into a blaze for a moment, though he held them in such a way that none of the light could fall upon his face.

Then a form came across the hotel veranda and rapidly across the street toward him. The starlight showed clearly enough that it was a woman. After her came a long-striding man, a queerly made, light-shouldered fellow who took immense steps.

The girl turned sideways from him and started to run. She thought better of it and turned suddenly to face him.

The two of them were close, by this time, and Silver had slipped back into the thicker shade of an inset doorway, where he was almost invisible.

He heard the girl saying: "You can't follow me. You can't bother me like this, Perry. It's no good! It won't do. I won't have it, Perry. You have no right!"

"Why, I don't know," said the man. "Maybe I have right enough. Maybe I have a sort of duty, Edith, to follow a woman who's run away from her husband the day of the wedding. Maybe I have a duty to show up a fraud. That's what the thing amounts to. Fraud, Edith! You deceived a man. You led him on to marry you, and then you ducked out. Plain fraud, and there are laws that deal with it!"

"You ought to see him," said the girl calmly. "Go see Ned Kenyon, and ask him to open suit against me."

"You're confident in him, are you?" said the other, sneering. "Edith, there's no shame in you, apparently!"

"Shame?" said the girl. "Shame, Perry Nellihan? Doesn't the word blister your tongue a little?"

"Why should it?" asked Nellihan. "I've done only what any man would do to protect my rights! I was robbed of my rights. And you know it!"

"Suppose," said the girl, "that my father had known what you are, instead of merely guessing—what do you think he would have done?"

"The old fool is dead," said Nellihan. "I don't have to think about him. The fact is that he raised me like his own son all my life, and then he cut me off without a penny! Practically."

"More than two hundred thousand dollars—is that only a penny?" she asked.

"Compared with what you're getting!" said Nellihan.

"If I had told father what I knew, he would never have left you even that."

"The point is that you didn't tell him what you knew. That's where you were a fool."

"Very well," said the girl. "Take your hand from my arm, Perry. I don't want you to touch me."

"I'm not good enough to touch you, eh?"

"You're not," said she.

"I've done my share of shady things, perhaps," answered Nellihan. "But I've never done a worse thing than you worked on that poor idiot of a Kenyon."

"I don't think you ever did," she agreed, with a sudden warmth that surprised Silver. "But you know why I had to do it. You know that you worked me into a corner from which I couldn't dodge! There was only that way out for me!"

"I arranged that pretty well," said Nellihan. And he laughed.

Everything about that man was offensive to Silver for more reasons than he could put into words. And the voice, high, thin, nasal, cut into his very brainpan and put his nerves on edge.

"Take your hand off my arm," she repeated.

And the striking muscles in the shoulder of Silver leaped into hardness that refused to relax.

"Where do you want to go?" asked Nellihan.

"That's my affair."

"Girl wandering alone in the middle of the night," Nellihan sneered. "Is your precious thug somewhere around here?"

Silver could see him turn his head suddenly from side to side in eager curiosity.

"If he were," said the girl, "you'd be shaking in your boots."

Nellihan laughed again. "You're wrong, honey," said he. "I'm no saint, but I'm not a coward, either. And when it comes to gun work, I'm not afraid of any man in the West. You ought to know that."

"I only know that you're detestable!" she exclaimed.

"Listen to me, Edith," said he. "You're trying a hard game, and I can spoil it for you. You'll have to talk turkey to me."

"You mean that I'll have to talk money to you?"

"That's what I mean."

"I'd rather give you my blood than a penny of father's money," she answered.

"No matter what you'd rather do," answered Nellihan, "you'll have to talk turkey. I've got you where I want you, and you're a poor fool if you think that I'll let you get out from under before you've ponied up the iron men."

"You haven't a finger's weight of hold on me," she told him.

"No?" said Nellihan. "Don't you suppose that I can put poor Kenyon on your trail? He can make plenty of trouble for you! You'll disgrace yourself and your family—and you won't be able to do a particle of good for the dirty rat you love."

Silver heard her sigh—a long, long breath of disgust and weariness.

"I've told you before," she said, "that you can't do anything with Ned Kenyon. He won't act against me!"

"He will, when I show him how much money he can get out of you. He hasn't enough brains to think in terms of millions, but I can teach him the way of it! I'll put a match to his imagination and set him on fire. Then he'll go after you! Before I did that, I wanted to have a talk with you. That's all. I wanted to show you that you're in my hands!"

"I'm not," said the girl. "For Ned won't act against me. It's hard for a poor, creeping snake like you, Perry, to understand that some men may be honorable!"

"Well," said Nellihan, overlooking the insults blandly, and going straight on, "let me tell you something. I have another hold on you. Do you know that Sheriff Bert Philips is in this town right now, looking for an escaped crook? Now, then, suppose that I tell him why you're here? Suppose I tell him that, suppose that he gets on your trail—why, what will happen then?"

"You won't do that, Perry," said the girl slowly. "I know that you're bad. But you're not as low as that! You know that my life is smashed to bits. You know that there's no future hope for me. And you won't take away my last chance to find a few minutes of happiness?"

"Won't I?" said Perry Nellihan. He began his snarling, savage, nasal laughter. "Oh, won't I?" he repeated. "Won't I squeeze you till I've got what I want out of you? Edith, don't be such a fool! You ought to know me better than that. The next thing I know, you'll be on your knees, begging. But words don't matter in my ear, Edith. Hard cash is the only thing that will talk to me!"

"It's true," she said. "And I am a fool to talk to you."

"On the other hand," said the man, "take a calm look at the business and see the simple and straight way out. I'm not going to try to take everything. I'm going to make a fair split with you. I'm only going to ask for what I should have by your father's will—one half of the whole estate. Your half will be more money than you can spend. You know that. Why should you grudge me my bit?"

The girl paused, and Silver waited, with tingling nerves, to hear her acquiesce.

Instead, she said in the same quiet way: "You don't quite understand, Perry. I've done one terribly bad thing. I've smashed the life of Ned Kenyon—for a little while, anyway. And that one bad thing is enough. I'm not going to do another. And the worst thing that I can think of would be to turn you loose on the world with money and power in your hands. The very worst thing! Better send a plague into a crowded city than put power in your hands!" She paused an instant. "I've told you what I think. Now get away from me."

"You're going to visit the sheriff with me, my dear," said he grimly. "You're going straight down the street with me till I find the sheriff, and I know where to look for him. Come along!"

He turned her with a violent jerk, so that she made a long, lurching step beside him. Then Silver came like a noiseless ghost behind them.

"Excuse me, señor," said Silver in Spanish.

Nellihan whipped about suddenly, and the force of his turn and the driving weight of Silver's fist combined to strike him down. He bent far backward and then dropped on his side with his arms flung out.

Chapter – 14

A MAN who falls like that does not rise suddenly. Silver gave him a single glance, and then said to the girl:

"Quickly, señorita! The two horses at this end of the hitch rack—the gray and the roan! Take the roan. I have shortened the stirrups for you!"

She nodded, saving her breath for her running. And, coming up with the hitch rack, she flashed into the saddle like a man, while Silver jerked loose the knot that tethered the ropes. In a moment he was jogging his horse beside hers down the street.

She had been about to break away at a mad gallop, when he cautioned her:

"Señorita, a slow horse is never seen, but a galloping horse is a bonfire. All eyes find it!"

They were turning the corner beyond the next saloon before Silver, looking back, saw the tall form of Nellihan stagger to its feet. They were out of sight around that corner before a sharp, wailing voice began to yammer for help.

The girl bent forward and turned her face to Silver, as though asking permission to gallop the horse. But he made a signal of denial.

That was why they went calmly, unseen through the town of Kirby Crossing. Only when they reached the upper valley road would Silvertip let the horses gallop. And as the windy darkness blew into his face, he set his teeth hard and tried to understand what he had just seen and overheard.

The whole problem remained vague and obscure in his mind, but he felt that this darkness might be that which goes before the dawn. Nellihan, it was plain, had been raised by the rich father of the girl as a member of the family, though it seemed that he had never been adopted. The man was a rascal, and Alton had suspected it; therefore Nellihan had been cut off with merely enough of an inheritance to support him in comfort. At the same time,

Nellihan had managed to use his influence so that the girl's own inheritance was embarrassed. And that embarrassment had forced her, it appeared, to marry Ned Kenyon.

At the thought of Kenyon, the hot anger poured through Silver again, and yet, in spite of himself, he was unable to detest the girl as he had done before. Contrasted with Nellihan, she seemed a saintly figure, almost. And furthermore, what the springs of her actions had been he could not understand, and perhaps when that understanding arrived, he would be able to forgive her, in part, even for the blow she had given to poor Ned Kenyon.

She loved a "thug," as Nellihan had phrased it. Her life, she had said, was wrecked. She was fighting now to salvage from the ruin a few moments of happiness!

As Silver turned these words and ideas in his mind, he was more and more darkly baffled. She was young, beautiful, rich. How could her life be wrecked?

They were almost at the end of the ride when another though struck like red fire through his brain.

Nellihan! There was a name that began with the letters he was searching for: "Nel—"

And why should it not have been Nellihan? The murderer of Buck must have been tied into this great tangle in some way. The whole thing seemed to possess minute inner relations. He ran over the names—Nellihan, Edith Alton, Ned Kenyon, Lorens, Buck, and finally perhaps some vague connections with the escaped convict, David Holman. These people had entered on the stage from various directions and at various points. When would they be combined in such a way that Silver would be able to understand the entire problem?

But one thing was clear in his mind. Nellihan, he could swear, was the man who had killed Buck. He had spoken of familiarity with guns. And he was exactly the type of slayer who would shoot from the dark of an open window.

These ideas, rolling across the brain of Silver, were ended by his arrival near the cabin where Lorens lived. He held up his hand as a signal to draw rein, and presently they were dismounting near the cabin of Lorens. He whistled, and Lorens himself came out, hurrying.

"Are you there?" he called.

"Here!" said the girl.

"Thank Heaven for that!" said Lorens.

He told Silver to unsaddle and hobble the horses. He even lingered a moment to look over the animals and he said:

"You got your money's worth, Juan."

Then he turned away beside the girl.

Silver heard her say breathlessly: "Is he here?"

"Not yet," answered Lorens, lowering his voice. "Not yet, but he ought to get here before the morning. Did you bring it?"

"I have it with me—plenty!" she said.

"Good!" said Lorens, very heartily, and they disappeared through the door of the cabin.

Silver went about the unsaddling of the horses, wondering who might the "he" whom the girl desired to see, and what was the "it" that she had brought plenty of?

He had hardly finished hobbling the horses when Lorens called him

"Juan," said the man, "can you navigate on very little sleep?"

"Senor," said Silver, "I can lay up sleep the way a cow lays up fat in summer for the winter."

"Can you keep your eyes open all night long?" asked Lorens.

"For three nights, señor, without closing my eyes."

"Good!" said Lorens. "Good man! The lady has told me about the way you handled Nellihan in the town. A very good bit of work, Juan. Come inside and have some coffee, and anything you want to eat."

"No, señor," said Silver. "I have had coffee enough; and I have eaten enough. Now I shall stay outside and watch."

"She wants to thank you, Juan," said Lorens. "Come in for that!"

It was the last thing that Silver wished to go through. He knew the clear, quiet eyes of the girl, and he did not wish to have them fall on him now. What men could not see, she would penetrate with her woman's glance, perhaps. However, there was hardly an easy way of refusing to face her, and he had to follow Lorens back into the cabin.

The girl sat at the wobbly little table in the centre of the room, eating cold venison steak with relish. She looked up at Silver, and smiled at him, while he stood with his head inclined, his feet close together, his neck thrust a little forward, and his shoulders bowed a trifle. There is nothing that confuses recollection more than a change of the habitual posture of a man. He could hope that she would never dream of the erect, straight-eyed, rather imperious "Arizona Jim," when she was talking to this awkward Mexican, with the shock of black hair falling down over his eyes.

"It was a very bad time for me, back yonder in the town, Juan," she said. "I want to thank you for helping me. Nobody could have done better. Nobody! For he's a dangerous fellow—that one, Juan. If you hadn't stunned him, he would have been shooting while he fell!"

Silver bobbed his head, made a vague, brief gesture with one hand, and then shrugged his shoulders, as much as to say that what was passed was forgotten, and that the whole affair was not really worth much consideration.

Her manner changed a little. Her head tilted a shade to the side. A certain quizzical look appeared in her face.

Then, rising, she held out her hand.

"Give me your hand, Juan," said she. "Because after we've shaken hands, you'll believe that I won't forget you. And when I find out what you like the most in the world, I'll try to get it for you."

Silver looked down at the palm of his right hand, shrugged his shoulders again, scrubbed his hand against the white cotton trousers he wore, and then glided forward to take the hand of the girl and make a little ducking bow above it.

When he tried to withdraw his hand, she kept a firm grip on it.

"It was something more than saving my life, that you did for me," she said. "It was giving me a last fighting chance for happiness, Juan!"

"He's tongue-tied," said Lorens, laughing. "Let him go. He's a strong devil, and brave as steel. Juan, you can go outside now, and stand watch. Keep your eyes open. What I expect is one man and one horse. If you find more than one coming this way, give me the alarm. You understand?"

Silver nodded, backed through the door, and was gone.

When he was at a distance, he whistled a bar of a song to register the amount of ground that separated him from the cabin; then he turned and ran for it like a silent shadow, and paused close to the door in time enough to hear her say:

"You're sure about him?"

"Why not?" said Lorens. "He's done enough to prove himself, I'd say! He's worked well for you. He's bought me two fine horses for half the money that I would have had to pay."

"His eyes are light," she answered.

"You find plenty of light-colored eyes in Mexico," said Lorens.

"They must be the exception, though," said the girl.

"Well, perhaps they are."

"So this man Juan is one of the exceptions," said she. "He's an exception in lots of ways. He's bigger than most men. He has heavier shoulders and longer arms. Most peons look stupid, but he has a thinking face. There is a sort of fire of fierceness in him, but when he was standing in front of me, he tried to cover up everything."

"Come, come," said Lorens. "You know how that is—just nervous, just embarrassed in front of the beautiful señorita!" He laughed a little.

"It wasn't embarrassment," she answered. "There wasn't any embarrassment in his make-up. There was no blood warming up to his skin. He was cool as a cucumber. And from the look or two I had at his eyes, it seemed to me that he was all set and intent on something, like a tightrope walker a thousand feet off the ground. He was watching his step."

"I don't believe that," said Lorens.

"I hope that I'm wrong," she answered. "But all the while it seemed to me that he was trying to prevent me from having a look at his mind. He hung his head and let his hair fall over his eyes. But it seemed to me that his natural position would be as straight as an arrow, and looking the world in the eye. That's what I felt about him. Perhaps I'm wrong. I know that I'm nervous enough to make mistakes. It's because I'm making my last play to win happiness, and I can't feel secure about anything. Perhaps I have an hour, or a day, or a week—if we're lucky, there may be a month for us. But that's the end! It's for that instant of happiness that I'm fighting and on the alert!"

"All right," said Lorens, his voice growing a little weary and cold. "I suppose I know what you mean. But this fellow Juan—he's all right. If he's not, I'll cut out his heart and take a look at the color of it!"

Chapter – 15

IT IS possible to be grateful even to a rogue. Silver was grateful to Lorens. He knew the man was a scoundrel, as dangerous as a snake with poisonous craft; still he was grateful because Lorens had defended him.

But as Silver drew back into the night again, he kept wondering what might be that happiness for which the girl was willing to do so much.

Now he began to make his rounds of the place, shadowy among the brush and through the trees, rousing up every animal instinct to the keenest pitch of alertness. Nervous hands, as it were, began to reach out from him, and make him aware of everything near by. And yet, for all his caution, for all his spying, when he saw the figure standing at the door of the shack, it was as though the form had risen out of the ground.

He started toward the cabin, swiftly.

For one thing, they had talked about a horseman arriving, and there had not been a hoofbeat even in the distance for a long time. Silver was halfway to the door of the cabin when the shadowy form slipped suddenly through the door into the lighted cabin. Silver had a sight of a man of middle height, of rather a strong build—and as the fellow disappeared from view, the voice of the girl split the very eardrum of Silver with a scream.

He came at the cabin as fast as a tiger runs at easy prey. Through the doorway he leaped with the Colt ready in his hand—and saw Edith Alton Kenyon wrapped in the arms of the stranger, while Lorens conveniently turned his back and had started toward the door.

When Lorens saw the drawn gun, he snapped out a revolver of his own with wonderful speed, but by that time it was apparent that Silver was simply amazed, not attacking. As for the stranger, his face was visible in profile, and it clearly showed the features of the escaped criminal, the pursued murderer, David Holman!

Silver drew back toward the door, entranced. Lorens was beckoning to him to go outside again. And the last he saw was that Holman had made the girl sit down, while he kneeled in front of her and kissed her hands, and looked constantly, hungrily, into her face.

Pale from the prison confinement, his eyes deeply sunk in shadow, it seemed to Silver that David Holman could easily be capable of a murder—but hardly a murder by stealth. It was as strong a face as Silver ever had seen. There was a stonelike quality about the flesh, and there seemed to be a stonelike quality about the stare which he fixed on the girl. He was not speaking. His jaws were hard set. But it seemed to Silver that he had never seen passion so mute or so powerful. That was the index and the key of the man—power, power, and more power!

Looking at him now, it was not at all strange that he had robbed a bank and killed two assistant thieves, but it was just a trifle odd that a sheriff and a posse ever had been able to take him alive, or that he should have told such a cock-and-bull story in his trial.

But there he was in the cabin—that happiness for which the girl had been working and praying; an hour, a day, a week, a month of David Holman had been her dream. And Silver, seeing her in the fulfillment of her wish, found her transfigured. She was crying with happiness; she was a child, and yet she was more profoundly a woman than any Silver had ever before seen in his strange life.

He went out through the door into the black of the night, dazed and confused. He heard Lorens saying, within:

"You two need to talk. Ill take the outer guard, and Juan will keep the door. You can talk right out. He only understands ten words of English."

He came out, calling: "Juan! Come here!"

Silver came slowly back to him.

"You stand here by the door, Juan," said Lorens. "You've made one mistake tonight—that is to say, it might have been a mistake if that had been any man other than Holman. Now, keep your eyes a little wider open. You won't find many as shifty as Holman, but there are others who have eyes, too."

"I shall watch," said Silver grimly. "But if I stay close by the door, I can see only half the night."

"Do as I tell you," said Lorens. "Stand right by the door, and be ready to shoot if anything strange happens. You know what this means, now, Juan. You know that Holman is hunted by the law, with a price on his head. But can you trust us to give you more than the law would give you?"

"Señor," said Silver, "the law has very seldom been my friend. Why should I work for it? And even if I could capture Señor Holman and bring him to the sheriff, ways would be found of cheating a poor Mexican like me. Besides, perhaps the law wants me, also!"

Lorens laughed. "You're a useful sort of a fellow, Juan," said he. "And you'll be paid your weight in gold, before you're through with this business. There's money to be had out of this affair, and trust me, I know how to get it. This whole business is dripping with coin—dripping! And you shall keep your share. Keep your eyes open. I'm going to walk in a big circle around the house."

He went off into the darkness, whistling under his breath, and Silver pursed his lips in silence.

It was clearly apparent that Lorens was in this for the money, only. He had been the agent, the go-between who had helped the girl to free Holman from prison, in some way. He had distributed the bribes in the proper places, perhaps. And now that the two were together, Lorens intended to watch over them, serve them, and continually squeeze the purse of the girl for his own gain.

In the meantime, it was unpleasant to be an eavesdropper at the door of the cabin, but he could not disobey Lorens. He walked back and forth and tried to shut the voices from his ears, but they kept penetrating his brain constantly.

She was explaining: "Lorens knew one of the trustees very well. He had to pour the man full of money, but at last the thing was done. Some of the bribes were handed out, here and there. And that was why the guards looked the other way when you were escaping. But I don't want to talk about that. The thing's done. You're here. Nothing else matters."

"I want to have everything clear in my mind," said Holman's voice. It was deep, resonant, and yet very quiet. "Where did the money come from? According to your father's will, you were not to have any real income until you married."

Light shot at last through the brain of Silver, as he listened.

The girl said nothing.

"Is that hard for you to answer?" asked Holman.

There was more silence.

"Do I have to tell you?" she asked at last.

"No," said Holman. "I don't want to put a finger's weight of pressure on you. Tell me only what you please."

"Then forget everything in the past!" she urged him. "You know that we haven't long together. They are going to hunt you down. Every minute is one of the last minutes. How can we waste them?"

"Secrets will make shadows between us—that's all," said Holman.

"If I tell you," said the girl, her voice breaking, "you'll despise me!"

A sudden fierce anxiety broke out in his next words: "What thing have you done?"

"I found a man who would marry me," she said. "I found—"

"You mean to say that you're married, Edith?" breathed Holman.

"Only in name, only in name!" said the girl. "Listen to me! There was no other way to get the money, and without money I couldn't help you. I found a man—the simplest fellow in the world, only interested in ranching and beef, and such things. I was going to marry him, and then disappear, and leave him a large sum of money, so that he could go ahead and lead the sort of life that he wanted to lead. And when I failed to appear again, he could get his divorce without the slightest trouble because of desertion. Don't you see? Wanted to do him no real harm, but actually to help him, and chiefly, to help you!"

"You wanted to do him no harm," muttered Holman. "And then what happened to him?"

She had to pause to rally herself for a moment, apparently, but at last she said: "He grew fond of me. And he—Listen to me! You have to listen. You can't turn away like this. I know it makes you sick at heart. I know that you would never have wanted me to do it. But I couldn't dream—"

"Before you married him," said Holman, "didn't you have an idea that he might be getting in pretty deep?"

"I couldn't know for sure. He was such a great, gaunt, simple creature—a caricature of a man. Everyone laughed at him—and I wasn't laughing at him. No, no, I was pitying him and liking him. I began to guess that he was fond of me, really. I couldn't tell how much, though."

Holman groaned. Silver heard the spat of a fist driven into the flat of a palm.

"David, what could I do?" cried the girl. "Look at me; tell me what I could do? I didn't dream poor Ned would be of such fine stuff. I thought he might feel one twinge of pain, and then forget all about me in the pleasure of having ten thousand dollars."

Holman's step began to pace the floor.

"What's his name?" asked Holman bluntly.

"Edward Kenyon. He—"

"I've kept my hands clean all my life," said Holman bitterly, "and only for this—to be a condemned criminal escaped from the death house owing to a fraud on the part of a woman. I'm a sponger—a sneaking, cringing cur! I live on a woman; I let her torture other men for me. Ah, that's a picture to remember!"

"If I'd opened my heart and told the whole thing to poor Ned," said the girl, "he would have gone through the form of the wedding. I know that, now, but at the time I was afraid that one whisper of the truth would get out and be the ruin of my plan to set you free, David."

"Hush!" said Holman. "I'm going mad. My brain's turning. I know you've done nothing for your own sake, and everything for mine. It seems that I'm put on the earth to make a fool of myself and a scoundrel of everyone else around me. I've put a curse on the people I love. I've made a sneaking, contriving, lying criminal out of you! Out of you!"

Silver heard her begin to sob, not wildly, but a deep, choked sound that told how she was fighting like a man against her weakness. But Holman did not console her.

"About the money," he said. "How much have you spent, so far?"

"I don't know, David. I don't want to think of it. The money doesn't matter. Heaven knows I would have given everything for these moments with you, even if you've begun to detest and despise me!"

"Despise you?" said Holman, in a voice that made Silver stop short in his harried pacing to and fro. "It's myself that's being poisoned by every word that you've told me. I want to know the whole story. How much have you spent?"

"You have to know? You command me, David?"

"I beg you, my dear!"

"It's something over forty thousand dollars."

Silver heard Holman gasp.

"You paid that out to whom?"

"To Lorens, of course. He's handled everything."

"And how much of it is left with Lorens?"

"Nothing, David. He had to spend floods in the prison, through the trusties."

"He used up the entire forty thousand dollars? He didn't put anything in his own pocket?"

"No, David. Not a penny. He has hardly a cent in his wallet, now. He told me only today. But I've brought more. I brought another fifty thousand out—"

"Fifty thousand?" cried Holman. "Don't you know that it's enough to get you murdered? Fifty thousand dollars, carrying it around like pebbles in your pocket? But wait a moment. How much does he get of that fifty thousand? How much does he expect?"

"Nothing for himself, David. All that he wants to do is to see you safe. He's had trouble with the law himself, and he took pity on us, David. He himself offered to do what he could. I've never been able to give him a single dollar for his own pocket."

"He sounds like an ideal character," said Holman dryly. "But he doesn't look like one. Not by a mile! Go on, Edith. Tell me how much you'll need to spend now?"

"Just for the moment, a good deal," said the girl. "Lorens is going to arrange everything for us. He knows a section of the mountains where we can be safe, he swears. Perhaps not for days and weeks, but for years. He knows the sheriff of that county, and he knows several others who can be bribed to close their eyes and not know that we're there. It will cost a good deal, to begin with, but then—"

"How much?"

"About forty thousand dollars."

"Forty thousand? Forty thousand dollars, did you say? For a sheriff—and a few others? Who are the others?"

"I didn't ask him. I know that we can trust him. Why are you glaring like that, David?"

"Because the thief is bleeding you! If he spent ten thousand to get me out of the prison, he was a fool. If there's a sheriff to be fixed, either the man can be bought for five thousand, or else he couldn't be touched for five millions. And that's more apt to be the case. Have you given him that forty thousand. yet?"

"Yes," said the girl. "Because he—What are you going to do, David? You're not—"

Holman came to the door of the shack.

"Oh, Lorens!" he called.

"Here!" answered Lorens, and came swiftly. "Anything wrong?" he asked cheerfully.

"I think there is," said Holman. "Come inside. I've been hearing about your money dealings with Edith. I've been hearing about your altruism, too. I've heard that you've just bled her for another forty thousand dollars, you cur! And I'm going to take that money away from you!"

Lorens flashed his hand for a gun.

Holman hit out with a strength that flung Lorens back against the wall and made him drop to one knee. He was half-stunned, but not enough to spoil his shooting at such a close range. And he meant murder. The snarling look in his face was like that of a wild cat about to put his teeth in red meat.

"You fool!" yelled Lorens, above the cry of the girl. "I've trimmed her. And now I'm going to trim you—and collect the blood money on your head!"

"No, señor," said Silver, and he shoved the muzzle of his Colt out of the darkness and into the verge of the light in the room.

Chapter – 16

THE whole scene was in nice balance. The girl had caught up a Winchester, but dared not swing the muzzle toward Lorens, knowing that she would be too late. So she stood with the rifle in her right hand, her left arm flung out, her face white with fear, and strained in every muscle. Holman, obviously unarmed, was on tiptoe to rush at the kneeling Lorens, but even Holman, though there was a savage fury in his face, kept himself from moving. And as for Lorens, he was tasting the kill beforehand, with an infinite relish.

But the gleaming of Silver's revolver was enough to change everything. It made Lorens glance to the side.

"You rat!" he yelled. Then he swung into smooth Spanish, saying: "Juan, you know the hand that feeds you. You know—"

"I know, señor," said Silver calmly. "And I know that it is the lady who will spend the money, and not you. Señor, I am sad, but if you don't put down that gun, I shall have to shoot you through the head! Quickly, amigo!"

Lorens turned on Silver a frightful look. Then, in silence, his right hand jerked down inch by inch until the gun lay on the floor. Still his fingers worked on the butt, yearning to snatch it up for action. At last his hand was clear of the Colt.

"Now stand up, señor," said Silver. "Forgive me—but if you make one quick move, my poor thumb on the hammer of this gun will be frightened, and the hammer will fall, and you will go up to join the sky people."

Lorens stood panting, silent. He obeyed Silver's instructions, and turned his face to the wall with both arms stretched high above his head, and in this position, Silver searched him from his hair to the soles of his boots. There was plenty to find, but what mattered most was not the hidden knife and the hidden little two-barrel pistol, but the wallets. One was a good pigskin and

344

rested in the inside coat pocket, but the others were simply a tissue of oiled silk inside the top of each boot.

In the first wallet there was intact exactly the forty thousand dollars which Lorens had been paid on this day. In the two silk swathings, there was almost thirty-two thousand more. Holman counted out that considerable fortune in greenbacks of large denominations.

In the meantime, Lorens was saying to Silver: "What a cursed fool I was! Tonight I argued on your side of the fence, too. But I'll tell you, Juan—I'll find a way to come back to you. How you'll pray to die—how you'll beg for hell itself when my hands get to work on you, one day!"

"You hear him, Juan?" said David Holman, in very poor Mexican dialect. "He means poison. You've given me a life that's not worth a rap, but I'm thanking you for it. That's all I can do—thank you. But the lady will try to choke you with a flood of money. Tell us, in the first place, what we can do with this fellow Lorens?"

"Señor," said Silver softly, "what do we do when we find a snake?"

"Kill him? Kill him out of hand?" asked Holman. "You mean that, Juan?"

He stepped back a little, not horrified, but looking at Silver with a sort of pitying curiosity.

"Listen to me, señor," said Silver. "If you try to take him with you, he will escape. If you set him free, no matter what he promises, he'll have the hunters on your trail very soon. I shall not murder him. Let him have back his revolver. We shall both put our guns away, and then it will be fair and even at the start!"

"Good!" said Lorens, with a sudden cry of relief. "I'll do that, Holman! I'll take my free chance with him, first, and with you, afterward!"

Holman shook his head. He lifted a finger at Juan.

"Tie his hands," said Holman. "Then we'll try to think the thing out."

Silver obediently bound the hands of Lorens. He could hardly believe the work that his fingers were doing.

He had found the trail of this adventure when he came out from the upper mountains into view of the plains. He had encountered poor Ned Kenyon and followed him into a maze of strangeness. He had outfronted Buck; he had seen Buck murdered on the verge of speaking the name which began with "Nel—" And he had become the "Mexican" servant of One-eyed Harry Bench, and then of Lorens, only to swing over to the aid of an outlaw with a price on his head!

"I'm wrong to keep him alive, perhaps," explained Holman to Silver, "because I know that he's no great gift to the world. But at the same time, we can't have people killed like that, Juan."

The girl came up close to Lorens.

"Why did you do it?" she pleaded. "I would have given you money. I would have given you anything you asked for. I trusted you. Don't you see, you were only harming yourself? Why did you do it?"

Lorens bared his teeth as he looked at her.

"Partly," he said insolently, "because I felt like doing it that way—because I wanted to make a fool out of you—because I intended to suck the blood out of your fortune and leave only a shell of it. And partly I did it because I hated the sight of your face, and the yammering about Holman. Is that enough reason for you?"

He was magnificent as is a fearless beast that is ready to fight to the last, and Silver dimly admired him for the savage that was in him. It was only strange, in the light of this wonderful courage, that the fellow had run away from him that day in the ravine, after firing the first shot. But perhaps that could be explained. There was no money, after all, in the murder of a stray rider, and why should such a man as the great Lorens needlessly leave dead men in his trail, so that the law could find them afterward?

"We'll have to talk things over," said Holman to the girl. "Come outside with me, and we'll make a decision. You, Juan—are you intending to help us?"

"And you shall have as much money—" cried the girl.

"Hush!" said Holman, lifting his hand. "There's something else. He's not doing this all for money."

"No," said Silver. "If they catch me with money, they'll soon know that Juan is a rascal. Let me be a poor man, señor, and when I leave you, give me only what you please. There is no spending of money when a man is buried, señor. And cold tortillas and stale beans are better to eat than lead; neither is it easy to swallow with a rope tight around the neck. Señor, they want you, and they have put a price on you. Señor, they want poor Juan, also. There are people who would pay a price for him, too. So I shall serve you, if you please. I only wish to run back into the town. In half an hour—in an hour, I come again."

"Very well," said Holman. "Trot along."

Lorens began to sneer.

"You see him now. When you see him again, he will have the head hunters along with him! Bah! When was there a greaser who could keep his tongue still?"

Holman merely said: "You can make a noise, Lorens, but you can't make a sound that any one of us wants to hear. Go on, Juan. I'll trust you. I'd rather be dead than give up the hope that there's an honest man somewhere in the world!"

That was what rang in the brain of Silver, as he raced down the valley toward the town again. The hope to find an honest man! It could hardly be mere hypocrisy. And was it true, therefore, that David Holman had been falsely accused, falsely sentenced?

Chapter – 17

I T SEEMED to Silver that he was in a labyrinth. Now and then he found or thought he found a glimmer of light, but whatever passage he took, led him eventually deeper into profound darkness. But he had the sense of one verity which measured with the simple honesty and gentleness of poor Ned Kenyon—and that was the passion that existed between Holman and the girl.

Silver ran straight on through the town. The dawn was commencing, and the edges of the river were streaked with fire. For this one hour in the day, work on the bridge almost seemed to have ceased. On through the silence of the town, and down the valley he went at full speed.

But when he was still at a distance from the lean-to, he saw the huge bulk of One-eyed Harry in front of the shack, and the smoke of the fire he had kindled rolling slowly off on the wind.

Silver leaned against the shack, panting out words.

"Harry, what's your limit? Are you ready for anything?"

"What are you up to?" asked Harry Bench, the beard puckering all over his face as he pressed his lips hard together.

"Taking an outlaw and his woman where the headhunters won't find him."

Harry Bench grunted. "That's a mean job," he said. "It's been tried, and it don't often work."

"This time it has to work," said Silver.

"What do you get out of it?"

"I get a barrel of fun out of it," said Silver grimly, "and a chance to put my claws into one or two people who need trouble. You get any sort of pay that you want."

"Well," said One-eyed Harry, considering. "I've worked a lot for a dollar and a half a day, and there's been times when I've got two and a half a day,

348

for a short job that was a hard one. But for a layout like this, I'd want double that. They'd have to come across with five dollars a day to me, brother!"

He shook his head to emphasize his demand.

"Ten dollars, call it," suggested Silver, smiling.

"Ten dollars?" said Harry Bench, his eyes gleaming. Then he shook his head again, but this time in denial. "It's too much. There ain't any man that's worth that much for the work he does with his hands. Five dollars a day does for me. No more, and no less. I ain't a hog, Silver!"

"Saddle up, then," said Silver. "Fix my outfit on Parade. Get everything together, and the pack saddle on Parade, and throw some dust on him to tame his color a little. I'm going to sleep a half hour, if it takes you that long."

He lay down on his back, closed his eyes, relaxed his body, his limbs. There was a nervous twitching of his right hand which presently stilled in turn, and as it ceased, Silver was asleep. Through the noise made by the heavy stride of Bench, through the squeaking of saddle leather, he slept on, until Bench called his name.

Then they went up the valley together, as Bench protested.

"It ain't right to start a long march on an empty stomach, partner!"

"You can live on your fat, for a few days," answered Silver. "We're not apt to have much time for cooking of fodder, or for the eating of it, either!"

"All right," said One-eyed Harry. "A gent can't expect to travel Pullman when he's collecting five bucks a day. Lead on, son!"

One-eyed Harry put his horse to a trot. Silver rode the mule with his own saddle on it, and Parade followed on a lead. That was how they got into Kirby Crossing just as the town wakened in earnest and the stores were opened. In the distance they could hear the shouting of voices, and the beating of hammers where the bridge was building.

"Go into the grocery store," said Silver. "We'll need more bacon and general grubstakes for four people. We're going to hit for the tall timber, and we won't be stopping to do any shopping on the way. Pick up what you want, Harry. I'll wait out here and hold the nags."

He sat down on his heels as Harry disappeared, made a cornucopia-shaped cigarette, and smoked with his back against a post of the hitch-rack, and his eyes half closed. As a matter of fact, he was half asleep when a voice said:

"Arizona, are you goin' to forget your old friends?"

He turned his head, suddenly, and found Ned Kenyon standing behind him, smiling a twisted smile.

Silver rose quickly to his feet.

"How did you spot me? Who told you that I'd be in this sort of get-up?" asked Silver scanning the street up and down.

"Nobody told me," said Kenyon. "But there was a kind of look about this here stallion. Four legs like those ain't put under every horse in the world, you know. And every man ain't got a pair of shoulders like yours, Arizona. Not shaking hands?"

"Do you shake hands with every greaser that you meet?" asked Silver.

The twisted smile of Kenyon appeared again. He was so worn about the eyes, his face was so sallow, that he looked as though he had barely dragged himself out of a sick bed.

"All right," said Kenyon. "No offense, Arizona. Shall I go along?"

"Wait a minute," answered Silver. "What brought you up here to Kirby Crossing?"

"There's a man by the name of Nellihan that I'm goin' to meet in a few minutes," said Kenyon. "He got in touch with me. I guess he's not much of a man, partner, but he has an idea about me making some trouble for Edith."

The eyes of Silver narrowed.

"Of course," went on the slow, weary voice of Kenyon, "I don't intend to do that. But I was thinking that through Nellihan, maybe, I'd be able to see her again. I managed to rake up five hundred dollars. I borrowed it here and there, and sold a coupla old saddles. And if Nellihan knows where she is, maybe for five hundred dollars he'd be willing to take me to her."

"Why do you want to see her again, Ned?" asked Silver, setting his teeth hard as pity for his friend mastered him.

Kenyon looked far off across the roofs of the houses. He pushed his hat back and scratched his head.

"Well, it's like this," he said. "If I could kind of tell her that there ain't any hard feelings on my part, and that I'm willing to go and get the divorce, if she wants me to, or keep on being married, if she wants me to, it would sort of ease me, a good bit. And more'n that, to tell you the truth, there's been some minutes—since that day—that I've sort of wished that I could see her. Just only that. To see her and not say anything, that would be better for me than venison steaks and church music, Jim!"

Silver swallowed hard.

"Nellihan," he said. "Where are you to meet him?"

"Right over there, in that little shack down the street—the one that's got white paint on the front of it and no paint on the rest of it."

"Are you going there now?"

"I'm going there as soon as you're through talking to me."

"Listen to me, Ned. Nellihan is a bad hombre."

"He has to be," answered Kenyon, "or he wouldn't want to make trouble for Edith."

"You don't need to talk to him, if you want to see her. I can take you to her."

"You?"

"Yes," said Silver. He waited for the flush to finish burning the face of Kenyon, and when the pallor had come over it again, as quickly, he said: "But I wonder if it's the right thing for you to do, Ned?"

"Maybe it ain't," agreed Kenyon gently. "I been thinking sort of selfish about it. But maybe it ain't the right thing to do. You know better. Jim. If you think that it would hurt her to see me, I wouldn't go."

He waited, tense with anxiety, for the judgment. He was only a child, thought Silver, but never in the world had a more honest child existed.

"If you want to see her, you shall," said Silver suddenly. "I'll take you out there to meet her. But I'd like to lay an eye on Mr Nellihan, first."

He said it in such a way that Kenyon started.

"What do you mean?" he asked. "You want me to take you over to him?"

"I want you to go over there and start talking to him," said Silver. "Because there's a chance that he knows the look of me, and if he does, he's likely to out with a gun and pepper me. I want you to go in and take his eye, and then I'll try to step inside and have a few words with him. Will you do that?"

"Does it mean guns?" asked Kenyon with a sigh. "I ain't any hero, Arizona. I ain't like you. I got nerves, and bad ones!"

"I don't know what it'll mean," said Silver. "I want to talk to him. You understand? I have something to say to him. That's all. He may start a fight. If he does, I'll have to try to finish it."

Kenyon bit his lip, then nodded.

"I'll go in first, then," said he. "You come when you're ready. So long, Arizona."

He went down the street with his long strides.

A moment later, big One-eyed Harry came out, singing from the bottom of his deep throat.

"Load up the stuff," commanded Silver abruptly. "Get the horses ready. And take them down the street, slowly, mind you. Don't go any farther than that white house, down there. When you get near that, find something to do about the saddle—a girth or something to fool with until you hear from me. Is that clear?"

"Clear as a bell," said Harry Bench. "What new kind of devilry is up now?"

"It's all a part of one pattern that I don't quite understand, but it's almost clear, now," said Silver. "Do what I say. Be ready to chuck the mule loose, because we may have to start moving faster than a mule gallop."

By this time, the tall form of Kenyon had disappeared through the front door of the white-faced shack, and therefore Silver followed on at once.

When he came to the steps that led up to the diminutive veranda, he was glad of the soft-soled sandals he wore. They carried him noiselessly to the door, and as he reached it, he could hear the voices inside.

The penetrating and disagreeable tone of Nellihan was saying: "Business is business, Mr Kenyon. But to go back to the beginning, you've endured a terrible wrong. That wrong ought to be righted. A fraud has been practiced on you. A terrible fraud. That marriage should not lead to a divorce. It ought to lead to an annulment. As though it never had been. It was a piece of trickery on the part of that girl. And she should be made to suffer for it. Any man with a right sense of his own dignity would be sure to see that she suffered for what she's done."

The gentle voice of Kenyon answered, drawling: "I suppose that a lot of people would agree with what you have to say, Mr Nellihan. But I dunno that I can see it that way. It ain't the money that—"

"Money!" said Nellihan his voice suddenly lowering. "Money? Do you know what I'm speaking about when I say money? Have you any idea of what you intend to throw out the window?"

"Not any clear idea," answered Kenyon.

"Then listen to me—and I know what I'm talking about. It's my business to know—and I know! It's a matter of between eight and ten million dollars!"

Kenyon gasped very audibly; even Silver was shocked by the amount of the fortune.

"I'm putting my cards on the table, Mr Kenyon," said Nellihan, "I have to say to you that I was made the victim of a crooked will, a piece of fraud engineered by that same girl, and I want you to know that if I can prove that her marriage was an act of fraud, I can have the estate sealed up, make her repay the money she's stolen from the bank, and have two chances out of three to have myself declared the full or the half heir of the whole business. There are my cards, sir. Now what do you think of 'em?"

His hand slapped the table, evidently, at this point.

"Well, partner," said Kenyon, "I dunno what I think. I only know what I feel when you tell me that you're goin' to accuse her of anything and try to prove it by something that I say or do. And I can tell you, man to man, with all the cards face up on the table, that you're an infernal rascal, and that I'll have nothing to do with you!"

"You fool!" gasped Nellihan.

And that was the moment when Silver pushed the door open and stepped inside.

Chapter – 18

THE gun of Silver appeared before his body, so the swift hand of Nellihan fluttered, but failed to complete its gesture. He stood in a rather ridiculous, namby-pamby attitude, as though he had been trying to shake mud off his fingers.

"Excuse me, señor, if you please," said Silver.

"Back up into the corner, Kenyon!" breathed Nellihan. "If we've got him between two angles, we'll make him jump! The greaser!"

Kenyon turned quietly to Silver.

"Shall I stay here?" he asked.

"Stand back here near the door," answered Silver, "and wait till I need you."

He kept his speech in Spanish, but Nellihan cried out in the same language:

"Is this a plot between the pair of you? Kenyon, are you a crook, after all? Here—you—what do you want?"

Silver looked at him with a curious penetration. He was seeing Nellihan clearly for the first time, and he thought the man's face was the most detestable he had ever seen. There was something about the entire makeup of Nellihan that was revolting—a sort of cross between the bird and the beast. He had a long, gaunt pair of legs with a pair of great feet on the end of them. He had a hunched back which forced his shoulders forward and kept his head thrust forward at a sharp angle. But no bodily deformity matched his face—a sickly yellow-gray.

The colour was not all. The features could be called handsome, in a way, and a smiling way, at that, but there was a birdlike intensity of brightness about the eyes that turned the blood of Silver cold. The man was something more and something less than human. And if this were the antagonist of Edith

353

Alton, Silver could pity her. It was no wonder that she had been driven to the wall.

"What do you want?" Nellihan was repeating.

"Señor," said Silver, "One night not long ago you killed, in a saloon in Mustang a man named Buck."

"You say I killed him," said Nellihan. "Is there any reason on earth why I should have done it?"

"Yes," said Silver. "The señor hired Buck to murder Señor Kenyon here. And when Buck was about to confess that he was hired, and who had bought him, the señor fired a bullet out of the darkness. He stood safe in the night, and killed this man. But Buck lived to write on the floor!"

"He wrote three letters on the floor, and because they're the first three letters of my name, d'you think that that's a proof against me?" asked Nellihan. "What would the law say to that? He might have been starting to write 'Nelson' or 'Nelly,' or I don't know what!"

"There are not very many names that begin with those letters," said Silver.

"You poor fool," exclaimed Nellihan, "you think that you'll get reward money if you take me back to Mustang and lay the charge against me? Why, the whole town would laugh. There's no motive that could be charged to me!"

"No?" said Silver. "There was first the motive of hiring Buck—to prevent the marriage of the señorita with Señor Kenyon—and then the killing of Buck to close his mouth."

Nellihan leaned over and gripped the edge of the table with both hands.

"That's the case you'll talk up, my Mexican friend, is it?" said he. "You might raise a mob—that's all you could do against me. You never would have a grip on the law. The law would laugh at you. The sheriff would refuse to make the arrest."

A change came over Silver. He stood straighter. The mop of black hair fell back from his eyes, and let the sheen of them strike into the very soul of Nellihan.

"The thing is outside of the law, señor," he said. "But, I, also, am outside of the law. I am going to put up my revolver. I know you carry one. If you can murder in the dark, perhaps you can fight in the light. Now, señor!"

Silver flashed his Colt back inside the looseness of his shirt, beneath the pit of the left arm.

But the fear that had been turning Nellihan to stone now was relieved, and the life gradually came back into his eyes. It had seemed to Kenyon, looking on at this strange scene, that the man had been taken into the hand of Silver's greater mind and greater emotion, and crushed. But now he recovered a little, rapidly.

"I see what you are," said Nellihan. "No more a peon than your eyes are black. No more a thug than a saint is. You're one of these romantic fools, are you? Well, I won't make a move to get my gun!"

"If you don't—" began Silver, and suddenly paused.

What could he do? There was nothing he wanted more than to rid the world of this poisonous monster. But he could not shoot down a man who refused to fight.

"I won't," said Nellihan, shaking his head, smiling and sneering. 'Some other day—perhaps. Perhaps when I'm myself. But I've had a small shock, and I'm upset. Another day, when I'm myself, I might have the pleasure of putting a bullet through you—whoever you are behind your skin! But not now. I won't lift a hand—and you won't do murder!"

Silver stared hard. If ever there had been a temptation toward murder, it was working now in his blood. His breath left him, in the passion of his anger and his disgust, and it would have been hard to tell what his next act might have been, when a footfall sounded on the steps of the little house, and the door was flung open by—Lorens!

The gun of Silver flashed toward him instantly, and seeing the full picture of Kenyon, Nellihan, and Silver gathered together, Lorens slammed the door again and bounded back down the steps, with a yell.

That yell went ringing through the air: "Help! Help! Guns this way!"

Silver rammed the muzzle of his Colt under the chin of Nellihan, and with a swift hand snatched away his two guns.

And he was saying as he "fanned" Nellihan: "There'll be another meeting, Nellihan."

"In which I'll send you to the devil!" said Nellihan.

He was perfectly calm about it. If there was no shame in the man, the lack of it was an added strength for him, it appeared.

"Get your horse!" called Silver to Kenyon. "Get your horse and ride like the devil after me. Keep the spur in its side!"

Then he leaped for the door and out into the street, in time to see Lorens darting into the hotel, still shouting.

The long legs of Kenyon bore him rapidly across the street, diagonally backward. Silver himself reached Parade, and as big Harry Bench mounted his own mustang, throwing the mule adrift, Silver flung himself on top of the pack.

He was working with both hands, as the great horse sprang away, and finally managing to reach down with his hunting knife, he cut the last strap that bound the pack and the saddle to the stallion.

The whole contraption fell crashing into the street, and left Silver on the smooth, rounded, powerful back of Parade.

Looking back, he saw Kenyon streaking a horse after him, with Harry Bench already midway between the two. Still farther back, there was a rout of men tumbling out of the hotel, and mounting their horses.

Silver thundered: "Harry, keep coming, I'm leaving you, but I'll meet you again in five minutes up the road!"

And he left them—yes, as though they were standing still, for at his call, Parade went away on wings. The green trees blurred together in walls on either side of the road, so great was his speed. It seemed hardly an instant before Silver found himself nearing the shack where Lorens had lived, and as he did so, he saw David Holman ride out on the grey horse into the trail.

Silver waved his arm frantically, as a signal for haste.

"The girl! The girl! Both of you start on the run!" he yelled.

Holman twisted that cow pony around as though he were an old hand on a cattle ranch, and as Silver checked the stallion opposite the shack, he saw Edith Alton swinging up onto the roan mustang. Then, in one well-formed sweep, the five riders broke away on the trail together.

Silver lingered near the front only long enough to call to Holman to learn how Lorens had escaped, and he was told that the man had been left securely tied, while Holman walked out with the girl for a few minutes. When he returned, just now, he found Lorens gone, and fearing that danger would come, he had saddled both horses and started to ride back a little down the trail to see that all was well.

The story was simple enough. The damage that was done by the fact that might be the end of them all, and Silver knew it.

He reined back beside the girl. She gave him a sidelong look of agony out of her pinched face. Her look said to him clearly: "You're Arizona Jim! You're the friend of Ned Kenyon, and you've brought him here like a curse on me!"

He answered that look by crying out: "I'm here to help you. So is Kenyon. We're for you, and for Holman, We'll see you through!"

He fell back still farther, and waved cheerfully to One-eyed Harry Bench, who gave him a tremendous scowl and a shake of the head, as though knowing that his weight would wear out any horse, in a long chase.

Still farther back, along the single file, Silver ranged up beside the white face and the shadowy, sunken eyes of Kenyon. That was what the sight of the girl had done to him.

But Silver shouted at him, almost savagely: "Go up into the lead! You know all of this country like a book. Go up and lay a trail for us that will shake off the men from Kirby Crossing! Go on up to the lead, Ned, if you're half a man!"

Chapter – 19

THERE were many doubts in the mind of Silver, as he fell back to the place of rear guard on that procession, with the dust raised by the others whipping into his face.

With Parade beneath him, he could sweep away from all danger, easily; and the girl and Holman were well mounted, also. But the weight of Harry Bench was a ponderous load for a horse to bear, and Kenyon was a clumsy rider, and his mustang not very fast of foot. The speed of the party would have to be the speed of the slowest member in it, unless he could devise a way to split the group into sections.

What the men from Kirby Crossing wanted, of course, was David Holman, and the price that was on his head. If Bench and Kenyon, being the worst mounted of the group, could be shunted aside, it was not likely that any of the men of Kirby Crossing would tail after them. But now they left the trees and entered a great ravine where there was not even a bush or a rock to make a hiding place, and no canyons opened on either side. Perhaps a glacier, in the dead ages, had plowed out this enormous trench. At any rate, it seemed to Silver that Kenyon was leading the party into a hopeless trap, for the pursuers were rushing out from the trees in turn, and racing up the gorge.

He looked back, and gauged them. There were a full score of head hunters who had answered the call of Lorens and joined in the chase. Except for Lorens himself, five thousand dollars, even if divided into twenty parts, would give a handsome sum to each of those fellows. And if Lorens despised a cash reward as small as this, he would be gratified by revenge.

They made a formidable couple, hunting together—Lorens and Nellihan. And behind them, no doubt, was a hardy assortment of fighting men. Silver, scanning them, thought that every one of the lot rode like a veteran horseman.

He ranged Parade forward to the side of Kenyon, who galloped in the lead.

"They're gaining on us, Ned!" he said. "Some of 'em are eating up the ground. We've got to get into cover or broken ground before long, or they'll scoop us up."

Kenyon pointed ahead.

"You can't see it yet," he said, "but half a mile ahead there's a ravine opening on the right. It twists back into the mountains, and it's filled with cover. Three men could hold off three hundred Injuns in that ravine."

Silver pulled back to the rear again. David Holman joined him.

"Go back to the girl!" Silver commanded him. "I don't need you."

"You've turned from Mexican into white, Juan, have you?" said Holman. "She tells me that she's recognized you at last—that you're Arizona Jim—that you're the friend of—of her husband!"

His face twisted as he said that.

"Whatever I am, and whatever Kenyon is," said Silver, "we're in here to help you. You get back beside the girl."

"While you stay back and catch the bullets that fly?" asked Holman.

He smiled a little then, then eased the Winchester that slanted in a saddle holster under his right leg.

"I'll stay back here with you," said Holman calmly.

Silver protested no longer. Those men from the town of Kirby Crossing were gaining too rapidly, and the mustang that carried the bulk of One-eyed Harry was beginning to labor and grow unsteady of foot. Loud yells came from the pursuit. Each man rode as if for a prize. And the cold sweat beaded the forehead of Silver as he heard the whoopings.

But there, on the right, opened the mouth of a narrow canyon. It looked not so much water-worn, as simply a crack in the rocks. Kenyon led the way into it, and from behind, Silver heard a redoubled shouting that seemed to be of triumph. He looked back. He saw waving hats and hands, and one of the punchers shooting a stream of bullets into the air.

That was the way men acted when they rejoiced, but why should they be triumphant now?

For the entrance to the ravine seemed to Silver to promise them an ideal retreat. The little canyon wound crookedly back into the highlands, and the floor was covered with shrubs and with rocks that had fallen from the walls. But as they turned the first elbow bend, a shout of woe went up from Kenyon.

Silver saw the trouble at a glance, and an explanation of the exultation of the men of Kirby Crossing. For the lofty wall on one side of the valley had been shaken loose by an earthquake, perhaps, and now the gorge was choked almost to the top with a mighty confusion of broken rock, great stones that had broken square or jagged, and were heaped in ten-ton fragments.

"Climb! Climb! Climb!" yelled Silver.

He took the lead to show them how to do it. There would be no time to dismount and gradually maneuver the horses up the face of that dangerous pile. The men of Kirby Crossing would be at them in no time, and Silver flew Parade right at the mighty barrier.

Right and left, like a mountain goat, Parade sprang up three-and four-foot stages. His feet were slipping; his iron shoes were striking fire at every move, yet he went on swiftly. Nothing but his seventeen hands could stretch from one footing to the next, perhaps. But up to the top he went, dislodging a great boulder near the crest of the barrier.

Silver, dismounting, shouted the order that would make the stallion lie flat on his side, safe from rifle fire. Silver himself turned, rifle in hand, and dropped to his knees, for his first purpose in riding up the wall had been to get into a position from which he could cover the climbing of the rest.

He saw the boulder that had been dislodged leap down an irregular step or two, then bound outward. It missed the head of Kenyon by a hair's breadth, and smashed to bits on the rocky floor of the ravine. Kenyon himself was struggling up among the rocks. He had given up trying to lead his horse, which had promptly balked. In fact, only one horse of the outfit was climbing, and that was the gray which Holman had been riding. The tough mustang seemed to be cat-footed as it followed, though far less swiftly, where Parade had showed the way with a rider on his back. Big Harry Bench was leading in the climb, close behind the mustang, and David Holman was a little below him, helping the girl.

That was the picture at the feet of Silver when the leaders of the posse came sweeping around the corner of the canyon wall. He hoped, in his heart, that Lorens and Nellihan would be among the first, for he wanted with all his heart to put lead into them. But they were not among the leaders, and Silver could not shoot point-blank at strange men, whose hands might be clean.

He could fan their faces with his bullets, however.

Lying flat, with his rifle on a rest, he pumped six shots in rapid succession among the riders, and every bullet made some one of them jump or duck as though it had actually whipped through his flesh.

They whirled their horses, yelling, swinging forward like Indians along the necks of their horses, to make themselves into smaller targets. In a moment they were out of view, at the same time that the grey mustang gained the crest of the rock pile. Silver caught the horse, threw the reins, and let it stand. Then he lay down once more to guard the climbing of his party.

Presently, guns began to ring out. The men from Kirby Crossing had dismounted, and lying behind rocks, or standing behind the edge of the elbow turn in the canyon wall, they opened fire. Two or three bullets sang in the air over Silver. Others thudded against the boulders farther down.

He answered that fire. He had only an occasional glance at the sheen of steel gun barrels, but a howl of pain answered his third shot.

An instant later, it was echoed by a cry of agony from Edith Alton. Silver looked down, in horror. It was not the girl that had been struck, however, but David Holman, who lay helpless, wedged between two rocks.

Kenyon saw that from beneath, and struggled up to help the wounded man. Greater help came from above, however, for huge One-eyed Harry sprang down, caught up Holman's body as though it were a sack of bran, and bore it unaided over the top of the rocks.

There was only one reason why every one of the climbers was not shot down, and that was the rapid fire which Silver opened on every glint of steel. Not a single rifle was answering him when Kenyon helped the girl up the last step, and the whole party ran stumbling forward into safety.

Silver looked back. He could see a red stain spreading over the back of Holman's coat, as Bench carried him trussed across his shoulders. The bullet seemed to have gone right through the centre of Holman's body! He marked the place where it had entered; he marked the white agony in the face of the girl as she ran to her lover. Then he shouted his orders.

They were to strip Holman to the waist and examine the wound, and dress it as well as they could. While the girl and Kenyon did that, Bench would clamber onto the high ground on the adjoining side of the rock heap, and cut down two straight, light-bodied saplings for the making of a litter. He, Silver, would try to keep the enemy back while these preparations were made for carrying Holman with them in their retreat.

No one answered him by word of mouth. Each dumbly set about the execution of his appointed task while Silver turned back with a freshly loaded rifle and gave his attention to the ravine below.

The men of Kirby Crossing were not apt to try to charge forward from their angle of concealment. They were more likely to try to climb the wall of the gorge at their left, and so come out on a level with their quarry. They would not be in very great haste however. For they knew that Holman had been shot, and they would not be likely to imagine that the other three men would attempt to take the desperately wounded man along with them in the retreat. No, Holman was their prize, and Holman they would soon have!

Silver could not help agreeing with that thought. Hope had dwindled in him to vanishing point, as he glanced back from his scanning of the valley and watched the girl and Kenyon at work. It was a strange sight to see the three together, the girl and the man she had wronged working with a single devotion to save her lover.

They had stripped Holman to the waist. He was still senseless. And now they were bandaging him with strips torn from shirts and the underskirt of the girl. Kenyon was lifting the body, and the girl was passing the long strips around it. She had made a pad over the wound where the bullet entered that body, and another over the more gaping mouth whereby it had torn its way out.

Were they bandaging a man already dead, or breathing his last?

Silver looked back toward the ravine again, when he heard the voice of Holman say distinctly:

"The rest of you go on. Arizona—and the rest of you. You'll get long terms if you're caught helping an outlawed man to escape. And I'm not worth it. The life's running out of me. In another hour it won't matter whether you've stood by me to the finish or not! Arizona, take charge—make the rest of 'em march on!"

Chapter – 20

SOMETIMES to a lucky father there comes a moment when his son reveals by some word or some act the promise of a mind and a soul worthy of taking its place among the good and the strong men of the world. And in that moment all the pain of labor that has been spent, the anxiety, the fear, the groaning time of disappointment, are repaid, and a calm happiness comes over him.

So it was with Silver when he heard Holman speak. Much had been ventured for this fellow. Not only Silver's safety, but Bench and poor Ned Kenyon were endangered exactly as the wounded man had pointed out. But that danger mattered nothing now, because the words of Holman proved that he was worth all that could be done for him.

He heard Kenyon saying: "There ain't any use talking. Arizona won't leave you. And I won't leave you. And I reckon that Harry Bench won't chuck you over, neither. Here he comes now!"

Bench had duly brought back the stripped sapling poles that Silver demanded. The ends of them were tied to the saddle of Parade and of the gray horse. Across the centre of them a blanket was lashed to complete the litter, and Silver helped lift the wounded man into it.

He made one final protest.

"Waste is a bad thing, Arizona," said he. "Why do you waste yourself and all the rest, Arizona? The life is running out of me. It's no good fighting when the fight's lost beforehand!"

He even turned to the girl, saying: "Tell them, Edith. Tell them that they've done enough already. If they try to go on with me, they'll simply be scooped in by Lorens and the rest. I'm what those fellows are after. They'll leave the trail if they get me!"

The girl said nothing. She kept her green eyes fixed upon the face of Holman and suffered silently.

"If you've got breath enough to chatter like this, you've got breath enough to live for a while," said Silver. "Harry, you can't lead Parade. He'd try to eat you. I'll have to take him along. Ned will see the gray doesn't pull back. Edith, you walk beside Holman. Harry, you're the rear guard. Watch yourself, because those fellows are going to be after us on horses before long!"

It was the logical danger. After the men of Kirby Crossing gained the high ground to which Silver's party was now passing, the pursuers would be sure to get at least some of their horses over the rocky barrier, and so be able to rush the fugitives.

There was one good feature. The whole of the upland was covered with boulders, with big brush, and with copses of pine; and if they could make a few trail problems, they might keep away from the pursuit until darkness gave them a real chance to slip away.

Behind them they heard not a sound as they began to climb the side of a mountain, and when they were well up, Silver looked back and halted Parade for an instant. They were among big pines, but through the trunks they had distant glimpses of the scene below, where the entire posse was at work bringing up unwilling horses to the top of the barrier. Already eleven horses were up. Two more came to the top, and instantly these were mounted, and the diminished posse rushed off in pursuit.

"Ned," called Silver, "they'll be on our heels in twenty minutes. Is there any way out for us?"

"There's no way except one that a horse can't walk!" said Kenyon. "There's nothing but the old rope bridge across Whistling Canyon. If the ropes ain't rotted away!"

No way except one that a horse could not take? It meant leaving the gray behind, then; above all, it meant that Parade would be lost. Silver, jerking his head suddenly back, looked up at the sky and groaned.

"You've done a grand piece of work and you've made a good try," called the voice of David Holman. "But it's no use. Put me down here, Arizona. Heaven bless you for what you've done, but drop me here and go on to clear your own heels before the fire gets at them!"

Silver answered harshly: "Save your breath, Holman. You may be needing it before the night! Ned, which way to the bridge?"

Kenyon called the directions. Silver led the way, and they went slowly around the side of the mountain—slower, it seemed, than the crawling of a snail—while behind them horses were galloping on their trail! But now they came out on the side of Whistling Canyon and saw the bridge. It was a thing to take the breath, a fifty-foot stretch of ropes sagging across a gulch a hundred yards deep. And those ropes not only looked small, but they were whitened by long weathering.

The floor of the bridge was a mere cross-lashing of small ropes, stiffened by sapling poles to give a steadier footing. There was a guide rope stretched three feet above the frail bridge, and the whole supple structure was swaying in the wind that had given the canyon its name.

Silver set his teeth and looked across the span. Then he stepped on the edge of the bridge and strained on the ropes with all his might. They gave very little as he pulled up the slack. But though their strength might sustain his single weight, how would it support two men in the centre with the burden of Holman borne between them?

He dared not risk that. Two at a time would be the greatest weight that he dared to put on the ropes, he felt.

Quickly the litter was unfastened from the stirrups, and, lifting Holman to a sitting posture, Silver said to him: "Hang your arms over my shoulders. I'm going to carry you."

"No!" cried the girl. "You can't balance yourself with Dave on your back. You'll both—"

Silver raised his hand.

Holman said gravely: "You know what you're doing. I'm only a fool if I try to stop you. But Heaven help you, Arizona, when you get out there in the center, if the wind starts the bridge pitching!"

Silver grunted. The fear of the thing was already a cold stone in his stomach.

"Go first, Ned," he commanded Kenyon. "Sneak across and try it out for us. If it holds one man, we'll chance it with two."

Kenyon, yellow-green with terror, cast one glance at the girl, winced back a step, and then marched straight out onto the ropes! Silver watched him, amazed at the nerve power that the poor fellow had managed to rouse in the time of need. Right out across the bridge went Kenyon, with stealthy, short steps, one hand gripping the guide rope. He reached the center. His weight there, fighting against the pressure of the wind, made the whole bridge shudder violently. But still he went on, perhaps for no other reason than because to pass on was easier than to turn back!

And now he had leaped the last yard or so and lay face down, safe on the farther side.

Big Harry Bench came grunting up, exclaiming: "They're milling around down there on the side of the mountain, but they'll find the trail again in a minute. What the devil is this here? I been told I was goin' to die by the rope, but I never seen this kind of a picture of my finish! Here, Silver! I'll pack him over! I can do it more easy than you!"

"Pack yourself over—and shut up," said Silver, and rose with the feeble arms of Holman hanging over his neck. He gripped those arms with one hand. The other he placed on the guide rope, and the last he saw before he stepped onto the peril of the bridge was the girl on her knees, her face buried in her hands, unable to look on.

No, there was one thing more he saw, and that was the beautiful head of Parade thrusting close to his face with pricking ears, and eyes filled with mild inquiry. He tried to speak, but no words came to Silver. It was the end of the horse for him, no doubt. Those men of Kirby Crossing would pick up the great horse as their rightful prize. And they would soon learn that it was a prize worth more than the blood money they could collect on poor David Holman.

He stepped straight past Parade and started out onto the bridge.

Step by step he went on, his teeth hard-set. And at his ear he heard the gasping breath of Holman, for, of course, the man was enduring the most frightful agony.

Silver tried to keep his glance only on the floor of the bridge, but that floor was hardly two and a half feet wide, and again and again his eyes slipped over the side and reached the bottom of the ravine, where the waters of Whistling Creek were churning themselves white and sending up an ominous voice into the shrillness of the wind. He saw a blasted pine, a naked trunk at the edge of the water, and it looked hardly larger than a walking stick.

One false step—

And he could not trust to the guide rope except for the most treacherous bit of aid in steadying himself. He had to keep his balance almost entirely by his feet alone. It was hard enough at the side; it was a desperate business in the center, for the wind came in gusts and struck the ropes hammer blows.

But the center had been passed, and now his courage and his hope revived together. He was moving forward more rapidly when suddenly the body he carried slumped down, the full weight jerking on his shoulders as the knees that had gripped his hips lost their hold.

He staggered. For one instant he swayed far to the right. The hands which clutched the arms of Holman shuddered and almost relaxed their grip. It seemed that they were already falling, the two of them together—and then the wind knocked at the bridge and seemed to put it again under the feet of Silver.

He walked on. The feet of the senseless man he carried were dragging behind him. But there was Ned Kenyon waiting for him, holding out both hands, shouting with a white, distorted mouth, words of encouragement. So he made the last steps and stretched his burden safely on the ground.

A dead man? No, the lips of Holman were moving, though they made no sound. Neither had there been a fresh hemorrhage. And Silver began to breath out loud groans of relief.

"Look at her!" he heard Kenyon saying. "There's no fear in her except for him. There's no care in her except about him, Jim! Look!"

She was already halfway across the bridge, moving more rapidly than any one who had passed before her. She seemed almost to run up the last bit of the way, and now she was dropping to her knees beside Holman.

Silver merely said: "He's living, and he's going to keep on living. I've forgotten the litter. No, there's Harry Bench bringing it. Ned, there's a man with a heart as big as his body!"

For Harry Bench, with the long poles of the litter balanced on his shoulder, was now coming steadily, smoothly across the bridge, and in a moment he was with them.

"Get him on the litter," commanded Silver. "Quick, Harry—take his shoulders—there we have him. Ned, cut the ropes at this end, and we'll leave a jump that the Kirby boys can't take!"

"Send him back!" shouted Kenyon. "Look, Jim! He's trying to cross the bridge to join you!"

Silver, whirling about, saw that the great stallion had actually started out on the bridge, and was already a little distance from the farther side. Crouching low, his head thrust far out and down, the golden horse was stealing like a cat across the bridge. And he could not be sent back; he was already committed to the crossing.

Chapter — 21

A STUPOR came over Silver as he watched. Love drew the great horse to him, he knew. But that crossing could not be made. Even if the ropes could endure the strain of that great body, Parade could not keep his balance against the battering strokes of the wind, whose force was increasing now. He had no hand to place on the guide rope and help him across the worst moments of the way.

He would fall, and the creek beneath would grind his glorious body to shreds. There would be one crimson flowing of the water, and there the end of Parade. And Silver thought of the other days when he had made the great march behind the starving wild horse, and how they had journeyed up the burning valley, and drunk together from the same spring!

He had not conquered Parade. It had been simply that in the end they had given their trust to one another. And because of that trust, Parade was crossing the bridge, trembling, crouching with terror, feeling his way like a cat, but always with his ears pricked.

Silver heard the voice of Holman saying: "His horse, Edith—he's giving his horse for me, too—and he'd rather give up half his life than that!"

Then the girl was suddenly at Silver's side, holding his arm with both hands, looking not at Parade, but at the master of the horse. She was saying:

"He's going to win across. God won't let him fall! God won't let him fall!"

Silver heard her words out of a dream. She believed them, perhaps.

Parade was coming to the center of the bridge, while the ropes groaned loudly under his great weight, and the wind screeched like an angry fiend as it smote that frail structure. With every gust the huge body of Parade shuddered, and the whole bridge swayed.

If there were some way to hearten him; if there were something that could be done!

For Parade had stopped in the very center of the bridge, at last totally overcome by fear. The slight twist of his head to the side made Silver know that the horse had given up hope and was thinking of the way back. Thinking of that—and staggering and swaying, his balance going. And every hair of his golden hide was drenched now with nervous sweat.

And Silver?

He broke suddenly forth with a hoarse singing, an old song that has comforted many a night herd when it was bedded down on the trail, a song that Silver had sung more than once when he and Parade were marching through the cold and the wind of some winter evening:

> *"Oh, I'm riding down the river,*
> *With my banjo on my knee;*
> *I'm riding down the river,*
> *And no one else with me.*
> *Strike up that banjo, strike her!*
> *A song has gotta be.*
> *Strike up that banjo, strike her!*
> *That banjo talks to me."*

As Silver worked into the song, his voice gained a ringing power and struck boldly across the canyon through the wind.

What meaning had it for Parade? Perhaps it meant for him as much as the touch of his master's hand on the reins, sending sure, calm messages from the brain of the man to the brain of the horse. For suddenly the stallion was no longer swaying, crouched till his belly almost touched the ropes. He was standing higher; he was moving forward with cautious steps; he was nearing the place where Silver stood with the agony in his eyes and the song on his lips. Now the outstretched hand of the master touched the head of Parade, and now the great horse stood shivering on safe ground!

The girl threw her arms around the wet neck of the stallion, but Silver merely laid his hand on the broad forehead of the horse and spoke words that had no meaning.

A moment later the knife of Kenyon had slashed the ropes, and the length of the bridge swished into the air and hung dangling from its moorings on the farther edge of the canyon.

After that Silver took up one end of the litter, and Harry Bench the other.

No one spoke. Something like fear was in their faces as they pressed forward among the rocks and the shrubbery, for they felt that they had been privileged to witness a miracle.

Hardly had the shrubbery closed behind them when they heard the beating of the hoofs of horses and the yells of angry men. The pursuit had reached the end of its tether for that day, at least!

They went on by slow stages to the end of the day, and so worked through the rough of the mountains to the projecting shoulder of a peak from which they could see foothills sloping down in diminishing waves to the plains beneath. In the sunset time they could see the faint golden sheen of the Tuckaway River that wound through the level and the windows of the town of Tuckaway itself glimmer like distant fire for a few moments before the sun went down.

It was necessary to rest at this point, for though the wounded man endured the pain of travel without a word, he would have to have sleep. It was certain, now, that the bullet had avoided injuring any vital organ; neither had there been any great loss of blood. He was simply weak from shock, and time would be needed for the healing of the wound.

It was the plan of Ned Kenyon, who knew the whole district perfectly, to leave the mountains before sunrise and trek out into the plains—chiefly because the pursuit would hardly expect such a move, and moreover because he knew of certain obscure shacks here and there where they could lie up with little danger of being discovered. As Kenyon put it: "We'll sit down right in front of their door, and they'll burn up their horseflesh combing the mountains for us."

The choice of that particular mountain shoulder was largely dictated by a lucky chance, for as they reached the ledge and put down the litter to take breath, a mountain sheep was seen far, far above them, looking out at the sunset. Silver's rifle clipped that prize through the head, and the sheep came pitching and rolling the great distance down to the flat, where the party waited.

Food was needed, and this was a prize. Kenyon and One-eyed Harry cut up the sheep rapidly while Silver arranged half a dozen small fires, which he fed with the wood of dead and dry brush. The changing half lights of this time of day would make it very difficult for an eye even close at hand to distinguish the misting breaths of smoke that rose from those small flames, each a mere handful of brightness. And presently there was mutton roasting on wooden spits at each of the fires.

They had not even salt; they had cold spring water instead of coffee; but ravenous hunger after the day of labor made them eat like wolves. And they were sheltered from observation for this one night, at least. Somewhere, perhaps not a mile away, the men of Kirby Crossing were bivouacking. Or had they turned back and given up the hunt? That was hardly likely—not with Nellihan and Lorens among their number to urge them on. But for this night it was almost impossible that they could close in on their quarry any farther. Tomorrow the peril would recommence. This was an interlude of peace to be enjoyed to the full.

Holman was the amazing man to Silver. With every hour he seemed to be gaining in strength. He ate a share of the roasted meat, and afterward he smoked a cigarette which Silver made for him. He had been bedded down on a soft pile of pine boughs, and after his wound was washed and fresh pads placed over the bleeding places, and the bandages again drawn into place, he seemed to be suffering no great pain. The girl sat beside him silently. There seemed to be no sky, no earth, no day and no night for them; they looked only at one another.

Holman tried to express thanks to Silver. He was cut off abruptly.

"If you've got any breath to waste," said Silver, "use it to tell me that the yarn I've heard about you is a lie. You didn't plan the robbing of the bank with 'em. What you told in the courtroom was the truth?"

Silver had discarded his black wig. He had scrubbed away the dark stain on his skin. And now, through the glimmer of twilight, the girl and Holman could see the points of gray in his hair, like an incipient horn growing up above either temple. That suggestion gave him a touch of wildness, and his ragged clothes intensified the strangeness—that and the way the stallion always grazed near by, sometimes coming over to sniff at the master, sometimes lifting a lordly head to study every scent that blew toward them on the wind. It was patent that this man was at home in the wilderness, and that he asked for no better companionship than that of the stallion alone. He seemed to Holman, particularly, like a wild, migratory animal which for a moment was crouched among them, and would presently be gone, no man could tell whither.

"What I told in the courtroom," said Holman, "sounded like cock-and-bull, but it was the truth. Truth has a silly face a good many times."

"Who was behind that pair of thugs, if you were not?" asked Silver.

"George Wayland. Buster Wayland."

"Who's he?"

"He used to be vice president of the bank. Simonson was the president, and Wayland the vice president. Now Simonson is out, and Wayland is the whole thing. He's the big boss."

"You hadn't robbed the bank of a hundred thousand or so before the safe was opened that night?"

"How could I have been such a fool?" asked Holman. "I have money enough of my own. I was working in that bank to get experience. That was all. I wasn't gambling. I wasn't buying stocks on a margin. As a matter of fact, my salary was small, but I lived inside of it."

"Who did rob the bank, then?" asked Silver.

"Wayland."

"Are you sure?"

"Yes. I saw him do it."

"When?"

"One night when they put guns at my head and made me go down to the bank. There were not just the two of them. Wayland was along."

"If he wanted to rob the bank, why didn't he do it without you?" asked Silver.

"Simonson and I were the only ones who knew the combination that unlocked the safe."

"And they picked on you instead of Simonson?"

"Simonson wouldn't be apt to rob his own bank. It was in good shape. And besides, Simonson would have fought back. They picked on me because they knew that I was yellow."

"That doesn't wash," said Silver. "You're not yellow."

"Perhaps not now. But I was then. And Wayland knew it. He'd bullied me in small things, and I had lain down. As a matter of fact, when they put guns to my head, I was so scared that I could hardly move. They had to carry me. When we got to the bank, my hands were shaking so that I could hardly work the combination. But I opened the door of the safe for 'em—and because of that, I deserved everything that happened to me afterward. Oh, I doubtless deserved even more."

"No!" whispered the girl.

Holman went on calmly: "Wayland had a small interest in the bank, even though he was vice president. He wasn't much of a banker. And he saw his chance to make a stake for himself. Right there in the bank, they split the loot into three parts. Wayland took one part. The two yeggs took two parts. It was an equal division, except that Wayland took most of the hard cash and gave the others more of the securities. Then the yeggs went on with me. You can see how the scheme would work out. The bank robbed, the door of the safe opened, and with me gone from town, the whole suspicion would point at me. When I was taken, I might shoot my head off accusing Wayland, but he would simply laugh at me. He could depend on the crooks to keep me away for a day or two, he thought.

"Well, matters went a little differently, but all the better for Wayland. The sheriff, happening by in the middle of the night, after Wayland had said good-by to the thugs and they'd started off with me, made things hard for them. Wayland got back home to his bed, but as he was turning in, the thugs were being run out of the town, and I was carried along by them. They were sticking to the promise they'd made to Wayland to the last. The posse came after us. Finally we got clear, and I saw that I was ruined unless I managed to do something.

"I got desperate enough to forget some of my fear. The two yeggs despised me. They had reason to despise me, you see. And so I had a chance to get a gun from one of them. I knew a bit about shooting. And I had them by surprise. I nailed them both, and then tried to get away with the loot they'd taken. My idea was that if I could get back to Tuckaway with the money, it would be proof that I'd been innocent. But when the sheriff and the posse hove in sight, I lost my head and tried to bolt again. I played the fool. They caught me. The money was on me, and when I tried to tell my story, I was laughed at.

"Now see how the thing worked out for Buster Wayland. As soon as I was brought in, he swore that if I had robbed the bank that night, I had been probably robbing it before, and covering up the thefts in my books. They made an accounting and found the bank terribly short. Of course, that was because Wayland still had his share of the loot! When the bank was found short, a run on it started. Simonson had no ready cash. When the funds in the safe were used up, Wayland was in a position to hold a gun to Simonson's head.

"Simonson had to sell out his shares in the bank for next to nothing. And Wayland simply stepped in and filled the breach with part of the stolen money. It gave him the name of a hero and a public benefactor, too. He wound up owning the bank; he'd established himself as an honest man and a strong one. The big ranchers and mine owners in the district, I understand, have been hauling their accounts out of other banks and depositing with the Wayland Bank in Tuckaway—because Wayland can now pose as the financial giant, the public-minded citizen, the man to whom honesty meant more than hard cash, the fellow who flung his private fortune into the breach and saved the widows and orphans. Simonson died of a broken heart. I was sentenced to die. And Wayland can loll back in his easy-chair and smoke some more of his fat cigars."

He ended without raising his voice. He had spoken rather as one who reads a story aloud than as one who tells it. It was almost pitch-dark, and out of the darkness came the voice of Silver, saying:

"I have to be taking a trip to Tuckaway tonight!"

Everyone protested, except One-eyed Harry. He said: "I ain't big enough to try to change his mind. Then how can the rest of you think that you got a chance?"

Holman said: "But I know the difficulties more than the rest of you. Arizona, let me tell you that Wayland keeps guards about him night and day. He knows how to win the faithful services of crooks, perhaps because he's such a crook himself. If it were Wayland himself—well, you might do something, though I don't see what!"

"I won't know till I'm on the spot," said Silver. "But I'm going to Tuckaway. Tell me one thing more. When the posse reached the second of the yeggs you had shot up, he was alive; and as he died, he confirmed the yarn that Wayland was to tell later. Why didn't he tell the truth as he died?"

"Because he wanted to be sure that he'd knotted the rope around my neck before he cashed in his chips. I'd killed him; he wanted to be the death of me; and he'd already gone over the story with Wayland in case of need."

"That's all logical," said Silver.

He went aside with One-eyed Harry and Kenyon, and said to them: "It's about an hour's ride from here to Tuckaway. That means two hours for going and coming back. Besides, I don't know how long I'll be in the place. It may be near to sunup before I arrive here again. Be on the watch. Lorens and Nellihan have brains in their heads, and they know how to use 'em. They're fighting men, too. And anything that a snake could do, they'll do. One of you had better keep on watch half the night, and one the other half. Ned, come and step away with me."

He led Kenyon aside and found his hand in the darkness.

"You're going through hell," said Silver, "but you're going through it like a man. I know you'll put up a fight if the pinch comes."

"I dunno," said Kenyon. "I ain't much of a fighting man, but I hope I'll do my best. And it ain't exactly hell that I'm going through, Arizona. The fact is, it's like bein' in the middle of a sort of a sad dream, but not wanting to wake up from it."

Silver wrung his hand and went to the girl. She moved slowly beside him through the darkness.

"Oh, have hope," said Silver. "There's luck with us, or we couldn't have lasted this long."

"We've had you from first to last," she answered. "You've saved us before, and I cannot help hoping, so long as you're in the fight!"

"Perhaps the whole thing is for the best," he said. "Tell me one thing— were you very fond of Holman before he got into this trouble?"

"I was always fond of him," she answered. "But he seemed a little weak and soft. He wasn't what he's grown to be. But when I heard what he was accused of, only one thing crashed into my mind—that he'd fought two criminals and beaten them with their own weapons."

"I almost knew it," said Silver. "He never would have discovered himself if the big pinch had not come. And you would never have discovered him, either. There's Nellihan, though? What about him? Is he as much of a snake as he seems?"

"The lowest creature in this world!" said the girl. "He was even able to put in my father's mind some doubts about me—to make it seem best to my father that I should not come into the money till I was married. That was because Nellihan knew that I loved David Holman, that David was sentenced to death, that if he died, I would never marry anyone. Don't you see? And Nellihan was the next heir."

"I understand," said Silver. "And in a short time he would have found a way to put you out of your misery. I have to leave you. Holman is going to live. Don't doubt that. And trust everything to Bench and Kenyon. I know how you feel about Kenyon, but I don't know what else you could have done. You tried to do a small wrong in order to do a great right. But I suppose that sacrificing one man for another is never a good business. However, that thing will be straightened out. Kenyon will do whatever you want. He'll get a divorce in Nevada, I suppose. And afterward I'll find ways in which you and Holman can manage to repay him."

"If you could do that!" cried the girl.

"Don't pity him too much," said Silver. "He's having his great chance to be a man just as Holman had his chance. Holman was remade. Kenyon is being remade, too. If he lives through it, he'll be able to respect himself for the rest of his life. He was simply a good-natured, haphazard, ramshackle cow-puncher and stage driver before this."

"And you?" said the girl suddenly. "What will you gain by all that you've done for Ned, for me, for David?"

"I'm having the fun of it," said Silver with a faint laugh. "And the rest of you are having the pain."

She did not try to answer him. He went back to Parade, saddled the horse, and rode him to the side of the wounded man.

"Heads up, Holman?" said he.

"Clear up in the sky," said Holman. "Arizona, I've tried to persuade you not to go near that devil in his own roost in Tuckaway. I know that you're going, anyway. But I want to say this last thing: Everything will be harder than you expect to find it!"

"Thanks," said Silver. "If you say that a thing is hard, I know that you mean it. But I've got to go. Holman, adios! We'll be together in a luckier time."

He turned Parade, and the stallion moved down the slope over the edge of the mountain shoulder. He went carefully, for the voice of his master was hushing him, and Parade glided through the brush like a hunting cat, making never a sound.

Chapter – 22

THE house of "Buster" Wayland had formerly been the house of the leading banker of the little town of Tuckaway. Simonson had taken an entire block, planted an evergreen hedge around the outside of it, and a grove of trees inside. Within the trees he had established a lawn, and within the lawn stood the house and the stables. The house itself was a frame dwelling, square, plain, and dignified, because Simonson had taste as good as it was simple.

Silver rode his horse right in through the big open gate, but turned aside from the driveway into a dark cloud of trees close to the lawn. There he dismounted and spent a few moments patting Parade and giving him those whispering injunctions which would make him stand fast until his master's whistle summoned him, or his master's voice.

In the meantime, Silver himself was taking breath, and clearing his wits, as it were, by deep breathing. He was still dressed, of course, in the ragged, stained white clothes which he had worn before. And therefore no eye could fall on him without suspicion. He would have to move invisible to the very moment when he began action. And even what that action was to be, he had very little idea. He was like an actor who walks out before the curtain to entertain a crowd, and who must improvise his speeches on the spur of the moment.

He left the horse at last and made a circle of the house. All along the front and rear and one side it was lighted. On the fourth side there was not a light showing.

The ground windows were low, and the first one that Silver looked through showed him the dining room, with Buster Wayland and three guests at the table, and a Chinaman, humpbacked with anxious effort, gliding about to serve them.

It was not hard to guess that the man at the head of the table was Wayland. All of his nickname of "Buster" showed in his big, florid face, in the sheen of his eyes, in his continual smiling or laughter. He was big. He was so big that he overflowed his armchair. His gestures and his voice were of the overflowing type, also, and as Silver looked at him, he could not help having a flash back at the wounded man who lay on the shoulder of the mountain with only the vaguest of hopes of giving him comfort.

As for the guests, they were men worth seeing. One of them was none other than Sheriff Bert Philips, whom Silver had last seen in the town of Mustang. The other two, it came instantly to knowledge, were deputies who were assisting Philips in the man hunt. They were talking of that, and of nothing else, and the banker was assuring the sheriff that there would be an adequate reward paid outside of the promise of the law once young Holman was accounted for.

"How he's kept away this long, nobody can make out!" declared Buster Wayland. He bumped the table with his fist. "But it's a certain sure thing he can't keep away much longer."

"It's nothing but Jim Silver, or Silvertip, or whatever you want to call him." declared the sheriff. "He's the fellow who has saved the scalp of Holman. And to think that I had him under my gun in Mustang, and didn't shoot."

"Aye, that was a mistake," growled the raw-boned young deputy whose fierce eyes faced Silver from the opposite side of the table.

"A mistake," agreed Wayland. "But I know how it is—a man wants to give the other fellow every chance, unless you're dead sure!"

"There's Silver's record, besides," said the sheriff. "He's been at outs with the law before this, but he always turns up right and the law turns up wrong. He proves his case, and it aint's always the law's case."

"One day he'll wake up dead before his proving is finished," said the deputy with the burning eyes.

"But there's money behind that crowd," said Wayland. "Silver, as you call him, may be honest most of the time, but that girl has money enough to bribe a saint."

"Maybe so—maybe so," said the sheriff. "But what counts with me is that Holman is still on the loose in the mountains."

"We'll hunt him out of there," said the second deputy, an older and a graver man, with a thick red neck and a bristling mustache.

"I think," said Bert Philips, "that maybe we'll do a good job if we simply keep a lot of men riding on the lookout down in the plains, not so far from Tuckaway. Remember that Ned Kenyon is with 'em, and Kenyon knows the lay of the land around here pretty good."

The truth of this remark pinched the memory of Silvertip. Whatever happened, he must get back to the party in time to warn them that Kenyon's suggestion would simply lead them into ruin. They must keep back among the mountains.

"If they're in the mountains," said Buster Wayland, "they'll soon come out on the run. That fellow Nellihan that came in and talked with me today, he's as keen as mustard, and he knows his business. He took all the best horses and the best riders out of this town when he scooted back for the hills. He'll work all night, if there's starlight enough to show him the difference between a rock and a bush."

"We'll get 'em," agreed the sheriff. "But only because Holman is wounded. It's a good thing that Lorens shot straight that time. Because if Silver's hands weren't tied down by the moving of a wounded man, I don't think that we'd ever see hide or hair of that party."

The second deputy put in: "What I wanta know is this—who had the nerve to tell the lie that a horse ever walked across the bridge in Whistling Canyon? I know that bridge. I've been across it, and it's made me sick at the stomach to go over. I've ridden twenty miles out of my way to keep from having to cross that bridge. And now some blockheads tell me that a big stallion up and crossed it—this fellow Silver's horse!"

"Aye, but that horse is Parade," said the sheriff. "You can't judge him by ordinary horses any more than you can judge Silver by ordinary men."

"How come?" asked Wayland.

"Parade was the hundred-thousand-dollar mustang that used to run wild up there in the Sierra Blanca Desert. Never hear of that?"

"Sure I have!" agreed Wayland.

"That's the one. Seventeen hands of thunder and lightning, and all gold and twenty-four carats. That's Parade. They say he'll stand up and cakewalk when his master whistles. And it's a sure thing that he did walk that bridge, because he wasn't left on the near side with the other mustang."

"We'll have a drink," said Wayland. "Hey, Sammy, bring in another bottle of that rye. We're going to have a drink to the lucky man that crashes a slug of lead through the brain of that scoundrel of a thief, that David Holman. The man that has that luck is going to collect an extra two thousand dollars from me, and you're all my witnesses!"

They looked at one another, and Silver gritted his teeth. To cowpunchers who worked for forty-five dollars a month, two thousand meant a huge fortune. Almost anything would be done for the sake of that money. Now it was stacked on top of the original five thousand that had been hung up as a prize, and nothing could save David Holman—nothing but some way of proving his innocence.

Silver kicked off his sandals. Even their light weight would be in his way now.

He rounded to the front of the houses, shimmied up one of the wooden columns that framed the Georgian porch, and so came to the second story of the big house. A balcony ran down the side of the building, and he could move at ease down this.

There were only two lighted rooms, one a big bedroom, and one an upstairs study with a big easy-chair in front of a fireplace, and a silk dressing gown and a pair of slippers laid out. Mr Buster Wayland would probably take his ease here after dinner had been finished.

But the furnishings of the room did not end here—there was also a big steel safe in a corner of the room. It was hardly a decorative piece, but it had more interest for the owner of the house, no doubt, than all the rest of the place that Simonson had built.

The safe was not all. There was also an element of human interest, for in a corner of the room, seated beside the only lighted lamp in the chamber, was a guard.

Holman had said that Wayland knew how to attach things to his interest, and certainly this fellow was a perfect example and type of ruffian. He was reading a magazine with such interest that his brutal head was thrust far forward on his neck, and his face snarled with the emotions that worked in him.

Something that Silver did not hear in the least reached the ear of the fellow. Instantly he was out of the chair, crouching, a gun in his hand. He went cat-like to the door, opened it, and then came slowly back, his mouth still working, his eyes glaring.

He was not a man. He was simply a formidable beast. Once back in his chair, he remained for a time alert, in a singular way, reading, or pretending to read, and suddenly flashing his glance up and around the room.

Then the truth was borne in upon Silver. It was the gaze that he himself kept fastened on the gunman that made the fellow uneasy, the insistent force of that regard constantly bearing in upon his unconscious mind, and vaguely sending messages of warning to the consciousness itself.

The man wriggled and stirred as though he were seated too close to a hot fire. Never had Silver seen instinct work more powerfully and on so slight a cause.

Presently the man sprang out of the chair and walked straight across the room and to the window where Silver was watching. Silver flattened himself close to the wall of the house, raising in his right hand a revolver which he grasped by the barrel, the butt offering as the club.

And after a moment a bullethead came out through the window, not slowly, but with a quick, dripping motion so fast that the blow that Silvertip aimed at the base of the man's neck found the very top of his head instead.

The weight of that shock drove his face down against the sill, but did not quite stun him. Silver, following his attack with wonderful speed, saw his man on one knee before the window, with a gun coming gradually into his hand. There was no need for another blow. Silver simply tapped him across the forehead and the gun slid to the rug.

The whole soul of the guard was striving to fight, but the numbed body and brain could not react. The face of the man was a frightful thing to see. It was like the twisted mask of an ape trying to bite.

He kept shaking his head to clear away the clouds that were gathering over his wits. Silver tied the vaguely struggling hands of the man behind his back before sense enough to cry out came to the thug. He tilted back his head, and his chest heaved before he let out the yell.

It was never uttered. Silver simply stepped in front of him and put the muzzle of the Colt into that open mouth. The apelike creature clamped his teeth down on the steel and gasped.

Silver removed the gun and looked over his captive.

"What's your name, brother?" he asked. "And talk soft when you answer."

"What the devil is my name to you?" snarled the captive. "What I'm goin' to do to a sneakin' slick of a second-story worker like you when I get my chance—" He paused, as though realizing the futility of threats at this moment. His breath came straining and rasping in his throat. The butt of the gun had cut his scalp a little, and a crimson trickle, having worked through the hair, spilled down beside his right eye, and gradually worked in a crooked course toward the chin.

"What's your name?" repeated Silver.

"Lefty some call me, and Soggy some call me," said the yegg.

"All right, Soggy," said Silver. "That name goes for me. Tell me when Mr Wayland comes up to this room?"

"Why should I tell you?"

"Because he's going to be wiped out of this town, Soggy," said Silver. "He may be wiped off the face of the earth. I don't know. The fact is that if I have to drop him, your own name will be mud around this neck of the woods. Am I wrong?"

"Soggy" said nothing. He merely lowered his head a little and glowered at Silver from beneath shaggy brows.

"It would be hard to explain," said Silver. "Wayland is a big man in this town. If anything happens to him, it might be tough on his hired gunman. Lynching parties work pretty fast around here."

Soggy pursed out his lips in thought. He said nothing.

"I'm going to tie you into that chair," said Silver. "If I have to, I'll choke you with a gag, but I'd rather give you a chance to breathe comfortably. Walk over there and sit down. Remember, I'm giving you a better break than you'd give me. And if you try to yell, I may have to sink a chunk of lead in you."

Chapter – 23

SOGGY, without a word of protest, let himself be tied into the chair. And Silver even made a cigarette, lighted it, and put it between the lips of his captive. Thereafter, by ducking his head far down, Soggy could manage to transfer the cigarette from his mouth to his right hand, which was tied out on the arm of the chair in which he sat. Silver stood back and grinned at him, and Soggy grinned back.

"Hard lines!" sympathized Silver.

"I've seen worse," said Soggy. "I've seen worse birds than you are, too. What's your monicker?"

"I work with quite a batch of 'em," said Silver.

"I'll bet you do," agreed Soggy.

"Arizona Jim, some call me."

"Arizona," said Soggy, "you're kind of white. What's the game on Wayland?"

"He's a thug and a crook," said Silver. "He has a lot coming to him, and he's going to get part of it, or all of it, tonight."

"I like to hear you, kind of," said Soggy. "The while I been workin' for him ain't been so sweet. Easy money—but he's a bum. He's a four-flusher."

"He can fight," said Silver tentatively.

"That's what he says," answered Soggy. He added: "If you hand him the rap, do you give me a break to get loose out of here?"

"If you don't bother me," said Silver.

"I'll sit like a bird in a tree," said Soggy. "Go ahead and blaze away, will you?"

"I'll go ahead, and I'll blaze away," agreed Silver. "Know anything good about this fellow Wayland?"

"No. Nothin'."

"Don't even know when he'll come up here?"

"No. Maybe in an hour. Maybe any time. He comes up here off and on to see how things go. He's got his heart and his liver and his lights locked up in the safe yonder. Some mug that cracks that safe open will get a hand-out worth havin'! And if—"

Silver raised a hand for silence. He heard something on the stairs beyond the room. He heard a rhythmic thing—a pressure rather than a sound—coming down the hall toward the door. Stepping close to the door, flattening his body against the wall, he saw the door suddenly swing open. Big Wayland, with a step surprisingly light and fast for a man of his size, strode into the room.

His first glance was for the face of the safe. But while he was taking it, he saw his gunman tied into the chair, and the ominous gun in the hand of Silver, just beside him.

There was good fighting stuff in Wayland, after all. With his right hand he reached for his gun. With his left he drove a long, straight, whipping punch at the head of Silver. The latter let the blow go past him. He stepped in and jabbed the muzzle of his Colt into the ribs of Wayland. With his left he caught the gun hand of the big fellow.

So for an instant they faced one another. Wayland glaring, the eyes of Silver utterly cold and remorseless. The thumb of his right hand was trembling with desire to let the hammer drop and ease this crooked life out of the world.

Wayland saw the expression and seemed to understand it. He said in a low, guttural voice: "All right. You've got me. Who are you? What do you want?"

"They've been talking about me down at your table," said Silver. "They call me Silver, or Silvertip, but names don't make much difference. This is a business call, Wayland. Give me that gun!"

He took the gun. It was the only weapon the banker carried, as Silver discovered by sliding his hand rapidly over the body of the man.

When he was disarmed, Silver stepped back from him and said calmly:

"You don't need to hoist your hands over your head. Just remember that I'm watching you, Wayland. Now take a sheet of that paper, sit down at the table, unscrew your fountain pen, and write a little letter for me."

"What sort? A letter of credit? Is that what you're driving at?" asked Wayland.

"A letter to whomever it concerns," said Silver. "Saying that you hired the two crooks who took young Holman down to the bank, that you went with them, that you helped yourself to one third of the loot, that when you saved the bank afterward, you were simply using money that you'd already stolen from it for that purpose, and for buying out poor Simonson before he died of a broken heart. Is that clear?"

Wayland showed not the least surprise.

"Write a little story that clears young Mr Holman. Is that it?" he asked.

Then he turned toward the tied-up gunman.

"You let yourself be brushed out of the picture, did you, Soggy?"

"He socked me," said Soggy. "But I dunno that I'm sorry, if I'm goin' to have a chance to see him sock you, too!"

"You can't go through with this," said Wayland to Silver. "I have men down there waiting for me. They'll be up to see what's wrong if I stay here. Besides, you're only making a fool of yourself. You're going to force a confession out of me, and a forced confession isn't worth anything, and I've got Soggy here as a witness to the force used. Look here, Silver, you're a fellow with a bright eye. You're the sort of a man who ought to be able to tell on which side your bread is buttered. And I'm an open-handed fellow, Silver, if people approach me in the right way. You could have a fair—"

He stopped. Something in the face of Silver told him he was wasting time—a cold and profound disgust.

"Sit down," said Silver, "and write. Begin with the date line, and go down to the finish. Understand? I know what the form should be, and so do you. Now write!"

The big man sat at the table, his face shining with sweat, the fatness of the fountain pen looking actually slender in his bulky hand.

"You can't bleed me," he gasped finally. "You can't do anything with a forced confession. I can laugh at this tomorrow."

"You won't be here tomorrow," said Silver.

"Murder?" said Wayland, steadily enough.

"I don't think so—unless you fail to write," said Silver. "To kill you wouldn't be murder, Wayland. But if you write the stuff out, I'm simply going to take you downtown and see you catch the freight that's pulling out of the station in about forty minutes. You'll catch that train, and Soggy will catch it with you. When the confession is found in here and you're found gone, I think it may do something, Wayland. But because I know you'd rather die than tell the truth and lose all your loot at the same time, I'm going to give you another sort of a chance with that. I'm going to let you open that safe and take what's in it along with you."

"To become a fugitive of justice, eh?" said Wayland, narrowing his eyes.

"You've been that before, or my eye can't read straight," said Silver. "Start writing!"

One desperate glance Wayland flung around the room. Then he compressed his lips and began to write. The room fell utterly silent, so silent that the scratching of the pen seemed to be growing louder and louder, and Silver became aware of the ticking of the big clock that stood on the mantelpiece above the chimney place.

He was aware of something else, too, after a time, and that was the approach of footfalls up the stairs. Big Wayland stopped writing, and his face lighted.

"If it's one of your guests," said Silver, turning the key in the door, "tell him that you're busy. That you'll be right down. Understand?"

Wayland nodded. But a fugitive hope was glimmering in his eyes all the time.

Presently a hand beat on the door firmly.

"Hello?" called Wayland, looking straight into the muzzle of Silver's gun.

"Hello, Wayland. This is Bert Philips. Wondered what was keeping you."

"Coming down in a minute," said Wayland. But there was a shaking huskiness in his voice that made Philips exclaim:

"Wayland! I want to see you, man!"

He rattled the knob of the door. He had found enough in the absence of his host, he had heard enough in the voice of that host, to alarm him. There was no doubt about it. Wayland would have to admit him; at least, see him face to face.

"You've been upset," whispered Silver to Wayland. "Tell him that. Go unlock the door and face him—but if you let him come into the room, I start shooting, and I shoot at you. You hear?"

Wayland rolled despairing eyes. Then he nodded, went to the door and turned the key. The door came instantly open, as though Philips were pushing against it. But Wayland held it by the knob, and the sheriff was saying:

"I'm worried about you, man. And you look green-gray. You're sweating. What the devil's the matter? May I come in?"

"I've been upset a little, is all. A little sick," muttered Wayland. "You go back and keep the boys entertained. I'll be down in a little while. Don't worry, I'm all right. Just keep the boys entertained for a bit, will you?"

"Well," said Philips uneasily, "well, I'll do that. But I'm worried about you. Sure that nothing's wrong?"

"No," said Wayland. "I'm all right!"

What torment it must have been for him to speak those words!

But they were spoken, the door closed against Philips, and the lock softly turned back.

Tottering in his step, his head hanging, Wayland went back to the table. Suddenly he said:

"Silver, I'll make you rich! I'll pay you—"

"Listen," said Silver sternly. "If you had ten millions in gold and you could give it to me with a wave of the hand, I'd still laugh at you!"

For one moment Wayland stared at that grim face. Then he resumed his writing.

As he finished it, Silver, looking over his shoulder, read the document, and knew as the signature went down that the thing was perfect. If anything could save Holman, this was it—if only Wayland could be removed, so that it would look as though conscience had forced a confession from him before he fled with a part of his loot.

He pushed the paper onto the center of the table, favored Silver with a scowl of the blackest hate, and then hurried to the safe. The combination wheel spun back and forth for an instant under his fat fingers. The heavy door opened with a faint puffing sound, and there was Wayland on his knees, at work.

He knew where every item of the highest value was to be found. Perhaps, crook that he was, he had the cream of his wealth collected there against just such an emergency as this. At any rate, in five minutes he was on his feet again, with his pockets stuffed. Silver, stepping to the side of Soggy, with a touch of the knife had made the thug free, merely whispering:

"Soggy, you're going to climb on board the same train with him. You know where the pies are. Maybe you'll be able to help yourself to some of 'em."

Soggy rolled up his face with a frightful grin distorting it, and a flare of the big, apish nostrils. Suddenly Silver knew that he could trust the man to work honestly with him during the rest of that adventure.

And he was right. He had no fear of the gun that he entrusted to Soggy. It was simply another proof that Wayland would not be able to get away. His figure was definitely settled.

They passed out along the balcony. Soggy went to the ground first. Wayland then with stifled grunts of effort followed, to slide down the pillar at the end of the porch, while Silver hung by his hands from the edge of the balcony above and then dropped lightly to the ground. That was how the trio reassembled, and started across the grounds. The thinnest sort of a whistle summoned Parade out of the trees to the side of his master, and now Silver walked behind the pair, occasionally spurring big Wayland forward with a word.

No one noticed the leading citizen of Tuckaway as he strode down alleys and across the little town toward the railroad station, or as he went under the guidance of Silver a little distance down the tracks to a point where a rising grade made it certain that the next freight could be boarded.

It was not until the train came groaning and thundering near, however, that Wayland realized a new feature of danger in his plight.

"You've given Soggy a gun!" he exclaimed. "It's the same as murder for me to get on board the train with him. He'll bump me off as sure as daylight! He's bound to!"

"I've got a spare gun for you, too," said Silver. "You can have it as soon as the headlight of the engine goes by."

"Hold on!" yelled Soggy. "Don't I get any edge on that big thug after I've—"

But the approaching thunder of the train drowned his voice. The headlight of the engine went by, printed the swinging shadows of the leaves of the bushes on the faces of the three men.

It was now that Silver put a Colt into the hand of Wayland.

"Now hop that train!" he shouted. "Because if you're still here after it goes by, you shoot it out with me!"

Then, kneeling at a gap in the brush, Silver, with poised gun, watched Wayland rush for the train. He saw Soggy leap like a monkey and catch with hands and feet. He saw big Wayland catch one of the iron ladders with almost equal agility. And then the train swayed on and passed out of view around the next turn, gathering speed all the while.

It was already shooting along with a speed which would break the neck of any man who tried to leap from it. And many and many a mile would be between Wayland and the town of Tuckaway before he could start the return journey. Day would have come again, and the news of his disappearance and of his confession, before he could get back. And with the news, there would be a run on the bank unless the directors of it closed the doors.

All the consequences were obscured before the eyes of Silver, except he knew that he had kept himself from shooting a rascal who needed killing—and that he had assured the safe return of David Holman to the ranks of the law-abiding citizens.

Chapter – 24

H E HAD assured the return of Holman—if only he could bring help to his friends in the mountains before the cruel wits of Nellihan and Lorens had located the wounded man and his companions.

Silver drove Parade like a golden streak straight back for the house of Wayland. He checked the stallion in front of the porch. Inside the house, he could hear a heavy battering at a door. Were they at last sufficiently alarmed to beat down the door?

He rapped on the front door, in his turn. The Chinaman opened it before him, and then winced back at the sight of the tall body and the white rags it was dressed in.

"Is the sheriff here?" asked Silver. "Then go tell him that Jim Silver is down here waiting to see him."

The Chinaman fled up the stairs, his hands outstretched to help him, like wings, his head jerking over a shoulder, now and then, to cast furtive glances back at the big man who waited in the hall.

Upstairs, the battering paused for an instant, and Silver heard the voice of one of the deputies exclaim: "Mr Wayland, if you don't open the door, we'll take it for granted that something has happened to you, and we're going to break it down!"

The voice of the Chinaman broke in on this. There was a sudden exclamation from the sheriff, then the stamp of his running feet on the hall floor above.

Silver sang out: "I'm down here, Philips, and I'm not fighting."

Yet the first thing that he saw come down the dimness of the stairs was the glimmer of a revolver, and then the dark outlines of Philips crouched behind the gun.

387

Silver put his hands up, shoulder high. "I'm not fighting," he said. "Tell me if you know that Wayland has run out of town with all the cash he could get together. And then come down here and pinch me, if you want to!"

"Break down that door, Gene!" called the sheriff to one of the deputies.

Then he came hurrying down and confronted Silver.

"Silver," he said, "keep those hands up till I've fanned you. You know you're wanted for knowingly and willingly and witting—or whatever the legal phrases are—helping that rat of a Dave Holman to escape!"

"Fan me, Bert," said Silver. "There's a gun under the pit of my left arm, and there's a knife on my left hip. Take 'em both!"

The door went down with a crash while he was speaking. Philips took him into the dining room, where the Chinaman remained quaking in a corner.

"It's the queerest layout that I've ever seen," declared Philips. "I've never known anything like it. I hope I never do know anything like it. Wayland has turned into a green-faced mystery. You say that he's gone out of town and—"

There was a loud shouting from above, and then the thundering of heavy feet on the stairs. The first deputy, he of the fierce eyes, rushed into the room, with the signed confession of Wayland fluttering like a white flag in his hand.

He slapped it onto the table in front of Philips and cried: "Bert we been ridin' all this way for nothin'. The scalp of this here gent, this David Holman, it ain't worth a damaged nickel—because the whole yarn about him robbing the bank was a lie. Here's the truth!"

The sheriff was not a slow-minded man, but when he had finished reading that paper for the third time, he said: "But what persuaded Wayland to confess? If he's been this much of a skunk, why should he ever have confessed?"

The deputy pointed at Silver.

"Him!" he said. "He must've done it!"

"We want Wayland, not Holman," said the sheriff. "Where did you say that Wayland is?"

"On a freight train bound east. You can telegraph ahead, but I don't think he'll arrive at the first station," said Silver.

"Why not?" asked Philips.

"Because he may have some trouble on the road," answered Silver. "Philips, if you don't want Holman, you don't want me."

"I don't want you," agreed Philips. "I might have known that you'd prove the law wrong, again! Poor Holman! Something ought to be done to make up to him what he's gone through!"

Silver had lowered his hands, slowly, while Gene watched him with starved, bright eyes, as though he hated to see this quarry slip through his hands.

"The great thing you can do," said Silver, "is to see that the men of Kirby Crossing don't mob Holman and the others during the night. Nellihan and Lorens are leading those men from Kirby, and you can bet your money that they'll keep moving all night. Philips, will you get on your horse and make a drive toward Kendal Mountain, yonder? That's where I left Holman and the other three—up on a shoulder."

"I know the place," said the sheriff. "I'll get there as fast as horseflesh is able to fetch me. I'll be with you in two minutes, as soon as we can saddle up."

Silver stepped to the window, and sent a whistle cutting into the outer night.

"I'm going on ahead," he said. "Parade will take me there ahead of you. There's enough moonlight for straight shooting, and I'm worried about what may be happening up there. So long! You know the place! Ride your horses to a finish!"

Hoofbeats sounded softly on the lawn, and came to a sliding halt on the gravel of the path beside the house. The sheriff saw the sheen of the golden stallion in the lamplight. Then Silver was through the window and into the saddle. He was gone in a flash into the night.

It was almost at that moment that on the shoulder of Kendal Mountain, Harry Bench laid his hand on his sleeping companion, Ned Kenyon. As Kenyon wakened, he heard Bench saying:

"They're coming, Ned! Get up and out of here, fast! They're not fifty steps away. Listen!"

Kenyon heard a soft crackling, as a twig snapped. He was up instantly, sweeping his blanket into a roll.

He saw, then, that the girl had not slept. She sat passively beside Holman. He had thrown out his hand, during his sleep, and she held it in both of hers. One gesture from Bench told her of the danger. She sprang up. Holman wakened with a start. In a moment Bench and Kenyon were carrying their wounded companion on the litter away from the little clearing.

The moon was less than half full, but it shed a light that seemed to be growing stronger and stronger, as though danger were brightening it. If those who hunted for them found the place where they had camped, might not they also be able to find the out trail they were following?

Kenyon carried the head of the litter and led the way. They went down the first slope until it entered the head of a ravine that wound on through the foothills, growing deeper every moment.

"This here—it's a trap!" said Harry Bench. "Suppose that they come down on us here, they'll just flood us away!"

"If we kept up there on the divides," said Kenyon, "they could see us miles away under this moon. We ain't in this valley because we like it, but because there ain't any better place for us to go!"

That was the sheer truth. They went on silently and had put a good mile behind them when a gun spoke from the cliff at their right.

No bullet came near them. Three times the rifle was fired in rapid succession, and looking up, their frightened eyes saw a horseman wheeling his mustang away from the edge of the cliff, and going out of sight at a dead gallop. His wild Indian yell came whooping dimly down to them.

The men of Kirby Crossing had found them. They could guess that, and it would not be long before the flood of fighters came sweeping down into the ravine, as fast as horseflesh could carry them. They put down the litter and stared at one another.

Holman said: "It's all right, boys. You've done more than any other men in the world could have done. The luck's against us, at last, and that's all. I can take the medicine. Stand back and hoist your hands if they sight you. Or better still, try to climb out of the canyon and get away. They may rough you up a little if they find you with me; but if you're not in sight, they'll be glad enough to get me, and they're not likely to keep on hunting for you."

The girl said nothing. As usual, she merely looked at Harry Bench, for she was rarely able even to glance toward Ned Kenyon.

It was Kenyon who made the answer to that last remark, however. He said: "Harry, we're in the narrows of the canyon. One man oughta be able to hold back a crowd for quite a spell, here. And while he's holding, the other man and Edith can fetch Holman along till you come to some cut-back at the side of the ravine—some place where you can hole up and hide."

He took out a silver dollar, new-minted, flashing in the moonlight, and laid it on the back of his thumb.

"Call, Harry!" said he, and spun the coin high into the air.

Harry Bench looked up at the rising of the coin with despairing eyes. It was life or death, he knew, that was being tossed for. The man who remained behind, as Kenyon had so calmly suggested, would check the flood for a time, but it was sure to beat him down and roll on, before any long time.

"Tails!" called Bench.

The coin spatted on the palm of Kenyon. Bench leaned forward to look at it, but instantly the long fingers of Kenyon furled over it.

"It's tails," said Kenyon. "It's tails, all right. You win, and I stay here."

"I won't stand for it!" groaned Holman. "Go and save yourselves, both of you, and take Edith."

Confusion of mind and doubt bred something like anger in the voice of Harry Bench.

"She won't leave you, you blockhead!" exclaimed Bench. "There ain't any other way about it than this. Heaven help Ned—but the luck was agin him. Edith, pick up the light end of the litter, there."

He himself picked up the head of the litter. But the girl had run to Kenyon.

"Come on with us, Ned!" she said. "If anything happens to you, even if the rest of us lived, would our lives be anything but a curse and a darkness?"

"I ain't going to be killed," said Kenyon. "I feel kind of calm, and lucky. Say 'Goodbye' and go fast."

"Come on!" cried Bench, "or I'll start draggin' him by myself!"

He began, in fact, to stride forward, trailing one end of the poles behind him.

"Go on," said Kenyon. "It's what I want you to do!"

Still, for an instant, she hesitated.

"Heaven will never forgive me for what I've done to you! But can you forgive me, Ned?" she asked him.

Holman was crying out wildly, ordering Bench to drop the litter, swearing that he would not accept a life given to him in this fashion. Kenyon took the girl by the arm and waved her toward Holman.

"He's a better man than me," said Kenyon. "Go help him. Forgive you? They're ain't anything to forgive. God bless you; goodbye!"

She seemed to Kenyon, suddenly, like a child that stared up with incredulous wonder, and awe. What she said, he could not understand, because her voice was choked. And then she was gone, and Kenyon stood looking down at the hand which she had kissed.

He saw her pick up the dragging poles of the litter, and so the group disappeared around the corner of the wall of the ravine, and the protesting voice of Holman grew faint. At the same time, the clanging hoofs of many horses came roaring into the upper end of the valley.

Kenyon looked up at the sky, where the moon made it pale with light. He looked down at the walls of the canyon, one black as ink, one shimmering softly with the moonshine. He felt that he was about to die, and this picture was in some manner entering his very soul.

There was only one bit of shelter for him—a fallen boulder that projected two feet or more above the sand. Behind that he stretched himself and put the rifle to his shoulder. And then he saw them come pouring—a great sweep of horsemen, darkly silhouetted against the moonlight wall of the ravine. He fired three shots and waited.

They were not aimed shots. He was no good with a rifle. Besides, he had no intention of shooting to kill. And he drew a great breath of relief when he saw the cavalcade split away to either side, suddenly, as though the prow of an invisible ship had cloven a way through them, pushing them back under the shadows of the cliffs. He saw one man dismount and begin to climb by a crevice up the sheer face of the ravine wall. That would be the end—when that fellow gained the top of the wall and could shoot down at an easy angle into the body of the man who blocked the passing of the ravine. But Ned Kenyon did not turn and run for his life. If there was fear in him, he could not recognize its presence, but all he felt was a calm happiness that had no regard whatever for the future.

Chapter – 25

IT TOOK one hour for a horseman to get from Tuckaway to Kendal Mountain. It took forty minutes for Silver to rush out from the town on the back of Parade. As he reached the abandoned camping place, he heard the rifles open in the ravine below. So he swept down from the heights like a hawk from the upper air, and came into the narrow ravine where the guns boomed like small cannon. Then, at an elbow turn of the wall, he had a chance to view the scene in detail, without being seen himself.

Close under the walls of the ravine, chiefly on the side where the shadow made a black apron, a dozen or fifteen men were taking shelter behind brush, or behind fragments of rock that had fallen from the cliffs above. Their rifles spurted little jets of fire, now and then. In answer to them there was an occasional shot from a point where the canyon narrowed until the wall of it seemed to be leaning together. Those solitary shots were fired by big Harry Bench and Kenyon, of course, and beyond the narrows of the ravine would be the wounded Dave Holman, and the girl.

Now Silver saw the greatest threatening danger—the small silhouette of a man who was climbing the eastern wall of the ravine, working himself up on the jags of a deep crevice. In a few moments, the fellow would be on the upper lip of the canyon cliff, and could destroy the defenders with ease and security.

Silver dismounted, and pressing close to the corner of the rock so that little of his body would show, he made his voice great and thundered:

"Kirby Crossing! Who's there to talk to Jim Silver? I've got news from Tuckaway. The sheriff's on the run to get out here. Buster Wayland has confessed he did the job of robbing the bank. Holman has clean hands. He's cleared."

There was a chorus of surprised shouts, and then a yell in which he recognized the snarling, high-pitched voice of Nellihan:

"He lies! It's a bluff! Why isn't the sheriff here before him? Boys, stand tight. We'll bag the whole lot of them in another minute. Lorens is on top, and we've got the lot of them!"

A yell of triumph ran in on the last of his words, for now the man who climbed the eastern wall had reached the top, and was running forward to gain a better position from which to shoot down into the ravine. That savage yell told Silver that he had come too late to use words. Only his rifle would help him now, and whipping it out of the saddle holster, he lay flat and drew a careful bead. First he ranged his eyes down the side of the ravine to estimate the range, then he caught the dark silhouette of the target in his sights, and began to squeeze his hand over the trigger.

At that moment, Lorens disappeared behind some upjutting rock on the verge of the cliff.

Sweat streamed down the face of Silver. But what could he do? If he rushed with Parade, he might escape the gauntlet of fire on either side of the ravine, but when he reached his friends in the narrows, he would simply be swallowed in the same trap that held them.

A moment later, the ravine was hushed, and immediately after that, he heard the clang of a rifle, fired from the top of the cliff. That shot had told, for Lorens, in excess of triumph, suddenly leaped to his feet with a yell that rang from far off, coming to the ears of Silver like the cry of a bird of prey from the central sky. It was a fatal mistake for Lorens. In rising to brandish his rifle so that it flashed in the moonlight, a meager, whirling streak of brilliance, he had jumped right into the sights of Silver's gun.

Nellihan's howling voice shrilled a warning, but it was heard too late. Silver fired. And the body of Lorens leaned slowly out. The rifle dropped before him. Then he shot out into the air in a graceful arc, like a high diver, and plunged from the height.

A great yell of rage and of horror came from the men of Kirby Crossing. Before it died out, Silver was in the saddle again and sending Parade down the ravine like a glimmering bolt of lightning.

The watchers were taken totally by surprise. A few turned their guns on him, but the shots they fired were random bullets, before he plunged into the shadows of the narrows. And as he went by, he saw the body of poor Ned Kenyon, spread-eagled behind the rock.

Dead?

He ranged Parade close against the canyon wall beyond the reach of the bullets; then he ran forward, stooping low, and gained the side of Kenyon.

A faint muttering sound came from the lips of his friend. He turned the limp body, and saw a patch of darkness high on the breast of Kenyon, a patch that grew.

"Arizona?" said Ned Kenyon faintly. "I might a' known that you'd get in on the thing before the wind-up. Have they blotted me?"

Silver thumbed the wound. The bullet had entered high on the shoulder, close to the base of the back of the neck; it had ranged forward and come out by the collar bone.

"Take one deep breath—and say one word!" said Silver.

Kenyon obediently breathed and said: "Damn!" clipping his teeth together as he spoke.

Silver sighed with relief. "If that bullet had got the lungs," he said, "there'd be bubbles of blood in your mouth when you talk. Ned, if I can get you out of this trap, you'll live! Try to lift your left arm. No? It's broken, then; the collar bone's broken, at least. But that's nothing. Where are the others?"

He had an answer from behind for that. They heard the crunching of a heavy footfall, and the great bulk of One-eyed Harry cast itself down beside them. He gasped:

"Thank Heaven you're here, Jim. I came back as soon as I got the girl and Holman stowed away in a little canyon that rips back from this here, a short ways down. Holman is raisin' the devil, and tryin' to break away and crawl back here, so's he can die with the rest of us; and the girl's praying for you out loud, Kenyon; and Holman says he never was worth one of your old boots. Who's that out there, looking at the moon?"

For not far in front of the rock there was the body of Lorens, stretched on its back and staring steadily up at the moon, which glinted on the dead eyes.

There was no chance for Silver or Kenyon to answer the question, for the voice of Nellihan, raised to an animal howl, was now urging the men of Kirby Crossing to close in and rush the defenders. And a great, bull voice made answer:

"Where's yourself, Nellihan? Close in and lead up, instead of talkin' from the back row of the church!"

"I'm here!" shouted Nellihan. "Boys, all together, now. Keep shooting as we go in on 'em. And then—"

"Wait a minute!" called Silver. "All you fellows from Kirby Crossing—if you rush us, we've got three rifles to blow the tar out of a good many of you. If Nellihan wants us, I'll stand out and fight him. If he drops me, you can have the rest of them. They'll surrender. If I drop him, you back up and take a rest till the morning. Does that sound fair to you?"

No one answered for a moment, because there was only one man who could speak, and that was Nellihan. Suddenly his long, misshapen body appeared, striding with long steps from out of the shadows near the wall. He was desperate, as Silver knew, for on this night he was playing his last cards to ruin the life of a girl and get his hands on the fortune.

"I'm here," said Nellihan. "Where are you? Stand out here and show us your face. Are you yellow?"

Silver rose and stood out before the eyes of all those enemies. His hands were empty, and so were the hands of Nellihan, who walked straight up to him and glared into his eyes with a hellish malice.

"You've spoiled everything for me. You've smashed every plan, and you've killed Lorens. You won't hang for that, because I guess he's wanted for more than one killing. But you wouldn't have a chance to hang, anyway. Because I'm going to split your wishbone for you tonight, my friend! Are you ready to start?"

Silver looked at him with a shrinking of the flesh. The man seemed neither old nor young. He was a thing of poisonous evil.

"I'm ready," said Silver. "We'll stand back to back, if you want, and walk away till somebody sings out to shoot. Does that suit you, Nellihan?"

Nellihan peered into his face, as though trying to find the source of the mysterious strength that sustained this man in the time of danger.

"Anything suits me," he said. "You're as good as a dead man, right now. Hey, Baldy! Sing out when you think we've walked far enough!"

They stood back to back. Silver, glancing down, saw that his shadow was sloping well out before him. That meant that when he turned, the moon would be in his eyes. But that was a small disadvantage—if only he could subdue the sick shuddering of his flesh, as he thought of this half-human animal, who would soon be whipping a gun from under his coat and turning to fire. To fight men, Silver felt himself capable; but it was impossible to think of Nellihan failing. The devil he served would support him.

"Start!" shouted the voice of Baldy.

The murmuring of many other voices died down like a wind passing out of trees. Slowly Silver stepped away, straining every nerve to an electric tension.

"Shoot!" screeched the voice of Baldy. Silver whirled, snatching his gun from beneath his arm. He saw Nellihan drawing a revolver and leaping far to the side at the same instant. Fast as Silver was, that snaky hand had been faster still. The gun in Nellihan's grip exploded. The brief breath of the bullet fanned the face of Silver as he fired in turn, with his gun hardly more than hip-high.

He thought he had missed, and that Nellihan had deliberately fired a bullet into the ground, for his second shot. It seemed almost—as he held his fire, with his man covered—that Nellihan was slowly dropping on one knee to take a more careful aim. But when he had come to one knee, his body continued to collapse, until he lay face down on the ground.

Death had simply laid its numbing hand upon him gradually.

And before this horror ended, or the silence after it had ceased, the ravine was echoing with the beat of the hoofs of horses. Out from the shadows at the upper end of the valley came three riders, and he who galloped in the lead was Sheriff Bert Philips, bringing up the authentic hand of the law, at last.

All was not as simple as Silver had hoped and even expected. It had looked easy enough on that night, when the men of Kirby Crossing gave up the prey that had baffled them so long, and even helped to take care of the two wounded men. There was no trouble afterward about Nellihan or Lorens, either. Because it was clear that Silver had represented law against mob violence. Furthermore, against Lorens, it was discovered that there were many counts; and when the character of Nellihan was exposed, the world looked on his death as deliverance from a plague.

Ned Kenyon, too, had a simple role. When he was well enough to ride, he went into Nevada to get the divorce that was necessary, and he went without any soreness of the heart. He said to Silver:

"The misery just kind of leaked out of me with my blood, after Lorens had sent the slug through me!"

"You're going to be sensible, I hope," said Silver. "You'll take the help that she and Holman want to give you?"

"Well," said Kenyon, "now that I've got over bein' foolish about her, I guess there's something in what she says—that I worked enough to deserve some pay. So I'm goin' to take the coin. She wants to give me a regular cattle king's layout. But I'll stick just to the ten thousand that she wanted to give me in the beginning. Small things are better for small men, Jim, and I never was as big as my inches."

All of these matters went very well, but it was a full six months before Holman was able to shake off the hand of the law. Not that anyone doubted his story, now, but there were complications which might never have been solved, had it not been that the governor of the State stepped in to cut all the red tape with a complete pardon.

But Silver was far away in the north-land when this happened, and he only heard of it through a letter that had followed him from one forwarding address to another.

It was from David Holman, and he said in part:

We've put our heads together, but we don't know what to do. We've owed our happiness to three people—one part to One-eyed Harry Bench, and nine parts to

Ned Kenyon, and ninety parts to you. Edith has been able to content Harry and Ned. But we are sorry we can't offer you hard cash, or even a ranch. If we could think of anything you need, we'd like to offer it. But a horse and a gun seem to make you a complete man. All that we can give you is gratitude.

Now that I'm free, and the divorce has been granted, we're going to be married quietly and go for a long trip. When we come back, we'll hope that one day you'll drop in on us. And stay the rest of your life, if you find the place comfortable. The best of all, would be to have you at the wedding. You saw Edith at a wedding once before. That was a marriage in the dark. We hope that this one will be in the sun, with not even a shadow on its future, no matter how much wretchedness may be in its past.

When you write to us, if you ever will, we wish that you could tell us where you are riding. Or do you know yourself, but simply drift with the wind or let Parade follow his fancy?

It was a cold day, and as Silver read that letter in the little post office and then crumpled the paper, he echoed that last question in his own mind. Where was he bound? He could not tell. The ancient melancholy descended upon him, and he fell into long reflections from which he awakened, suddenly, remembering that he had left Parade shivering in the street.

SILVERTIP'S STRIKE

CONTENTS

1 – Wycombe Ranch

WHEN Jim Silver came over the last divide, he could see the ranch house among the low foothills, and beyond the foothills was the desert. It looked like a green smudge, an olive-green drab; but he knew that at close hand the green would thin out to a sparse scattering of shrubs, all of which were arrayed in foliage which was no more than a mist, the leaves turning their edges up so as to split the full heat of the sun that would have withered them. He knew that only the toughest grass would be found yonder, and that in occasional tufts which keep a cow steadily walking as it grazes all day long.

Yet in the distance the effect of the rolling desert was green, though it was not the luminous sheen of well-watered country, but rather as grasslands appear under cloud or seen through a fog of dust. To look at that desert made the day seem overcast, though a brilliant sun was shining. The burning weight of it on the shoulders of Jim Silver told him with what force it was shining, and so did the little white streaks of salt that appeared all over the hide of his chestnut stallion where the sweat had sprung out and dried as it began to run.

The band of his sombrero was hot and soggy. He took off the hat, pulled out a bandanna, and mopped the leather band, then dried his forehead and the back of his neck. Now that his hat was off for a moment, one could see the two marks of gray hair above his temples, like small horns breaking through. He had gained his name of Silver or "Silvertip" from those spots of white hair. He was called "Arizona Jim" and other names as well, but his real name was as much a secret as the wellspring of that quiet smile which was found more often in his eyes than about his lips.

He had the look of a man who is sufficient unto himself and who relies upon greater strength than even that which appeared in his long arms and in his heavy shoulders. Or perhaps it was the stallion—a great, glimmering sheen of gold—that made him seem as much at home on the verge of the mountains and the desert as any hawk afloat in the sky.

The smile which was habitually his disappeared as he marked the gray-white of the ranch house among the hills. For he had no need to pull the letter out of his pocket; he could remember every word that Steve Wycombe had written:

DEAR SILVER You've always hated my heart.

That's all right, because I've always hated yours, too. But now there's a chance that we can use one another. I'm asking you to come over to see me because I've got as big a job as you ever tackled in your life—and I know that you've had some big ones. Hard cash is what I'm talking about. I pay, and you take, and your job is the sort of hell fire that you prefer to breathe.

Just by accident I've heard that you're drifting north, and that's why I'm leaving this letter in Rusty Gulch in the hope that you may call for mail there.

I want you to try to forget the old days and believe that I'm talking the sort of business that you always like to hear.

Adios,

steve wycombe

Silver recalled the words of the letter, now, as he settled the hat again on his head. And, as the shadow fell over his face, the hazel of his eyes lightened to a flicker of yellow fire, as certain types of hazel eyes can do. For he could remember very well a few of those old days when he had known Steve Wycombe before the inheriting of a ranch had removed Steve from the ranks of the professional gamblers and gunmen.

Wycombe had been half fox and half wolf. He had both teeth and cunning, plus what Jim Silver hated more than anything else in the world—the smooth and ingratiating manner of the born hypocrite.

However, the letter had called Silver across the mountains. He knew that Wycombe might be setting a trap for him, but a great part of Silver's time was spent in avoiding the traps which his enemies laid for him. Besides, there was a ring of sincerity in the words of Wycombe that led Silver to believe that the man might have fallen into a need greater than his hatred; it might be just possible that Steve was willing to forget that day when Silver had shamed him before many men in Gold Gulch.

So, for the moment, Jim Silver balanced the question nicely in his mind. At last, he rubbed the tips of his gloved fingers down the arch of the stallion's neck and murmured:

"Parade, it looks like trouble, it feels like trouble, and it probably is trouble. But all oats and no trouble would make us too fat to work."

He spoke again, and the stallion started down the easy slope at a trot. His rider kept no rein; but, having selected a direction, gave his mind to other things while the horse picked out the way that suited him best. He was not compelled to go over hard beds of rock if he saw going more to his taste to the right or the left; he was not forced straight on through stifling dust if he wished to take a higher route; in all things he was allowed to do pretty much as he pleased, so long as he sailed by the right star, so to speak.

If the man and the saddle had been removed and the horse considered by itself, one might have said that Parade was running wild, such was the height of his head and the free fire in his eye. There was not even a bit between his teeth, of braided horsehair. But, though he picked his own way, he remained true to the direction which had been given to him, as though from the first he had seen the low, sprawling line of the ranch house with the spider-webbing of corral fences near it.

As he went over a winding trail out of the clean brown of the sun-burned mountain slopes and into the dry mauve of the desert, Jim Silver took heed of the grazing cattle, true desert types rather roached of back and down of head; lean, active creatures which could forage actively and use their legs to go from pasture to water, even at a gallop. Off to the left, four or five miles from the house, he saw the sheen of a body of water where the spring rains had been dammed up in a "tank," and trailing out of the distance were dust clouds that rapidly approached the lake. Those were cattle on the run for moisture, and the sight of them at once told Silver the dimensions of the Wycombe ranch.

As far as the eye could reach, all of this land belonged to Steve Wycombe, and, no matter how many acres were needed to support a cow, there was enough mileage to give pasturage to a big herd. Therefore, one important fact was assured—that Wycombe had enough money to be in big trouble. For, if money is the root of all trouble, the size of the root is apt to gauge the size of the trouble.

The hands of big Jim Silver slid up inside his coat and touched the handles of the two oversize Colts which hung in spring holsters under the pits of his arms. He glanced down, also, at the Winchester which fitted into the saddle holster that sloped down under his right knee.

The ranch house was split into two wings, one section to give bunks for the hired hands, and the other for the occupancy of the owner; the kitchen was in the small link that joined the two. A windmill, whirring, moaning, clanking, arose on great skeleton legs of iron.

The possibility of digging down to water was enough to explain the presence of the house on this site. As he came closer, Silver could hear the plumping sound of the stream as it fell with a regular pulsation into the galvanized-iron tank near the mill. He thought instinctively of the days of calm when that wheel would not turn and when the long-handled pump would have to be used instead. Just inside the first corral there was a long line of troughs. If the tanks that held spring rain went dry, the cattle could be watered—in part, at least—from these troughs.

Silver went into that corral and slipped the hackamore off the head of the stallion. Parade was instantly eye-deep in the sparkle of the water. Silver watched the boluses of water glide rapidly down the throat of the horse. Again and again the dripping head of the horse was tossed up so that he could look around him, certain proof that he had known what it meant to run wild and fend for himself.

Silver put his hand on the neck of the horse, smiling, and after that Parade drank steadily, with eyes at peace, switching his tail and shrinking his hide to get off the flies that came swarming. As he finished drinking, the door of the house jerked open. A man with a pearl-gray sombrero on the back of his head, wearing a bright-yellow shirt and an unbuttoned vest, stood on the threshold for an instant; then he shouted, "Silver! Hi!" and came hurrying.

That was Steve Wycombe. Silver, watching him, knew that he could have remembered the man by the swagger of his walk and the cant of his head. A woman appeared in the dimness of the interior of the kitchen, from the door of which Wycombe had gone out. She stood close enough to the sunshine for Silver to see that her hair was bright and that her face was young. Then she closed the door.

Perhaps she was Mrs Steve Wycombe, poor girl!

Wycombe came up with his head to one side, nodding, smiling. He had projecting upper teeth so that he could only grin broadly with a great flash of the teeth or else hang his upper lip in a crooked sneer. The grin was very broad, just now.

There is something about buckteeth that makes a man look young and innocent. That was the appearance of Wycombe, in the main, except that his eyes could be pocketed up in wrinkles that were not always lines of mirth. He was not bad looking, but he wore his hat like a tough, and he had his blond hair combed down over his forehead so that he had to keep tossing his head to throw back the lock out of his eyes.

"Old boy Jim Silver!" he said with emphasis.

He came up and took Silver's hand and held it through a long moment. He was one of those fellows who stand close when they speak to a man, and use their eyes up and down. That was the way he scanned Silver.

"You haven't shrunk any!" he said. "Come on in and put yourself outside a drink. I've got some seventeen-year-old rye. When I say seventeen, I don't mean seven. I'm glad to see you, you big steer!"

"I'm putting up the horse first," said Silver. "That the shed? Or do you keep all your saddle stock out?"

"That's the shed. Come along," answered Wycombe. "This is Parade, eh? He looks as though he could move. That's a shoulder! That's as fine a shoulder as I ever saw on a thoroughbred!"

"Watch yourself," said Jim Silver. "He'll take your arm out by the roots, if you don't."

"Savage, eh?" asked Wycombe. His step back was as swift as that of a dancer. The whole man became suddenly quick and light, and that reminded Silver of sundry unlucky fellows who had discovered the deftness of Wycombe's gun hand too late. Doctors were of very little use after Wycombe had made his play.

They put up the horse in the shed. Silver unsaddled Parade, rubbed him down with some big twists of straw, and selected the best hay he could find in the mow of the shed. There were no oats; he poured crushed barley into the feed box.

"I don't know," commented Wycombe. "Take a slick horse like that, and it's like a slick woman. Needs a lot of caring for. I don't know that it's worthwhile. Take a mustang, you throw a rope and climb on and ride as far as you want. If the bronc is used up, throw it away; it doesn't cost anything."

"Parade will stand the rough use, too," answered Silver. "But a horse is like a gun. It's better clean."

"Yeah. But when you need a gun, you need it," observed Wycombe.

"Times when I've needed Parade," said Silver, smiling.

Wycombe looked at him with a sudden seriousness, his upper lip crookedly suspended on his buckteeth.

"You've been through it, all right," he said. "You've seen everything that a man can see."

He added, rather sharply: "You used to hate my heart. What about it, Jim?"

"We can all be wrong, Wycombe," said Silver coldly.

They went back to the house in a silence, with a shadow between them; but when they reached the place, Wycombe winked and nodded.

"Want you to see something," he said, and opened the door to the kitchen.

The girl with the bright hair sat in a corner by the window, peeling potatoes. She had one pan in her lap, another on the floor beside her. She stood up, holding the pan between her elbows, smiling at the stranger the way Western girls are supposed to do. She had a good, straight smile, and her eyes were a stain of blue in her face. To Silver she seemed almost beautiful, which was as much as he seemed able to say about any woman.

"This is Esther Maxwell," said Wycombe. "Shake hands with her, Jim. She don't need an introduction to you. She knows about Jim Silver. Everybody knows about you. How big does he look to you, Esther?"

She kept right on smiling at Silver, as he stepped forward.

"My fingers are all sloppy from the potatoes. I can't shake hands," she said.

"How big does he look to you?" insisted Wycombe.

Silver glanced sidelong at his host.

"He looks so big," said the girl.

Wycombe, laughing, led the way into the next room, put his back against the door as he closed it, and winked and nodded at Silver.

"That doesn't wear the Wycombe brand, yet," he murmured, "but it's going to, boy! Pretty slick, eh? You see her dolled up for a dance and you see something. Works like a Chinaman, too."

He walked on, tapping himself on the chest, his teeth flashing.

"All for me, brother," he said.

He led the way into the next room.

"Office," he said. "All the papers and everything. Here's where little Steve works the brains; the cowboys have to work the hands."

He kept on laughing as Silver ran his glance over the square box of a room. There was one overstuffed chair in it that looked out of place, like a fur coat on a summer day.

"Sit down there while I crack open the hooch," said Wycombe. "It's going to open your eye for you, brother. But tell me first what you think of that."

He hooked his thumb over his shoulder.

"She's a pretty girl," said Silver.

"She's pretty and she's handsome. She's a performer, is what she is. All mine, brother. All for me!"

He continued to chuckle as he took a bottle out of a cupboard and filled two whisky glasses. "Just take a sock at this," he said.

Silver tasted it with his eyes studiously aslant. He smiled in honor of that noble liquor, not of his host; then they drank together.

"Now what?" asked Silver. "This is good stuff. But now what?"

Wycombe slowly thrust out his lower jaw as he answered: "Two hombres want to lift my hair. Two real bad boys. They've already started on the way. They might arrive here any old time. But when they come, they're going to find your guns working for me!"

2 – The Foreman

WYCOMBE held the glass in his right hand with his forefinger pointing out from it at Silver, fixing him in place, preventing speech.

"Don't talk," he said. "Wait till I get finished. Don't say 'No' till you understand why you ought to say 'Yes'! You remember me out of the old days. But I'm different now. I'm no tinhorn gambler, these days. I can play for stakes. And what do you think that life is worth to a rich man?"

"You're handy with a gun," said Silver. "Take care of yourself."

"I'm handy. You bet, I'm handy. But I'm bright, too. I'm so bright that I know when the other fellow has the high hand. And two high hands are going to be sitting in against me, before long."

"How high?" asked Silver.

"Straight flushes!" said Wycombe.

Silver sat up in his chair a little.

"I'm all right in a fight, but I'm not that right," said Wycombe. "I know it, and they know it. That makes it bad. I know they can beat me, and they know it, too. None of us are in the dark. That's what makes it bad."

"That makes it bad," said Silver.

"They're coming for me with all the cards in the world," went on Wycombe, "and they think that they've got the pot already; but I'm switching things on 'em. They're going to find me sitting against their two straight flushes with a royal flush. And that's you!"

He kept on jabbing his forefinger in the direction of Silver.

"If you see white water ahead, take a trip," said Silver. "For my part, I'm busy."

"Busy doing what?"

"I'm traveling."

"You are always traveling. Where?"

"Up the line," said Silver, with a vague gesture.

"No, you're not. I've got it in my pocket."

"What?"

"Your price."

"Perhaps you have," said Silver coldly.

"First, I've got you because you love a fight," said Wycombe. "I'm talking right out at you, you see? You love a fight for the fight's sake. A lot of people say that you're never in trouble till fools put you in it. But nobody ever killed your list without liking the feel of that last part of a second before the guns are going to be pulled. Answer me straight in the eyes. Do you like it? I mean, when the other fellow's eyes turn red, and he begins to show his teeth at you, and bunch his shoulders over, and his hands start working. Do you like that?"

Silver sighed and shrugged his shoulders.

"Go on with it," he said.

"Well, I'm going to hook you with the names of the hombres that are coming to lift my hair. Because, when you hear those names, your mouth is going to water. It's the sort of meat you like. It's high! The two of 'em are crooks from away back. They've both done their killings and plenty of 'em. They're stake runners. They start from scratch when it comes to guns, and one of 'em is Morris Delgas. You know Delgas?"

"I know him," said Silver.

"He killed Rex Walters and Lefty Markham; those are about the best two he killed. But there's others."

"I know what Morrie Delgas has done," answered Silver.

"A nice fly for a trout to rise at, eh? But the other's a shade better, even. The other's that devil of a Harry Rutherford! I don't need to ask if you know that little drink of poison! It wouldn't be healthy for you not to know! A little left-handed streak of misery, is what he is. Some people say he's the slickest hand with a gun that ever fanned a Colt. That's what a lot of people say. I don't know. I'd back you against him. That's all I know. And the money I put down goes into your pocket. Listen to me, Silver. When I say money, I mean it. Big money."

Silver shook his head and stood up slowly.

"Hey!" cried Wycombe. "Don't act that way. Wait a minute. Listen."

"I don't want to listen," said Silver.

"Wait! I'm talking something like this—five thousand apiece. I know you, Jim. You're not small time. For each one of those hombres, five thousand bucks paid on the spot."

"I don't want it," said Silver.

A moment of silence struck between them. Silver heard the ticking of a clock that was not in the room. He heard the buzzing of a big bluebottle that circled around and around the room. He smelled the aromatic sharpness of hot varnish, and knew that his body was covered with sweat, also. Wycombe was staring at him.

"Have I banked on a lame horse? Have you lost your nerve?" whispered Wycombe.

Then his voice came out with a bang. "I said five thousand. I mean it. I'll give you five thousand on account, Jim! Those hombres mean to murder me, I tell you. I'll pay you five thousand advance just to be the bodyguard!"

"I don't want the money," said Silver.

"You mean," shouted Wycombe, "that you don't want any part of my game. You don't want me!"

Silver was silent. He knew that anything could happen now, and he was ready for it, looking fixedly into the eyes of Wycombe and watching the trembling of the upper lip that hung crookedly over the buckteeth.

"I've missed!" whispered Wycombe. He cried out suddenly: "Listen to me. I can't slip up. Listen to me, Jim. I've got ten thousand dollars right here in this room. It's yours!"

Silver shook his head. A whole storm of rage and darkness poured over the eyes of Wycombe. His body trembled. His mouth kept working vainly around the prominence of those big front teeth.

"All right," he said at last, and, turning on his heel, he walked out of the room.

Silver followed him, looking left and right as he stepped cautiously through each doorway. As he went toward the back of the house, he heard the voice of Wycombe ring out ahead of him:

"What the devil do you mean by coming up here and hanging around the kitchen? Get out on the range, where you belong. Foreman? You're no foreman. You're no good. I've got a mind to fire you on the spot. I'm sick of the pretty face of you."

Silver, stepping into the kitchen, saw Wycombe in the middle of the floor, shaking his fist at a tall, brown-faced youth who stood with his sombrero in the tips of his fingers, his back to the door. On the floor he had just laid the quarters of a deer. Anger had marked the cheeks of this fellow with white, and pure rage was about to burst out of his lips when the girl intervened. She was behind the back of Wycombe, so that only Silver saw her frightened gesture of entreaty. Both hands remained for an instant pressed against her throat while her eyes talked to the foreman.

He took a great breath.

"I thought you folks might want some fresh venison, was all," said he.

He began to turn toward the door. It was very hard for him, Silver could see that, to swallow the string of insults that had just been poured at him. In a sense, Silver felt guilty, because it was plain that Wycombe felt himself enough of a gun fighter to handle this honest cow-puncher, and the wrath which he had accumulated during his interview with Silver was to be poured out now.

It was the girl who had stopped the retort that might have meant gunfire. And, if she had stopped it, most assuredly it had not been because her great concern was for Wycombe.

"I'm going to teach you," shouted Wycombe, beside himself with rage as he saw the other giving way, "I'm going to teach you that your place is out where—"

"Wait a minute, Wycombe," said Silver.

Wycombe spun about with his shoulders suddenly against the wall, the very attitude of a man who fears that he may be attacked from two sides at once.

"Hey—well, what you want?" he barked.

"I've been thinking things over," said Silver.

He felt the eyes of the girl suddenly on his face; he felt the wonder in them.

Wycombe was instantly changed. He seemed to forget his foreman in a flash.

"You mean that, Jim?" he cried. "You're going to stand by me and take a chance to—"

"I'll stand by you, I suppose," said Silver.

"Come on back in that room," urged Wycombe. "I'm going to pay you now to—"

"Wait a moment," said Silver.

He walked slowly toward the young foreman, who was closing the door. The latter paused, opened the door again.

"Wycombe's temper is not worth much," said Silver, "and sometimes he talks a lot."

He held out his hand with a smile.

"My name is Jim Silver," he said.

The white face of the foreman turned crimson. He knew, it was clear, that this gesture on the part of Silver was purely in token that the stranger had overheard but had not lost respect for the foreman because he had taken water in the row. Never was a stronger grasp laid on the hand of Silver.

"I'm Dan Farrel," said he. "And—thanks. It's great to meet you, Silver. It's great!"

He went out, closing the door hastily behind him, as though he wished to conceal something that was coming into his face.

Silver, turning, saw Wycombe beckoning impatiently at the other door of the kitchen. He saw, also, one flash of gratitude and astonishment in the eyes of the girl. Then he went on through the door with Wycombe and back into the study.

"You gave me a turn, Silver." Steve Wycombe laughed. "You can throw a bluff with anybody I ever saw. I thought for a minute that you meant what you said. Wait a minute. Ten thousand, I said, and ten thousand it's going to be."

He started to unlock the door of a big square-faced safe that filled a corner of the room.

"No," said Silver. "I don't want the cash."

"You don't want what?" shouted Wycombe.

"I don't take blood money," said Silver.

Wycombe straightened his body with jerks and finally faced his guest with a frown.

"I never was able to figure you out," he said. "You beat me—but that's all right. As long as you're with me, anything's all right! Only—"

He paused, and then shrugged his lean shoulders twice.

"About that fellow Farrel," he said. "Why did you make that funny play about him? Going up and shaking hands with the bum when he'd just backed down and taken water like a cur?"

"He's not a cur. He's a man," said Silver. "And I'd rather murder a man than shame him."

3 – Silver Listens

THEY sat for a time in the office. Wycombe drank more of the old rye whisky. Silver smoked cigarettes and did the listening, as a rule.

He had merely said: "Let's find out why the pair are after you. It's quite a time since you were in the games where you rubbed elbows with the pair of 'em. Two or three years, I should say."

"All that matters," said Wycombe, "is that they're after me, and that you know what they look like."

"No," said Silver. "I need to know more."

Wycombe curled his upper lip to speak, and once more the lip stayed curled on the projecting teeth while Wycombe changed his mind about the words he was to have spoken.

"Well," he said at last, "you won't be a hired man. You're going to have your full share in the show."

He struck out his jaw after the way he had, and tossed back the blond hair.

"I'm sorry I got sore in front of the girl," he said suddenly. "You think she noticed?"

"She noticed," said Silver.

"What did she look like?" asked Wycombe.

"Frightened," said Silver.

Wycombe lolled back in his chair, suddenly at ease.

"It don't do any harm to throw a scare into a jane," he declared. "Let 'em know that there's a real man around, and they like it all the better. You know what I mean."

"I know what you mean," said Silver, probing the dark and mean soul of the man with a steady eye.

But Wycombe failed to understand the glance. He went on: "You know how it is. A girl likes to see a man that's up to something. She doesn't want to have a yellow pup around. She's always liked that foreman of mine pretty well. She'll hate his heart from now on. Eh?"

"Perhaps," said Silver.

"They know my record, around here," went on Wycombe. "They know that I'm no soft-handed baby. Eh?"

"They ought to know that."

"But, going back a little—I'm kind of beat by you, Silver. You throw ten thousand dollars out the window?"

Silver shrugged his shoulders.

"I want to be my own man," said he. "I want to do as I please. And I don't want blood money. I never took any, and I don't want it."

"But you'll hire out—you'll stay here, I mean—and keep an eye out for me?"

"I'll stay here—for a while. If Morrie Delgas and Harry Rutherford show up, I'll try my hand fighting for you. I'll work for you as though you'd paid me the money, Wycombe—unless you start kicking things around."

"Kicking you around?" said Wycombe, laughing. "I'm not a half-wit, old son."

"Let's hear the story of why the pair are on your trail."

"Why pick on that? Why does it matter?"

"Because," said Silver, "the cause that puts a man on a trail is the grindstone that sharpens the edge of him. I want to know what sort of a temper and edge these fellows are wearing."

Wycombe considered gloomily. He made himself a cigarette and then remarked:

"You know Gold Gulch?"

"Yes."

"Know Fourth Street?"

"Yes."

"Know the pawnshop on the corner?"

"Pudge Wayland used to run it."

"That's right. Know anything more about Pudge?"

"He was a crook and a fence."

"He was a crook and a fence, all right," said Wycombe. "Know what happened to him?"

"He was shot."

"By whom?" asked Wycombe.

"I never heard."

"Nobody else did, except a few. I'm the fellow that killed him."

Silver actually sighed with relief.

"Is that what's behind this trail that Morrie Delgas and Rutherford are on?"

"That's it!" said Steve Wycombe, brightening. "I ought to have a medal and a vote of thanks for getting that fat Gila monster out of the world, instead of inheriting trouble about it, eh?"

"It seems that way. How did the thing happen?"

"I'd had words with him. It was a couple of years back. I'd had words with him. About nothing much. Just about a loan he'd made me on a gold watch. I was sore. The next time I saw him, I was coming out of the mouth of an alley. It was night. I saw the fat back of Pudge Wayland come across the street. I sang out and swore at him. He whirled around. I was drunk. I was on a mean drunk. You know, the kind when you don't know what you're doing. I thought I saw a gun in his hand. I shot him dead. That's all."

He stuck out his lower jaw and stared at the floor.

"That's all—except that he wasn't even wearing a gun?" suggested Silver.

"The fool," said Steve Wycombe, "should a' had one on, anyway. There was a witness, y'understand? A sap of a no-good sneak thief. He saw everything. He spotted me. I had to give him a regular pension to keep his mouth shut. And he went off into Mexico, where he'd be safe in case I decided to pay him the rest of his pension with a chunk of lead. He stayed down there and collected my checks. Just like that. And then the blockhead goes and gets into a row, a while ago, and gets himself knifed up, and the doctors say that he's going to die, and he lies there on the floor of a saloon and tells what he knows to the fellow that knifed him. Makes a confession, d'you see? And the fellow that knifed him is Harry Rutherford, and with Harry is that Morrie Delgas.

"Well, this is how the thing all hitches together. That Pudge Wayland was a fence, and you know it. And he'd done a lot of work for Delgas and for Rutherford, both of 'em, because they were working hand in glove. And when Wayland died, he had a whole slew of stolen goods on his hands, and a big pile of it belonged to those two thugs.

"You see what had happened? I bump off Pudge Wayland. His heirs get everything in his shop—and it's a ton! They clean out his safe. They get themselves rich, and gyp Morrie and Harry out of a whole little fortune in honest stolen goods they'd given to Pudge. That must have been the way of it.

"Anyway, my man lies there on the floor of the cantina and talks his fool head off, and he sees that pair shake hands over him and swear that they'll go and bump off Wycombe, just to even the account. They'd always hated me, anyway, since a little poker game we once played together. And then the fool fellow, he doesn't die, after all; but he gets better, and he's honest enough to write me a letter and tell me how he happened to put those two bloodhounds on my trail. But you see the funny part?"

"I don't know what part would be funny to you," said Silver.

"Why," said Wycombe, "ain't it a scream that'd curdle your blood to think of me bumping off a fat fool like Pudge Wayland and then getting a pair of wildcats like those two dropped right down my back?"

4 – Silver Gives Warning

THE evening came on, and Jim Silver was glad of a chance to get out of the tobacco reek and whisky smell of the closed house into the open. Besides, there was something unusual—rain promised over the desert, and thunder bumping and rumbling in the sky just like carts going over iron bridges.

Steve Wycombe went off by himself for a few moments, and Silver was gladdest of all to be alone. He wanted to do some thinking. He had come to the hardest moment of all, which is when a man tries to untangle his own actions and discover the motives of them. He kept telling himself that he was a fool to have bound himself to fight for this fellow Wycombe and, above all, to have bound himself against such formidable men as Morris Delgas and that ravenous ghost of a man, Harry Rutherford.

Certainly it was not compassion for Wycombe that kept him on the place. He could hardly put his finger on the cause until he saw young Dan Farrel walk from the first corral toward the bunk house. Then he could remember and be sure that it was something about Farrel and the girl that had turned the scales and induced him to stay. Why?

Well, he could not say exactly. He was simply a prospector in the land of trouble, and there seemed to be a rich strike of danger and complications straight ahead of him.

A pair of cow-punchers came away from the horse shed and ran sneaking up on their foreman. They were almost on him when he sidestepped. There was a swift flurry of action, an uproar of laughing voices, and the foreman went on, leaving his two men to pick themselves up from the ground. Jim Silver was pleased enough to smile. He waved Farrel over to him.

"What do you say about rain, Farrel?" he asked.

418

Farrel shook his head. "It's the wrong season," he declared. "You don't know how rain comes here—just a few drops at a time—just enough to keep the lips wet and the patient from dying. Just enough water to keep the grass from dying clear down to the bottom of its roots. This is a dry ranch, Silver!"

He nodded and smiled as he spoke.

"You like it." said Jim Silver. "There's something about it you like, or that you expect to like later on."

"Why do you say that?"

"Because you'll put up with a good deal in order to stay on it. Why, Farrel? There are plenty of jobs everywhere for good cowmen."

Farrel stared at him. Then turning toward the foothills, he waved his hand west and north and east.

"You see how those mountains are heaped up in three bunches? Over there to the east are the Rendais—that's old Mount Kendal back there in blue and white, just on the right. Over here, straight north, that second bunch make up the Humphreys Mountains. I don't have to tell you which is Mount Humphreys itself. Look at the way it goes jump into the sky! Now, yonder on the left, right over there bang against the west, you see the biggest of the three bunches? Those are the Farrel Mountains."

Silver looked not so much at the silhouette of ragged blackness in the west, not so much at the three vast masses of cumulus clouds which were blossoming over the three groups of mountains, as he did into the lean, brown face of Dan Farrel. For it seemed to Silver that some of the fire and grandeur of the sunset mountains was reflected in the face of the cow-puncher.

"I see," said Silver. "They were named after one of your tribe?"

"Great-grandfather. Ever since his day there's always been a Farrel on this ground."

He hooked his thumb over his shoulder.

"It isn't the house that matters. I don't give a hang about that. It's the ground that counts. I've gone away and worked on other places—places on the ledge of the desert, like this, with mountains close by that were a lot bigger and finer than those three outfits—but I never found a place that fitted into my head the way this one does. Every time I lay an eye on those mountains, it's as though I'd daubed a rope on a maverick and added it to my herd. I tell you what, Silver—it may seem a funny thing to you, but it's true—it seems to me that I know every wave of the ground off there to the south from the ranch house. I know just where the waves of the land are running, every one of 'em."

"How did the Farrels lose the place?" asked Silver.

"My old man gambled it away to Wycombe's old man, that's the whole story."

"You hate to leave it?"

"The way you'd hate to stop breathing."

"Well," said Silver, "it looks as though you'd have to go."

"Does it?"

"On account of the girl."

"What d'you mean?"

"I've been talking to Wycombe, and he wants her. If he thinks you're in his way, with her, he'll cut your throat. He'll fire you off the ranch, at least."

"What makes you think that there's anything between the girl and me?" asked Dan Farrel.

"I saw her turning white and pink, today in the kitchen. Farrel, you'll have to move."

Farrel took off his hat, mopped his forehead, and then stood with the hat crushed in his two hands. Slowly his glance went across the mountains from the east to the west, until he was facing the last fire of the sunset. He said nothing but, after a moment, he walked away and left Silvertip in profoundly gloomy thought. Tragedy was not ten steps away from the Wycombe ranch, he felt, and it was probably even nearer than those expert gunmen, Morrie Delgas and Harry Rutherford; in fact, it probably was stepping in the boots of Dan Farrel.

Nothing like this had ever come into the ken of Jim Silver.

Through the open kitchen window, he saw the girl moving back and forth rapidly, with the haste of a cook who is making the last preparations for the service of a meal. He went to the window and leaned an elbow on the sill. The girl was pouring the water off a pot of boiled potatoes; a cloud of steam rushed up from the sink about her shoulders and head. Then she spilled the potatoes into a great dish.

"Suppose," said Silver, without an introductory word, "that a fellow had a good pair of hands, plenty of work anywhere he wanted to find it, and a girl willing to travel anywhere in the world with him; couldn't he be happy off the home ground?"

She had turned half toward him, though without looking into his face. It was as if his words had arrested her whole mind so that a greater and a greater tension was put on her. He saw it in the stiffening of her body, in the way her head lifted. Afterward, she came to the window to confront him closely.

"How much has Danny told you?" she asked.

"Not as much as I told him," answered Jim Silver. "Do you know how close you are to trouble?"

"From Steve Wycombe?" she asked.

"He's going to ask you to marry him. How long can you put him off? He's used to having his own way."

She took a deep, quick breath. The shake of her head was a shudder through her entire body.

"I don't know," she answered. "I can't get Danny to leave the place."

"You'll have to," responded Silver. "You'll have to persuade him fast, too. Wycombe wants you. He wants you as much as he can want anything. If you put him off, he'll be suspicious. If he grows suspicious, he can't help finding out that there's something between you and Farrel. And if he guesses that—" He paused.

"I know," said the girl. "He'd murder Dan in a moment, I suppose. I'm going to leave! I'll leave tonight. I'll leave now!"

"You'd better," said Silver. He pitied her, suddenly, more than he had ever pitied any other human being. The trouble which faced her seemed so totally unfair. "There's only one other thing to do—and that's to persuade Danny to live in another place."

"It's no good. He has desert fever, and the only desert he can live in is this one. He's tried to go away before this. But he came back looking like a ghost. It's the sort of homesickness that doesn't fade out."

"Have you got a horse of your own?" Silver asked her.

"I have."

"Have you money?"

"No. Only a little."

"I can help you out with some cash."

"If I have to step out of his life—out of Danny's life—forever—" she murmured.

Then she straightened herself and smiled wanly at Silver.

"I can't even say good-by to him, I suppose," she said.

"No, I suppose not," said Silver.

He reached for his wallet and opened it.

"Take this," said he, and offered a sheaf of bills. But she only shook her head.

"I can't do it," she told him. "I can manage with what I have."

Silver put the money back into the wallet, stared at her, and then walked away into the dusk. His thoughts were so baffled, so gloomy, that he kicked aimlessly at the ground over which he walked. He had been in tangles before, but none so thoroughly complicated as this one. The chief anger he felt was directed toward Farrel. The fellow looked as hard as nails, but his weakness was what is the strength of other men—an overmastering love for one place.

Into the darkening north Silver looked, toward the mountains. They were new enough to him, and yet already they began to stand in his mind like old, familiar faces. He remembered how Farrel had pointed to them; he remembered the reverence and affection with which the voice of Farrel had uttered the names. After all, a man cannot be blamed for passions which are bigger than himself.

He went to the pump and sloshed a tin pan full of cold water. There was soap, yellow and strong, to wash with, and a big, coarse scrubbing brush. He worked on his finger tips until he had got the leather grease out from under the nails. The rest of his washing took very little time. He managed to find a clean spot on one of the big roller towels and dried himself.

The cow-punchers were all around him, sputtering in the water, swearing as the soap got into recent cuts. One of them was red-headed, the clown of the lot. He squared off in front of Silver, swaying thick shoulders.

"He ain't so big," said Red. "I'll take you on for a couple of rounds, big boy."

He began to dance on the tips of his toes, easing his hands back and forth in readiness to strike or to parry. Silver finished drying his own hands and smiled.

"Come on!" said Red, as the others began to crow and whoop. "Come on!" said Red. "Nobody gets by on reputation in this man's ranch. Let's see what you've got, Jim Silver!"

He was dancing, still swaying himself from side to side a little, when Silver made a flashing gesture with both arms and caught the two hands of Red. He kept on smiling as he crushed those hands until he could feel the supple bones springing and giving.

"In my part of the world, we shake before we fight," said Silver.

He released the hands and stepped back. Red began to open and close his fingers, laughing.

"In my part of the world, when a gent shakes hands like that, we don't fight him," said Red.

The other punchers were laughing, too. The supper gong rang. Silver went in with the rest, and by the brightness of their eyes he knew that he would have no more signs of trouble from them. They had accepted him as something more than a large bubble of reputation.

5 – Guns in the Dark

A S THE punchers entered, their employer was revealed walking up
and down at the head of the dining room. He had dressed for dinner
by buttoning his vest, sleeking the blond forelock with water, and slipping
a pair of brilliant elastic garters over his sleeves to leave his wrists supple
and free. As the spurs jingled and the heels thundered on the wooden floor,
Mr Wycombe made a movement of his hand that stopped everyone. Then
he said:

"You waddies have gotta know that there are two thugs steering for this
ranch, right now, and aiming to collect my scalp when they arrive. If they
look in through the window and start blazing away while we're having supper,
they might smash up a lot of crockery. So one of you stand guard outside.
Red, you take a turn. Ten or fifteen minutes and you can come back inside
and somebody else will take the beat. The hombres I talk about are Morrie
Delgas and that skinny little streak of murder, Harry Rutherford. If they start
raising the devil, maybe my friend, Jim Silver, will help my song and dance.
That's all, boys. Set down and feed your faces."

Red took a handful of biscuits, wedged some butter into them, and left the
room to stand guard. The other punchers sat down. The chairs rumbled like
thunder. Dishes and cutlery began to clatter. Someone asked Wycombe what
Delgas and Rutherford had against him.

"Just old chums gone wrong," said Wycombe.

There were heaps of food—venison steaks, two great bowls of baked
beans with a rich scum browned over the tops of them, heaps of biscuits
with snowy flanks and crusty tops, mountains of potatoes, huge dishes of
gravy. Forks and spoons dug into these treasures. Presently heads were
seriously bent; the girl came in and filled the ponderous drinking cups from

423

a pail of coffee. She wore a faint, fixed smile. She reminded Silver of a prize fighter sick with punishment but smiling to show that everything is all right.

When she came by Wycombe, he lifted his head and smiled like a calf at her. Then he resumed his former position, his brow reclining in the palm of his left hand while with the right he casually and in the most disinterested fashion scooped food toward his face. A profound loathing began to work at the very roots of the soul of Jim Silver.

The better the food, the swifter the eating on a Western ranch. Those punchers walked through the provisions on the table and then rolled cigarettes and sipped a second beaker of coffee. They said things to Esther as she went the round, pouring it out. "Regular good stuff," said one, and another: "Where you cook, this cowboy camps." Some of them said: "How's things?" Every one muttered something; up to that time no one had seemed aware of her existence, except Wycombe.

The second round of coffee was finished. Whirls, clouds, long streaks of cigarette smoke hung in the air as the punchers rose, one after another, and went out. Their footfalls boomed through the room, then grew dim and muffled in the dust outside. The smoke seemed to be collecting around the two lamps that stood on the table. There remained at the table only the foreman, Silver, and Wycombe, as the girl came in to clear the dishes away. When she went past Wycombe, he put out his arm and gathered her suddenly into the hollow of it.

"How's things?" asked Wycombe, smiling up at her.

She only smiled down at him vaguely. Danny Farrel grew rigid in his chair.

"I've got to finish my work," said Esther Maxwell. "Please, Steve."

"Maybe you're going to stop working, pretty soon," said Wycombe. "Maybe there's going to be a Chinaman or something for you to boss. Maybe—"

"Esther!" barked Farrel.

Wycombe released her suddenly. She stepped back.

"Eight o'clock and all's well," drawled the puncher who walked on guard outside the windows.

Farrel and Wycombe were staring at one another, Farrel still rigid, and Wycombe leaning loosely forward. In the middle of a smile, his upper lip had caught again over his projecting teeth and stayed there in a snarl. The girl hurried out of the room with a pile of empty dishes. Silver folded his arms, because in that position his hands were close to his guns. It seemed strange to him that the girl should have left the room, unaware that there was murder in the air. He himself could hear the bumping of blood against his temples as his heart beat faster and stronger.

"You've got the say with her, have you?" said Wycombe.

Farrel was as straight as a stick and pale as a stone; he had his two hands on the edge of the table. The hands of Wycombe were out of sight.

"I hate to see a girl mauled around," said Farrel.

"You hate to see it, do you?" answered Wycombe.

He worked his lips until they closed; he moistened them with the swift red tip of his tongue.

Farrel pushed back his chair.

"I'll be going on," he murmured slowly.

He stood up.

"Wait a minute," commanded Wycombe. "I'm going to find out something."

Farrel halted, halfway to the door.

Wycombe had pushed back his chair and sat forward on the edge of it with his hands still out of sight.

"I wanta know," said Steve Wycombe, "what that girl is to you, Farrel."

"Never mind. Nothing!" said Farrel.

"I'm not to never mind, eh?" said Wycombe. He laughed suddenly, turning all white around the mouth and with a devil in his eyes. "Why, Farrel, who are you?"

Farrel said nothing.

Wycombe gasped: "You're going to tell me what to do and how to act in my own house, are you? You're going to tell me how to treat a girl, are you? You dirty rat, what's the girl to you?"

"I'm going to marry her, that's all," said Farrel.

The door opened. The girl came back, not in time to hear anything, but in time to see the attitudes of the two men. She cried out in fear.

"Listen to me—you, Esther," said Wycombe. "Have you been fooling me? Have you been making a fool of me? This bum of a secondhand foreman says that he's going to marry you. Is that straight?"

"Oh, Danny!" mourned the girl.

The way she put out her hands toward Farrel told Steve Wycombe enough.

"You sneaking thief!" he yelled, and came out of his chair with a gun in each hand. "I'm going to—"

"Back up!" called Silver, and shot the left-hand gun out of the grasp of Wycombe.

"You? You, too?" screamed Wycombe." I'll get you both. I'll—I'l—"

He dived under the table and heaved up the side of it with a lift of his shoulders. The whole mass of crockery went to the floor. The lamps were dashed out. Darkness blotted the room, and the scream of the girl made a red zigzag like lightning across the brain of Silver.

It was not complete darkness. The flame of one lamp had ignited the oil that spread out from it in a thin layer on the floor. A blue welter of fire began to play, keeping the room awash with uncertain ebbing and flowing of shadows. Outside, the guard was shouting; the girl had not stopped screaming.

Silver, flat on his stomach in a corner of the room, extended two guns before him and waited. A gun spat fire twice from close to the opposite wall. The voice of Farrel, near the windows, cursed briefly.

"I've got one of you!" screamed Wycombe.

There was the loose impact of a falling body against the floor. The guard was shouting, near the door:

"What the devil's up? What's happening?"

He was afraid to come in, of course.

The gun of Wycombe flashed again, and Silver shot at the glint of the face that he saw behind the little red tongue of fire. He almost felt the impact of his bullet tearing through flesh and bone.

A voice said, "Ah!"

That was Wycombe. There was no vocal strength to the sound; he simply breathed the word out. "Light!" said Wycombe. And now his voice had a great weakness of shuddering in it. "Light! I'm dying! I'm sick—"

The screaming of the girl was ended. That was one good thing. Farrel said nothing. Perhaps he was dead.

Silver went across the room to where Wycombe lay. The burning oil gave only the dimmest sort of a light, but it was enough for him to see that Farrel had been kneeling against the wall between the two windows; the body of the girl lay flat near the kitchen door; and Wycombe had slipped down with his head pressing at a breaking angle against the wall.

"Get a lantern, Farrel," said Silver.

"Esther's dead!" shouted Farrel. "Help! He's murdered her."

Other voices, many footfalls were heard outside the door. Someone carried a lantern, its light swinging wildly across the windows and intercrossing swift shuttles of brightness over the ceiling.

The lantern was brought into the room, and showed Farrel holding the limp body of the girl in his arms. Her head hung down; her arms and legs trailed toward the floor. The wave of cow-punchers advanced in a solid mass.

"Wycombe, did you shoot at the girl?" murmured Silver.

"No!" said Wycombe. "I wish I had. I'm dying. You got me, you sneak, you traitor! I wish I'd killed you all!"

The lantern light came close and flooded over him. His whole breast was flowing with blood, it seemed. The blood ran down to the floor and gathered in two pools. The body of Wycombe grew still. His arms lay limply at his sides, with the hands turned palm up. But his face was working violently, the lips covering and uncovering the gleam of the teeth.

"Take Silver!" he said. "Red, Joe, Lefty, Mack, take Silver. He murdered me. He killed me right here. The skunk—he killed me! Shoot him to pieces!"

They looked at one another; they looked at Silver; they looked vaguely back at their employer.

One of the lot helped Farrel with the girl. She had only fainted, it appeared, and now she began to moan. They carried her out of the shambles.

Silver said: "Wycombe found out that Farrel is going to marry Esther. He went crazy and pulled his guns on Farrel. I knocked one gun out of his grip. He threw the table over and tried to shoot up the lot of us. That was why I plugged him. A dirty business, but it had to be done."

He kneeled beside Wycombe in an effort to feel his pulse.

"Don't touch me. Keep your murdering hands away from me," said Wycombe, in a horrible, bubbling voice. "Boys, don't believe him. He's lying. Tear him apart. Let me see you split him open. I've got a thousand dollars for the man who—"

"Shut up, Steve," said a voice from the doorway. "He only stole a march on us."

Silver saw two men at the entrance of the room, one a great, hairy brute, and the other small and dapper, with a pale face. He knew that Delgas and Rutherford had arrived too late.

6 – Wycombe's Will

SOME of the men threw sand on the burning oil and put it out. At the directions of Silver, two more dragged in a mattress, with the blankets folded to lift Wycombe's head and shoulders, for when he lay flat his own blood choked him.

Silver cut away the clothes, tried to stop the bleeding in chest and back with handfuls of dust, and bound a thick bandage made of a torn sheet around and around the scrawny body. Hollow-chested, lean of shoulders and arms, Wycombe looked no more than a boy. It had only been his spirit that made him dangerous, and the same spirit was still green in his eyes. He kept rolling his glance from Delgas to Silver to Rutherford.

"Give me a shot of hooch," he said. "I've got some thinking to do."

Silver tilted his head and applied a bottle of whisky to the lips. Wycombe drank it like water. Afterward he closed his eyes for a long moment, but he was not dead. Silver could see the pulse beat in the scrawny hollow of the throat.

"I wanta have a pen and paper," said Wycombe. "Silver, you write down what I say. I'm going to make my will."

One of the men ran off to get what was needed.

Rutherford sat down on the floor beside Wycombe.

"I'm sorry to see you this way, Steve," said he. "I hoped that you'd be up and about when we arrived. You're not much use to us this way, Steve. We've been killing you every day for a long time. Now that you're passing out on your own hook, there doesn't seem to be anything left for us to do. The world's a hollow place for us, with you out of it!"

"Yeah?" murmured Wycombe. "He shot me in the dark. He sided with that rat of a Farrel of mine. And I'd hired Silver to keep the two of you away from me."

"Had you?" said Rutherford.

He turned his thin, handsome face toward Jim Silver and smiled.

"Old Jim Silver," he said softly. "Always up to something."

Delgas came and put his hands on his knees. The hair grew like fur down to the second knuckles.

"How d'you feel, kid?" he asked.

"There's hands inside of me tearing me apart," said Wycombe.

"Too bad," said Delgas, and began to grin widely, nodding at Wycombe. "We had lots of hell, but it's better than nothing to get a flash of you when you're like that."

"You swine!" breathed Steve Wycombe.

"Let him alone, Delgas," said Silver. "Get up and stand back from him, Rutherford. He's a dying man."

"Oh," said Rutherford. "You don't like my manners, Silver?"

He rose slowly, still smiling.

"I don't like your manners," said Silver.

He looked at them calmly.

"Now!" whispered Wycombe, his eyes burning. "Are you going to take water from him, the pair of you? Jump him—blow him to pieces, boys! I'll thank you, and I'll pay you for doing it! It'll make a red-letter day in your lives, the cash I'll give you!"

"And be mobbed by this gang when we open up? We're not such fools," said Rutherford.

He stepped back. Wycombe glowered at Silver.

"I've got no luck," he said.

"You'll be hearing from us, Silver," said Delgas.

"Thanks," said Silver. "Come and take tea with me, one day. Any old time would suit me."

The paper and ink and pen arrived. Silver sat down cross-legged and dipped the pen and poised it above the writing pad.

"Go ahead, Wycombe," he suggested.

"I want this to sound like law," said Wycombe. "Write like this. Put the date down and the place, first. Then say: 'I, Stephen Wycombe, being in my right mind and the full possession of my faculties, make this my last will and testament.' How does that sound to you, boys? Legal?"

The cow-punchers formed an outer semicircle. Some of them were standing. Some were sitting on their heels, watching.

"It sounds like a book," said one of them.

"That's the way you gotta sound, or else the lawyers will take you all apart," said Wycombe. "Somebody wipe my mouth. I don't seem to have any hands."

Red came close and wiped the bloody lips with a bandanna. He gave Wycombe another taste of the whisky.

"It's hard," said Wycombe, "to think of losing out on all of that seventeen-year-old rye! Go on writing, Silver. 'Last will and testament. It takes the place of, and makes null, all other wills and testaments that I may have made.' You see, I haven't made any other wills; but you've got to talk like that in a will."

He went on: "I give, devise, and bequeath to my dear friend, Morris Delgas, one third of all the bulls, steers, cows, and calves in my possession."

"Hey," said Delgas. "What's this?"

"Shut up!" whispered Wycombe. "I gotta keep enough breath to finish. Go on writing, Silver. 'One half of all my land, except as shall hereinafter be excepted.' How's that for fancy talk? I was educated all right. A lot of good my education has done me! Go on: 'And to my dear friend, Henry Rutherford, I give, devise, and bequeath one third of all the livestock in my possession, together with one half of my land, except as shall be hereinafter excepted.' Have you got that?"

"I have it," said Silver, working with a rapid pen.

"Well," murmured Harry Rutherford softly, "this is the richest thing that I ever heard of. Where does the poison come in, Wycombe?"

"Wait a minute. He's having his joke," said Delgas. "The catch is going to come now."

"Go on writing," urged Wycombe. "And to my dear friend called variously Arizona Jim, Silvertip, Silver, Jim Silver, and other aliases—I mean the man who caught the famous wild horse, Parade—I give, devise, and bequeath all the cash in my possession, together with the debts which I owe and one third of all the livestock on my place. In addition I give, devise, and bequeath to Jim Silver, alias Arizona Jim, alias Silvertip, all the water rights to the big tank called Johnson's Lake, and I give him outright the house and the corrals and all the ground in every direction for one half mile from the ranch house.' There, boys, that looks like a pretty even split, to me. Silver don't get any land to speak of, but he gets cash and water. Give me that to sign, Jim, will you?"

Silver held the pad before him. Wycombe, with a twitching mouth, scratched on his signature.

"That look all right and legal, Silver?" asked Wycombe.

"It looks right enough to me," said Silver.

"Sign it, then. Everybody in the room sign it. Silver, write down: 'Witnessed this day by me,' and then the rest of you sign under that place. Understand?"

The paper was accordingly passed around. Wycombe lay back, nodding a little as he heard the scratching of the pen. Once Silver found the eyes of the dying man fixed upon him with a deathless malice and hatred.

"The gent that should have guarded me, he shoots me down!" said Wycombe. Then, suddenly, he asked: "Where's the girl and where's Farrel? Go call 'em in, will you? I wanta say goodbye to them. I gotta remember my manners and say goodbye to all of my old friends."

He closed his eyes. His mouth opened. Silver could no longer see the beat of the pulse in the hollow of the throat. When he touched the face of Wycombe, he found the skin clammy with cold sweat.

One of the punchers came back, bringing the girl and tall Dan Farrel. She held back. Farrel had an arm about her, supporting her forward. Her eyes were doubly large in the pallor of her face.

So the two of them came before the dying man.

"They're here," said Silver.

The eyes of Wycombe fluttered and then opened. He frowned to bring his attention on the pair.

"Farrel and Esther. Fine-looking pair, eh?" he muttered. "The two of you—I want to say something to you. You're the ones that knifed me. Except because of your pretty mug, Esther, I'd be all right now. I'd be drinking rye and taking it easy, instead of going where I'm bound. I—" He gasped.

"Whisky!" he whispered.

Silver poured a large dram down his throat. He coughed and strangled feebly over it. The bubbling of his voice became greater, as though some of the liquid were in his lungs.

He said: "I never wasted time on girls before I saw you, Esther."

"Steve," cried the girl, "I never wanted to lead you on. I never said a word to you. The only reason that I didn't tell you right away that I loved Danny was because I was afraid that he'd be fired, and he can't live away from this place."

"Yeah? Can't he?" murmured Wycombe. "He'll damned well live away from it, now that these three hombres have the place. And this is what I wanta say to the pair of you: I hope you have nothing but rotten bad luck. I hope the pair of you get sickness and meanness. I hope you start in hating each other. If you have kids, I hope that they're halfwits and that they're sick every day of their lives. I hope you're broke and stay broke. I hope you have to beg, and folks kick you out of their way. If there's anything in the curse of a dying man, I put it on—"

His head dropped back. The girl, with her hands pressed before her eyes, shut out the grisly picture of the dying man.

"Take me away, Danny!" she murmured.

"I put—a curse," muttered Wycombe, "on—on—"

He bit at the air, writhed his legs together, and sat bolt upright.

"I can't breathe!" he gasped. "Give me air—whisky. I—"

Blood bubbles broke on his lips. He twisted suddenly, fell on his side, and lay still.

Silver leaned close above him for an instant, then turned him on his back and closed the eyes. Wycombe was smiling in death as in life, with his upper lip caught crookedly across his projecting teeth. Silver, with a fold of the blanket, covered that repulsive face.

He stood up and faced the silence of the group.

"Friends," he said, "the law is going to put an eye on all of this. You fellows jot down everything that you can remember of exactly what's happened. You'll have to answer questions. One thing is straight—I killed Wycombe. I shot him to keep him from murdering Farrel—and myself. Farrel, were you hurt?"

"A graze along the ribs," said Dan Farrel. "It's nothing."

"Lemme tell you all something," boomed the great bass voice of Morris Delgas. "I dunno just how it's going to work out, but this here Wycombe was always a poison rat. It looks like he's done something for us, but before we get through we'll find out that he's put a knife through us, every one. I'm going to go out and get some fresh air."

7 – The New Manager

A CORONER came out from Pepper Gulch the next morning and made an examination. He was an old-timer with a dull-blue eye and tobacco-stained blond mustache. His examination lasted not more than half an hour, after which he pronounced over a glass of rye whisky, aged seventeen years:

"The way it looks to me, it would be pretty hard to kill a gent like Steve Wycombe without doin' it in self-defense. I dunno that you could pick up any jury around this part of the world that would accuse a man of nothin' more than self-defense even if there was eye-witnesses that seen somebody bash Steve over the head when his back was turned."

The reputation of Wycombe was in this manner its own reward. The body was carted to the town to be buried in the plot where other and hardly more honorable ancestors had lain before him, and the will which he had signed was promptly recorded and filed.

The result was that the three to whom the inheritance had so strangely come could enter upon the possession at once. It was not many days later that they held a conference in the very room that had formerly been the office of the dead man.

Morris Delgas, because he was the oldest and the largest of the trio, presided. He sat not in a chair but on the desk, with his shirt open and his sleeves rolled up. The man was everywhere furred over with black hair. His forehead was wide and very low, with a knob at either corner of it to match the cheek bones beneath. He looked like a perfect specimen for the prize ring, now grown a little overweight.

He wore new boots, graced with golden, spoon-handled spurs; but otherwise he showed no token of the sudden good fortune that had come to him, for his clothes were those which any cow-puncher might have donned as

433

a working outfit. His shirt was blue flannel, in spite of the heat of the weather; his hat was a very battered old felt, and the only other evidence of wealth lay in the great fat cigar into which he had sunk his teeth.

He liked the feel of it so well that he could not relax the grip of his teeth for an instant. The oily stain ran across his mouth. The tongue with which he licked those lips became stained, also. But he never touched the cigar with his hand. He smoked it rarely in puffs, but let it burn slowly with the movements of his breath, and when he changed its position, it was done by manipulations of the teeth and the tongue. In fact, he was a formidable brute of a man. His body looked too gross for activity, but his eye was as bright as the eye of a wild cat.

Sitting there on the desk, with his huge back turned to the windows, he literally cast a shadow over the other two men.

"Gents," he said, "we gotta get together. We gotta find out what was in the crazy bean of Steve Wycombe when he passed us this ground, and then we gotta see how we can pull together. Because look at the lay of the land. Me and Harry have got half the acres. And, believe me, there's some acres! I been out and rode all around the place, and it's a long day's ride. And we each got a third of the live stock, along with you, Silver. But there's another way of lookin' at the thing. We got the land and our shares of the stock. But you got the most part of the water, if not all. Except for some shallow kind of pools that stand a while around in the spring rains, there ain't no water on the rest of the place. The cows have gotta come in to the big tank or else they've gotta come right in here to the home place. It's a funny business, and I guess that the brains must have run with the blood right out of poor old Steve! Now's the time for us to talk a spell and keep shut up afterward."

"Wycombe wasn't crazy," said Harry Rutherford. "Not a bit."

"What was he, then?" asked big Delgas.

"He was out for blood, that's all," said Rutherford.

"Go on, handsome, and tell me what you mean," said Delgas.

"Aw, you tell him, Silver," said Rutherford. "He can't see it. Poor old Delgas is so gentle and trusting that he doesn't know how to look around the corner and see the devil in what people do."

Silver smiled, his faint, faint smile. "As Wycombe lay dying," he said, "there were three men in the world that he wanted to kill. Name 'em, Delgas."

"You first, because you'd sunk a shot in him between wind and water," said Delgas presently. "And I suppose that me and Rutherford would come on the list, too."

"Very well," said Silver, "and to whom did he leave his land?"

"Well, the same three. But how's he goin' to kill us by givin' us the land?"

"Because he hoped that we'd not be friends. He hoped that you and Rutherford would hang together and that you'd be against me, and that we'd start a war and fight to a finish."

"Hey!" exclaimed Delgas. "You mean that, Silver? You think that's the straight of it, Harry?"

Harry Rutherford waved a slender hand.

"Of course that's it," he said. "Don't be so dumb, Brother Morris. Wycombe set us up for a battle royal. What else could he have had in his mind? Think that he wanted to reward us for being after his scalp?"

Delgas champed noisily on the butt of his cigar, the smoke squeezing out of the burning end of it in little rapid puffs.

"I begin to see," said he. "We can starve out Silver because we've got the land, and he can starve out us because he's got the water. The minute one shuts down on the other, there's bound to be trouble. It's a fight to the finish, and a mighty quick fight."

"There's only one way out," said Rutherford.

"Name it," said Delgas.

"Not to fight," said Rutherford.

"Sure! And that's easy," said Delgas. He turned to Silver. "You got a kind of an upstage way about you," he declared. "And maybe you ain't been very friendly toward the pair of us, now and then. But that don't matter to me so much. I can get on with anybody. My skin is thick enough. And I got a place in my system where I could use the dough we're goin' to pull down out of this business."

"So have I," said Rutherford. "All we need to do is to lay down a scheme to run the ranch. One of us has to run it, and the others stand by, and make a few suggestions."

"It won't work," said Silver.

"Why not?" asked Rutherford sharply.

Silver turned up the palm of his right hand.

"Do the same thing," he said to the others.

They obeyed him, frowning with curiosity.

"We've got soft hands," said Silver.

"Now, what the devil does that mean?" asked Delgas.

"Why, it means that we don't know enough about the business to run a ranch, any of us," answered Rutherford shortly.

He left his chair and walked rapidly back and forth through the room. He seemed to be angry. Now and then he swore softly under his breath.

"Well," he exclaimed suddenly, stopping right in front of Silver, "what's the solution?"

"I haven't any," said Silver.

"What have you got, then?"

"Only an idea."

"Let's have it, Silver. Nobody accuses you of being a fathead. Fire away with the idea," urged Rutherford.

"My idea is that we all step out and let a fourth man run the place," suggested Silver.

"What man?" snapped Rutherford and Delgas in one voice.

"Any man we can all agree on," said Silver.

"Name one," said Rutherford.

"I haven't any names on the tip of my tongue," said Silver. "How about you?"

"It's all a funny business," said Delgas. "I dunno. I got no ideas. I only got a hunch that maybe Wycombe was right and a lot of trouble is likely to grow out of this here deal. Dead men don't enjoy the money they spend."

There was such truth in this remark that a short silence followed.

"How's the place running now?" demanded Rutherford.

"Pretty well, I suppose," said Silver. "The foreman knows his business. If he could suit a hound like Wycombe, he ought to suit us."

"There is something in that," agreed Delgas instantly.

"Make him the manager?" asked Rutherford.

"You fellows think that I'm sure to be against you, and that I'm sure to try to put one over on you," said Silver. "Get that idea out of your head. If you don't want Farrel, take anybody you like—if I like him, too."

Delgas and Rutherford looked fixedly at one another.

"Well, that sounds all right to me," said Delgas.

Rutherford shrugged his narrow shoulders. He sat down, made a cigarette with the fingers of a conjurer, and lighted it. He spoke, breathing out the smoke through nose and mouth.

"Make it Farrel till we vote him out," suggested Rutherford. "A majority vote puts one ranch manager out and a new one in. This is a democratic country, and the majority ought to rule."

"You've got your voters all in a lump," answered Silver. "No. One vote has to be enough to put out the manager. And a new one can't go in until every one of the three of us is satisfied."

There was another silence.

"Well," said Rutherford, "that might mean never. We might never hit on the kind of a fellow who would please all of us. I'm for putting this whole ranch on sale and getting rid of it."

"You couldn't get a quarter of what it's worth," complained Delgas. "I asked a couple of bankers what this here place is worth. The money they talked made me sick, I can tell you! They don't want to pay nothing. Nothing at all! There ain't any market for desert land, like this. People are afraid of a big drought when even the well might go dry, and then the cows would starve before they could be drove to the nearest water hole. And all we could do would be to sell the cattle and call it quits. And I ain't ready to be robbed like that!"

"Nor I!" said Rutherford. He turned to Silver, saying: "We'll start out with Farrel, then. Your man Farrel will make a start. If any of us don't like him, he's fired on the spot. That suit you?"

"That has to suit," answered Jim Silver.

He stood up.

"You boys," he said, "have been talking about building a shack up in the foothills. You don't have to. You can stay right here and live in the house. It belongs to me, but you're mighty welcome to room in it."

He walked out of the room and into the kitchen, where he saw the girl. She had had sleepless nights since the death of Wycombe, and now there were black shadows inlaid around her eyes.

"It's all right," said Silver. "Farrel stays on. He's not the foreman, but the manager."

He went out to the place where Farrel was nailing some new shakes on the roof of the big shed. At the signal he gave, Farrel came quickly down to the ground.

"You're to stay on as manager," said Silver.

"Thanks," said Farrel. "I know you did that for me, Jim. It's not the first good thing you've done for me, though. Are things going to be all right?"

"All right?" echoed Silver, laughing a little. "Why, man, one of these days there's going to be an explosion big enough to blow up everything."

"Then why do you stay?" asked Farrel, agape. "Two of 'em to one of you. I'd be on your side, but I'm no gunman. Why do you stay, Jim?"

"Because," said Silver, "I don't know when the explosion will come, and I like to hear the fuse burn."

8 – Trouble's Sign

SINCE Jim Silver looked for a storm, he was by no means deceived by the perfect peace and quiet of the first few days that followed, when big Morris Delgas and Harry Rutherford were both the perfection of consideration, as far as they knew how to be.

For one thing, they seemed to be taking very seriously their new-found duties as ranchers, for they were hardly ever at the ranch house, except for meals. The lunch hour they often missed completely when they went off on a whole day of exploration—"a day's hunt," as Morrie Delgas used to say, "to find mountain lions, mountain sheep, or mountain suckers."

Morrie Delgas was very gay. His loud voice boomed through the house. His heavy step thundered on the floor. Rutherford, beside him, was like a cat beside a horse, speaking little, keeping himself neat always, with a pale smile on his pale face. But, by the shifting lights in his eyes, it was plain that his mind was never still.

There was only one sign of trouble, a few days after Delgas and Rutherford came to live at the house. At the breakfast table, after Delgas had had his "eye opener" of rye, he boomed out to Silver:

"You've got the ready cash, Silver. You've got heaps of it, and we're just about broke. How about a couple of thousand on account?"

Silver looked across the table and permitted his smile to broaden a trifle.

"You mean a couple of hundred, Morrie, don't you?" he asked.

Delgas stared back, not at Silver but at Rutherford.

"He says that I mean a couple of hundred, not grands," quoted Delgas.

Rutherford nodded. Nothing further was said, no gesture made to accept the money. Delgas seemed to be hearing what he expected, and Silver knew by a thrill in his bones that trouble had been brought still closer to him.

Two days later, Farrel reported quietly to Silver that he was beginning to have trouble with the men.

"They look me in the eye and swallow their grins," said Farrel. "I feel their eyes following me, too, and their grins when my back is turned."

"What's wrong?" asked Silver.

"You know," said Farrel, "one bad apple will spoil a barrel. And this gang was always a tough lot to handle. Wycombe wanted them that way. He never employed a man that hadn't done time."

"You mean all the lads on the place have a prison record of some sort?" asked Silver.

"That's what I mean," answered Farrel. "Wycombe always felt that he might get into a pinch where he'd want tough fellows around him, to back him up. So he collected this crew. Only, when he heard that both Delgas and Rutherford were on the trail after him, he lost his nerve and sent for you. He needed a bigger gun than any he'd ever hired, so he got hold of you. But there's not a man on the place that isn't pretty good with guns, in one way or another. Wycombe knew I hadn't been in jail, and that suited him because he wanted an honest foreman to handle accounts."

"How have you managed to handle this gang?" asked Silver curiously.

"I'm a little better with my hands than they are," said Farrel. "Besides, I know one end of a gun from another. They don't want trouble with me unless it's worth their while; but, if it is worth their while, any one of the lot would be glad enough to rip into me, I suppose."

"What bad apples were dropped into the barrel?" asked Silver.

"You guess," answered the foreman.

"You mean Delgas and Rutherford?"

"They're not too busy riding the range for the sake of hunting," said Farrel. "They never bring any game in. And they don't need all of this time to look over the lay of the land on the ranch. But I've spotted one of them time and again, off on the sky line, talking to one of the punchers and then fading out of the picture. They got up into the foothills, too. I don't know for what."

"Any guesses?" asked Silver.

"Yes. But nothing I can back on."

"Fire away."

"I think that they're in touch with crooks who'll buy a lot of cattle if they can get 'em at the right price. The other day I bumped into Sam Waring riding across our range. You know Sam?"

"No," said Silver.

He leaned back in his chair and let the sun flow over his body while his eyes were closed.

Farrel regarded the placid calm of his "one-third" boss with a troubled eye. He stepped closer as he added:

"Sam Waring is a tough hombre. He's as tough as they come. He's done plenty of time, and he's been up for counterfeiting. You know that they're tough when they handle the green goods."

"That's Federal business. Yes, they're tough or crazy when they handle the green goods," agreed Silver, opening his eyes drowsily.

"Waring," said Farrel, "isn't up here for his health. He's in on some deal or he wouldn't be around. He told me that he was just passing through on a line for the other side of the Farrel Mountains. But I think he was lying. He'd make a good running mate for Delgas and that ghoul of a Rutherford. If he's that close to them, it'll be strange if they don't get together."

"You don't like Rutherford?" said Silver.

"Do you?" asked Farrel.

"He's a handsome fellow," said Silver. "Go on and think out loud, Danny." Farrel hesitated.

Then he exploded: "In two days the punchers on this place could sweep every sound head of cattle right off up the valleys in the foothills and turn 'em over to anybody with the cash to pay half value on the nail! And Waring always represents plenty of money. My hunch is that he's been sent for to take the cows—at a price."

"Why does this burn you all up?" asked Silver lazily.

"Why?" cried Farrel. "Because I've put in my years building the herd. When I came here, there was a scratch lot of worthless beef too weak to cover ground for fodder and get back to water again. I've traded and bred and fought and prayed to make this herd what it is. I came onto the job when I was a kid. I'm not very old now, but, believe me, I've done a lifetime's work already, I think.

"This herd is what it ought to be—long and rangy, with enough bone to carry flesh when the cattle go north to fatten on good grasslands. It's my work. It's the sort of a herd that used to run on the place when my father had the ground. You can't build the right sort of a herd in a minute. It takes years. Once it's wiped out, you have to go clear back to the start, and that's hard. Maybe you'll never hit just the right combination again. And now a pair of crooks are likely to wipe out all the work that I've done. That's why I'm burning up! That's why I want to know what you intend to do about it."

"Nothing," said Silver.

"Nothing?" cried Farrel.

"Not a thing—yet," said Silver.

"Then you're not worth the powder it would take to blow you up!" shouted Farrel.

Silver closed his half-opened eyes again.

Farrel's footsteps strode to the door and halted there.

"I've said too much," he growled. "You saved my hide, the other night. I forgot that for a minute. I remember it now. Silver, does it make any difference if I say I'm sorry?"

"Sure. It's all right," said Silver. "Don't worry about me. Just tell me why Delgas and Rutherford should want to sell all the stock off at about half price, will you?"

He kept his eyes closed, but he could feel young Farrel coming back toward him. The voice of the foreman grew louder, more vibrant again.

"Because," said Farrel, "if your share is thrown in with theirs and sold, they won't be losing so very much. Because fellows like that always prefer hard cash to anything else in the world. Finally, because, once the cattle are gone, they'll soon have you off the ranch—and they hate your heart. I've seen them looking at you when your back was turned. They hate your heart."

Silver, without opening his eyes, took a sack of tobacco out of a breast pocket, together with a little battered pack of wheat-straw papers. Deftly and blindly he made his cigarette, a trick very worthwhile to one who often must ride at night. He crimped one end of his smoke, put the other between his lips, took out a cube of sulphur matches, and scratched one of them under the arm of his chair.

He allowed that match to burn for an instant so that the sulphur fumes would clear away. Then he lighted his cigarette and threw the match into the air. The flame fluttered out. The match left in the air a little irregular-curving streak of blue smoke. And still the eyes of Silver were not open as he smoked.

Farrel, biting his lips, took heed of all of these details.

"They want me out of the way?" said Silver. "How does having the cattle wangle that for them?"

"Don't you see?" argued the other. "That's your hold on them in this bargain about the leaving of the ranch?"

"I've got the house and the water rights."

"The house doesn't matter. And the water rights don't matter if there aren't any cattle to need the water. You'll be stuck here with nothing on your hands except the hard cash that you pulled down in the deal. You'll have ho land; you'll have no cows; you'll have to clear out; and then they will manage to sell off the land. They'll pull the wool over the eyes of some fool of a tenderfoot buyer and make him think that he gets the water rights with the land. Isn't that clear?"

Silver whistled.

"I hadn't thought of all that," said he.

"And now," urged Farrel, "tell me what you're to do about it, will you?"

"I'm going to think," said Silver, and continued to smoke with closed eyes.

Farrel endured the picture of indifference as long as he could. Then he turned without a word and strode out of the room.

* * *

Silver continued to lead the life of an idler, rarely leaving the house. He was in bed early. He was up very late. As he sat alone at his breakfast, he could sometimes feel the eye of the girl fixed upon him with a melancholy appeal, but neither she nor Farrel spoke a word to him about the subject of Farrel's anxiety.

It was two days after this that the next step was made toward tragedy. Farrel came into the house in the middle of the day.

Through the window of his room, where he lounged in the easy-chair, Silver saw the foreman come from the corral with bowed head. In the kitchen, Farrel paused for a moment, and Silver heard the girl cry out sharply with pain.

By that, Silver knew what had happened. He knew still better when Farrel stood before him in the room, looking years older, wrinkled about the eyes, drawn, battered of face like one who has faced a great storm for many hours.

"Delgas and Rutherford have fired me," said Farrel. "They sent me to you for my pay."

9 – Nine Against Two

FROM the expression in the face of Silver, it seemed that he was hearing of a thing with which he had been long familiar.

He took out a wallet.

"What's owing?" he asked.

"I've had fifty from them. You owe me twenty-five."

Silver passed out the amount and replaced his wallet in his pocket. Farrel went back to the door and made a farewell speech.

"I thought it might be that we could make a fight to save the herd," he declared. "I thought you might be the one man in the world to beat those crooks. But I guess you're too tired. I'm thanking you for the life that I still walk around with—and—so long, Silver."

He was half through the doorway when Silver, his hands folded beneath his head, his eyes lazy, turned a little in the chair and asked:

"Where you going, Danny?"

"Going?" answered Danny. "I don't know. I don't care. Just somewhere."

"Why not stay here?"

"Here? I'm fired, I tell you. I've been paid off."

"You've been paid off by the ranch. Now I hire you again at the same rate of pay," said Silver.

At this, Farrel gripped the edge of the door so that the knob of it jangled suddenly. Then he made a quick step back inside the room. He pulled the door shut as carefully as though death were in the making of a sound, and there he stood before Silver, staring with incredulous eyes.

"Sit down and rest your feet," said Silver.

"Tell me what's in the air?" asked Farrel.

443

"I'm retaining a good man because I might need him. You've got a room in the house. Go upstairs and use it."

"How?"

"Go up and lie down and rest."

"Rest? I don't need to rest."

"Do what I tell you," said Silver quietly. "There may be a time ahead when you won't rest for quite a spell. So long, Danny. Go take it easy while you can."

Farrel looked at him with blazing eyes. "I might have known," he said, with a trembling voice. "I might have known that you wouldn't lie down and take it—like a dog! I don't care what pops. I'm with you to the finish." He went out of the room. The keen ear of Silver, afterward, heard the excited babbling of voices in the kitchen, and he smiled.

Delgas and Rutherford came in before supper time, and Delgas said carelessly: "That bum of a Dan Farrel, I gave him the rush today. He's no good."

"He's a tramp," said Rutherford.

Silver, reclined in his chair, looked over the two of them casually. The face of Rutherford, which generally was the color of a cellar-grown plant, was now patched with sunburn, and his lips were gray from the chapping wind raised by a galloping horse. Dust had reddened the eyes of both men. Delgas had fortified his greasy skin by letting a week's beard darken his face. They sat down uninvited in the room of Silver and lighted cigars.

"Not much cow sense—Farrel?" asked Silver gently.

"Cow sense? No sense at all," said Delgas. "I been watching him. I been out and around, since I came onto this place. You been layin' low and takin' things easy. That's all right if it's your way, but I mean to make a real ranch out of this dump. Know that, Jim?"

"I'm glad of that," said Silver.

"I even got Harry Rutherford interested," said Delgas. "He thinks that some of my ideas are pretty good, eh, Harry?"

Rutherford shrugged his shoulders. He sat on the base of his spine and inhaled the strong smoke of the cigar and then blew it in a swift stream high toward the ceiling.

"What we gotta do is use some brains," said Delgas. "That's what we gotta do. And I'll tell you the trouble with Farrel. Know what it is?"

"Well?" said Silver.

"No brains," said Delgas. "Eh, Harry?"

"No brains," said Rutherford.

"I'm sorry about that," said Silver. "He looks to me like a decent sort."

"Yeah. Clean hands," said Delgas. "Yeah, clean hands and a washout for a brain, eh, Harry?"

"Washout," said Harry Rutherford, coldly, to the ceiling.

"Just a dumb kind of an hombre," said Delgas. "It's lucky that we been out and watched him workin' the men. That's the main trouble. The men don't care a thing about him. Eh, Harry?"

"Not a thing," said Rutherford.

"He looks like something," went on Delgas, clearing his throat, "and he stands like something, and he sticks out his chest like something. But he ain't nothing at all. He's a blank. So we gave him the bum's rush. Just thought we'd tell you, though."

"Thanks," said Silver. He made a cigarette in his unconcerned way.

"You're having a rest, Silver, eh?" said Rutherford, suddenly curious. "From what I knew about you, I thought you were the sort of an hombre that never ran dry, never got out of patience, never knew what it was to quit. That all wrong?"

"I only do what I have to do," said Silver, smiling.

Rutherford was sitting straight up, his eyes lighted with keen concentration, a focused brilliance.

"You're different from what I thought," admitted Harry Rutherford.

"Sorry," said Silver, still smiling.

Rutherford's eyes were darkened by a frown.

"Unless you're putting on a front for me," said Rutherford.

"Aw, quit tryin' to get behind everything," protested Delgas, pulling out a flask and putting it to his lips for a long swig. "You take a bird like Harry, that's got brains, and the trouble with him is that he's always trying to use 'em. Know that? Never contented. Always got to keep hammerin' away at people. Give a gent a chance to rest, will you, Harry?"

"Shut up, will you?" answered Rutherford softly. And still he peered at Silver and at the steady, dull-eyed smile with which Silver looked back at him.

Suddenly Rutherford rose, went to the door, paused there, and finally left the room.

Delgas looked after him, his grin gradually widening on both sides of his cigar, his brown-stained lips shining with the juice from the tobacco.

"Funny, ain't he?" he said to Silver. "He's got something in his head, has that bird Rutherford. He is like a bird—just like a bird, always cocking his head around and looking at something. He don't give you no peace, not when you're his partner. Now I tell you what—I gotta go and corral him and find out what's made him so shifty on his pins, all at once. See you later, brother."

He in turn paused at the door.

"You paid off your third to Farrel?" he asked.

"I paid him," said Silver.

"Good riddance," said Delgas. "Cheap at twice the price, I say." He was smiling more broadly than ever as he turned and left the room.

Before supper time, as Silver lay quietly in his chair and watched the evening rise like blue water among the canyons of the mountains, Farrel tapped at the door and came in again. He said uneasily:

"There's going to be an explosion if I walk into that dining room after the pair of them have fired me off the place."

"Well," said Silver, couching his big head in his hands again, "there's got to be an explosion some time, and you've had a long rest, this afternoon."

Farrel went to the window and looked out as though something had suddenly taken his eyes, but Silver knew that he was looking at nothing but the sweetness of life. It might well be that both of them were hardly an hour from the end of everything.

"There has to be a show-down," said Silver.

"You told 'em that you'd keep me on?"

"No," said Silver, and watched his man wince. Farrel stepped back from the window and turned a gray face to Silver.

"What's the good?" he asked. "Seven and two make nine. There's nine of 'em. Nine against two. That's not funny."

"No, that's not funny," said Silver lazily, yawning out the words.

Farrel suddenly pointed a hand at him and said: "I think you like this sort of a business! It's fun, for you."

"I don't know," said Silver. "It just has to be done. That's all."

Farrel cleared his throat, made a turn through the room, confronted that placid face again.

"Two men can't kill nine. Not nine like them. Not in a closed room. There's no chance."

"There's no chance," said Silver, nodding.

"Then what the devil?" demanded Farrel.

"We've got to keep the devil out, I'd say. Keep the devil out of their heads and the guns out of their hands."

"How?"

"You come in after everybody else has sat down. Will you do that?"

Farrel drew a long breath. His right hand doubled into a fist and then slowly relaxed again.

"Yes," he said slowly. "I'll come in—after everybody else is at the table."

"Good boy," said Silver. "You'll be heeled, eh?"

"I've got a gun. So have all the rest of those tramps."

"Carry two guns, and then you'll be one up on some of them."

"I thought you said the thing was for us to keep this from coming to a fight?"

"I did," answered Silver. "But if the fighting starts, we want to scratch them up a little, eh? We want to make a few dents."

"Silver," murmured the other, "we may both be dead men, in half an hour!"

"We certainly may," said Silver. "But there has to be a show-down, or else they're apt simply to pick us up and throw us off the ranch. If they once have us on the run, they'll keep us there."

Farrel looked out the darkening window and muttered: "Well, it's better than chucking in our hand. I'll walk in—with two guns on me. And then?"

"Well," said Silver, "after that we'll have to watch the play of the cards. That's all. Just see how they fall."

Farrel smiled a twisted smile, saying: "And follow the lead?"

Silver sat up and suddenly caught the hand of the cow-puncher.

"That's it, Danny," he said. "Play all your cards—and follow the lead!"

10 – The Show-Down

TROUBLE was so thick in the air of the dining room, that night, that the girl seemed to sense it long before the men came in. Perhaps she had been watching their faces through the window, and listening to their voices. At any rate, she had a sick, pale face when Silver walked through the kitchen as the gong sounded. She stood back with a great platter of corn bread to let him pass, and her frightened eyes turned up silently to his face.

"What's the matter, Esther?" he asked her.

She shook her head.

"Say it," persuaded Silver. "It's better to talk a thing out."

"What will happen?" she breathed, with a tremor of hysteria in her voice. "What will they do to Danny—and you?"

"What does Danny think?"

"He hasn't said anything. But I know he was fired, and that you took him on again. You don't think—"

"Everything is going to be all right," said Silver. "Enough has happened in that dining room already. It ought to be peaceful the rest of its life."

He walked on into the dining room, where there was a great scuffling of feet and groaning of chair legs as the punchers took their places. One thing was instantly noticeable: Delgas sat at the top of the table, which hitherto had been Silver's place, not because he had any essential right to that chair but because the weight of his name was greater than the repute of either of the other owners of the ranch. Now Delgas was there, squaring his great shoulders.

Silver went down toward the foot of the table and took a vacant chair. Delgas looked at him flat in the eye, saying:

"Turn and turn about, eh, Jim? I thought I'd try the fit of this place."

All eyes flashed toward Silver. When they saw him merely smile, one of the men burst out with loud laughter. He choked it off suddenly.

It was Red, who was in the act of hanging his sombrero on a peg of the wall; now he changed his mind and put the hat on the back of his head before he sat down. He sat a little sidewise, as though he were ready to talk rather than to eat. And his mischievous, bright eyes went back and forth across the other faces around him.

The clatter of the crockery and the clashing of the knives and forks had begun in another moment when tall Dan Farrel walked quietly through the door.

"Hey! There's the big stiff now!" shouted a puncher.

Farrel got to the vacant chair which had not been noticed before. He was pale. He wore a wooden, brittle smile that made Silver bite his lip. For, without help, he knew that he could never win through the scene that was to come.

All the banter had disappeared from the eyes of the men about the table, as they saw Farrel sitting down. Rutherford looked straight at Silver, and seemed to wait. It was Delgas who heaved himself to his feet and bellowed:

"You bum, you ain't wanted. Get out of that chair! You're fired. Get off the ranch, you namby-pamby blockhead! You ain't wanted. Get out before I throw you out!"

"I'm hired again," said Farrel, with a barely audible voice. He cleared his throat.

"Hired? You lie!" yelled Delgas, throwing his head from side to side. "You lie and you lie loud! Who hired you again?"

"Jim Silver," said Farrel, sitting stiffly erect on the edge of his chair.

The words struck a silence through the room. Every man at the table stirred a little, and all eyes centered on Silver, as though Farrel no longer existed.

"You?" called Delgas in a mighty voice. "You hired that fool again?"

"You know, Morrie," said Silver, "that what's a fool to you might be a wise man to me. We don't all want the same things."

Delgas looked aside at Rutherford, but Rutherford stared only at Silver, like a hungry cat. He was not paler. He was simply set and ready. Silver folded his arms. He smiled straight back at Delgas.

"We don't want the same things, eh?" said Delgas. "I wanta know what there is around here that you'd like to change?"

The arms of Silver unfolded, and two oversized Colts winged in his hands. One of them pointed at Rutherford. With the left-hand gun he shot the hat off the head of Red.

From the corner of his eye he saw that two guns were now in the hands of Farrel, and he breathed more easily. With that backing, he might win.

Out of the kitchen came a scream, and Silver surmised that the girl was watching through the dining-room doorway. Rutherford sat with his right hand deep beneath his coat, motionless. He had been fully prepared, and yet he was a thousandth part of a second too late, and knew it. Delgas, too, had flung a hand back to his hip and kept it there. Not a man at the table that had failed to make a move towards a gun, only to have the firing of the shot make each one realize that he was too late and that he, perhaps, would be the next target.

As for Red, he had ducked his head forward and looked at Silver as if at a hangman who was about to drop the trap.

All of this Silver saw by the time the hat of Red had flown into the air, struck the wall, and flopped loudly against the floor. All noises were loud now. With a little care, one could distinguish the breathing of every man at the table.

"One thing I'll change at the start," said Silver, "is the wearing of hats at the table. The second thing I'll change is cursing out any man that works for me. Delgas, watch yourself!"

For the shoulder of Delgas had twitched a little.

"All right," said Morris Delgas in a barely audible voice.

Silver stood up slowly. If he made a swift move, he knew that every man at the table would grab at a gun. So he rose slowly. He seemed to be watching everybody, but in reality he had his eye on Delgas and Rutherford only. Rutherford, he knew, was his chief care. However formidable Delgas might be as a great brute of a man, he was nothing compared to the catlike speed and surety of Rutherford.

"Stand up, Farrel," commanded Silver. "Start at the end of the table with Delgas and go around the line. See how much hardware you can collect and pile it on the floor."

"If you do that—" began Rutherford, and then stopped himself. He was pale enough now. All the heat and color of his body had gone into his eyes as he stared at Silvertip, and Jim Silver knew that before the end of the game one of the two of them would have to die. This moment in the dining room was only the first trick. Others would inevitably follow.

"I'm going to do that," said Silver. "Start in, Danny. I'll try to entertain the rest of you boys while you wait. Go slow and be sure, Danny. We ought to collect quite a lot of valuable stuff, this way. Anybody would be glad to see it—a sheriff particularly. Now, the rest of you fellows, I know that you're only a lot of cheap rats. You've followed Rutherford and Delgas, and you've burned your fingers with the first trick. Other tricks are going to come. Perhaps I'll have a chance to see the lot of you dead or jailed as a pack of dirty cattle rustlers and horse thieves. I don't know; I'm just hoping. Keep your hands on the table; make no quick moves; and you can start eating as soon as you've let Danny take a weight off your mind."

Farrel had reached a long-drawn, lean-faced cow-puncher who said gently: "I'm goin' to cut your heart out for this, Farrel."

Farrel said nothing. He went on with his collection. There was not a man at the table who carried less than one revolver. A good many had knives, also. The collection went on gradually.

"Come down here and take my place," said Silver. "Down here, Delgas. I thought you might fit at the head of the table, but I see you're not man enough."

Delgas, breathing like a steam engine, walked silently down the room.

"I ain't hungry," he said. "I'm goin' to go outside."

"To get a rifle and start shooting through the door?" asked Silver, smiling. "No; wait a while, and maybe your appetite will come back."

Delgas took the vacated place where Silver had been sitting. The man seemed to be suffering from a fit that contracted the muscles of his body and twisted his face into a horror. He was insane with a rage which he dared not express in action, but his hands gripped the edge of the table so hard that his arms shuddered with the might of that grasp.

When the crew had been disarmed thoroughly, from first to last, Silver said: "Some of you boys may have a decent streak in you. If you have, stay in the room after the rest go out. That's all. I can use a right man who thinks that he can use me. Now those of you who want to finish supper, stay right in your places. The rest of you can file out. Danny, pull down the blinds of those windows and watch the door."

He paused. Every man arose. Only Red seemed to find it hard to get out of his chair, as he kept his fascinated eyes upon the face of Silver. But Delgas, in passing, spoke one word to him, and Red nodded and followed.

They went out the door with Rutherford, as might have been expected, the last one through—a rear guard to see that the rest did the right thing for him.

For his own part, he turned and bowed to Silver, a little, short jerk of head and body, as though he were acknowledging an introduction.

"Silver, you're quite a fellow," he said. "When the time comes for the finish of you, it ought to be a party I'll want to remember. So long!"

And he stepped out into the dark of the night.

11 – Besieged

ROUTED troops need a time for rallying, even if they have fallen back without loss. After the sinister face of Rutherford had disappeared from the doorway, the two men and the girl inside the house could hear the scattering of voices drawing gradually together, increasing in loudness. It left one moment for consultation to the three.

Silver, as he turned toward the frightened girl, saw that she was carrying a double-barreled shotgun that dragged down her arm with its weight. But, no matter how white her face or how big her eyes, it was clear that she was not near fainting. She had meant business with that powerful weapon so long as her lover was in danger.

Tall Dan Farrel locked the door swiftly. As he turned, he was saying:

"Silver, if we get into the kitchen side of the house, we could stand a siege, maybe. They're not through with us. There are other guns they'll get their hands on. This heap isn't all that they have. They'll come back at us."

Silver was gathering the weighty heap of revolvers; he let the big knives lie.

"You're right," he told Farrel. "They may try to rush us, but I doubt it. There's no use in trying to watch all sides of the house. We can't do it. Better get into the kitchen and wait there. It has windows looking on two sides."

What he said was law. They got into the kitchen, locked and braced chairs against the doors from it leading into the dining room and the main body of the house, and hastily threw open the windows to either side and the kitchen door which faced the big shed.

For, as Silver said, it was necessary for them to look out on the ground nearby. The lamp in the kitchen was out. The girl sat in a chair against the wall, facing the stove. Silver had for his province the window and door toward the big corral. Farrel had the surveillance of the opposite window.

452

Farrel sat in a chair near the window with a rifle across his knees. Silver lay flat on the floor with another rifle beside him. The girl still kept her double-barreled shotgun. If it came to a sudden rush, that weapon might do more execution than a dozen rifles. Silver expected no mass attack simply because there was little practical value behind such a move. It would gratify the spite of the offended men, but it would put no hard cash into the pockets of their leaders.

Inside, a big-lidded kettle was muttering and hissing on the stove, from which red pencils of light flowed through the darkness. But the outer night was more fully illumined. Silver could see the upward flow of the mountains against the northern stars, and the gaunt legs of the windmill, and the great, rounded mass of the iron tank which seemed suspended in the air without support. He could make out portions of the fence, also, and guess at the position of the two haystacks. The shed itself was, of course, clearly discernible as to the roof, but the rest of it merged toward the shadows of the ground. It seemed easier to look into the distance and make out the objects near the horizon than to study things close at hand.

There seemed to be a motion of the ground toward the house. The surface seemed to be pouring slowly toward his watchful eyes.

He tried his rifle sights at big objects and small. He drew a bead on the wavering streak of a fence post, even; but the star sheen along the barrel troubled him a little. He went to the stove, got some of the blacking on his fingers, and smeared that along the top of the rifle barrel. He went back and lay down.

"If they put fire to the house—" said the girl.

"Silence!" commanded Silver.

She was quiet. Farrel cleared his throat softly, very softly.

Out of the distance, now, they heard outbreaks of loud, arguing voices. These noises were interspersed with moments of silence; there followed a considerable time when not a sound was heard except from the windmill. A breeze was turning the wheel slowly; at intervals the stream from the pump dropped. The water in the tank was so low that the water fell like a hand on a brazen drum, with splashings and reverberations. This noise seemed to grow louder and louder. Sometimes it was as if the windmill and tank were moving toward the house. Silver kept on taking sights at everything he could see, making his vision small enough to grasp the least possible targets.

Then a tumult broke out in the dining room. The door went down with a crash—that door, it seemed, which communicated with the outside. Footfalls boomed on the floor. A ray of light worked fitfully around the edges of the door that closed the kitchen away from the dining room. A hand shook that door. Silver promptly put a bullet high up through the woodwork.

He had fired high on purpose. To shoot even at hostile men with nothing but blind chance to guide the bullet was against his nature, and the force of necessity had little control over his instincts. But, though he purposely had fired the warning shot high, a yell of derision came from the men in the next room. There seemed to be three or four of them, at least. Their footfalls rapidly retreated; they made no further effort, for the moment, to get into the kitchen.

After that, a portion of them, at least, were heard leaving the dining room. Perhaps one man was left there as a guard and spy to hem in the maneuvers of the three.

Silver saw a dim silhouette of a man move out toward the big corral and the shed. Another and another stealthy figure followed. Parade was out there in the shed, either munching hay or lying down at ease. Parade was there, but Silver would not fire at the unknown men on account of any hope of preserving the stallion. He had, in fact, a strong hope that the horse would be able to preserve himself.

Then Farrel fired a shot. The boom of the gun was thunderous in the small kitchen. It seemed to bring a jingling echo out of the iron-work of the stove. Outside, there was silence. Then voices stirred far away at the horse shed, followed by an outcry of curses at the farther end of the house.

"I missed that one, all right," Farrel said. "I won't miss the next, I hope."

They heard doors flung open, and heavy feet trampling across floors. At last there were men in the next room, where Silver had lounged all those recent days.

Someone bawled out: "We got you! We know you're in the kitchen. We're goin' to blow you to pieces, Silver! We're goin' to smear you all over the place."

Silver said nothing.

He could make out the rumbling voice of Delgas saying: "This is where the hound has been takin' it easy. This is where he's been sleepin' away his days. Oh, ain't he goin' to eat his heart—ain't he eatin' it now, to think what a fool we've made of him?"

One of the others laughed. Someone burst out in a tirade. Silver got up and went quietly to the door that opened on this room. He began to move away, silently, the chairs that were braced against it.

Then the girl reached for him and found him in the darkness. "Don't do it! Don't do it!" she said.

"What?" whispered Silver.

"You want to throw that door open and sweep them out of the house. Don't do it, Jim. Please don't go mad!"

He realized that he was mad, that an overmastering hunger to destroy them like reptiles had made a blackness of his brain. He put the chair soundlessly back in place and went back to lie on the floor at the door.

Some day, he knew, he would be led to throw his life away by the headlong sweeping of one of those fighting impulses of his that throttled his good sense and judgment. He grew afraid, as he lay there, not of all the danger that lay in the outer night but of himself. He began to forget the whole situation and wonder about himself; but all the while he was as alert as a wild cat hunting over strange ground.

From the horse shed came a crashing and snorting.

It raised him to his feet. The girl was beside him again, with her hand on his arm. He struck it away and strode for the door. She gripped him again.

"They're waiting for you to go out, when you hear Parade!" she warned him. "They're watching this door and the window, hoping that you'll come out. They're watching from each side, I know. They want to murder you, Jim!"

He thought of the soft gold of Parade and of the flexible steel that underlay the surface; he thought of the great wise brain of the stallion and the heart without fear. He began to tremble. The girl's hands kept pulsing against him, not strongly, but with a steady rhythm.

"No," he whispered at last. "I won't go. I'm ashamed. I'm only a fool and a baby. And you see through me. But I won't go."

He made himself get down on one knee, and then she went back to her place against the wall.

"She's the captain, the leader, the brain, and I'm only a pair of blind hands working by direction," he told himself.

He began to see her with clearness. He saw her more clearly in the darkness than ever he had seen her before in the light of the day, for he could place his memory on every bit of her.

She wore rubber gloves to keep her hands from puffing and reddening in the dishwater, but nevertheless, potatoes and onions and the handling of meat had stained her skin. Her hands were small and well-made but they were not pretty. Hands of a woman ought to be smooth and brown; they don't need to be very little, but the skin should be perfectly kept, thought Silver. And her hands would never be right because all her life she would be working away at sewing or cooking or scrubbing floors. She got right down on her knees and went after a floor with might and main. He had seen her making the suds fly. She scrubbed a floor white, like the deck of a ship. And if she were not doing work like that for a husband, she would surely be doing it for hire.

Silver decided, suddenly, that it was the matter of her hands that kept her from being beautiful, in his eyes. Her face was well enough. And her eyes were a blue stain in it. When she looked at Silver, her eyes and her mouth were still with awe; when she looked at Farrel, a smile kept dawning and dying on her lips and eyes. She kept taking gentle possession of him with her glances.

It might be a woman something like that who would one day, for the first time, fling open the door to Silver's heart and walk in and take command. Men said that when the moment came, they were helpless. They resisted, they fought against the thing, they fled from it. But they always fled in a circle and came back to the starting point. He would be like all the rest— one day!

Out of the shed figures moved again. A door opened with a crash.

"Ride him, cowboy! Ride him!" yelled a chorus of voices.

He heard the brazen neigh of Parade. It made him think of days of long ago when he had followed the great horse across the endless desert. That neigh had been the challenge that rung in his ears in those times until by chance and fortune and kindness, more than strength, at last he made the great horse his own. But it was not possession. He belonged to Parade as much as Parade belonged to him.

Now he was fighting against the mastery of another man, out there in the darkness. Silver heard the thumping of the hoofs on the ground, then a form exploded upward, vaguely spread-eagled against the horizon stars.

"Get the rope! Hold him! That's it!" shouted voices. "Now, Rutherford, if you can ride anything that wears hair, you take your turn!"

They might wear down Parade among them, taking him turn after turn. A whistle trilled suddenly out of the mouth of Silver. It brought as an echo a wild tumult, an outcrying. A gun barked, and another weapon spat fire. Then a mighty form winged over the corral fence.

Silver stood up, and called. Right to the kitchen door raced Parade, skidded to a halt, then entered, crouched low, feeling his way over the sagging, creaking boards, with bended legs. Like a monstrous cat shuddering on unknown ground, surrounded by the fear of traps, the big horse entered to the voice of Silver. At another word he lay down. His great breathing filled the room. The shouting outside was a dim and vague and distant thing to Silver, as he ran his hand over the body of the stallion, feeling for blood.

He found nothing. Blood was not running onto the floor, either. The hand which gripped the heart of Silver gradually relaxed. He drew his hand slowly over the face of the horse, reading the features of it with well-remembering finger tips. Then he went back to lie down at guard in the doorway again.

Out by the shed, men were cursing, blaming one another. And Silver began to laugh, a mere soundless vibration in the darkness.

For toward the east he saw the gleam of an increasing pyramid of light on the horizon and he knew that before long the moon would be riding above the desert. The instant its bright rim was up, all of those men would be in peril around the ranch house, and they must know it by this time. A very little longer and they probably would withdraw.

12 – Farrel's Decision

THE most alarming outburst of all came afterward. Perhaps it was the loss of the great horse that maddened the gang, but suddenly in the house broke out a great crashing and smashing as if men with axes were breaking all they could put their hands on. Voices came into the next room and bawled out curses. Other voices shouted in triumph as various bits of loot were found.

And then Rutherford was saying in his calm way: "You've won the second round, too, Silver. But the end of the fight hasn't come yet. Something tells me that I'm going to have the killing of you, Jim, and ride your horse afterward."

Although he did not lift his voice, he seemed to be speaking right there in the kitchen beside Silver. It was an uncanny thing. It sent strange shudders of apprehension through the body of Silver.

After that, the gang withdrew. In the distance behind the corral there were noises of the snorting horses as they were saddled and bridled. A few loud whoops were raised by the chorus, and after that they heard the beat of the departing hoofs.

Silver went out first, made a tour around the house, and then through the darkness of all the rooms inside it. For it was not impossible that a man or two might have been left behind to take him by surprise after he had counted on the retreat of the entire body. However, he found nothing except the smashed furniture and the ruined rooms where the thugs of Rutherford and Delgas had wreaked their angry disappointment.

It was only after he had completed his tour that Silver came back into the kitchen, called Parade into the open with a word, and gave permission for the kindling of a light. He asked for bacon and corn bread and coffee. He gave one glance at the girl and her sweetheart, their faces still pale and set from the ordeal that had been passed. Then he said:

458

"I'm going outside to have another look around and try to think out the next step. Whatever it is, you'll probably have to ride with me and leave Esther behind. Say goodbye before I get back. That is, if you still want to see this business through, Farrel."

He went outside and watched the rising of the moon as it puffed out its swollen yellow cheeks and then, climbing higher in the sky, drew into a smaller, brighter sphere of silver. It was one of those nights when a man thinks that he can see not the flatness of the disk but the roundness of the orb. As Silver watched the progress of the moon, he saw it strike a cloud into transparent spray and emerge on the farther side, sweeping along as though a stronger wind were in that billowing, bright sail.

He could not help wondering what that moon would see of him before the sun came up to turn its brilliance into no more than a pale-azure cloud in the Western sky. Delgas, and the crowd of punchers who had all done time, and above all, the pale, thoughtful face of Rutherford—they would have to be encountered, perhaps, before this single night had ended.

He went back, finally, into the kitchen, and as he entered, he heard young Dan Farrel laughing with the girl. The smoke and steam of cookery made a bright mist in the room. He felt a tang of appetite greater than he had known for a week. The anxiety since the supper gong sounded had been like a day's labor to build hunger.

They sat together, the three of them, while the stallion wandered back and forth outside, now and then putting his head through the doorway to watch his master, recoiling again because of the offensive smell of cooked meat and steaming coffee.

"He'd rather have oats," said the girl. "I'll get him an apple. Will he eat apples?"

Silver said vaguely: "I remember a time when he ate raw meat. Raw meat, wrapped up in fat, and stuffed down his throat. He ate a lot of it. He ate nothing else for four days—and he kept on going!"

"On a diet of meat?" cried Farrel, agape. "How did that happen? In a desert somewhere?"

"Pretty much in a desert. Away down south in Mexico, where the mountains are all scalped and where the sun burns the grass down to the roots Sometimes I found a cactus and pared the thorns off of it and shredded the fibers and gave some of that to Parade, too. It was filthy stuff. It was like offering him dry rope. But he'll eat anything in a pinch. He ran wild, you know, and wild horses know the point of eating or dying. Parade will always eat!"

"What was happening?" asked the girl. "Had you just got lost in the desert? How terrible!"

"Lost?" said Silver, more vaguely than before. "Well, that's one way of putting it. I had to be lost to the eyes of a lot of hombres who were riding after me."

"After you? But they never caught up with you?"

Silver looked at her with a very faint and very grim smile.

"Yes," he said. "Some of them caught up with me, too. But after a time that gang stopped following and turned back."

"All that were left of 'em?" suggested Farrel eagerly.

"Well," said Silver, as he finished eating and confined his attention to coffee, "there's still a job ahead. Farrel, you don't own a hair of a cow or an acre of land in the deal. Do you still want to ride with me?"

"I do," said Farrel.

Silver looked at the girl.

"Do you think that he ought to?" asked Silver.

She kept looking at Silver with great eyes of fear while she reached out for Farrel and blindly found him. Then as her hand tightened on him, she said:

"Yes. I think he ought to go."

"You've made up your mind?" asked Silver.

"I'd rather," said she, and paused, but went on again: "I'd rather remember him dead in a way like that—than dodging."

Silver said nothing. He began to frown into his coffee. It was almost unprecedented in his life. He had been with plenty of men who were willing to fight most desperately, but always because they had as great a goal as he, or a greater one. It was a novelty to him to find a fellow who was willing to throw himself away out of friendship, or gratitude for a past service.

Perhaps he should not permit that sacrifice. And yet he had in mind a reward that would repay Farrel for every effort, in the end. There was a battle to fight, first, and in that battle the odds were exactly nine to two—unless Sam Waring and perhaps sundry others were enlisted in the fight before the end.

He made a cigarette, lighted it, and tried to see the right course more clearly through the smoke.

"You talk, Farrel," he commanded suddenly. "You tell me what we ought to do."

"Go to town," said Farrel. "That's the best way, and get a whole mob of gunmen to come out here and mop up the thugs."

"How far to town?" asked Silver.

"Ten hours, I suppose."

"And then two or three hours, anyway, to get together enough of the right sort of men and mount them. Another ten hours to get back. That's one day."

Farrel nodded, frowning.

"It won't do," said the girl.

"Why not?" asked Farrel. "It's the best thing that we can do."

"What will Rutherford do now?" asked Silver of the girl.

She made a sweeping gesture.

"He'll have the men clear off the whole place. He'll have them clear off every cow on the place and all the horses. Every head of livestock will be up there in the foothills, somewhere, within four or five hours. Because Danny says that the men have been drifting everything north for days. They have them ready, now, for a quick push."

Silver nodded. "That's what Rutherford will do," he agreed.

Farrel looked painfully down at the table, before he began to shake his head.

"You're right," he said. "There's not time enough to let us get to town and back. There never was time enough for that. There's only the pair of us against the nine of them—plus a lot of others that we don't know anything about!"

He took a good swallow of coffee. The girl was watching him with a peculiar anxiety. Silver watched him, too. Farrel was no lover of danger. That was clear. But he had two senses. One was of honor and one was of duty. They pinched and whitened his face, but at last he was able to lift his head.

"All right," he said quietly to Silver. "I didn't see, at first, just what I was heading for. Now I see and I'll go through with it if I can."

"You know the lay of the land," said Silver. "What ought we to do, Danny?"

Farrel brushed his knuckles across his forehead and left three parallel streaks of white from the greatness of the pressure.

He flung out a hand behind him, pointing north.

"They'll scoop 'em all up and throw 'em into one of the two valleys," he declared. "They'll sweep 'em into the gap between the foothills of the Farrel Mountains and the hills below Mount Humphreys. Or else they'll drive through between the Humphreys Mountains and the Kendal Hills. That's the easiest way."

Silver nodded. "After that?" he suggested.

"Well," said Farrel slowly, as though he were willing to let his mind dwell on the details, "after that they'll have no trouble. They'll split the big herd into little sections and wind 'em through the mountains. You can depend upon it, if I'm right and they're ready to make their sale, somewhere up there in the mountains there are a lot of punchers ready to grab the herd for Sam Waring and push it away to markets that we don't know anything about. You could sprinkle ten million cows through those mountains and make it hard for anything but hawks to find 'em!"

"That's what they'll do then," said Silver calmly. "I believe every word that you say. But what about the pair of us? What can we do to stop 'em?"

Farrel stirred uneasily in his chair.

"Well," he said at last, "I don't know. First, we'll have to spot the way they're taking. That means that we'll have to separate. You go to the head of the valley between Humphreys and Kendal. I'll go to the head of the valley between Humphreys and Farrel Mountain. The one who sees the drift of cattle coming can climb the high hill at the foot of Humphreys. Know that hill?"

"No."

"You'll spot it easily enough. It stands up like a spur, all by itself. A fire lighted on that hill can be seen in both valleys. It will be the call which tells the other fellow that he's wanted. And when the herd comes—and you and I are both together—well, then Heaven alone can tell what we'll be able to do!"

13 – The Signal Fire

IT WAS not so much the courage of Farrel that moved Silver, though it was a stirring thing to see the way the man drove his unwilling mind, as it was the strength of the girl. Not once did she falter.

The horses had been cleared out of the big corral, as a matter of course, by the retiring men of Rutherford and Delgas. But there were others in more distant fields. Silver went out on Parade and daubed a rope on a strong-looking mustang that led its herd in the effort to escape but could not lead fast enough to run away from the devouring stride of Parade. He brought that horse back and saddled it while Farrel said goodbye to the girl.

She was as steady as a rock, saying goodbye. Silver, when he took her hand, said:

"You have to stay alone, here, and I know that's hard to do. You have to let Dan go with me. And that's harder still. You're a brick, and I'm not forgetting it."

That was all. He made her no promises of reward because he felt that such talk would be an insult to a spirit like hers. Then he rode off at the side of Farrel. They were well-armed, well-mounted, and they had their wits about them. But as they got under way and as the outlines of the foothills drew nearer to them under the brightness of the moonlight, the thing looked more and more hopeless to Silver.

Farrel drew up his horse presently and pointed off to the right.

"That's your way, Jim," said he. "Ride up the valley there between the foothills. When you get to the head of it, you can wait. If my idea's right, those punchers are sweeping in the cows right now, out of the desert behind us. Once they get the herd together and start it rolling, it will move fast because these cows can run and keep on running like horses. They can be

463

pushed like a big gang of mustangs. You'll hear 'em coming before you see 'em, maybe. And when you hear 'em pointing up your valley, climb the hill that will be off to the side—you won't miss it—and light the fire. If I don't see the red of the fire in this moonlight, I'll spot the rising of the smoke. Is that all straight?"

"That's all straight," said Silver. Then he added: "I'd very much like to know the top thing in your mind, right now."

"Why," said Farrel, "I'm thinking about Steve Wycombe. Wherever he is, if he knows what's happening on earth, he must be laughing. See the way it's all working out for him! He split up his land among three men, and now he's got a first-rate chance that they'll cut each other's throats for the sake of his land. He's got a ten-to-one chance that you'll go down, anyway. And you're the one that bumped him off. Oh, Steve's laughing good and hard now, all right."

Silver nodded. "Let him laugh," he murmured. "One chance in ten isn't bad, when the stakes run high. Every man bets on a long shot, now and then. That's the spice of life."

Farrel stared back at him. Silver could feel the eyes under the black mask of shadow that fell across the forehead of his companion.

"I'd like to know one thing, Jim," said Farrel. "What's the top layer in your mind, just now?"

"The white of Rutherford's face," said Silver instantly. "And the blue of the eyes of your girl. I hope that you get back to her. But—so long, Danny!"

He shook hands with Farrel, and saw the puncher jog his mustang off to the left until it was out of sight beyond the first of the low-rolling hills that descended from the mighty knees of Mount Humphreys.

It was a bitter business, and he wondered how he could be justified by any sense of higher right in allowing this man to ride into the danger. Yet something sure and strong in the nature of Silver told him that he was right. If all worked out as he faintly hoped it might, there would be a reward for his friend, and such a reward was worth working for.

He kept telling himself that.

A wolf howled from the hillside, unseen. The doleful sound roused Jim Silver to action. He spoke, and Parade stepped out into a trot, then into a long and sweeping gallop that started him up the wide mouth of the valley, with the hills walking slowly back behind him to either side.

Nothing lived around him, and yet everything seemed at wait, the cactus with its black spot of shadow beside it, the crouching shapes of the hills themselves, and the narrow mouths of the ravines that opened ominously toward him as he went by. It was a moment not easy on the nerves; he wondered how big Dan Farrel was handling the thing.

He thought of Steve Wycombe, too, who had planned his revenge on his enemies so cunningly, as he lay dying. Poison was usually put in food; this was poison placed in rich possessions. Truly Farrel was right, and the soul of Wycombe must be laughing at thought of the evil he had left behind him on earth.

When Silver got up to the head of the valley, where the hills pinched together, he dismounted, let Parade graze on the dusty tufts of grass, here and there, and smoked a cigarette while he walked up and down.

The night was perfectly still now. It seemed as though the slightest sound must necessarily trouble and dim the pure outline of the hills against the moonlight in the sky.

He fell into a mood of absolute quiet. This sort of a time of stillness was, after all, nearer and dearer to him than anything else in life. Neither man nor woman could enter his heart so deeply. So he sat like a stone, only his eyes moving, as he heard Parade crop the grass with slight ripping noises like the tearing of bits of cloth.

He had been there for a long time when, looking up the slope toward the isolated hill of which Farrel had spoken, he saw a red flower bloom in the steep shadow of a rock high above. He knew that it was the signal fire by which Dan Farrel was calling to him for help.

14 – A Reception Committee

DAN FARREL, when he trotted his horse away from Silver and up the shallow mouth of the valley that lay between the sprawling hills of the Farrel Mountains and those that descended from Mount Humphreys, felt with every beat of the mustang's right forefoot that he must rein the little horse around and return to tell Silver frankly: "I'm not in this game. I haven't the nerve. I can't do it. The cattle don't belong to me. The land doesn't belong to me. I'm out of the picture."

That would have been talking the way he felt. And finally he swung the mustang sharply around only to find that the lower foothills from the Humphreys range had crawled between him and Silver. He was alone. With the moonlight gleaming in the desert dust, he seemed to be sitting in a thin, ground mist. The hammering of his heart made it hard for him to breathe; it was as though he were submerged in water.

The air was warm enough. He knew that. And yet there was cold inside him. It seemed to come out of the moonlight and run into the marrow of his bones.

"You're a yellow dog," he told himself.

His throat worked on the words. He remembered how he had sat at the table, that night, and how Jim Silver had drawn guns to protect him.

"You're a yellow dog!" he said, out loud.

The bigness of his own voice amazed him. He turned his horse around and made it walk up the flat of the valley. As for fellows like Silver, why should they be praised for courage when, as a matter of fact, the God that made them had given them different nerves, different capacities? Does one praise a cat for its skill in catching a bird? No, one simply admires the delicate craftsmanship of nature which can bring foot and eye to such perfection. Does one eulogize the hawk that blows on an easy wing across the heavens?

466

Then why should Silver be worshiped like a glorious thing when he was simply one of nature's special products, one of her fine elaborations? His eye was surer, his hand was swifter. He could take a fellow like that husky lad, Red, and paralyze him with a grip. At a single gesture he showed himself to be beyond the ken of ordinary people. And as a type of his superiority there was the horse he rode which, to other mustangs, was as an eagle to a crow. From the pursuit of Silver no man in open country could escape. From the pursuit of others, he could easily drift away.

So Farrel kept telling himself over and over again that he was a fool, that he had no business trying to follow the seven-league strides of Jim Silver. And yet, all the while something inside him made him know that he would not give up this fight until bullets or blows had forced him out of it.

He got up to the head of the valley, dismounted, threw the reins off the mustang, and started walking up and down. He was caught, he felt. He was enslaved by an idea, a sense of pride and duty. Was there not a story of the Roman sentinel who kept at his post as the city burned, simply because no orders had come relieving him? And he, Danny Farrel, was like that. He was being a blind and automatic machine. He would get no glory for it, only a hard-nosed bullet out of a Winchester to nudge the life out of him and turn him into food for buzzards.

He looked up the slope of the signal hill, again and again, each time half expecting to see the fire. He was not sure that he would be able to spot the flame. It was perhaps only the dim shimmer of the smoke as it rose through the moonlight that he would be able to distinguish. Or would Silver light the fire in the shadow of a certain tall rock, so that the flames would lock out with a redder eye?

He walked up to the top of a low hummock from which he had a better view of the lower valley. He could look out onto the desert itself, which appeared as a thicker streak of mist in the distance.

He came down again to the horse. There was a sudden bond between him and that roach-backed, ewe-necked gelding. He could remember it as a yearling, as a two-year-old. A good set of legs and a body that was like a question mark. Just an ordinary dull-witted, stubborn, headstrong, savage little animal, but now the pressure of fear brought Farrel close to the horse.

The stock of the Winchester that protruded out of the saddle holster was another comfort like the face of a friend. He pulled the gun out, and after handling it a moment, he put it back inside the cover.

If he had had any sense, he would have spent time every day practicing. He would have known that, sooner or later, his life might depend upon his marksmanship. He would have known that it was better to waste a few cartridges for half an hour a day than it was to come to a moment like this. He told himself that therein lay the difference, in part, between himself and men who got on in the world. Fellows like Delgas and Rutherford, for instance, were willing to practice their card tricks and their gun work for hours every free day. That meant that they were prepared when the pinches came, the golden opportunities which so often went hand in hand with terrible dangers.

But as for himself, what was he, and what had he done? He was merely a growth from the soil and attached to it by a blind affection and yearning. He was a thing all root and no tree, like the twisted mesquite. And his labors had been given to riding herd, building fences, doctoring sick cows, tailing them out of mud-holes, keeping the night watch, singing to the dogies, breaking mean, down-headed horses, patching sheds. Why, when he died and went over the rim of things into the other world, the ghosts of real men would laugh at him when he tried to describe the still, strange beauty of the desert and the way the three mountains climbed up the northern sky.

He sighed, and then went up to the top of the hummock from which he could look out to the desert. It was just the same with some difference that he could not spot, some small difference.

Then, his mind clearing, he knew what the change was. The sheen of desert dust under the moon was no longer a low, thin streak. It rose much higher, as though a wind were blowing straight up the valley. But something more than the wind might cause the dust to rise.

He looked up at the sky and studied the thin patches of clouds for a moment. No, there was no wind.

So he hurried to his horse, with his heart beating very fast. Still, he must not merely guess, in this fashion. He must not call to Silver with an entirely false alarm.

He threw himself down on the ground and pressed his ear to it. At first he thought that he could hear a distant sound, but finally he knew that it was only the rushing of the blood through the arteries of his head. That noise grew dim, disappeared. Then he could really listen and make out a subdued murmuring. No, it was a rhythm, a pulse, and nothing more. He lay there still, holding his breath, and strained every nerve.

Then he distinguished it clearly—the noise of many, many hoofs trampling.

He was on the back of the mustang in a moment, staring under the shadow of both hands. Now, clearly, he could see the rising of the dust. He thought that he could even make out the twistings of the upper layers of it as the herd entered the mouth of the valley. Perhaps, if the men riding point had sent out a scout well ahead, the puncher in the lead might not be far from him at that moment.

But he gave only a casual glance to the floor of the valley about him. Anger such as he could hardly believe in himself was surging and rising in him He cast a glance toward the mountains, and marked the jet-black, zigzag traceries of the innumerable canyons against the brightness of the smoother slopes. Once the herd reached that hole-in-the-wall country, pursuit would simply be ridiculous. And therefore, all the early work of his life would be wiped out. It would more than be wiped out. It would be cast into the hands of the two scoundrels, Delgas and Harry Rutherford.

The heat of his anger dissolved all fear. He put the mustang at the slope, and the little horse went up the rough and graveled surface with perfect certainty, straining, throwing itself into its labor as though it perfectly understood.

Right up toward the top they went until they reached that high rock which the glance of Farrel had picked out before this. There was plenty of brush for the kindling of a fire. However, he did not want a great deal. Even the smallest eye of red was likely to meet not only the eye of Silver, in the valley beneath, but also the attention of the men handling the herd, and on a night like this they would be on edge with nervous suspicions.

The brush was tough sage. He tore up some small bushes. The wood resisted his hands when he stripped off the branches. However, he rapidly made a small pile. The leaves which he had shaken off he swept together in a heap, and put a match to them. The flame caught in them. There was a crinkling sound. The red of the fire disappeared. A thickening white smoke went up. The breath of it was pungent and sweet to him. It reminded him of a thousand open camp fires that he had kindled before this, but never had he struck a match that might lead to what would follow now!

The flame burst up through the center of the leaves in a small volcanic eruption of red. He put on little branches of the sage. It burned with a greasy crackling. He put on the larger brush. He stood back and watched the red flower bloom in the shadow of the rock.

He had built it right on the farther edge of this little shoulder, yet it seemed to him that the feeble glow of the flame could not possibly walk so far through the moonlight as to come to the eyes of Jim Silver, in the valley beneath.

He could see that valley. Yes, and now he thought that he could see Silver, far away. A moment later, he was certain. He could not spot man and horse so well, but he was sure of the shadows which they cast on the ground.

Now, as he watched, the man mounted, and began to move straight up the slope toward him. Relief in a warm wave swept through the body and the brain of Dan Farrel. To be alone on such a night was terrible, but to be with such a man as Jim Silver would be exciting, almost glorious, perhaps.

He knew, as he stared down at the climbing form, that he had made no mistake—that he would never regret having ridden out on this night to fight for the herd. Then he thought of Esther and how she had let him go, willingly enough. People like Esther, he felt, always are right. They know how to pick between the easy way and the way of honor and duty and just pride.

After that, he muttered aloud: "Good old Jim Silver."

Something jammed into the small of his back as he stood shaking his head with a new-found affection.

"Yeah," said the voice of Delgas. "He'll be good and old, before very long. Come here, Red. Fan this bird and get his guns. We're goin' to be a reception committee, son. Because that's Jim Silver that's climbin' his horse up the way!"

15 – The Ambush

FARREL was backed up from the edge of the little plateau. If they could see Silver, it was just possible that Silver might be able to spot them. Red stood in front of Farrel and laughed.

"What a simp you are, Danny!" said he. "Why didn't you turn around and look behind you, a couple of times?"

It was strange to Farrel that he felt neither fear nor shame. There had been only a blinding moment of terror when the voice first spoke behind him, but now he could look steadily into the eyes of Red. He had always known the fellow was little good.

"I'm not clever at this sort of work," said Farrel. "I've never spent much time with crooks."

Red had just taken Farrel's Colt. Now he laid the barrel suddenly along the head of Farrel and knocked him staggering.

"Quit that, you fool!" exclaimed Delgas. "We don't want any noise up here. The first thing you know, Silver will hear something. He's got ears like a cat. That's what he is—a cat!"

Delgas was tying the hands of Farrel behind his back. Red, tying a double knot in a big silk bandanna that he folded across, suddenly thrust it between the teeth of Farrel. It made an efficient gag.

"He won't do any yelling to warn Silver. Not just now," said Red.

"Good work," answered Delgas. "You've got a brain, kid. We can use you, maybe—Rutherford and me."

"Jake with me," answered Red. "You know how it is. There ain't any use in punching cows. Ever seen an old cow-puncher? What becomes of ' em, then? They fade away, I tell you."

471

"They do," agreed Delgas. "The way of it is like this: Those that have got the coin keep it. The poor stiffs that try to work up, they're just playin' into the hands of the millionaire. There's something in the Bible, even, about that. About them that have the goods are going to get the extras, too."

"Yeah, and I've seen it, and I've read it," said Red.

He stepped cautiously across the face of the rock to peer down at the progress of Silver.

"It'll take him a minute," muttered Red. "It's a steep path, and even Parade can't fly that slope. They gotta zigzag up the face of it."

"Sit down," ordered Delgas. "Sit down and rest yourself, kid."

Farrel sat down with his back to the rock.

"What about putting the fire out?" asked Red.

"Sure," agreed Delgas. "That'll make Silver think that Farrel sees him comin'."

Red kicked the fire over the ground. The flames stopped dancing; a broader smudge arose.

The two sat on their heels and waited.

Delgas began to utter his philosophy. "A gent with a bean," he said, "is a gent that knows how to make the easy money. Anybody knows that. And where does the easy money lie? Why, it lies in the other fellow's pocket. And how are you goin' to get it out? By talkin', by turnin' a key, or by usin' a gun. Those are the three ways. There ain't any others. A kid like you, Red, could learn a lot. You could learn to crack a safe, do some confidence steerin', and pack a gun for the pinches."

"Yeah," said Red. "A fellow just has to learn his line. That's all. I guess Rutherford has a line, eh?"

"Thing to listen to," said Delgas, "is that smooth little devil talkin' his way into the confidence of a female. That's where he shines. With a flower in his buttonhole and a hard hat on his head, and with a walkin' stick in his hand and a shine of his shoes, doggone me if it don't do your heart good to see the way he walks right into the heart of a girl. He's slick, is what he is. Understand? He's as slick as they make 'em!"

"Yeah, yeah," muttered Red eagerly. "Wouldn't I like to hear him work, though? Maybe I could do something with the ladies myself. I ain't such a bad hand."

"It's the way he's got of saying the simple things. That's what counts with the females," said Delgas. "You take a woman, they ain't never got more'n the half of a brain in their head. Kind of nutty and foolish. You can't argue with 'em none. You gotta let 'em have their own way or else just sock 'em and let 'em drop. Or else you gotta make love to 'em. That's where Harry shines. He's gotta brain, is what he's got."

"Yeah, he's got a brain," agreed Red, grinning and gaping with admiration.

"Lemme tell you another thing," said Delgas. "A great dodge of Harry's is bein' a recovered consumptive. A lunger that's gone and got well, and he's a millionaire, you see, and he wants to contribute a lot of money to make a big resort where other lungers can go and get well. That's the line he uses in some small town in the Southwest. Anywhere in the Southwest. He gets the whole town all boiled up. He's goin' to build a great big hotel. He's goin' to bring business and lungers on the jump into the place.

"The storekeepers and the ranchers and everybody chips in and raises a nice lot of money. All they gotta do is to deposit as much as the check that Harry puts into the hands of the treasurer of the company, and while Harry's just put in a check, the rest of 'em put in cash. Y'understand? They put in cash and when they've got in the fifteen or twenty thousand dollars which is to show that the town is behind the big idea and willing to help on the street improvements and all of that, then one night the treasurer and Harry disappear, and the town has to sit on its heels and cuss."

Red chuckled softly. "You been the treasurer?" he asked.

"Yeah. I been the treasurer," said Delgas. "Doggone me if I don't laugh till I cry, when I think about some of Harry's stunts. He's gotta brain, is what he's got."

"Look here," said Red. "Whatcha mean by talkin' all these things over in front of Danny?"

"Why," said Delgas, "I got an idea that maybe Danny ain't goin' to live to talk. I got an idea that maybe he'll be lyin' out here mum as a stone, before very long. I just want Harry's O.K. on the job."

Even Red winced a little at this suggestion.

"You're going to—knock him right over the head?" he asked huskily.

"Yeah, and what difference would that make to you? Is he your long-lost brother, or something like that?" asked Delgas, sneering.

"No, no," muttered Red. "Only—well, what Rutherford decides is all right with me."

"He don't go in for the red-handed stuff," agreed Delgas. "Harry is gentle—except when he makes up his mind to be the other thing. What Harry says is that it's a dumb play to go and collect scalps when what you want is wallets. If somebody's gotta be sunk, he'll lay 'em colder'n a stone, all right. But he dodges the trouble. He's that way. He dodges the blood. And I don't blame him. It gets people stirred up when they find blood on the trail. They don't like it. They begin to raise posses. Posses ain't so hard to handle but sometimes they make a little trouble."

"It was a posse that grabbed me and threw me in the can," observed Red thoughtfully.

"You were only a kid and didn't know how to handle yourself," suggested Delgas.

"Yeah. I was only a kid. I hadn't gone to college, at that time. But now that I'm a graduate from the pen, you can bet that I'm wiser. Only, I took a whirl at trying to go straight, till you and Harry come along and showed me that I was making a fool of myself."

"Gents like Rutherford and me, that uses the bean, we don't sit down and take a kick in the face," declared Delgas. "We stand up and kick somebody else."

"Yeah, you do, and you get away with it," said Red, nodding his head.

He began to look with open eyes at Delgas, a sign that his mind was as open as a summer's day, also.

"It's better to kick than to be kicked," said Red.

"Ain't it, though?" agreed Delgas.

"Listen!" said Red.

Over the edge of the hill, Farrel heard the clank of an iron-shod hoof against a stone.

"He's comin' closer," said Delgas. "Listen, kid. This is the greatest chance that you ever had in your life."

"You mean you ain't goin' to take a try at him?" asked Red quickly.

"Sure I'm goin' to take a try at him. We're both goin' to take a try," said Delgas. "But there's enough glory in bumping off Silver to spread thick on two slices, lemme tell you. We're goin' to be known, from now on, as the birds that killed Silvertip. People are goin' to say: 'There goes the birds that bumped off Jim Silver. Those are the ones that killed Arizona Jim.' We're goin' to be pointed out. Understand?"

"Yeah. Sure," said Red. "But he ain't dead yet."

"He's goin' to be dead. Now listen to me. When we sneak up to the edge of the hill, yonder, poke your head over dead easy. Understand? And have your rifle out in front of you. And what you shoot at is the hoss."

"Parade?" said Red. "Morrie, you wouldn't take and kill the finest hoss in the world, would you?"

"Shut up and don't argue," said Delgas, drawing out a pair of Colts from which the sights and triggers had been filed away. "I know best. The job that we got is to bring him down and kill him. And the first stir of anything, that stallion is goin' to jump twenty feet sideways. He's that way. The reason that Silver has got through so many tight holes is mostly that Parade is eyes and ears for him, and a jumpin' fool of a jack-in-the-box, besides. He can smell trouble a mile off down wind, too.

"No, kill that stallion, and Silver is half dead right then. You use your rifle. Make sure. Shoot straight. I'm goin' to use a Colt because I'm sort of more used to it, and if I miss at a cinch of a target like that, call me an old woman and slap my face for me!"

He put down his left-hand gun not far from the feet of Dan Farrel and began to do something to his other Colt.

"It's time!" said Red.

"Wait a minute," commanded Delgas. "Don't rush it. We wanta get there to the ledge just at the right second. I'll tell you when to start. My ears are measurin' the sound and the distance like a tape. I'll tell you when."

He went on: "You gotta learn to fan a gun, kid, and I'm goin' to teach you. It turns loose the bullets like drops of water out of a hose. Now shut up and don't talk. He's too near. And the stallion can hear like a telephone receiver."

So they crouched there, hushed.

Dan Farrel, tied, gagged so that he could hardly breathe, listened to the frantic bumping of his heart. He was wet with sweat. It trickled from his forehead and ran into his helpless eyes. But he saw neither of the men before him clearly; rather he was seeing the big head and shoulders of Silver, swaying a little against the moonlight as Parade carried him lightly up the slope—a perfect target black against the moonlight! One uproar of guns and one thudding of bullets, and that would be the end of him.

It seemed to Farrel like the fall of mountains. He thought of Parade and the death of the great horse was even more impossible than the death of the man. But life can be let out by the prick of a pin. Somewhere he had found that—in a church or in a book.

He wondered if, by a great effort, he could make around the gag some sort of a strangling noise that might be a sufficient warning for Silver. But he knew that he could not manage it. His will was right. He felt that he was willing to die if he could send the message to the man who rode so helplessly into ambush. But he could do nothing.

He twisted in agony, and one foot touched the Colt which had been laid on the ground by Delgas. The electric spark of an idea leaped instantly through his brain. For the hair-trigger weapon was set so that the merest flick of the thumb on the hammer would discharge it, and if he could get his toe on the hammer for an instant—

Vaguely he saw Red begin to crawl forward, easing the rifle along the ground, moving like a great hunting beast. And over the edge of the hill he distinctly heard the clattering fall of a stone which Parade had dislodged.

The rider was close now. Soon he would be looming above the ledge.

"Now!" whispered Delgas to Red, and reached a hand for the Colt he had put down.

Farrel could not be sure that he would accomplish his purpose. He could only reach out rather blindly and flick back his toe. He felt no resistance more than a mere scratch against the sole of his boot, but a deep explosion boomed instantly in his ear. He had touched the hammer by the grace of chance!

He saw Delgas turn on him like a tiger; he heard the startled snort and plunge of the horse that could not be seen. Then Red had risen to his feet and run forward. On the verge of the ledge, big against the moonlight sky, Red leveled his rifle from the shoulder and fired.

Delgas was instantly beside him, turning loose a stream of bullets.

Both stopped shooting. To look at the dead bodies tumbling down the slope?—wondered Farrel. No, for Delgas was exclaiming:

"Wait—when he comes out from behind the rock—steady—get your bead to the right. I'll watch the left—now—now!"

And again the guns boomed.

Delgas began to spring up and down, cursing. He threw his empty gun on the ground. His yells of rage were like the howling of a beast. But Red, rifle at the ready, was still peering at the distance, trying to get in a final shot.

Farrel took a great breath. Death would be easy to face, he felt, for he had done enough to make his life worthwhile.

Then Delgas turned and rushed snarling back at him.

16 – The Herd

ELGAS meant murder. The moon was behind his head, but enough of his features showed to let Farrel see the twist and stretch of them, and the catfish gape of his grin. The big fellow took Farrel by the throat. He could not even curse. He could only gasp with the completeness of his rage. With the butt of a revolver he offered to beat Farrel over the head, then to bash in his face.

He could not make a choice when the rifle of Red cracked again and Delgas dropped Farrel flat and ran back to see what had happened.

"I've got him!" yelled Red. "I've got him! Oh, no, he's gone! He's gone. He's made of moonshine, Delgas. Bullets just slide right through him and don't do no harm."

"He'll moonshine you when he lays his hands on you!" said Morris Delgas. "He'll show you what moonshine can do, you flathead! What you got a rifle for? What you good for, you four-flusher, you fake of a wooden Injun?"

Red gradually straightened under the pouring of the abuse. At last he said: "That's about enough out of your trap, Delgas."

"It's enough, is it?" shouted Delgas. "I'll show you what's enough! I'm goin' to see what's inside you! I'm goin' to take a look at your lining!"

He put his great grasp on Red, who slid one hand behind him as if to get at a knife. For a moment, they faced each other. Then Delgas cursed and took his hands away from Red.

"I oughta eat your heart," he vowed, "but it'd be that much the better for the skunk that's lyin' yonder laughin' at us! It'd be fine for him if we choked each other and rolled down the slope here and bashed our heads in. Wouldn't that be slick for him?"

"I done the best shootin' I could," said Red. "But that hoss was maneuverin' all the time like a snipe flyin' down wind. There wasn't no regularity about

477

nothin' he did. He didn't keep to no straight lines, the fool. You seen that for yourself, Delgas. You had a pretty close shot at him, but you couldn't hit him."

"It was Farrel that give him a couple of winks of head start," argued Delgas. "The shootin' off of the gun was what started that hawk flyin', and two flaps takes a bird like that a long ways. Red, I'm sorry I started in to manhandle you. It wasn't your fault. But for a second, all I could think of was that Jim Silver had been inside our hands—and that we let him slip!"

"I know," said Red. "I know how you feel. Don't I feel the same way, though? It's hell, is all that it is!"

They went back to Farrel and stood over him. The hands of Morris Delgas worked at his sides. They looked to Farrel like the jaws of two fish biting at the air. He kicked Farrel in the ribs.

"Get up!" he commanded.

The pain of the bruised flesh sickened Farrel. The weight of the blow made it difficult for him to breathe, but he got slowly to his feet. He realized that the least hesitation might hasten his time of dying.

So he stood and confronted the pair of them. And suddenly, Delgas reached out and removed the bandanna that gagged Farrel.

"You done the noble thing, didn't you?" asked Delgas. "Hey? It was noble, wasn't it?"

Farrel said nothing.

"Answer me!" shouted Delgas. "You was being noble, wasn't you?"

Farrel said nothing. He saw Delgas swing back a fist and how the punch traveled right at his head. He had an idea that he might be able to duck the blow, but if he avoided it, he was reasonably sure that he would be murdered. It was what Delgas wanted—the least additional excuse so that he would not be killing a helpless man in cold blood. So Farrel stood still and let the fist strike him in the face.

Once he had been struck down when the massive shoulder of a hay wagon nudged him. The fist of Delgas was like that. It seemed to be faced with brass and to have a ton of driving weight behind it. It took him right off his feet and slammed him down on the back of his head. He could hear the whack of the fist against his flesh as though two hands had been clapped together. Afterward, he heard his head pound solidly against the rock.

When his wits cleared, a second later, the left side of his face was numb, with liquid trickling over the skin, tickling it. Then he realized that his cheek bone had been laid open and the blood was running down from that.

Big Morris Delgas got him by the hair of his head and jerked him to a sitting posture. He swung back his other fist.

"I asked you, was you being noble?" shouted Delgas. "I asked you was you a dirty hound that was being noble, shooting a gun by a kick of your foot, giving Jim Silver warning. I asked you was you a dirty rat, a dirty noble rat? Was you?"

He kept jerking the head of Farrel back and forth, and his right hand oscillated with terrible eagerness to beat again into the face of the prisoner.

Red broke in suddenly: "Aw, back up, Delgas. Let him be."

Delgas dropped Dan Farrel and whirled about.

"You want something?" he yelled.

Red had backed up a little. He had his hand behind him again, and Farrel could see how the fingers were looped over the handle of a knife. He seemed to mean business, though he kept on backing up, slowly, before the truculent advance of Delgas.

"I won't take water from you, Delgas," he said.

"You're butting in, you fool!" shouted Delgas, wavering with the wind of his fury. "You're butting in and you're tryin' to tell me what's what. I'm goin' to smash you!"

Red kept on backing up, more and more slowly.

"I won't take water from nobody," he said.

He stood still, suddenly.

"I won't take water from you, Delgas," he said.

His hand came around from the small of his back. The moonlight winked along the blade of the sharpened steel.

Delgas strode close and measured himself against Red. He was so big that he had only to throw out his arms in order to embrace the smaller man. The whole body of Delgas worked in his passion, just as the entire body of a vast cat might work, as it sharpens its claws.

"You poor fool," said Delgas, "d'you think your toad sticker can stop me?"

"I don't think nothing," said Red. "I just think that I won't take water from nobody."

"I got a mind to bash your head in," said Delgas.

"All right. I guess you're big enough to bash me," said Red, "but you gotta prove it. I ain't taking water from nobody."

"What's the matter with you, kid?" demanded Delgas. "Are you nutty or something? What you butting in for?"

"I don't care about him," said Red. "You can take and drill him through the head, for all I care, or open him up with a knife, and it's Jake with me. But I hate you to be beating up a bird that can't lift his hands."

"What's the matter with you? You ain't takin' the socks, are you?" asked Delgas.

"I dunno. It sort of makes me sick," said Red.

Delgas laughed. "You are funny," he said. "That is what you are. You're just a funny hombre. I bang him in the mug and you take and get sick. You're just a funny hombre, is what you are, Red."

"All right," said Red. "I can't help it."

"Sure you can't help it, if you're built that way," said Delgas. "Besides, I dunno that it's a good idea to smear up this gent too much. Maybe it's better to wait till Harry Rutherford has a look at him. Harry might have some ideas about the way to handle him, I guess."

"Sure he might," agreed Red. "Now you're talking, old son. We'll get him back to Rutherford, down yonder, and see what Harry has to say about him."

Delgas nodded. He concluded the argument on which the life of Farrel had depended by saying: "He thought he was being noble, was what made me sore. Reaching out and shooting the gun to warn his friend—you know, kind of being noble and giving himself away to the Injuns for the sake of his partner—you know, regular story stuff. That was what made me sick, him playing noble, like that. That's why I asked him was he trying to be noble. If he'd said yes, I would a' bashed him to a pulp!"

They mounted Farrel on his horse, tying its lead rope to the pommel of Delgas's saddle, after the other two climbed on their own horses, which had been left a little down the slope. And Farrel found himself looking down to a great wave of turmoil that swept up through the valley gradually.

Over it, a great billowing mist came up in waves. There seemed to be no wind, and yet the dust kept on rising. The acrid taint of it began to stain the air around Farrel. He could look down into the thin fog and see through it the swaying, pouring multitudes of the herd. Right across the valley they spread.

They moved as a front of water moves. Sometimes a pressure of some sort caused one section to roll swiftly out ahead of the rest of the front, and then that section was delayed, as though the dry sands were drinking up the current, and another portion of the front lurched into the lead. Waves like those of water passed through the herd, also; vague perturbations and disturbances of the living mass. And the clatter and rattle of the clashing hoofs and the striking horns beat up to Farrel like a vast cymbal chorus, while the calves bawled high and the bulls roared low.

And he was the maker of that great herd. He could remember the day when he talked to old Wycombe, that cunning fox who had been the father of the dead man. He had said: "Mr Wycombe, I'm fifteen. That's why I'm willing to start small and work big. You wait and see. I know the right sort of a steer to run on this sort of land. I can breed 'em, and I can buy 'em, too. I know beef as I know the flat of my own hand."

Old Wycombe had listened, and smiled, and listened. That was the day Farrel began to be a slave to an idea, and to the Wycombe family, and finally he had built up his herd, in actual fact. The size of it seemed to be magnified by the moonlight. It was flooding through his heart and soul. The mountains seemed to be trembling with the thunder of the multitude. He kept on saying to himself soundlessly: "I did all of that. I raised that herd. And now it's going to be wasted. Now it's going to be wasted."

Big Delgas, reining close to him, said: "Your face is all swelling up, kid. I'm sorry that I socked you like that. But you made me sore. It makes me sore to see a gent trying to be noble. It makes me mad, is all it does."

Farrel shrugged his shoulders.

"He's thinking about the beef. He's not thinking about himself," remarked Red, with a touch of both curiosity and of sympathy in his voice.

"What you mean, he's thinking about the beef?" said Delgas.

"Down there," said Red, gesturing. "He's not so sorry for the beating he got, but he's sorry to see his herd break up."

"He never owned no part of it," answered Degas.

"He built it, brother, is what I mean," said Red. "You gotta understand how you'd feel if you'd built something and seen it go smash."

"Like a toy house. I know," said Delgas. "My big brother built a kind of a toy house, one day. I come along and took and give it a shove, and it goes in a pile. Was he sore? He was sore, lemme tell you. He up and after me. And I went high-tailin' through the house and outside, and he took and made a high dive off the back porch and caught me, and then did he pretty near kill me? I'll tell a man he done just that. He was kind of sore because I'd spilled his house. But this guy is funny, that wants to cry when he sees his herd break up—his herd that he don't own no hair of."

Suddenly Farrel found himself, quite outside of his own expectations, making an explanation.

"Suppose you had a big stretch of land," he said. "Suppose you have a big stock of water behind a dam. Feed it out slow, and you've got water for the whole year through. Bust the dam, and it's all gone in a day, and the ranch is thrown away. That's the way I feel. Those cows are going to spill away through the hills and split up into a hundred different sections. Who's buying them? Sam Waring?"

The heads of both Red and Delgas jerked suddenly.

"Never mind who's buying them," said Delgas. "Worry about the coin that's comin' into your own pocket, not what's comin' into mine!"

17 – Sam Waring

THEY talked for a moment as to which end of the herd they should aim at—the rear of it or the point. Because the cattle were not being pushed ahead into the mountains. There was no very great hurry, for that matter, and, since the herding by daylight would be more assured work than herding them by night, perhaps the herd would be kept here until close to daylight, which was not very far off in any event.

Finally it was decided to go down the slope to the point of the herd, where it was held by several riders at the head of the valley. They descended rapidly, and, coming out into the open, they were assailed by angry cries that ordered them to get to work. The punchers were working short-handed, in trying to hold that confused mob of steers. But one puncher, coming near enough to identify faces, raised a whoop of excited triumph at the sight of Farrel. He went off, waving his hat in circles and yelling like a wolf.

"Your punchers don't seem to think much of you, kid," said Delgas, laughing.

Farrel made no answer. Now that he was at close range, even through the rolling and thick, fog-white outpouring of the dust, he could recognize steer and cow and calf that he had handled himself. And he ran his eyes with a strange love over the long shanks of the cattle, and the straight, lean bellies, and the high, lean backs. No sign of roaching in those backs, and no sign of weakness in the quarters. They were built like deer. They could move to forage. They could run a whole day for water after they had lived on dry feed for two days.

That line of cattle was not his discovery. The Spanish had bred it in a small version centuries before; the Texans had bred it big in more recent times; but he knew the particular brand and type that suited this special bit of desert range. He knew it like a book, and he had made it. Now it was to go. It was to pour away through the mountain canyons and be dissipated like water running through a sieve. He turned his head away. He could not face the wretched thought of all that wasted labor.

He knew now, suddenly, that a man lives not for the sake of putting hard cash into his own pocket, but for the sake of some sort of creation—a store, a poem, a herd of cows. It was all the same. To build up something where there was nothing before—that was the feeling that drove decent men. And now, in stealing the herd, they were stealing a portion of his life that could never be returned to him. The dollars could go to the devil. But time is more priceless, and it was time which they would be wasting.

Delgas aimed for a flicker of firelight that was visible at the very point of the valley, where the foot of a hill was splintered into a great shagginess of rocks. When they drew closer to the firelight, a man stood up, and they saw the sheen of the long barrel of a rifle.

This fellow, who seemed to be a guard, sang out:

"Yeah? Yeah? Which way, waddies?"

"Delgas speakin'!" called Delgas.

"That don't mean nothin' to me," said the other.

"One of the others," said Red. He added loudly: "Is Rutherford around?"

"Rutherford is here," said the puncher with the rifle. "If that means much to you, he's here and he's busy."

"Take this hombre," said Delgas.

He dismounted, threw the reins of his horse to Red, and walked ahead. After a few words with the guard, he called for the others to come, and Red led Farrel to the verge of the rocks.

The fire was blazing merrily behind them. A pair of unshaven fellows had drawn off portions of the main blaze, and on these smaller fires they were frying bacon and bringing coffee to a boil. The scent of the food was good in the nostrils of Farrel. He told himself that he would remember this—that even in the midst of misery he was able to feel hunger and desire food as though he had simply come to the end of a long, hard, successful day's work.

Tethered close by, here and there, stood several good-looking horses, and a mule whose pack was being unloaded.

"Go easy with that pack, you fool!" sang out a voice.

"There's dynamite in that!"

Everyone raised a shout at the word.

Rutherford alone did not stir. He was sitting cross-legged in front of a flat slab of rock, counting out stacks of greenbacks and weighing them down, one after another, with stones. Beside him stood the big, rounded paunch and the fat face of Sam Waring, crook extraordinary.

After the confusion caused by the word about dynamite had died down, Delgas came close up and leaned over Rutherford.

"We've got Danny Farrel," he said. "We nearly got Silver, too."

"You nearly got hell," said Rutherford, without looking up, continuing his count.

"Farrel was signaling him," said Delgas. "We waited, and Silver came right up the hill, but Farrel managed to kick the hammer of my gun, and the shot scared Silver away like a wild duck."

"You talking about Arizona Jim? You talking about Jim Silver?" demanded Waring, shifting the butt of his cigar rapidly across his wide mouth.

"That's the hombre," said Delgas.

"I don't want any part of him!" said Sam Waring hastily.

He threw out both hands in a great gesture to emphasize his point.

"I don't want any part in him at all!" he shouted.

"I told you he was on deck," said Rutherford.

"You told me you'd have him under cover," answered Waring.

"The fool ought to be," said Rutherford. "We left him under cover, and he should have stayed there; but—well, I've felt in my bones that I'd have it out with him, before long."

"Have it out with him by yourself," remarked Waring. "I don't want any part of him. He's 'Mr Silver,' and 'your honor,' and anything he wants, so far as I'm concerned."

"Oh, shut up, Waring," said Rutherford. "You're not going to pull out because of Jim Silver."

"If I'd known he was to be on the loose," said Waring, "I'd never a' worked into this here deal. I'm a peaceable man. I don't want any hell for pepper in my soup, thanks. I'm no fightin' man, Rutherford, and you know it."

"You've got plenty of thugs along to do your fighting for you," said Rutherford.

"I'm an old man," answered Waring, who looked about fifty by the gray of his hair and the lines in his face. "But there's still a mite of life in me, and I don't want to drain it out. One small bullet hole will let a million dollars' worth run out and go to waste in half a second, brother. And I know it."

Something else took the attention of Waring, a moment later, and, before any one could comment on his last speech, he pointed silently at Farrel.

"That! Who brought that man in here?" said Waring.

"What's the matter with him?" asked Delgas.

"He's not in on the deal!" exclaimed Waring. "What are you fellows trying to do? Advertise me in the newspapers?"

He was very excited, and began to beat a fist into the fat palm of his hand.

"Keep your hat on," advised Delgas. "He ain't goin' to do you no harm."

"What's the matter, Sam?" asked Farrel.

"It's Danny Farrel," said Waring, "and he knows me as well as I'd know my own father. You fellows are crazy loons! Why'd you bring him in here, anyway?"

Rutherford looked up from his counting.

"Maybe he knows too much, anyway, before he saw you. If he knows too much, maybe we'll have to make him forget it, Sam."

"What you mean?" asked Waring.

Rutherford slid a forefinger, slowly, across his scrawny neck.

"Oh," groaned Waring, "do we have to have that kind of dirty work?"

"Yeah?" said Delgas. "It's your laundry that we're worryin' about, Sam."

Waring snapped his fat fingers high above his head. He was very impatient.

"It's a bad business," he said.

"Worse for Farrel than for you," added Delgas.

Waring turned his back and began to walk up and down, puffing rapidly at his cigar until a veil of white formed about his head, and he kept striding back and forth through it, making gestures of protest and annoyance.

Rutherford continued his counting, laying small stones on the heaps that he put out on the rock.

"That's a lot of kale you been carrying around with you, Waring," observed Delgas.

"Cash is better than carry," said Waring shortly.

He stopped in his pacing and pointed at Farrel.

"Something's gotta be done," he said.

"Do it yourself, then. I guess that nobody would stop you," said Delgas. "I don't love him none. My knuckles are what cut him up, the poor sucker."

"Come out with it," urged Rutherford. "You want him bumped off now, Waring?"

"Wait a minute," said Waring. "Let's think it over. Maybe something can be done with him."

The heart of Farrel, which had turned to ice, began to beat again.

"Get that canvas sack away from the fire!" suddenly shouted some one. "That's the dynamite, you fools!"

The man who was carrying the tarpaulin almost dropped it, and when he had lowered it to the ground, he jumped a rod.

"Why didn't you say so before?" he yelled. "I got a good mind—"

"You got a good mind to back up, and that's what you're goin' to do," said an unshaven brute, swaying to his feet from beside the fire.

Waring turned and raised one hand.

"Stop!" he commenced. "Brick, take that dynamite back from the fire."

"Brick," who had just risen ready for fight, snarled under his breath, but he picked up the tarpaulin and carried it to a crevice between two of the rocks.

"The point is," said Waring, "that we've got this fellow Farrel on our hands, and Jim Silver ready to poison us somewhere in the open, loose and freehanded! Silver's enough to have on the mind. And you have to tell me if Farrel can be handled."

"He can't be handled," said Rutherford, still counting. "He's one of the fools who prefer to be honest if they have to die for it."

"He's the kind of a fool," broke in Delgas, "that wants to do something noble. That's the kind that he is."

And Farrel knew that he was listening to his death sentence.

18 – A Cool Bird

ONE MAN more than those who could be counted around the fire had heard the last speech. That was Jim Silver, who had fled from the warning sound of the shot as he rode toward the signal smoke, and who had rounded through the upper shoulder of Mount Humphreys and come down again toward the face of the herd that was now in full view, sweeping into the valley.

Farrel was gone, that was clear. His own single pair of hands could probably do nothing; but, nevertheless, he did not turn back or ride for help in the town. He kept on toward the perils of one more "last chance."

A long, sharp-sided ravine gave him a good slant toward the head of the valley. When he came out of that ravine, he was low down the slope and he could see the fluttering of the firelight among rocks at the base of the hill.

Therefore, he left the great stallion behind him and came on foot, worming his way here and there, never knowing when the upthrust of a hand of fire might show him to hostile eyes. And sometimes it seemed to Silver, as he came in closer, that the light was focused upon him out of a lantern, and that eyes were fixed upon him. It seemed as though voices were raised in laughing mockery while he drew nearer. Guns must be watching him. Fingers must be curling contentedly around the polished curve of triggers.

But he came on up until the blackness of the shadows at close hand shielded him from the light of the fire, and there was only the moon to consider. That was comparatively simple, because the shadow of the next hill now sloped across half of the rock nest inside of which the fire was burning. That was why Silver was able to draw so very close up to the point of danger and of interest.

He had arrived in time to see and hear all that had recently passed. He had had the uncomfortable experience of seeing the sack of dynamite placed right before the spot where he cowered. He used it, afterward, as a better cover which enabled him to draw nearer.

So he heard the death sentence passed on Farrel, in simple words.

"Look, Farrel," said Sam Waring, striding suddenly up to the prisoner. "Don't you go and be a fool. You come along with us. I'll take care of you. You come along with me. I'll give you a regular split in the job. I'll take care of you. I don't want the blood of any kid on my hands."

"It ain't any good," argued Delgas. "There we had him tied and gagged and stretched all out, and the fool, he wants to be noble and kicks my gun and makes it go off and scare away that bird, Silver. A gent that wants to be noble," said Delgas, "ain't any use to birds like us. You know that, Sam."

"Shut up, Morrie," said Waring. "I know plenty. I'm asking the kid. It's up to you, Danny. Will you play with us?"

Silver risked being seen, as he lifted his head to stare into the face of Farrell. That face was puffed and blood-streaked. It was set, too, in hard lines of endurance. The eyes glistened as Farrel stared back at Waring.

"We've all gotta die once," said Farrel.

"Oh, hell!" said Waring, turning on his heel.

He threw up his hands, as though to ask the world's attention to the effort that he had been willing to make on behalf of this young fool.

"I told you," said Delgas.

"Yeah, you told me," said Waring. "I wouldn't believe anybody'd be such a fool. Look here, Danny!"

He whirled and faced Farrel again.

"Everybody's laughing at you, you half-wit," said he. "Don't hold out on us, Danny. Come in and play the game, will you? What's the matter with you?"

"He's nuts about a girl that cooks back there on the ranch," said Delgas. "Look at, kid," said Delgas, stepping suddenly close to Farrel. "She don't care about you. She was only givin' you a play, that's all. She'd pick up anybody. She give me the sweet eye, is what she done. She's just stringing you along."

"You lie!" said Farrel.

"You see?" said Delgas, stepping back and turning his hands palms up. "He's goin' to be noble, that's all. He's nuts about the girl, and he's goin' to be noble. She'll be married to some other sap about a week after the coyotes finish lickin' his bones, but he's goin' to die noble and believe in her to the finish."

"Shut up, Morrie," commanded Waring again. "Let me talk to him. Listen to me, kid, will you?"

Farrel looked straight a Waring and said nothing.

"I'm giving you a break," said Waring. "Wake up to it, hombre. I'm giving you a break, and you don't know it. Will you take a hand in our game?"

"Thanks," said Farrel.

"Thanks what? Yes, or no?"

"Thanks—no," said Farrel.

The hair prickled on the head of Jim Silver, as he heard that. He took out both revolvers and made his calculations. There was plenty of cover all around. He might get two or three of them before the rest were out of sight. He might even let Farrel have a chance to get to him. But after that?

Well, after that, they'd be done for. Nothing could save them—not when fellows like Delgas and Waring and Rutherford were around. For all the pretended strength of his hatred for blood, Waring was the sort of a marksman who cannot miss, and Silver knew it very well.

It was not of Rutherford's pale face that Silver thought most, now. It was of the bucktoothed smile of Steve Wycombe, his upper lips caught and hanging. That was the way he must be smiling now. For it began to look a good bet that all the men he wanted to get would go down—Rutherford, Delgas, and Jim Silver, all three.

Decent men, it seemed to Silver, have fewer brains than rascals. Otherwise, such an inspiration could never have come into the head of Steve Wycombe.

"You won't play with us?" repeated Waring.

"He won't," said Delgas. "He's scared stiff, and he's dyin' on his feet with fear; but he's gotta be noble, the sucker! Give him the works and get rid of him, will you?"

"You talk as if you'd like the job," Waring said. "Take it, Delgas. I give you my share in him."

"Am I goin' to stick pigs for you, Sam?" demanded Delgas. "Since when, I'd like to know!"

"All right," said Waring. "It'll have to be fixed some way. One of my boys will turn the trick, I suppose. Too bad, though, because he's a pretty good kid."

"Sam," said the voice of Rutherford.

"Keep your eye on Farrel," said Waring to the man called Brick. "He needs plenty of watching. One fellow like that, loose in the world, could spoil my future for me."

"Your future's like a fish a week out of water," said Brick gloomily, but he took up his post beside Farrel.

"What is it, Harry?" Waring was asking, while Silver breathed more easily for the moment.

He began to cudgel his brains. He had a conviction that, no matter how tight the pinch, no matter how hopeless a situation might be, there was always some way of solving it, some way of cutting the Gordian knot. Now he felt fairly baffled, but baffled he must not be.

He began to strain his wits. Then he told himself that ideas would not come in that fashion. Instead, he must lie still, passively, and wait for whatever would come to him. So, little by little, he relaxed.

There was a promise that he might gain a little time, for Rutherford and Waring were wrangling hotly.

"Sorry, Sam," Rutherford said. "Looks as though you're just fifty-seven hundred dollars short in the payment."

"Hey!" shouted Waring, starting violently.

Rutherford was not in the least moved. He lifted his pale face and studied Waring with a calm interest.

"What you mean by fifty-seven hundred short?" demanded Waring.

"I mean five thousand and seven hundred dollars and no cents," said Rutherford. "I mean that money's short."

"It was in the pile when I handed it to you," declared Waring.

Very gradually a smile spread over the features of Rutherford. He shook his head.

"It was in the satchel when I handed it to you," said Waring.

Rutherford kept on smiling.

"What the devil's the matter, Harry?" asked Waring "You don't think that I'd try to cheat you, do you?"

"You know, brother," said Rutherford, "that we all look for a little inside profit. You wouldn't call it stealing."

"Why, Harry," said Waring, "I'm kind of shocked by this here. It couldn't be that Ferris would a' hooked a handful of dough out of that satchel, could it? You don't really mean that the coin's missing, though? You're just laughin' up your sleeve at me."

Rutherford continued to smile.

"When you get through talking, Sam," said he, "just grab the extra cash and hand it over."

"You don't understand," said Waring. "Where would I get that much loose cash out of a crowd like this? Every bean that I've got is right in there. But I'll see you in a couple or three days."

"I won't be around," said Harry Rutherford. "But don't you worry about the extra money, Sam."

"No? Thanks," said Waring. "I knew you wouldn't try to hang up a deal like this on account of a measly little five or six thousand. I'll fix it with you, one day, as straight as a road."

"Of course you will," said the quiet voice of Rutherford. "You'll fix it now. I'll just take that big rock you wear in your necktie, brother."

"I'm not wearing that diamond now, Harry," said Waring.

"Not at your neck in the bandanna," agreed Rutherford. "You have it pinned under the lapel of your coat."

"What?" exclaimed Sam Waring. "How did you—"

He broke off his protesting argument and shouted with laughter.

"Hey, but you're a cool bird, Harry," he said. "Did anybody ever put anything over on you?"

"Not one, except Steve Wycombe, and he's wearing the scars of the good turn he did for me. Let's see the hard cash, brother."

"Sure," said Waring.

And the brazen cheat instantly pulled out a wallet and counted the extra cash into the hand of Rutherford.

19 – Stampede

By this time, clouds of dust raised by the milling cattle were pouring in rapid drifts across the camp fire, turning into grit the food which the men were eating, scumming the surface of the coffee. All complexions became gray in a moment. It was a fog, and not a thin fog, that surrounded the fire and that made the moon dim.

Silver, with the razor edge of a knife, slit the tarpaulin that covered the dynamite. Inside was a quantity of sawdust; inside the sawdust lay the corded sticks of the explosive, each one carefully wrapped. He took out half a dozen of them, short lengths, and found a quantity of fuse, also. That was what he wanted. He hardly dared to look at Dan Farrel, in the meantime, for the moment of Dan's death was close at hand, plainly.

He heard Red make a feeble protest.

"This here is a fellow that would keep his mouth shut," said Red. "You could trust him, Waring. If he said he wouldn't talk about you, he'd keep his word."

Waring went up to Red and laid a fatherly hand on his shoulder.

"My dear young feller," said Waring. "You're just in the make and you ain't finished, yet, or else I'd be bothered about you. I'd say that maybe you had a lot to learn about the way folks act when they're under temptation.

"Now, you take young Farrel here. I'd say that he's a fine lad and an honest lad and a lad that means well, but I wouldn't be able to tell what he might do after givin' us his word here. He might be tempted—"

Here Farrel broke in, his voice dry and harsh: "If I ever had a chance to hang the whole crew of you, I'd do it. I'd give my life to do it."

The words fell like a blow on Jim Silver. He barely heard the voice of Waring continuing: "There! You can see for yourself what things are like.

You can see for yourself that he ain't the sort of a fellow that would make a nice, reasonable bargain, is he?"

"I dunno," said Red. "I'm kind of sick, is all I know."

That was the last that Silver heard as he withdrew like a snake among the rocks. The sweeping of the dust from the herd covered him, and the thickness of the uproar of clashing hoofs and horns, the pounding, the bellowing seemed to conceal him under a blanket of noise. The sound of a cataract draws down all eyes into it, and in the same manner, perhaps, all looks would be centering now upon the milling of the herd.

So he took chances of being seen as he hurried back toward the stallion. At any moment, even in a few seconds after he turned his back on the camp-fire scene, the thrust of a knife or the explosion of a gun might be the end of Farrel.

If Farrel died, he swore that he would spend the rest of his days tracking down every man who had appeared around that fire. But all that quantity of revenge would not bring back life to Danny Farrel or ease the heart of the girl who had sent him away to do his duty on this night.

So Silver worked with frantic haste, as he kneeled beside Parade, at last, attaching to each of the dynamite sticks a fuse of the length he had decided upon. He had three sticks and three fuses, each a little longer than the other, when he finally mounted. He proposed to save Farrel, if he could, not by shooting down the men who stood around him—there were too many of these—but by sweeping the whole gang away in the current of an action that promised to carry out from their hands the entire profits of the adventure on which they had embarked.

So he rode Parade right down the gulley to the point where it shelved off to meet the valley floor and the sweeping dust clouds which drove up above the herd and circled in the light wind toward the moon. He was doubly glad of that screen of dust now.

Closely as he harkened, he had not distinguished the sound of a gun during the interim. Perhaps Rutherford and Delgas and Waring were patching up the last details of their agreement; perhaps they intended to wait until the final moment before the herd was pushed up into the hills before they killed Dan Farrel and left him on the ground to be battered by the trampling hoofs beyond all recognition.

Silver scratched a match.

"Hey, Ferris, is that you?" yelled a voice not far away. "Cut in there and do your bit! Climb into it, kid!"

Silver touched the flame of the match to the ends of the three fuses, one quite short, the others longer. He had three portions of death in his grasp then. Even Parade, steel-nerved under most circumstances, now began to dance uneasily as he saw the sparkling blue fire run sputtering up the fuses.

Silver, with a yell, drove the stallion straight at the herd.

Off to his right, he saw a rider phantom-gray in the dust, and heard the man cursing with bewildered surprise. The sweep of the outer flank of the milling cattle came into clearer view. He saw the dull sheen of their eyes, the tossing of the horns like crooked spears continually stabbing at the air, and full at the mass of them he threw the dynamite with the shortest fuse attached.

It had seemed to him that he had waited until the fire was fairly kissing the dynamite, and yet there was no uproar of an explosion. Instead, the dynamite rolled under the feet of the first steers and was instantly out of sight.

He turned the stallion, with a groan, to try again farther down the head of the crowding cattle. Then, behind him, he heard the explosion and felt the weight of it in the air about him, a soft and ponderous blow that made Parade leap like a hare.

Glancing back, he could see several of the steers down, struggling. Those poor, mangled creatures would never rise again. But from about them the rest of the cattle were pressing back, throwing up their heads, trying to climb over the backs of the steers which still were surging up from the depths of the valley. It seemed to Silver that he had done no more than throw a bucket of water against the sweep of a sea, so small was the reaction.

But he went on, yelling like a fiend.

The second fuse had burned short. He set his teeth, counted three, and flung it. It burst in the very air, flattening several animals. He went on and cast the third stick far over against the farther side of the valley's head, into the thick of the steers.

Again some of the poor creatures went down. But the rest were turning rapidly to escape these thunderbolts. With a frantic bawling the entire front of the herd wheeled and pressed back. It was slow work. The mass of the cattle remained before the terrified vanguard, a living wall against retreat unless the panic should spread to them.

Right and left, now, Silver saw riders making toward him. He heard the shouting of the many voices. He thought he could make out the tremendous uproar of Delgas above the rest, thundering like a wounded bull.

For his own part, Silver was pushing close in behind the van, close into the stifling fog of dust through which he was only vaguely aware of the twisting, swirling masses of confused backs, and of swaying horns. It made him dizzy, like looking into the fling and leap of water as it runs down a cataract.

He shouted; he yelled; he fired guns in the face of any beast that chanced to turn back toward him. Far before him, he could hear the rear guard of cow-punchers shooting their Colts to keep the cattle near them from turning in a stampede.

Close beside him, a voice drove in, screaming out curses. A bullet touched his hat, jerked at it with a small but deadly touch. He shot that fellow out of the saddle and saw the frightened cow pony go crash into the wall of the herd.

But it was no longer quite a solid wall. It was splitting up. A shudder was working through the mass of the steers; the solidity of the throng opened into cracks that filled, closed, opened again. It was like watching a quicksand at work. Then all that quicksand began to flow, slowly, more quickly, as fast as a man could run, as fast, almost, as a horse could gallop.

Parade followed close to the swinging tails.

It was dangerous work. The dust streamed back at them in dense up-pourings that blinded the eyes. But eyes were needed to see the crumpled, red-washed bodies that lay on ground, here and there, where some unlucky steer had fallen and been beaten instantly to death by heavy hoofs.

Through rifts in the flying dust, Silver, muffled to the eyes in a bandanna so that breathing could be possible, saw the walls of the ravine, one black with shadow, one gleaming with the moon.

That gleaming wall he saw thrust out a straight-faced bluff where the valley narrowed a trifle. It was easy to see and easy to avoid, with the moon striking the front of it as if it glanced from white marble; but the steers could not turn, no matter what they saw through the blindness of their fear. There was no shifting inward, because the little valley was blocked from side to side, jammed with the sweep of the running cattle. There was no halting or turning back, because the rearward cattle picked up those in front and hurled them forward.

So Silver saw a living wave strike the face of that bluff, pile instantly high on it, bank the angle full with the dead, and so shunt the remnant safely past the danger point.

It was enough to break a man's heart to see good beef wasted in this fashion, but in a moment like that the salvation of the entire herd was what Silver had to think of.

Then, before him, he saw the herd thinning. He knew by that that they were approaching the mouth of the valley. Presently the dust cloud thinned away. Breaths and puffs of sweet, fresh air came to him like a salvation. The myriad beating of the hoofs no more kept the ground quivering beneath him, but scattered far and wide.

He rode off to the right, drawing up Parade to a canter. He was off to the side of the valley's mouth when he saw other riders fly by him, half revealed through the dust, sweeping on to head off the stampede, if possible.

But Silver, drawing back into a corner of the hills, observed the onward course of the living avalanche which he had started and was content. Stampeding steers are not easily turned, and they do not easily lose their momentum. Far, far away across the desert the dust cloud blew, rolled small and smaller, dwindled, seemed no more than an obscure smoke that was barely visible beneath the moon.

After it had dwindled like this, he saw, from his shadow-filled cranny, the thing that he had hoped to see.

Out of the valley's mouth proceeded a small group of riders, among whom he recognized Rutherford, Waring, and Red. With them came a tall fellow who sat with his hands tied behind his back and had his horse's lead rope attached to Waring's saddle.

That was poor Danny Farrel. The stampede had given him the grace of a little more life, but in a way it seemed to have made his death almost the more sure. For every one of the group would be savagely hungry for blood after the disappointment of that night.

20 – Waring's Proposition

MOONLIGHT swallows things quickly, even when there is the clear air of the desert for it to shine through. That cavalcade disappeared and left an ache in the back of Silver's brain as he recalled the straight back and the high head of poor Dan Farrel.

Why had they saved him? Perhaps—it had been Silver's hope from the first—because with the cattle scattered and Jim Silver abroad to make further mischief, Rutherford and the rest would be glad to have him alive as a bargaining point.

It was in this hope that he calmly unsaddled Parade that night, wrapped himself in slicker and blanket, and, with the saddle for a pillow went to sleep.

Twice Parade wakened him, snuffing close to his face and stamping to give the alarm. Once it was merely a wolf that had come out on the shoulder of the hill to look down on man. Once it was for some taint that had blown to Parade on the air; but, when Silver could see nothing, he lay down again and slept peacefully until the sun put a warm hand on his face.

He got up, washed his eyes and mouth with water from his canteen, swallowed a few drops of the liquid, and then pulled up his belt two notches to take the place of breakfast. Parade, grazing the tough gramma grass at a short distance from his master, came back and stood with downward head, dozing, while Silver smoked a cigarette.

After a time the stallion went off to graze again, while Silver waited through the hot hours. For once in his life he had no plan beyond that waiting.

A glad man was Jim Silver when, late in the morning, he saw a rider jog toward him across the sands from the direction of the ranch house. He watched the little puffs of dust that squirted out from the feet of the horse as the rider drew nearer. Then he made out the bulky form of none other than

Sam Waring, who stopped at a considerable distance and waved a white rag or handkerchief slowly back and forth.

Silver grinned as he watched. He took out a bandanna and waved that in answer. Waring seemed still in doubt, but finally he came on slowly. Twice and again he paused for further thought, but at length he rode straight up to the place where Silver sat on a rock, inhaling the smoke of a cigarette.

The hesitation that had appeared in Waring's actions was not in his speech. He summoned a broad smile and waved his hand at Silver.

"All safe and friendly, brother, eh?" he asked cheerfully.

Silver made a noncommittal gesture.

"It seemed a good time for a little talk," said Waring, "so the boys sent me out to find you. They thought you'd be around this valley, somewhere—and here you are."

"Get off the horse and sit down, Waring," suggested Silver. "You don't look happy there. You're too high in the air."

Waring laughed as he got down to the ground.

"I ain't what I used to be in a saddle," he confessed. "There was a day when I fitted onto a hoss like a clothespin onto a line. But that day's gone, and now I'm kind of swelled up and wabbling with fat."

He sat down on a rock near Silver, took off his hat, mopped his fleshy brow, and went on:

"I've come to talk about young Farrel, of course."

Silver nodded.

"Being a friend of yours," said Waring, "nacherally you want him out of hock."

Silver nodded again.

"And the fact is," said Waring, "that he's been in a good deal of danger."

"Has he?" said Silver.

"There was a time last night," said Waring, "when some of the boys wanted to bump him off before he had a chance to get loose and spread the news around about the way they'd been cutting up. If it hadn't been for me talking on his side, something bad would sure a' happened to him."

"Thanks," said Silver. "I was behind a rock near the dynamite sack, Waring, when you were interceding for him. I know the kind things you said."

He looked into the eyes of the fat man, but Waring merely laughed.

"You're a fox, Silver," said he. "A regular silver fox, is what you are, and it would take a brighter man than poor old Sam Waring to put anything over on you. But, all jokes aside, young Danny Farrel is in a heap of hot trouble."

"He is," agreed Silver.

"So doggone much trouble that something had oughta be done about it, and that's why I'm out here to talk to you, Jim!"

"Make your proposition," said Silver.

"It's this way," said Waring. "Everybody knows that Silver ain't the sort of a fellow to turn down a friend. Everybody knows that you're the sort who sticks by a partner to the finish. Well, then, this is what we've got in mind: On the one side there's a few cows. On the other side there's a friend. You can make your choice, and I know what choice you'll make."

"It's this way," said Silver. "If I agree to let you fellows get away with the cattle, you'll let me have young Danny Farrel—and his girl beside him."

"Aw, the girl don't count. We throw her in. Sure, you can have her," said Waring. "You don't think that we'd make trouble for a woman, do you, Jim? Do you think that we're that sort of snake?"

"I think," said Silver, "that you'd throttle a baby in a cradle if you could make a hundred dollars out of it."

"Come, come, come!" protested Waring, holding up a fat, soft hand. "You wouldn't wanta talk rough, Jim, would you? The fact is that you and me have to talk business, and it don't help business along to start calling names. You know that, I suppose?"

"I suppose I do," said Silver. "But I've named the proposition, haven't I?"

"Exactly," said Waring. "We've got your young friend. A fine, manly, honest kid, Silver. As manly and honest as I ever seen. It would do me good to see a kid like that wearing my name, matter of fact. But, when all's said and done, business is business. How does it sound to you?"

Silver rubbed his toe in the dust. "I could spoil your business for you, Waring," said he. "I could get to town and gather in plenty of men in a posse to wreck the job for you before your boys will ever be able to gather those cows out of the stampede."

Waring scowled at him with a sudden loss of his cheerful veneer.

"You've raised hell already," said he. "You've spilled more'n a thousand dollars of good beef out of the cup already. It's lying dead back there in the valley to feed the buzzards, and that's your work. What put it into your head to use dynamite to start the stampede?"

"They laid the dynamite down in front of me," said Silver. "You can't expect me to refuse a gift like that, can you?"

Waring stared.

"And then you rode right in through the bunch and got at the cows. Ferris is laid up bad. He's shot inside the shoulder, and he might not pull through."

"I'm sorry for that," said Silver, frowning.

Sam Waring answered suddenly: "Why lie about it, Silver? You're glad that you nicked one of the boys. It pleases you the same's it would a' pleased them to put a slug in you. I ain't wrong about that."

"You are," said Silver. "I've seen men that I'd like to drift some lead into. But I hate to shoot at a man I don't know."

Waring grunted his disbelief as he rolled a cigarette.

"How did you happen to have that dynamite along?" asked Silver.

"Ferris again!" exclaimed Waring. "The fool only got what he deserved. He was on a prospecting trip, him and a mule. We come across him in the hills, and we picked up him and our bad luck and brought 'em both along to help out. A lot of help he was. But come on, Silver. Make your bargain."

"I give up a third of the cattle for the sake of one man?" said Silver.

Waring winced, as though he felt the force of this argument.

"Well," he said, "that's the proposition, and I gotta stick to it."

Suddenly Silver nodded. "I'll make the exchange," he said.

Waring heaved a breath of relief.

"Well," he said, "that's great. I gotta admit that you're a reasonable gent to do business with. Mighty reasonable. We'll just run the cows out of the desert and off the ranch into the hills, and then you can have your partner. You can have him safe and sound."

Silver smiled.

"Hey, what's the matter?" asked Waring.

"You keep him till you've got the cattle where you want 'em, eh?" queried Silver.

"What's the matter with that? Mean that you don't trust us, old son?"

Silver shook his head. "If I let you get the cattle through the hills, you may turn Farrel over to me, but he'll be a dead man when I find him."

"I swear," said Waring, lifting one hand and rolling up his eyes with a solemn shake of his head. "I swear—"

"Don't do it," said Silver. "Take your hand down and don't swear. It doesn't work with me, Waring."

The fat man slowly dropped his hand. A faint stain of red crawled up his throat and over his face. He said nothing.

"I'll have to make another sort of deal," said Silver. "I'll have to have security that you'll turn Farrel over to me if I let the herd go."

"What sort of security?" asked Waring.

"A man for a man. If Delgas or Rutherford will put themselves in my hands, I'll take 'em as bail for Farrel."

"Delgas—Rutherford—you ain't crazy, Silver, are you?" shouted Waring.

"It's the only way I'll talk business," said Silver.

Waring stared at him, started to talk, changed his mind. Then he stood up. "How long before you expect an answer?" he asked.

"Sunset," said Silver. "If one of 'em rides out from the house at sunset, I'll know that he's come to be bail for Farrel, and the deal goes through."

Waring, his head fallen in thought, rode off without another word.

21 – Trapped

SILVER waited out the hours of that long afternoon among the sun-baked hills. He was very hungry, and a big jack rabbit obligingly poked its foolish head up above a rock to make a dinner for him. He took off the head of the rabbit with a .45 caliber slug and broiled the flesh over a small fire. He ate it slowly, because he had very little water to wash it down. Parade was now so thirsty that he had stopped grazing altogether, so Silver took him across country to the verge of the big tank and let him drink from that muddy water.

In the sunset he came back toward the ranch house and stopped five hundred yards from it, where he began to drift the horse forward and backward. Nearer he dared not come, for there were men in that outfit to whom even five hundred yards was not impossible with their favorite rifle. He depended on the flare and uncertainty of the light at this time of the day.

In the meantime, he scanned the horizon and saw from south and east and west approaching clouds of dust which told him that some of the punchers were bringing up the cattle that they had collected across the face of the desert. All of those dust clouds moved toward the ranch house as a focus. Some time during the night, perhaps, the big herd would be assembled, and the drift toward the mountains would start.

Already it was rather late. He had waited long, and, if he rode to get help, they might have most of the cattle deep in the ravines before he returned.

He had thought of that all during the day, but he had not dared to ride for a posse. By that means he would be able to save the herd, of course, but he would never be able to save Danny Farrel. They would shoot him out of hand at the first sign of approaching danger, of course.

But what a quandary Delgas and the great Rutherford must be in at this moment, risking, as they were, the value of both land and cattle. For, though

502

they might rush the cows through, they would certainly lose their landed acres as men outlawed for their crime.

It could only be that they hoped against hope that they would be able to sell the herd and deliver it, and then that they could dispose of Farrel and leave Silver with empty hands.

If afterward Jim Silver appeared in the law courts—though that was not his wont—then a staunch agreement between themselves would swear down his testimony in nearly any court of the law.

He thought of this grimly, as he saw the sun go down beneath the horizon without sign of anyone coming toward him from the ranch house.

A number of the punchers had gathered near the house, staring out toward the shimmering, golden figure of the stallion. Silver could see them watching, pointing, gesticulating. He could hear the dim tremors of their voices. He could hear a man calling from the bunk house, a sound like a bird in the far-away sky. But increasing dimness of the twilight thickened the air. And at last, as only a dull band of orange burned along the horizon, he knew that no one would come out to him.

The house disappeared in darkness, then was marked by a single ray of yellow light, which told him of poor Esther at work in her kitchen with ice in her heart.

He looked around the black immensity of the earth, and it seemed to him that his mind was as empty of all resources as the darkening vault of the sky. Still he could hear voices, the slamming of doors, from the house, though he could no longer make out individual figures. But some of the men were probably still there, staring across the night at him, wondering what he, poor fool, could do about it.

That was the thing. What could he do?

He could only grit his teeth and pray for an idea. So long as they held poor Danny Farrel, they held Jim Silver, also, and they were clever enough to know this. That was what forced him to make up his mind to the impossible. He would go straight into the house of the enemy and there do what he could for Farrel.

He rode back through the night slowly, trying to sketch a plan. The house was fairly well in his mind, but now he wished that he had drawn a print of every room and every window. He had to plan, and yet there was not much to plan about. It seemed almost better to advance blindly and leave everything to chance when he came in contact with the Rutherford and Waring men.

What worried him most of all was Rutherford. The others might be surprised, taken off their feet by a sudden move; but the imagination of Rutherford was of the capacious sort which understands what other men are likely to conceive.

The shallow draw which ran out of the desert toward the house gave Silver such good cover that he could ride the gold stallion within a very short distance of the place. There he dismounted, made the tall horse lie down, and prepared to go ahead on foot.

He turned himself into a ragamuffin for the purpose. Coat, sombrero, boots, socks went into the discard. He rolled his riding trousers to the knee. He had with him the weight of his two Colts, and that was all, when he came over the edge of the draw and started for the house.

The windmill offered some sort of cover for his advance, but it was the sort of skeleton protection which would be watched by the men on guard without actually making a shield for a spy. So he gave up the thought of the windmill and went straight at the house. He had on the straight line only the almost imperceptible undulations of the ground and one good-sized cactus. It was not protection. It was hardly a hint at protection. What he would have to rely upon was the fact that people do not look for men working like snakes in the dust, as he was working now.

He was almost at the cactus, blessing the size of its three large leaves, when lantern light began to wash across the black earth around him. Not one, but several lanterns were brought, and, while he lay there behind the wretchedly imperfect shadow of that cactus, he saw a lantern nailed up at every corner of the house!

That was Rutherford. He was the fellow who would think of bathing the house with light to expose all who approached, whereas most people would have kept their eyes open in darkness and so would have hoped to trap the invader. But Rutherford had a brain.

Not only was there a light at each corner of the irregular building, but there appeared to be a man on guard there, also.

Silver lay sweating in the dust, and it was by no means the heat of the ground that caused the water to pour.

For his position seemed to him most perfectly helpless. To worm his way forward in the darkness had been dangerous and hard enough. To worm his way backward through the light until he reached the edge of the draw would be worse than madness, he was certain. Then what remained for him to do?

In his excitement, he drew a breath that was chiefly dust, and had to lie, strangling, choking, stifling, for whole minutes, controlling the convulsions of his body with a mighty effort of the will to keep from drawing a single gasping breath.

When at last he was able to breathe again, he could give his mind to an insoluble problem. He was more and more convinced that he was hopelessly trapped. There was not even a thing to hope for, except a rain and hailstorm so tremendous that it would blot out the light of the lanterns and give him a chance to crawl away through the mud, but to pray for rain under the starry sky of the desert was like praying for a miracle. Ten months might pass, here, before so much as a shower fell.

The Rutherford men were ideally placed. They had light by which to spy him out if he so much as stirred, and they had their saddle horses at hand if the least suspicious sign appeared to their eyes. They could be in the saddle and away like bullets at the first signal. The mustangs, with thrown reins to anchor them, stood in three groups near the house, four or five in a bunch. There were more than were needed, for the reason, perhaps, that Rutherford had decided to be forehanded and equipped in every possible particular.

Silver, lying flat on his face, could have groaned with despair. He heard one of the men at the nearer corners of the house saying:

"One way of looking at it, this here is a funny business—we hang out a light for a gent to shoot at us by."

"He won't shoot," said the other. "Silver ain't that kind. There ain't no Injun about him. He don't take no advantages."

"Ain't he a gunman?" asked the other.

"Sure, he's a gunman."

"Then what you mean he don't take advantages? He's faster with a gun than other folks are, and he's straighter with his shooting. That means that he's got all kind of advantages."

"I mean, he don't play 'em. When they crowd him, he fights back, and that's all there is to it."

"You sound kind of nutty to me," said the other. "Here's a gent with a list of dead as long as my arm, and you say he don't take advantages? How could he have such a record if he didn't go out for scalps?"

"You dunno the kind of a fool this bird is. He goes where the water is likely to have fish in it, and then he waits for a fish to show. He don't drop a line in. He waits for the fish to bite him, and then he bites back."

"That sounds like fool talk."

"Does it? What I mean is that he waits for the other gents to crowd him. If they won't crowd him man by man, they'll crowd him in couples or gangs. There ain't many stories of Silver hunted by single men. There's plenty of stories of him hunted by a whole crew."

"It looks to me as though Rutherford and Delgas and Waring have got him beat to a frazzle in this here business."

"Nobody's got him beat till he's ten feet buried underground, and even then he's likely to claw his way out. But there's numbers and brains against him now. There's Waring and Rutherford, to say nothin' of Delgas, that's worth a little speech all by himself."

"What is goin' to happen to Danny Farrel?"

"The same as always happens to a gent that tries to go straight when going crooked is the way the others around him are walking."

A shadow fell over Silver as he listened to the last words. That shadow struck his brain like a bullet. He hardly dared to look up, but then he saw that it was only one of the horses which had edged close to smell at the tempting green and the bristling thorns of the big cactus. If the brute suddenly took notice of a man lying on the ground and jumped away with a snort, it was apt to bring the attention of the guards to Silver.

Then he saw that the thing might be a sort of act of Providence to give him deliverance from his danger of the moment.

Someone called out at the other end of the house. One of the nearest sentries turned to watch; the other sang out in reply.

That moment Silver used to rise slowly to his feet.

He could not sit in the saddle, of course, but he fitted his knee into the stirrup leather just above the stirrup, and, with his weight resting on that support, he slid the other leg far back, hooking his toes around the pony's quarter. With his hands he gripped the saddle flaps. He was embarked. Neither his feet nor his body showed, for the moment. He was something suspended in empty air, as it were.

22 – In the House

THE great advantage was that Silver was at last off the ground. The black shadow of the body of the horse was as a blessing to him, but that mustang was not bestowing more than one blessing at a time. He reached around, got a good grip, and took a bite at the shoulder of Jim Silver. The tough flesh slipped from under the teeth of the horse, but it was agony for Silver. He dared not move to beat the head of the horse away, at that moment, for his knee threatened to slip out of the stirrup leather and let him down with a crash in the dust.

Having taken one nip, the horse seemed content. It began to drift on away from the cactus, moving with very short steps. And Silver discovered that the brute was moving not away from the house but toward it!

It seemed to be trying to steal away from the other animals, by the shortness of its steps deceiving the eyes of the men who watched it.

One of them sang out, "What's the matter with that fool of a hoss?"

"That's Jerry's hoss. He's gone and cinched it up loose. Look at the way that saddle's turned over!"

"I better fix it. If that hoss has to be used, it's gotta be used fast and used hard."

Steps came toward Jim Silver. He loosened the grip of his right hand, though thereby he made his hold on the horse very precarious.

"Wait a minute. Let Jerry do his own work. He's always sliding out from trouble," said the other sentry.

The footfall paused.

"Yeah, maybe you're right," said the second speaker, and turned back.

"I never seen a freckle-nosed son that was any good, anyway," said the other. "And Jerry's all over freckles."

"He's a lazy hobo," said the other sentry.

Silver, using his right hand to pluck at the mane of the mustang, tried to pull it away from the house and turn the head of the horse in another direction. But the mustang was perceptibly braced against this weight which lay along its side and therefore it naturally moved in the opposite direction. That happened to be toward the house, and nothing that Silver could do would make the pony change his mind. He dared not reach for the reins, of course.

They were now steering past the corner of the house.

"That hoss is sure a drifter," said one of the watchers. "He sure aims to stir around."

"It's Jerry own fault," said the other. "He oughta train a hoss to stand when the reins are once throwed on it."

"Yeah, he'd oughta do that. I wonder, is Delgas socking that old rye on the nose, right now?"

By this time the mustang had gone past the corner of the house. As it moved in closer to the wall, a new danger came to Silver, which was that he might now be seen by either of the guards if they chanced to make a single pace out from the wall. But now they were right beside the wall.

Silver softly dropped his feet to the ground, ducked under the neck of the mustang, and stood in front of the black, square mouth of an open window. The blaze of the lanterns struck full on him. He saw the guard off at the right, turn his head and apparently look straight at him. Yet the man in a moment turned his head once more and looked straight before him, whistling! He had seen nothing because he expected to see nothing.

Silver, the next instant, was through the black of the window and kneeling in safety on the floor of the room inside.

Safety? He could hardly call it safety to be in a house where every hand was against him, and where no hands were weak. He heard, very distinctly, the deep voice of Delgas, which was booming in another portion of the house. What a windfall it would be to Delgas and Rutherford if they could get their hands on him!

He smiled a little, as he thought of that.

Then, just outside the window, he heard a voice exclaim: "Look here! Here's a footmark in the dust. Look at it. Right where the mustang was standin'!"

Silver moved like a snake into a corner of the room and lay still.

"Yeah," said the second sentry, joining his companion. "It looks like a footprint, all right."

Then a silence followed in which the imagination of Silver conceived of the truth entering the brains of those fellows.

But presently one of them said: "Well, there ain't any footmarks leadin' up to it. You can see that for yourself."

"Sure I can. But I wanta know how this here mark came."

"I dunno. Maybe it dropped down out of the sky."

"Don't talk like a fool. There ain't anybody around this house that'd be likely to go without boots, is there?"

"Well, how would a mark like that come there? You think that Silver made it?"

"I dunno. I ain't thinking."

"I reckon you ain't, Slim."

"All I know is that it's a funny thing that that mark's on the ground. I dunno what to make of it."

"Maybe an angel made it. Jumped down out of the sky and stamped on the ground, and jumped up into the sky ag'in. Maybe there's an angel laughin' at us right now."

"Aw," said Slim gruffly, "shut up, will you?" His voice entered the room, as he spoke, and now he scratched a match. Silver, curled up in a corner behind a chair, covered his man with a Colt and prayed that he would not have to shoot.

The flame of the match revealed a long, sallow, evil face, and a gaunt neck with an Adam's apple that moved up and down like a fist.

Slim presently tossed the match over his shoulder and straightened.

"I was just thinking," he said.

"That's likely to be kind of hard on you," said the other.

"Leave me be," said Slim. "I'm goin' to go and report this here."

"Are you? You'll catch it if you do. There's some of the boys that think you ain't too bright already, Slim, and if you start in talkin' about angels that leave their footprints on the ground—well, there'll be trouble!"

"Hold your trap," said Slim, "or I'll slam it shut for you. I'm goin' to tell Rutherford and see what he'll have to say."

The footfall departed with a soft jingling of spurs.

Silver looked desperately about him in the dark of the room. He could not stay there. Where could he stay in the place when once the word was brought to the great Rutherford? The active wit of that man would not fail to hitch importance to the mystery of that footprint in the dust.

Silver found the knob of a door and opened it upon the dark of a hall. Through the darkness, voices came to him intimately, dwelling in his ear. He saw the long yellow-red slit of lamplight that showed where a door fitted poorly to its jamb.

Then, in farther distance, he could make out the sharp, high-pitched voice of Slim saying words which he did not understand, but which were undoubtedly about the mystery of that footprint. A moment later the house would be searched. There would be nothing for him except to fight as well as he could until they decided to burn him out. It would not take them very long to decide that, of course.

Another door, just a step down the hallway, yawned suddenly with a low groan of hinges. As he jerked back his head, he saw a lamp carried in the hand of Esther Maxwell, its light close to her tired face and the red blotches of her eyes.

He drew back from her sight still farther, but he called softly out of the darkness of his room, as the light walked toward him in regular pulsations down the hall.

"Esther! Esther! Do you hear me? It's Jim Silver."

He heard the catch and the long take of her breath, like a soft moan. Then he ventured to step out before her. The lamp wobbled out of her hand. He caught it. He took her by the wrists and crushed them together.

"Take hold of yourself!" said Silver savagely.

She nodded, breathless.

"They'll be hunting for me through the house in another minute," said he, returning the lamp to her hand. "Hide me somewhere. In your room is as good as the next place."

He heard the voice of Rutherford calling: "Billy! Mike! Whisky Joe!"

"Quick! Quick!" he urged her.

She tried to run past him up the stairs to show the way, but he checked her. Whatever happened, no running footfalls must be heard by those who would soon be hunting through the place for him.

They went up the narrow stairway. It had no railing for safety or comfort and it was simply bracketed out from the wall, so that squeaking was unavoidable even when he walked close to the supporting wall.

There was no hallway, only a single landing and door at the head of the steps. He opened that and glided through in the lead as a trampling of many feet came into the hall beneath and the voice of Delgas boomed:

"Who's that?"

"It's I," said the girl. "What's wrong?" Delgas imitated her stammering voice and roared with laughter.

"The little fool's goin' to fall down on her bean," said Delgas. "She's scared pink and blue, already. Well, honey, there ain't nothing wrong—yet—but if there turns out to be a man in the house, there's goin' to be a whole lot wrong. Come on, boys!"

The girl entered the room behind Silver and closed the door behind her, the light staggering in her frightened hand. She turned and looked with ghostly eyes at him.

"What can we do?" said her soundless lips.

He went across the floor like a cat, took the lamp, and put it on the center table.

Then he looked around him.

For a window there was only a pair of square holes punched into the roof, each about a foot wide. The furniture consisted of a small wardrobe, the little center table, the washstand, two narrow chairs, and an iron bedstead. There was no paint on the floor, walls, or ceiling. It was simply a bare box. The air was hot. The sun of the long afternoon had turned the room into an oven. And as the sweat trickled down the face of Silver, seeing how perfectly he was trapped, he thought once more of dead Steve Wycombe who was reaching so strongly out of the grave to draw down after him the man who had taken his life.

Then Silver turned back to the white, staring face of the girl.

"There's nothing for me to do but hide," he whispered. "There's no place for me to hide except under that bed. You do something. Sit down and write a letter. Do anything to show that you're occupied, and if they want to come in to search—don't oppose them!"

23 – The Search

H E slid under the bed. It was sufficiently wide and the shadow the lamp threw was sufficiently steep so that he would be hidden from the gaze of any except a man who leaned over and peered for him. But if they searched in the room at all, were they not sure to look carefully under the bed?

He could see the girl sitting at the center table. He could see her as far as her elbows; he could hear the rapid scratching of her pen.

"Where's Danny?" he whispered.

"Don't talk!" she gasped.

"They can't hear, if you whisper. Where's Danny?"

"In your room. With Mr Rutherford."

"What are they going to do with him?"

"Keep him. They're going to keep him to make sure that you do nothing and then—"

Even her whisper was more than she could maintain, at that point.

And Silver understood. They would keep Dan Farrel with them until the drive into the mountains had been completed and then, instead of giving him freedom, they would put a bullet through his head and leave him for the buzzards and coyotes. They would be reasonably sure that Jim Silver would not interfere so long as his friend was in their hands. It seemed to Silver, as he lay there and ran his swift eye back over the pages of his life, that all his troubles had sprung from his friendships, and yet all of those labors had not yielded him a single friend whom he cared to take with him on his adventures. Where he met a man, there he left him. His partners remained where he had found them, fixed in his memory like the mountains; only Silver went on.

He heard the girl say: "I know what you've done, and no man ever did more for a friend. I've prayed for you when I prayed for Danny."

512

"Hush!" breathed Silver, as he heard a footfall coming up the stairs.

It was a heavy step, stamping down on the boards, making the flimsy wood groan and squeak under the pressure.

Delgas beat once on the door, heavily, and then flung it open.

"Hello. What's in here?" he roared.

He came thumping into the room with the jingle of the spurs at his heels. The reek of his cigar was instantly in every corner.

"Just takin' a quiet little minute by yourself, eh?" said Delgas to the girl. "You ain't seen nothing of a long streak of poison called Jim Silver, have you?"

She said nothing. She must have been shaking her head.

"Scared stiff, eh?" said Delgas. "So doggone scared that she dunno what to do about it? Can't talk? Just stand there and wag your head? Well, I guess he ain't in here, unless he's under the bed."

The big feet of Delgas crossed the room, and he kicked at the empty space under the bed. That maneuver came so unexpectedly that Silver barely flinched his face back in time enough to escape from catching the blow.

Delgas turned again.

"There ain't anything for you to be so shakin' about," said Delgas. "He can't do you no harm, this gent Silver. Not while gents like me are around. You know why? Because I'd take care of you. You're an uncommon pretty girl, Esther, and I been noticin' you. You'd be a help to a gent. There's only one funny thing about you, and that's why you cotton to a doggone common gent like poor Danny Farrel. I'll tell you why. It's because there ain't anything to a feller like that. There ain't any sand to him, and there ain't any brains. He's in the soup, and the best way for you is to forget him and take a look around for something else in the way of a man. And when you're lookin', stop your eye a minute on Morrie Delgas. He ain't pretty, but he's got a silver lining!"

When he finished, he broke into a great, bawling laughter that filled the room and half deafened Silver. Then, still braying, Delgas went out of the room and creaked down the stairs, slamming the door behind him.

Through the flimsy partitions, Silver could hear Delgas saying: "No sign of him up there. No sign of nobody. It ain't likely he'd be fool enough to come into this house anyway, is it?"

"When you know enough," answered the voice of Rutherford, "to read the mind of Jim Silver and say what he's likely to do and what he's not likely to do, I'll take my hat off to you and go to work for you, Morrie. You weren't long enough in that room to search it."

"That's a lie," answered Delgas. "I was long enough to search the room and kiss the girl and come back again."

And the long uproar of his laughter went quivering through the house once more.

"Steady, now!" whispered Silver. "That's Rutherford coming, and he's twice the danger that's in Delgas."

There was a polite rap at the door.

"Come in!" called the girl.

The door opened.

"Sorry to bother you, Esther," said Rutherford, "but I ought to glance over this room. Delgas is a little careless."

"I've been right here," said the girl.

"He was in the house before you went up to your room," answered Rutherford.

He paused.

"I don't see where he could be, though," said Rutherford. There was another pause.

Then he asked: "Writing letters through all the excitement, Esther?"

"I had to do something," said the girl. "I've been half hysterical. Is Jim Silver in the house?"

"Excuse me a moment," said Rutherford. "I hate to do this, but little things are sometimes important."

Paper rustled. He read:

"Dearest Mother: It's high time that I should write you a letter because I haven't written for a long time and if—"

There was another pause.

"Yes," said Rutherford quietly. "I should say that you have been half hysterical—or else that you were simply scratching words down on paper for the sake of seeming occupied. It isn't that, my dear, is it?"

"Seeming occupied?" the girl stammered.

"There's nothing but the bed that could hide anything," said he.

And he walked straight toward it.

Silver hesitated a tenth part of a second. He could kill Rutherford, easily enough, but the report of the gun would bring the others, and nothing in the world could save him then.

He hooked his toes inside the cross rod at the head of the bed; he grasped the cross rod at the foot of the bed; and in that manner he was able, with a great effort, to heave himself up until his back touched the springs.

He saw the slender, pointed toes of the boots of the great Rutherford approach, shining like quicksilver. The boots paused. There was the deadly gleam of a Colt six-gun beneath the hanging edge of the coverlet. Then he saw the shadow of Rutherford sweep over the floor as he bent down.

He tensed himself to receive the shock of the bullet.

Instead, Rutherford straightened again, and walked back across the room.

"Well," said he, "I'm sorry that I've bothered you, Esther. In a time like this, with a fellow such as Silver in the offing, I have to take precautions. You understand that?"

She failed to answer. And he laughed as he said:

"You look as though a glance under your bed was worse than murder, my dear."

He went out; the door closed; and Silver relaxed once more on the floor beneath the bed.

He could not believe his escape. His brain was still spinning with the sensation of imminent death, as he watched the feet of the girl go stumbling to a chair into which she fell.

He whispered. There was no answer for a long moment.

Then, very dimly, from the outside of the house he heard a man exclaiming: "He's a regular Robinson Crusoe, old Slim is. He seen a footprint in the dust and he went and raised hell about it, was what he did. Good old Slim, he's the kind of a gent that don't let none of the small change slip."

There was laughter, after this, and then the small voice of the girl close to Silver murmured:

"We're saved, Jim Silver."

Silver slid out from beneath the bed and got to his feet.

"You'll be safe here," she said. Her face was shining. "And in the morning when they start the herd, you can get out of the house with no trouble at all."

Out of the distance, as though fulfilling a part of her words, he heard the bawling of cattle.

"And Danny?" he asked her.

The joy was struck out of her face. But she shook her head, answering: "You've tried to do more than any other man in the world would try. You can't do more. You've got to hide and be quiet."

He looked at the narrow windows.

There was no way through them, of course. There was no possible exit from the room except down the narrow, squeaking stairway. But he was determined, in some manner, to get to Danny Farrel on this night.

"There's nothing more you can do," whispered the girl urgently. "Don't try anything."

"I've got to think," said Silver.

He sat down in a chair, made a cigarette, remembered himself, and dropped the makings of it into his pocket. There was a wall of darkness before his brain, and it would not lift.

He looked at the girl.

She had grown older. She had been very pretty, before, but she was almost ugly, now, to the eye. What she had gained for Silver was a touch of inward beauty. If she were doddering in wrinkled age, she would never be less than beautiful to him, knowing what he knew of her.

And he whispered to her suddenly: "I think that I'll have luck. I don't know how. But I think that I'll have luck."

One of the cow-punchers on guard outside the house began to sing loudly. Another sentinel exclaimed:

"Shut up! Don'tcha know some of the boys are tryin' to get a wink of sleep now?"

Silver stood up from the chair. He took the hand of the girl in silence.

"Don't make a noise," he told her. "I understand what I'm about. Nobody can do anything without luck, anyway, and I'm just going to ask for an extra slice of luck now."

Then he opened the door and looked down into the black well of the hallway.

24 – Rutherford's Opinion

THE girl came after him. She dared not so much as whisper, now that the door of her room was open, but she grasped his arm with both hands.

He removed her grip and closed the door in her face. Then he lay down on his side, close to the wall, and began to work his way down the stairs, feet first. In that way, his weight was distributed over a number of the steps. He was close to the wall where his poundage would exercise the least leverage on the supporting brackets. And so, inch by inch, he wormed his way down toward the hall below.

He was nearly to the bottom when a door swung open, a broad flash of light entered the hall and streamed into the eyes of Silver. On the threshold stood Red, the light glancing through his tousled hair. After a moment he closed the door softly.

What had he heard to bring him there? What had he seen when he looked through?

Silver, standing now on the floor of the hall with a gun in each hand, waited breathlessly, but he heard no alarm given, no lifting of voices, no scurrying of quick feet. Red, it seemed, had seen nothing. Once more it was proved that a man sees only what he expects to see, and a man prone on the stairs was not what a man expects to see.

Silver went to the door of that room which he had used for lounging while he was in the house. The voices inside were those of Waring, Delgas, Rutherford, and young Danny Farrel.

They were still talking about the print of the naked foot, with Waring saying:

"The way I aim to live, gents, I don't get no dyspepsia about things that don't bother me none and ain't in my way. If there was ten thousand footprints

517

in the dust and a chance to grab ten bucks off a table, I'd take the ten bucks and let the ten thousand footprints go."

Delgas laughed at this viewpoint, heartily.

"I say the same," said he.

"Look here, Farrel," said Rutherford. "You're a lad with a brain. Whatever you think, you can't help your partner, Silver. Suppose you tell me what you think made that footprint."

"One of your own men trying to string the rest of you along," said Farrel instantly.

"You're all against me then," answered Rutherford. "And I'll tell you what I think."

"Blaze away," said Delgas.

"I think," said Rutherford, "that Jim Silver made the mark."

"Hey!" said Delgas. "Watcha mean, Harry? You mean that Jim Silver's been that close to the house and not come inside? What kind of reason have you got for it, anyway?"

"I know something about Silver," said Rutherford. "I have to study fellows like that. And it's an old saying with every man West of the Mississippi who has to live by his wits that it's better to have a sheriff and his posse after you than it is to have Jim Silver on your trail. I've thought that I'd always be clever enough to keep out of his way—but this time he's after me!"

"You don't like it, Harry, do you?" asked Waring.

"I hate it like the devil," answered Rutherford frankly.

"Got the wind up?" asked Waring, chuckling.

"I have," said Rutherford. "So would the rest of you, if you had any sense."

"Go on, brother, and clear that up for us," suggested Delgas. "Why ain't we got any sense?"

"Because if you knew Silver, you'd be as sure as I am that he left that footprint behind him."

"Go on and open up," urged Waring.

"Silver's like a sailor," said Rutherford. "When there's dangerous work ahead, he likes to go at it with bare feet. Bare feet are the best on a slippery deck. They're more silent than shoes, too."

"They ain't so good in a fire," Waring chuckled.

"Silver's are," said Rutherford.

"Wait a minute," broke in Delgas. "You mean, Harry, that Silver has the habit of going around in bare feet when he's about to raise the devil?"

"If he's going to enter a house where he wants to be as quiet as a moving shadow—yes, he'd be in bare feet."

"But he's not in the house, Harry."

"That's what you say."

"Why, man," said Waring, "ain't we looked the place over from head to heel? We ain't seen a thing!"

"Not a thing," echoed Delgas. "Not a thing, and I looked over every inch of the house myself."

"Nobody has seen anything," answered Rutherford. "Nobody saw a man come up to the house. There were four guards out there and plenty of lantern light. But one minute that dust was clear, except for horse tracks, and the next minute, there's the print of a naked foot. Do you think it was a ghost that made the mark, Delgas?"

"I dunno," said Delgas. "It beats me, is what it does."

"Somebody came up to this house and made that mark before he got through the window—or climbed up to the roof!

"Aye, the roof!" cried Delgas. "I never thought of that!"

"I did, though," said Rutherford. "I thought of the roof and ran a ladder up and climbed up to the top, but there's nothing to see on the top of the house."

"He's not on the roof, and he's not in the house. And if he came up and made his mark in the dust, then he went off again the same way he came," said Delgas. "That's the long and the short of it."

"It's the long of it and the wrong of it," answered Rutherford. "A fellow like Silver went through a lot of danger to get that close to the house, and he wouldn't turn away again before he'd accomplished something. You fellows ought to see that."

"I don't get what you're drivin' at. You have me beat," said Waring. "It kind of sounds like geometry to me, and I never was no good in funny things like that."

"Well," said Delgas, "let Harry blaze away and tell us what's what. He'll be talkin' about ghosts walkin', before long. Even Harry can be wrong, I guess."

"You think that Silver is a ghost?" asked Rutherford.

"I don't say that I think that," answered Delgas.

"Well," said Rutherford, "I can't tell you any more reasons, unless you count the feeling in my marrow bones as a reason, but I'll tell you that I'm sure that Jim Silver is in this house at this moment!"

"Hi!" yelled Waring.

Somebody started up out of a chair and crossed the room with heavy steps and stood at the door.

"You mean that, Harry?" said Delgas. "What makes you say so?"

"I've told you my reasons, and you say they're no good. I say that Jim Silver made that print in the dust, and that Jim Silver made that print just before he slipped through the open window into the house. We searched the place and we couldn't find him, any more than our guards outside were able to see him walk right up to the house through the lantern light. But in spite of that, he's somewhere in this house."

"Where?" shouted Delgas.

"I don't know. Outside that door, perhaps—from the feeling that's inside my spine!" said Rutherford.

"Doggone if it don't begin to scare me—it's a regular ghost story!" exclaimed Waring. "It makes me sweat, though I feel pretty cold. Is that fellow in on it? Farrel, have you got a hand in this?"

"How could he have a hand in it?" asked Delgas. "Waring, you're nutty."

"What Harry says is enough to make any man nutty," cried Waring. "We been over this place with a fine-toothed comb, and now we start in talkin' about ghosts. I ain't no hero even when it comes to fightin' men, and I lay off when it comes to ghosts. I don't want no part of 'em!"

"If you got this idea in your head," said Delgas, "what you want us to do about it, Harry?"

"I don't know," said Rutherford. "We've got the house guarded. There's nobody asleep except in the bunk house, and they're ready to turn out and ride at any minute. I don't very well know what more we can do."

"Except to keep our eyes open," suggested Delgas.

"That's it," said Rutherford. "We've got to keep on the alert, my friends."

"It makes me nervous, though," said Waring. "Delgas, get away from that door. You act like you was afraid that somebody would walk in through it. If Jim Silver can do what you gents say, he don't need to open the door. He'll slide in through the keyhole, and turn out of a mist into a man, like they do in the fairy tales."

"Yeah?" said Delgas. "I dunno."

The door jerked open so rapidly that the gesture was almost too fast for Jim Silver, even. He had barely time to snatch out a revolver as the door pulled wide and Delgas stood scowling on the threshold.

Silver beat the heavy butt of a revolver into the center of that scowl. As Delgas fell senseless on his back, Silver stepped over the body and took the remaining pair under the muzzles of his guns.

25 – A Beaten Crew

RUTHERFORD'S first gesture was a flick of the fingers that nearly touched the handles of his gun beneath his coat. But his thought was faster still. It saw that he was well-covered, and his second thought brought the hand away again. He sat leaning forward a little in his chair, looking not at the leveled Colt but into the steady, gleaming eyes of Silver. They were worth seeing. A changing yellow light glowed and sank and rose again in them.

Big Waring had got his hand as far as the gun on his hip, and there his grasp froze.

It was strange that a face could change so suddenly. All his jowls and the hanging flap of the flesh beneath his chin were struck stone-white, and all about his mouth was white, too. His upper lip began to work. And his great red nose stood out like a thing painted with blood, and his eyes were as bright as the eyes of a hawk. One could tell by the look of them that the spirit in the man was greater than any professions he made of courage. Whatever his faults were, he was a fighting machine.

"Here we are again," said Silver.

He kicked the door shut behind him.

"Stand up and come over here, Danny," he commanded.

Farrel rose. He was shaking from head to foot. He was the only man in the room who seemed close to a break-down.

"Don't get between me and either of them," said Silver.

Farrel edged around the wall as though a great fire were blazing in the center of the room. He had to take short steps because of the rope that was fastened about his knees. His hands were tied behind his back.

"You two," said Silver, "turn and face the wall."

521

He added: "Hoist your hands, first. And see that the hand you lift from that hip is empty, Waring. I'm watching you a little harder than I'm watching Rutherford, in case you're in doubt about it."

Starting to turn, Waring and Rutherford looked at one another. They paused and seemed to consult with glances. Then they kept on turning until they were facing the wall. They lifted their hands high above their heads and stood rigid. The tail of Waring's coat was hitched up almost to the small of his back, and his big-handled revolver showed.

Silver said: "I'm going to shift one gun into my pocket and keep you fellows covered with the right-hand gun only. If you want to try a sudden break, that'll be your opportunity."

He slipped one gun down between his legs, as he spoke. A shudder went through the body of Waring. Rutherford, who seemed to read the mind of his companion, barked suddenly:

"Don't be a fool, Waring. You'll get the pair of us killed out of hand, the first thing you know."

So Waring stood fast, but the noise of his heavy breathing was loud through the room.

Silver took out a knife, pressed the spring that made the blade fly out, and, without taking his eyes from his double target, found the ropes that tied the hands of Dan Farrel.

When Farrel was free, he snatched the knife from Silver, cut the tie rope that bound his knees together, and leaned over Delgas.

"This fellow first, Jim?" he asked.

"Take him first," agreed Silver.

He gave one glance downward to the bleeding face of Delgas. It sagged as though the blow on the forehead had smashed all the other bones of the countenance so that the features were as soft as putty.

Farrel threw the man's coat open and took away the guns from the holsters beneath the pits of the arms. He took a bit of the rope which had been used on him and trussed Delgas hand and foot. The fallen man was coming to. He breathed like one out of breath after being in water, making a heavy puffing sound.

Still his eyes were not open when Farrel left him and went across the room to the other pair. They had not stirred. Only, as the shadow of Farrel swept across the wall, Waring said half aloud:

"Somebody gets it, for this."

His big, fat body was still quivering. His pretended humility left him. He was the fighting beast pure and simple, overlaid with certain layers of blubber.

Farrel got the guns, and from Waring a long, straight-bladed knife that could apparently be used for throwing as well as for handwork.

After that, he procured more rope and made the two fast. He had finished that task and armed himself with a pair of guns when the voice of Red came down the hallway, softly singing. His hand fell with a respectful knock at the door.

"Come!" called Silver.

The door opened, with the voice of Red coming cheerfully through the gap before the way was clear to his eyes.

"The herds are coming up," he said, "and we're ready to start running 'em at the—"

He had the door open by this time. He could see his three leaders helplessly tied, and the guns of Silver were hardly a yard from his breast. He put out his head in a queer way, like a rooster stretching his neck before crowing. Then he began to hoist his hands. They were level with his shoulders before Silver said:

"You see the lay of the land, brother?"

Red nodded convulsively.

And he whispered immediately afterward, under his breath: "I had the hunch right from the start. I had the hunch that I wouldn't be able to push the thing through. I knew from the start that the crooks would go down—fool that I am!"

"Jim, don't do him any harm," said Danny Farrel.

He moved up a hand toward his own bruised face.

"Except for Red, I'd have every bone in my body broken," said Farrel. "I'd be dead by this time, I guess, or worse than dead, if Delgas had had his way with me, but Red stood in between."

"Did he?" asked Silver.

His cold eye ran slowly over the body and then over the face, over the frightened, staring soul of the cow-puncher.

"Talk up for yourself, Red," said Silver. "Any reason why you shouldn't go where the other three are going?"

Red started to speak, thought better of it, locked his jaws. He thrust out his head still farther and looked Silver suddenly in the eyes.

"You go to the devil," said Red.

At that, Silver laughed.

"Not going to make any excuses, Red?" he asked.

The thick shoulders of the cow-puncher shrugged.

"Well," said Silver, "I'll tell you what. You just ease yourself outside the door and go tell the other boys that the game's up. We've got the three of 'em. We've got them, but if the rest of the boys want to take their horses and high-tail out of these diggings, nobody will stop 'em. Understand?"

Red nodded.

"Get out!" commanded Silver.

Red hesitated one longer moment. Then he backed through the door with his hands still held high. He kept on backing till the dark of the hall was about to swallow him, and Silver slammed and locked the door in his face.

He turned and sat down.

Delgas woke up with a start and began to babble: "Come on, boys! Come on! Down with 'em!"

"Oh, shut up," said Rutherford. "Don't you know you're licked with the rest of us?"

Delgas sat up, and started at Silver.

"It's no good," he said. "You done some mind reading, Harry—and Silver was in the house all the time."

"Sure he was in the house," snarled Rutherford.

Waring sank his big chin on his chest and stared down at the table. His rage had not grown less. When his eyes stirred, they showed smoking fire.

"Beaten," he said, "like three curs."

"It looks to me as though we can send you fellows up for close to life," Silver said. "Cattle rustling doesn't go down very well in this state."

Rutherford was staring at Silver in silence. His eyes could not move from the face of the big man.

But Delgas said: "We'll find our way out of that."

"It looks to me," said Silver, "that we can make some sort of an agreement out of this thing."

He was interrupted by a sudden outburst of yelling from the men beyond the house. Someone fired three shots through the outer wall of the rooms and roared:

"Rutherford! Rutherford! Speak up and let's know the truth about it!"

"Hello!" called Rutherford calmly. "That you, Lefty?"

"It's me, and what—"

"Shut up," said Rutherford. Lefty was still.

"I'm tied hand and foot," said Rutherford. He took out the words one by one, like a showman exhibiting his wares. The deliberation with which he spoke was apparently a sign of the exquisite agony of shame which he was enduring. He could not grow paler, because his face was normally as pale as a bone, but his mouth kept working slightly at the corners.

"You're tied hand and foot?" howled Lefty. "Where's Delgas then? Is what Red tells us the straight of it?"

"Red tells you the straight," said Rutherford.

A torrent of cursing came from Lefty, who finished: "What's happened?"

"I've been a fool," said Rutherford. "I've been handled like a baby. There's nothing I can do. You boys take care of yourselves, because Jim Silver has won once more!"

Lefty departed. He bade no farewell, but his going was announced by the diminishing volume of his voice as he went off, cursing at every step A moment later, with a wild whooping, the whole body of the cow-punchers started to circle the house, and the louder they yelled, the faster they fired their revolvers into the building.

Nearly every one of the bullets ranged through the house from side to side. One struck the table and split it clear across. Another peeled a great splinter off the floor, slapping it up against the wall. Another smashed the knob of the door, striking out a chime as if from a bell. Still another slug took the hat off Waring's head.

Danny Farrel shrank into a corner. It was notable that not one of the other four so much as stirred in his place. Silver occupied himself, during the uproar, with making a cigarette for Delgas. He put it between the lips of Delgas and lighted it. Delgas nodded his thanks as the horde of cow-punchers and ex-convicts ran yelling off across the desert.

"All right," said Silver, "we can talk business now. The boys have gone. Waring, I suppose you're the most poisonous of the gang. We'll take enough of your money to pay for as many steers of mine as are missing, but I don't think we'll take your scalp. Rutherford, you and Delgas have one easy way out. You've tried to do more harm, here, than you've managed to wangle, but—"

A door slammed. The steps and the voice of the girl rapidly approached the room.

Silver's nerves for the first time showed that they were ragged. He jerked a thumb over his shoulder.

"Go and stop that noise!" he commanded Farrel.

Dan Farrel left the room. As he opened the door, Silver could hear the girl crying out in a frenzied panic.

The door shut, and Silver sighed with relief. He found that Waring was looking at him with a queer, twisted smile.

"You don't like the females, Silver, eh?" he asked. "Maybe not," answered Silver.

"That's a weakness," said Waring. "And I'm glad to know that you've got one. But, believe me, brother, the bigger you are and the longer you take, the harder you'll fall for 'em, one of these days. Go on and talk your business. I've lost a lot on this job, and I'm going to call myself lucky to get out without losing more blood than dollars."

26 – The Hand from the Grave

THE END of the thing was in sight. Silver was quick about it. He merely said: "Delgas, you and Rutherford got in on this thing for nothing. It was Steve Wycombe's idea to hook the three of us. Well, you almost snagged me, and just slipped up."

"Where were you?" said Delgas.

"Hanging onto the rods under the girl's bed," said Silver, and smiled on them.

They heard in silence. Rutherford swayed his pale face from side to side.

"Yeah," said Delgas. "All the big things come easy."

"Now, then," said Silver, "I've plenty of stuff on you, out of this deal. I can have you sent up. But I'm giving you a break."

"Show me the break, and then I'll believe it," answered Delgas.

"Listen and learn," said Silver calmly. "Delgas, all you need to do is to sign a little paper that I'll draw up for you. That paper deeds your share of the ranch to Danny Farrel. Understand?"

"Hey," said Delgas, "why should I deed my share to that bum. He ain't the one that handed me the rap! Deed it to you, you mean?"

"To Farrel," said Silver. "Except for him, the job would never have gone through."

He himself sat down at the table and took pen and paper. Rapidly he wrote, in a hand strangely small and swiftly flowing. When he had ended, he passed the paper to Delgas.

"How does that sound to you?" Silver asked.

"Yeah, I'll sign," said Delgas. "Same for Harry?"

"Ask him," said Silver.

"Same for you, Harry?" asked Delgas.

Rutherford merely smiled. "The big hombre knows me better than I thought," he declared.

"What's that mean?" asked Delgas. "Have I gone and missed anything? I won't sign, then. I ain't signed it yet, anyway."

"You'll sign, you flat-faced fool!" said Rutherford. "I mean, the big boy knows what's in my mind. I don't take anything but lead from him."

Silver opened the door and called. Danny Farrel answered at once with a joyous voice, and the girl's cry of triumph joined with the sound.

"Danny," Silver said, "get a pair of horses. Put Esther on one of 'em, and clear out. Don't come back to this place before morning. Stay five mile away from it, unless you want to take a chance on your hide. Get out fast."

The girl's voice began to protest, but Farrel could be heard to say:

"Whatever he says is good enough for me. Come on. We'll ride when Silver tells us to."

"I dunno what the gag is," said Delgas, agape.

Waring had closed his eyes. The motion of his lower jaw against his chest made his head sway up and down.

"They're going to have it out, first," he said. "They're going to shoot it out, brother. Those two hombres ain't made to live and circulate. Not on one little earth like this. The continents is too frequent, and the oceans is just wet places to step across, for birds like them."

"I guess we can agree, Harry," Silver said.

"I guess we can," said Rutherford. "I'll sign if you'll fight for it afterward, Silver."

"I'll fight for it," said Jim Silver.

He sat down to write, once more, and completed the second paper, by which Mr Harry Rutherford legally transferred his rights to the Wycombe ranch to Daniel Farrel. When he had ended, he took two revolvers, laid one at each end of the table, and set Rutherford free from the ropes. He kept a gun in his hand until Rutherford had signed his name.

"Funny thing," said Waring, as he looked on. "Now you've done the job for him, he could let the daylight into you, Harry."

"He's an honorable man, though," answered Rutherford. His malice twisted his smile as he flung the pen down on the floor.

"What happens?" he asked.

"Go back to that opposite wall," said Silver.

Rutherford went back to the opposite wall. Silver faced him. The table was exactly between them, and in front of each, a stride away, was a loaded gun.

"Stand a few inches away from the wall," said Silver.

Rutherford obeyed.

"That's to even things up," said Silver. "I'm taller than you are and I could reach farther. Now, Harry, I'll just toss this gun aside, and when I do that, we'll both go for the guns. Is that right?"

"Right!" said Rutherford.

He looked aside at Waring, and then he said: "Silver, killing you is going to be the sweetest thing in my life!" He had put so much passion into the words that his breath was exhausted. He drew it in again with a drinking sound. And his eyes devoured Silver. His head was back. The eyelids were half lowered. He had almost the look of a man staring at a thing of surpassing beauty. There was the same sort of a smile on his face.

"Are you ready?" asked Silver.

"Ready," said Rutherford.

"Are you on edge?"

"On edge!"

"Then go!" said Silver, and threw his gun aside.

He leaped for the other weapon at the same instant, and saw the flash of Rutherford's hand, bright with speed like a bit of metal.

Then, before Silver's eyes, he saw the table heel over and the Colt spill off to the side. It was Waring, who with his long leg had managed to reach the foot of the table and hook it suddenly toward him, spilling both weapons at Rutherford and away from Silver.

He saw Rutherford bending, picking a falling gun out of the air. But Silver did not dodge. He went straight on, and with the lift of his shoulder caught the edge of the table, hurling it before him right at Harry Rutherford.

Catching the gun from the air with unfailing hand, Rutherford had tried a snap shot even before he straightened his body. The bullet slit open the shirt along Silver's left side. Then, with his bulk behind it, the table crashed against Rutherford.

The gun spoke again, but there was no whir of a bullet in the air. Waring was up, kicking at Silver with his spurs, using them as a game-cock fights. But Silver, bare-footed and swift as a cat, was on the other side of the table in an instant and had caught up a fallen Colt—his own. One gesture with that gun sent Waring crowding back into a corner.

Most of the body of Rutherford was hidden under the table, but his head and shoulders, jammed up against the wall, were visible. He had both arms pinned down, and he was not struggling to get free. Something about the eyes of the man told Silver just what had happened.

He jerked the table away and saw on the breast of Rutherford the spreading red stain of the blood. As the table struck him, a bullet from his own gun had penetrated his body. No doctor on earth would be able to heal that wound.

Still, with a nerveless hand, he was trying to pick up the fallen revolver from the floor, but the weight of it slid through his fingers.

Rutherford began to smile.

"Poor Steve Wycombe thought he could make it three for one," said he huskily. "But the poor devil was out of luck. He only got an even break. He only got—me!"

He seemed to nod a confirmation of his last words, but Silver knew that the head would never lift again. He picked up the body. It was hardly more heavy than the body of a child. Silver laid it straight on the floor and closed the eyes. He stood up and turned to Waring. Delgas, all this while, had sat entranced. Events had moved a little too fast for his comprehension.

"I ought to put you there beside him on the floor," said Silver to Waring. "But you've a little too old. Besides, I need you for a witness, on both those little documents. But the law will do the rest of the talking to you, partner. You're old enough to need a rest, and the state will take care of you free of charge."

That was how Steve Wycombe finished off his deal. He had, most surely, put a hand from the grave and taken one living man from the face of the earth. Delgas, a discredited man among his own kind, was turned loose; and Waring went up for a long term.

As for Mr and Mrs Daniel Farrel, they wanted Jim Silver to stay on with them indefinitely because, as Farrel said, he would never consider that two thirds of the ranch really belonged to him. He was really holding it merely in trust for Silver. They followed Silver as far as the corner of the corral and watched him saddle Parade and mount, and still they poured out arguments.

Silver looked down at them and smiled. He had said goodbye before.

"I can't stay," he said. "I'm awash with cash that needs spending. Besides, it's not the sort of a place for me."

"Why not?" asked Farrel. "You stay here for a while, Jim, and you'll love it the way I do. Those three mountains will be like three friendly faces to you, every day of your life. What's wrong?"

"It's the air," said Jim Silver. "There's too much honesty in it, now, and not enough action." He smiled, and added: "You see, when I came here, it was simply as a prospector in a land of trouble, with the chance of a rich strike of danger straight ahead."

"Well, Jim," said Farrel, "you surely made a big strike of what you were looking for. So I suppose you're satisfied."